The MUSICAL

The M

A CONCISE HISTORY

NORTHEASTERN UNIVERSITY PRESS
BOSTON

USICAL

KURT
GÄNZL

Northeastern University Press

Library of Congress Cataloging-in-Publication Data

The musical : a concise history / Kurt Gänzl
 p.   cm.
Includes index.
ISBN 1-55553-311-6 (alk. paper)
1. Musicals—History and criticism. Title.
ML1700.G322   1997
782.1′4′09—dc21   97-3008
                                                             MN

Designed by Janice Wheeler

Composed in Electra by Blue Heron, Inc., Lawrence, Kansas.
Printed and bound by Thomson-Shore, Inc., Dexter, Michigan. The paper is Glatfelter Offset, an acid-free stock.

MANUFACTURED IN THE UNITED STATES OF AMERICA

01 00 99 98 97   5 4 3 2 1

For John Franceschina

and his classes at Penn State University . . .

CONTENTS

LIST OF ILLUSTRATIONS

PREFACE

The musical theater: it's an endless source of fascination and enjoyment for those of us who work in it, who watch it, or who even just listen to it. But the musical theater isn't, of course, just those few shows that we work in, watch, and listen to today, at the end of the twentieth century. It's all those other thousands and thousands of variegated entertainments that have sung and danced their way across thousands and thousands of stages, all round the world, for hundreds of years. They've been a dazzling and disparate lot, those entertainments, and the story of how, where, when, and why they won their hours or years of glory in the theater is an equally dazzling and disparate one. And it's the story that I'm going to try to tell you—concisely (as my subtitle says)—here.

Over recent years, as the hugely popular body of entertainments that we call musical theater has become a more and more popular subject for scholarly and academic study, and as an awareness and knowledge of the shows of earlier years, their music, and their texts has become more widespread, a number of substantial studies of the musical stage in various countries and cities have appeared: Florian Bruyas's *L'Histoire de l'opérette en France*, dealing with the great days (and the not so great ones) of the mostly Parisian musical theater, Otto Schneidereit's chatty tales of the musical entertainments of the Berlin stage, Anton Bauer's careful listings of Viennese musical productions through the centuries, Gerry Bordman's classic chronicle of the New York musical stage, *The American Musical Theater* (soon to be supplemented by Richard Norton's impeccably detailed volumes of credits and song listings), and my own hefty two volumes on the thousand or so original shows produced in the last 150 years in *The British Musical Theatre*. Each of us, however, dealt almost entirely with the product of the country about which we were writing and, although we—or some of us—tried to put our area of musical theater history a little into a general, wider, and even wholly international context, the accent of each of our works was, naturally, very firmly on its declared subject and area.

But, of course, the history of the musical theate—as opposed to "the history of the musical theater *in* New York, *in* Britain, *in* Vienna" or whatever—is no one-nation or one-center affair. It is a history that's knitted together from strands drawn from hither and yon, in a rich, crazy-quilt kind of pattern of languages and theatrical or musical styles whose diversity only helps to give it its own wonderful diversity. To chronicle that whole history in its fullest details would be a five- or ten-volume effort—large volumes, too. Someday, perhaps, some brave person may get down to the monumental lifetime of work that would be needed to complete such an opus in such a way. But I am going to be, as my subtitle says, "concise" . . . even though those of you who know my other books on this subject might find this a little hard to believe.

So, what I have tried to do here is to pull together all the main strands which go to make up the history of what we nowadays call "the musical" and combine them in one all-in history of the musical stage. Not the history of the musical theater "in" or "from" any-one-where, but just plain "the history of the musical theater"—in the world, if you like. Someone called it "the Big Picture." Someone else, taking the novelist's phrase, referred to it as "the eye of God technique." Anyway, what I've tried to do is stand outside and away from any one central place (not so difficult for someone who comes from New Zealand!) and tell the roller-coaster story of the musical stage of the past centuries, down to today, in such a way as to place the major chronicles I referred to in their proper positions on the full stage, and in their context in the whole of history—musical theater history, that is.

Anyone dealing with "musical theater" has, of course, first to state his definition of what he understands by that term. I can only repeat what I said in the preface to my *Encyclopedia of the Musical Theatre*:

I have chosen to stick with what I know about. I deal only with the book musical. That is to say, I cover the original musical play in all its shapes, forms and sizes—any original piece with a continuous libretto, lyrics and music, whether it be a sung-through five-act romantic operetta, a Germanic Posse with a half-dozen numbers, or a little farcical piece illustrated by some tap-dancing high-jinks and a tiny bookful of squeaked-out excuses for songs. I draw my line around that area, and in doing so I regretfully—but necessarily—exclude from my survey all such contiguous and/or related forms of musico-theatre entertainment as opera, pantomime (in both the original and the Anglo-Christmas senses of the word), revue, minstrelsy, compilation shows, paste-up-musicals (mostly), dance shows, concerts, musical hall/variety/vaudeville and so forth, as well as musical film and television. This doesn't mean there is no mention of these areas in the book. They just aren't the subject of the book . . .

I'll actually take that a bit further on this occasion. Here, I have stuck not only with the book musical, but with the successful book musical. The (hi)story that I tell in these pages is the history of that part of the genre that has entertained most of the people most of the time, in most places where musical theater is played: musicals for all. Is "mainstream" the right word? This means that we will encounter together here only those musicals bred and boarded in the four areas which have, at various times, been the most effective purveyors of such shows to the international stage—France, Britain, America, and the Austria/Hungary/Germany area of Central Europe. Such mainly for-home-consumption traditions as the zarzuela of Spain, or the operetta of Italy, and such barely traveling musicals as the product of Russia, New Zealand, or South America, which never belonged to the successful mainstream, must be left aside. Similarly, it means that—as we follow the straight(ish) and narrow(ish) path taken through the years by the great hit entertainments—there will be no delving into the sidestreets inhabited by those "special interest" groups of musicals which have become favorite and fashionable areas of study in our own divisive and divided age: such subjects as the specifically socialist, feminist, gay, and black musical theater have their own specialist historians, and musicals from these areas impinge on our story only when they not only entertain their own devotees but also measure up to my yardstick by entertaining "most of the people most of the time . . ."

This yardstick also means that there will be precious little mention (to use again that much-used theatrical word) here of favorite flops. Well, maybe just one or two of *my* favorite flops, but then I'm writing the book, and everyone's allowed their little weaknesses. In general, though, shows that were less than successful (and even, given the hundreds of successes there have been through the years, quite a few that were really pretty successful), and writers, composers, and songwriters whose work was a little less than internationally popular, may not appear in these pages. Broad lines are broad lines, and that's what I'm drawing here.

As I take those broad lines, I've done my best to give an even-handed treatment to the various eras and areas of musical theater, featuring in each period the shows and the writers (these are my main care: performers, producers, directors, et al. get altogether less attention) which and who had the widest and greatest success. This means that the shows produced in the various areas quoted above when they were not providing the world with its favorite entertainments usually get short coverage. For example, the first attempts to make mostly mock-European musicals in America—even including that long-running (but otherwise pretty insignificant) melodramatic legshow *The Black Crook*—have to ease over and out to make space for the big, international hits of the 1860s and 1870s theater, and—even more dramatically—Continental Europe, as a creative center, almost disappears from our story after the Second World War. The "broad lines" in question, and the factual-figure tables with which I've occasionally illustrated the text, may turn up the odd surprise for some readers. In fact, over the years, a handful of shows and of writers (usually thanks to an enthusiastic publicist, an heir with a royalty to earn, or a writer with a thesis to prove) have had a prominence and a significance claimed for them which I think is not altogether in keeping with what really happened. I've tried to even out some of these what I see as historical bumps, to put the proportions back to something a bit more fair and historically correct, and to give their share of the credit back to some undeservedly now-forgotten-by-all-but-the-experts men.

You'll see the word "international" used quite a lot, not only in this preface but also in the book. That's natural enough when you're doing a "Big Picture" or "Eye of God" sort of history. But you will also see those shows which succeeded or were seen on an international basis featured much more firmly than those which were seen or succeeded only in their home areas. This isn't to say that those shows which went round the world are necessarily better shows than the ones that got left at home (sometimes they undoubtedly weren't, but I'm not presuming subjectively to judge "worth" here, just to chronicle fairly objectively what happened), but they are certainly more relevant to the sort of story I'm relating. For they were seen by more people, in more parts of the world, and so forth. And that's been my central criterion in writing a history that's meant to be a Big Picture.

Before I close down this little Declaration of Intent, I should add a few little remarks about usage and layout. Those of you who've come across my other books will be used by now to the mid-Pacific way I talk (write, that is), but here I've gone in for one particular usage throughout which might be confusing to anyone unwarned. We're dealing with the product of four main centers here, and we're also dealing with four different languages. The only thing is, the four don't pair off. Both America and Britain speak and sing in English, Austria and Germany perform in German, and only France and Hungary keep their languages to themselves. So, very often through these pages you will see the word "English" used when I mean "English-language" and "German" when I mean "German-language," even though I may be talking about the product of the American or Austrian stage. I started off putting "English/German-language" or "-speaking" or "-singing" every time the expression or occasion turned up, but it turned up so frequently and sounded so cumbersome that I gave up.

Most of us, of course, are not fluent in all of the four languages that raise their heads throughout the book (my German is—in spite of my name—little better than basic, and my Hungarian is stumble-through-with-a-dictionaryable), but I found that translating every title in the running text broke up its easy-to-read-ness dreadfully. So, what I've done is to translate each title in brackets—and it's a translation, not the show's equivalent English name—after its listing in the summary of "notable musicals of the period" that follows each section of the narrative. I'm afraid I haven't done the same thing for the foreign-language song-titles—you'll have to do as I do and get out a dictionary! Or the score.

Those songlists, by the way, have been appended to each example of what I intend to be a little self-sufficient encapsulation of the most important and successful shows in musical-theater history. I know a song-title alone means very little, even attached to a story—a song has to be sung and/or heard to mean something—but, hopefully, some readers will be encouraged to dip into the repertoire of songs from the shows of yesteryear and find out just what they were. I promise you, it's a dip worth the taking. These songlists have been taken from printed scores and/or programs. The two sources very frequently don't agree in their details, so I've sometimes been forced to do a bit of do-it-yourself carpentry to complete a listing—with the help of my friends. Thanks, everyone.

As I said at the start of this preface, this is a concise history, a study of the mainstream and the hits in the international musical theater of the past centuries. As such, it cannot of course take time to go deeply into any one particular show or the career of one particular person. If, as I hope it will be, your interest in some person or play is whetted sufficiently by reading this story that you want to know more about him, her, or it, I'd direct you—first and foremost—to the score, the text, and (where relevant) the recording of the piece in question, but also to a handful of works on the international musical theater which should at very least point you out the way to further knowledge. Er . . . they're actually by me.

You will find the largest collation of international facts and figures, including references to available biographies and studies (which aren't by me!), recordings, and so forth in my two-volume *Encyclopedia of the Musical Theatre*. You will find the full plot synopses with in situ song-titles of most of the "boxed" shows of this book, as well as a good few more, in the London-published *Gänzl's Book of the Musical Theatre* (written in collaboration with Andrew Lamb) and its more recent American counterpart *Gänzl's Book of the Broadway Musical*. And you will find a discussion of the LP recordings of shows and show music put out through the years (in a book where I actually get to give opinions!) in Blackwell's guide to *The Musical Theatre on Record*. But the literature of the musical theater is getting larger and richer seemingly by the minute, and there is a wealth of material to get into both for the student of history and facts, and for the lover of a good anecdotal—and perhaps rather less factual—read. Though I'm sure I'm not the only one to think that it's a pity they've stopped publishing scores.

But the best part, of course, even in this often overamplified and too often sing-the-scenery age, is always going to be going to the shows.

Merry musical-theater going!

KURT GÄNZL

1 THE EARLY DAYS

he musical. That inventive person who first decided to turn a hard-working adjective into a nice new noun, thus leaving us with the nearly new word that nowadays describes—and not just in the English language—the world's most popular form of theatrical entertainment, did us all a favor.

The bastard but beautiful term that he fathered has various virtues but, to me, the most important among them is that it is so gloriously unspecific, so thoroughly and promiscuously all-embracing. Under the umbrella of that nice new noun there shelters an almost endless variety of theatrical entertainments: comical ones, dramatic ones, romantic ones, as well of course as those that opt for being all three at the same time. Shows with finely plotted libretti, others that have no real plotline to speak of, pieces with dropped trousers or dramatic death-scenes (though only rarely both), with realistic, farcical, improbable, and/or happy beginnings and middles and endings, and with characters colorful, grotesque, swashbuckling, sighing, overwhelming, or side-splitting. There are those that tend to the historical, the biographical, the satirical, the hysterical, the sentimental, and/or the spectacular, to the fantastical and/or preachy, the extravagant, imaginative, parodic, pretentious, the strivingly relevant or gloriously irrelevant, shows light, dazzling, dark, or shadowy, shows with tales original, borrowed, or even sometimes stolen, but all of them—in their diversity—have in common that sine qua non: they all have music.

Like the subject matter and the style of this terrific rainbow of musical plays, that music, and the part it fulfills in the show, can vary hugely. It may consist of just a handful of little songs, new or even second-hand, sung to an accompaniment provided by a minimum of musicians as a mere and incidental decoration to a piece whose spoken text is its raison d'être. Or it may be a full-blown score of richly written and expansively orchestrated music, designed to be sung by voices of range and powerful expression, and the element around which all the rest of the entertainment is constructed. But, whether a show belongs to one or the other of these two extreme categories, or whether it takes on any one of the many shades of musical coloring that go in between, the result of this combining of song, ensemble, dance, and/or incidental music and a story text is the same: it gives us that species of theater that recent decades have chosen to call "the musical."

In earlier theatrical decades, in earlier theatrical centuries, in the days before our unknown benefactor coined his useful bit of terminology, many or all of the kinds of show we revel in as "musicals" today did, of course, already exist and flourish. But they existed and flourished under different labels. For, in those earlier days, the description that followed a musical's title on the playbill was normally intended to give an audience a slightly specific idea of what they could expect from their evening's entertainment. So, a musical wasn't just "a musical," it was "a musical comedy," "a romantic musical play," "a burlesque," "a farcical comedy with songs and dances," an "operetta," or even occasionally something more individual and flavorful. A musical-theater bill or title-page in nineteenth-century France might have carried the mention "opéra-bouffe" or "opéra-comique," "vaudeville" or "comédie mêlée d'ariettes," while the German-language theater of the same era proffered such categories as "komische Oper" (comic opera, i.e., music-based play with spoken text), "Lebensbild" ("picture-from-life") or "Posse" ("homely" musical play) "mit Gesang und Tanz" (as an alternative to those Possen and Lebensbilder which had no Gesang und Tanz), "Operette" (light or small-in-subject opera), "Zauberspiele" (magical or fairy-tale play, fantasy), "Volksmärchen" (folk-story), or "Singspiel" (musical play). Each and every one of these subtitles had its own specific shade of meaning, often bordering on and sometimes crossing one other, and their audiences had a pretty good idea what they signified.

But the fashion for the kind of more-or-less-precise labels that the writers and producers of past times chose to put on their shows, in a way our present generation has preferred not to, has had a dubious effect on those of us who like to look back at the wealth of musical theater produced in years gone by. It has led folk in the days of "the musical"—and at no time more so than in fin-de-siècle today—to regard those shows, with their unfamiliar descriptions, as being somehow different, as belonging to another genre, another world, than the one inhabited by the "musicals" of the last decades of the twentieth century. And that idea is—of course—quite wrong. They don't. They differ only as much as a person born in one decade, a novel written in one era, a building built at some time in the past, differs from a person, a novel, or a building of nowadays. They are no less a person, a book, or a building, just because of their date of birth. And the same goes for all those shows. No matter what description they sported in their young days, they are no less "musicals" than the ones which just happen to have been, thanks to that mid-twentieth-century turn in terminology, called "musical" from their birth.

Since this is so, how far back do we have to go to find the show that might be worthily deemed "the first musical," in the manner that Jacopo Peri's *Dafne* of 1597 is so neatly taped and ticketed as "the first opera"? The answer is undoubtedly "very much further than that." It may not be a very convincing or precise answer, but history is like that. It doesn't lay itself out in nice, straight, clearly defined lines, with little red rosettes glued on to "the first this" and "the first that" to point out a path that will lead us through the centuries like Hänsel and Gretel's crumbs. And theatrical history is no exception.

One thing that can safely be said is that there has been music in the theater for as long as the theater has existed. And not only our "theater" of the bricks-and-mortar era, but that of the days of set-ups and booths, and of performances of a very different kind from those which we enjoy today. There were certainly "musicals" of a kind to be seen and heard in the theaters of ancient Greece and Italy. Were they the first? Probably not. But who knows? We don't, and it is unlikely that we ever shall.

I am not going to attempt to delve into musical-theater archeology in this survey, in some kind of hopeless search for the archetypal musical. Neither am I going to enter into the special study that is the stage and music in classical antiquity, or that of the performances and plays of the sixteenth, seventeenth, or even much of the eighteenth centuries of this modern era. Rather than spread myself margarine-thinly through thousands or even hundreds of years, I am going to limit the body of this chronicling of the history of the entertainment we know as the musical to just the last one hundred and fifty.

I am not, however, proposing to come out of this particular set of historical starting blocks without good reason. The years around the middle of the nineteenth century saw a significant change come over the musical theater. In those years it blossomed forth with a new style and a new spirit, sweeping crazily round the world and its many-languaged stages in what, if it was not actually that very beginning of the career of "the musical," which lies buried somewhere in the sands of time, was at least something that can be argued to be the beginning of the era of the "modern musical" that has entertained the Western world so lavishly in the century and a half since.

THE MUSICAL STAGE BEFORE 1850

So, what was this new style and spirit? What was this new world-wowing direction that the musical took? To understand it, of course, we first have to look at what it was a direction away from, at what the musical-theater entertainments on view in the most theatrically active and creative parts of the world—Italy, France, Germany, Austria, and Britain and their colonial outposts—had been like during the previous decades.

By and large—as is the case in most subjects, the theater and its history turn up exceptions to each and any rule and every generalization, but by and large—those entertainments fell into two distinct categories. They don't have nice neat titles so, for better or for worse, I'm going to call them the Popular and the Operatic. And what was it that divided these two categories the one from the other? Well, when all was totted up and tallied, it was very largely a question of emphasis.

The Popular entertainments—farcical plays shot through with musical numbers, rustic romances decorated with songs and dances, song-studded burlesques of the theater's more high-flown genres and mannerisms, merry musical tales of marital mix-ups, magical and mythological romps, or little (and even not so little) pieces called "burletta" or "comic opera" by their authors—were shows that were built soundly on their text, a text to which the variously sized musical part of the entertainment was simply a divertissement and a decoration. Very often, in fact more often than not, the music in question wasn't even new. The sung part of such an entertainment was made up of lyrics that suited or slipped easily into their story stuck on to arrangements of ancient folksongs, on to the melodies of the popular songs of the day, or even on to those of pieces pinched from other shows, from the loftiest to the most cheerfully lowbrow, from the oldest to the still running. The most favored of these melodies, indeed, quite simply went from show to show to show, and in some cases they ultimately came to signify a particular mood or a moment in the action, just as their equivalent "signatures" would do, many years later, in the scores to the silent movies.

The Operatic entertainments, as a contrast, made a proud feature of their musical part, a musical part that was not second- or tenth-hand, but which consisted of a score specially composed for the show in which it was displayed, just like the scores for the serious and tragic grand operas which were at the time considered the summit (if then, as now, not necessarily the most popular manifestation) of musical-theater art. Sometimes the libretti of the "operatic" shows told much the same kind of tale that the "popular" ones did. As in the non-musical theater, a very large percentage of musical play plots were set on the rutted road to marriage, in tales romantic, or comical, or both. Sometimes, too, the words to these operatic pieces were skillfully written, but—as was evidenced in the eighteenth century by the number of times the same libretti and stories were set and reset with fresh scores of original music by a series of musicians in a series of languages and countries—it was the musical score that was the heart of the matter. The book was there merely to serve as a setting for the songs and the ensembles provided by the composer.

In the first part of the eighteenth century, both sides of this dogmatic division produced some highly successful works, a number of which would even outlive their own times and go on to many decades of representations on the world's stages.

POPULAR ENTERTAINMENTS OF THE EARLY EIGHTEENTH CENTURY

On the popular side, the London theater notched up one of the musical theater's most memorable and enduring hits when it welcomed *The Beggar's Opera* (1728), a bitingly funny piece of lowlife comedy, spiked with all kinds of easily appreciable topical, social, and personal jibes, which—following the fashion of the booth entertainments of the French fairs—doubled its appeal by taking a musical sideshot at the modish artificialities of the newly fashionable everything-stops-for-an-aria Italian opera. The score, arranged by Dr Johann Christoph Pepusch (1667–1752), was made up of songs and ensembles that were based on a whole array of common and popular melodies and second-hand song-tunes, from the "anon" folksong to the polite arietta, and those tunes made up into a funsome series of altogether less pretentious set-piece musical moments than the florid and repetitive showpiece arias, with their emphasis on vocalization rather than on dramatic value, that made up the backbone of the Italian scores. As the years went on, *The Beggar's Opera*—which emphasized this parallel with the Italians both in its incongruous title and by taking on itself the novel appellation of "ballad opera"— naturally found all its topical and many of its burlesque points blunted, but this jaunty show, with its oversexed thug of an anti-hero and its merry mixture of musical styles, still stands up, a quarter of a millennium later, as a jolly, mudslinging bit of thoroughly musical comedy, and the text which John Gay (1685–1732) provided has served as the basis for a series of remakes all around Europe.

THE BEGGAR'S OPERA, a ballad opera (comic opera) in 3 acts by John Gay. Lyrics by Gay and others. Music selected and arranged by Johann Christoph Pepusch. Produced at Lincoln's Inn Fields Theatre, London, 29 January 1728.

Characters: Mr Peachum, Mrs Peachum, Polly Peachum, Captain Macheath, Filch, Lockit, Lucy Lockit, Matt o' the Mint, Jenny Diver, Suky Tawdry, &c.

Plot: Mr Peachum, a prospering London thiefmaster and fence, and his helpmate wife are aghast when they hear that their daughter Polly has unadvisedly married one of their suppliers, the swaggering, womanizing road-thief known as Captain Macheath. The couple fear that their new son-in-law will now betray their operation to the law so that, as next of kin, he may inherit all of their soiled savings. So, with the help of a willing and jealous whore and a useful jail boss, the Peachums hastily get their son-in-law condemned himself, and although one of his many less official "wives," the jailer's daughter Lucy, helps him temporarily to escape, he has made it to the gallows tree before he is improbably reprieved to go home to his lawful wedded wench.

Principal songs: "Through All the Employments of Life" (Peachum), "'Tis Woman That Seduces All Mankind" (Peachum), "Virgins Are Like the Fair Flow'r in Its Lustre" (Polly), "Our Polly Is a Sad Slut" (Mrs Peachum), "Can Love Be Controlled by Advice?" (Polly), "O Polly, You Might Have Toy'd and Kissed" (Peachum, Mrs Peachum), "O Ponder Well, Be Not Severe" (Polly), "Pretty Polly, Say" (Macheath), "My Heart Was So Free" (Macheath), "Were I Laid on Greenland's Coast" (Macheath, Polly), "Let Us Take the Road" (Matt), "If the Heart of Man Is Depress'd with Cares" (Macheath), "When You Censure the Age" (Lockit), "How Happy I Could Be with Either" (Macheath), "Cease Your Funning" (Polly), "Why, How Now, Madam Flirt" (Lucy), "I Like the Fox Shall Grieve" (Lucy), "When a Wife's in a Pout" (Lucy), "Thus I Stand Like the Turk" (Macheath).

The piece that stands out as probably the most internationally successful example of a musical comedy to come out in this period also began its career in London. With an eye to the fashion created by its already famous predecessor, *The Devil to Pay* (1731), written by Irishman Charles Coffey (d 1745), which saw stage-light just three years after The *Beggar's Opera*, was

called a "ballad farce." This piece was an adaptation of an even earlier comedy, illustrated by sixteen (later slimmed to eleven) musical numbers, and it told the story of a nagging aristocratic wife and a brutally macho cobbler who are, thanks to a bit of timely magic, temporarily and salutorily given to each other as partners. The libretto for the show was full-steam-ahead comedy, with just a little moral in its happy (for the protagonists' battered spouses) ending, for, unlike *The Beggar's Opera,* Coffey's musical did not strive to make any points, parodic or otherwise, in either its text or its music. It was simply a farcical musical comedy thoroughly worthy of the name. The musical part of the show consisted of the same kind of pasticcio or collage of not-so-new tunes that the earlier show had sported, but the "ballad" part of this "ballad farce" took a firm second place to the action and the fun of the farce. And that farce proved enormously successful, going out from London to make itself a hit, in a whole series of versions, all round the world.

In Germany it became *Der Teufel ist los* (1752) and, set with a replacement score of original music, a landmark in the German musical theater as its first major musical-comedy or Singspiel hit; in France, set with a fresh pasticcio of French music, it became *Le Diable à quatre* (1756); in Vienna, an Italian version called *Poche, ma buone* (1800), with an original score by Ferdinando Paër (1771–1839), became a thorough hit; and, more than a century on, after what the *Biographica Dramatica* of 1782 called "as many transformations as the Banjans of the East Indies fable their Deity Wistnon to have passed through," not to mention one of the first musequels in musical-theater history, Coffey's libretto made it all the way back to Britain to be set by the celebrated operatic composer Michael Balfe (1808–1870) as *The Devil's in It* (1852), and back to Vienna as a "komische Zauberposse," or magical musical comedy, adapted by top playwright Karl Costa (1832–1907) and freshly composed by Franz von Suppé (1820–1895), as *Die Frau Meisterin* (1868).

THE DEVIL TO PAY, or The Wives Metamorphos'd, a ballad farce in 3 acts (later 6 scenes) by Charles Coffey, based on the farce *The Devil of a Wife* by Thomas Jevon. Music uncredited. Produced at the Theatre Royal, Drury Lane, London, 17 August 1731.

Characters: Sir John Loverule, Lady Loverule, Zekel Jobson, Nell Jobson, Doctor, Lucy, Lettice, Butler, Coachman, Cook, Footman, &c.

Plot: The uncouth cobbler Jobson is "a true English heart" who boozes with the boys and beats and bullies his dutiful wife, Nell. Lady Loverule is a haughty termagant who treats all—including her generous husband—with scalding rudeness. One day she turns away from her door a benighted Doctor, who finds hospitality instead with the bedrudged Nell, and in grateful return the Doctor—who is nothing of the kind—brews a little sorcery. Gentle Nell turns up in Sir John's home and bed, and on the receiving end of his kindnesses and his household's love, while Lady Loverule finds herself in the Jobsons' cot and on the receiving end of Zekel's strap. But only the two women are aware of the switch—everyone else just sees an amazing character change. When the magic is finally undone and the women return home, both the cobbler and the Lady have been thoroughly chastened by the experience.

Songs: "He That Has the Best Wife" (Jobson), "Come, Jolly Bacchus" (Jobson), "Here's a Good Health to the King" (Jobson), "Ye Gods, You Gave to Me a Wife" (Sir John), "My Little Spirits Now Appear" (Doctor), "Of All the Trades from East to West" (Jobson), "In Bath a Wanton Wife Did Dwell" (Jobson), "I Will Come in Spite, She Said" (Jobson), "Though Late I Was a Cobbler's Wife" (Nell), "Was Ever Man Possess'd?" (Sir John, Nell), "Let Ev'ry Face with Smiles Appear" (ensemble).

Burlesque—the extravagantly ridiculous parody of things overly serious, and in particular of the more dramatically pompous and pretentious parts of the theater—had been a popular pastime on European stages for many years, and *The Beggar's Opera* was only one (and far from the first or the most brutally direct) of many madcap attacks that were made on the early eighteenth-century stages on the manners and mannerisms of the eminently attackable Italian opera, with its coloratura and castrati and its vastly exaggerated and melodramatic sentiments and action. Debunking the highflown was a popular theatrical sport, and French producers, in particular, were liable to have direct parodies of the latest grand operas on the boards within a remarkably short time of their première. These parodies, of course, included a significant helping of music. In fact, they often used chunks of the score of the burlesqued opera itself, set to grotesque words and sung with very different emphases and style, but no one minded: after all, to get the most out of a burlesque you had first to buy a ticket to see the opera that was being burlesqued.

Among the most successful burlesque operas of the period on the English-language stage were two shows that were not one-to-one burlesques of specific grand operas but rather parodies of the whole idea of opera, its conventions, and its extravagant staging: a musicalized version of Henry Fielding's already popular parody of the fiorature of the melodramatic stage, *Tom Thumb*, "set to music after the Italian manner" as *The Opera of Operas* (1733), and a gloriously nonsensical piece, written by Henry Carey (d 1743), "a musician by profession, and one of the lower order of poets," and composed by J. F. Lampe (1703–1751), which combined the tale of a ridiculous and raunchy old English ballad called *The Dragon of Wantley* (1737), full of common and even low or lewd language, with a score of the utmost operatic pomposity.

THE DRAGON OF WANTLEY, a burlesque opera in 3 acts by Henry Carey. Music by John Frederick Lampe. Produced at the Theatre Royal, Covent Garden, London, 6 November 1737.

Characters: Moore, Margery, Mauxalinda, The Dragon, Gubbins, &c.

Plot: A dragon has been laying waste a chunk of rural Yorkshire, gobbling up the children's breakfast bread and butter before they can gobble it up themselves, so the incredibly valiant local knight, Moore of Moore Hall, is called in to dispose of the beast. He agrees to do so, for the love of pretty village Margery, which makes pretty village Mauxalinda, whom he'd wooed last Christmas, see scarlet. Having first put a stop to the jilted one's attempt at a pretty village murder, Moore dons his heroic armor, dispatches the dragon by means of a well-aimed pointed toe-piece up the beast's fatally vulnerable rectum, and returns home in splendid operatic triumph.

The Dragon of Wantley: "Oh! oh! oh! The devil take your toe." A mortal blow by an armored toe, in a place where a gentleman's toe shouldn't go.

Act III —Scene 1.

Songs: "Fly, Neighbours, Fly!" (chorus), "Poor Children Three" (Gubbins), "But to Hear the Children Mutter" (Margery), "He's a Man Ev'ry Inch" (Mauxalinda), "Zeno, Plato, Aristotle" (Moore), "Oh, Save Us!" (chorus), "Gentle Knight! All Knights Exceeding" (Margery), "If That's All You Ask" (Margery), "Let My Dearest Be Near Me" (Margery, Moore), "By the Beer as Brown as Berry" (Moore), "Pigs Shall Not Be" (Moore, Mauxalinda), "Sure, My Stays Will Burst with Sobbing" (Margery), "Insulting Gipsy" (Mauxalinda, Margery), "Oh! Give Me Not Up to the Law" (Mauxalinda), "Oh! How Easy Is a Woman" (Mauxalinda, Moore, Margery), "Fill, Fill the Mighty Flagon" (Moore, chorus), "Dragon, Dragon, Thus I Dare Thee" (Moore), "Oh, Oh! Mr Moore, You Son of a Whore" (Dragon), "My Sweet Honeysuckle" (Moore, Margery), "Sing, Sing and Rorio"/"Huzza!" (chorus).

Raunchiness was also often a feature of what the eighteenth-century French enjoyed as their favorite kind of popular musical-theater entertainment, under the name of opéra-comique. "Opéra-comique" was an expression that would effectively change its meaning several times over the years, as the genre—or at least its name—went steadily upmarket, but at this point in time the sort of show that was so described actually had more in common with the British ballad farce or its German equivalent, the Singspiel, than with anything approaching what we would today call opera. For the "opéra" here didn't mean "grand opera" and the "comique" didn't mean "funny": all that was signified in the expression was that the "opéra" or musical part of the show was attached to a "comédie," a play, instead of being written in the sung-through "opératique" style of the Italians. Not necessarily a comic play either, but any sort of play. However, as brought to its happiest heights in the 1730s and 1740s by the enormously successful author-actor Charles Favart (1710–1792), this brand of opéra-comique was most often a lively, sexy piece of humorously pointed theater, illustrated by a bevy of brief musical cuts—little lighthearted lyrics set to combinations of a whole list of popular tunes and familiar musical phrases. Favart's jolliest hit of these years was undoubtedly the typical tale of the dense but country-clever lass who is *La Chercheuse d'esprit* (1741). A saucy, rustic piece with a simple story of rural matchmaking and unmaking, set with a series of musical numbers that were made up from bits of no fewer than seventy tunes, it remained a feature on the French musical stage for well over a century.

LA CHERCHEUSE D'ESPRIT, an opéra-comique in 1 act by Charles S. Favart. Music uncredited. Produced at the Théâtre de la Foire Saint-Germain, Paris, 20 February 1741.

Characters: Madame Madre, Monsieur Subtil, Monsieur Narquois, Nicette, Alain, L'Éveillé, Finette.

Plot: The widowed magistrate, Subtil, in search of a more amenable (than the first) second wife, asks her mother, Mme Madre, for the hand of dopey, fourteen-year-old Nicette. Madame, in return, will marry his equally naive and moldable son, Alain. Mother frets that Nicette's lack of "esprit" (brains/personality/know-how) will lose her this fine match, and she orders the girl to go out and find herself some of this drastically missing quality. The learned Narquois tells her it can't be got if you haven't got it, the jolly L'Éveillé, who is about to wed the village chatterbox, Finette, gets caught trying to teach her his version of it, and Finette archly tells her to go and learn from silly Alain. So she does. The two youngsters quickly comprehend that it's each other they like, and Nicette turns out to have more than enough native wit and know-how to mow down her mother's plans and bring things to a happy youth-weds-youth ending.

Songs: "Je veux être son époux" (Subtil, Madre), "Sa taille est ravissante" (Subtil), "Que diriez-vous donc, ma chère?" (Subtil, Madre), "Craignez-vous l'artifice" (Madre), "Je viens de vous choisir" (Subtil, Nicette), "Cela me prouve son honneur" (Subtil, Nicette, Madre), "Allez chercher de l'esprit" (Nicette, Subtil, Madre), "Quelle désespoir" (Nicette), "Finette avec moi s'engage" (L'Éveillé), "Et pourquoi non, mon biau tendron" (L'Éveillé), "Me donner tout l'esprit qu'il a" (Nicette, L'Éveillé), "Avec ce tendron" (Finette, L'Éveillé), "Tout le monde m'abandonne" (Nicette), "Hé bien, qu'est-ce qui vous chagrine?" (Alain, Nicette), "On trouve de tout à Paris" (Alain), "Alain, ou voulez-vous aller?" (Madre, Nicette), "Il faut l'aborder joliment" (Madre), "Tu ne feras plus le dragon" (L'Éveillé, Finette), "Me promenant, à l'écart" (L'Éveillé), "Les soins, les soucis, l'embarras" (Finette), "Hola, belle Nicette!" (Alain), "On prend la main encore" (Alain, Nicette), "C'est raisonner fort prudemment" (Alain), "Hé bien, hé bien, mariez-moi ma mère" (Nicette), "À présent je ne dois plus feindre" (Nicette), "Bon effet ça viant de produire" (Alain), &c.

OPERATIC ENTERTAINMENTS OF THE EARLY EIGHTEENTH CENTURY

La Chercheuse d'esprit came out in Paris less than a decade after a musical-theater conflict that had caused a considerable stir. At the heart of that conflict—a virtual contest for supremacy between the popular and operatic styles in musical theater which actually had members of the royal family aligned on one side or the other—was the same frantically fashionable Italian opera which had so stirred up English sensibilities, and most particularly a little Italian intermezzo called *La serva padrona* (1733), the biggest hit of its kind—both in Italy and abroad—to date.

The intermezzo was a curious invention. Apparently, even at this early stage in its history, the mythologico-tragic, politico-tragic, romantico-tragic nature of the Italian opera seria had proven limited in its appeal: a little bit of a downer for that general public which the now increasing number of for-the-public theaters were trying to attract. So, in order to pick the audience's jowls up off the floor after an actful of gloomy sentiments and castrato trills, before it was time to launch into a second, third, or even fifth actful of the same fare, someone invented the intermezzo: a jolly little comic opera which was played as light relief between the acts of the gloomico-tragic one. Since it was still an opera it was, of course, all sung, with what would have been the dialogue given in recitativo secco, a curious sort of conversational sung-speech in which the vocalist didn't have to climb off the top of the stave or do anything ornamental as he did in the arias, and in which the words weren't repeated ad infinitum as in the set-piece numbers, but instead given in relatively normal speech patterns. But sung.

Pieces such as *Il marito giogatore* (1718) and *La serva padrona*—their titles, the gambling husband, the maid become mistress, already show the classic comic strain that they followed—established this kind of entertainment to such good effect that it was eventually able to move out of its position as a supporting act, and into one as its own master: Italy's version of the comic opera. Comic opera of this kind, sometimes with recitative, sometimes with spoken dialogue, and, of course, lengthened to proportions that would fill a full evening in the theater, was duly copied in the other main centers, and this musically ambitious, "operatic" kind of musical play went on to have a memorable career during the next century or so, peaking in the production of an array of enduringly popular pieces with music by composers who were sufficiently skilled and "upmarket" to shine equally brightly in the world of the grand and tragic opera: Mozart's *Die Entführung aus dem Serail* (1782) and *Le nozze di Figaro* (1786), his dramma giocoso *Don Giovanni* (1787) and *Cosí fan tutte* (1790), Rossini's *Il barbiere di Siviglia* (1816) and *La Cenerentola* (1817), and so forth. In the twentieth century, the product of this era of Italianate comic opera has made its way firmly and finally into the world's opera houses, joining there not only the opera seria but such later and thoroughly composed soi-disants opéras-comiques of the French stage as the tragic, rather than humorous, but spoken-dialogued *Carmen* and *Faust* as an important part of the operatic repertoire. In the early decades of their existence, however, these pieces were firmly dubbed "comic operas," a genre apart from the serious opera, and they were often played by touring "operatic" companies in repertoire with burlesques, opéras-bouffes, and pasticcio entertainments.

THE RISE OF THE ORIGINAL MUSICAL PLAY

During the second half of the eighteenth century and the first years of the nineteenth, much of what was produced as musical-theater entertainment followed the lines that had been established in these early years. Little by little, however, the popular pieces began to undergo some important changes. Most importantly, they began regularly rather than exceptionally to take in original rather than recomposed music: music that was of a "popular" bent, in the same style as the favorite songs and tunes previously used as musical-theater song-fodder, but freshly baked in a virtual imitation of the pasticcio songs. At first, as the expression "composed and arranged by . . ." became a regular one on musical comedy playbills, it was mostly a matter of only some new or specially written numbers being included in a score that was largely pasticcio, but as time went on the "composed" began sometimes to outweigh the "and arranged" and, in the long run, popular musical plays were produced that boasted a whole custom-made set of popularly musicked songs.

In Britain, during the later years of the eighteenth century, such men as playwright and popular-songwriter Charles Dibdin (1745–1814), librettist Isaac Bickerstaff (1733–?1812), and musicians Thomas Arne (1710–1778), Samuel Arnold (1740–1802), and William Shield (1748–1829) came to prominence in this kind of musical theater, and they were responsible for turning out a number of musicals which would have a long and healthy life. Bickerstaff and Arne combined on two merry English musical love stories, the freshly composed *Thomas and Sally* (1760) and the "composed and arranged" *Love in a Village* (1762), and the librettist worked with Dibdin on what was to turn out to be not only the most widely popular English musical comedy of the time, but the most successful such piece since the triumphant *The Devil to Pay*: *The Padlock* (1768), with its famous low comedy character of the drolly dialected West-Indian servant Mungo.

THE PADLOCK, a comic opera in 2 acts by Isaac Bickerstaff, based on *El celoso extremeño* by Cervantes. Music by Charles Dibdin. Produced at the Theatre Royal, Drury Lane, London, 3 October 1768.

Characters: Don Diego, Leonora, Ursula, Mungo, Leander, two scholars.

Plot: Wealthy, more-than-middle-aged Don Diego has brought the teenaged Leonora from her poor parents' home to pass three months in his lofty mansion on approval as a potential, if taken rather late in life, wife. Now he has decided that she will do, so leaving the girl securely padlocked behind his mansion gates, watched over by the duenna Ursula and his negro servant Mungo, he sets off to finalize the betrothal. But while he is gone, a pretty young fellow called Leander clambers in past the padlock, woos his way around the susceptible spinster and the wine-sodden slave, and when the would-be groom comes home he finds a youthful love-scene that makes him come to his senses.

Songs: "Thoughts to Council" (Diego), "Say, Little, Foolish, Fluttering Thing" (Leonora), "By Some I Am Told" (Diego), "Were I a Shepherd's Maid" (Leonora), "Hither Venus, with Your Doves" (Leander), "Dear Heart, What a Terrible Life I Am Led" (Mungo), "O Thou, Whose Charms Enslave My Heart" (Leander, Leonora, Mungo, Ursula), "Let Me, When My Heart a Sinking" (Mungo), "In Vain You Bid Your Captive Live" (Leander), "Oh Me! Oh Me! What Shall We Do?" (Leonora), "Oh, Wherefore This Terrible Flurry?" (Diego), "Then Must I Go?" (Leander, Leonora), Finale: "Go Forge Me Fetters That Shall Bind" (Diego, Mungo, Leonora).

The intrigue of *The Padlock*, with its young lovers overcoming parental preferences and routing the older, richer, and generally objectionable bridegroom planned for the heroine, was one that was repeated over and over in varying disguises and dresses during this period. Pieces such as Sheridan and Linley's comical musical play about *The Duenna* (1775) who helps true love to triumph over a stern parent and a Portuguese Jew pretendant, and Dibdin's cautionary tale of a pair of overly self-centered country lovers who misjudge the good heart of *The Quaker* (1777) whom the young lady is supposed to wed, treated almost precisely the same plotline. However, a considerable range of other subjects also got a showing. The successful Stephen Storace/Prince Hoare "comic opera" *No Song, No Supper* (1790), with its homely story of a randy and rascally lawyer tricked out of cash, sex, and his leg-of-lamb dinner, and others of its kind may have concentrated humorously and similarly on other aspects of the marriage/sex and money that were central to the *Padlock* kind of story, but not all musicals of the period insisted on comic imbroglios as their text. Shows such as John O'Keeffe and Samuel Arnold's venture into comic-opera-banditland with the colorful *The Castle of Andalusia* (1782), or the aristocratic love-and-lucre tale of a usurped title, a lost heir, and a counterfeit Lady that comes to a climax in *The Haunted Tower* (1789) which was the setting for the full-blooded libretto concocted by James Cobb, took more romantically colorful backgrounds and more momentously romantic events as their raw material. However, in spite of the considerable popularity of musicals of this more extravagantly painted kind on English-language stages in these years, the most enduring comic opera to come out of Britain in the last part of the eighteenth century was not a romantic piece with aristocratic characters and lofty settings, but a humorous little musical on the marriage-and-mother theme that found its people and its songs as near as could be to home. Dibdin's tiny tale of *The Waterman* took place alongside the River Thames, and the lively and long-loved numbers that he wrote for its musical part were supplemented in production by such eternal favorites as "The Bay of Biscay" and "Rule, Britannia!"

THE WATERMAN, or The First of August, a ballad opera in 2 acts by Charles Dibdin. Music composed and arranged by Dibdin. Produced at the Little Haymarket Theatre, London, 8 August 1774.

Characters: Mr Bundle, Mrs Bundle, Tom Tug, Robin, Wilhelmina, &c.

Plot: Wilhelmina, the daughter of the peaceable, garden-loving Mr Bundle and his overbearing, snobbish wife, is the object of the affections of two young men: the waterman, Tom Tug, and the dandified, prolix Robin. Mr Bundle is all in favor of her wedding Tom, but the girl's pretentious mother is determined that Robin shall be her son-in-law. Wilhelmina wavers to and fro, but when Tom goes out and wins the Thames watermen's race and its coat and badge in her name, she finally sees clearly enough to prefer the man of action to the man of words. And Bundle revolts long enough to put his wife gaspingly in her place.

Songs: "Labour, Lads, 'ere Youth Be Gone" (ensemble), "My Counsel Take" (Mrs Bundle), "Two Youths for My Love Are Contending in Vain" (Wilhelmina), "And Did You Not Hear of a Jolly Young Waterman?" (Tom), "Then Farewell, My Trim Built Wherry" (Tom), "Bid the Blossoms Ne'er Be Blighted" (Robin), "Too Yielding a Carriage" (Wilhelmina), "In Vain, Dear Friends, Each Art You Try" (Wilhelmina), "Indeed, Miss, Such Sweethearts as I Am" (Tom), "Cherries and Plums Are Never Found" (Robin), "I Vow'd for the Prize" (Tom), "Ne'er Let Your Heart, My Girl, Sink Down" (Tom, Wilhelmina, Bundle, Mrs Bundle).

Alongside these original and semi-original musical plays, pasticcio shows still throve thoroughly, and burlesque—which remained resolutely a pasticcio affair through the years—throve as well as any. In fact, the genre throve to such good effect that the success and longevity of *The Waterman* on English stages was at least equaled by that of its most successful eighteenth-century example, a happy Irish burletta called *Midas*. The events and plot of *Midas* might not have been that different from those used in the "real life" kind of musical comedy—rich old man chases young, pretty, and unenthusiastic lass—but the use of mythological characters and a fantasy setting, instead of here-and-now ones, allowed the author all those extra latitudes that helped make burlesque and extravaganza so attractive and so popular. He could propel his nubile nymphs and satyrical immortals into much more grotesque situations than he could "real" people, he could allow them songs and rhyming-coupleted speeches of a much more extravagant nature, and he could let his imagination run rife much more merrily than was possible in the kind of true-to-real-life musical comedies turned out by Bickerstaff, Dibdin, or Sheridan, or in the romantic and dramatic shows of O'Keeffe and Cobb.

MIDAS, a comic opera in 2 acts by Kane O'Hara. Music uncredited. Produced at the Crow Street Theatre, Dublin, 22 January 1762.

Characters: Jupiter, Apollo, Pan, Mercury, Momus, Juno, Midas, Damaetas, Sileno, Mysis, Nysa, Daphne, &c.

Plot: Banished to earth for spying on his Olympian Papa's amours, the god Apollo gets mixed up there in the attempts of squire Midas and his pimp Damaetas to lay a couple of local lassies. Both girls fall for the newcomer, and the irritated Midas, unable to make any headway in his lecheries, resolves to get rid of the attractive stranger by having him beaten in a singing contest by his crony, Pan. Since Midas is the judge for the contest, Pan is given as the winner, but then the angry God of Music reveals his real identity. The crooked Midas is changed to an ass and virtue is rewarded all round before, in a final tableau, Apollo ascends to Olympus.

Songs: "Jove in His Chair" (chorus), "Think Not, Lewd Jove" (Juno), "Be By Your Friends Advised" (Apollo), "Since You Mean to Hire for Service" (Sileno, Apollo), "Girls Are Known to Mischief Prone" (Mysis), "Pray, Goody" (Apollo), "Mamma, How Can You Be So Ill-Natured?" (Mysis, Nysa, Daphne, Sileno), "Shall a Paltry Clown" (Midas), "Jupiter Wenches and Drinks" (Pan), "All Around the Maypole" (Damaetas), "Sure I Shall Run with Vexation Distracted" (Mysis), "He's as Tight a Lad to See" (Daphne), "Lovely Nymph" (Apollo), "My Minnikin Miss" (Daphne, Nysa), "O, What Pleasures Will Abound" (Midas), "Ne'er Will I Be Left in the Lurch" (Nysa), "If into Your Hen-Yard" (Midas), "In These Greasy Old Tatters" (Nysa), "Master Pol" (Midas, Pan, Mysis), "If a Rival Thy Character Draw" (Sileno, Damaetas), "Mother, Sure You Never" (Daphne, Nysa, Mysis, Sileno, Damaetas), "What the Devil's Here to Do?"/"I'm Given to Understand" (Midas), "Now I'm Seated" (Midas), "A Plague on Your Pother" (Pan), Apollo's Competition Song: "Ah! Happy Hours" (Apollo), "See, Triumphant Sits the Bard" (Chorus), "Dunce, I Did But Sham" (Apollo), Finale: "Thou a Billingsgate Quean" (Apollo), &c.

Alongside repeated performances of homegrown pieces such as *The Padlock*, *The Waterman*, and *Midas*, the London stage of the later eighteenth century also featured a very large number of musicals that were "taken from the French." This was in no way surprising, for during the second half of the eighteenth century the vast bulk of the most substantial musicals that were produced in Europe did indeed come out of the French theater. The Italian-style versus French-style battle that had raged in the comic-opera world in the Paris of the 1750s had resolved itself, and it had resolved itself not by one kind of show ousting the other from the stage, but by each type going its own way. And while the Italian-style comic opera ended up finding its apotheosis in the hallows of the world's opera houses and in the hands of musicians such as Mozart and Rossini, the French-style opéra-comique made itself a separate and barely less important existence in the hands of a group of solidly French musicians whose names would be pinned to a long series of musical-theater hits during the years up to the Revolution.

Ironically enough, the first of these musicians to make a mark was actually an Italian, Egidio Duni (1709–1775), whose *Le Caprice amoureux, ou Ninette à la cour*, a pasticcio burlesque, to a text by Favart, of a successful Italian comic opera by Ciampi and Goldoni, was a considerable hit in 1755 Paris. Duni went on to further successes, composing rather than collecting scores for such varied pieces as Favart's *Le Peintre amoureux de son modèle* (1757), his rustic story of a long-lost heroine rescued from among *Les Moissoneurs* (1768), and the remade Chaucerian fantasy *Le Fée Urgèle* (1765), but more considerable works of this kind from more considerable musicians soon followed, and, as the years went on, the opéra-comique began effectively to establish itself as the most substantial and appreciable kind of musical play yet to have been seen on the world's stages.

The most prominent among the musicians whose work made this period of French opéra-comique so much more enterprising than the earlier scissors-and-paste one had been were André Danican Philidor (1726–1795), Pierre Alexandre Monsigny (1729–1817), and André Ernest

Tom Jones: A happy ending to a picaresque opéra-comique. After many wenchful adventures on the roads of southern England, Tom Jones finally gets his Sophia.

Grétry (1741–1813). They were musicians who worked in an altogether more classical idiom than that used by the likes of the cheerfully popular-songmaking Dibdin, and, as a result, even if the libretti which they set often varied little in subject and in style from the British ones, their comic operas had an entirely more classically "operatic" ring to them than such lively little pieces as *The Waterman* or *Midas*.

Philidor, after making a gentle entry into the field with an arranged score for a version of *The Devil to Pay*, had his first notable success as a theater composer with the one-act opéra-comique *Blaise le savetier* in 1759, and he then went on to turn out such successful musicals as *Le Maréchal Ferrant* (1761), the fairy-tale about what happened to *Le Bûcheron* (1763) when he got his three wishes granted, and a particularly well-received version of Henry Fielding's picaresque English novel *Tom Jones* (1765). Monsigny made his début in the same year as Philidor, and in the next two decades he turned out the music for a long run of opéras-comiques, including the little rustic *Rose et Colas* (1764) and, his best-known work, the story of the soldier who thinks he's lost his girl, so admits almost fatally to being *Le Déserteur* (1769).

Grétry did not make his mark until nearly a decade later than the other two but, after the production of his noble-savage parody *Le Huron* in 1768, he more than made up for lost time, turning out during the rest of his career some fifty opéras-comiques of all styles and flavors, from the Beauty-and-the-Beastly comédie-ballet *Zémire et Azor* (1771) to the modern comedy of *Les Fausses Apparences* (1778), the rustic *L'Épreuve villageoise* (1783), the horrid tale of the uxorious *Raoul Barbe-Bleue* (1789) and, above all, the romantic little history built around the episode of the rescue of *Richard Coeur-de-Lion* (1784) from the castle of Linz by the minstrel Blondel.

RICHARD COEUR-DE-LION, an opéra-comique in 3 acts by Michel Sedaine. Music by André Ernest Grétry. Produced at the Théâtre-Italien, Paris, 21 October 1784.

Characters: Richard king of England, Blondel, Le Sénéchal, Florestan, Guillot, Williams, Antonio, Marguerite countess of Artois, Laurette Williams, Béatrix, &c.

Plot: Blondel has come to Austria disguised as a blind musician and discovered that King Richard is imprisoned in the castle of Linz. When Florestan, the governor of the castle, sends a love-letter to a Welsh lass who lives nearby, the minstrel—who, by his singing, has let his king know of his presence—concocts a plot. He lets himself be captured and, brought before the governor, he tells him that little Miss Williams will meet him at the rustic wedding party being held that night at her father's house. When the governor comes for what he hopes is an amorous rendezvous, he is taken prisoner, his castle is attacked by the bodyguard of the Countess of Anjou, and Richard is released and restored to that lady's fond embraces.

Songs: "Chantons, chantons!" (chorus), "La danse n'est pas ce que j'aime" (Antonio), "O, Richard! ô, mon roi!" (Blondel), "C'est de la part du gouverneur" (Blondel, Williams, Guillot, Laurette), "Je crains de lui parler la nuit" (Laurette), "Un bandeau couvre les yeux" (Blondel, Laurette), "Que le sultan Saladin" (Blondel), "Si l'univers entier m'oublie" (Richard), "Une fièvre brulante" (Blondel, Richard), "Sais-tu, connais-tu?" (Blondel, soldiers), Finale Act 2: "Pour le peu que tu m'as dit," "Il faut, il faut, il faut que je lui parle" (Blondel, servants), "Oui, chevaliers, oui, ce rempart" (Blondel, Marguerite, knights), "Le gouverneur, après la danse" (Williams, Laurette, Blondel, servants), "Et zig, et zog" (A peasant), Finale Act 3: "Dieu! quelle trahison!"/"C'est l'amitié fidèle."

A good number of these new-style, new-weight opéras-comiques were seen outside France following their hometown successes, but they were seen only rarely in their original and unspoiled state. In the usual manner of these non-copyright times, they were grossly ill-treated by foreign managers and performers, arriving almost invariably on other stages and in other tongues in a well and truly botched state. Their libretti were localized and peppered with hometown jokes, their musical part was chopped up and about and stuck full of local songs—old and new—with a popular ring, and sometimes, indeed, the entire score of the French composer was simply turfed out and replaced by home-made numbers that were of quite a different level of ambition and musical quality. Britain, for example, clearly had no taste for musicals that mixed this kind of story with that kind of music, and the part they preferred to retain "from the French" was not the elegant music of Messieurs Philidor, Monsigny, and Grétry, but the more like-home-style texts. The German-language theater also helped itself to just as much of the French shows as it pleased, and some of the most popular Singspiele of the day, such as Weisse and Hiller's *Die Jagd* (1770), were, as the same team's hit version of *The Devil to Pay* had been, simply remusicked versions of the most popular shows from abroad. And so, in this way, the libretti of such writers as Favart or the most effective of his successors, *Richard Coeur-de-Lion* librettist Michel Sedaine (1719–1797), generally got a better showing beyond their home shores, in variously made-over versions, than did the work of their musicians. Except, of course, that the French composers' scores were heartily pillaged to provide numbers for the pasticcio musicals of those same other countries!

THE RISE OF THE ROMANTIC

In the decades after the Revolution, the character of the musical theater in France began to change once again, and the kind of show that the early part of the nineteenth century called opéra-comique was one that, reflecting the escapist needs and moods of those uncertain times, more and more renounced the jolly intrigues and ingenuous lovemaking that had been the subject-matter for the musicals of the Favartian years in favor of stories featuring the dramatic, the swashbuckling, the highly colored, the exotic, and the romantic. The music that accompanied these tales—music from the pens of musicians who were often equally adept at turning out scores for the grandiose serious operas of the day—was fitted to the temper of these libretti, and by the time the nineteenth century moved towards its third decade the opéra-comique could be seen to have become a much more richly romantic and musically full-blooded affair. But this kind of opéra-comique proved to be internationally the most successful to have so far come out of France, and the works of such of its outstanding writers as librettist Eugène Scribe (1791–1861) and composers Adrien Boïeldieu (1775–1834), Daniel Auber (1782– 1871), Adolphe Adam (1802–856), and Ferdinand Hérold (1791–1833) spread themselves throughout the theatrical world as the modern opéra-comique established itself as one of the favorite musical-theater entertainments of its time—and, this time, no one dumped their music in favor of the latest thing in popular ballads or sea shanties.

The biggest successes in this romantic opéra-comique style began to appear in the 1820s, and one of the earliest and the biggest was the chef d'oeuvre of Boïeldieu, who had already triumphed with such light-hearted pieces as the delightfully sparkling and wholly comical piece of royal teasing that is *Jean de Paris* (1812), and who, in 1825, turned out the thoroughly romantic history of *La Dame blanche*. This tale of a long-lost heir, a greedy steward, and an apparently haunted Scottish castle provoked memories of the early British hit *The Haunted Tower*, but Scribe's text was illustrated by the French composer with an original score rather than the earlier show's pasticcio selection, and the result was one of the classic romantic musicals of the opéra-comique stage.

Eugène Scribe also co-provided the text for another 1825 hit in *Le Maçon*, a rocambolesque, dramatic tale of a Parisian workman whisked away from his wedding night by mysterious Turks in order fatally to wall up an unhappy odalisque and the Frenchman who would carry her off from their embassy. The music for this piece was the work of Auber, and he would go on not only to turn out an important grand opera in *La Muette de Portici*, but to combine with Scribe on a series of the most successful opéras-comiques of the period: the swaggering tale of the bandit known as *Fra Diavolo* (1830), with its expert and even surprising mixture of the vicious and the farcical, the lavishly féerique story of *Le Cheval de bronze* (1835), the swirling, glamorous tale of the convent lady who hides herself behind *Le Domino noir* (1837), and the courtly history of *Les Diamants de la couronne* (1841).

Adolphe Adam, best known nowadays as the composer of the music to the ballet *Giselle*, also scored in tandem with Scribe on the pretty, countrified *Le Châlet* (1834). However, he found his most far-flung success with the romantic tale and tenorious music of *Le Postillon de Longjumeau* (1836), the story of a top-D singing coachman who abandons his country bride to go off to the big city and become a fashionable opera star. Ferdinand Hérold had two first-class hits with the dramatic tale of the horrid pirate called *Zampa* (1831), whose lusts are curtailed by a statue no less vengeful than Don Giovanni's Commendatore, and the dungeons and duels piece *Le Pré aux clercs* (1832), and Donizetti followed his classic Italian *L'Elisir d'amore* with the triumphant French *La Fille du régiment* (1840), before the distinction between opéra-comique and opéra began taking on that shadowy substance that would, in years to come, end with the opéra-comique darkening into thoroughly operatic modes with the advent of such pieces as *Mignon*, *Faust*, and *Carmen*.

FRA DIAVOLO, or L'Hôtellerie de Terracina, an opéra-comique in 3 acts by Eugène Scribe. Music by Daniel Auber. Produced at the Opéra-Comique, Paris, 28 January 1830.

Characters: Marquis de San Marco (otherwise Fra Diavolo), Lord Cokbourg, Lady Paméla Cokbourg, Lorenzo, Mathéo, Zerline, Giacomo, Beppo, &c.

Plot: The merciless bandit known as Fra Diavolo is tracking the wealthy English Lord and Lady Cokbourg through Italy with intent to rob, and if necessary kill, but his plans come unstuck at an inn in Terracina when lovesick Lorenzo, the local carabinier brigadier, slaughters his brigand band;

when Fra Diavolo and his lieutenants get stuck in a cupboard while a pretty maidservant undresses in front of the door that leads to the travellers' room and their jewels; and when, after moments both farcical and fearsome, misunderstandings and mayhem, the highwayman is himself finally led into a trap, thanks to the incompetence of his newest recruit and the energies of Lorenzo.

Songs: "En bons militaires" (chorus), Nocturne: "Cher Lorenzo, conservons l'espérance" (Lorenzo, Zerline), "Au secours, au secours" (Milord, Milady), "Je voulais bien, je voulais bien" (Milord), "Un landau qui s'arrête" (Mathéo, Milord, Milady, Zerline, Diavolo), "Voyez sur cette roche" (Zerline), "Le gondolier fidèle" (Diavolo, Milady), "Combien moi, j'aimais la musique" (Milord, Milady, Diavolo), Finale Act 1: "Victoire! Victoire!," "Allons, ma femme" (Milord, Milady, Zerline), "Agnès, la jouvencelle" (Diavolo), "Oui, c'est demain" (Zerline), Finale Act 2: "N'était-il pas prudent?," "Je vois marcher sous mes bannières"/"Nous ne demandons rien aux belles"/"Il faut se hâter, le temps presse" (Diavolo), "C'est aujourd'hui Pâques fleuries" (chorus), "Pour toujours, disait-elle" (Lorenzo), "Allons, allons" (ensemble), Finale Act 3: "Grands dieux!"

The English- and German-language stages took up the fashion for the romantic musical play enthusiastically, and in the mid-1800s Britain welcomed a small group of "romantic operas," by a small group of composers, which quickly became the most popular musical shows that that country had ever produced. Irishman Michael Balfe, who like Auber and others of the Continental composers of opéra-comique had proven himself in the field of grand opera, was responsible for two successful English remakes of French texts, *The Rose of Castille* (1857) and *Satanella* (1858), but he made easily his most memorable success of all with his score to the long-lost heiress tale of *The Bohemian Girl* (1843) and its megahit soprano song "I Dreamt That I Dwelt in Marble Halls." A second Irishman, Vincent Wallace (1814–1865), was responsible for the other major hit show of the period when he turned out yet another variation on a French text, the celebrated drama of *Don César de Bazan*, with its plot based on a blindfold marriage of convenience, under the title *Maritana* (1845). *Maritana* had its hit numbers too— "Ah! Let Me Like a Soldier Fall" and "Scenes That Are Brightest" rendered nothing to Balfe's best songs in enduring popularity—and, like Balfe, Wallace also succeeded in following up his biggest triumph with another popular piece: the romantic fantasy of the Rhinemaiden *Lurline* (1860) and her love for mortal man. Julius Benedict's musicalization of the famous Dion Boucicault play *The Colleen Bawn* as *The Lily of Killarney* (1862), John Barnett's fairy-tale *The Mountain Sylph* (1834), Edward Loder's retelling of the tale of *Giselle* as *The Night Dancers* (1846), and George Macfarren's version of the *Robin Hood* story (1860) were among other successes on an English opera stage where *The Bohemian Girl*, which went on to find more success in lands and languages further afield than any British musical to date, and *Maritana* would remain hardy annuals for many, many years.

THE BOHEMIAN GIRL, an opera in 4 acts by Alfred Bunn, based on the ballet-pantomime *La Gipsy* by J. H. Vernoy de Saint-Georges. Music by Michael Balfe. Produced at the Theatre Royal, Drury Lane, London, 27 November 1843.

Characters: Thaddeus, Arline, Gipsy Queen, Arnheim, Florestein, Devilshoof, &c.

Plot: The child Arline, daughter of Arnheim, the Austrian governor of Pressburg, is stolen by gipsies in a revengeful raid on her father. Among those gipsies is Thaddeus, a noble Polish exile, who, as she grows to adulthood, falls in love with the "gipsy" girl. The jealous Queen of the Romany band contrives to have Arline arrested by the governor on a charge of theft, but he recognizes his long-lost child from an old scar and, returned to her rightful place, Arline is able to wed the reinstated Thaddeus.

Songs: "Up with the Banner" (chorus), "A Soldier's Life" (Arnheim), Hunters' Chorus: "Away to the Hill and Glen," "'Tis Sad to Leave Your Fatherland"/"Without Friends" (Thaddeus), "In the Gipsy's Life You May Read" (chorus), "Comrade, Your Hand" (Devilshoof, Thaddeus), "Is No Succour Near at Hand?" (Florestein), Waltz, Finale Act 1: "Down With the Daring Slave," "Silence! Silence—the Lady Moon" (chorus), "There's a Deed to Do Whose Gains" (Devilshoof), Gipsy Chorus, "I Dreamt That I Dwelt in Marble Halls" (Arline), "The Wound upon Thine Arm" (Thaddeus, Arline), "Listen, While I Relate"/"Happy and Light of Heart" (Arline &c.), "In the Gipsies' Life" (chorus), "This Is Thy Deed—Seek Not to Assuage" (Queen, Devilshoof), "Come with the Gipsy Bride" (Arline), Fair Chorus, "From the Valleys and Hills" (Arline, Queen, Thaddeus, Devilshoof), Gipsy March, "The Heart Bow'd Down" (Arnheim), Finale Act 2: "Hold! Hold!," "When Other Lips and Other Hearts" (Thaddeus), "Through the World Wilt Thou Fly" (Thaddeus, Arline, Devilshoof), Finale Act 3: "Welcome the Present," "To Shame and Feeling Dead" (Arnheim, Florestein, Arline, Thaddeus, Queen), "When the Fair Land of Poland" (Thaddeus), "Let Not the Heart for Sorrows Grieve" (Arnheim, Arline, Thaddeus), "Oh! What Full Delight" (Arline).

In Central Europe, too, the fashion for the thoroughly composed romantic comic opera took over, and the hits of the late 1700s, such as the comically complex Romeo and Juliet–style tale of the children of a mutually mistrusting *Doktor und Apotheker* (1786), the "dramma giocoso" *Una cosa rara* (1786), with a text by Mozart's librettist Da Ponte and music by the Spanish composer Martin y Soler (1754–1810), or the jolly Singspiel goings-on around *Der Dorfbarbier* (1796), were succeeded by the romantic works of such as Carl Maria von Weber, on the one hand, and, on the other, by komische Opern from Albert Lortzing (1803–1851)—*Zar und Zimmermann* (1839), with its story of Russian royalty disguised as a shipyard-worker and officialdom's clumsy failure to identify him, and *Der Wildschütz* (1842), a tale of a merry poacher mixed up in the amorous intrigues of the aristocracy—by Friedrich von Flotow's enduring marriage-market musical, *Martha* (1847), and by Otto Nicolai's musicalization of Shakespeare, *Die lustigen Weiber von Windsor* (1849).

However, while the romantic, operatic style of musical triumphed throughout Europe, the popular musical plays and burlesques did not fade away. On the contrary, the vaudeville, now developed from a rather low comedy with signature musical refrains into a much more sophisticated comedy with songs, was highly popular on Parisian stages, and the various forms of theater with songs had reached a memorable high point in Austria, where a veritable flood of Possen, Zauberspiele, and the other local variants on the play-with-songs theme from the hands of such authors as Ferdinand Raimund (1790–1836) (*Das Mädchen aus den Feenwelt*, 1826; *Alpenkönig und Menschenfeind*, 1828) and Johann Nestroy (1801–1862) (*Der bose Geist Lumpacivagabundus*, 1833; *Das Mädel aus der Vorstadt*, 1841; *Einen Jux will er sich machen*, 1842) and a merry mass of up-to-date burlesques crowded onto the Viennese stage.

In Britain, where the musical play or "comic opera" of the kind that Dibdin and his contemporaries had produced had now rather faded away, the extravaganza and burlesque tradition had risen to its greatest popularity ever, as writers such as James R. Planché (1796–880), the brothers William (1826–1870) and Robert Brough (1828–1860), and Francis Talfourd (1827–1862) turned out regular musical-theater versions of a long list of favorite fairy stories and mythological subjects, or took whimsical pot-shots at pieces from the classic or modern theater repertoire to the accompaniment of pasticcio scores which were availing themselves for their tunes a little less of folksongs and rather more of the up-to-date melodies of the opéra-comique stage.

So, as the mid-point of the nineteenth century hove to, all three of the principal musical-theater centers of Europe—and that meant, at this time, of the world—were thriving on a double diet of popular and usually pasticcio musical comedy and burlesque on the one hand, and romantic, operatic musical plays on the other. If the popular pieces, by and large, each found their popularity in their own country, or at least in the language of their original, the more substantial musical pieces often proved—in one version or another—internationally successful, and many of them were played and imitated in countries and languages both near (Hungarian, Spanish) and sometimes far from their birthplaces and tongues. But soon that would change. Soon that gap between the two kinds of entertainment would be filled by a new brand of musical theater—one which had all the musical substance of the operatic shows, yet all the lively spirit and style of the popular entertainments. This new kind of entertainment had its birth in France, and that naturally meant that it was given a French sobriquet. That sobriquet was "opéra-bouffe."

SOME NOTABLE MUSICALS 1700–1849

1708   PRUNELLA (pasticcio/Richard Estcourt) Theatre Royal, Drury Lane, London, 23 February

1718   IL MARITO GIOGATORE [The gambling husband] (Fernando Orlandini/Antonio Salvi) Teatro San Angelo, Venice, 24 December

1728   THE BEGGAR'S OPERA (arr. Johann Christoph Pepusch/John Gay) Lincoln's Inn Fields Theatre, London, 29 January

1731   THE DEVIL TO PAY, or The Wives Metamorphos'd (pasticcio/Charles Coffey) Theatre Royal, Drury Lane, London, 17 August

1733   THE OPERA OF OPERAS (Thomas Arne/Henry Fielding) Theatre Royal, Haymarket, London, 31 May
LA SERVA PADRONA [The mistress who is a maidservant] (Giovanni Battista Pergolesi/Gennaro Antonio Federico) Teatro San Bartolommeo, Naples, 28 August

1737   THE DRAGON OF WANTLEY (John Frederick Lampe/Henry Carey) Theatre Royal, Covent Garden, London, 6 November

1741   LA CHERCHEUSE D'ESPRIT [She's looking for wits] (pasticcio/Charles Favart) Théâtre de la Foire Saint-Germain, Paris, 20 February

?1750   IL FILOSOFO DI CAMPAGNA [The country philosopher] (Antonio Galuppi/Carlo Goldoni) Milan, and Teatro San Samuele, Venice, 26 October 1854

1752   DER TEUFEL IST LOS, oder Die verwandelten Weiber [The Devil's abroad, or The changed women] (Johann Hiller/Christian Felix Weisse) Leipzig, 6 October

          LE DEVIN DU VILLAGE [The village sage] (Jean-Jacques Rousseau) Fontainebleau, 18 October

1753   LES TROQUEURS [The tricksters] (Antoine Dauvergne/Jean-Joseph Vadé) Opéra-Comique, Paris, 30 July

1755   LE CAPRICE AMOUREUX, ou Ninette à la cour [Love's fancies, or Ninette at court] (arr. Egidio Duni/Charles Favart) Comédie-Italienne, Paris, 12 February

1759   BLAISE LE SAVETIER [Blaise, the shoemaker] (André Danican Philidor/Michel Sedaine) Opéra-Comique, Paris, 9 March

1760   LA BUONA FIGLIOLA [The good little girl] (Nicola Piccini/Carlo Goldoni) Teatro delle Dame, Rome, 6 February

          THOMAS AND SALLY, or The Sailor's Return (Thomas Arne/Issac Bickerstaff) Theatre Royal, Covent Garden, London, 28 November

1761   LES TROIS SULTANES, ou Soliman II [The three Sultanas, or King Soliman II] (Gilbert/Charles Favart) Théâtre-Italien, Paris, 9 April

          LE MARÉCHAL FERRANT (André Danican Philidor/Antoine François Quétant) Opéra-Comique, Paris, 22 August

          LE CADI DUPÉ [The tricked cadi] (Christoph Willibald Gluck/Pierre René Lemonnier) Burgtheater, Vienna, December

1762   MIDAS (pasticcio/Kane O'Hara) Crow Street Theatre, Dublin, 22 January

          LOVE IN A VILLAGE (comp./arr. Thomas Arne/Isaac Bickerstaff) Theatre Royal, Covent Garden, London, 8 December

1763   LE BÛCHERON, ou Les Trois Souhaits [The woodcutter, or Three wishes] (André Danican Philidor/Jean-François Guichard, Castet) Comédie-Italienne, Paris, 28 February

1765   TOM JONES (André Danican Philidor/Antoine Poinsinet) Comédie-Italienne, Paris, 27 February

1765   LA FÉE URGÈLE, ou Ce qui plaît aux dames [The fairy Urgèle, or What women want] (Egidio Duni/Charles Favart) Fontainebleau, 26 October

1768   LES MOISSONEURS [The harvesters] (Egidio Duni/Charles Favart) Comédie-Italienne, Paris, 27 January

          LIONEL AND CLARISSA (Charles Dibdin/Isaac Bickerstaff) Theatre Royal, Covent Garden, London, 25 February

          LE HURON [The huron] (André Grétry/Jean-François Marmontel) Comédie-Italienne, Paris, 20 August

          THE PADLOCK (Charles Dibdin/Isaac Bickerstaff) Theatre Royal, Drury Lane, London, 3 October

1769 LE DÉSERTEUR [The army deserter] (Pierre Monsigny/Michel Sedaine) Comédie Italienne, Paris, 6 March

1770 DIE JAGD [The hunt] (Johann Hiller/Christian Felix Weisse) Weimar, 29 January

1771 ZÉMIRE ET AZOR (André Grétry/Jean-François Marmontel) Fontainebleau, 9 November

1774 THE WATERMAN, or The First of August (Charles Dibdin) Little Theatre, Haymarket, London, 8 August

1775 THE DUENNA, or The Double Elopement (comp./arr. Thomas Linley, Thomas Linley jr./Richard Brinsley Sheridan) Theatre Royal, Covent Garden, London, 21 November

1777 THE QUAKER (Charles Dibdin) Theatre Royal, Drury Lane, London, 7 October

1778 LES FAUSSES APPARENCES, ou L'Amant jaloux [Things aren't what they seem, or The jealous lover] (André Grétry/Thomas d'Hèle) Versailles, 20 November

1782 DIE ENTFÜHRUNG AUS DEM SERAIL [The rape from the harem] (Wolfgang Amadeus Mozart/Christoph Friedrich Bretzner) Burgtheater, Vienna, 16 July
      IL BARBIERE DI SIVIGLIA, ovvero La precautzione inutile [The barber of Seville, or Useless precautions] (Giovanni Paisiello/Giuseppe Petrosellini) St Petersburg, 26 September
      THE CASTLE OF ANDALUSIA (comp./arr. Samuel Arnold/John O'Keeffe) Theatre Royal, Covent Garden, London, 2 November
      ROSINA (William Shield/adapted by Frances Brooke) Theatre Royal, Covent Garden, London, 31 December

1783 THE POOR SOLDIER (William Shield/John O'Keeffe) Theatre Royal, Covent Garden, London, 4 November

1784 L'ÉPREUVE VILLAGEOISE [The country trial] (aka *Théodore et Paulin*) (André Grétry/Pierre Jean Baptiste Chouard Desforges) Versailles, 5 March
      RICHARD COEUR-DE-LION [Richard the Lionheart] (André Grétry/Michel Sedaine) Théâtre-Italien, Paris, 21 October

1786 DER SCHAUSPIELDIREKTOR [The theater director] (Wolfgang Mozart/Gottlieb Stephanie] Schönbrunn, Vienna, 7 February
      NINA, ou La Folle par amour [Nina, or The maid maddened by love] (Nicolas Dalayrac/Benoît Joseph Marsollier) Comédie-Italienne, Paris, 15 May
      DOKTOR UND APOTHEKER [Doctor and apothecary] (Karl Ditters von Dittersdorf/Gottlieb Stephanie] Kärntnertor-Theater, Vienna, 11 July
      UNA COSA RARA, o sia Bellezza ed onestà [Something rare, or Beauty and honesty] (Martin y Soler/Lorenzo Da Ponte) Burgtheater, Vienna, 17 November

1789 RAOUL BARBE-BLEUE (André Grétry/Michel Sedaine) Comédie-Italienne, Paris, 2 March
      THE HAUNTED TOWER (Stephen Storace/James Cobb) Theatre Royal, Drury Lane, London, 24 November

1790 NO SONG, NO SUPPER (comp./arr. Stephen Storace/Prince Hoare) Theatre Royal, Drury Lane, London, 16 April

1791 THE SIEGE OF BELGRADE (Stephen Storace/James Cobb) Theatre Royal, Drury Lane, London, 1 January

1792   IL MATRIMÒNIO SEGRETO [The secret marriage] (Domenico Cimarosa/Bertati) Burgtheater, Vienna, 7 February

LES VISTANDINES (François Devienne/Louis Benoît Picard) Théâtre Feydeau, Paris, 7 July

1796   DER DORFBARBIER [The village barber] (Johann Schenck/Joseph Weidmann) Burgtheater, Vienna, 30 October

1802   UNE FOLIE [A crazy thing] (Etienne Nicolas Méhul/Jean Nicolas Bouilly) Opéra-Comique, Paris, 5 April

1803   MA TANTE AURORE, ou Le Roman impromptu [Auntie Aurora, or The off-the-cuff romance] (Adrien Boïeldieu/Charles de Longchamps) Opéra-Comique, Paris, 13 January

1808   LES VOITURES VERSÉES [The crashed-up coaches] (Adrien Boïeldieu/Emanuel Mercier-Dupaty) St Petersburg, 26 April

1810   BOMBASTES FURIOSO (pasticcio/William Barnes Rhodes) Haymarket Theatre, London, 7 August

1811   HAMLET TRAVESTIE (pasticcio/John Poole) New Theatre, London, 24 January

1812   JEAN DE PARIS (Adrien Boïeldieu/C. Godard d'Aucour de Saint-Just) Opéra-Comique, Paris, 1 April

1817   DON GIOVANNI, or A Spectre on Horseback (pasticcio/Thomas Dibdin) Royal Circus and Surrey Theatre, London, 12 May

1821   LE MAÎTRE DE CHAPELLE, ou Le Souper imprévu [The church musician, or The unexpected supper] (Ferdinando Paër/Sophie Gay) Opéra-Comique, Paris, 29 March

1823   CLARI, or The Maid of Milan (Henry Bishop/John Howard Payne and/or James Robinson Planché) Theatre Royal, Covent Garden, London, 8 May

1825   LE MAÇON [The mason] (Daniel Auber/Eugène Scribe) Opéra-Comique, Paris, 3 May

LA DAME BLANCHE [The white lady] (Adrien Boïeldieu/Eugène Scribe) Opéra-Comique, Paris, 10 December

1826   DAS MÄDCHEN AUS DEN FEENWELT, oder Bauer als Millionär [The girl from fairyland, or The millionaire peasant] (Josef Drechsler/Ferdinand Raimund) Theater in der Leopoldstadt, Vienna, 10 November

1828   ALPENKÖNIG UND MENSCHENFEIND [Mountain-king and misanthropist] (Wenzel Müller/Ferdinand Raimund) Theater in der Leopoldstadt, Vienna, 17 October

1829   OTHELLERL, DER LUSTIGE MOHR VON WIEN, oder Die geheilte Eifersucht [Little Othello, the merry moor of Venice, or Jealousy cured] (Adolf Müller/Karl Meisl) Theater an der Wien, Vienna, 6 June

1830   FRA DIAVOLO, ou L'Hôtellerie de Terracine [Fra Diavolo, or The inn at Terracina] (Daniel Auber/Eugène Scribe) Opéra-Comique, Paris, 28 January

1831   OLYMPIC REVELS, or Prometheus and Pandora (pasticcio/John R. Planché, Charles Dance) Olympic Theatre, London, 3 January

ZAMPA, ou La Fiancée de marbre [Zampa, or The marble bride] (Ferdinand Hérold/A. H. J. Mélesville) Opéra-Comique, Paris, 3 May

1832   ZAMPERL DER TAGDIEB, oder Die Braut von Gips [Little Zampa, the thief of light] (Adolf Müller/Johann Nestroy) Theater an der Wien, Vienna, 22 June

LE PRÉ AUX CLERCS (Ferdinand Hérold/François A. E. de Planard) Opéra-Comique, Paris, 15 December

1833   DER BOSE GEIST LUMPACIVAGABUNDUS [The wicked spirit Lumpacivagabundus] (Adolf Müller/Johann Nestroy) Theater an der Wien, Vienna, 11 April

ROBERT DER TEUXEL (Adolf Müller/Johann Nestroy) Theater an der Wien, Vienna, 9 October

1834   LE CHÂLET (Adolphe Adam/Eugène Scribe, A. H. J. Mélesville) Opéra-Comique, Paris, 25 Setpember

1835   LE CHEVAL DE BRONZE [The bronze horse] (Daniel Auber/Eugène Scribe) Opéra-Comique, Paris, 23 March

1836   LE POSTILLON DE LONGJUMEAU (Adolphe Adam/Adolphe de Leuven, Léon Lévy Brunswick) Opéra-Comique, Paris, 13 October

1837   LE DOMINO NOIR [The black mask] (Daniel Auber/Eugène Scribe) Opéra-Comique, Paris, 2 December

ZAR UND ZIMMERMANN, oder Die zwei Peter [Czar and carpenter, or The two Peters] (Albert Lortzing) Leipzig, 22 December

1840   LA FILLE DU RÉGIMENT [The daughter of the regiment] (Gaetano Donizetti/Jean-François Bayard, Jules Vernoy de Saint-Georges] Opéra-Comique, Paris, 2 February

1841   LES DIAMANTS DE LA COURONNE [The royal diamonds] (Daniel Auber/Eugène Scribe, Jules Vernoy de Saint-Georges) Opéra-Comique, Paris, 6 March

DAS MÄDEL AUS DER VORSTADT [The suburban girl] (Adolf Müller/Johann Nestroy) Theater an der Wien, Vienna, 24 November

1842   EINEN JUX WILL ER SICH MACHEN [He will have his joke] (Adolf Müller/Johann Nestroy) Theater in der Leopoldstadt, Vienna, 15 January

FORTUNIO, or The Seven Gifted Servants (pasticcio/James Robinson Planché) Theatre Royal, Drury Lane, London, 17 April

1843   THE BOHEMIAN GIRL (Michael Balfe/Alfred Bunn) Theatre Royal, Drury Lane, London, 27 November

THE FAIR ONE WITH THE GOLDEN LOCKS (pasticcio/James Robinson Planché) Theatre Royal, Haymarket, London, 26 December

DER WILDSCHÜTZ, oder Die Stimme der Natur [The poacher, or The voice of nature] (Albert Lortzing) Leipzig, 31 December

1845   LA BICHE AU BOIS [The fawn in the forest] (pasticcio/Théodore Cogniard, Hippolyte Cogniard) Théâtre de la Porte Saint-Martin, Paris, 29 March

UNDINE (Albert Lortzing) Magdeburg, 21 April

MARITANA (Vincent Wallace/Edward Fitzball) Theatre Royal, Drury Lane, London, 15 November

1846   DER WAFFENSCHMIED [The armourer] (Albert Lortzing) Theater an der Wien, Vienna, 31 May

THE INVISIBLE PRINCE, or The Island of Tranquil Delights (pasticcio/James Robinson Planché) Theatre Royal, Haymarket, London, 26 December

1848   DON QUICHOTTE ET SANCHO PANÇA [Don Quixote and Sancho Panza] (Hervé) Théâtre National, Paris, 5 March

LE VAL D'ANDORRE (Fromenthal Halévy/Jules Vernoy de Saint-Georges) Opéra-Comique, Paris, 11 November

MARTL, oder Der Portiunculatag in Schnabelhausen [Little Martha] (Franz von Suppé/Alois Berla) Theater an der Wien, Vienna, 16 December

CAMARALZAMAN AND BADOURA (pasticcio/Robert Brough, William Brough) Theatre Royal, Haymarket, London, 26 December

1849 DIE LUSTIGEN WEIBER VON WINDSOR [The merry wives of Windsor] (Otto Nicolai/Hermann Salomon Mosenthal) Opernhaus, Berlin, 9 March

*O*péra-bouffe came of age in the year 1858. It had effectively been born some years before that, but this new kind of musical had taken a number of years to grow to its majority, hampered, as it were, by doing its growing up on the wrong side of the tracks and under the severely inhibiting eye of the French legal system.

Theaters in mid-nineteenth-century France were subject to strict licensing regulations. Not only were their numbers limited, but the kind of show that could be played in each house was rigidly and precisely defined by the law. This created a very particular situation insofar as the musical theater in Paris was concerned, for although several of the city's eight secondary theaters were permitted to play various kinds of comedies with patchwork songs, or burlesques with similarly pasticcio scores, the effect of these controls was to give a virtual monopoly on the production of original, full-length musical plays to the Opéra-Comique. It was, however, permitted under a lesser, concert type of license to play original, two-handed musical sketches in what passed for concert rooms rather than genuine theaters, and it was in this form, and under these restrictions, that the opérette-bouffe came into being.

The real name of the man who, single-handed, first manufactured, produced, and popularized this type of entertainment was Florimond Ronger (1825–1892), but he worked—whether as composer, musician, chef d'orchestre, singer, comic actor, director, or producer, or sometimes all these things at once—under the name Hervé. And the show with which he launched both his own career and the budding opérette-bouffe tradition was an extravagantly comical little "tableau grotesque" depicting his pixilated versions of the famous characters of *Don Quichotte et Sancho Pança* (1848)—and, of course, given the restrictions, no one else. Originally written as an occasional piece for a suburban benefit program, Hervé's super-silly slice of over-the-edge *Don Quixote* was subsequently taken up in several regular Paris theaters, but when he attempted to follow it up with another little piece, produced this time in the wholly official purlieus of the "Comédie-Français No. 2," the Théâtre de l'Odéon, the bully boys of the Opéra-Comique (who'd had their own chance to produce it, and tergiversated) jumped jealously in and had the show banned. But Hervé persisted, and finally he won through. In 1854, thanks to friends in extremely high places, he was given official permission to open his own little concert room-cum-theater. And there, at this tiny Folies-Concertantes (soon dollied up and renamed the Folies-Nouvelles), he launched a whole series of the crazy little burlesque musicals that were his speciality. Pieces built on the most beautifully bizarre ideas, with crazy characters, dippy, incoherent dialogue, and plots that ranged from the surreal to the stupefying, the whole decorated with that bristling, melodious, and eminently singable—not to say whistleable—kind of music that would soon characterize the opéra-bouffe genre to the whole world. And the public came.

Hervé had not been eighteen months in business when another musician, who'd had equally little joy out of the gentlemen at the Opéra-Comique, followed his example and got the go-ahead to set up his own independent theater. German-born Jacques Offenbach (1819–1880) and his libretto-writing colleagues jumped happily on that bouffe bandwagon of which Hervé had so thoroughly cut the brake-cable, and the three- or four-part programs that were played nightly at the composer's Théâtre des Bouffes-Parisiens included, alongside the less way-out rustic romances, comic scenas, and wordless pantomimes, some splendidly loopy little musicals in the new bouffe manner. Musicals which, thanks to a relaxing of the law, now sported not two but three characters. As well as some of the most deliciously light-footed, laughing music ever to have been heard in a theater: music which sparkled with the dance rhythms of court and country and such up-to-date outrageries as the can-can, music which, while glitteringly melodious, fell easily into voices of charm and character rather than the booming vocalizing of the Opéra, music which, while indubitably "well-written" in both its soli and its ensemble work, had all the catch and appeal of the popular song.

The Folies-Nouvelles and the Bouffes-Parisiens prospered alongside each other for a little over two years, with the authors and producers inventing all kinds of hilarious means of out-witting the legislation on cast numbers through ingenious and sometimes outrageous plotting (characters were temporarily "killed"; two halves of a camel conversed though it was "one" character; a "mute" character who'd had his tongue cut out still grunted a vocal line!) in a way that only added to the far-fetched humor of the entertainment, until finally the restrictions in question were, first, eased further, and then abolished. Now, at last, the tradition of musical theater which had already produced so many enjoyable and enjoyed entertainments—from the semi-autobiomusical *Le Compositeur toqué* of Hervé through such pieces as the comic duolog *Les Deux Aveugles*, the mad chinoiserie *Ba-ta-clan*, the mock banditland musical *Tromb-al-ca-zar*, and the madly medieval *Croquefer* of Offenbach—could finally develop into something more substantial. The opérette-bouffe could grow into the opéra-bouffe.

The show that marked the taking of this memorable step was produced at the Bouffes-Parisiens (a second, and more central, theater of that name to which Offenbach had quickly progressed following his first big successes) and, of course, it had a score by its manager. Hervé had temporarily missed the train, for, hacked down by the overwork involved in his hectic producing-writing-performing schedule at the Folies-Nouvelles, he'd suffered a breakdown and been forced to give up his theater. When that first opéra-bouffe, Offenbach's *Orphée aux enfers*, was produced, he was playing in one of his little opérettes, under someone else's management, at the Folies-Marigny, the theater which had formerly been the Bouffes-Parisiens and Offenbach's original smaller-scale home.

Orphée aux enfers was a piece thoroughly in the burlesque tradition, though it was scarcely as wild or as obviously incoherent in its bouffe improbabilities as had been some of the little musicals that Hervé and Offenbach had previously produced. The show took for its subject the famous Greek myth of the musician Orpheus and his tormented quest to Hell in search for his dead wife, and, most specifically, the version of that myth as retold in Calzabigi's libretto for Gluck's celebrated opera *Orfeo ed Euridice*, and treated it in a light-hearted, up-to-date style and tone, instead of with the usual operatic reverence. If this kind of a ridiculous remake of mythology seems a wholly harmless practice to us today, it wasn't considered so at the time. It was even considered blasphemous in some quarters to thus make fun of the "noble perfection" of the ancient world. Co-librettist Ludovic Halévy (1834–1908) kept his name off the bills in fear that his career in the diplomatic service would be harmed if he were known to be connected with such an irreverent exercise, and newspaper umbrage was taken at the writers' unseemly trivializing of the lofty, on behalf of both the classics and the opera. But audiences adored it. *Orphée aux enfers* was a triumph, and the adult, full-grown opéra-bouffe was well and truly launched.

ORPHÉE AUX ENFERS, an opéra-bouffon in 2 acts by Hector Crémieux (and Ludovic Halévy). Music by Jacques Offenbach. Produced at the Théâtre des Bouffes-Parisiens, Paris, 21 October 1858.

Characters: Aristée/Pluton, Jupiter, Orphée, John Styx, Mercure, Bacchus, Mars, Eurydice, Diane, L'Opinion Publique, Junon, Vénus, Cupidon, Minerve, &c.

Plot: Pluton, ruler of the dead, has been up from the nether regions on a nymph-hunt and, while trolling about the Ancient Greek city of Thebes disguised as an Arcadian shepherd, he's taken a taste for Eurydice, the dissatisfied wife of the local music teacher, Orphée. A bit of godly magic with an asp, and zap! the lady is dead and transported to Hades. She's happy, he's happy, and her husband is relieved to be rid of his flighty spouse. But alas! that ghastly busybody called Public Opinion gets wind of this latest bit of Theban marital affairing, and determines that Morality must triumph. She drags Orphée all the way up to Olympus to demand of Jupiter, King of the Gods, that he get Pluton to give his stolen wife back, and Jupiter, whose own sexual forays to earth are threatening to get Olympus a bad press, announces that he will go down to Hades and inspect the situation. When he finds the lady, he's decidedly taken with her, and is all prepared to set her up as a bit on the side for himself. However, even though he disposes in turn of the furious Public Opinion, the delighted Orphée, and a petulant Pluton (who is miffed at Jupiter's changing the myth's traditional ending), he finally decides that this troublesome female would be too much even for him, and so he hands her over to Bacchus to end her days as a Bacchante.

Songs: "La Femme dont le coeur rêve" (Eurydice), "Ah! c'est ainsi?" (Orphée, Eurydice), "Moi, je suis Aristée" (Aristée), "La mort m'apparaît souriante" (Eurydice), "Viens! c'est l'honneur qui t'appelle!" (L'Opinion Publique, Orphée), "Dormons, que notre somme" (Gods, Vénus, Cupidon, Jupiter), "Quand Diane descend dans la plaine" (Diane), "Aux armes! dieux et demi-dieux!"

(ensemble), "Pour séduire Alcmène la fière" (Minerve, Diane, Cupidon, Vénus, Pluton), Finale Act 1: "Il approche! il s'avance," "Quand j'étais roi de Béotie" (John Styx), "Il m'a semblé sur mon épaule" (Eurydice, Jupiter), "Vive le vin! Vive Pluton!" (chorus), "J'ai vu le dieu Bacchus" (Eurydice), Menuet et Galop infernale (ballet), Finale Act 3: "Ne regarde pas en arrière"/ "Bacchus! mon âme legère." Alternative and additional numbers include "Voici la douzième heure" (chorus), Ballet pastorale: "Ah! rien n'égale mon tourment" (Diane), "Eh hop! Eh hop! place à Mercure" (Mercure), Air en prose (Pluton), Couplets des regrets: "Personne encore!" (Eurydice), Septuor du Tribual: "Minos, Éaque et Rhadamante" (judges), Ronde des policemen: "Nez au vent" (chorus), Couplets des baisers: "Pour attirer du fond de sa retraite" (Cupidon), Petit ronde du bourdon: "Le beau bourdon" (chorus), Ballet des mouches, &c.

In the dozen years that followed the production of *Orphée aux enfers* a whole series of similarly sparkling, saucy, and glitteringly tuneful opéras-bouffes was produced on the stages of Paris, and from Paris they would set out round the theaters of Central Europe, the works of Offenbach leading the rout, creating both a sensation and a fashion in musical theater in such key theatrical cities as Vienna that was no less than those they had created at home.

The fashion and the sensation did not, however, occur overnight. And neither did Offenbach simply sling in his other variegated areas of writing and devote himself utterly and wholly to composing full-length burlesque operas. In the years after the production of *Orphée*, he not only continued to turn out a regular supply of the short pieces with which he had made his earlier success, and which still filled many a highly popular bill at the Bouffes-Parisiens, but even composed the score for a show mounted (unsuccessfully!) at the Opéra-Comique. And although the three most important full-length opéras-bouffes for which he did compose the scores, among a welter of other work, over the next half-dozen years—a zany parody of the grim medieval history of *Geneviève de Brabant*, a dizzy bit of melodramatic daggers-and-doges burlesque set in the Venice of *Le Pont des soupirs*, and a less extravagant (and less successful) piece about a Turkish harem-stocking raid among *Les Géorgiennes*—each did fairly well to pretty well, none of them caused the kind of stir, in Paris or such other European capitals as picked up on the newest examples of this newest kind of musical theater, that the first one had done.

It was the mid-1860s before the really momentous opéra-bouffe successors to *Orphée* started to put in an appearance, and their moment came when Offenbach joined forces with producer Hippolyte Cogniard (1807–1882) of the Théâtre des Variétés, and with a new librettist, Henri Meilhac (1831–1897), who had teamed up with the now less shy and thoroughly established Ludovic Halévy. The first piece produced by this group was, once again, a burlesque of classical antiquity, a particularly Parisian look at the behaviour of *La Belle Hélène*, the Spartan Queen whose elopement with a princeling from Asia Minor was the excuse and the occasion for the Homeric excesses of the Trojan war. Meilhac and Halévy's Helen was a fairly flighty queen, one with very little real objection to the Goddess of Love making it Olympianly obligatory for her to cuckold her funny little royal husband with a particularly handsome shepherd.

And that the shepherd should turn out to be a prince in disguise, ready to whisk her back to Asia for regular repeat performances, was just the cherry on the cupcake. The Kings of Greece were depicted as an ensemble-singing bunch of comics who played parlor games in a burlesque of the French court; the seer Calchas was little more than an Olympian pimp who cheated to win at snakes-and-ladders; Orestes, a wild-oat sowing lad of loose morals, was impersonated (as had been the juvenile men of both *Geneviève de Brabant* and *Le Pont des soupirs*) by a leggy lass in a short tunic; and Paris—disguised as a glittering grand priest—carried off Helen to the strains of a sexy tyrolienne, yodeling routine and all. Deliciously ridiculous and divinely bouffe, it was illustrated by a score of music which ranged from the most beautifully lilting—as in the numbers for Paris and Hélène—to the puffingly and poundingly parodic in those pieces given to the comical kings, and it was a very big hit.

LA BELLE HÉLÈNE, an opéra-bouffe in 3 acts by Henri Meilhac and Ludovic Halévy. Music by Jacques Offenbach. Produced at the Théâtre des Variétés, Paris, 17 December 1864.

Characters: Paris, Ménélas, Agamemnon, Calchas, Achille, Ajax premier, Ajax deuxième, Philocome, Euthycles, Hélène, Oreste, Bacchis, Léæna, Parthénis, &c.

Plot: Prince Paris of Troy has given the title of Miss Olympus, and the golden apple that goes with it, to Vénus, Goddess of Love, and, in return, she has promised him the most beautiful woman in the world all for himself. Even though she's already married to someone else—King Ménélas of Sparta, to be precise. Paris goes to Sparta, where he routs the local Kings in a kind of gameshow quiz, and then gets into Hélène's bed by pretending to be a dream, but he gets caught with his tunic down when Ménélas returns unexpectedly and Vénus has to be called in to help out. The Goddess sends down a plague of wifely infidelity upon Greece, and soon poor Ménélas doesn't have an ally left among his nation's husbands. The frantic King writes to Vénus's headquarters in Cythère for an exorcizing priest, and the priest prescribes a sacrifice as the cure. Hélène must go to Cythère with him. Of course, the priest is a drolly disguised phoney. It's Paris all the time and, once the lady is safely aboard his ship, the two set off merrily for Troy. The Trojan war can now take place.

Songs: "Vers tels autels" (chorus), "Amours divins!" (Hélène), "Au Cabaret du Labyrinthe" (Oreste), "Au mont Ida trois déesses" (Paris), "Voici les rois de la Grèce" (Ménélas, Agamemnon, Ajax I & II, Achille), Finale Act 1: "Gloire au berger"/"Pars pour la Crète," "O reine, en ce jour" (Hélène, chorus), "Dis-moi, Vénus" (Hélène), Marche de l'Oie, "À moi les trois talents" (ensemble), "En couronnes tressons les roses" (chorus), "C'est le ciel qui m'envoie" (Hélène, Paris), Finale Act 2: "En couronnes tressons les roses"/"Un mari sage"/"Je ne vous crains pas"/"File, file, file," "Dansons, aimons" (chorus), "Vénus au fond de notre âme" (Oreste), "Là, vrai, je ne suis pas coupable" (Hélène), "Lorsque la Grèce est un champ de carnage" (Agamemnon, Calchas, Ménélas), "La galère de Cythère" (chorus), "Et tout d'abord, ô vile multitude" (Paris), Finale Act 3: "Elle vient! c'est elle"/"Va, pars pour la Crète."

The same team who were responsible for *La Belle Hélène* in 1864 followed her up in 1866 with an opéra-bouffe version of Perrault's once gory and melodramatic tale about the lustfully murderous potentate known as *Barbe-Bleue*. The original Bluebeard of legend, whose nasty habit of disposing of the remains of his used wives in a disused room in his castle is discovered by his latest bride and put an end to by her avenging family, underwent the same kind of bouffe metamorphosis as had been imposed on Homer's heroes and heroics. Meilhac and Halévy's *Sire de Barbe-Bleue* is a belligerent, tenorious braggart who can't keep his pants up or his preferences in order, and the ex-wives of their version are no longer dead. They are merely kept hidden downstairs by Bluebeard's susceptible executioner-cum-alchemist for his own entertainment, and are thus able to come conveniently back to life to confound their horrid husband in the last act. Much of the fun of the piece was contained in the rôle and the subplotting of the local king, Bobèche, an excessively touchy monarch who has the habit of executing any courtier who he fancies is making eyes at his dragonistic queen. He, too, has a susceptible underling, so there are just enough unexecuted courtiers in the basement at the final curtain to pair up with the polygamized wives. Once again, the libretto drew a good deal of slightly daring topical fun from digs at things royal and courtly—a satirical song about bootlicking minions was the hit of the night—and once again Offenbach supplied a glitteringly merry score, which parodied the pomposities of the grand operatic at one moment and provided some superbly sweet melody the next. And *Barbe-Bleue* established itself as a far-and-wide hit.

BARBE-BLEUE, an opéra-bouffe in 3 acts by Henri Meilhac and Ludovic Halévy. Music by Jacques Offenbach. Produced at the Théâtre des Variétés, Paris, 5 February 1866.

Characters: Le Sire de Barbe-Bleue, Le Roi Bobèche, Le Comte Oscar, Popolani, Le Prince Saphir, Alvarez, Boulotte, La Reine Clémentine, La Princesse Hermia (formerly Fleurette), Barbe-Bleue's wives, &c.

Plot: Having wedded, bedded, and ridded himself of five wives in three years, the ravenously randy Sire de Barbe-Bleue takes a burstingly sexy and distinctly bossy country wench called Boulotte for his sixth, and then decides, almost immediately, to dump her for a long-lost local Princess whose hand he demands from her father—his own overlord—by force of arms. But Barbe-Bleue's alchemist, Popolani, doesn't poison Boulotte as ordered. Instead, he and she lead all the displaced wives up to Bobèche's palace, disguised as gipsy entertainers, and when they are admitted to jolly up the tantrum-stained wedding of the villain and the unwilling Princess, Barbe-Bleue's wicked past is poured out in full view of the royal family. The sextigamous wedding is annulled, the Princess is returned to her sweethearting Prince, and the contritish knight is sent home to what will undoubtedly be a thoroughly henpecked life with Boulotte.

Songs: "Dans la nature, tout s'éveille"/"Tous les deux, amoureux" (Saphir, Fleurette), "Y'a p't-être des bergèr's dans l'village" (Bouloutte), "Vous toutes et vous tous qui vous trouvez ici" (Popolani), "V'la z'encor' de drôl's de jeunesses" (Boulotte), "Saperlotte, c'est Boulotte!" (chorus, Oscar), "Montez sur ce palaquin" (chorus, Fleurette), "Ma première femme est morte" (Barbe-Bleue), Finale Act 1: "Honneur, honneur"/"C'est un Rubens!"/"En recevant ce témoignage"/"Allons marchons," "Notre maître va paraître"/"C'est un métier difficile" (Oscar, chorus), "On prend un ange d'innocence" (Clémentine), "C'est mon berger!" (Hermia), "Ran, plan, plan, plan, plan!" (Bobèche, Clémentine, Hermia, Saphir), Finale Act 2/1: "Voici cet heureux couple"/"J'ai la dernière semaine"/"Partez, partez, emmenez-la!," "Le voilà donc le tombeau des cinq femmes"

Barbe-Bleue: A grand bit of nineteenth-century casting. You can see that this Broadway Boulotte isn't easily going to become the latest turnover in Bluebeard's list of wives.

(Barbe-Bleue), "Vous avez vu ce monument" (Barbe-Bleue, Boulotte), "Holà! holà! Ça me prend là!" (Boulotte, Barbe-Bleue, Popolani), Finale Act 2/ii: "Salut à toi, sixième femme," "Madame! ah! madame!" (Barbe-Bleue), "Hymenée, hymenée" (chorus), "J'ai pas bien loin dans la montagne" (Barbe-Bleue), "Nous arrivons à l'instant même"/"Nous possédons l'art merveilleux" (Boulotte, chorus), Finale Act 3: "Idée heureuse."

Up till the time of the production of *Barbe-Bleue*, Offenbach and his librettists had stood alone as the suppliers of opéra-bouffe to the world, but in 1866 they found competition for the first time. It was scarcely new competition, because the composer who illustrated the merry burlesque book that had been written by two new authors, Henri Chivot (1830–1897) and Alfred Duru (1829–1889), on the subject of King Arthur and the knights of his round table, was none other than the man who had started it all, nearly two decades earlier, Florimond Ronger *dit* Hervé. *Les Chevaliers de la table ronde* did not even begin to approach *Barbe-Bleue* or *La Belle Hélène* in success, but Hervé—after spending some eight years recovering, performing, conducting, and writing music and/or texts for many a short opérette while his rival took the genre he had "invented" to new heights—was now thoroughly back on the scene, and in the next few years he was to prove that the old spark was still as bright as ever, and that France had more than one able and notable musician interested in writing opéra-bouffe.

In 1867, while Offenbach and his partners at the Variétés replaced *Barbe-Bleue* with a vastly popular parody on people in power and the military called *La Grande-Duchesse de Gérolstein*, and the composer reorganized his oddly under-appreciated 1859 piece *Geneviève de Brabant* for a new showing, Hervé penned both book and music for the almost equally successful and far more extravagantly burlesque mixture of bits of *William Tell* and *Der Freischütz* and so forth that he called *L'Oeil crevé* for the Folies-Dramatiques. In 1868, while Offenbach eased back from opéra-bouffe and turned out the sentimental musical comedy tale of *La Périchole*, Hervé dove deeper into the waters of the burstingly bouffe and turned out a marvelously extravagant medieval burlesque on the bloody history of the Merovingian king *Chilpéric*. Then, in 1869, as the opéra-bouffe tradition moved to its peak and to what were to be its last great moments, the Variétés trio produced a sparklingly complex bit of burlesque opera on the eternally favorite subject of the bad habits of bandits, *Les Brigands*, while Hervé submitted a bouffe version of the Faust legend and of Gounod's opera thereon, which, as *Le Petit Faust*, would prove his most popular opéra-bouffe of all.

Thus, in just four years between 1866 and 1869, years that also saw the production of such successful pieces as Émile Jonas' *Le Canard à trois becs*, a very large part of the basic opéra-bouffe repertoire first saw the light of stage. Yet the end of that prolific period was also the end of the heyday of the genre. The Franco-Prussian war of 1870–71 put an end to the French Second Empire, and it also put an end to its favorite kind of entertainment. When the war was over, and the battered and besieged Paris started to get itself together again, it was in no mood for the zany frivolities of opéra-bouffe. The entertainments of the new German-imposed Republic were entertainments of a different type, and the great writers and composers who had manufactured the best of the opéras-bouffes were obliged to change their tone and their tune accordingly.

However, if the opéra-bouffe had had its best days in France, it still had many more outstanding days to come further afield. Vienna, and the other chief theatrical cities of Central Europe, had not been too slow to pick up the stunning new shows coming out of Paris, and *Die schöne Helena*, *Blaubart*, and *Die Grossherzogin von Gérolstein*, in particular, had quickly become German-language favorites. And that in spite of the howlings of those Germans who, with something of an echo of the stuffier Parisian reaction to *Orphée aux enfers*, accused the makers of opéra-bouffe of being nothing less than part of a Jewish conspiracy to undermine tradition, order, and family values by means of ridicule of all that was admirable and holy.

The English-language stage on both sides of the Atlantic was less swift to react, and it was not until the end of the 1860s that opéra-bouffe caught on in Britain and America. When it did catch on, however, it did so with a bushfire brilliance. America succumbed first, under the influence of a touring company brought out from Paris with the less-than-a-year-old *La Grande-Duchesse* as its chief offering. The show, even though given in French, caused a sensation. Within weeks the first translated Duchess was winking across the footlights of Broadway, and the rage for the new breed of French musical was launched across America.

LA GRANDE-DUCHESSE (DE GÉROLSTEIN), an opéra-bouffe in 3 acts by Henri Meilhac and Ludovic Halévy. Music by Jacques Offenbach. Produced at the Théâtre des Variétés, Paris, 12 April 1867.

Characters: La Grande-Duchesse, Fritz, Le Prince Paul, Le Général Boum, Le Baron Puck, Le Baron Grog, Népomuc, Wanda, Iza, Amélie, Olga, Charlotte, &c.

Plot: The powerful and noble of Gérolstein are worried because their adolescent Grande-Duchesse is coming of an age where she might start interfering with their running of the state. They need to find her a hobby and a husband to keep her otherwise occupied. The husband they propose is a manageable Netherlandish Prince, but the Duchess is not interested. Then she spots a pretty soldier called Fritz and she is so interested that—sacking her horrified general—she promptly promotes the lad to be commander-in-chief of her army. But Fritz is too thick to catch the right end of his sovereign's amorous hints, goes ahead and marries his village Wanda, and soon finds himself thoroughly demoted. The Duchess switches her gaze instead onto a nice Netherlandish envoy, but he turns out to have a wife and four children back home, so in the end she settles resignedly for the timid Prince Paul, as politics and positions in Gérolstein plummet safely back to the status quo.

Songs: "En attendant que l'heure sonne" (chorus), "Allez, jeunes filles" (Fritz), "À cheval sur la discipline" (Boum), "Me voici, Fritz! . . . j'ai tant couru" (Wanda, Fritz), "Portons armes!" (chorus), "Ah! que j'aime les militaires" (Duchesse), "Ah! c'est un fameux régiment" (Duchesse, Fritz), "Pour épouser une princesse" (Paul), Finale Act 1: "Nous allons partir pour la guerre"/"Voici le sabre de mon père" (Duchesse)/"Je serai vainqueur," "Enfin la guerre est terminée" (chorus), "Je t'ai sur mon coeur placée en peinture" (Olga, Amélie, Iza), "Madame, en quatre jours j'ai terminée la guerre"/"En très bon ordre nous partîmes" (Fritz), "Dites-lui qu'on l'a remarqué, distingué"/"Ma fortune en dépend" (Duchesse, Fritz), "Max était soldat de fortune" (Boum, Puck, Paul), "O grandes leçons du passé" (Duchesse, Boum), "Nous amenons la jeune femme" (ensemble), "Faut-il, mon Dieu, que je sois bête" (Wanda, Fritz), Finale Act 3/I: "Ouvrez, ouvrez, dépêchez-vous," "Au repas comme à la bataille" (ensemble), "Il était un de mes aïeux" (Duchesse), "Eh, bien, Altesse, me voilà!" (Fritz), Finale Act 3/II: "Enfin, j'ai repris la panache."

London had seen English-language adaptations of several Offenbach musicals before *La Grande-Duchesse* arrived there, but their translators had failed to capture the French "bouffe" quality in their rather drastic remakes, and—although Offenbach's music was all the rage on

La Grande-Duchesse de Gérolstein: Fritz enjoys the company of his rustic Wanda, even though he's supposed to be unapproachably "en garde."

the city's stages and in its music-halls—the shows had failed to catch on. So the less hamfisted British version of *La Grande-Duchesse* was given only a limited London season, then bundled out onto the road. It was still on the road, two and a half years later, when opéra-bouffe finally and genuinely achieved lift-off in London. It was 1870, the show responsible was *Chilpéric*, and, undoubtedly not at all coincidentally, it was directed by and starred a man who had no equal when it came to getting across every nuance of thoroughly French bouffing: Hervé himself. London's *Chilpéric*, with its crazy story and its extravagantly too-dramatic characters and text and staging, with its hilarious can-can, such breathtaking numbers as its crazy, colorful first-act finale with druids and courtiers capering about in a loopy legs-up under colorful umbrellas, its merry but very obviously well-made music, and its rows of choice and underclad young show-girls, was opéra-bouffe as opéra-bouffe was intended to be, and, not surprisingly, this time it worked.

CHILPÉRIC, an opéra-bouffe in 3 acts by Hervé. Produced at the Théâtre des Folies-Dramatiques, Paris, 24 October 1868.

Characters: Chilpéric, Siegbert, Ricin [Senna], Le Grand Légendaire [Fatout], Landry, Frédé-gonde, Diviaticus, Don Nervoso, Galsuinthe [Galusinda], Brunehaut, Alfred, Fana, &c.

Plot: King Chilpéric of Neustria and Soissons is out hunting one day when he spies a sexy shep-herdess who seems worth taking home for some après-sport sport. Frédégonde is dumb enough to think being shacked up in the palace means she's in line for a crown, but the King's brother Sieg-bert and his machinating Spanish wife Brunehaut are—for all sorts of dynastically complex and po-tentially murderous reasons—plotting to wed Chilpéric to Brunehaut's sister, Galsuinthe. Which means Frédégonde has to go. And that's just the beginning. The plotting winds up to such a melo-dramoperatic height that, on the night of the royal wedding, the conveniently thick curtains in the royal bedchamber hide no fewer than three murdering men, each out to kill a lady on behalf of an-other lady. And then a little war breaks out. And then someone presses a button and the (occupied) royal bed plunges to the dungeons, and then—well, eventually there's an end to it all.

Songs: "Prêtres d'Ésus" (Diviaticus), "Voyez cette figure" (Chilpéric), "Que nos voix dans les Bois" (chorus), Le Chanson du Jambon (Chilpéric), "Divine Frédégonde" (Chilpéric, Frédégonde, Brunehaut, Siegbert), Finale Act 1: "Dans les combats," "Je suis nerveuse, il est grincheux" (Frédé-gonde), "Il est dix heures" (chorus), "Petit papillon bleu volage" (Chilpéric), "En tout affaire, le sage flaire" (Ricin), "Sur les côteaux, pauvre pastour" (Brunehaut, Landry), "O ciel! que vient-on de m'apprendre" (Frédégonde, Chilpéric), "C'est la princesse" (chorus), "À la Sierra Moréna" (Galsuinthe), Ballet (Polka Mazurka, Polka des Martels), "Loin de ces lieux" (Frédégonde), Finale Act 2: "Ah! que c'est donc amusant," "Chantons! buvons! vidons les flacons" (chorus), "Passerez-vous la nuit tranquille" (Alfred), [later "Te souvient-il du temps tranquille" (Landry)], "De Singapour à Kamatchka" (Ricin, Grand Légendaire, Landry), "Nuit fortunée" (Frédégonde), "Loin des armes, du bruit," "De Pampelune à Saragosse" (Galsuinthe), "O surprise, ô crainte" (chorus), Marche Gauloise: "L'ennemi fuit éperdu" (chorus), Finale Act 3: "Cors et cymbales."

Chilpéric remained a favorite on the English-singing stage for many years, but, more impor-tantly, it also set the manner for opéra-bouffe productions in Britain in the future and secured their place on the British stage. Undoubtedly the most successful among such productions was another piece which, while it did well enough at home, had and has never been regarded there as among the few most favored opéras-bouffes. Like *Chilpéric*, *Geneviève de Brabant* was a bur-lesque of things medieval, like *Chilpéric* it was more hilariously extravagant in its plotting, its sit-uations, and its characters than a piece like *La Grande-Duchesse*, but unlike its predecessor it was not by Hervé. The score to *Geneviève de Brabant* was by Offenbach, and it would give him his greatest-ever success on the British stage. In fact, the *Geneviève de Brabant* which proved such a hit throughout the English-speaking world was a rehash. After the show had proved only a so-so proposition on its initial production in 1859, it had been put through a serious rewrite before being given a second chance, eight years later. The rewrite, which introduced the stand-up comic and topical number which would become famous as the Gens d'armes duo ("we run them in, we run them in . . ."), again did only quite well in Paris, but it was enthusiastically received in America, and—produced with all the Gallic gaiety, glamor, girls, and good singing (and the odd song that wasn't by Offenbach!) that had been such features of *Chilpéric*—caused a sensation in Britain, confirming the fashion for opéra-bouffe in English, just at the same time that the next and newest brand of French musical theater that would cause a furor on the international musical stage was beginning to raise its head on home stages.

GENEVIÈVE DE BRABANT, an opéra-bouffe in 3 acts by Hector Crémieux and Étienne Tréfeu, based on the 2-act original by Tréfeu (19 November 1859). Music by Jacques Offenbach. Produced at the Théâtre des Menus-Plaisirs, Paris, 26 December 1867.

Characters: Sifroy, Geneviève, Golo, Drogan, Brigitte, Christine, Charles Martel, Grabuge, Pitou, Burgomaster Vanderprout, Narcisse, Péterpip, Isoline, L'Eremite du Ravin, &c.

Plot: The subjects and courtiers of Sifroy, Duke of Curaçao, are so anxious for him to produce a son and heir that they have offered a reward to whoever might help put the required light in his eye and/or lead in his pencil. It seems that the prize may be won when the little pastrycook Drogan produces a Virility Pie which has instant and visible effects, but the Duke is put off his unaccustomed stride, just as he is getting into it, by his favorite courtier, Golo. You see, Golo knows that, if there is no heir, his dear friend the Duke will make him the heir, so he spends his days doing everything he can to stop Sifroy and his lady Geneviève from doing anything they can that might result in an heir. By the end of Act 1, he has sent Sifroy off to the crusades with Charles Martel, and by the beginning of Act 2, the threatened Geneviève, guarded by the faithful Drogan, is in operatically dramatic flight into the local forests. But the crusaders don't get to Palestine, they only get to Asnières, and there the Golo-less Sifroy is busy discovering what a good time he's been missing all these years when Drogan arrives with news of the drastic dynastic happenings back home. Everyone hurries back to Curaçao for a series of splendidly melodramatic revelations and accusations and, of course, a happy (for everyone but Golo) ending.

Songs: "Flamands de tous pays" (chorus, Christine), Rondo du Pâté: "Salut! noble assemblée" (Drogan), "En passant sous la fenêtre" (Drogan, Geneviève), "Curaçoiens, que la victoire couronne" (chorus), "Une poule sur un mur" (Sifroy), "Travaillons comme des fées" (Ladies in waiting), "Cet habit-là ne lui va point" (Brigitte), "Grace à vous, mesdemoiselles" (Drogan), "Ah! Madame . . . Vous qui brillez" (Drogan, Geneviève, Brigitte), "De mon coeur un trouble s'empare" (Sifroy, Geneviève), "Je ne connais rien au monde" (Sifroy), "J'arrive armé du pied en cap" (Martel), Finale Act 1: "Ciel! qu'ai-je appris!"/Depart pour la Palestine, "Fuyons, fuyons l'orage" (Drogan, Geneviève, Brigitte), Duo des gens d'armes: "Protéger le repos des villes" (Grabuge, Pitou), "Je suis l'Eremite du ravin" (Eremite), "Allons, madame, il faut mourir" (Grabuge, Pitou, Geneviève, [Drogan]), "Chantez, chantez, cocodettes" (ensemble), "Pour combattre les infidèles" (Sifroy, Martel, Isoline), Tyrolienne, Ballet et Farandole (ensemble), "Geneviève était blonde" (Drogan), Finale Act 2: "Amis, faisons vibrer sous ces dômes brillants," "Quand on possède une biche" (Geneviève, [Brigitte]), "Partons en chasse" (Drogan, hunters), "Je viens de la Turquie"

(Sifroy, [Martel]), "Golo, monstre plein de crime" (Drogan). Additional and alternative numbers include "Vos Echevins, vos édiles" (Vanderprout), "Il m'a mis sur le front le toque de satin" (Golo).

This handful of genuine opéras-bouffes, which was to go round the world to such effect, was not, however, the only successful musical theater to come out of France in the 1860s. The other kinds of musical theater which had prospered in their mini versions at the Bouffes-Parisiens also grew up to full size, along with their more extravagant fellows. But even if such merry farcical pieces as *Le Voyage en Chine*, with its comical story of a hasty young husband who hijacks his father-in-law on a ship allegedly heading for the Orient in order to win his after-the-event consent, or fantasy in the vein of *La Cour du Roi Pétaud*, with which Léo Delibes made his one attempt at a full-length musical, still called themselves opéra-comique, others, thanks to the enormous currency given to the term opéra-bouffe by the vivacious success of *Orphée aux enfers* and its fellows in France and around Europe during the last years of the Empire, called themselves opéra-bouffe, without in fact strictly earning that appellation contrôlée. Some of these pieces, indeed, came from the masters of the opéra-bouffe genre themselves: Meilhac, Halévy, and Offenbach's sentimental musical comedy centered on the South American street-singer *La Périchole* (later revised with an extra and determinedly "bouffe" act), the far-fetched bit of musical comedy about *Le Voyage des MM Dunanan père et fils*—a phoney journey to Venice staged to fool a pair of provincials—written for Offenbach by Jules Moinaux (1815–1895) and Paul Siraudin (1812–1883), the merry comicalities surrounding the waxworks doll representing *La Princesse de Trébizonde* who "comes to life" in Charles Nuitter (1828–1899) and Étienne Tréfeu's (1821–1903) libretto to a third Offenbach musical, or, most successful of all, Meilhac and Halévy's farcical skate through a handful of sexy adventures in up-to-date Paris as related in *La Vie parisienne*, a thorough-going musical farcical comedy, littered with impersonations but with barely an element of genuine burlesque in either its text or its music.

LA VIE PARISIENNE, an opéra-bouffe in 4 (originally 5) acts by Henri Meilhac and Ludovic Halévy. Music by Jacques Offenbach. Produced at the Théâtre du Palais-Royal, Paris, 31 October 1866.

Characters: Le Baron de Gondremarck, La Baronne de Gondremarck, Bobinet, Raoul de Gardefeu, Un Brésilien/Frick/Prosper, Alfred, Urbain, Joseph, Gabrielle, Métella, Pauline, Alphonse, Léonie, Clara, &c.

Plot: Having had his susceptibilities dented in a non-exclusive (on her part) affaire with one Métella, a Parisian lady of limited virtue, fashionable young Raoul de Gardefeu has decided to find his future pleasures with a less wounding breed: women of society. Pretending to be a tourist guide, he picks up a Swedish baron and his attractive wife, lodges them at his home on the pretence it is a hotel, and gets his friend, and former rival, Bobinet to mount a juicily girl-studded evening to distract the dying-to-dip-his-wick baron while he lays siege to the baroness. The baron has a wow of a time romancing Bobinet's "society ladies"—who are nothing more than his servants in disguise—but Métella has decided she wants her paramour back, and she not only pre-warns the baroness about what's going on, but manipulates everything so that the contrite baron is returned, undipped, to his wife, and that she herself gets back not just one but both her admirers.

Songs: "Nous sommes employés de la ligne de l'Ouest" (chorus), Choeur des voyageurs: "Le ciel est noir" (chorus), "Attendez d'abord que je place" (Métella), "Elles sont tristes, les marquises" (Bobinet), "Ce que c'est pourtant que la vie" (Gardefeu), "Jamais, foi de cicérone" (Gardefeu, Baron, Baroness), Finale Act 1: "À Paris nous arrivons en masse"/"Je suis Brésilien, j'ai de l'or" (Brésilien)/"Entrons, entrons dans la fournaise," "Entrez, entrez, jeune fille à l'oeil bleu!" (Frick, Gabrielle), "Autrefois plus d'un amant" (Gabrielle), "Dans cette ville toute pleine" (Baron), "Vous souvient-il, ma belle" (Métella), "Pour découper adroitement" (Frick), "Nous entrons dans cette demeure" (chorus), "Je suis veuve d'un colonel" (Gabrielle), Tyrolienne: "On est v'nu m'inviter" (Gabrielle), "Donc, je puis me fier à vous" (Bobinet, Pauline, Prosper, Urbain, &c.), "L'amour, c'est une échelle immense" (Pauline, Baron), "On va courir, on va sortir" (Gabrielle), "Votre habit a craqué dans le dos" (sextet), Finale Act 3: "Soupons, soupons, c'est le moment"/"En endossant mon uniforme"/"Il est gris, tout à fait gris," "Bien bichonnés et bien rasés" (waiters), "Avant toute chose il faut être" (Alfred), "C'est ici l'endroit redouté des mères" (Métella), "En avant, les jeunes femmes!" (chorus), "Hier, à midi, la gantière" (Gabrielle, Brésilien), Finale Act 4: "En cherchant dans la ville."

In the giant shadow of Offenbach and Hervé, and the theaters which they provided with their work, other composers—Jonas, Frédéric Barbier, Laurent de Rillé, Jean-Jacques de Billemont—and theaters—the Théâtre des Menus-Plaisirs and the Fantaisies-Parisiennes at their head—also strove to turn out Parisian musical plays in the latest manner and mode, and it was this last-named house, a shoestring affair run by the eccentric writer William Busnach, which finally succeeded in producing one of the few winners to come from outside the most famous circles. It was, however, a winner that was heavy with pointers for the future. *Fleur de thé*, a soi-disant opéra-bouffe with something of the exotic flavor popularized by such little musicals as Offenbach's early hit *Ba-ta-clan*, but really more of a sex farce about French folk caught up with funny oriental folk with funny oriental habits in a funny oriental country, had a libretto by the same young writers, Chivot and Duru, who had authored *Les Chevaliers de la table ronde* for Hervé, and it had a score by one of Busnach's music staff, the young Charles Lecocq (1832–1918). Within a few years, as *Fleur de thé* did the rounds of the world's stages, all three writers would be rising steadily to the top of their profession in postwar France. And riding highest of them all would be the composer, the new bright star of the new bright postwar style of musical.

But during the 1860s, during those years that the Parisian stage was producing the musicals that would fill foreign theaters for many years to come, what was happening in those other main theatrical centers? What in the way of full-scale musical plays was being produced in the German-speaking and English-speaking theater? The answer was, and is, not a great deal that was anything but resolutely backwards looking—antique comic operas, pasticcio burlesque, and chunks of melodramatic and/or fairy-tale spectacle—and almost nothing that would prove internationally interesting and enduring in the way that the French musicals did. However, slowly and surely the ground was being prepared, and those writers and players were starting to put in an appearance who would, in the next decade, allow both London and Vienna to turn out outstanding musical plays of their own.

It was Vienna which was the quickest and most efficient of the other main centers both in picking up on the new musicals coming out of France and in making its own attempts to turn out something of the same kind. At first these Viennese pieces were little ones, made in the mold of the early successes at the Folies-Nouvelles and the Bouffes-Parisiens—Erik Nessl and Carl Friedrich Konradin's "tragi-komische Operett" *Flodoardo Wuprahall* and their burlesque Indian Operett *Rabuzikokoatl,* Krone and Niemetz's little tale of Prince Absalon "the pigtail-cutter," *Der Zofpabschneider,* and the girlie displays of *Das Pensionat* and *Zehn Mädchen und kein Mann* set to music by Franz von Suppé (1819–1895). Some of them, notably the best of Suppé's works (*Flotte Bursche, Leichte Kavallerie, Die schöne Galathee*) and those by the Croatian composer Giovanni von Zaytz (1831–1914) (*Mannschaft an Bord, Fitzliputzli der Teufelchen der Ehe, Der Meisterschuss von Pottenstein*), found more than a little favor at home, and even the occasional bit of exposure further afield, but efforts at producing a full-sized German opéra-bouffe proved less successful. The Julius Sixtus/Julius Hopp "Parodie-Burlesk mit Musik und Tanz" of *Faust, Fäustling und Margarethl,* found some success, but neither Suppé's full-length attempt with a parody of the opera *Dinorah,* nor von Zaytz's *Die Hexe von Boissy,* nor Hopp's *Die Donauweibchen und der Ritter von Kahlenberg* turned out to have the appeal of the imported opéras-bouffes, or to be the show needed to give an impetus to a German Oper-Burlesk tradition.

In Britain, virtually no attempt was made to imitate the successful product of the French stage. British burlesque remained staunchly what it had been for years, coming to a peak of popularity with such pasticcio pieces as Henry J. Byron's (1835–1884) rhyming and punning versions of *Cinderella* and *Aladdin,* with F. C. Burnand's merry Olympian legshow, *Ixion,* and with the same author's record-breaking burlesque version of the nautical drama *Black-Eyed Susan.* In 1865, Burnand (1836–1917) was part of a temporary try at displacing the old glued-together scores of burlesque with original music when he worked on two such pieces—parodies of the novel *Windsor Castle* and of the opera *L'Africaine*—for the Strand Theatre. He also penned the libretti for two pieces which attacked the area from the opposite end when he combined with the young composer Arthur Sullivan on a slightly bouffe bandit-land comic opera called *The Contrabandista* and on the adaptation of a long-favorite playlet as a little comical musical "triumviretta" called *Cox and Box.* Both these latter pieces did well on their first showings at off-the-mainstream venues, but they did not provoke anything more in the way of a follow-up than the Strand burlesques had done, and the possibility of an English strain of opéra-bouffe didn't catch on any more than a Viennese one had. Not for now, anyhow. As in Vienna, it was a case of waiting for the seventies.

SOME NOTABLE MUSICALS 1851–1869

1851   BONSOIR, M PANTALON [Good evening, Mr Clown] (Albert Grisar/J. P. Lockroy)
Opéra-Comique, Paris, 19 February

1852   LA POUPÉE DE NUREMBERG [The Nuremberg doll] (Adolphe Adam/Adolphe de
Leuven, Arthur de Beauplan) Théâtre Lyrique, Paris, 21 February
GALATHÉE [Galatea] (Victor Massé/Jules Barbier, Michel Carré) Opéra-Comique, Paris,
14 April

1853   LES NOCES DE JEANNETTE [Jeannette's wedding] (Victor Massé/Jules Barbier,
Michel Carré) Opéra-Comique, Paris, 4 February
LES FOLIES DRAMATIQUES [Crazy moments in the theater] (Hervé/Clairville,
Philippe Dumanoir) Tuileries, Paris, 1 March
PÉPITO (Jacques Offenbach/Léon Battu, Jules Moinaux) Théâtre des Variétés, Paris,
28 October

1854   LE COMPOSITEUR TOQUÉ [The nutty composer] (Hervé) Folies-Concertantes, Paris,
11 April

1855   LES DEUX AVEUGLES [Two blind men] (Jacques Offenbach/Jules Moinaux) Théâtre
des Bouffes-Parisiens, Paris, 5 July
LE VIOLONEUX [The violinist] (Jacques Offenbach/Eugène Mestépès, Émile Chevalet)
Théâtre des Bouffes-Parisiens, Paris, 31 August
BA-TA-CLAN (Jacques Offenbach/Ludovic Halévy) Théâtre des Bouffes-Parisiens, Paris,
29 December

1856   TROMB-AL-CA-ZAR (Jacques Offenbach/Charles Dupeuty, Ernest Bourget) Théâtre des
Bouffes-Parisiens, Paris, 3 April
LES PANTINS DE VIOLETTE [Violet's toys] (Adolphe Adam/Léon Battu) Théâtre des
Bouffes-Parisiens, Paris, 29 April
LA ROSE DE SAINT-FLOUR (Jacques Offenbach/Michel Carré) Théâtre des Bouffes-
Parisiens, Paris, 12 June
LE 66 [Ticket number 66] (Jacques Offenbach/Pittaud de Forges, "Laurencin") Théâtre
des Bouffes-Parisiens, Paris, 31 July
LES DRAGONS DE VILLARS [The dragoons of Villars] (Aimé Maillart/J. P. Lockroy,
Eugène Cormon) Théâtre Lyrique, Paris, 19 September

1857   CROQUEFER, ou Le Dernier des paladins [Croquefer, or The last of the paladins]
(Jacques Offenbach/Adolphe Jaime, Étienne Tréfeu) Théâtre des Bouffes-Parisiens, Paris,
12 February
LE MARIAGE AUX LANTERNES [Wedding by lanternlight] (Jacques
Offenbach/Michel Carré, Léon Battu) Théâtre des Bouffes-Parisiens, Paris, 10 October

1858   MESDAMES DE LA HALLE [Ladies of the marketplace] (Jacques Offenbach/Armand
Lapointe) Théâtre des Bouffes-Parisiens, Paris, 3 March
THE MAID AND THE MAGPIE (pasticcio/Henry J. Byron) Strand Theatre, London,
11 October
ORPHÉE AUX ENFERS [Orpheus goes to hell] (Jacques Offenbach/Ludovic Halévy,
Hector Crémieux) Théâtre des Bouffes-Parisiens, Paris, 21 October

1859   GENEVIÈVE DE BRABANT (Jacques Offenbach/Étienne Tréfeu) Théâtre des Bouffes-Parisiens, Paris, 19 November

FLODOARDO WUPRAHALL (Carl Friedrich Conradin/Erik Nessl) Carltheater, Vienna, 14 December

1860   LURLINE (Vincent Wallace/Edward Fitzball) Theatre Royal, Covent Garden, London, 23 February

DIDO (arr. Hayward/Francis C. Burnand) St James's Theatre, London, 23 March

DAS PENSIONAT [The boarding school] (Franz von Suppé/"C. K") Theater an der Wien, Vienna, 24 November

CINDERELLA, or The Prince, the Lackey, and the Little Glass Slipper (pasticcio/Henry J. Byron) Strand Theatre, London, 26 December

1861   LA CHANSON DE FORTUNIO [Fortunio's song] (Jacques Offenbach/Hector Crémieux, Ludovic Halévy) Théâtre des Bouffes-Parisiens, Paris, 5 January

LE PONT DES SOUPIRS [The bridge of sighs] (Jacques Offenbach/Ludovic Halévy, Hector Crémieux) Théâtre des Bouffes-Parisiens, Paris, 23 March

ALADDIN, or The Wonderful Scamp (pasticcio/Henry J. Byron) Strand Theatre, London, 1 April

MONSIEUR CHOUFLEURI RESTERA CHEZ LUI LE . . . [Mr Cauliflower requests the pleasure . . .] (Jacques Offenbach/Hector Crémieux, Ludovic Halévy, "Saint-Rémy") Présidence du Corps-Legislatif, Paris, 31 May

1862   MONSIEUR ET MADAME DENIS (Jacques Offenbach/Laurencin, Michel Delaporte) Théâtre des Bouffes-Parisiens, Paris, 11 January

THE LILY OF KILLARNEY (Jules Benedict/John Oxenford, Dion Boucicault) Theatre Royal, Covent Garden, London, 8 February

LE VOYAGE DE MM DUNANAN PÈRE ET FILS [The Dunanans, father and son, take a trip] (Jacques Offenbach/Paul Siraudin, Jules Moinaux) Théâtre des Bouffes-Parisiens, Paris, 23 March

THE DOCTOR OF ALCANTARA (Julius Eichberg/Benjamin Woolf) Boston Museum, Boston, 7 April

PRINCE AMABEL, or The Fairy Roses (pasticcio/William Brough) St James's Theatre, London, 5 May

FÄUSTLING UND MARGARETHL [Little Faust and diddy Marguerite] (Julius Hopp/Julius Sixtus) Strampfertheater, Vienna, 20 September

ZEHN MÄDCHEN UND KEIN MANN [Ten unmarried ladies and not a single man] (Franz von Suppé/W. Friedrich) Theater am Franz-Josefs-Kai, Vienna, 25 October

1863   LES BAVARDS [The chatterboxes] (revised) (Jacques Offenbach/Charles Nuitter) Théâtre des Bouffes-Parisiens, Paris, 20 February

FLOTTE BURSCHE [Jolly young chaps] (Franz von Suppé/Josef Braun) Theater am Franz-Josefs-Kai, Vienna, 18 April

LISCHEN ET FRITZCHEN (Jacques Offenbach/Paul Boisselot) Ems, 21 July

IXION, or The Man at the Wheel (pasticcio/Francis C. Burnand) Royalty Theatre, London, 28 September

MANNSCHAFT AN BORD [The crew at sea] (Giovanni von Zaytz/J. L. Harisch) Carltheater, Vienna, 15 December

1864   LE JOUEUR DE FLÛTE [The flute-player] (Hervé/Jules Moinaux) Théâtre des Variétés, Paris, 16 April

LA BELLE HÉLÈNE [The beautiful Helen] (Jacques Offenbach/Henri Meilhac, Ludovic Halévy) Théâtre des Variétés, Paris, 17 December

PAN Y TOROS [Bread and bulls] (Francisco A. Barbieri/José Picon) Teatro de la Zarzuela, Madrid, 22 December

1865   WINDSOR CASTLE (Frank Musgrave/Francis C. Burnand) Strand Theatre, London, 5 June

DIE SCHÖNE GALATHEE [Gorgeous Galatea] (Franz von Suppé/"Poly Henrion") Meysels Theater, Berlin, 30 June

LE VOYAGE EN CHINE [The trip to China] (François Bazin/Eugène Labiche, Alfred Delacour) Opéra-Comique, Paris, 9 December

1866   BARBE-BLEUE [Bluebeard] (Jacques Offenbach/Henri Meilhac, Ludovic Halévy) Théâtre des Variétés, Paris, 5 February

LEICHTE KAVALLERIE [Light cavalry] (Franz von Suppé/Karl Costa) Carltheater, Vienna, 21 March

THE BLACK CROOK (comp./arr. Thomas Baker et al./Charles M. Barras) Niblo's Garden, New York, 12 September

LA VIE PARISIENNE [Life in Paris] (Jacques Offenbach/Henri Meilhac, Ludovic Halévy) Palais-Royal, Paris, 31 October

LES CHEVALIERS DE LA TABLE RONDE [The knights of the round table] (Hervé/Henri Chivot, Alfred Duru) Théâtre des Bouffes-Parisiens, Paris, 17 November

BLACK-EYED SUSAN, or The Little Bill That Was Taken Up (arr. Hermann/Francis C. Burnand) Royalty Theatre, London, 29 November

1867   LA GRANDE-DUCHESSE (DE GÉROLSTEIN) (Jacques Offenbach/Henri Meilhac, Ludovic Halévy) Théâtre des Variétés, Paris, 12 April

COX AND BOX (Arthur Sullivan/Francis C. Burnand) Adelphi Theatre, London, 11 May

L'OEIL CREVÉ [Bang! in the eye] (Hervé) Théâtre des Folies-Dramatiques, Paris, 12 October

THE CONTRABANDISTA, or The Law of the Ladrones (Arthur Sullivan/Francis C. Burnand) St George's Opera House, London, 18 December

1868   FLEUR DE THÉ [Tea-flower] (Charles Lecocq/Henri Chivot, Alfred Duru) Théâtre de l'Athénée, Paris, 11 April

THE FIELD OF THE CLOTH OF GOLD (pasticcio/William Brough) Strand Theatre, London, 11 April

L'ÎLE DE TULIPATAN [Tulipatan Island] (Jacques Offenbach/Henri Chivot, Alfred Duru) Théâtre des Bouffes-Parisiens, Paris, 30 September

LA PÉRICHOLE (Jacques Offenbach/Henri Meilhac, Ludovic Halévy) Théâtre des Variétés, Paris, 6 October

CHILPÉRIC (Hervé) Théâtre des Folies-Dramatiques, Paris, 24 October

1869   LE CANARD À TROIS BECS [The duck with three beaks] (Émile Jonas/Jules Moinaux) Théâtre des Folies-Dramatiques, Paris, 6 February

LA COUR DU ROI PÉTAUD [At the court of King Pétaud] (Léo Delibes/Adolphe Jaime, Philippe Gille) Théâtre des Variétés, Paris, 24 April

LE PETIT FAUST [Little Faust] (Hervé/Adolphe Jaime, Hector Crémieux) Théâtre des Folies-Dramatiques, Paris, 28 April

LA PRINCESSE DE TRÉBIZONDE (Jacques Offenbach/Charles Nuitter, Étienne Tréfeu) Baden-Baden, 31 July

AGES AGO (Frederick Clay/William S. Gilbert) Gallery of Illustration, London, 22 November

LES BRIGANDS (Jacques Offenbach/Henri Meilhac, Ludovic Halévy) Théâtre des Variétés, Paris, 10 December

LES TURCS (Hervé) Théâtre des Folies-Dramatiques, Paris, 23 December

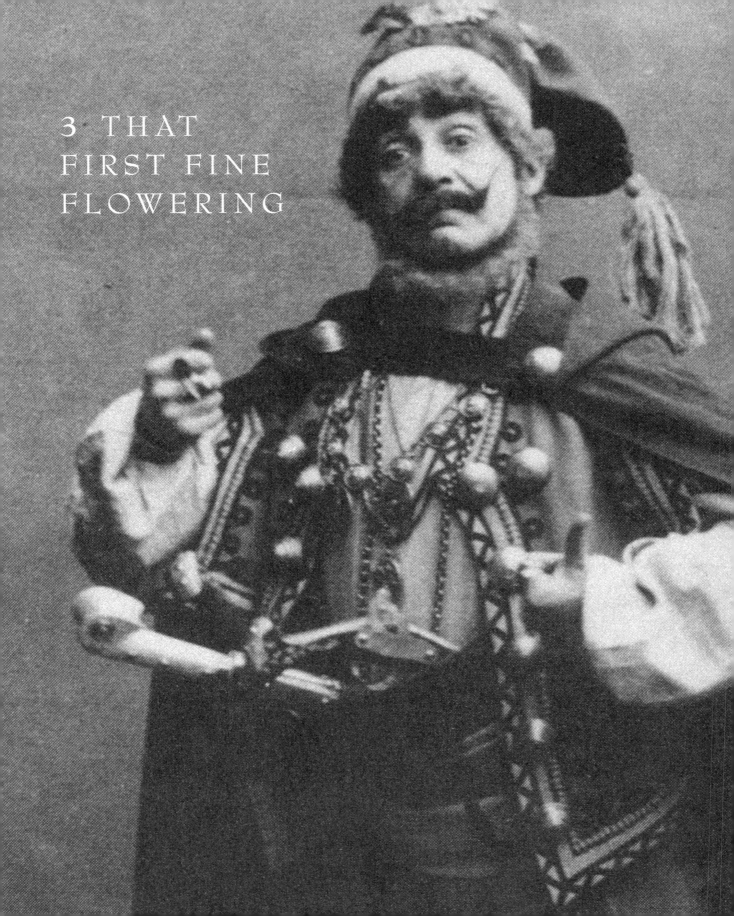

3 THAT
FIRST FINE
FLOWERING

The 1870s saw the world-wide blossoming of the musical theater, as the German- and English-language stages began tardily, but soon distinctly successfully, to follow where the French theater of the 1860s had marked out the trail, and by the end of the decade Paris, Vienna, and London were each turning out a regular supply of fine and internationally played shows. But they were not shows like those of the sixties. The very specially flavored opéra-bouffe tradition, with its sophisticated incongruities, its way-out humor, and its dazzlingly light and bright music, withered away in post–Prussian-War France, and although some of its extravagances remained fuzzily visible in some of the Parisian hits of the earliest years of the seventies, by and large the Second Empire's favorite breed of entertainment gave place on French stages to a more measured, less flyaway kind of comical musical play.

In Vienna, Budapest, Prague, and Berlin, a homegrown equivalent to the French opéra-bouffe never succeeded in making itself a place on local stages. The German-language theater welcomed translated and adapted versions of the French opéra-bouffe hits with enthusiasm, but that was it. Musicals written specifically for the Vienna stage by French writers and composers Offenbach and Jonas failed, a musicalization by local composer Karl Millöcker (1842–1899) of a text by Moinaux, librettist of several successful Parisian opéras-bouffes, did no better, and neither Suppé's opéra-bouffe on *Lohengrin, Die Jungfrau von Dragant,* nor the most famous Viennese opéra-bouffe flop of all, the attempt by the popular dance-music composer Johann Strauss II (1825–1899) to set a *Ba-ta-clan*nish libretto about Ali Baba and a bunch of Viennese interlopers as *Indigo und die vierzig Räuber,* proved the keystone show from which a German-language opéra-bouffe tradition might take off. Very soon after the failure of *Indigo,* the Viennese musical or Operette was actually to launch itself on its first great period of productivity and prosperity. But when it did, it was under the influence of a different kind of French theater, and with a kind of comical musical which owed little or nothing of its flavor to the individualities of opéra-bouffe. What it did owe to that generation of crazy Gallic shows, however, was its creators: for each member of the writing team on Vienna's first big Operette success had cut at least some of his theatrical teeth on trying to turn out opéra-bouffe.

In Britain, however, where the opéra-bouffe had taken so long to take root, things went differently. Among the imported, adapted (and, most often, cruelly de-sexed) Parisian opéras-bouffes, among those ruinously spectacular scenery-ballet-and-fairy-tale pieces which called themselves "grands opéras-bouffes féeries" (*Le Roi Carotte*, *La Biche au bois*, *The Black Crook*, et al.) and which were for some years a feature of stages world-wide, and among a continuing flood of old-fashioned British rhymes-puns-and-pasticcio burlesques, a genuine English opéra-bouffe tradition did eventually succeed in getting off the ground. As in Vienna, some of the earliest efforts at growing this brand of "French" musicals in Britain involved the importation of French musicians—not a difficult thing given conditions in wartime and postwartime Paris—and so the early 1870s saw Hervé, Jonas, Offenbach, Gaston Serpette, Jean-Jacques de Billemont, Jules Rivière, and others all contributing original work to the London stage. But then, in 1877, a young producer called Richard D'Oyly Carte mounted a wholly original and entirely English burlesque musical play. The piece was called *The Sorcerer*, its merrily tongue-in-cheek text was written in a cockeyed, burlesque prose of as much individual character as the works of the great French librettists, and its music was light operatic music which had the sparkling virtues of the work of an Offenbach or an Hervé but yet retained a very specifically English character. The writer of *The Sorcerer* was W. S. Gilbert (1836–1911), a playwright whose previous musicals had included traditional, rhymed burlesques, magical musical plays of the Zauberposse kind, a burlesque bandit musical, and even Ancient Greek extravaganza, and the composer was Arthur Sullivan (1842–1900), one of the country's most admired young musicians and more than a decade back the writer of those early English musicals *The Contrabandista* and *Cox and Box*. Gilbert and Sullivan would, with a little help from their friends, make their special brand of English burlesque opera a feature of the English-language stage of the 1870s and 1880s, and they would keep the flag of opéra-bouffe flying at the top of the mast in the English-speaking theater long after it had drooped in favor of saner entertainments on the other side of the English Channel.

It was on that other side of the English Channel, however, that most of the most important and internationally successful musicals of those twenty years were created. Paris, once she and her theaters had found their feet again after the pounding handed out by the Prussians, leaped quickly back into the saddle, and a brilliant new brand of French opéra-comique or opérette soon forged forth, a brand of musical which would quickly take over where the hits of opéra-bouffe days had left off at the forefront of the musical theater, as its favorite examples ran round the world, showing themselves off on stages from St Petersburg to Sydney.

In fact, the first and the most important of the postwar shows did not start their stage-lives in Paris, but over the Belgian border in Brussels. Brussels, in the earliest 1870s, was the home of a particularly go-ahead musical theater, the Fantaisies-Parisiennes, run by an enthusiastic producer and manager called Eugène Humbert (?1835–1886), but also, more temporarily, of Charles Lecocq, the composer of that merry bit of Chinese musical-bedding called *Fleur de thé*, which had been one of the last successes of the prewar Parisian musical stage. Manager and musician came happily together, and Lecocq and his *Fleur de thé* librettists, Chivot and Duru, teamed this time with one of Paris's most versatile theater-writers in Clairville (1811–1879), presented Humbert with an extraordinarily funny and tuneful musical comedy, a piece which had enough of the zany about it that it did not entirely sail under false colors when it presented itself as an opéra-bouffe.

Les Cent Vierges—and even that title, which characterized the show so well, would give foreign producers cold feet—found its fun not in burlesque effects but in the brightest of situation comedy, as it followed, to a threatened fate almost worse than bigamy, a couple of French demoiselles who get mistakenly carried off to a women-less English colony in the Pacific Ocean on a bride ship and also, more extravagantly, their husbands, who get into frocks to follow and rescue them, and who end up "wedded" to and very nearly bedded by the local governor and his side-kick. High and distinctly low comedy mixed with the brightest and most tuneful of music to great effect, and *Les Cent Vierges* was a first-class hit in Brussels, on the stage in Paris within weeks, and on its way to be seen by a whole range of foreign audiences, in variously deodorized versions, as *Hundert Jungfrauen*, *The Island of Bachelors*, *Szaz szüz*, and *To the Green Isles Direct* within the next couple of years.

But even though *Les Cent Vierges* was both a splendid musical comedy and a world-wide success, it was small beer in comparison with the second musical which Humbert, Lecocq, and Clairville turned out, less than nine months later, on those same Belgian boards. *La Fille de Madame Angot* was not described as an opéra-bouffe by its author, and with good reason. In tone, in tale, in scenes, in characters, and in music it had nothing of the bouffe in it at all, nothing comically exaggerated, nothing burlesque, nothing over-the-top. Clairville's libretto (for which two ideas men took co-credit and of course co-royalties) was a masterly work—a mixture of sex and politics and comedy, of real and feeling characters and situations no less humorous for being realistic, all set in the colorful but thoroughly real days of the post-revolutionary Directoire government—while Lecocq's music, although not indulging in the more brilliant fireworks of the opéra-bouffe register, was in the most melodious and effective vein of light-hearted theatrical music: swirling waltzes, gentle ballads, and even such special-effects pieces as a hammering exchange of insults-to-music or a whispered conspiratorial bit of chorus work, two pieces which would both become enduring world-wide favorites.

LA FILLE DE MADAME ANGOT, an opéra-comique in 3 acts by Clairville, Paul Siraudin, and Victor Koning. Music by Charles Lecocq. Produced at the Fantaisies-Parisiennes, Brussels, 4 December 1872.

Characters: Clairette Angot, Mlle Lange, Pomponnet, Ange Pitou, Larivaudière, Trénitz, Louchard, Amaranthe, Javotte, Cadet, Babet, Hersilie, Buteux, Thérèse, Guillaume, Cydalise, &c.

Plot: The market folk of Les Halles who have brought up the orphaned Clairette Angot have arranged for her to marry the little hairdresser Pomponnet. But Clairette has been romancing the dashing, demagoguic poet and street-singer Ange Pitou and, rather than wed Pomponnet, she purposely gets

herself arrested on what should be her wedding day for singing one of Pitou's anti-government songs in the marketplace. Clairette is released from jail thanks to the influence of her old schoolfriend Lange, who is now the mistress of the powerful politician Barras, and she finds herself in the middle of a conspiracy. Lange and Barras and their friends are not what they seem; they are key members of a group which is secretly plotting to restore the monarchy. She also discovers that Lange is not only amorously double-crossing her partner with another conspirator, the important and absurdly jealous financier Larivaudière, but is also angling towards an affair with a not at all indifferent Pitou. She tricks Lange and Pitou to a rendezvous in a Parisian pub garden, exposes all the amorous coming-and-goings-on, and then returns to the good Pomponnet, leaving the political and sexual waltzing of the powerful and the plotters to carry on without her. For the meanwhile, anyhow.

Songs: "Bras dessus, bras dessous" (chorus), "Aujourd'hui, prenons bien garde" (Pomponnet), "Je vous dois tout" (Clairette), "Marchande de marée" (Amaranthe), "Certainement j'aimais Clairette" (Ange Pitou), "Pour être fort on se rassemble" (Clairette, Ange Pitou), "Eh quoi, c'est Larivaudière" (Ange Pitou, Larivaudière), Finale Act 1: "Tu l'a promis, tu chanteras"/Chanson politique: "Jadis les rois, race proscrite" (Clairette), "Non, personne ne voudra croire" (chorus), "Les soldats d'Augereau sont des hommes" (Lange), "Gloire au pouvoir exécutif" (Trénitz), "Elle est

La Fille de Madame Angot: "Jadis les roi, race proscrit . . ." Clairette gets herself arrested to avoid getting married and Mlle Lange gets down to a bit of plotting.

tellement innocente" (Pomponnet), "Jours fortunés de notre enfance" (Lange, Clairette), "Voyons, monsieur, raisonnons politique" (Lange, Ange Pitou), "Oui je vous le dis, c'est pour elle" (Lange, Larivaudière, Clairette, Ange Pitou, Louchard), Finale Act 2: "Quand on conspire"/"Tournez, tournez" (Lange), "Vous aviez fait de la dépense" (Clairette), "Je ne sais plus ce que j'éprouve" (Pomponnet), "Prenez-donc garde!" (Pomponnet, Larivaudière), "Je trouve mon futur charmant" (Clairette, Pomponnet, Larivaudière), "Chère ennemi que je devrais haïr" (Ange Pitou, Lange), Finale Act 3: "Ah! c'est donc toi, Madam' Barras" (Clairette, Lange).

La Fille de Madame Angot followed *Les Cent Vierges* to Paris, and then to all corners of the musical-theater world, but it followed its funny forerunner with a truly unequalled vigor. In fact, so great was the triumph of Lecocq and Clairville's musical, not just in its original language but throughout the entire world, that it became and it remains arguably the most successful piece of work to have come out of the whole tradition of musical theater created in nineteenth-century France. But that was not all. The show also set, or at least confirmed in a definitive way, the French musical theater on what would be its postwar course, a course that it would follow through the later seventies and the eighties, and through the creation of a whole body of internationally triumphant musical plays, to enormous effect. Now, the burlesque extravagances and pixilated plots of the Empire years were a thing of the past. They were replaced by highly crafted comical libretti with all the value of a classic French farce—and, of course, inevitably hinging on the same thoroughly sexual imbroglios as those farces—libretti that were usually set in a recognizable corner of period France or some other nearby European country rather than in the fantastical lands and fairylands once so popular as settings for musicals, and which dealt with characters of the real world rather than the grotesque and oversized personalities of burlesque or of the worlds of magic, mythology, and imagination.

Lecocq composed a third piece for Brussels, another opéra-bouffe which was rather more in the madcap comic strain of *Les Cent Vierges* than of *La Fille de Madame Angot*, and he came out with a third international hit. For *Giroflé-Girofla*, Eugène Leterrier (1842–1884) and Albert Vanloo (1846–1920) provided their colleague with an even more sex-based tale than that of the earlier show—the dilemma facing a nervous Spanish governor and his family when, on the day when one twin daughter is to secure her father's finances by marrying his banker's son, and the other his frontiers by marrying the belligerent moor next-door, one girl gets carried off by pirates. While the gubernatorial navy chases after the pirates, the other little bride has to deputize for her sister and cope with the duties and pleasures of two simultaneous wedding nights without being precisely adulterous. Set with some of the composer's merriest music, this piece proved a huge international hit. As this team, and then Lecocq in tandem with other librettists, including both the Chivot/Duru partnership and the famed Meilhac/Halévy pairing, went on to turn out a whole series of mostly successful shows for the Paris of the next seven or eight years, the plots they worked on became a little more "reasonable," if by no means more modest, but they happily became no less full of farcical twists and turns.

The libretti of such Lecocq shows as *La Petite Mariée*, *La Marjolaine*, *Le Jour et la nuit*, and *Le Coeur et la main*—big hits all—were almost entirely based on the now-he/she-gets-it-now-he/she-doesn't (they never actually DID) kind of tale that had been used in both *Les Cent Vierges* and *Giroflé-Girofla*, they were mostly set in some kind of aristocratic or royal circle, and they invariably told their saucy stories with wit, hilarity, and sometimes marvelously complex plotting, but some other Lecocq opéras-comiques tended very much more to the sentimental and the romantic. *Les Prés Saint-Gervais* and *Le Petit Duc*, this latter the most enduringly successful of Lecocq's post-Brussels musicals, were both period pieces which dealt with young French courtly characters and, of course, their young French sexual problems, but they dealt with those sexual problems with a gently amused and encouraging hand rather than a hilarious one, and Lecocq echoed that gentleness and sweet amusement in his music. *Le Petit Duc*, for example, contains some of the composer's, and of the opéra-comique's, most lovely love duetting. Elsewhere, too, things historical and political were given a further airing. *La Camargo* had the famous dancer outwitting the historical bandit Mandrin, the seventeenth-century French heroine of *La Petite Mademoiselle* went through a series of disguises in pursuit of political rather than amorous intrigues, and the plot of *La Princesse des Canaries* concentrated on discovering which of two nubile maidens was the heiress to the title in question. However, needless to say, each and every one of these apparently and basically romantic and/or political plots had plenty of seams to let out, seams in which the regulation amount of comical and sexual-comical scenes and situations, not to mention that barrage of songs both merry and charming of which Lecocq had proven himself the modern master, could be held.

LE PETIT DUC, an opéra-comique in 3 acts by Henri Meilhac and Ludovic Halévy. Music by Charles Lecocq. Produced at the Théâtre de la Renaissance, Paris, 25 January 1878.

Characters: Le Duc de Parthenay, Blanche duchesse de Parthenay, Montlandry, Frimousse, Diane de Château-Lansac, Navailles, Bernard, Montchevrier, Tanneville, Champvallon, Mérignac, Nancey, Roger, Gérard, Julien, Gontran, Henri, Gaston, Hélène, &c.

Plot: The teenaged Duke of Parthenay has been conveniently wed by his courtly elders to an equally young Duchesse, and is adoringly ready to begin real married life. But although he insists that "you're old enough to wed when you're old enough to bed," their elders decide the pair are too young to be allowed to consummate their marriage, and send the little wife off to boarding school and the little husband to the army. So the little Duke leads his regiment to Lunéville to besiege the school. Disguised as a peasant girl, he infiltrates the schoolroom, defended tooth and nail by its aristocratic headmistress, but he has to give up his siege when his men are called to fight a real battle. Risking the royal wrath, the Duchess Blanche runs away from school and finds her little husband on the battlefield, but all is forgiven when the little Duke wins his battle and proves himself a man, deserving of his bride.

Songs: "Il est l'heure" (chorus, Roger, Gérard), "Le savant part, tenant un livre" (Frimousse, Montlandry), "Enfin nous voici, ma petite" (Duc), "Objet d'espoir et de la crainte" (chorus), "C'est pourtant bien doux" (Duc/Duchesse), "La petite femme" (Duc), "Il a l'oreille basse" (pages), Finale Act 1: "Mon colonel," "L'amour seul est le bien suprème" (schoolgirls), "Les voici les parlementaires" (ensemble), "Vous menacer? À Dieu ne plaise" (Montlandry), "La guerre! la guerre!" (Montlandry, Diane), "Mes bell' madam', écoutez ça" ("une paysanne," i.e., Duc), "Ils ont c'qui nomm'nt des sabretaches" ("paysanne," Diane, schoolgirls), "C'est une idylle" ("paysanne," Frimousse), Finale Act 2: "À sac! à sac! la ville est prise," "Tambour et trompette" (chorus), "Il était un petit bossu" (Montlandry), "Ah! mon Dieu, que deviendrons-nous?" (ensemble), "La guerre, c'est donc ça, la guerre!" (Duc), "Pas de femmes" (ensemble), "Décidemment mon cher mari" (Duchesse, Duc), "Mon épée! ah! l'ordre est sévère" (Duc), "Le plus bel officier du monde" (ensemble).

During the decade in which Charles Lecocq was the dominant musician on the Paris stage, he did not by any means have the scene as largely to himself as Hervé and Offenbach had done in earlier days. During the 1870s and the 1880s a goodly number of fine and favored French musicians made notable appearances as composers of opéra-comique, and their works imitated those of Lecocq in following up their Parisian careers by taking a trip round the theaters of the world in a manner, and with a success, that no other body of contemporary musical theater—either from Britain or from Vienna—could equal.

Among these exportable musicians of the moment were Edmond Audran (1842–1901), Léon Vasseur (1844–1917), Louis Varney (1844–1908), Francis Chassaigne (1848–1922), Paul Lacôme (1838–1920), Firmin Bernicat (1843–1883), and André Messager (1853–1929), as well as the still decidedly present and producing Offenbach and Hervé, but the biggest single winner of the era—a success which rivalled even that of *La Fille de Madame Angot* in size, in endurance, and in traveling power—came from the music-pad of Robert Planquette (1848–1903), a musician whose success up to the time of his début on the opéra-comique stage had been made with café-concert songs and popular marches. The show with which Planquette forever made his mark was actually a surprisingly old-fashioned one in its subject matter and its plotting.

The story of *Les Cloches de Corneville*, as invented by a Parisian policeman called Charles Gabet, was one that with its phoney haunted château and its long-lost heiress went right back to the old *The Haunted Tower/La Dame blanche* type of show. There was none of the blistering "suggestiveness" and sexual gallimaufry of such texts as *La Petite Mariée* or that most outrageously blushmaking of all French musicals, the 1872 *La Timbale d'argent*, there was none of the political or military maneuvering which was a feature of so many of the best and most popular musicals of the time, there was none of the sophistication of a *La Fille de Madame Angot*: the backbone to this almost naively comic-romantic libretto was nothing more than the ages-old disguised-heir-finds-long-lost-heroine tale. But *Les Cloches de Corneville* had two big advantages. Gabet's libretto was remade by the same Clairville who had been responsible for *La Fille de Madame Angot*, with undemanding humor, endearing and even interesting characters, and some surprising moments of pathos, and the whole was set by the theatrically all-but-unknown Planquette with music that was both enormously catchy and attractive. Those com-

ponents more than did the trick. And, thanks to them, after *Les Cloches de Corneville* had triumphed at home, it was—like *La Fille de Madame Angot*—able to go on to the rest of the world without undergoing the kind of bowdlerization which had turned so many a risqué Paris hit into a gelded shadow of its original self before it could be seen on politer stages. In London, in particular, the local version of *Les Cloches de Corneville* proved an enormous hit. It set up a West End long-run record and established itself for decades of touring round the English-speaking world. In France, the show is still regularly played today, alongside *La Fille de Madame Angot*, as one of the most important items in the very slim repertoire of French musicals which have survived as the classics of its nineteenth-century heyday.

Les Cloches de Corneville: "C'est le marché de Corne-Corneville." Even in the dramatic moments there's always time for a jolly bit of highish kicking.

LES CLOCHES DE CORNEVILLE, an opéra-comique in 3 acts by Clairville and Charles Gabet. Music by Robert Planquette. Produced at the Théâtre des Folies-Dramatiques, Paris, 19 April 1877.

Characters: Germaine, Serpolette, Gaspard, Henri, Le Marquis de Corneville, Jean Grénicheux, Le Bailli, Le Tabellion, Manette, Jeanne, Gertrude, Suzanne, Catherine, Marguerite, Cachalot, Grippardin, Fouinard, &c.

Plot: The old steward Gaspard holds two trusts. For years, since the exile of the Marquis of Corneville, he has hoarded the profits of his master's estates in a room in the abandoned castle, putting about the rumor that the place is haunted to keep prying eyes away. He has also brought up the daughter of another noble exile as his own niece, and in his fanatic desire to keep "his" castle and treasure safe, he is planning to wed her to an aging local magistrate. Germaine, however, feels obliged to give her hand to the peasant Grénicheux, who saved her from drowning. Then Henri, the son of the old Marquis, returns from exile, and soon the secrets of Corneville begin to open up. It comes out that it is Germaine, not as first thought the saucy peasant girl Serpolette, who is the missing heiress, it was Henri not Grénicheux who pulled her from the sea, and Gaspard—who went out of his mind when the young Marquis descended on his hideaway clad in the armour of his ancestors—is relieved of both his trusts as the curtain falls.

Songs: "C'est le marché de Corneville" (chorus), Le Chanson des "on dit" (Serpolette), "Dans ma mystérieuse histoire" (Germaine), "Va petit mousse" (Grénicheux), "Même sans consulter mon coeur" (Germaine, Grénicheux), Légende des cloches: "Nous avons, hélas, perdus d'excellents maîtres" (Germaine), "J'ai fait trois fois le tour du monde" (Marquis), Finale Act 1/I: "C'est affreux, odieux," "Je ne sais comment faire" (Grénicheux), "Sur le marché de Corneville" (chorus), "Vous qui voulez des servantes" (Serpolette), Finale Act 1/II: "Jeune fille, dis-moi ton nom," "À la lueur des flambeaux" (chorus), "Fermons les yeux" (Grénicheux, Serpolette, Le Bailli), "Ne parlez pas de mon courage" (Germaine), "J'avais perdu la tête et ma perruque" (Le Bailli), "Sous les armures à leur taille" (Marquis), "Vicomtesse et marquise" (Serpolette), "C'est elle et son destin le guide" (Henri, Germaine), Chanson des "oui" et "non" (Germaine), "Gloire au valereux Grénicheux" (sailors), Finale Act 2: "C'est là, c'est là, qu'est la richesse," Chanson des gueux (Gaspard), "Oui, c'est moi, c'est Serpolette" (Serpolette), Chanson du cidre (Serpolette), "Je regardais en l'air" (Grénicheux), "Une servante, que m'importe" (Marquis, Germaine), Finale Act 3: "Pour ce trésor."

Planquette went on to compose the scores for a number of other fine works—notably a highly successful musical based on Washington Irving's story of *Rip van Winkle*, a piece which again featured a ghostly element, mixed here with both a touch of US–UK politics and the usual ladleful of marital moments, and another which used the historical pirate *Surcouf* as the hero of a comical and romantic tale set against a Britain versus France wartime background—but his first full-sized musical remains the one for which he is remembered.

Another musician of this time whose earliest works proved to be his biggest successes was Edmond Audran, whose first opéra-comique, *Le Grand Mogol*, came out in Marseilles in the same year as *Les Cloches de Corneville* did in Paris. Even though its action was set in the nebulous East, Chivot's libretto for this piece still used a set of variations on the most popular plot elements of the moment: it dealt with the struggle for a royal crown which, so tradition says, will be lost should the pretender fall from virginity before succeeding. There is, of course, a lady—nay, two ladies—in the affair. And one of them is a French snake-charmer. Audran's music—educated, light-hearted, and ineffably melodious—quickly assured both its success and a commission for its composer to write a show for Paris, and in rapid succession he turned out the scores for two of what would prove to be the most widely popular musicals of the era: *Les Noces d'Olivette* and *La Mascotte*.

Both these opérettes (as the term now currently went, in preference to either "opéra-bouffe," which was a thing of the past, or "opéra-comique," which had returned to describing the kind of entertainment found at the thus-named theater) had books, written by the now top-rated Chivot and Duru, which were typical examples of the farcical, sexual, courtly/military/political libretti of the time, and both were equipped with musical scores that would launch a series of favorite songs around the world.

The first of them, *Les Noces d'Olivette*, followed the malheurs and mishaps experienced by one Valentin on the way to—and beyond—his marriage with his Olivette. Having accidentally invaded the bedroom of the local countess in an élan of pre-wedding passion, he is flung in jail, escapes in disguise as his own uncle, and then finds himself forced—as the uncle—to wed his own bride, under orders from the countess, who has decided she fancies Valentin for herself. A conspiracy against her highness-ship, her kidnapping, and many a bit of sexual on-the-spot-putting intervene before the evening ends with the usual happily-ever-afters and no one having actually put a foot (or any other piece of anatomy) wrong. *Olivette* (as it was mostly known outside France) was one of the very biggest hits of its time on both French- and English-language stages, and its merry song "The Torpedo and the Whale" became the show-song of the era in America. But, even so, the piece was outpointed, particularly in the long run, by its writers' own next offering.

La Mascotte reprised, in a way, the theme of *Le Grand Mogol*, basing its plot on the need for its heroine (instead of the earlier piece's hero) to maintain her virginity or pay a dreadful price. However, Chivot and Duru wrapped up their central theme in a bedroom- and throne-room-farcical series of comical scenes and situations far cleverer than those of the earlier show, and their bristlingly funny book and what is perhaps Audran's most thoroughly winning score of music, topped by an ingenuous "Glou-glou" duet for the turkey-girl heroine and her shepherd sweetheart which outdid even "The Torpedo and the Whale" in world-wide popularity, combined to make *La Mascotte* the most widely and lengthily popular of all the merry series of "indecent" musicals that characterized this period.

The word "indecent" was, of course, not used (by any except the crabbed or the crusading) to describe the show in France, any more than it was used to describe any one of those of its kindred musicals, from *La Timbale d'argent* in 1872 up to *Le Coeur et la main* in 1883, that were produced at a time and in a place where sexual maneuverings—in and/or out of marriage (especially someone else's)—were considered splendid and smileworthy sport, where a breast-beating or whimpering cuckold or done-down wife who didn't go out prospecting themselves was a figure of anything from fun to amused pity, where social and financial promotion by marriage or any degree of quasi-marriage was considered at least OK and more often than not admirable, where a would-be gallivanter who worked his way to the green but failed to sink his putt was looked on as a loser, and, most importantly, where slim-waisted, taut-thighed youth and beauty was an excuse for absolutely anything, and sagging middle-to-old-age still accompanied by the urges of earlier years was the butt of absolutely everything.

Such sentiments and dramatic works based on them had been the mainstay of comic theater in the seventeenth-century England of the years after the Restoration of the monarchy, but two hundred years down the line, with morality—or at least the permitted public display of morality—having been given a stiff dip in a barrel of bleach, they were considered way beyond the pale, and a piece like *Les Noces d'Olivette* or *La Mascotte* had to be "cleaned up" before it was considered suitable for delicate English-hearing ears. Oddly enough, though, *La Mascotte* got a much lighter whitewashing than most of its contemporaries, and it went on to triumph on foreign stages just as it had at home.

LA MASCOTTE, an opérette (opéra-comique) in 3 acts by Henri Chivot and Alfred Duru. Music by Edmond Audran. Produced at the Théâtre des Bouffes-Parisiens, Paris, 28 December 1880.

Characters: Le Prince Laurent XVII of Piombino, Pippo, Le Prince Fritellini, Bettina la Rougeade, La Princesse Fiametta, Rocco, Mathéo, Sergent Parafante, Francesca, Antonia, Paola, Luigi, Beppo, Carlo, Angelo, &c.

Plot: The turkey-girl Bettina is a "mascotte," which means she brings good luck to whoever employs her . . . as long as she remains a virgin. When the local Prince—who has lost an awful lot of wars on the trot—discovers this, he whisks Bettina away from Rocco's farm and from her shepherd boyfriend Pippo, carries her off to court, and determines that, to keep her there, he will wed her. No problem about the virginity bit—the old chap is impotent. Pippo will be safely married off to his daughter, the Princess Fiametta. But Bettina and Pippo escape, Prince Laurent's luck in the field goes instantly sour, and he finds his princedom attacked by his daughter's indignantly displaced lover, the neighboring Prince Fritellini. Since Bettina and Pippo have run straight to the protective Fritellini, who is perfectly willing, nay delighted, to see them wed, he now has all the luck. But Rocco discloses to the younger Prince the caveats on Bettina's sex life, and Fritellini then joins the farmer in trying everything possible to stop the shepherd getting into bed with his new wife and depriving her of the talent that is so useful to them. But Laurent gives Pippo a leg up through a handy window, the deed is done, and all the two princes can do is settle down to wait till the resultant child, which it seems will inherit its mother's lost gift, is born. It had better be twins.

Songs: "La vendange est terminée" (chorus), Légende: "Un jour le diable, ivre d'orgeuil" (Pippo), "N'avancez pas ou j'tape" (Bettina), "Les gens sensés et sages" (Laurent), "Ah! qu'il est beau, l'homme des champs" (Fiametta), "Le je ne sais quoi poétique" (Fritellini), Duo des bé-bé: "Je sens, lorsque je t'aperçois" (Pippo, Bettina), Finale Act 1: "On sonne, on sonne," "Qu'elle est belle et qu'elle a de grâce" (chorus), "Que je regrette mon village" (Bettina), "Spectacle charmante" (chorus), "C'est moi, c'est moi Saltarello" (Pippo), "Sais-tu que ces beaux habits-là" (Pippo, Bettina), "Mon cher que vous êtes naïf" (Fritellini), "Chasser le cerf au son du cor" (Laurent), Finale Act 2: "C'est le futur de la princesse"/"Un jour un brave capitaine" (Bettina), "Verse, verse, verse à boire" (soldiers), "De nos pas marquant la cadence" (Fritellini), Chanson de l'Orang Outang: "Le grand singe d'Amérique" (Fiametta), "Je touche au but" (Pippo), "Quoi! Pippo quand je vous réclame" (Bettina, Pippo, Laurent, Rocco), Finale Act 3: "Et pourquoi donc crier ainsi."

If the world-wide success of *La Mascotte*—not to forget *La Fille de Madame Angot* and *Les Cloches de Corneville*—was in some part owing to their escaping, or not needing, too much in the way of a textual bromide for overseas consumption, there were other contemporaneously "indecent" pieces which wholly failed to export beyond France for little other reason than that they were quite simply unbleachable. The most notable example of such a piece was the first and most successful (at home) work of the composer Léon Vasseur. His opéra-bouffe *La Timbale d'argent* came out in 1872, hard on the heels of *La Fille de Madame Angot*, and it provoked some gasps even in Paris with the merry lechery of its reverse *Lysistrata* kind of story. That story, written by Adolphe Jaime (1824–1901), co-author of *Le Petit Faust* and the crazy little *Croquefer*, and by Jules Noriac (1827–1882), was another that drew its fun from the pangs of unnatural celibacy and the path to the soothing of those pangs. The hero—a lad from a "foreign" village— wins the hand of the soubrette everyone wants in a singing contest, but his chief rival discovers that his superior singing skills have arisen thanks to an oath of sexual abstinence, and so all the men of the village take to zipping up, tarting up their top notes a treat, and winning prizes. The women, the newly wed Molda at their head, rebel, and go to work to get their status quo and marriage rights back. As in so many of these shows, it wasn't just the plot that rippled with glorious "indecency," but the dialogue and the song-words, and even the music: when the heroine sang "v'là que ça gli-sse!" ("see it slip u-u-p"), to suitable musical accompaniment, it was fairly obvious she wasn't just talking about a little singing trophy. *La Timbale d'argent* almost equalled *La Fille de Madame Angot* in first-run popularity, and it won revivals in Paris for a quarter of a century; however, it never established itself further afield, and Vasseur—although he scored several more successes in France—won scant showing for his works abroad.

If a show could have its prospects damaged by too much sex, the same apparently didn't go for politics. Very many of the shows that followed *La Fille de Madame Angot* to success on the Paris stage had plots and characters that were centered on historical eras or personalities, on military escapades or other famous French events. The delicious *Jeanne, Jeannette et Jeanneton*, written by Clairville and another of France's top comic playwrights, the same Alfred Delacour (?1815–1883) who had teamed with Hennequin on the megahit farce *Les Dominos roses* and with Labiche on *La Cagnotte* and *Le Voyage en Chine*, and set to charming music by Paul Lacôme, was one such. It followed the fortunes of three country girls come to Paris to make good. One ends up as the famous dancer La Guimard, another as Mme du Barry, and all three get involved in a spaghetti-tangle of affairs of the heart and of state which ends with the trio wreaking awful vengeance on a doubly faithless nobleman. The one big opérette by the ill-fated composer Firmin Bernicat, *François les bas-bleus*, was another: it used the antique long-lost-noble-child syndrome as its principal plotline, but the piece took place before a background of eve-of-Revolution Paris, and its deus ex machina was the historical storming of the Bastille prison. Even such a piece as *Les Mousquetaires au couvent*, a merry musical comedy built around the age-old situation of a couple of lovestruck lads loose in a girls' school, taken by Paul

Ferrier (1843–1920) and Jules Prével (1835–1889) from an old vaudeville and remade with a fresh score by the first-up Louis Varney, availed itself of a solid historical background. The key to the happy ending was the uncovering of a plot against the deeply unfictional Cardinal Richelieu.

Two of the most notable pieces in this line, however, came from no less a composer than Jacques Offenbach. Offenbach had by no means faded away with the end of the Empire and of opéra-bouffe. He had just lost his way a little, and wandered from the path of success. In the first part of the 1870s he had dallied with all kinds of shows, attempting to prolong the days of bouffe-flavored musicals with such pieces as *Madame L'Archiduc*—a disappointing reverse-sex *La Grande-Duchesse*—or a parody of Verne in *Le Docteur Ox*, subjugating his music to scenic values and spectacular staging in such shows as *Le Roi Carotte* or *Le Voyage dans la lune*, or following the newest trends with a sex comedy musical, *La Jolie Parfumeuse*, composed to a libretto by his *Orphée aux enfers* partner Crémieux and Ernest Blum (1836–1907), and put the little perfume-shop lady of the title triumphantly through a frustrating (for the would-be seducer) series of perils to her virtue to the accompaniment of some charming songs. Offenbach also set a typically hectically plotted and endlessly funny libretto by the faithful Meilhac and Halévy as *La Boulangère a des écus*, but this piece—which would surely and easily have outdone *La Jolie Parfumeuse* in prewar Paris—was clearly not in the style of the moment, and it was the tale of the virtuous and canny perfumeress which proved the best liked of Offenbach's musicals, around the world, between 1870 and 1877.

In 1878, however, he hit the bullseye again, with more than a little aid from those habitués of the bullseye, Messieurs Chivot and Duru. The evergreen pair of writers supplied him with a splendid, farcical libretto, which featured a magnificent rôle à tiroirs (a part allowing the performer to go through the whole register of her art) for its leading lady as the celebrated, historical French actress *Madame Favart*. Like the little perfumeress, Madame Favart spent the evening keeping one step ahead of a pursuing male who was convinced that his high position made her his lawful prey. The lady pops in and out of various disguises, old, young, high, and low, and the odd bit of real history, until the king himself discovers what his army chief is up to, and does the decent thing. The final act included a scene where Madame Favart performs—as she did in real life—her very real husband's famous musical *La Chercheuse d'esprit*.

Madame Favart did particularly well in Britain, where it became one of the longest-running musicals in up-to-then stage history, but wider success was reserved for the same writers' and composer's next—and last—work together, the lively story of *La Fille du Tambour-Major*. This time, Chivot and Duru renounced the pursued-damsel motif in favor of a thoroughly semi-historical piece, set in the context of the warring between Italy and France at the turn of the eighteenth century, in which the fate of the long-lost child of the title was really subsidiary to the comical, marital, political, and military maneuverings and situations that went on around her and which were put an end to by the French army invading Milan, rather like the cavalry arriving in the last reel of a western. If the text in *Madame Favart* had had just a little tendency to overwhelm the music in importance, this time round there was no such imbalance, and the show went on to give the composer his greatest latter-day success.

LA FILLE DU TAMBOUR MAJOR, an opéra-comique in 3 acts by Henri Chivot and Alfred Duru. Music by Jacques Offenbach. Produced at the Théâtre des Folies-Dramatiques, Paris, 13 December 1879.

Characters: Monthabor, Le Duc della Volta, La Duchesse della Volta, Stella, Griolet, Claudine, Le Marquis Bambini, Clampas, La Prieure, Gregorio, Le Sergent Morin, Zerbinelli, Del Ponto, Francesca, Lorenza, Lucrezia, &c.

Plot: A regiment of the French army forays into northern Italy, finds young Stella locked in the detention room of her abandoned school, and then billets itself in the château belonging to the girl's horrified parents. But Stella, it turns out, is not really the child of the Duc della Volta, but of his wife's first husband, the French drum-major Monthabor, and now she refuses to wed the Duc's preferred suitor, the rich and effete Bambini, for she has fallen for Robert, the baritonic lieutenant of the invading regiment. Stella runs away, the Duc pursues, the Duchesse finds old sentiments stirred anew, and after some farcical situations of disguise and mistaken identity have ended with our friends apparently cornered in Milan, Robert, Stella, and their Francophile friends are saved by the arrival of the main body of the invading army.

Songs: "Reçois, sainte madone" (schoolgirls), Légende du fruit défendu: "Prenez les grappes empourprées" (Stella), "Par un chaleur aussi forte" (chorus), "Nous courrons tous après la gloire" (Robert), "Ce n'est pas une âne ordinaire" (Claudine), "De grâce, ayez pitié de moi" (ensemble), "Tout en tirant mon aiguille" (Griolet), "Puisque le couvert est mis" (chorus &c.), "Petit français, brave français" (Stella), "Il était une grande princesse" (Griolet, Claudine), Finale Act 1: "Messieurs les militaires"/"Pour recevoir un régiment" (Stella), "J'ai ma migraine!" (Duchesse), "Ah! vraiment je le déclare" (Stella), "C'est un billet de logement" (Robert, Monthabor, Duc, Griolet), "Vlan! vlan! mets-ça dans ta poche" (Claudine), "Dansons et valsons" (ensemble), "J'ose vous le dire" (Robert, Stella), "Il est là ce bel uniforme" (Griolet), Finale Act 2: "Par devant monsieur le notaire"/"Oui, c'est mon père"/"La fille du tambour-major," "Chut! chut! il faut de la prudence" (chorus, Clampas), "Nous étions à Novare" (Robert), "Je suis l' petit cocher" (Stella), "Quoi! c'est vous mes amis?" (Robert, Stella, Monthabor, Griolet), "Devant moi, contre tout attente" (Duchesse, Monthabor), "Un mariage s'apprête" (chorus, Clampas), Finale Act 3: "Clampas . . . ah! mon ami."

If Offenbach was a long time coming up with his biggest postwar successes, Hervé took even longer. The "crazy composer" was undoubtedly less happy than his fellow musician working outside the flamboyantly nonsensical world of opéra-bouffe and unable, unlike Offenbach, to be at home working with the pursued-damsel kind of text, he didn't succeed in turning out a major opéra-comique or opérette hit in the 1870s. But Hervé was ultimately to come back to the very top, and to come back with a set of shows that not only outshone the most successful of his most famous contemporary's latter-day shows, but which have become—in these days when the most far-fetched of opéra-bouffe seems to be beyond the comprehension of most producers and performers—the most enduring part of his entire opus.

These successes came in a different area of the musical theater from that which had been all and everywhere supreme over the last fifteen or twenty years, an area of the musical theater which, while always popular, had never been given the same consideration or achieved the same profile as the opéra-bouffe, the opéra-comique, or the opérette: the vaudeville. In the 1870s, vaudevilles—lively, up-to-date, and often quite complex comical plays with music, the descendants of the old comedies of the fair-booth days with their "signature tune" musical part—still flourished on the Paris stage, but they were more often played in the comedy theaters than in those which devoted themselves seriously to opérette in all its forms and under all its names. Their musical part had changed little: it was still simple and still very often made up from that same basic bundle of familiar and frequently recycled "ponts-neufs" that had been used as vaudeville tunes for years. But now the vaudeville was in for a dose of upmarketing, a dose that would gradually lead it to becoming, by the 1890s, the most appreciable and real "musical comedy" to be found anywhere on the world's stages.

The process began in the year 1877, and the folk responsible were producer Eugène Bertrand of the Paris Théâtre des Variétés and his resident star Anna Judic—the very same star who a few years earlier had made such a sensation performing the *Timbale d'argent* song that claimed "it slips up, like this . . ." Judic (1850–1911) had starred in a number of opérettes since *La Timbale d'argent* without finding another part that allowed her the same opportunities, and Bertrand, on the look-out for a vehicle for his slightly wasted top-biller, decided to try a vaudeville that had been submitted to him by two experienced writers. It was called *Niniche*, and its title-rôle seemed thoroughly made for Anna Judic. He attempted to put a shine on the piece by getting Offenbach to compose original melodies for the show's musical numbers, but Offenbach, in spite of being at an all-time low, wasn't interested in going "down" to writing for the vaudeville stage so, instead, the theater's former musical director put together a "composed and arranged" set of a dozen of the usual kind of tunes to do duty as the musical part of the show. And the saucily comical *Niniche*—scissors-and-paste score and all—turned out a triumph. In a year that saw *Le Petit Duc, Madame Favart, La Camargo*, Vasseur's *Le Droit du seigneur*, and other fine opérettes first brought to the boards, *Niniche* was quite simply the most remarkable international musical-theater hit to come out of France. Judic (who created a sensation by appearing at one stage in the action in a bathing suit) would play the show, and its megastar central rôle, all round the world for a quarter of a century, as it was remade over and over, in all kinds of shapes and with all kinds of replacement scores, in both English— where the first attempt at translation failed to get past the censor—and in German (and probably in all kinds of other languages), launching the vaudeville on a whole new career during which it would drop the old ponts-neufs in favor of original music, and eventually mutate into what the 1890s called, with fine regard for the genre's new and nicer stature, the vaudeville-opérette. But which, more than any kind of show to date, really deserved to be called quite simply "musical comedy."

NINICHE, a vaudeville [pièce] in 3 acts by Alfred Hennequin and Albert Millaud. Music composed and arranged by Marius Boullard. Produced at the Théâtre des Variétés, Paris, 15 February 1878.

Characters: La Comtesse Corniska otherwise Niniche, Grégoire, Le Comte Olympus Corniski, Anatole de Beaupersil, Desablettes, La veuve Sillery, Georgina, Narcisse, Dupiton, Baptiste, Coquet, Cora, Castagnette, Annette, Amanda, Caro, Simonne, &c.

Plot: The Parisienne courtesan Niniche wed a Polish diplomat, gave up work, went off to married life in the deepest north, and there she met up with an old client for whom she'd had a mutual very soft spot. Only now he was about to be promoted to King, and since people in power risk all sorts of poisonous, petulant, politically motivated press paragraphs or worse should anything more enjoyable than perfectly pure be found in their past, her old friend and his representatives are very anxious to get back the unfettered letters he once wrote to the now non-existent Niniche. Unfortunately, they were left in a Parisian drawer when Niniche transmuted into Comtesse Corniska, and that drawer is part of the now non-existent Niniche's furniture which is being sold off to cover some still existent debts. So the Comte and Comtesse Corniska, the helpful de Beaupersil, and the ambitious Grégoire all set off south to recover those dangerous letters. It takes two acts of delicate situations, disguises, and comedy before the curtain can fall on a well-arranged ending.

Songs: "Sur la plage allons prendre l'air" (chorus), "Si j'avais suivi les voeux de mon père" (Grégoire), "En frisonnant je me hasarde" (Niniche), "C'est, je vous le jure" (Niniche), "En revenant après six mois" (Niniche), "Avec ce costume, Anatole" (Niniche), "Si vous connaissez la comtesse" (Niniche, Grégoire), Couplets du Commissaire: "Je viens de chez le Commissaire" (Niniche), Couplets du masseur: "Certes, Monsieur doit plaire aux dames" (Grégoire), Finale Act 3: "Voici la minut' délicate."

Needless to say, the first and the most enthusiastic follower-up of Niniche was producer Bertrand, and in the next half dozen years he put onto the stage of the Variétés — under all sorts of appellations from "pièce" to "comédie-opérette" — the circus-land tale of the disappearing *Le Grand Casimir* and his bigamous problems with the brigands of Corsica, the comical *La Femme à Papa*, which featured Judic as the lightish lass intended by a po-faced son to control his frisky widower of a father, the comic and romantic comings and goings of the search for the long-lost *La Roussotte* (Judic again) and her brother, the through the years blighted-love-story of *Lili* (with Judic in a bravura rôle as mother and daughter), and pieces featuring the theater's star as the naughty schoolgirl *Mam'zelle Nitouche* and the runaway Russian aristocrat known as *La Cosaque*. The music for *Le Grand Casimir* was composed by Lecocq, that of *La Roussotte*, through circumstances, was a three-handed affair, but otherwise, from *La Femme à Papa*, with its famous Chanson du Colonel, onwards, it was Hervé who supplied the ever-growing amounts of music for this enormously popular series, and Hervé who reaped the musical rewards of its greatest hits — *Lili* and, the most enduring of all, the (for the composer) semi-autobiographical *Mam'zelle Nitouche*, with its central character of a convent music master who doubles secretly as a composer for the theater.

MAM'ZELLE NITOUCHE, a comédie-opérette in 3 acts by Henri Meilhac and Albert Millaud. Music by Hervé. Produced at the Théâtre des Variétés, Paris, 26 January 1883.

Characters: Denise de Flavigny, Célestin, Major Château-Gibus, Corinne, La Supérieure, Champlâtreux, Loriot, La Tourière, Sylvie, Lydie, Gimblette.

Plot: Denise de Flavigny is considered the angel of her convent school, but she isn't. Butter would boil in her mouth. And when she discovers that the music-master, Célestin, leads a double life, piously teaching young ladies by day and working at a theater at nights, she blackmails him. The blackmail is necessary because Denise's parents have decided to marry her, and little Miss Innocence isn't going to have that. She will, with Célestin's help, run away. Her running away leads her first to the theater, where she encounters the dishy young officer Champlâtreux, then to a military barrack, amid a barrage of events and accidents, and finally back to base and a happy ending—because Denise has discovered that her parents' choice as her husband is . . . guess who? So Little Miss Innocence dutifully obeys her parents commands, and only her husband and her music-master need ever know what almost happened.

Songs: "Pour le théâtre Floridor" (Célestin), "En sortant de matines" (chorus), "Sous les vieux arceaus gothiques" (Denise), "Le grenadier était bel homme" (Denise, Célestin), "Pardonnez-moi, mademoiselle" (Champlâtreux), "Ce n'est pas une sinécure"/Allélujah (Denise), Finale Act 1: "Eh, quoi, Denise, notre orgeuil"/"Ah! mes soeurs que cela m'afflige," "Buvons, rions, chantons" (chorus), "Un mariage de raison" (Champlâtreux), Rondeau de l'escapade: "La voiture attendait en bas" (Denise), "Babet et Cadet" (Denise), "Je suis de Saint-Étienne" (Loriot), "Floridor, vous avez raison" (Denise, Célestin, officers), "Au gai soleil" (Denise), Légende de la grosse caisse: "Le long de la rue Lafayette" (Denise), "Est-il possible?" (Denise), Invocation à Sainte-Nitouche: "Je te plains, ma pauvre Denise" (Denise), "Quand vous êtes venu" (Denise, Champlâtreux), Finale Act 3: Allons, voyons, mam'zell' Nitouche."

While the latest version of the vaudeville was establishing itself as a favorite form of entertainment, however, the opérette—that ever more civilized daughter of the opéra-bouffe and the Lecocqian opéra-comique—was beginning to undergo a bit of a sea change, one that would not be—in the end—very good for its health. Although comedy and a comic element were still featured as an important part of almost any musical play, it seemed now as if the most real and rib-wrenching comedy was being left to the vaudevilles and comédies-opérettes (or whatever their authors chose to call their comical plays with new music), and that the opérette, which had so long survived and sparkled on farcical, fast-moving, comic libretti, was on its way to becoming more romantic and sentimental in character. Certainly, some of the same situations appeared in new shows as in old ones, but they were made and played in a rather different tone. When the heroine of *Madame Boniface* went through the pursued-damsel routine in 1883, for example, she didn't do it with quite the libidinous gallivantry that her very close sister *La Jolie Parfumeuse* had done ten years earlier (or the heroine of the old opéra-comique *Les Porcherons* well before that). A piece such as the 1886 *La Cigale et la fourmi*—undoubtedly the most internationally successful French opérette of the late eighties—sported as its libretto a nearly tragic version of the "cricket and ant" tale of a country girl brought to ruin by the temptations of the town. In spite of the introduction of some light-comic subsidiary characters and moments, it was distinctly short on laughs, although not on attractive tunes. And when another musical from the same season, *Les Noces improvisées*, was taken to Britain and America after a weak showing in Paris, its romantic road-story about the exiled Hungarian patriot Rákóczi, his loved lady, and their battle against the horrid Austrian oppressor had to be jollied up by the wholesale introduction of a big, bill-topping low comedy part before the show could become a success.

The renunciation of vigorous comedy in favor of sentiment and romance as the heart of the French opérette effectively signaled the beginning of its end. In the 1890s that trend would continue and deepen, and, while the vaudeville-opérette took over as France's most satisfying and exportable form of musical theater, only a tiny handful of the pretty pieces produced as opérette proved able to find a comparative success. France and the French-language theater's hour as the dominant force in the musical theater would be over, never to return.

OPERETTE

It took fifteen years, from the first Viennese attempt to follow in the fiacre-tracks of the new French fashion in musical theater with the little *Flodoardo Wuprahall*, in 1859, for the German-language musical theater to find its own first full-sized and full-scale hit. Fifteen years in which there were turned out some agreeable and effective smaller pieces but which failed to produce that one, keystone show which is always needed to provide the first foundations for a theatrical tradition.

When it did come, that show—like so many of its predecessors, and like innumerable of its successors—did, indeed, firmly follow the French fashion. More, in fact, for, again like so many of both its forerunners and its successors, it went straight to France and to the French comic theater for its raw textual material. However, this is not to say that the Operetten of Austria were simply grown-away-from-home French opérettes. If the libretti of the first and many of the most famous among them were little more than made-over pieces of French theater, the music that was attached to them—the songs and dances and ensembles that made up an Operette score—was certainly not French. It was what we, with a fine disgregard for the rest of Austria, call Viennese music, the waltzing, polka-ing, merrily marching music of the Austrian cafés and dance-halls as purveyed down through the earlier years of the nineteenth century by such composers as Josef Lanner, Johann Strauss, and, more recently, his son, the younger Johann Strauss.

In fact, it was the younger Strauss who was responsible for the musical part of that keystone Austrian Operette. Having been tempted from the world of the orchestra and the dance-hall into the potentially lucrative purlieus of the theater by his singer wife and the eye-for-a-big-name manager of the Theater an der Wien, he had made several attempts at writing a musical in the French mode, but without success. Neither his first musical actually to get completed and onto the stage, a Viennese-style opéra-bouffe called *Indigo und die vierzig Räuber*, nor the more coherent but slightly stiff-necked romantic musical play *Carneval in Rom* which followed it a little over a year down the line, proved, in spite of some charming music, to be keystone— or even particularly staying—material, any more than a variety of early attempts at a major musical by such composers as Franz von Suppé, Giovanni von Zaytz, Julius Hopp, or Karl Millöcker had done. But, third time round, Johann Strauss hit the gold.

Die Fledermaus had an excellent pedigree. Its libretto was not original: a departure already from the French way of life where musical-theater books were almost always freshly brewed material and only very rarely any kind of adaptation. It was a remake of a fine and funny Parisian comedy called *Le Réveillon*, and the authors of *Le Réveillon* were none other than those stars of the opéra-bouffe firmament, Henri Meilhac and Ludovic Halévy. Meilhac and Halévy, however, had more than one chamber to their theatrical guns. As they had shown over and over again, both on the comic stage and in such musical pieces as *La Vie Parisienne* or *La Boulangère a des écus*, they could turn out the briskest of situation and character comedy equally as well as they could burlesque works, and it was into that line of straight comedy that *Le Réveillon* fell. The second bloodline in the *Die Fledermaus* pedigree was its adaptor: Richard Genée (1823–1895). A composer and conductor himself, Genée was able to mold his lyrics expertly and happily to the music of the theatrically wobbly Strauss, and as a deft author he was able—while maintaining large pieces of Meilhac and Halévy's original dialogue—to transmute the very largely male comedy of *Le Réveillon* into a conventional musical-theater piece with two sizeable and showy female star rôles. To this text, already so very much stronger than anything he had worked with before, but also so very much more suitable to the light-footed melodiousness of his favorite style of music than the bouffe or romantic books he had set previously, Strauss added a delightful score, turning a decidedly French comedy into an ineffably Austrian musical with marked success.

DIE FLEDERMAUS, a komische Operette in 3 acts by Richard Genée (and Karl Haffner), based on *Le Réveillon* by Henri Meilhac and Ludovic Halévy. Music by Johann Strauss. Produced at the Theater an der Wien, Vienna, 5 April 1874.

Characters: Gabriel von Eisenstein, Rosalinde von Eisenstein, Frank, Prinz Orlofsky, Alfred, Dr Falke, Dr Blind, Adele, Frosch, &c.

Plot: As the consequence of a very minor misdemeanour, Gabriel von Eisenstein has been sentenced to a very little stay in prison. However, the prospect held out by his buddy Falke of a particularly promising party on the very evening when he is due to present himself to the prison governor for his little period of incarceration proves too much of a temptation. The dissembling Eisenstein bids a prisonwards goodnight to his wife and, instead of heading for the penitentiary, goes off partying chez Prinz Orlofsky. He isn't missed down at the jail though, for the prison governor is taking a night off at the same party, and his underlings mistakenly incarcerate in his place the amorous gentleman who has invited himself to supper with the lonely Madame Eisenstein. Eisenstein and Gov-

ernor Frank aren't the only folk who arrive at Orlofsky's masquerading under false names and titles. The Eisenstein's maid, Adele, turns up pretending to be an actress, and Rosalinde herself puts in an appearance in the guise of a Hungarian countess. Thus disguised, she flirts heavily with her own husband and wins from him his chiming watch as a later proof of his attempted infidelity. It is the following morning that things come to their farcical peak. Eisenstein turns up tardily at the prison to find his carousing partner of the night before back at his gubernatorial post, and "himself" already in prison! But what looks like his wife's infidelity has, of course, been no more real than his own, and the ghastly moments of suspicion he has gone through have actually all been arranged by old buddy Falke as revenge for a practical joke of yesteryear.

Songs: Introduction: "Täubchen, das entflattert ist" (Alfred, Adele, Rosalinde), "Nein, mit solchen Advokaten" (Eisenstein, Blind, Rosalinde), "Komm' mit mir zum Souper" (Falke, Eisenstein), "So muss allein ich bleiben" (Rosalinde, Adele, Eisenstein), Finale Act 1: "Trinke, Liebchen, trinke schnell"/"Mein Herr, was dächten Sie von mir?"/"Mein schönes grosses Vogelhaus," "Ein Souper heut' uns winkt" (chorus), "Ich lade gern mir Gäste ein" (Orlofsky), "Mein Herr Marquis" (Adele), "Dieser Anstand, so manierlich" (Rosalinde, Eisenstein), "Klänge der Heimat" (Rosalinde), Finale Act 2: "Im Feuerstrom der Reben"/"Brüderlein und Schwesterlein"/"Ha, welch' ein Fest!," "Spiel' ich die Unschuld vom Lande" (Adele), "Ich stehe voll Zegen" (Eisenstein, Rosalinde, Alfred), Finale Act 3: "O Fledermaus, o Fledermaus."

Die Fledermaus may have been the Operette which stirred the Austrian musical stage into life and drove it onto the road leading to its first period of greatness, but, in spite of that, it was not the show which carried the Operette out from Vienna to the rest of the world to the best effect. In fact, although it did splendidly in a series of mostly German-language productions around Central Europe in the years following its Viennese début, the show had a decidedly muted early career on both the English- and French-language stages. It was not until a gaudy twentieth-century remake, splashily mounted with the well-remembered name of Strauss floating gaily over it, brought it tardily to the attention of folk further afield that that rehabilitation began which has made *Die Fledermaus* the best-known representative of nineteenth-century Viennese Operette to fin-de-twentieth-century audiences, in preference to and even to the exclusion of other works which were generally both better-liked and more widely and frequently played first time round.

It was, however, undoubtedly the success won by *Die Fledermaus* at the Theater an der Wien that was responsible for those other shows being written and staged. The reception given to Genée and Strauss's show encouraged a number of other musicians to launch themselves on composing a similar, full-sized Operette—a similarly "French" Operette—and, in the seasons following the launching of *Die Fledermaus*, several of these put in an appearance on the Viennese stage: Austrian Operetticized versions of the old Scribe libretto to *La Circassienne*, of Bayard and Dumanoir's aged but still popular *Le Vicomte de Letorrières* and *Le Capitaine Charlotte*, and of the old vaudeville *Nanon, Ninon et Madame de Maintenon*, as well as others which vaguely admitted to being "based on an old work," or "based on Scribe" or "on Bayard," or others among the popular writers of yesteryear, or the year before yesteryear. No one was, it seemed, yet willing—as Genée and Strauss had been—to tackle more up-to-date subjects and styles in French comedy. Or was it just that stealing texts from living authors was more hazardous than plundering dead ones? Still, old or not, old-fashioned and even unsophisticated or not, the French texts that were carried off and done over by Austria's librettists in the 1870s proved to be the bases for some extremely successful shows.

Two of the most successful came from Genée. Genée the composer, this time, rather than Genée the lyricist-librettist, although he took a share in the writing of the text too, alongside his longtime partner "F. Zell"—otherwise Theater an der Wien manager Camillo Walzel (1829–1895). The first of their hits was *Der Seekadett*, the *Capitaine Charlotte* remake, a period piece set in courtly Portuguese circles which had its uncourtly French heroine getting into seaman's clothes to go south and find her lost lover. He's actually got lost on purpose, because he's been morganatically married to the local queen, so—after the usual ration of farcical quiproquos, including the queen's taking a decidedly embarrassing shine to the pretty "sea cadet"—the heroine goes off instead with a jolly, wealthy Peruvian. *Der Seekadett* did extremely well both at home and abroad, finding a particularly warm welcome, under the title *The Royal Middy*, in America, but Genée and Zell's second success, *Nanon*, a romantic musical comedy which pitted tavern-keeper Nanon against aristocratic Ninon de l'Enclos for the favors of a two-or-three-timing Marquis, was an even bigger one, and, with this pair of triumphs under his belt, this versatile writer and composer notched himself up a reference as one of the biggest stars of the German-language musical stage.

Of course, Genée's success was not limited just to his two most successful written-and-composed Operetten, for he was involved, as librettist and/or lyricist, in a long list of the earliest hits of the Operette traditon.

Among those encouraged towards the three-act Operette—or, in this case, encouraged back to it—by the success of *Die Fledermaus* was Franz von Suppé, already the composer of several unrewarded attempts at both full-sized opéra-bouffe and at comic Operette in the years since he had led the way in the Viennese musical theater with his shorter Operetten. Now Suppé finally and fully hit the mark, teaming with Zell and Genée on the two "French" Operetten which would be the biggest international hits of all among the shows of these early days of the Operette.

The first of the two was the *Circassienne* remake, *Fatinitza*. In Zell and Genée's version of Scribe's story Fatinitza was a she who was a he. Lieutenant Wladimir Samoiloff dresses up as a girl so as to be able to romance his not-very-understanding general's niece, Lydia, under his very nose. But first the general takes a decidedly awkward fancy to Fatinitza, and then the Turks invade and carry both Lydia and Fatinitza off to the harem of Izzet Pascha. Just to make this male-female business all the more confusing, the rôle of Wladimir/Fatinitza was written for a mezzo-soprano in pants! The comedy of *Fatinitza* was droll and merry, if scarcely of the degree of sophistication of the *Fledermaus* text, its situations and settings were highly colorful, and Suppé supplied a delightful score of romantic and comic, sometimes military, and even vaguely Turkish music to go with the comedy. The result was a success which rivaled that of Strauss's hit at home, and quite outflanked it in theaters and adaptations further afield. America, with its large German-American theater-going public, proved a particularly enthusiastic taker, and the success won by the 1879 Broadway production of an English version of *Fatinitza* was responsible for launching the Central European Operette on the English-language stage.

FATINITZA, an Operette in 3 acts by Richard Genée and F. Zell, based on the libretto *La Circassienne* by Eugène Scribe. Music by Franz von Suppé. Produced at the Carltheater, Vienna, 5 January 1876.

Characters: General Timofey Gavrilovitch Kantschukoff, Lydia Iwanova, Lieutenant Wladimir Samoiloff, Julian von Golz, Izzet Pascha, Captain Vasil Starieff, Wutki, Lieutenant Osipp Safonoff, Steipann, Hassan Bey, &c.

Plot: General Kantschukoff has taken a violent fancy for his niece's friend Fatinitza, unaware that "she" is actually a "he"—Lieutenant Wladimir Samoiloff, who has donned feminine disguise so as to be able more easily to court his Lydia. The General's passion has to take a hitch when both Lydia and "Fatinitza" are captured by marauding Turks, but when—with the help of the journalist van Golz—the "girls" are recovered, "Fatinitza" vanishes. She has, of course, turned back into being Wladimir. Kantschukoff agrees to allow Wladimir to wed Lydia if he can produce the missing apple of his bloodshot eye. Of course, nothing could be easier.

Songs: "Halt, wer da?," "Liegt der Schnee so weiss" (Steipann), "Wutki, Wutki, Wutki wenn die Flaschen leer" (Wutki, soldiers), "Erwache frei von allem Kummer" (soldiers), "Sie, die ich darf nie nennen" (Wladimir), "Was gibt da?" "Ein Spion!" (Wladmir, Steipann, Julian, chorus), "Ein Reporter ist ein Mann, dem man nicht vergeben kann" (Julian), "Aber deswegen niemals verlegen" (Julian, soldiers), "Himmel, Bomben, Element!" (Kantschukoff), "Woll'n sie mich lieben" (Kantschukoff, Fatinitza), "Teuer Oheim, länger konnt ich diesem Drang nicht wiedersteh'n"/"Eine Influcht winket dir" (Lydia, Wladimir, Kantschukoff, Julian), Finale Act 1: "Nur kein Geschrei," "Den Gebieter zu entzucken" (wives), "Reformen tun Not" (Izzet Pascha), "Ein bissel auffrischen" (Izzet Pascha), "Mein Herz, es zagt" (Fatinitza), "Ha! ein Mann" (wives, Wladimir, Lydia), "Jeder Trinker ist anfangs nüchtern" (Julian, Izzet Pascha), "Silberglöckchen rufen helle" (wives, Julian, Izzet Pascha), Finale Act 2: "Zwei Russen, der Spass ist gar nicht schlecht," "Glockenklänge künden Frieden" (Lydia), "Um Fatinitzas Spur zu finden" (Julian, Kantschukoff), "Dich wieder zu seh'n" (Lydia, Wladimir, Julian), "Vorwärts mit frischem Mut" (Julian, Lydia, Wladimir), Finale Act 3: "Jubelsang ertönt dem Fremden zum Empfang."

Johann Strauss did not manage to turn out another successful musical during the seventies—*Cagliostro in Wien*, *Prinz Methusalem* (with an original libretto especially ordered from France), and *Blindekuh* went progressively further and further down the pan—but Suppé, flushed with the fame garnered by *Fatinitza*, did. Not only did he follow up his first big hit, he actually topped it . . . with the single most successful work to come out of the nineteenth-century Viennese musical theater. *Boccaccio* was, like *Fatinitza*, *Nanon*, and *Der Seekadett*, built on the bones of an aging French play, one in which Bayard, the co-author of the original of *Der Seekadett*, had again had a hand. Again like *Fatinitza*, it featured a hero who was played by a sexy mezzo-soprano in tights—but there was no getting into a frock for this hero, for to the poet who was made the central character of this randy romp "getting into a frock" meant something quite different: the frock needed to be on someone else's wife.

BOCCACCIO, an Operette in 3 acts by Richard Genée and F. Zell, based on a play by Jean-François Bayard, de Beauplan, and de Leuwen. Music by Franz von Suppé. Produced at the Carltheater, Vienna, 1 February 1879.

Characters: Giovanni Boccaccio, Pietro, Scalza, Beatrice, Lotteringhi, Isabella, Lambertuccio, Peronella, Fiametta, Checco, Fresco, Leonetto, a bookseller, &c.

Plot: The fashionably saucy writer Boccaccio prides himself on taking his tales of wifely infidelities from real life—his own gallivantingly real life—but, alongside the amorous escapades in which he leads his band of bawdy bachelors, he has also actually found time to fall in love. The object of his heart's desires is the grocer's foster-daughter Fiametta. Fiametta, however, is in truth the baby-farmed-out daughter of the Duke of Tuscany, and it eventuates that she is royally scheduled to become the bride of the young Prince of Palermo. It also eventuates that the said young Prince is none other than the same "Pietro" who, in unroyal and wild-oat-sowing disguise, has been one of the more enthusiastic of Boccaccio's followers during the course of the evening's free-cuckolding antics. At the end of the affair, and in spite of the presence of some of the Florentine families among whose womenfolk he has sown his oats in the first two acts, Boccaccio somehow convinces everyone that he's really an awfully moral fellow at heart, and succeeds in persuading his pal to forego his bride. Instead of Princess of Palermo she will be Signora Boccaccio.

Songs: "Heut' am Tag des Patrons von Florenz" (Checco, Leonetto, chorus), "Neuste Novellen" (bookseller, chorus), "Holde Schöne" (Scalza, Lotteringhi, Lambertuccio), "Ha, sie sind's, sie kommen schon heran" (Beatrice, Scalza, &c.), "Ich sehe einen jungen Mann dort stehn"/"Das ist doch jedem klar" (Boccaccio, Leonetto, chorus), "Die Glocken läuten hell und rein" (Peronella, Fiametta), "Hab' ich nur deine Liebe" (Fiametta, Boccaccio), "Ein armer Blinder"/"Nur ein Wort" (Boccaccio, Fiametta), Finale Act 1: "Ehrsame Bürger dieser Stadt"/"Er ist ein Prinz"/"Was wir verdammen," "Beim Liebchen, beim Liebchen" (Boccaccio, Pietro, Leonetto), "Ein Stern zu sein" (Boccaccio, Pietro, Leonetto), "Tagtäglich zankt mein Weib" (Lotteringhi), "Wie pocht mein Herz so ungestüm"/"Wonnevolle Kunde, neu belebend" (Peronella, Isabella, Fiametta), "Um die Spannung zu erhöh'n" (Pietro), "So oft man mich nach 'Neuem' fragt" (Boccaccio), Finale Act 2: "Benützen wir den Augenblick"/"Lotteringhi, Lambertuccio, macht doch auf!"/"Ich bin hier nicht von ungefähr," "Erfrische Quellen sind seine Novellen" (ensemble), "Um des Fürsten Zorn zu meiden" (Lambertuccio), "Mia bella Fiorentina" ["Florenz hat schönen Frauen"] (Fiametta, Boccaccio), "Ihr Toren, ihr wollt mich hassen?" (Boccaccio &c.), Finale Act 3: "Der Witz, die Laune, die Wahrheit."

Boccaccio, with its merry story, comical situations, and sufficient but never overwhelming romantic moments, its finely written mixture of lively and lovely music, and its series of grateful rôles, was a major hit in Vienna, and it went out from Austria, in the footsteps of *Fatinitza* and *Der Seekadett*, to establish itself in almost every country where musical theater was then played as the most important hit to have yet come from the Operette stage. It was a position it would keep—with only very few challengers—for nearly thirty years, as a succession of later Viennese Operetten followed it to stages around the world.

While this run of from-the-French pieces was establishing the new breed of Operette both at home and round the world, the more traditional kinds of German-language musical play—the Possen, Singspiele, and so forth—with their lively, comic, here-and-nowish libretti and their rather more simple and short-winded musical part, still held their place. Shows such as the musical-comedy remake of Karl Görlitz's *Drei Paar Schuhe*, with its merry tale of a shoemaker's wife who pops about delivering footwear and solving her customers' problems, and Karl Costa's *Ein Blitzmädel*—the impersonation-filled adventures of a telegraph girl and a tenor out to stop some naughty nepotism in high places—not only scored fine first-up successes, but went on to become favorite items in the revivable repertoire.

Before very long, in the natural course of things, the Posse and the Singspiel started to snuggle up to the Operette, in the same way that the French vaudeville had crept over to share a blanket with the more musically substantial opérette, and there were born on the Viennese stage some Operetten which sported little or no French influence in their bloodlines. One of the earliest successful examples of this kind came from the same pair of writers who had so successfully made over *Drei Paar Schuhe* in 1871. Two years later, playwright Alois Berla (1826–1896) and composer Karl Millöcker turned out *Abenteuer in Wien*, labeled—in a neat blend of terminologies—as a "Lokale Operette" in three acts and five scenes. The adventures in question involved a Viennese chemical manufacturer-cum-perfumer, his new young wife's sprightly godmother, a Hungarian knight, and a widow-woman from Serbia, and they all came to their peak in the local Grand Hotel and in nothing less dramatic than a "murder"!

Other Operetten with original, homegrown texts followed, some written in what was virtual imitation of the French shows, some persisting with the burlesque or the fantastical, and others finding their subject matter anywhere from Cromwellian Scotland to seventeenth-century Saxony, but the most successful among them was another piece by Berla and Millöcker which again took the present day and Austria for its settings. *Das verwunschene Schloß*, described (as *Die Fledermaus* had been) as a komische Operette, had a principal plotline that concerned itself with the wine-women-'n'-song goings-on of the libertine aristocracy, but it was its heavily accented Austrian peasant-comic characters, a pair straight out of the Posse kind of theater, who were both the stars of the "haunted castle" entertainment and its backbone.

DAS VERWUNSCHENE SCHLOSS, a komische Operette in 5 scenes by Alois Berla. Music by Karl Millöcker. Produced at the Theater an der Wien, Vienna, 30 March 1878.

Characters: Der Graf von Geiersberg, Coralie, Grosslechner, Mirzl, Sepp, Andredl, Trauderl, Regerl, Lamotte, &c.

Plot: The young Tyrôlean dairyman Sepp doesn't believe the tale that his local castle is haunted but, when he says so, his employer and prospective father-in-law throws him out of the house for impiety. Sepp and his servant Andredl repair to the hillside hut of old Trauderl and her servant Regerl, and from there they look down over the castle and its mysterious lights. Then Sepp decides he will check out these "ghosts." Andredl is terrified by the devilish folk they find at the end of their expedition but, when Sepp is drugged and carried away into the castle, he leads Regerl to the rescue. The "devils" finally turn out to be only the local Count and his friends having a little orgy, and when the villagers discover the truth they turn thoroughly mutinous. Trouble is averted by the Count's dancer mistress, who assures the locals that the festivity is a wedding: she is becoming the Gräfin von Geiersberg. Since everybody loves a wedding, the naughty Count is forgiven in time for an all-round happy ending.

Songs: "Von der Alm, von der Alm" (chorus), "Droben hoch von Geierstoan" (Mirzl), Finale Act 1: "Hört, hört, das Blasen und Frohlocken" (chorus)/"Grüsse die Gott mein Heimaththal" (Sepp)/"Da bin I schon" (Andredl), "Schirlingskraut beim Mondschein g'hohlt" (Regerl), "Wie glanzt der grüne Wlad" (Regerl, Sepp, Andredl), Polonaise, Coralie's Lied (Coralie), "Gespenster, so heisst man uns mit Grauen" (Coralie, ensemble), "Nur fein stad und fein Schleuni" (Sepp, Andredl), "Schau I di an so is ma frei als I' s'erste Mal" (Sepp, Coralie, Andredl), Finale Act 3: "No, Andredl, Schau"/"Oh, do himmelbaluer See" (Sepp, Andredl, Coralie, et al.), "Ah! Dirn! gibst ka Ruah?" (Andredl), "Die Menschen muss ma kenna" (Coralie), "I Woas net wia's kennt"/"A bisserl Liab und a bisserl Treu" (Regerl), "Mirzl wart' lass' mi vowan dass I lachten heflen kann" (Mirzl, Andredl), Schlussgesang: "Wir sind jetzt froh."

Unlike the vaudeville-opérette, this kind of Lokal Operette or Posse-Operette arrived not at a time when its elder sister was starting to show a wrinkle or two, but just as she was blossoming into maturity, and—in spite of the success in Central Europe of such pieces as *Das verwunschene Schloß*—its success would remain limited in an Operette world where the highly colored, Frenchified libretti of Genée and Zell went on from success to success.

Another who went from success to success was the composer Millöcker. After *Das verwunschene Schloß*, Millöcker took a hitch in the voluble illustration of Possen which had always been his chief occupation as a composer, and moved across to try his hand at the increasingly fashionable Genée-ial kind of Operette. In the late seventies and early eighties he set two libretti drawn by Zell and Genée from French vaudevilles—the history of the lowly lass who rose to become a king's mistress as *Gräfin Dubarry* and the less historical story of the naughty lassie who was *Die Jungfrau von Belleville*, as well as *Apajune der Wassermann*, a more Berla-ish and, apparently, original text by the same pair which nevertheless took for its hub that favorite French topic of the droit du seigneur and a young couple's attempts to avoid it. If the first of these pieces, which insisted it was a "komische Oper," had limited success, the other two—which allowed that they were frankly Operetten—both had fine careers. Both were, nevertheless, totally eclipsed when the fourth collaboration of Genée, Zell, and Millöcker appeared on the Vienna stage in 1882. *Der Bettelstudent* didn't actually admit the ancestry of its libretto at all, but those who knew the product of the European stage of past years were able to recognize without too much difficulty the bones of Bulwer Lytton's celebrated *The Lady of Lyons* and of Victorien Sardou's *Fernande* under the smooth skin of the new show. But, whether the book of *Der Bettelstudent* was built on borrowed parts or not, its mixture of the romantic and the comic, of sexual and political plotting and counterplotting, came together in the most effective libretto that the dominant librettists of the Vienna stage would ever turn out, a libretto which was comparable both in its tone and its effectiveness to that of the all-conquering *La Fille de Madame Angot* in France. Millöcker's score—which bubbled as it soared, catching the mixture of the merry and the romantic in a fine balance—only underlined the value of the libretto, and *Der Bettelstudent* went out from Austria to become the principal challenger to *Boccaccio* and to its record as the world's most popular Operette.

Der Zigeunerbaron: Life's a pig. It certainly is for Kálmán Zsupán. He farms them. And his disobedient daughter won't marry the "gipsy baron" next door.

DER BETTELSTUDENT, an Operette in 4 acts by F. Zell and Richard Genée. Music by Karl Millöcker. Produced at the Theater an der Wien, Vienna, 6 December 1882.

Characters: Palmatica countess Nowalska, Laura, Bronislawa, Colonel Ollendorf, Symon Rymanowicz, Jan Janicki, Bogumil Malachowsky, Cornet von Richthofen, Enterich, Onuphrie, Wangenheim, Schweinitz, Henrici, Eva, Piffke, Puffke, &c.

Plot: One night, at a party, Colonel Ollendorf of the occupying German army kissed the pretty and invitingly décolletée Polish Countess Laura Nowalska on the shoulder, and got whacked in the face with a fan for his unwelcome attempts at international osculation. By way of revenge on this proud but penny-pinched little aristocrat, Ollendorf releases a pair of beggar students from the local jail, dolls them up as a rich count and his secretary, and sets the false Count Wybicki to woo and win in marriage the uppity girl who had so publicly spurned him. Wybicki—otherwise Symon Rymanowicz—does his job to perfection, but at the same time he falls in love with Laura. Ollendorf fools him into thinking that she is willing to go ahead with their marriage, even knowing that Symon is no rich count, and when he looses the inmates of the local jail on their post-wedding celebration as the bridegroom's "best friends," it seems that his revenge has wholly succeeded. But the "secretary"—otherwise Jan Janicki, and an officer in the Polish army—has profited from his unexpected freedom, and, while Symon has been building Ollendorf's revenge, he has been organizing an uprising by the Poles and their much-sought (by the Germans) Duke. With the broken-hearted Symon's selfless help, he keeps Ollendorf diverted and on the wrong track long enough for the Poles to attack the unprepared occupying forces and triumph. By the time the evening ends, Symon Rymanowicz has been dubbed a real count for his part in the restoration of the Polish monarch.

Songs: "Ach, unsere Lieben sperrte man ein"/"Ach guter Meister Enterich"/"Beim Trinken, Essen fliehet der Verdruss" (ensemble with Enterich), "Ach ich hab' sie ja nur auf die Schulter geküsst" (Ollendorf), "Die Welt hat das genialste Streben" (Jan, Symon), "So leb' denn wohl, du enge Zelle" (Jan, Symon), "Juchheissa! hurra! die Messe beginnt!" (chorus), "Einkäufe machen" (Palmatica, Laura, Bronislawa, Onuphrie), "Das ist der Fürst Wybicki mit seinem Sekretär" (ensemble), "Ich knüpfte manche zarte Bande" (Symon), Finale Act 1: "Du bist die Seine?"/"Höchste Lust und tiefstes Leid"/"Bei solchem Fest," "Einen Mann hat sie gefunden" (Palmatica, Laura, Bronislawa), "Nur das Eine bitt' ich dich, liebe mich" (Jan, Bronislawa), "Ich setz' den Fall" (Symon, Laura), "Glückliche Braut" (ensemble), "Schwamm drüber!" (Ollendorf), Finale Act 2: "Klinget, Feierglocken, klinget!," "Lumpen, Bagage, Bettelstudent" (chorus), "Der Fürst soll nur ein Bettler sein" (Bronislawa), "Ich hab' kein Geld, bin vogelfrei" (Symon), Finale Act 3: "Still man kommt!"/"Aus den wichtigen Papieren"/"Jetzt lach' ich jeglicher Gefahr"/"Befreit das Land!"

By and large, the composers of the handful of the most successful Operetten of the 1870s and early 1880s remained the musical stars of the German-language musical stage during the rest of the century, though Genée—the busiest of them all—devoted himself in later years very largely to texts rather than to music. Suppé did not come up with another *Fatinitza* or *Boccaccio*, but he nevertheless turned out a half dozen more musicals—at first with Zell and Genée, later with such of their successors as Moritz West (1840–1904), Ludwig Held (1837–1900), and Victor Léon (1858–1940); *Donna Juanita* (yet another tale of a man disguised as a woman), *Der Gascogner*, the more freewheelingly funny *Die Afrikareise* with its comical adventures in the North African desert, a sort-of-biomusical of the Swedish poet *Bellman*, and the rather more soberly moving but musically mature from-the-French *Die Jagd nach dem Glück* all had at least a degree of success at home and/or abroad.

Millöcker's post-*Bettelstudent* works more than confirmed their composer's now second-to-none reputation as a theater composer. After two more successes with Zell and Genée, on the smugglers-and-stolen-jewels tale of *Gasparone* and the shipful of Spanish disguises that made up the story of a phoney *Der Viceadmiral*, and a happy collaboration with Hugo Wittmann (1839–1923) and Alois Wohlmuth, on the farago of false identities and romances in the field that comprised the history of *Der Feldprediger* (a big hit in America under the title *The Black*

Hussar), he teamed with Wittmann and Julius Bauer (1853–1941) on a set of musicals for the Theater an der Wien which, between 1887 and 1896, produced two respectable successes in *Die sieben Schwaben* and *Das Sonntagskind,* as well as his biggest hit since *Der Bettelstudent* in the very largely comical story of *Der arme Jonathan,* the poor cook who changes places with his rich, world-weary master and sets off with his girl to Monte Carlo. By the end, of course, everyone has happily returned to the situation in which they started. *Der arme Jonathan* performed extremely well at home, but it found its greatest accolades on the other side of the Atlantic, clocking up one of the longest Broadway runs achieved by any Viennese show of the time.

While Suppé and Millöcker turned out this regular supply of reasonably successful to distinctly successful musicals—with only the rare full-grown flop—Johann Strauss continued his saw's-edge career in the musical theater. He found some success with *Das Spitzentuch des Königin,* an Operette composed to a very old-fashioned kind of text (which Genée had cobbled up from a piece submitted by an inexperienced would-be librettist) about a greedy regent and a little king and little queen who need to be helped to take up both their crown and real married life together, but then—seven years after *Die Fledermaus*—the composer got thoroughly on target again in another collaboration with the Zell/Genée partnership on another "French" Operette. The book of *Der lustige Krieg* was a remake of a twenty-four-year-old comic opera script originally set by the French composer Reber, but its almost bouffe story of a phoney war, and the phoney marriage which it occasions, was decorated with some funny and some charming characters and some sparkling situations. This was far from the contemporary comedy of *Die Fledermaus* where—in his only ever attempt at illustrating a humorous, middle-class story set in the recognizable here and now—the composer had found himself so well suited, but it was, at least, full-blooded comedy, and Strauss's vigorously tuneful and momentarily melting music proved ideal as an accompaniment to its "lustige" ins and outs.

DER LUSTIGE KRIEG, an Operette in 3 acts by F. Zell and Richard Genée, based on the libretto *Les Dames capitaines* by Mélesville. Music by Johann Strauss. Produced at the Theater an der Wien, Vienna, 25 November 1881.

Characters: Princess Artemisia Malaspina of Massa-Carrara, Violetta, Marchese Filippo Sebastiani, Colonel van Scheelen, Balthasar Groot, Else Groot, Umberto Spinola, Ricardo Durazzo, Carlo Spinzi, Fortunato Franchetti, Panfilio Podestà, &c.

Plot: The rulers of Massa-Carrara and Genoa had a little quarrel which grew and grew until it became a little war, and eventually the all-female army of the first and the all-male army of the second drew up battle lines. Princess Artemisia of Massa-Carrara, deciding that reinforcements were in order, struck a bargain with the bachelor Duke of Limbourg, and Violetta, her widowed and exceedingly eligible cousin, was despatched in the direction of Limbourg in exchange for troops. But, owing to a little indiscretion, Violetta didn't make it to her rendezvous with the Duke's marital proxy. She was intercepted by the Genoese. But the marrige went ahead. The Genoese commander, Spinola, having fallen in love with Violetta at first sight, pretended to be the Limbourgoise proxy, a little Dutch tulip-grower who had wandered unwittingly into the battle-lines was forced to pretend to be the Duke, and the bride and her new "allies" proceeded to Massa-Carrara. There the truth eventually came out—Massa-Carrara had, horror!, married Genoa—but Violetta was proving so thoroughly contented with her new husband that it seemed easier just to call off that "jolly" war which had never actually begun.

Songs: "Keinen Kampf, keinen Sieg bracht bisher dieser Krieg" (chorus), "Wie schlüg' ich mich gern ein wenig herum" (Spinola), "Der klügere gibt nach"/"Mit meinen Feinden dejeunieren" (Sebastiani), "Ein Blitz, ein Knall" (Spinola), "Wir machten zusammen aus Holland die Reise" (Balthasar, Else), "Umsonst! Ich kann nicht fort!"/"Für diese Kriegzugs Wohl und Wehe" (Violetta), "Bitte! Bitte! 's ist ganz unmöglich"/"Von einem Mann liess ich mich küssen" (Violetta, Spinola), "Kommen und gehen" (Violetta, Sebastiani, Spinola, Fortunato, Carlo), Finale Act 1: "Was lange währt, wird gut"/"Schlagt ein, Herr Substitut!," "Die Fürstin lud zum Café und Kriegsrath heute uns ein" (chorus), "Mit Ihre Haltung bin ich zufrieden"/"Den Feind den möcht' ich seh'n der da kann weidersteh'n!" (Artemisia), "Durch Wald und Feld" (Else), "Heil! Heil der Gräfin Lomellini" (ensemble), "Es war ein lustig Abenteuer" (Violetta), "Nur für Natur" (Sebastiani), "Der Langersehnte, den fern man wähnte traf ein schon heut," "Me frown, ick wensch u gooden dag"/"Was ist an einen Küss gelegen" (Balthasar, Else), Finale Act 2: "Schon dunkelt rings die Nacht" (Spinola)/"Herr Herzog, riechen Sie mir den Arm"/"Sei's bei Tanz, bei Politik," "Die Commandantin kam an" (chorus), "Was ich erstrebt durch lange Zeit" (Violetta et al.), "Zwei Monat sind es schon" (Balthasar, Else), "Mein ist das Commando noch für heut"/"Süsse Friedensglocken" (Violetta, Spinola, Sebastiani), Finale Act 3: "Mag um Ruhm und um Ehr."

Strauss, Zell, Genée, and France all got together just one more time after *Der lustige Krieg*, on a remake of another two-decades-old French opéra-comique which was altogether less felicitous than the last. *Eine Nacht in Venedig* was poor stuff made from poor stuff, and, although Strauss provided some pieces of delightful music as an illustration to this umpteenth tale about a randy aristo and the little sweethearts who stop him getting his kneebreeches off through three whole acts, the show wasn't in the same class as *Der lustige Krieg*. As a result, Strauss, who by this time had became a touch neurotic about his libretti, got cross with the men who'd been responsible for the texts to his two biggest hits (but not for his two biggests flops), and yet who had supplied Suppé so recently with the libretto for *Der Bettelstudent*, and he severed connections.

At first, it looked as if he might have made a wise decision. For his first new Operette after *Eine Nacht in Venedig* gave him his third big success. *Der Zigeunerbaron*, however, was a piece decidedly different in flavor from the first two. Where they had both been "French" comic pieces, glittering with fun and sprightly melody, this one was Hungarian—drawn from a Hungarian novel by a Hungarian journalist-cum-dramatist and set in the gipsylands of Temesvár—and it was, above all, romantic and sentimental. The story of the "gipsy baron" Sándor Barinkay and his restoration to his lands and titles and to the arms of a real live princess was, needfully, decorated with a set of comical characters and incidents in parallel to its main plot, and indeed the rôle of the bourgeois pig-breeder Zsupán turned out to be one of the prize low-comedy parts of the era, but, in spite of that, this Operette—as witnessed by the much richer, darker, and less mobile music that Strauss composed for it—moved much further into the realm of the romantic musical than its predecessors had done.

DER ZIGEUNERBARON, a komische Oper in 3 acts by Ignaz Schnitzer, based on the novel *Sáffi* by Mór Jókai. Music by Johann Strauss. Produced at the Theater an der Wien, Vienna, 24 October 1885.

Characters: Sándor Barinkay, Kálmán Zsupán, Graf Peter Homonáy, Conte Carnero, Arsena, Mirabella, Sáffi, Czipra, Ottokar, Pali, &c.

Plot: When Sándor Barinkay is brought by the government official, Carnero, to have restored to him the Temesvár farmlands of which his father was dispossessed, the pig-farmer, Zsupán, is quick to promote a marriage between his new neighbor and his daughter, Arsena. Arsena has, however, given her heart elsewhere and she refuses the match—she will marry no man less than a baron. Barinkay soon discovers the truth and, to Zsupán's fury, plights himself instead to the gipsy maid, Sáffi. Sáffi and her mother, Czipra, lead Barinkay to the ruins of his family home, and there they discover the treasure hidden by his fleeing father. Zsupán and Carnero both do all they can to get their hands on the money, but when a recruiting officer comes by, raising troops for the war against Spain, Barinkay—distraught at the revelation that his gipsy girl is in truth a Hungarian princess—offers both himself and his fortune to the cause. Accompanied by Zsupán and Arsena's beloved Ottokar, who have accidentally drunk the wine which enlists them, he goes off to the war, and when he returns in the final act, covered in glory, all can finally come to a rich and romantic ending.

Songs: "Das wär' kein rechter Schiffersknecht" (chorus), "Jeden Tag, Müh und Plag" (Ottokar), "Als flotter Geist" (Barinkay), "So täuschte mich die Ahnung nicht" (Czipra &c.), "Verloren hast du einen Schatz" (Czipra, Carnero), "Ja, das Schreiben und das Lesen" (Zsupán), "Just sind es vierundzwanzig Jahre" (Mirabella), "Dem Freier naht die Braut" (chorus), "Ein Freier meldet sich" (Arsena &c.), "Hochzeitskuchen, bitte zu versuchen" (chorus), "Nachbar Zsupán" (ensemble), "Ein Falter schwirt ums Licht" (Arsena), "So elend und treu" (Sáffi), Finale Act 1: "Arsena! Arsena!"/Zieguener-chor/"Hier in diesem Land," "Mein Aug' bewacht" (Czipra, Barinkay, Sáffi)/"In dieser Nacht" (Barinkay), "Ein Greis ist mir im Traum erschienen" (Sáffi, Czipra, Barinkay), "Ha, seht, es winkt" (Barinkay, Sáffi, Czipra), "Auf, auf, auf, vorbei ist die Nacht" (Páli, chorus), "Wer uns getraut" (Barinkay, Sáffi), "Nur keusch und rein" (Carnero), "Her die Hand, es muss ja sein" (Homonáy), Finale Act 2: "Noch eben in Gloria," "Freuet Euch!" (chorus), "Ein Mädchen hat es gar nicht gut" (Arsena), "Von des Tajos Strand" (Zsupán), "Hurrah, die Schlacht mitgemacht" (chorus), Finale Act 3: "Reich ihm die Hand."

In the dozen years that followed *Der Zigeunerbaron*, Strauss turned out five more Operetten, but although his waltz-famous name ensured—as it does today—that several of these pieces, in spite of indifferent or dreadful Viennese showings, were seen around Central Europe, none even got near to being accounted a success.

A number of other writers and composers also contributed texts and scores to the German-language musical stage as it grew into the 1880s as an ever more thriving institution. The percentage of imports from Paris dropped steadily as the principal theater managers of Vienna instead mounted new works by local writers and by composers such as Carl Zeller (1842–1898), Alfons Czibulka (1842–1894), Pepi Hellmesberger (1855–1907), Alfred Zamara (1863–1940), Josef Brandl (1835–1913), the younger Adolf Müller (1839–1901), Carl Michael Ziehrer (1843–1922), Carl Weinberger (1861–1939), or Germany's most successful stage musician, Rudolf Dellinger (1857–1910). Very few of these works succeeded in even approaching the success of the hits written by the four most prominent Austrian theater-musicians of their era, but several of them scored well at home, and a smaller number were tried on the other side of the Atlantic—always more appreciative of the produce of Central Europe in the nineteenth century than either London or Paris—to varying reactions.

Thriving? Well, it certainly looked like it. But, as is so often the case, a handful of very bright stars actually obscured, by their very bright light, the fact that there was less than there seemed behind them. The Viennese musical stage which looked so prosperous in the eighties, housing the new tradition that could turn out a *Der Bettelstudent*, a *Der lustige Krieg*, and a *Der Zigeunerbaron* and still, at the end of the decade, produce a *Der arme Jonathan*, actually took a nosedive almost immediately after that. Between 1892 and 1897 not a single successful Operette came along to add itself to the hit-list established in the twenty previous years. And, one by one, the small circle of men who had made the nineteenth-century heyday of the Vienna stage what it was began to disappear. But the Austrian musical theater had one more enduring hit to deliver before it went into virtual hibernation for nearly a decade. It was a piece which, like *Der Zigeunerbaron*, didn't have the taste and sound of the most successful shows of the previous decade or so. In fact, *Der Vogelhändler*, with its countryfied tale of the country birdseller and his girl, whose love-lives get all muddled up when they become entangled with folk from the big city, and the particularly free-lilting pieces of open-fields-flavored melody with which Carl Zeller illustrated it, in some ways came over more like the merry little Possen of earlier times.

DER VOGELHÄNDLER, an Operette in 3 acts by Moritz West and Ludwig Held, based on *Ce qui deviennent les roses* by Charles Varin and de Biéville. Music by Carl Zeller. Produced at the Theater an der Wien, Vienna, 10 January 1891.

Characters: Adam, Christel, Kurfürstin Marie, Adelaide, Baron Weps, Graf Stanislaus, Süffle, Würmchen, Schneck, Jette, &c.

Plot: The birdseller Adam is to wed Christel from the Post, and if he could win the job of Royal Menagerie Keeper it would make their married life much easier. So, when the local Prince comes by on a hunting jaunt, Christel goes to his private tent to ask for the royal favor and support. Adam, unfortunately, gets the wrong end of the stick, becomes jealous, and ends up spitedly throwing himself, in what looks like a fairly final way, at a pretty stranger called Marie. But Marie is actually the local Prince's wife, come out from the city in a dirndl to check up on what her husband is up to. It eventuates—after a couple of acts of misunderstandings—that the flirty Prince isn't actually her Prince after all, but only a minor noble giving himself out-of-town airs. By the final curtain, after a whole series of rural and courtly complications has intervened, Adam has his job and his bride, and harmony is restored in high places as well as low.

Songs: "Hurrah! Hurrah! Her die Gewehr" (chorus)/"Ihr habt gestohlen niederträchtig" (Weps), "Grüss enk Gott, alle miteinander" (Adam &c.), "Als dir die Welt voll Rosen hing" (Stanislaus, Weps), "Schnell kommt nur alle!" (chorus), "Fröhlich Pfalz" (Marie), "Ich bin die Christel von der Post" (Christel), "Ach, Ihre Reputation ist just die beste nicht" (Christel, Stanislaus, Weps), Finale Act 1: "Vivat! Hoch! Hurra! Nun gilt's loyal zu sein"/"Schenkt man sich Rosen in Tirol" (Adam), "Haben Sie gehört?" (chorus), "Ich bin der Prodekan" (Süffle, Würmchen), "Beschedien, mit verschämten Wangen" (Christel, Marie, Adelaide), "Schau mir nur recht ins Gesicht" (Christel, Stanislaus), Finale Act 2: "Wir spiel'n bei Hof gar heut'"/"Wie mein Ahnl zwanzig Jahr" (Adam), "Nein, nein, nein, nein, das ist uns gemein," "Als geblüht der Kirschenbaum" (Marie), "Kom' ih iazt wieder ham" (Adam), "Kämpfe nie mit Frau'n" (Christel, Stanislaus, Adam), Finale Act 3: "B'hüt enk Gott, alle miteinander."

Zeller followed up *Der Vogelhändler* with another piece of a similar flavor in *Der Obersteiger,* which came nearer than most to making a success in the fading years of the century, but thereafter he gave no more new shows to the stage, and in 1898 he died. Genée, Walzel, and Suppé had all passed on in 1895, and Millöcker and Strauss would follow in 1899; by the turn of the century not one of those writers and composers who had been the strong men of the Austrian Operette stage through its twenty years of flourishing was still alive. And no one had put in an appearance who seemed likely to take their place.

It was actually only a case of waiting a few years. It wasn't that there was no one to take up the baton: it was simply that they weren't ready. And, anyway, musical tastes and styles were changing. Popular dance music, which had been the basis of so much of the best and most successful music of the Operette, as of the opérette, was changing. The twentieth century would soon see the Viennese musical stage raise its head again, but to music which moved its feet with a rather lighter and looser grace than it had in the nineteenth century. And then, the shows and show-music of Vienna would go forth and find even greater success than they had in their first period of prominence.

THE ENGLISH MUSICAL STAGE OF THE 1870s AND 1880s

When Gilbert and Sullivan's *The Sorcerer* made its first appearance on the stage of London's Opera Comique in 1877, the modern British and English-language musical theater already had more than a decade of existence and a number of not unsuccessful shows to its credit. There were those, such as the Gaiety Theatre's *Aladdin II* and *Cinderella the Younger,* the Alhambra's *The Demon's Bride* and *Whittington,* or the grossly scenic fairy-tale spectaculars *Babil and Bijou* and *The Black Crook,* that were home-made from a mixture of English and French contributions, but authors such as Robert Reece (1838–1891), Harry Paulton (1841–1917), and Gilbert,

composers including Freddie Clay (1839–1889), Alfred Cellier (1844–1891), and Sullivan, and musicals such as *Cattarina*, *The Sultan of Mocha*, and *Princess Toto* had all done their bit to help launch the tradition which finally found itself a voice that would well and truly carry with the production, first, of Gilbert and Sullivan's little bouffe "cantata" *Trial by Jury* in 1875, and then with their first full-length burlesque opera.

The Sorcerer, a tale of a clumsy necromancer who—like the Dulcamara of Gilbert's earlier burlesque of the opera *L'Elisir d'amore*—spreads a love potion about in a sleepy English village, to hectic effect, was a deliciously amusing piece. It wasn't funny with the belly-laugh fun of the old British burlesques, or with the shriekingly hilarious craziness of a *Chilpéric*, but instead it sported a more contained and wittily precise kind of humor. The author's happy and crisply individual style of dialogue—a style which maintained a refined version of the special tone of burlesque without indulging in its wilder extravagances, and which limited the rhymes and rhythms of the old style of show to its lyric part—combined with the composer's melodious, English but eye-

HMS Pinafore: A "big, big, D." When Captain Corcoran catches his coloratura daughter running away with a tenorious tar, he cracks and out comes . . . a socially unacceptable word.

twinkling music in a mixture which proved both attractive and well-liked. *The Sorcerer* had a good first run in London, but it was nevertheless slow to attract further attention, and it was not until the following year, when its producer, Richard D'Oyly Carte (1844–1901), mounted a second burlesque opera by the same team, that the English-language musical theater found its keystone show, the musical that would establish itself as an international hit, the fountainhead for a whole series of like pieces, and the most important landmark to date in the English musical theater.

HMS PINAFORE, or The Lass That Loved a Sailor, a comic opera in 2 acts by W. S. Gilbert. Music by Arthur Sullivan. Produced at the Opera Comique, London, 25 May 1878.

Characters: The Rt. Hon. Sir Joseph Porter, KCB, Captain Corcoran, Ralph Rackstraw, Dick Deadeye, Josephine, Little Buttercup, Hebe, Bill Bobstay, Bob Becket, &c.

Plot: Able Seaman Ralph Rackstraw is in love with his Captain's daughter, Josephine, but she is too far above him in social standing for him to hope to regularize the attachment. In fact, her father has offered his weddable child in marriage to no less a gentleman than the First Lord of the Admiralty, and he, all condescension and wet lips, insists that a difference in rank can be overlooked when love is concerned. But Josephine has a soft spot for the tenorious tar, and—fortified by her lofty suitor's maxim—she forgets propriety long enough to prevent Ralph blowing his brains out by telling him so. Alas! as the young pair prepare to elope, they are betrayed by an unprepossessing seaman, and prospects look dark for them until the local bumboat woman comes up with a confession. She used to be a wet-nurse, and as such she suckled both poor Ralph and the well-born Captain. Only, when it came to delivering the babes back to their families, she mixed them up. In verity, it is Ralph who is "related to peer," and the Captain and his daughter who are thorough commoners. So, since birth and rank are in all things primordial, the job of Captain has to change hands, and the new foremast-hand's daughter has delightedly to give up pretensions to a titled husband.

Songs: "We Sail the Ocean Blue" (sailors), "I'm Called Little Buttercup" (Buttercup), "A Maiden Fair to See" (Ralph), "I Am the Captain of the Pinafore" (Corcoran), "Sorry Her Lot Who Loves Too Well" (Josephine), "Over the Bright Blue Sea" (chorus), "I Am the Monarch of the Sea"/"When I Was a Lad" (Sir Joseph), "A British Tar" (Ralph, Bob, Bill, sailors), "Refrain, Audacious Tar" (Josephine, Ralph), Finale Act 1: "Can I Survive This Overbearing"/"Oh Joy, Oh Rapture Unforeseen"/"This Very Night with Bated Breath," "Fair Moon, to Thee I Sing" (Corcoran), "Things Are Seldom What They Seem" (Buttercup, Corcoran), "The Hours Creep on Apace" (Josephine), "Never Mind the Why and Wherefore" (Corcoran, Josephine, Sir Joseph), "Kind Captain, I've Important Information" (Dick), "Carefully on Tiptoe Stealing" (ensemble), "Farewell, My Own" (ensemble), "A Many Years Ago" (Buttercup), Finale Act 2: "Oh Joy, Oh Rapture Unforeseen."

HMS Pinafore was burlesque, in that it burlesqued the conventions of the dramatic stage, the operatic stage, and most especially the nautical stage, but it was also both topical and satirical, with the author using exaggeration and ridicule to take general pot-shots at the conventions of a well-established and distinctly layered society, or—more particularly—at the upper layer of that society: the British aristocracy, its traditions, and its inherited positions (a favorite butt of Gilbert's later rather bilious envy through the years). It also targeted specific public figures. The *Pinafore* character of the First Lord of the Admiralty who has never been to sea was, for example, a direct jab at Disraeli's current First Lord, the newsagent-cum-politician W. H. Smith—a man with no aristocratic or maritime past. Immortalization in *HMS Pinafore* didn't do him any harm, however, for he went on to become First Lord of the Treasury and Leader of the House of Commons, as well as a megachain of stationery-cum-a-few-books-shops. Mostly, however, the show was simply witty and tongue-in-cheek good fun. Gilbert's mock melodrama and posingly polysyllabic or super-nautical dialogue brought forth laugh after laugh, and the songs—from a mock operatic scena for the heroine to a harmonized patriotic glee for the tongue-in-cheeky seamen, a pattering curriculum vitae for the unlikely First Lord, and (the highlight of the evening) a grotesque minuettish dance performed to a jaunty little melody as Sir Joseph and Corcoran try to convince Josephine of the unimportance of rank where true love is concerned, ran the gamut of English theater music to the very best and most smiling effect.

HMS Pinafore went on from a London success which almost if not quite equaled that of its record-breaking contemporary *Les Cloches de Corneville*, to find a welcome even greater than that received by any of the most favored of the French musicals of the age all around the rest of the English-speaking world, but it had its greatest triumph in America. As of yet, the American stage had itself produced little in the way of durable musical-theater plays. Over the last decade in particular, it had lived largely on a diet of imported and/or adapted foreign shows, from opéra-bouffe, opéra-comique, and Operette to British leg-show burlesque, and its own original product had been mostly in the vein of the broadest of burlesque, of star-vehicle musical-comedy-dramas built on the lines of the German Possen, and of fairy spectaculars, many of them still relying on "composed and arranged" scores. The arrival on the scene of a substantial and original English-language musical, with custom-written words replacing the often hacked about, hack-written, and disinfected scripts of the local versions of Continental shows, and with music of rather more quality that the cheerfully popular songs of burlesque, caused a sensation. *HMS Pinafore* became the hottest musical in Broadway history.

However, in spite of the enormous success garnered by Gilbert and Sullivan's show, very few other writers—on either side of the Atlantic—leaped onto the partners' pillion and started turning out classy English opéra-bouffe. Gilbert and Sullivan were very largely followed up by Gilbert and Sullivan. After *HMS Pinafore*, with its cod nautical air, they turned out a bristling burlesque of the melodrama stage in the tale of a bunch of disaffected young peers who have become *The Pirates of Penzance*, a cockeyed tale of an ingenuous romantic triangle, with a milkmaid called *Patience* at its apex, set against a background of the craze for that kind of too-too-medieval-my-dear aestheticism which is personified to us today by the posturings of such devotees as Oscar Wilde, and a tongue-in-cheek (but also rather more sentimental) piece called *Iolanthe*, which found its fun in confronting a very Victorian vision of fairyland with the inmates of the British House of Lords. All three works dazzlingly confirmed the success of *HMS Pinafore*, as the Gilbert and Sullivan shows established themselves as the backbone of the newly thriving English musical theater.

In those five years between 1878 and 1882 which saw these four outstanding Gilbert and Sullivan pieces first come to the stage, the English musical theater did produce at least one other original musical that was fit to challenge them. *Billee Taylor* was a burlesque musical based on an old British ballad which had already and often been used as the subject-matter for pantomimes or old pasticcio burlesques. Its libretto was the work of the journalist Henry Pottinger Stephens (1851–1903), and its music was composed by the young conductor of *Les Cloches de Corneville*, Teddy Solomon (1855–1895). Stephens caught the bouffe tone to a nicety in a splendidly comical, tongue-in-cheek libretto which had fun—as *Pinafore* had done—most particularly at the expense of the nautical-dramatic stage of the *Black Eyed Susan* kind, with its Jolly Jack Tar "heart of oak" hero, its determinedly virtuous heroine, and its pawing, grasping, landlordly villain. In *Billee Taylor* the sailor hero is an opportunistic prig and a coward, the heroine a doughty little battler who shows him up for what he is, and the shamefaced villain a no-hoper who is not even up to pulling off a decent bit of villainy. Solomon's music was fit to put alongside Sullivan's, and—even though there were recognizable equivalents of pieces from *Pinafore*, *La Fille de Madame Angot*, and other musical hits among the show's songs—some parts of it became distinctly popular, with the jolly number about the comical press-ganger who went to sea "All on Account of Eliza" becoming perhaps the biggest show-song hit of its time.

Unfortunately, *Billee Taylor*'s career was hamstrung when D'Oyly Carte recognized it as competition, and got a colleague to start making the authors all sorts of offers. Money soon brought discord, the show's London producer closed his original production, and it was left to a multitude of often pirated versions, which quickly appeared all round America, to win *Billee Taylor* its widest showing.

BILLEE TAYLOR, or The Reward of Virtue, a nautical comic opera in 2 acts by Henry Pottinger Stephens. Music by Edward Solomon. Produced at the Imperial Theatre, London, 30 October 1880.

Characters: Captain the Hon. Felix Flapper RN, Sir Mincing Lane, Kt, Billee Taylor, Ben Barnacle, Christopher Crab, Phoebe Fairleigh, Arabella Lane, Eliza Dabsey, Susan, &c.

Plot: The exceedingly virtuous gardener Billee Taylor is to be virtuously wed to the little charity girl, Phoebe. This upsets both his boss's daughter, Arabella, who has her covetous eyes on the pretty fellow, and the dying-to-be-villainous schoolmaster Crab, who has eyes on the lovely lass, so this plotful pair arrange with Captain Flapper of the "Thunderbomb" (who is himself not indifferent to Phoebe's charms) to press-gang the boy at the altar. Two years pass. Sailor Billee has risen in rank and been decorated for valor, and he is now more inclined to listen to the cooings of lofty Arabella than to ponder marriage with a charity girl. But where is Phoebe? Why, on the day of his enlèvement, she and all her girlfriends disguised themselves as jolly jacqueline tars, and took to the sea to find Billee. Now she returns to find the fellow faithless! And finally it all comes out: it was "Richard Carr," otherwise the disguised Phoebe, who really performed the deeds that won Billee his rank and decoration. He is a fraud and a phoney! So Billee is reduced to the ranks, while Phoebe gets both his vacant Lieutenancy . . . and the hand in marriage of jolly Captain Flapper.

Songs: "Today, Today Is Holiday" (chorus), "The Virtuous Gardener" (Billee), "Ifs and Ans"

(Arabella), "We Stick to Our Letters" (Charity Girls), "The Two Rivers" ["Yesterday and Tomorrow"] (Phoebe, Susan), "The Self-Made Knight" (Mincing Lane), "A Guileless Orphan" (Phoebe), "Revenge, Revenge and Retribution" (Flapper, Arabella, Crab), "The Gallant Thunderbomb" (sailors), "All on Account of Eliza" (Ben), "Hark! the Merry Marriage Bells" (chorus), Finale Act 1: "'Tis Hard Thus by Fate to Be Parted," "Back Again, Back Again" (chorus), Ballet & Black Cook's Dance, "The Poor Wicked Man" (Crab), The Ballad of the Billow (Arabella), "By Rule of Three" (Mincing Lane, Billee, Arabella), "The Faithful Crew" (Phoebe, chorus), "In Days Gone By" (Billee, Phoebe), "Trim Little Phoebe" (Flapper, Phoebe, Susan), "With Fife and Drum" (chorus), "Don't Go for to Leave Us Richard Carr" (ensemble), "Love, Love, Love!" (Flapper), "See Here, My Lads, What Would You Do?" (Phoebe, Ben, &c.), "Stay, Stay, for I Am No Man"/Quarrelling Duet (Phoebe, Arabella, &c.), Finale Act 2: "This Is a Statement Most Untoward."

Stephens and Solomon wrote several other musicals together, but Stephens largely failed to find the same happy humorous touch again, their shows veered towards the romantic rather than the burlesque-comic, and—although they did score again as a team—Solomon had to wait for a dozen years and a new librettist before he once more turned out a piece as good as *Billee Taylor*.

Gilbert and Sullivan, however, continued vigorously on their merry way and, after a small hiccup with a slightly awkward remake of an old Gilbert burlesque script as *Princess Ida*, they turned out what would be their most successful show of all. *The Mikado* was a real landmark in the English musical theater, more so even, in a sense, than *HMS Pinafore* had been for, if it was *Pinafore* that had taken and transplanted the British musical so soundly and resoundingly throughout the English-speaking world, it was *The Mikado* which launched it into spheres and theaters and languages further afield. It was to become the first wholly English musical to triumph from one side of the European continent to the other, finding notable success on those stages which had previously exported shows to the English theater rather than received them therefrom.

The Mikado was, like *HMS Pinafore*, a burlesque opera, although its burlesque character was by now more that kind of general flavor that had permeated such latter-day French pieces as *Giroflé-Girofla* than any kind of direct parody. Officialdom, of course, came in for its ration of Gilbertian pummeling, and Sullivan drew up his first-act finale to magnificent burlesque-operatic proportions, but the Gilbert-Sullivan style—the author's quaint and witty dialogue and situations and the musician's sparkling, English music—was by now well established, and their oriental musical shared neither the zany extravagance of such early oriental opéras-bouffes as *Ba-ta-clan* nor the sexy comicalities of a *Fleur-de-thé*, but sported English opéra-bouffe qualities all its own.

THE MIKADO, or The Town of Titipu, a comic opera in 2 acts by W. S. Gilbert. Music by Arthur Sullivan. Produced at the Savoy Theatre, London, 14 March 1885.

Characters: The Mikado of Japan, Nanki-Poo, Ko-Ko, Pooh-Bah, Pish-Tush, Yum-Yum, Pitti-Sing, Peep-Bo, Katisha, &c.

Plot: Threatened with marriage to the dragonistic Katisha, Nanki-Poo, the son of the Mikado of Japan, has fled the paternal court and is hiding out in the town of Titipu disguised as an itinerant musician. There he falls in love with little local Yum-Yum. Unfortunately, little local Yum-Yum is scheduled to be imminently wed to Ko-Ko, the Lord High Executioner. But the Executioner is in a spot: he hasn't been executing and he stands to lose his job. Suicidal Nanki-Poo offers to be the needed victim if he can have a month of wedded bliss with Yum-Yum first. The wedding goes ahead, but then Ko-Ko isn't able to do the deed, so—with the Mikado on the horizon—an execution is faked. But Ko-Ko has gone from hot into boiling water. He's admitted to removing the head of a man who is—horror!—none other than the heir to the Japanese throne, and the heir to the Japanese throne refuses to come back to life while Katisha is in a state of suspended spinsterhood. So Ko-Ko has to sacrifice himself to what seems like the lesser of two evils. Marriage—even with Katisha—rather than something lingering with boiling oil.

Songs: "If You Want to Know Who We Are" (chorus), "A Wandering Minstrel, I" (Nanki-Poo), "Our Great Mikado, Virtuous Man" (Pish-Tush), "Young Man, Despair" (Pooh-Bah), "Behold, the Lord High Executioner" (chorus, Ko-Ko), "As Some Day It May Happen That a Victim Must Be Found" (Ko-Ko), "Comes a Train of Little Ladies" (chorus), "Three Little Maids from School Are We" (Yum-Yum, Pitti-Sing, Peep-Bo), "So Please You, Sir, We Much Regret" (Yum-Yum, Pitti-Song, Peep-Bo, Pooh-Bah), "Were You Not to Ko-Ko Plighted" (Nanki-Poo, Yum-Yum), "My Brain It Teems" (Ko-Ko, Pooh-Bah, Pish-Tush), Finale Act 1: "With Aspect Stern"/"O Fool That Fleest My Hallowed Joys" (Katisha), "Braid the Raven Hair" (chorus), "The Sun, Whose Rays" (Yum-Yum), "Brightly Dawns Our Wedding Day" (Yum-Yum, Pitti-Sing, Nanki-Poo, Pish-Tush), "Here's a How-de-do" (Yum-Yum, Nanki-Poo, Ko-Ko), March of the Mikado's Troops, "From Every Kind of Man" (Mikado, Katisha), "A More Humane Mikado" (Mikado), "The Criminal Cried, as He Dropped Him Down" (Ko-Ko, Pitti-Sing, Pooh-Bah), "See How the Fates Their Gifts Allot" (Mikado, Katisha, Ko-Ko, Pooh-Bah, Pitti-Sing), "The Flowers That Bloom in the Spring" (Nanki-Poo, Ko-Ko), "Hearts Do Not Break" (Katisha), "On a Tree by a Willow" (Ko-Ko), "There Is Beauty in the Bellow of the Blast" (Ko-Ko, Katisha), Finale Act 2: "For He's Gone and Married Yum-Yum."

While the English opéra-bouffe lived out its greatest days of popularity, other kinds of English-language musical theater prospered alongside it, on both sides of the Atlantic, and none prospered more fruitfully than the "French" romantic musical. The first real hit to come from this area was genuinely semi-French—the *Rip van Winkle* commissioned for London by *Cloches de Corneville* producer Alexander Henderson (?1829–1886) from that show's Parisian composer, Planquette—and the second very little less. *Les Manteaux Noirs*, French title and all, was quite simply a remusicked version of the popular opéra-comique *Giralda*, a piece still being played in the repertoire of Paris's Opéra-Comique! However, it was given a particularly lively and comical remake by star comedian Harry Paulton, and became, in its new version, far more popular on the English stage than the original ever had. But the success of *Les Manteaux Noirs* had a greater importance than this. It encouraged Paulton to adapt another well-known French work as a comical-musical vehicle for his own clowning talents, and this time

round he came out not just with a success, but with a megahit: the musical which would become Broadway's most outstanding comic opera success of the century.

Erminie was a remake of the famous old melodrama *L'Auberge des Adrets*, with its laughably scoundrelly pair of thieving "heroes," Robert Macaire and Jacques Strop. Paulton was Strop (here renamed Cadeau), the low comic side-kick to the dashing Macaire (now called Ravannes), and the evening contained rather more incidental comedy than dashing thievery in the scenes that filled out the gaps in the show's requisite and spinal light-operatic love-and-marriage story. The text was accompanied by a pretty, light score by a young English composer, Edward Jakobowski (1858–1929), who'd been studying on the Continent, and that score produced from its pages one of Broadway's most outstanding show-song hits of the century in the odd little lullaby "Dear Mother, in Dreams I See Her," as *Erminie* gamboled on to record-breaking heights in New York before having a long, long life on the road and a whole swatch of revivals in decades to come.

ERMINIE, a comic opera in 2 acts by Harry Paulton and Claxson Bellamy. Music by Edward Jakobowski. Produced at the Comedy Theatre, London, 9 November 1885.

Characters: Marquis de Pontvert, Erminie de Pontvert, Eugène Marcel, Cérise Marcel, Vicomte de Brissac, Ravannes, Cadeau, La Princesse de Gramponeur, Chevalier de Brabazon, Dufois, Simon, Delaunay, Javotte, Marie, Clémentine, &c.

Plot: Two escaped jailbirds, Ravannes and Cadeau, steal the clothes and papers of the Vicomte de Brissac, and present themselves at his destination, the Château de Pontvert, as Brissac and his friend "the Baron." Brissac—son of an old family friend—was coming to Pontvert to be betrothed to Erminie, the daughter of the house, and the evening's celebrations will give the thieves the chance to rifle the jewels of the rich house-party present for the occasion. But Erminie is in love with her father's secretary, Eugène Marcel, and, as her nuptial ball dances on and Cadeau entrances the old ladies with his ability to make pieces of jewelry "vanish," she determines to escape this unknown bridegroom. With discovery and the real Brissac now nigh, Ravannes agrees to help her elope with Eugène that very night, meaning at the same time to get his thieving done and disappear. However, some farcical goings-on in the darkened castle corridors end with the thieves' charade being unmasked, and they and the love story are both satisfactorily tied up before the curtain falls.

Songs: "Around in a Whirl" (chorus), "Vive le Marquis" (chorus), "When Love Is Young" (Erminie), "Past and Future" (Erminie, Eugène), "A Soldier's Life" (Marquis), "Downy Jailbirds of a Feather" (Ravannes, Cadeau), The Dream Song: "At Midnight on My Pillow Lying" (Erminie), "The Blissful Pleasure, I Confess" (ensemble), Finale Act 1: "Away to the Château," "Here on Lord and Lady Waiting" (Marie, chorus), "Woman's Dress" (Marie), "Darkest the Hour" (Eugène), "Joy Attend on Erminie" (chorus, Erminie), "The Sighing Swain" (Erminie), "What the Dicky Birds Say" (Cadeau), "Join in Pleasure" (chorus), Lullaby: "Dear Mother, in Dreams I See Her" (Erminie), "To Supper" (chorus), "Good Night" (ensemble), Finale Act 2: "Should We Gain, Ev'ry Heart Is Gay."

In the wake of *Erminie,* London got another piece on similar—but this time non-French—lines which would prove even more popular on home ground. In fact, the so-called comedy opera *Dorothy* would turn out to be nineteenth-century London's longest-running musical of all—ahead of *Les Cloches de Corneville,* ahead of each and every one of the Gilbert and Sullivan works, ahead of anything that the West End would mount in the decade and a half of the century that was left. It was a truly strange phenomenon, for *Dorothy* was, to put it mildly, an oddly old-fashioned piece of work. It was equipped with a period libretto relying on that oldest of plots—the unwilling bridegroom mistakenly wooing the very girl he is intended to wed—built up with a comedy subplot involving a lowly bailiff disguised as a gentleman's secretary who romances a foolish elderly widow in pretty much the same way that *Erminie*'s Cadeau had flirted with his aged Princesse, and the whole was decorated with a musical score that had previously been part of a provincial flop. But it worked, and with a vengeance. It set its West

End record, made its favorite song—an old-fashioned parlor ballad called "Queen of My Heart"—into a huge hit, and then went on to share the country roads and provincial stages of Britain with *Erminie* and with the musicals of Gilbert and Sullivan for countless years.

Perhaps the successes of *Erminie* and *Dorothy* had something to do with Gilbert and Sullivan also being tempted to try a "French" romantic comic opera. For the pair atypically put aside their usual bouffe style when they ventured with the umpteenth musical version of the famous *Don César de Bazan* tale (the same that had served as basis for *Maritana*)—a version that was, nevertheless, decorated with many of the characteristics and characters which had made their earlier pieces such favorites. *The Yeomen of the Guard* had a fine run at the Savoy Theatre, and, if it didn't find the same kind of super-success as *Erminie* or *Dorothy* had, nor indeed the wide popularity of *The Mikado*, it found a particularly fond following with light-opera lovers and has remained in the revivable repertoire for a century.

Alongside the English opéra-bouffe and the romantically inclined "French" musical, the more popular kinds of entertainments also flourished. Pasticcio burlesque was still a favorite—both in Britain, where the Gaiety Theatre, in particular, featured a long run of such pieces on its programs, and in America, which not only welcomed such ambassadors of British burlesque as the famous Lydia Thompson troupe of "British Blondes" (some of whom were neither) or the all-women *An Adamless Eden* company, but also manufactured a number of successful extravaganzas of its own. Several, such as the 1873 *Evangeline* and the 1884 *Adonis*, followed their home-town successes with forays onto overseas stages, but there they were dismissed as virtual variety shows. The first international hit to come out of the American musical theater was not for yet.

There were, however, a number of shows which did come out of America during these years and make themselves a home on, in particular, the British touring circuits, and they were the kind of show which, at this period in time, the American stage seemed to concoct better than any other: the Posse. These local comedies with songs, even if they owed something to the old German tradition, were nevertheless far and away the most "American" and individual pieces being turned out on a Broadway which had, until now, mostly just adapted or imitated. They traveled successfully, however, very largely because the stars around whom they were written traveled successfully—Joseph K. Emmet as *Fritz, Our Cousin German*, searching for his lost sister and confounding a moustachio-twirling melodrama villain while plunking a long series of songs out of his guitar, Johnnie Sheridan's impersonation of the prospecting (for a man) Widow O'Brien in *Fun on the Bristol*, the eternally teenaged Minnie Palmer's gallivant through the melodramatic trials and tribulations and ever-changing list of musical numbers that beset *My Sweetheart*, or Charles Arnold's comico-tragico-musico-weepie tale of *Hans, the Boatman*—and it was not by any means the best of them which found the widest exposure.

The best came very largely from the pens of two energetic author-managers, Ned Harrigan (1845–1911) and Charles Hoyt (1860–1900), both of whom would find fairly continuous success on the American stage through some dozen years. Harrigan was also a performer, and he and his shows originated in the world of the minstrel show and of variety and the sketches that he had played there with his double-act partner, Tony Hart (1855–1891). Harrigan and Hart became popular enough to set up their own theater in New York, and there they produced a lengthy series of farcical musical plays of a character very different from anything to be found on the English stage. The people of Harrigan's shows were new Americans—German-Americans, Irish-Americans, black Americans—all out to make a profit from the new freedoms of the new world in their own native way, while yet making sure that no one else profited in their native way. Harrigan made fun of the lot of them, of their exaggerated rivalries and their emphatic attempts at one-upmanship, in an uncompromising, free-speaking manner that would shrivel up today's fascists of the "politically correct," as the Mulligans and the Lochmullers and the Skidmores struggled for supremacy on the streets and in the striving parlors of immigrant New York, alternately bashing each other over the head or doing each other down, and stopping to deliver one of the tuneful ditties with which Harrigan and house musician Dave Braham (?1838–1905) decorated the action. The most successful shows among the nearly forty that Harrigan provided for the New York stage were those that he wrote featuring himself as Irish-American Dan Mulligan and Hart as the family's sassy black maid, Rebecca Allup. That little soap-operatic series climaxed in 1884 with *Cordelia's Aspirations* before the Harrigan/Hart team broke up, but Harrigan continued with more of the same kind of fare and with a certain success for a further half-dozen years before finally fading from the scene.

If Harrigan had the continuing New York presence, however, it was Hoyt who turned out the single show that would have the biggest and widest individual success. Hoyt's plays were less wholly local in their character and their characters. Where Harrigan concentrated above all in his pieces on the people and found his fun largely in them, Hoyt went in for pure low, action comedy. His earliest works were gutsy, knockabout comedies of the most blatant kind, decorated with music gathered from hither and yon, but they were put together with a know-how and an understanding of things theatrical and of his audiences that found shows such as *A Bunch of Keys*, *A Parlour Match*, and *A Texas Steer* (advertised proudly as "an American play by an American author based on American peculiarities") vigorous lives on the country circuits. In 1890 he turned out a less horse-playing kind of musical which was to have a much more upmarket life than these. *A Trip to Chinatown*—which had more than the occasional ring in it of the famous Nestroy Posse *Einen Jux will er sich machen*—was a comical piece about a group of young folk and their seemingly strict but woman-chasing bachelor uncle who go out—separately—for a night on the town. The folk and the fun and the mixture of songs, old, remade, and new, that they found there made up the entertainment. *A Trip to Chinatown* spent a year on the touring trails that its predecessors had trod so happily before it ventured into New York, but, when it did, it proved a first-class hit. Then, having set up one of the longest runs in Broadway history, launched the not-so-new "After the Ball," the remade "Reuben and Cynthia," and the brand new "The Bowery" as popular hits, it set off for Britain and—as songs came and went, and words and scenes or even whole acts were altered to suit whoever happened to be saying or playing them—it settled in on the British circuits with equal felicity. It even played a good 125 nights in the West End.

A TRIP TO CHINATOWN, an Idyll of San Francisco (musical trifle) in 3 acts by Charles Hoyt. Music composed and arranged by Percy Gaunt. First produced in 1890, played at the Madison Square Theatre, New York, from 9 November 1891.

Characters: Mrs Guyer, Welland Strong, Ben Gay, Rashleigh Gay, Tony Gay, Norman Blood, Willie Grow, Noah Heap, Hoffman Price, Slavin Pain, Turner Swift, Isabel Dame, Flirt, première danseuse.

Plot: The young "bohemian" folk of the Gay family are out for a jolly night on the town, with their chaperone, Mrs Guyer, "a widow from Chicago—not too strenuous on culture, but making up for it on 'biff.'" Unfortunately her letter confirming their meeting falls into the hands of old uncle Gay, who thinks it is an invitation to a romantic rendezvous. Off he goes to the Riche Restaurant, where he finds himself landed with a bill he can't pay and no lady, as the comedy and the setting progress to Cliff House and to a merry and musical climax.

Principal Songs: "The Pretty Widow" (by Hoyt & Gaunt), "Out for a Racket" (music by Gaunt), African Cantata: "Push Dem Clouds Away," "Love Me Little, Love Me Long" (music by Gaunt), "Crisp Young Chaperone" (music by Barton), Trio, burlesque of Italian opera (arr. Gaunt), medley including "There Will Never Be Another Like You," "Naughty, Sporty Boys," "I Will Be True," "Reuben and Cynthia," Amorita Waltz, Whistling Extraordinary, "You Did That," Toe Dance and Flower Girl Dance, "The Bowery" (by Hoyt & Gaunt), and a varied selection of others.

During the 1880s and the very earliest 1890s, while these imported pieces knocked up multi-year tours through the provinces, the British musical theater also produced some new and original "popular" entertainments. They did not, however, spring from the same roots as this kind of musical farce-comedy, but from burlesque. The burlesques at the Gaiety had for many years past been an important and highly profitable part of the entertainment there. But they were, nevertheless, only a part, for these pasticcio pieces, with the famous foursome of comedian Edward Terry, "boy" specialist Nellie Farren, and dancers Kate Vaughan and Teddy Royce as their inevitable stars, were less than a full evening's entertainment. But in 1885, the same year that saw *The Mikado* and *Erminie* make their débuts on the London stage, George Edwardes, the new manager of the Gaiety Theatre, launched a full-length burlesque. A full-sized, evening-filling burlesque with dialogue in prose rather than in the traditional rhymed and punned couplets, and with original music, even though that music was gathered from all sides by house conductor Meyer Lutz (1829–1903), the man who had been in charge of composing and arranging burlesque scores for the Gaiety almost since its opening, seventeen years earlier. The show was a burlesque of Harrison Ainsworth's tale of London skulduggery, *Jack Sheppard*, with Miss Farren playing the titular *Little Jack Sheppard* and young comedian Fred Leslie as the crooked thieftaker, Jonathan Wild, and both it and its new star team turned out to be enormously successful. Over the next half dozen years and more Edwardes brought to the stage a non-stop succession of similar pieces, with Lutz soon supplying all the music, and two companies—one headed by Fred and Nellie, and the other by a swiftly popular set of other new stars—rotated between London and the provinces with such shows as the Victor Hugo parody *Miss Esmeralda*, done-down Dumas as *Monte Cristo jr*, garbled opera in *Faust Up-to-Date* (with its famous Barn Dance, Lutz's biggest ever show-tune hit) and *Carmen Up-to-Data*, more French drama parody in *Ruy Blas and the Blasé Roué*, or fussed-up fairy-tale in *Cinder-Ellen Up-too-Late*. Under these nominal titles, the shows presented their stars with a variegated host of opportunities for comedy scenes and virtual sketches, for cheery up-to-date songs and pretty ballads, without worrying too much about coherence or dramatic integrity or accurate parody: after all, this was burlesque and incongruity was one of the characteristics of burlesque.

The fashion for New Burlesque, as Edwardes's new kind of show became subtitled, naturally spread out beyond the walls of the Gaiety, and it was not long before burlesque pieces with prose dialogue and modern music began popping up at other London houses. They proved a hugely popular breed of entertainment, and Edwardes soon had his companies traveling as far as America and Australia with repertoires of New Burlesques, but, in spite of all the enthusiasm they provoked, their fashion would last only eight years or so. Then fate and George Edwardes together put an end to them. Fate brought the death of young Leslie and the retirement from the stage of Nellie Farren, suffering from locomotor ataxy, which made the middle fall right out of the Gaiety Theatre's burlesque Milky Way. And Edwardes? He plumped for a switch in production values, and chucked out the fanciful costumes and scenery and fairy-tale/foreign trimmings of the burlesque Cinderellas and Don Juans in favor of fashionable modern dresses and here-and-now stories and settings. New Burlesque—burlesque of any kind—was out, and what was to be called "musical comedy" was in. In with a vengeance. During the course of the 1890s George Edwardes and his new brand of musical play would lead the English musical theater to the very front line of the international entertainment scene. As the traditions which had prospered so magnificently in France and Austria over the past decades started to stutter and fade, and while America still searched for that keystone show which would give its native theater international lift-off, the British musical play would step in to take over as the world's preferred form of musical theater.

SOME NOTABLE MUSICALS 1870–1889

1870   FRITZ, OUR COUSIN GERMAN (comp. & arr. various hands/Charles Gayler)
        Wallack's Theatre, New York, 11 July
        ALADDIN II (Hervé/Alfred Thompson) Gaiety Theatre, London, 24 December
1871   DREI PAAR SCHUHE [Three pairs of shoes] (Karl Millöcker/Alois Berla) Theater an der
        Wien, Vienna, 5 January

INDIGO UND DIE VIERZIG RÄUBER [Indigo and the forty thieves] (Johann Strauss/Max Steiner, Hugo Felix, et al.) Theater an der Wien, Vienna, 10 February

1872   LE ROI CAROTTE [King Carrot] (Jacques Offenbach/Victorien Sardou) Théâtre de la Gaîté, Paris, 15 January

LES CENT VIERGES [The hundred unmarried maidens] (Charles Lecocq/Henri Chivot, Alfred Duru) Fantaisies-Parisiennes, Brussels, 16 March

LA TIMBALE D'ARGENT [The silver chalice] (Léon Vasseur/Adolphe Jaime, Jules Noriac) Théâtre des Bouffes-Parisiens, Paris, 9 April

DES LÖWEN ERWACHEN [The lion's awakening] (Johann Brandl/Julius Rosen) Carltheater, Vienna, 26 April

LA FILLE DE MADAME ANGOT [Madame Angot's daughter] (Charles Lecocq/Clairville, Paul Siraudin [Victor Koning]) Fantaisies-Parisiennes, Brussels, 4 December

1873   ABENTEUER IN WIEN [Gallivant in Vienna] (Karl Millöcker/Alois Berla) Theater an der Wien, Vienna, 20 January

CARNEVAL IN ROM [Roman carnival] (Johann Strauss/Josef Braun) Theater an der Wien, Vienna, 1 March

NEMESIS (comp. & arr. John Fitzgerald/H. B. Farnie) Strand Theatre, London, 17 April

EVANGELINE (Edward Rice/J. Cheever Goodwin) Niblo's Gardens, New York, 27 July

LA JOLIE PARFUMEUSE [The perfumer's pretty wife] (Jacques Offenbach/Hector Crémieux, Ernest Blum) Théâtre de la Renaissance, Paris, 29 November

1874   GIROFLÉ-GIROFLA (Charles Lecocq/Henri Chivot, Alfred Duru) Faintaisies-Parisiennes, Brussels, 21 March

DIE FLEDERMAUS [The bat] (Johann Strauss/Richard Genée [Karl Haffner]) Theater an der Wien, Vienna, 5 April

MADAME L'ARCHIDUC [Madame the Archduke] (Jacques Offenbach/Alfred Millaud, Ludovic Halévy) Théâtre des Bouffes-Parisiens, Paris, 31 October

LES PRÉS SAINT-GERVAIS [Saint-Gervais Park] (Charles Lecocq/Philippe Gille, Victorien Sardou) Théâtre des Variétés, Paris, 14 November

THE SULTAN OF MOCHA (Alfred Cellier/anon.) Prince's Theatre, Manchester, 16 November

EL BARBERILLO DE LAVAPIÈS [The Barber from Lavapiès] (Francisco A. Barbieri/Luis Mariano de Larra) Teatro de la Zarzuela, Madrid, 18 December

WHITTINGTON (Jacques Offenbach/H. B. Farnie) Alhambra, London, 26 December

1875   ROBINSON CRUSOE (Francisco A. Barbieri/Rafael Garcia Santestiban) Teatro Circo, Madrid, 18 March

TRIAL BY JURY (Arthur Sullivan/William S. Gilbert) Royalty Theatre, London, 25 March

LA BOULANGÈRE A DES ÉCUS [The bakeress has cash] (Jacques Offenbach/Henri Meilhac, Ludovic Halévy) Théâtre des Variétés, Paris, 19 October

LE VOYAGE DANS LA LUNE [The trip to the moon] (Jacques Offenbach/Albert Vanloo, Eugène Leterrier, Alfred Mortier) Théâtre de la Gaîté, Paris, 26 October

LA PETITE MARIÉE [The little bride] (Charles Lecocq/Albert Vanloo, Eugène Leterrier) Théâtre de la Renaissance, Paris, 21 December

1876   FATINITZA (Franz von Suppé/Richard Genée, F. Zell) Carltheater, Vienna, 5 January

DER SEEKADETT [The naval cadet] (Richard Genée/F. Zell) Theater an der Wien, Vienna, 24 October

JEANNE, JEANNETTE ET JEANNETON (Paul Lacôme/Clairville, Alfred Delacour) Théâtre des Folies-Dramatiques, Paris, 27 October

1877 LA MARJOLAINE (Charles Lecocq/Albert Vanloo, Eugène Leterrier) Théâtre de la Renaissance, Paris, 3 February

EIN BLITZMÄDEL [A lightning girl] (Karl Millöcker/Karl Costa) Theater an der Wien, Vienna, 4 February

LE GRAND MOGOL (Edmond Audran/Henri Chivot) Théâtre du Gymnase, Marseille, 24 February

NANON, DIE WIRTHIN VON "GOLDENEN LAMM" [Nanon, the hostess at the "Golden Lamb"] (Richard Genée/F. Zell) Theater an der Wien, Vienna, 10 March

LES CLOCHES DE CORNEVILLE [The bells of Corneville] (Robert Planquette/Clairville, Charles Gabet) Théâtre des Folies-Dramatiques, Paris, 19 April

THE SORCERER (Arthur Sullivan/William S. Gilbert) Opera Comique, London, 17 November

L'ÉTOILE [The star] (Emmanuel Chabrier/Albert Vanloo, Eugène Leterrier) Théâtre des Bouffes-Parisiens, Paris, 28 November

1878 LE PETIT DUC [The little duke] (Charles Lecocq/Henri Meilhac, Ludovic Halévy) Théâtre de la Renaissance, Paris, 25 January

NINICHE (comp. & arr. Marius Boullard/Albert Millaud, Alfred Hennequin) Théâtre des Variétés, Paris, 15 February

DAS VERWUNSCHENE SCHLOSS [The haunted castle] (Karl Millöcker/Alois Berla) Theater an der Wien, Vienna, 30 March

HMS PINAFORE (Arthur Sullivan/William S. Gilbert) Opera Comique, London, 25 May

THE MULLIGAN GUARDS' PICNIC (David Braham/Edward Harrigan) Théâtre Comique, New York, 23 September

LA CAMARGO (Charles Lecocq/Albert Vanloo, Eugène Leterrier) Théâtre de la Renaissance, Paris, 20 November

LE DROIT DU SEIGNEUR (Léon Vasseur/Paul Burani, Maxime Boucheron) Fantaisies-Parisiennes, Paris, 13 December

MADAME FAVART (Jacques Offenbach/Henri Chivot, Alfred Duru) Théâtre des Folies-Dramatiques, Paris, 28 December

1879 LE GRAND CASIMIR (Charles Lecocq/Jules Prével, Albert de Saint-Albin) Théâtre des Variétés, Paris, 11 January

BOCCACCIO (Franz von Suppé/Richard Genée, F. Zell) Carltheater, Vienna, 1 February

LA PETITE MADEMOISELLE (Charles Lecocq/Henri Meilhac, Ludovic Halévy) Théâtre de la Renaissance, Paris, 12 April

LES NOCES D'OLIVETTE [Olivette's wedding] (Edmond Audran/Henri Chivot, Alfred Duru) Théâtre des Bouffes-Parisiens, Paris, 13 November

LA FEMME À PAPA [Daddy's wife] (Hervé et al./Albert Millaud, Alfred Hennequin) Théâtre des Variétés, Paris, 3 December

LA FILLE DU TAMBOUR-MAJOR [The drum-major's daughter] (Jacques Offenbach/Henri Chivot, Alfred Duru) Théâtre des Folies-Dramatiques, Paris, 13 December

1880   LES VOLTIGEURS DE LA 32ÈME [The men of the 32nd regiment] (Robert Planquette/Edmond Gondinet, Georges Duval) Théâtre de la Renaissance, Paris, 7 January

DONNA JUANITA (Franz von Suppé/Richard Genée, F. Zell) Carltheater, Vienna, 21 February

DIE NÄHERIN [The seamstress] (Karl Millöcker/Ludwig Held) Theater an der Wien, Vienna, 13 March

LES MOUSQUETAIRES AU COUVENT [The musketeers in a convent school] (Louis Varney/Paul Ferrier, Jules Prével) Théâtre des Bouffes-Parisiens, Paris, 16 March

FUN ON THE BRISTOL (pasticcio/George Fawcett Rowe) Newport, Rhode Island, n.d., 14th Street Theatre, New York, 9 August

DAS SPITZENTUCH DER KÖNIGIN [The Queen's handkerchief] (Johann Strauss/Bohrmann-Riegen, Richard Genée) Theater an der Wien, Vienna, 1 October

L'ARBRE DE NOËL [The christmas tree] (Charles Lecocq/Albert Vanloo, Eugène Leterrier, Arnold Mortier) Théâtre de la Porte-Saint-Martin, Paris, 6 October

BILLEE TAYLOR (Edward Solomon/Henry Pottinger Stephens) Imperial Theatre, London, 30 October

APAJUNE DER WASSERMANN [Apajune, the river-sprite] (Karl Millöcker/Richard Genée, F. Zell) Theater an der Wien, Vienna, 18 December

LA MASCOTTE [The Goodluck-bringer] (Edmond Audran/Henri Chivot, Alfred Duru) Théâtre des Bouffes-Parisiens, Paris, 28 December

THE PIRATES OF PENZANCE (Arthur Sullivan/William S. Gilbert) Fifth Avenue Theatre, New York, 31 December

1881   LA ROUSSOTTE [Miss Redhead] (Hervé et al./Albert Millaud, Henri Meilhac, Ludovic Halévy) Théâtre des Variétés, Paris, 28 January

DER GASCOGNER [The Gascon] (Franz von Suppé/Richard Genée, F. Zell) Carltheater, Vienna, 22 March

PATIENCE (Arthur Sullivan/William S. Gilbert) Opera Comique, London, 23 April

DIE JUNGFRAU VON BELLEVILLE [The lass from Belleville] (Karl Millöcker/Richard Genée, F. Zell) Theater an der Wien, Vienna, 29 October

LE JOUR ET LA NUIT [Day and night] (Charles Lecocq/Eugène Leterrier, Albert Vanloo) Théâtre des Nouveautés, Paris, 5 November

DER LUSTIGE KRIEG [The jolly war] (Johann Strauss/Richard Genée, F. Zell) Theater an der Wien, Vienna, 25 November

1882   LILI (Hervé/Albert Millaud, Alfred Hennequin, Ernest Blum) Théâtre des Variétés, Paris, 10 January

LES MANTEAUX NOIRS [Black cloaks] (Procida Bucalossi/Harry Paulton, Walter Parke) Avenue Theatre, London, 3 June

MY SWEETHEART (comp. & arr. various hands/Willie B. Gill, Clay Greene) Haverley's Fourteenth Street Theatre, New York, 14 September

RIP VAN WINKLE (Robert Planquette/H. B. Farnie) Comedy Theatre, London, 14 October

FANFAN LA TULIPE (Louis Varney/Paul Ferrier, Jules Prével) Théâtre des Folies-Dramatiques, Paris, 21 October

GILETTE DE NARBONNE (Edmond Audran/Henri Chivot, Alfred Duru) Théâtre des Bouffes-Parisiens, Paris, 11 November

IOLANTHE (Arthur Sullivan/William S. Gilbert) Savoy Theatre, London, 25 November

DER BETTELSTUDENT [The beggar-student] (Karl Millöcker/Richard Genée, F. Zell) Theater an der Wien, Vienna, 6 December

AN ADAMLESS EDEN (Walter Slaughter/Henry Savile Clarke) Opera Comique, London, 13 December

1883   MAM'ZELLE NITOUCHE (Hervé/ Albert Millaud, Henri Meilhac) Théâtre des Variétés, Paris, 26 January

LE DROIT D'AÎNESSE [The privileges of the firstborn] (Francis Chassaigne/Eugène Leterrier, Albert Vanloo) Théâtre des Nouveautés, Paris, 27 January

DIE AFRIKAREISE [A journey through Africa] (Franz von Suppé/Richard Genée, Moritz West) Theater an der Wien, Vienna, 17 March

THE MERRY DUCHESS (Frederick Clay/George Sims) Royalty Theatre, London, 23 April

EINE NACHT IN VENEDIG [One night in Venice] (Johann Strauss/Richard Genée, F. Zell) Friedrich Wilhemstädtisches Theater, Berlin, 3 October

LE COEUR ET LA MAIN [Heart and hand] (Charles Lecocq/Charles Nuitter, Alexandre Beaumont) Théâtre des Nouveautés, Paris, 19 October

MADAME BONIFACE (Paul Lacôme/Charles Clairville, Ernest Depré) Théâtre des Bouffes-Parisiens, Paris, 20 October

CORDELIA'S ASPIRATIONS (David Braham/Edward Harrigan) Théâtre Comique, New York, 5 November

FRANÇOIS LES BAS-BLEUS [François the bluestocking] (Firmin Bernicat/Ernest Dubreuil, Paul Burani, Eugène Humbert) Théâtre des Folies-Dramatiques, Paris, 8 November

1884   GASPARONE (Karl Millöcker/Richard Genée, F. Zell) Theater an der Wien, Vienna, 26 January

LA COSAQUE (Hervé/Henri Meilhac, Albert Millaud) Théâtre des Variétés, Paris, 1 February

LA PRINCESSE DES CANARIES [The Princess of the Canary Isles] (Charles Lecocq/Henri Chivot, Alfred Duru) Théâtre des Folies-Dramatiques, Paris, 9 February

AZ ELEVEN ÖRDÖG [The living devil] (József Konti/Ántal Deréki) Budai Színkör, Budapest, 8 August

ADONIS (Edward E. Rice et al./Willie B. Gill) Bijou Theatre, New York, 4 September

DER FELDPREDIGER [The fieldofficer] (Karl Millöcker/Hugo Wittmann, Alois Wohlmuth) Theater an der Wien, Vienna, 31 October

1885   THE MIKADO (Arthur Sullivan/William S. Gilbert) Savoy Theatre, London, 14 March

DON CESAR (Rudolf Dellinger/Oskar Walther) Carl-Schultze Theater, Hamburg, 28 March

DER ZIGEUNERBARON [The gipsy baron] (Johann Strauss/Ignaz Schnitzer) Theater an der Wien, Vienna, 24 October

ERMINIE (Edward Jakobowski/Harry Paulton, Claxson Bellamy) Comedy Theatre, London, 9 November

LA FAUVETTE DU TEMPLE [The nightingale of the Temple district] (André Messager/Paul Burani, Eugène Humbert) Théâtre des Folies-Dramatiques, Paris, 17 November

LA BÉARNAISE [The girl from the Béarn] (André Messager/Albert Vanloo, Eugène Leterrier) Théâtre des Bouffes-Parisiens, Paris, 12 December

LITTLE JACK SHEPPARD (Meyer Lutz et al./William Yardley, Henry Pottinger Stephens) Gaiety Theatre, London, 26 December

1886   LES NOCES IMPROVISÉES [The unexpected wedding] (Francis Chassaigne/Armand Liorat, Albert Fonteney) Théâtre des Bouffes-Parisiens, Paris, 13 February

JOSÉPHINE VENDUE PAR SES SOEURS [Josephine, sold by her sisters] (Victor Roger/Paul Ferrier, Fabrice Carré) Théâtre des Bouffes-Parisiens, Paris, 20 March

LA GRAN VÍA [The main street] (Federico Chueca, Joaquín Valverde/Felipe Perez y Gonzales) Teatro Felipe, Madrid, 2 July

DOROTHY (Alfred Cellier/B. Charles Stephenson) Gaiety Theatre, London, 25 September

LA CIGALE ET LA FOURMI [The cricket and the ant] (Edmond Audran/Henri Chivot, Alfred Duru) Théâtre de la Gaîté, Paris, 30 October

DER HOFNARR [The royal jester] (Adolf Müller/Hugo Wittmann, Julius Bauer) Theater an der Wien, Vienna, 20 November

MONTE CRISTO JR (Meyer Lutz, Ivan Caryll, et al./"Richard Henry" [i.e., H. Chance Newton, Richard Butler]) Gaiety Theatre, London, 23 December

1887   RUDDIGORE, or The Witch's Curse (Arthur Sullivan/William S. Gilbert) Savoy Theatre, London, 22 January

L'AMOUR MOUILLÉ [Damp Cupid] (Louis Varney/Jules Prével, Armand Liorat) Théâtre des Nouveautés, Paris, 25 January

SURCOUF (Robert Planquette/Henri Chivot, Alfred Duru) Théâtre des Folies-Dramatiques, Paris, 6 October

MISS ESMERALDA (Meyer Lutz et al./"A. C. Torr" [i.e., Fred Leslie], Horace Mills) Gaiety Theatre, London, 8 October

DIE SIEBEN SCHWABEN [The seven Swabians] (Karl Millöcker/Alois Wittmann, Julius Bauer) Theater an der Wien, Vienna, 29 October

1888   PEKING RÓSZÁJA [The rose of Peking] (Jenö Sztojanovits/Miksa Ruttkay) Népszinház, Budapest, 7 April

THE YEOMEN OF THE GUARD, or The Merryman and his Maid (Arthur Sullivan/William S. Gilbert) Savoy Theatre, London, 3 October

FAUST UP-TO-DATE (Meyer Lutz et al./George R. Sims, Henry Pettitt) Gaiety Theatre, London, 30 October

1889   DORIS (Alfred Cellier/B. Charles Stephenson) Lyric Theatre, London, 20 April

RUY BLAS AND THE BLASÉ ROUÉ (Meyer Lutz et al./"A. C. Torr" [i.e., Fred Leslie], Herbert F. Clark) Gaiety Theatre, London, 3 September

THE RED HUSSAR (Edward Solomon/Henry Pottinger Stephens) Lyric Theatre, London, 23 November

THE GONDOLIERS, or The King of Barataria (Arthur Sullivan/William S. Gilbert) Savoy Theatre, London, 7 December

4 THE 1890S

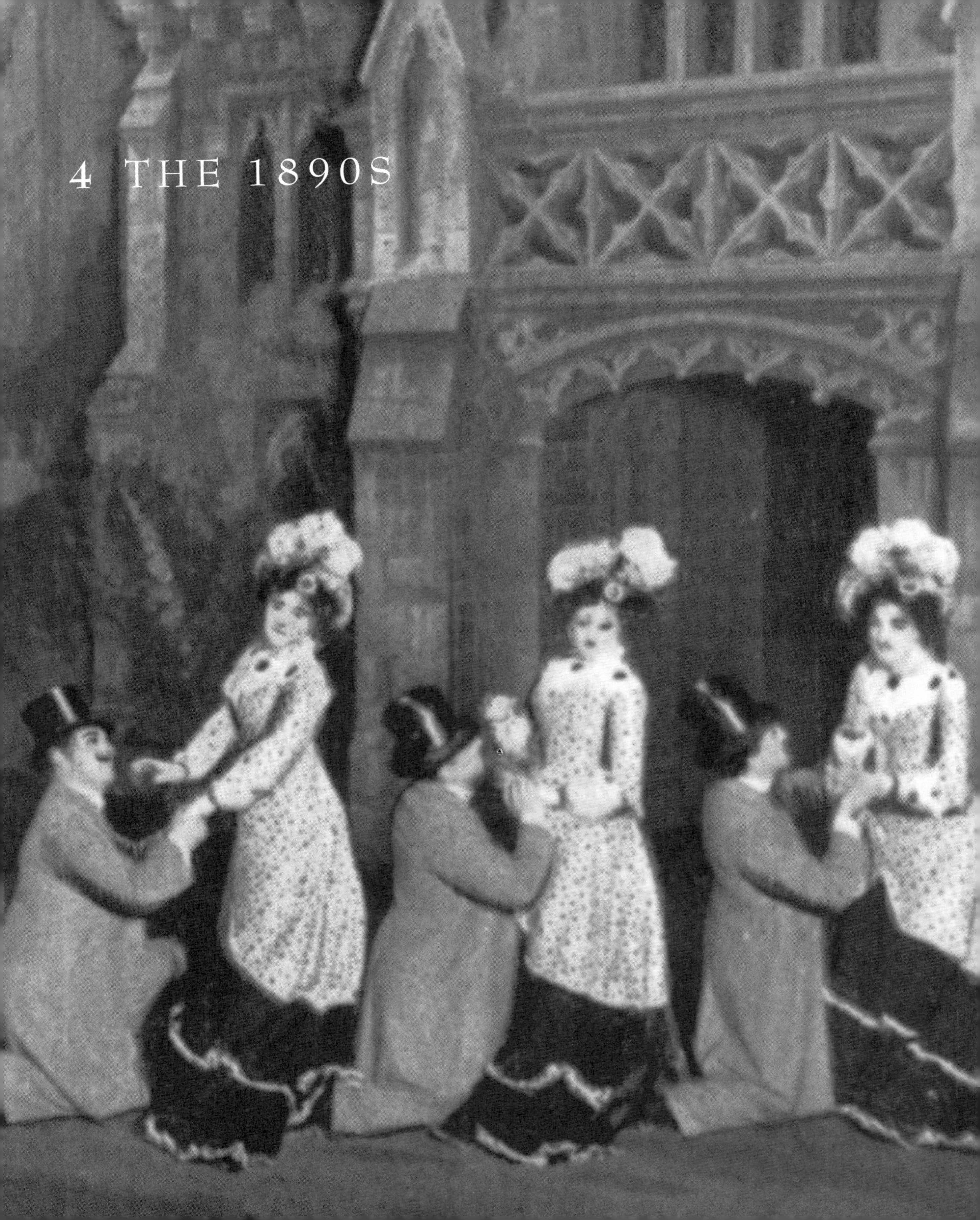

The 1890s saw a new look appear on the playbills of the world's most important musical-theater centers, from Vienna, Budapest, Paris, and Berlin to London, New York, Boston, San Francisco, and Sydney, Australia. It was a new look that had a lot to do with the fact that now, at last, the English-language musical had built itself a highway into Europe, and as the decade progressed its most successful examples moved happily in to fill the gap left by the shrinking of those native French and German traditions which had up till now been so prolific and popular, not only on English-language stages but throughout the world.

Of course, neither of those two soundly established traditions just disappeared overnight. If the French stage saw the once all-conquering opérette pale away in a flurry of prettiness with such charming but essentially soft-spined pieces as the extremely successful *La Poupée, Les P'tites Michu, Véronique, and Les Saltimbanques* — shows with plenty of sweet melody, but none of the vigor and fun of the musical theater of *Les Cent Vierges* or *Giroflé-Girofla* days — it did not mean that those qualities of vigor and fun were lost to the French musical. Far from it. Both were sidewound, along with the merry sexual imbroglios that had been at the heart of so many of the best shows of earlier years, into what would be the most successful part of the French musical stage of the turn-of-the-century decades, the more-flourishing-than-ever tradition of the vaudeville-opérette, the genuine musical comedy of its time.

In Central Europe, things went a little less well. After *Der Vogelhändler* in 1891, Vienna launched only a couple of isolated Operetten which would win any attention on a wider scale — the "French" *Der Opernball* (a version of the famous comedy *Les Dominos roses*) and the merrily Posse-like *Die Landstreicher* — during the rest of the decade. Budapest, which had pointed its nose promisingly with its most successful "French" musicals, József Konti's *Az eleven ördög* and *A suhanc*, in the 1880s, turned out several more on similar lines, topped by György Verö's remake of Favart's *Les Trois Sultanes* as *A szultán*, while Berlin's best effort was a couple of little one-act pieces — *Venus auf Erden* and *Frau Luna* — mixing local and topical songs and stories with fantasy and grand spectacle, which were written by Heinrich Bolten-Bäckers (1871–1938) and composer Paul Lincke (1866–1946) to be part of the program at a variety theater. It was more than slightly disappointing total, and there was little to suggest that, in just a few years' time, it would be the Viennese musical theater that would again spring to the forefront to dominate the musical stages of the world as never before.

But if, in the nineties, Europe had little more than the bristling French vaudeville-opérette and that very small handful of opérettes and Operetten with which to keep up its export rate, that slackening was little noticed abroad. For the English-language musical stage was not only becoming steadily more self-supporting, it was also producing musical plays that would lead it into Europe in an unprecedented way, as they spread to all corners of the earth in the same way that the Continental musicals of the past three generations had done.

The musical plays that made this "invasion" possible came from London, and a very large proportion of them came from the theaters run by one producer, the same George Edwardes who had taken over the Gaiety in the mid-1880s and there launched the New Burlesque series with such swinging success. In 1892 Edwardes took a determined step away from New Burlesque when, abandoning the colorful frills of the burlesque tradition, he launched his first "modern dress" musical, *In Town*, at the Prince of Wales Theatre. In essence, *In Town* had many points of similarity with the New Burlesques—the star-serving comic scenes were laid out in the same way, and the songs, topical, comical, and balladic, that served for one might have served for the other—but it was the differences that mattered. The slight story of the new show was set in modern-day London, its characters were recognizable modern types, their dialogue was recognizable modern chat, their clothes were the height of 1892 fashion, and they were worn by shapely girls who showed them off to the feminine part of the audience with more skill than a shop model could ever do. When a topical joke surfaced, it didn't come incongruously from the lips of a bespangled oriental houri, as it might in the burlesques, but from a smart society lady or an up-to-date dude. And that, somehow, brought its point much closer to home.

In Town was constructed around two top-billable stars, comic Arthur Roberts and soprano Florence St John. He played a jokey, social layabout-about-town called Captain Coddington deputed by an aristocratic youth to show him the sights of London. Like the Baron of *La Vie parisienne*, the sights that the boy wants to see are, of course, those connected with wine, women, and (if necessary) song. She played the leading lady of the Ambiguity Theatre—whose greenroom, with its off-stage chorus-girls, is one of the exciting "sights" in question—a girl who, before her rise to stardom, was sacked by noble mama from the post of governess to the same youth's sister for having aroused the lusts of noble papa. Noble papa and noble mama both arrived in time for a second act of backstage and on-stage frolics, which included a bundle of stand-up material, notably a big chunk of play-within-a-play burlesque, and which was later expanded with regularly changed speciality acts and new or newly popular songs. *In Town* was scarcely a copybook "musical farce"—in comparison with the vaudeville-opérettes of the same period it was desperately lacking in sophistication and in coherency in both its plotline and its characters—but it was a success, and its nearly 300 performances on the London stage confirmed Edwardes in the way he was going to take over the next decade and more, followed and imitated, of course, by a whole line of other writers and producers.

In fact, the modern dress musical—soon to be known as "musical comedy"—developed in more than one way, partly by design, and partly by accident. Edwardes led off in one direction with his second such musical, *A Gaiety Girl*, a second piece launched at the Prince of Wales Theatre but one constructed in a rather different way and with rather different emphases from the first. *A Gaiety Girl* had no above-the-title stars around whose versatility everything had to be woven. Instead, it stuck to its telling of a more vertebrate if nevertheless microscopically tiny garden-party story of class-distinction and marriage-angling of which the crux was an accusation of theft by an aristocratic lady against the girl of the title. Of course, she didn't do it—it was the naughty, foreign French maid—but that barely mattered, for what was important in the book of this show was its dialogue. Smart, slicing, society talk, spiced with all kinds of indiscretions and suggestions, which soon came under the censor's hand. But that book—the work of a first-up librettist, the bohemian Jewish occasional lawyer, dangerous journalist, and outrageous man-about-town Jimmy Davis (nom de plume "Owen Hall") (1853–1907)—was an eye-opener. The text of *A Gaiety Girl* wasn't, however, its only asset. The libretto was teamed with a set of de-lightful songs and ensembles in the popular vein which had been composed by another neo-phyte, conductor and musician Sidney Jones (1861–1946). Some of these numbers actually re-lated specifically to the story going on, and one of them—"Sunshine Above"—even turned out a hit, but the whole set of them added up to a fine and popular musical score that did much to help *A Gaiety Girl* to a run of more than 400 nights in London. And by the time that run was done, the show was already on its way through America and Australia, and had made its first European appearance, on the stage of Berlin's Adolf-Ernst Theater.

If *A Gaiety Girl* took the musical comedy a step forward from *In Town* insofar as a coherent book, characters, and score were concerned, there were other shows which latched on, in pref-erence, to the merrily movable "variety" element that had been such a prominent part of the earlier show's second act. The first of these was a piece punningly called *Morocco Bound*. In the new manner, it took for its principal characters some smart—and some not so smart—folk of the here and now, but it hedged its bets by whisking them out of England and down to the burlesque-days Pasha-lands of northern Africa for its second part. This was reasonably reason-able, for the plotline of *Morocco Bound* was concerned with the ins and outs of its main char-acters' securing of a concession to run a music-hall in Morocco. It was also smart, for such a plotline allowed almost the entire second half of the show to be filled up with a concert by the various principals, "auditioning" music-hall material for the Moroccan high-ups who will grant the privilege. Since the music-halls were out of bounds to much of polite society, the show had the extra advantage of offering nice, respectable theatergoers the chance to hear some of the "naughty" stuff that went on in those dens of iniquity. They didn't have to know that those "naughty" songs were the work of two young University graduates—Adrian Ross (1859–1933) and Frank Osmond Carr (1858–1916)—both of whom would make a notable mark on the English musical stage.

Morocco Bound was a definite success through nearly 300 nights in London, and it toured for several years thereafter in the British provinces and even into Europe, giving a great boost to the development of the kind of "variety musical" which was to become so very popular—especially in provincial houses—in years to come: a show where a reasonable, modern story was set up in the first act, but which in its second act—for some reason, or for very little at all—fishtailed away into little more than a series of songs and turns, with the plot and characterization returning just long enough before the final curtain for everyone to get his deserts, and her rich and handsome husband. The most remarkable piece of this kind was actually launched just a few months after *Morocco Bound*, and a month before *A Gaiety Girl*, and not in London but at the Theatre Royal in provincial Northampton. *The Lady Slavey* was authored by George Dance (?1865–1932), a clever theater writer who had shown his colors very successfully when called in to supply a new Savoy Theatre musical—vice W. S. Gilbert—a couple of years earlier. *The Nautch Girl* had proved to be a delicious piece of witty and well-constructed writing, but Dance's great talent lay not in manufacturing quasi-Gilbertian comic opera, but in more popular areas of the theater. Over the next years he turned out a number of musical comedies which would catch the general public's ear to a staggering degree, giving him a record which not even "Owen Hall" would outdo. The original musical score for *The Lady Slavey* was a "composed and arranged" one, with such favorites as "Daisy Bell," "The Man Who Broke the Bank at Monte Carlo," and "Wotcher" finding their way into its second-act concert, but the show was recomposed when it went into the West End, being equipped instead with a mixture of mostly new songs from a bevy of songwriters, and it was that score that held its place when the show went back on the road for a tour that would last for some fifteen years.

THE LADY SLAVEY, a musical go-as-you-please in 2 acts by George Dance. Music by John Crook and others. Produced at the Theatre Royal, Northampton, 4 September 1893. Produced at the Avenue Theatre, London, in a revised version with new music by John Crook, 20 October 1894.

Characters: Major O'Neill, Maud, Beatrice, Phyllis, Roberts, Vincent A. Evelyn, Lord Lavender, Flo Honeydew, Mlle Pontet, Mlle Louise, Bill, Captain FitzNorris, &c.

Plot: The tinned-tomato millionaire Vincent Evelyn is in the market for a bride, and he is coming to stay at the home of impoverished Major O'Neill and his three daughters. The O'Neills actually already have one visitor, for they are down on their uppers and the bailiff Roberts is in possession. To give a bit of tone to the place, and promote the chances of Beatrice or Maud catching the marital prize, the youngest sister, Phyllis, volunteers to be "the maid" and Roberts is persuaded into being "the butler" for the duration of Evelyn's visit. Unexpected competition arrives in the person of the music-hall's Flo Honeydew, but Evelyn tastefully falls for "the maid." The others are led to believe that it is Roberts who is the real millionaire, craftily disguised so as to see and not be seen, and while Vincent and Phyllis get on with their wooing, the bailiff is royally entertained (mostly with a concert!) until it is time for the final curtain with its explanations and deserts for all.

Songs: "We're Sorry to Trouble You" (chorus), "St Patrick Was an Irishman" (Major), "Sing Hi! for the Cake and the Ring!" (ensemble), "What's a Poor Girl to Do?" (by Joseph & Mary Watson)

(Phyllis), "The Tears Rolled Down His Cheeks" (lyric by Willie Younge) (Roberts), "Why Love in Secret?" (by Henry J. Wood, Joseph Hart & Dance) (Beatrice, Vincent), Finale Act 1: "Five o'Clock Chimes"/"Wanted a Wife" (Vincent), "Nature Doth Fashion" (chorus), "'Tis Hard to Love and Say Farewell" (music by Frank Isitt) (Phyllis), "It's a Very Wise Child That Knows" (Roberts, Phyllis and later Flo, Lord Lavender), "Each Bird and Beast" (Roberts, Phyllis), "Welcome, Welcome, Millionaire" (chorus), "The Big Boss Dude from O-hi-o" (Roberts), "List, oh List" (solo & chorus), "The Land of Dreams" (by Alfred Cammeyer/Herbert Walther) (Phyllis), "Dorothy Flop" (by Letty Lind/Adrian Ross) (Maud), "Gee Up, Gee Up Whoa!" (Phyllis), Finale Act 2: "My Darling Phyllis." Added, alternative, and interpolated songs included: "Whoop de dooden do" (Flo), "I Must Look a Bit Higher Than That" (Phyllis), "When You and I Are Wed" (Vincent, Phyllis), "Paddy Malone" (Roberts), "In Friendship's Name" (music by Charles Graham) (Vincent), "The Sunshine of Paradise Alley" (Flo), "I Want Yer My Honey" (Flo), "My Sweethearts" (Lord Lavender), "Henry Did" (music by Joseph Hart) (Lord Lavender), "The Ole Banjo" (Vincent), "He Stole McCarthy's Wife," and many others.

Although it had taken in the tag end of the run of *In Town*, it was not until 1894, with *Morocco Bound*, *The Lady Slavey*, its almost as incredibly successful successor *The Gay Parisienne*, and *A Gaiety Girl* all well on their way, that the Gaiety Theatre produced the first of the series of musical comedies with which it would become so securely identified. Curiously, for *The Shop Girl* Edwardes didn't go back to the team that had supplied him so felicitously with *A Gaiety Girl*; instead he got his libretto from an American journalist called Henry Jackson Dam (1859–1906), and, in traditional in-house manner, had it decorated musically by the Gaiety's new musical director, Ivan Caryll (1860–1921), who had scored his first full-scale musical theater hit the year before with the tunes for a new burlesque named *Little Christopher Columbus*. *The Shop Girl* was, perhaps, not very original in its plot, and its dialogue didn't have quite the cutting edge that Hall's had had, but that plot and the dialogue came together superbly with Caryll's melodies—supplemented, in what would become the up-to-date manner, by some made-to-catch, music-hally numbers, freshly brewed or occasionally second-hand, from other sources—and as played by the new set of performers that Edwardes had gathered from all corners of the stage and music-hall world, the show turned out to be a great success.

THE SHOP GIRL, a musical comedy in 2 acts by Henry Jackson W. Dam. Music by Ivan Caryll. Additional lyrics by Adrian Ross. Additional music by Lionel Monckton. Produced at the Gaiety Theatre, London, 24 November 1894.

Characters: Mr Hooley, Charles Appleby, Mr Miggles, Miss Robinson, Ada Smith, Bessie Brent, Bertie Boyd, John Brown, Sir George Appleby, Lady Appleby, Lady Dodo Singleton, Count St Vaurien, Colonel Singleton, Mr Tweets, Faith, Hope, Charity, Maud Plantaganet, &c.

Plot: Miner John Brown went to America and made himself a fortune, and now he has advertised to try to find the daughter he left behind in England. The search has been narrowed to Mr Hooley's store, and it seems that the plump and pouting shopgirl Ada Smith may be the lost heiress. Big-boss Hooley quickly proposes marriage, and Ada dumps her little shopman sweetheart Miggles to grab the

better offer. But then Brown turns up. The advertisement misprinted the child's age—Ada is ten years too old, and the real Miss Brown is another Hooley's shopgirl—ingénue Bessie Brent. Now she can wed the aristocratic Charlie whose parents and lineage were previously insuperably ranged against her, while Miggles finds consolation for his weighty loss in duets with a glamorous lassie from Sales.

Songs: Opening chorus: "The Royal Stores" (chorus), "By Special Appointment" (Hooley), "We'll Proceed to Search for Ada" (Hooley, Count, Colonel, Sir George), "Stage Beauties" (chorus), "Superfluous Relations" (Charlie), "Over the Hills" (Dodo), "The Shop Girl," later "The Song of the Shop" (Bessie), Perambulator Duet: "Hush-a-bye" (Bessie, Charlie), "Foundlings Are We" (octette), "The Vegetarian" (Miggles), "The Foundling" (Ada), Finale Act 1: "Farewell, Farewell," "Charity, Charity" (chorus), "The Smartest Girl in Town" (Maud), "My Lousiana Lou" (by Leslie Stuart) (Bessie), "Love on the Japanese Plan" (Miggles, Miss Robinson), "Brown of Colorado" (Brown), "Too Clever by Half" (Colonel, Count, Sir George), "We Are Now to Have Some Mystery" (chorus), "Her Golden Hair Was Hanging Down Her Back" (by Felix McGlennon/ adapted by Ross) (Charlie), "The Man in the Moon" (by Teresa del Riego) (Dodo), "Nothing's So Good for the Agonised Heart" (quartet), "Beautiful Bountiful Bertie" (lyric by George Grossmith) (Bertie), Show Song: "The Show, the Show," Finale Act 2: "Now Joy Is in the Air." Other interpolated numbers included: "What Could the Poor Girl Do?" (by Emilie Alexanda/adapted by Adrian Ross), "I Want Yer My Honey" (by Fay Templeton) (Bessie), "Oh! My Dummy" (Miggles), "The Little Mademoiselle" (by Leslie Stuart) (Charlie), "The Simple Maiden" (by T. Merton Clark/ E. W. Bowles), "The Honeymoon" (lyric by Harry Greenbank) (Bessie).

The Shop Girl was greeted happily by public and press, the general opinion being that the show nicely struck the balance between just enough, but not too much, story and some merry, but not extravagantly music-hally, numbers (even though the hit solo of the night, the hero's "Her Golden Hair Was Hanging Down Her Back," came precisely from the music-halls), that its characters were entertaining, its dances delightful, its gowns gorgeous and the girls who wore them—now established forever as the Gaiety Girls—no less so, and that it was, in any case, way above anything the burlesque theater had ever provided. The show stayed 546 performances at the Gaiety before going on to fields afar, and the die was set. Or almost. Edwardes clearly recognized that although *The Shop Girl* had the formula fairly right, it had yet to be perfected. With his next show, *My Girl,* he tried to inject a little more body and complexity into the story and dialogue of what he and his house librettist, James Tanner (1858–1915), called "a domestic musical play," and Adrian Ross supplied a bookful of clever and frequently topically pointed lyrics which were set by his *In Town* partner Frank Carr with music rather less loose-limbed than some of that which they'd written for *Morocco Bound. My Girl* did well, but there were distinct mumbles from those who wanted the Gaiety to continue with nothing but feather-weight entertainment and Edwardes listened. For his third show, the thoroughly uncomplicated *The Circus Girl,* he teamed Tanner ("assisted by the chairman of the Gaiety board"!) with Ross, the ill-fated young lyricist Harry Greenbank (1865–1899), Caryll, and his "additional numbers" colleague Lionel Monckton (1861–1924), and what would become in effect "the Gaiety team," turning out the light, bright, girl-studded shows for which the theater would be famous during the years to come, was in place. Various other writers and musicians would have a supporting hand in those shows, but the run of "musical comedies" which saw out the nineteenth century and the days of the original Gaiety Theatre—*The Circus Girl* (1896, 494 performances), *A Runaway Girl* (1898, 593 performances), *The Messenger Boy* (1900, 429 performances), *The Toreador* (1901, 675 performances)—each bore the names of at least some of Edwardes's most trusted Gaiety musical-makers.

What made up a Gaiety musical? Well, first of all it had to have a framework of plot—one, preferably, that allowed its characters and its scenic and costume artists to get themselves into some unlikely and picturesque spots. *The Circus Girl* took its English folk to the gaieties of Paris, its artists' ball, and even into a circus ring, *A Runaway Girl* was chased around southern Europe with an emphasis on Corsica and its bandits and modern-day Venice, *The Messenger Boy* was sent off to coffee-colored Africa with the rest of the cast behind him, and the little chap who wasn't really *The Toreador* had his adventures around the Spanish border. Even more importantly, however, that plot had to be able to hold characters to suit the artists who very quickly became the Gaiety's regular stars—or in their absence the nearest clone available: little-chap comic Teddy Payne and his soubrette partner Katie Seymour, dude comedian George Grossmith, portly comedienne Connie Ediss, a pair of sparky young lovers—Seymour Hicks and Ellaline Terriss—who didn't sigh and pine and sing ballads like musical heroes and heroines of yore but who tit-for-tatted and sang light, bright popular songs. A Gaiety show was constructed around its audience's favorite folk, in rôles made to their measure just as the regulars of the Savoy company were fitted, from show to show, by the Gilbert and Sullivan team.

Alongside the principals there were also, of course, the Girls. The Girls had always been a part of the Gaiety and its shows, right from the earliest days of the theater's activity when Lardy Wilson, Kate Love, Alma Egerton, and a small bouquet of other elegant beauties had been gracefully displayed in what were smilingly called "thinking rôles." But the Gaiety musical comedy brought the Girls much more to the fore, and some of them even got to do more than "think." A handful were promoted to speaking or even singing rôles. But a Gaiety Girl was not first or foremost an actress or a singer; she was an elegant young woman who could wear modern clothes effectively, and move gracefully and with a polished seductiveness in them through the routines provided. A serious dance training was not necessary, for the chorus dances of a Gaiety musical were gentle affairs made up of dainty stepping rather than the energetic leg-flinging of the opéra-bouffe girls, the bone fide ballet (the graceful Italo-French variety, the Russian gymnastic strain being not yet popularized) of the Alhambra's soloists, or the acrobatics of the specialist comedy dancers who had long been a feature of both theater and music-hall in England.

The scenes in which the plot progressed were, by and large, progressive. They actually went forward in a connected way. The slicing and scathing and smartness that Owen Hall had gone in for in his dialogue were now tempered into something a little less aggressive and more comfy as the young lovers made unsoulful young love, the comedians cracked topical jokes and got themselves in and out of fixes to the accompaniment of a rather lower kind of bantering than that indulged in by the sweethearts and soubrettes, and everybody regularly took time off—no matter what they were doing—to indulge in the musical part of the show, its songs, its dances, and its stage pictures, but the thread of plot didn't ever vanish for long in the way that it did in the latter stages of the variety musicals.

The musical part of a Gaiety show was paramount, and Edwardes had the luck—or the skill—to fall upon two of the most delightfully light-fingered songwriters of the day as his principal composers. Ivan Caryll, the theater's chief conductor, was a Belgian, thoroughly musically educated in France, and with a great theatrical flair, while Lionel Monckton was an Englishman with a remarkable gift for melody. At the beginning, Monckton supplied just the odd "pop" song to be featured, in a variation of musical style, in Caryll's score, but his success was such that he was soon moved up to equal billing and a larger representation, although Caryll needfully kept the job of writing the concerted music.

The music of the Gaiety shows was popular music, for if such concerted pieces as there were—the choruses and truncated (by comparison with the comic opera) finales and the occasional trio or quartet—carried a tiny perfume of the "operatic" theater, the songs that were the features of the score were mostly made in the same vein as those of the new burlesque days had been, and as those of the politer music-halls still were. Many of them were slotted into the plot, situation, and characters of the piece, but—just as in the variety musical—very often, in the second act, a little group of numbers which had a minimal reference to anything would be popped in. Thus, in *A Runaway Girl*, after a comical piece about "Barcelona," a pair of numbers heralding the scene change to "In Venice," and the plotful number "We Have Left Pursuit Behind Us"—and before things got back to the subject in hand with a Gondola Song, a Carnival Chorus, and the call to "Comrades All, Come See the Sight"—time was taken out for a secondary lassie to grab her big moment and sing a jaunty Lionel Monckton number about a very English bunch of "Soldiers in the Park." Then the star ingénue came up with a childish little ditty called "The Boy Guessed Right" before it was time for the comedy duet of the night—Payne and his partner blacked up as "The Piccaninnies"! But that was all right: they were blacked up in an attempt to escape the bandits, which was more than one could say in plotful justification of the other two songs. But those two songs were the two takeaway hits of *A Runaway Girl*. Precisely the same thing happened in *The Messenger Boy*: the score progressed through "Hooker Pasha" and "Up the Nile'—and then the same sort of little lassie stepped forward to coo out the assertion that "Maisie is a daisy . . . ," and yet another had her moment and her "spot" singing a coon song—the then-fashionable imitation of the American plantation song. And this time Payne and Miss Seymour managed to find an excuse to get dressed up as "Mummies" as a means of escaping their pursuers! And what was the song hit of *The Messenger Boy*? Why, "Maisie," of course.

During the course of the run of a Gaiety show, the score would inevitably undergo changes—partly to please an audience which repeated its visits regularly, and partly to keep up to date: when the Boer War hit, for example, *The Messenger Boy* sang about "When the Boys Come Home Once More" and "How I Saw the CIV." Normally, the plotful numbers held their place, alongside such Gaiety-musts as the character duos for Payne and Miss Seymour, and it was the ballads, the point numbers, or the little bunch of tacked-on songs that were overhauled. Sometimes no cutting was done either and the musical part of the entertainment just grew, with the addition both of new numbers and even occasionally of songs that had been picked up somewhere else and were now brought to prominence at London's favorite musical theater.

Fun of all kinds, catchy tunes, and gorgeous girls in gorgeous frocks were the keynotes of a Gaiety musical, and the audience who went to the Gaiety—including those who swanned in and out of the stalls seats just for their favorite part of the show, or in time to catch a particular artist, or perhaps just a little late and lit-up after having dined rather wetly—knew that that was what they would find there. And, until his box-office showed him signs that this was no longer what they wanted there, George Edwardes kept right on providing just that.

THE MESSENGER BOY, a musical play in 2 acts by James Tanner and Alfred Murray. Lyrics by Adrian Ross and Percy Greenbank. Music by Ivan Caryll and Lionel Monckton. Produced at the Gaiety Theatre, London, 3 February 1900.

Characters: Tommy Bang, Rosa, Mrs Bang, Hooker Pasha, Cosmos Bey, Clive Radnor, Captain Pott, Professor Phunkwitz, Tudor Pyke, Comte le Fleury, Lord Punchestown, Lady Punchestown, Nora Punchestown, Isabel Blyth, Daisy Dapple, Captain Naylor, Mr Gascoigne &c.

Plot: Nora Punchestown accepts a proposal of marriage from Clive Radnor, and Clive sets off for Egypt to get the consent of her aristocratic papa. But Nora's rejected suitor, Tudor Pyke, fights back. He hires a messenger boy to head for Egypt and aristocratic papa bearing a promissory note which will ruin Radnor's reputation. He has two instructions: he must get to Lord Punchestown first, and he must guard the precious paper with his life. But when little Tommy has set off, Pyke discovers he has given the boy the wrong paper . . . a compromising letter from Lady Punchestown! Pyke sets off to stop Tommy, and Nora, put wise, sets off to stop Pyke. But Tommy and Lady P's maid, Rosa, succeed after many an escapade and disguise in escaping all their pursuers on the way to what is ultimately a happy Egyptian ending.

Songs: "To Our Charity Bazaar" (chorus), "The Merry Marriage Market of the East" (Cosmos Bey), "What Would Society Say?" (Lady Punchestown, Pyke), "Tittle-tattle" (Nora), "Ask Papa" (Nora, Clive), "Bradshaw's Guide"(Cosmos Bey, Daisy, Gascoigne, Le Fleury, Phunkwitz), "The Messenger Boy" (Tommy), "Aspirations" (Tommy, Rosa), Tarantella: "We're a Troupe of Merry Dancers" (chorus), "Mary, Mary, Quite Contrary" (Clive), "Off to Cairo" (Naylor, Pott, Cosmos Bey), "In the Wash" (Mrs Bang), "Ask the Advice of the Captain" (Pott), Finale Act I: "Cast the Moorings Free," "Sheltered from the Noonday Glare" (chorus), "Hooker Pasha" (Hooker), "Up the Nile" (Clive, Daisy, Gascoigne, Le Fleury, Phunkwitz), "Maisie" (Isabel), Dervish Dance, "Co-ee, Ma Girlie" (Rosa), "It's Got to Be Done" (Lady Punchestown, Mrs Bang, Pyke, Hooker), "They're All After Pott" (Pott), "Let the Trumpets" (chorus), "Mummies" (Tommy, Rosa), "When the Boys

Come Home Once More" (Nora), "Comme ci, comme ça" (Mrs Bang), Finale Act 2: "We Will
Take Our Wedding Trip." Added and interpolated numbers included: "A Perfectly Peaceful Person" (by Paul Rubens) (Clive), "The Boys of London Town," "President Doppen," "A Little Bit
Further On" (Tommy, Pott), "The Pretty Petticoat," "How I Saw the CIV" (Mrs Bang), "I'm Tired
of Being Respectable" (by Melville Ellis) (Pott), burlesque on "Tell Me, Pretty Maiden" (by John
Stromberg/Paul Rubens) (sextet), "Hold Tight, Mother" (Tommy, Pott, &c.), "The Paris Exhibition" (chorus), "I'm a Little Dutch Maid" (lyric by Paul Rubens) (Rosa, Tommy).

Edwardes, however, did not only offer Londoners of the nimble nineties the petal-weight kind
of entertainment purveyed at the Gaiety. In parallel to the enormously successful series of
musicals played at the merry little house in the Strand, he mounted a second series, not very
far down the road, in Leicester Square. Leicester Square was the home of Daly's Theatre, a
house built by Edwardes on a time-share agreement with the New York impresario Augustin
Daly. Daly didn't share for long, so Edwardes ended up taking over the management of the
new house alone, and transferred A Gaiety Girl there for the last part of its run. It, of course,
did very well, so the producer planned to replace it with more of the same. Owen Hall, Harry
Greenbank (the young lyricist who, with Adrian Ross, helped to put the profession of lyricist, as
opposed to all-in-textwriter, on the map or, at least, the playbill) and Sidney Jones were put to
work on a repeat show, built around a little tale about a runaway schoolgirl in Paris and the English antics of her pursuing family: it was to be called A Naughty Girl. A Naughty Girl would
have been—give or take its Owen Hall dialogue—pretty much like what would become known
as a Gaiety-style show, only it never made it to the stage. Edwardes got the chance to sign up
the soprano Marie Tempest, recently returned from a successful stint in comic opera in America, and—since there was no chance of the distinctly soprano Miss Tempest impersonating a
naughty teenager—A Naughty Girl was put in for rewrites. Owen Hall didn't fiddle with his text.
He quite simply glued a whole new subplot into it—one featuring a rich widow, once an artist's
model, now returned to Paris and to the artist she always really loved. Sidney Jones supplied
the lady and her richly baritonic boyfriend with some lushly romantic music, and what had been
once A Naughty Girl was produced instead as An Artist's Model with Miss Tempest teamed with
handsome vocalist Hayden Coffin, and pretty little Letty Lind of skirt-dance fame featured as
the schoolgirl who had once been the sole center of attraction but who was now only a co-plot.

An Artist's Model proved to be an even bigger hit than A Gaiety Girl had been, and its trio
de tête of stars—the soprano, the baritone, and the dancing soubrette—complemented each
other, and the swatch of supporting comedians, superbly. And so, the "Daly's team" was born:
Hall, Greenbank, Jones, Miss Tempest, Miss Lind, and Coffin, a group topped up by a fourth
star performer, the little comedian Huntley Wright, and the inveterate "additional numbers"
man, Monckton, as they moved on and into more musicals made on the same, originally acci-
dental, now purposeful lines, and to a kind and volume of success that would outshine even
that of the Gaiety musicals on the international stage.

An *Artist's Model* was followed by *The Geisha* (1896) and *A Greek Slave* (1898) before holes started to appear in the team. For *San Toy* (1899), Edwardes had to dispense with the services of the skilled Hall when a powerful journalist offered him a libretto (which was all but rewritten in rehearsal), then young Greenbank died aged only thirty-three, Miss Lind decamped, and Marie Tempest was persuaded to break her contract and quit the show partway through the run. But in those four shows, and in just five years or so, the Daly's musical had become established as a highly important and effective kind of musical theater.

Even though the same writers occasionally worked on both, "a Daly's musical" differed from "a Gaiety musical" in several fundamental ways. As at the Gaiety, of course, the libretto had to be written in such a way as to give good rôles and opportunities to the theater's flagship stars, but at Daly's the script was expected to be noticeably more substantial both in plot and dialogue. Whereas drama and real romance were altogether foreign to a Gaiety plot, a Daly's one was expected to have both. Soprano Miss Tempest and baritone Coffin had to lead their love affair through difficulties as well as duets to a happy ending at the final curtain. And they did not conduct that love affair in the light-hearted fashion that Ellaline Terriss and Seymour Hicks and their successors at the Gaiety did. Although Miss Tempest, in particular, was allowed her light-hearted moments during the show, her romance was real and heartfelt. And the music that accompanied it was music of a range and depth which was hardly ever heard at the Gaiety—and certainly not from any of its resident stars. Letty Lind's soubrette performances as an English miss (*The Geisha*) and an ancient Roman maidservant (*A Greek Slave*), had a touch more of the Gaiety about them, but the comedy purveyed by Wright and by such other established comedians as Harry Monkhouse and Rutland Barrington was of a kind that was as near to that of the Savoy as to that of the Strand.

The music which Jones composed for his shows was of a markedly different character and weight from Caryll's music for the Gaiety. The percentage of lyric music was high, the amount of ensemble work was perceptibly greater, and the show's acts were equipped with full-scale concerted finales made up of music that the Gaiety casts wouldn't have got within a mile of tackling. The first-act finale of *The Geisha*—which takes place at the show's dramatic height, with tenor, soprano, and soubrette all in a hole, baritone clamoring heroically to the rescue, and everyone else in a ten-part harmony pother—and of *A Greek Slave*—a splendid phoney séance with an apparition of a soaringly baritonic God of Love—were masterpieces of romantic musical theater that rendered nothing in quality and effectiveness to such classics of the genre as Sullivan's *Mikado* first-act closer. As at the Gaiety, the principal composer's score was leavened with Monckton ditties for, most especially, the soubrette, and the mixture of contrasting styles proved to be as effective as it was in the lighter scores.

Daly's Theatre did, of course, also have its girls. The Parisiennes of *An Artist's Model* gave way to fashionable English ladies, to geisha girlies, to Ancient Roman puellae and matronae. But the girls of the Daly's Theatre chorus weren't just the elegant clotheshorses that their companions at the Gaiety were. To start with, the majority were required to sing, and sing well enough to make something out of Jones's thoroughly singable music. A handful of girls from the Gaiety put in appearances at Daly's—more often than not when a dancer or a particularly elegant lady was required—but, by and large, the two theaters bred their own kind of chorine: at the Gaiety style and glamour were paramount, at Daly's a good voice was inclined to come above other charms.

San Toy had the longest London run of the four Daly's musicals of the nineteenth century, but it was by no means superior in quality to the others, and it was by no means the most generally and widely successful. That honor went unchallengeably to *The Geisha*.

Owen Hall's libretto to *The Geisha* was skillfully crafted to give the three equally billed stars of Daly's equally prominent rôles, and he even worked it so that the title applied both to Miss Tempest (who played a real Japanese) and to Miss Lind (who played a phoney one). Coffin was the white-uniformed English naval officer who is engaged to one and taken with the other, and in a neat (but politically correct, for the times) twist he was paired off at the final curtain not in a miscegenous match with the oriental soprano, but with the soubrette. There were splendid rôles, too, for Wright as Wun-Hi, the funny little proprietor of the tea-house where Mimosa is indentured, thrown into ruin when the local potentate (a glowering rôle for Monkhouse and later Barrington) sells him up; for another in the line of smart society ladies, initiated by the librettist with enormous success in *A Gaiety Girl*, as the meddling aristocrat whose arrival in Japan sets the cat amongst the amorous naval officer's peacocks; and also for one of London's newest imported stars, the young French girl Juliette Nesville who had featured in both *A Gaiety Girl* and *An Artist's Model*.

Jones, too, provided of his best—both brilliant soprano music and piquant point numbers for Miss Tempest, soulful balladry, martial moments and flirtatious duos for Coffin, a jaunty "Chin-Chin-Chinaman" for the down-in-the-dumps Wun-Hi, variegated soubretteries for Miss Lind, including one of the coy little animal songs ("The Interfering Parrot") with which she had scored so well in her previous outing, and saucy French numbers for the saucy French lass, the whole topped off by some splendid concerted music, notably that effective finale to the first act. Monckton added a couple of choice bits with a sailor song for Coffin and a takeaway hit about "The Toy Monkey" for Miss Lind, and one of the Gaiety's occasional conductors came up with the song that would be his claim to fame in an extra solo in which Miss Tempest claimed to be "The Jewel of Asia."

Following its 760 West End showings, *The Geisha* triumphed wherever it went: first around Britain and the rest of the English-speaking world, but then also in Europe. In Europe, in fact, it became a sensation. Never before had an English-language musical scored such a success. From Vienna and Berlin to Budapest, Milan, and St Petersburg the show went and, by the time it had done so, not only had it established itself as far and away the most internationally successful imported-into-Europe musical of all time—way, way ahead of *The Mikado* and never even to be approached till the advent of *No, No, Nanette*—but it had established the English romantic musical play, that genre half-way between light opera and musical comedy, in such a way that *A Greek Slave*, *San Toy*, and others would find a much easier and wider welcome than they had before.

THE GEISHA, a Story of a Tea-House, a Japanese musical play in 2 acts by Owen Hall. Lyrics by Harry Greenbank. Music by Sidney Jones. Additional music by Lionel Monckton and James Philp. Produced at Daly's Theatre, London, 25 April 1896.

Characters: O Mimosa San, Juliette Diamant, Lady Constance Wynne, Molly Seamore, Reginald Fairfax RN, Dick Cunningham, Wun-Hi, Marquis Imari, Nami, O Kiku San, O Hana San, O Kinkoto San, Komurasaki San, Ethel Hurst, Mabel Grant, Louie Plumpton, Arthur Cuddy, George Grimston, Captain Katana, Takemine, Tommy Stanley, &c.

Plot: Reggie Fairfax, out on duty in far-off Japan, whiles away his leisure hours in the company of the tea-house geisha O Mimosa San. The voyaging Lady Wynne feels he is whiling altogether too enthusiastically, and telegraphs Reggie's fiancée, Molly, to head out east in a proprietorial hurry. But the local Marquis also has his eye on Mimosa, and he forces the tea-house into bankruptcy, meaning to buy Mimosa's indentures at the dispersal sale. Lady Wynne puts a stop to that by out-bidding the lubricious Marquis at the break-up auction, but he doesn't quibble—he happily buys the next girl instead. Unfortunately, that next girl is Molly, who's arrived in town and got herself into Japanese dress as a sort of come-on to her Reggie. Since she doesn't want to be a Japanese Marquise, everyone gangs up and goes to her rescue, and finally—thanks to a bit of veil and a traditional canopy—the Marquis is fooled into wedding the tea-house interpreter, little French Juliette, who is delighted to be promoted to the nobility, Japanese or not. Reggie goes back to his Molly, and Mimosa is free to wed her longtime tenor lover.

Songs: "Happy Japan" (chorus), "Shall We Sing You?"/"Here They Come" (geisha), "The Dear Little Jap-Jap-Jappy" (Dick), "The Amorous Goldfish" (Mimosa), Kissing Duet (Reggie, Mimosa), "If You Will Come to Tea" (geisha), Lamentation chorus: "O Will They Sell Our Master Up?" (chorus), "We're Going to Call on the Marquis" (ensemble), Toy Duet: "When I Was But a Tiny Tot" (Molly, Reggie), "A Geisha's Life" (Mimosa), "Jack's the Boy" (music by Monckton) (Reggie), "Attention Pray" (Takemine), "Chivalry" (Reggie), "Chon-kina" (Molly), Finale Act 1: "Though of Staying Too Long You're Accusing Us," "Day Born of Love" (chorus), "The Toy Monkey" (music by Monckton) (Molly), "Ching-a-ring-a-ree" (Juliette, Wun-Hi), "Geisha Are We" (geisha), "Star of My Soul" (Reggie), "If That's Not Love—What Is?" (Juliette), Japanese March, "With Splendour Auspicious" (chorus), "Chin-Chin-Chinaman" (Wun-Hi), "Love! Love!" (Mimosa), "Hey Diddle Diddle, When Man Is in Love" (Cunningham), "The Interfering Parrot" (Molly), "What Will the Marquis Do?" (Mimosa, Reggie, Cunningham, Wun-Hi), Finale Act 2: "Before Our Eyes." Alternative and interpolated numbers included: "Jolly Young Jacks Are We" (Reggie, Cunningham, & sailors), "The Jewel of Asia" (music by James Philp) (Mimosa), "I Can't Refrain from Laughing" (music by Napoleon Lambelet), "The Wedding" (lyric by Adrian Ross) (Imari), "Molly Mine" (Reggie), "C'est moi" (Juliette), "Love, Could I Only Tell Thee" (by G. H. Clutsam/J. M. Capel), "It's Coming Off Today."

The Gaiety and Daly's were not, of course, the only British theaters producing the new brand of musical comedy and romantic musical plays during the 1890s. Both the London and the

Florodora: "Tell me, pretty maiden, are there any more at home like you?" Sidney Ellison's routine to this double sextet became one of the greatest dance hits of an era.

provincial theaters were quick to follow where *In Town, A Gaiety Girl, Morocco Bound, The Lady Slavey, The Shop Girl,* and *An Artist's Model* had so very successfully led, and they followed with such enthusiasm that, by the last part of the decade, barely a translated musical was to be seen on that London stage which not long since had been simply overflowing with French shows.

Among the most successful of these shows were a number which came from the same two librettists—Owen Hall and George Dance—who had been responsible for the very earliest hits in the new vein. Hall, who suffered from a quite maniacal gambling habit, was always in need of ready cash, so he always worked—for anyone—for a fee down and no royalties. As his successes mounted, those fees were, of course, able to rise considerably, and Owen Hall in all his career only really turned out one and a half shows that weren't a success. His biggest success, apart from *The Geisha,* came when he teamed up with a fellow gambler, the highly successful popular songwriter Leslie Stuart (1864–1928), on the musician's first attempt at writing a piece for the stage. Hall's plot for *Florodora* was a fairly routine comico-romantic one about soprano-baritone love and comical skulduggery in the picturesque Philippine Islands and a not-quite-haunted Welsh castle, but he repeated the trick that had worked so well in *An Artist's Model* by opportunistically adding to this basic tale one of his smart society-dame rôles for out-of-work soubrette Ada Reeve—the original shopgirl of the Gaiety's musical—a gambit which gave the show a much more Hall-ian flavor, and the writer the opportunity for much more of the spiky dialogue in which he specialized. Stuart, in his turn, provided a set of slightly idiosyncratic songs—his songwriting style, with its long lines and odd rhythms, was not quite like any other—but, to his indignation, he found it punctured through with the now regular sprinkling of "additional numbers" by the much less proficient, but indubitably catchy, Paul Rubens

(1875–1917). Rubens, who specialized in straightforward tunes and baby-blue lyrics, supplied most of the material for Miss Reeve, and, as had happened with Monckton's extra numbers in Caryll's and Jones's scores, these more obvious numbers proved to be some of the takeaway tunes of the night. However, Rubens did not score the big song hit of *Florodora*. That went— to general surprise—to a little ensemble called "Are There Any More at Home Like You?" Six dapper chorus boys squired six fashionably dressed front-line ladies back and forth across the stage in a droll little Sidney Ellison dance routine, and the town went wild. Soon the number, rechristened by its first line as "Tell Me, Pretty Maiden," was one of the biggest song hits in musical comedy history, as *Florodora* made its way to a memorable career on Broadway, another in Australia, and a swath of productions throughout the rest of the world.

FLORODORA, a musical comedy in 2 acts by Owen Hall. Lyrics by Ernest Boyd-Jones and Paul Rubens. Music by Leslie Stuart. Additional songs by Paul Rubens. Produced at the Lyric Theatre, London, 11 November 1899.

Characters: Cyrus W. Gilfain, Frank Abercoed, Leandro, Captain Arthur Pym, Anthony Tweedlepunch, Dolores, Angela Gilfain, Lady Holyrood, Valleda, Donegal, &c.

Plot: Cyrus Gilfain runs a flower plantation in the Philippines, making Florodora perfume, but he is, in fact, not the legal owner of the plantation. When we see him making marital advances at the local girl Dolores, who works for him, we can guess why. But Dolores is in love with the overseer Frank Abercoed, the man whom Gilfain had usefully earmarked for his own daughter, Angela, who is in any case sighing over a little English Captain. Gilfain tries to force his preferred combinations to the altar by bribing a traveling phrenologist to "suit" them, but Abercoed refuses thus to be coerced and leaves for his family home in Wales. Unfortunately, his family has gone bust and their castle has been sold to be the European base for . . . Florodora perfume. And Cyrus G. has installed himself there. With the help of the clever, managing Lady Holyrood, the young people and Tweedlepunch the phrenologist stage a ghostly attack and force the guilty magnate into confession, restitution, consent, and a generally happy ending.

Songs: "Flowers a-blooming So Gay" (chorus), "The Credit's Due to Me" (clerks), "The Silver Star of Love" (Dolores), "Somebody" (Abercoed, Dolores), Welcome Chorus: "Hail from the Storm" (chorus), "Come and See Our Island" (chorus), "When I Leave Town" (Lady Holyrood), "Galloping" (Angela, Donegal), "I Want to Marry a Man, I Do" (Lady Holyrood, Tweedlepunch, Gilfain), "The Fellow Who Might" (lyric by J. Hickory Wood) (Angela), "Phrenology" (Gilfain), "When an Interfering Person" (Lady Holyrood, Angela, Donegal), "The Shade of the Palm" (Frank), Finale Act 1:"Hey! Hey! Alack-a-day," "Come Lads and Lasses" (chorus), "Tact" (Lady Holyrood), "The Millionaire" (Gilfain), "Tell Me, Pretty Maiden" (clerks, English girls), "Whistling" (Angela), "I've an Inkling" (Lady Holyrood), Finale Act 2: "At Last Prosperity Comes Shining." Additional and interpolated numbers included: "Mysterious Musicians" (Dolores, Tweedlepunch), "The Queen of the Philippine Islands" (Dolores), "We Get Up at 8 A.M." (Leandro, Valleda), "I Want to Be a Military Man" (lyric by Frank Clement) (Donegal), "He Loves, He Loves Me Not" (Dolores), "Willie Was a Gay Boy" (lyric by Alfred Murray) (Angela), "When We're on the Stage" (Dolores, Tweedlepunch), "The Island of Love" (by Ivan Caryll/Aubrey Hopwood) (Dolores), "He Didn't Like the Look of It at All" (Donegal), "Such a Don" (Dolores), "Land of My Home" (Abercoed).

If the career and hit average of Owen Hall were remarkable, those of George Dance rendered them little on either front. Dance, however, worked in a different register. The sort of so-
ciety-page chat with which Hall so effectively peppered his scripts was outside Dance's range:
he contented himself with a merry, straightforward story, full of enjoyable characters and lively
songs aimed not at a "sophisticated" London audience but at the more straightforward theatergoers of the rest of the country. And—as he had done in *The Lady Slavey*—he did so with the
most unfailingly popular touch. A year after launching *The Lady Slavey* on its multi-year career,
he provided the libretto for *The Gay Parisienne*, another initially musically "composed and borrowed" piece which went on to count its tours in decades rather than years and—recomposed
by Ivan Caryll—also scored fine runs both in the West End and on Broadway. He followed up
with the not dissimilar *The Gay Grisette*, another musical which notched up many years of touring around the British Isles, and then, in 1899, he produced what was scheduled to be his latest contribution to the vast and enormously profitable touring circuits—a comical little piece,
with echoes of *The Geisha* and *The Mikado*, set in the fashionable Orient, and with songs
composed by Howard Talbot (1865–1928), an Anglo-America-Irish musician and conductor
whose London theatrical record to date ran to two quarter-successes in five years. *A Chinese
Honeymoon* changed all that with a vengeance.

A CHINESE HONEYMOON, a musical comedy in 2 acts by George Dance. Music by Howard Talbot. Produced at the Theatre Royal, Hanley, 16 October 1899. Produced at the Royal Strand Theatre, London, 5 October 1901.

Characters: Emperor Hang Chow, Soo Soo, Chippee Chop, Hi Lung, Tom Hatherton, Mr Samuel Pineapple, Mrs Marie Pineapple, Fi Fi, Mrs Brown, Florrie, Violet, Millie, Gertie, &c.

Plot: Tom Hatherton has thrown in his commission in the Royal Navy so that he can stay out east in Ylang Ylang and sigh over a pretty singing girl. Of course, Soo Soo is not actually a singing girl at all, but the niece of the local Emperor, out in disguise. The Emperor, a middle-aged gent of small attractions, is currently in search of a wife, but he insists that postulants must not know of his august position, and therefore his Admiral Hi Lung is having a devil of a job finding candidates for the post. But now an English couple, Samuel and Marie Pineapple, arrive in China on their honeymoon. Pineapple is a jolly, flirty sort of fellow, and his new wife is so watchful of him that she's brought her bridesmaids on the honeymoon equipped with instructions and warning whistles. Pineapple flirts, the girls whistle, and the piqued Marie accepts a kiss from the Emperor in retaliation. By Ylang Ylang law, that makes her his bride. And since Pineapple has been caught giving a kindly peck to Soo Soo, it looks as if the honeymoon is going to turn into two very unexpected honeymoons. It takes the whole of the second act to sort things out, but ultimately all the Brits escape from the threatened Chinese tortures and Chinese weddings thanks to the timely arrival of . . . the British Consul. Ta-ra!

Songs: "In Ylang Ylang" (chorus)/"Roly Poly" (Hi Lung), "A Paper Fan" (Soo Soo), "The Emperor Hang Chow" (Hang Chow), "A Chinese Honeymoon" (Mr & Mrs Pineapple, bridesmaids), "The à la Girl" (Mrs Pineapple), "Roses Red and White" (lyric by Harry Greenbank) (Soo Soo, Tom), "Nursery Rhymes" (music by Ernest Vousden) (ensemble), "The Twiddly Bits" (by Ernest Woodville/J. Adams & Dance) (Fi Fi), Finale Act 1: "A Royal Honeymoon," "With Weary Hearts" (chorus, Soo Soo), "I Want to Be a Lidy" (music by "George Dee") (Fi Fi), "Daisy with the Dimple on Her Chin" (by Ivan Caryll/Alfred Murray) (Soo Soo), "That Happy Land" (Hang Chow), "You Pat Me" (ensemble), "Welcome, Official Mother-in-Law" (chorus), "But Yesterday" (music by Ernest Vousden) (Tom), "Tit-Bits from the Plays" (Tom, Mrs Pineapple), "Click, Click" (Emperor, Fi Fi), "Martha Spanks the Grand Pianner" (Fi Fi), Finale Act 2: "He Is the Bridegroom." Alternative and interpolated songs included: "Follow Your Leader" (music by Ernest Vousden) (sextet), "Mandie of Ohio" (by Ernest Vousden/Fred Oliver), "I Hear They Want Some More" (by Ernest Bucalossi/Ernest Cosham), Chinese Cakewalk (music by Vousden), Two-Step (by Alfred Aarons/Richard Carle & Dance) (Mrs Pineapple), "Penelope" (sextet), "Chow Chow's Honeymoon" (Soo Soo, Tom), "The Maid of Pekin" (Soo Soo), "Egypt" (by Clare Kummer) (Tom), Parasol Song, "The Art of Making Love" (Tom, Mrs Pineapple).

A *Chinese Honeymoon* was distinctly more loaded with plot and story than the Gaiety musicals, but most of that plot and construction were contained in the bulging bit of entertainment that was the first act. In the second, in the fashion of the variety musical, that plot was allowed to wander off at will, and the action consisted of little more than a series of comical scenes containing the disguised or plotted efforts by the unwillingly to-be-wed Englishfolk to escape their Chinese honeymoon. In the midst of these antics, of course, came the songs and, as in the

Gaiety shows but perhaps rather more so, some of those middle-of-the-second-act numbers had precious little to do with what was going on. When the low comedienne of the evening, the little Chinese waitress Fi Fi (who is really Arabella from Acton, come East in search of a strayed sailor), delivered the hit song of the night, a thoroughly music-hally ditty about her cockney family's weekend music-making called "Martha Spanks the Grand Pianner," it was theoretically to prove that she is indeed what she is disguised as: a Chinese street singer. And at one stage of the show's career the actress playing Mrs Pineapple interpolated a coon song . . . for which she burnt-corked-up!

A *Chinese Honeymoon* didn't bring Dance wallet-filling triumph just in the country. This time he hit gold in town as well. The musical was picked up by producer Frank Curzon (1868–1927), and after a handful of rewrites (adding Fi Fi's rôle and its music-hally songs, for the "sophisticated" city!), it was mounted at London's Royal Strand Theatre. There, this joyously comical romp with its merry musical mélange of a score stayed for 1,075 performances, becoming in the process the first musical, anywhere in the world, to top the 1,000 performance mark in one metropolitan venue. From London, while its provincial touring record mounted and mounted, it then went round the world. The neophyte American producers the Shubert brothers scored their first big Broadway hit with A *Chinese Honeymoon*, it broke records in Australia, Germany saw two rival adaptations, Budapest got it in Hungarian, and the show even made its way to Shanghai—in English—as A *Chinese Honeymoon* joined the very vanguard of that army of musicals which were in the process of making the product of the English-language stage the most popular and omnipresent musical plays of their time.

Not quite all these musicals, however, came from London or from the British provinces. Now, slowly, the musical theater in America was getting itself into gear, and—as burlesque, fairy spectacular, and farce-comedy gave way to post-*Pinafore* comic opera and Gaiety-style musical comedy—the 1890s saw the first genuinely international success come out from the Broadway stage to entertain the rest of the world.

The comic-opera area produced the first successes at home, but those shows were doomed to provoking very limited interest further afield. This was, perhaps, not surprising for, like the very first success of the American musical stage, the 1862 *The Doctor of Alcantara*, they were backward-looking pieces whose usually competent but clichéd libretti could not wholly be redeemed by some capable and sometimes fine operettic music. *Robin Hood*, the first among them, was produced in 1890 by the touring troupe known as The Bostonians, a group whose repertoire was largely made up of Gilbert and Sullivan, anglicized Operette, and the choicest French pieces of the earlier decades. Their "new and original" piece, in fact, looked even further back in time than these and, like *Dorothy* in Britain, imitated the comic-opera fashions of the middle of the century, in the days before the spirit of opéra-bouffe or Gilbertian comic opera had illuminated the musical stage. The score, by Reginald De Koven (1861–1920), was written in much the same elderly vein, but it nevertheless produced some attractive concert-platform type numbers—notably a basso Armourer's Song and a contralto Wedding Song, "O Promise Me"—which became familiar favorites around America. Harry Bache Smith (1861–1936), the librettist of *Robin Hood*, also teamed on several comic operas with the new-American musician Victor Herbert (1859–1924), but although the Ruritanian *The Fortune Teller* and the intermittently rather more amusing and occasionally almost bouffe *The Serenade* also produced several songs that would have their turn as favorites, as stage pieces they proved to have a limited appeal, and the same team's shot at a livelier and less operatic subject in the comical history of the phoney rainmaker who was supposed to be *The Wizard of the Nile* was much better liked beyond America's shores than these romantic shows.

There was rather more spirit and skill on view in a merry musical called *El Capitan*, written by Charles Klein (1867–1915) and composed by John Philip Sousa (1854–1932), the then comic-opera conductor better known today for his march music. Klein's text, while in no way particularly original or inventive, was much better made than Smith's were, and rather more touched with "esprit," Sousa's music was well-made and attractive, if perhaps less catching than Herbert's, and *El Capitan*—with patented star De Wolf Hopper in its title-rôle—was a fine home-town success. But abroad, in spite of a season in London, no one took very much notice.

It was, however, with a patent imitation of overseas styles that the American musical would break through. Not with a comic opera, though, but with an example of the more modern and distinctly more joyous musical comedy. In the 1890s, several of the Gaiety musical comedies had been imported to Broadway both by Edwardes and by Daly, and other producers had also happily latched on to the new transatlantic musical comedies that quickly became as much the rage of Broadway as they were of Britain. Naturally enough, Broadway soon had its own go at turning out its own version of this lively type of entertainment, and it wasn't too long before success came—even if it didn't necessarily go to the most deserving piece of theater.

The most interesting among Broadway's 1890s musical comedies was an 1896 piece which ranged very close to the French vaudeville in its manner. *Lost, Strayed or Stolen* was, in fact, a musicalized version of a successful French comedy, *Le Baptême du petit Oscar*, with all that signified in the way of fine farcical construction. Adapter John Cheever Goodwin (1850–1912)— the same man who'd been responsible for the meandering low jinks of *Evangeline* two decades earlier—didn't try to localize the crazy chase after a lost baby, and the cavortings of the plot still went on in gay Paree, but he and musician Woolson Morse (1858–1897) decorated their genuine musical comedy with some jolly, un-French songs and the show not only did well at home—it even got a brief showing in London.

It was not, however, a stoutly constructed musical play such as this one which would win the honors, but a much more go-as-you-please piece put together for the Casino Theatre, formerly the main home of Operette and opéra-comique productions in America, but now purveying much lighter fare. *The Belle of New York* was an altogether more "American" piece than *Lost, Strayed or Stolen*. It was set in New York, its characters were a colorful group of the

American types seen in so many local comedies and musicals over recent years, and its tiny plot was threaded with lively variations on the most popular kinds of American songs which—in the Gaiety way, or even the variety musical way—came into their own in a last scene which was pretty much a concert. New York was fairly unimpressed with *The Belle of New York*, and the Casino company were soon on their way to Boston—and then to Britain. Australian manager George Musgrove (1854–1916), in trouble at the West End theater he had rented, took the risk of importing the *Belle of New York* company to London in toto to fill his sagging theater, and his risk paid off. Those American characters and American songs which had failed to impress an America surfeited with both one and the other proved delightfully different to Londoners who had seen little of either, and the buxom, energetic American chorus girls were an eye-opening novelty after the elegant strollers of the London stage. Everything combined to make *The Belle of New York* a big, novelty hit. And, naturally, the European theaters, eager for the latest success from the London stage which had recently provided them with a selection of merry hits, followed London's choice. *The Belle of New York* was produced around Europe, and Europe—whose previous tastes of American work had been limited to American imitations of European styles—reacted in the same way. For all that there were undoubtedly better shows that didn't get out of America, this one that did, this easy-going Gaiety-gone-American mixture of songs and dances and comedy (and virtually no "romance"), proved to be a delightful and thoroughly appreciated change in diet for the folk on the right-hand side of the Atlantic.

THE BELLE OF NEW YORK, a musical comedy in 2 acts by "Hugh Morton" (C. M. S. McLellan). Music by Gustave Kerker. Produced at the Casino Theatre, New York, 28 September 1897.

Characters: Ichabod Bronson, Harry Bronson, Karl von Pumpernick, "Doc" Snifkins, Blinky Bill McGuire, Kenneth Mugg, Count Ratsi Rattatoo, Count Patsi Rattatoo, Violet Gray, Fifi Fricot, Kissie Fitzgarter, Cora Angélique, Mamie Clancy, Pansy Pinns, Billy Breeze, &c.

Plot: Harry Bronson is living it up in New York, spending his father's money lavishly on a crowd of hangers-on and a selection of girlfriends-cum-fiancées, when Papa turns up in town. The scapegrace is disinherited, and Papa's money settled instead on the daughter of his old partner, the pretty Salvation Army lassie Violet Gray. Old Ichabod isn't, of course, half as strict as he makes out, and after Harry has done a stint as a soda jerk, during which time the hangers-on and the mercenary floozies have, of course, vanished, he gets together with the one person who has tried to help him in his disinherited disgrace. As Papa intended all along, it is Violet.

Songs: "When a Man Is Twenty-One" (chorus), "When I Was Born, the Stars Stood Still" (Cora), "Little Sister Kissie" (Kissie), "Teach Me How to Kiss" (Fifi), "We Come This Way" (chorus), "The Anti-Cigarette Society" (Ichabod), "Wine, Woman and Song" (Harry), "La Belle Parisienne" (Fifi), "My Little Baby" (Ichabod), "Pretty Little China Girl" (chorus), "They All Follow Me" (Violet), "We'll Stand and Die Together" (Billy Breeze), "She Is the Belle of New York" (Blinky Bill), Finale Act 1: "Your Life, My Little Girl," "Oh! Sonny" (chorus), "When We Are Married" (Harry, Fifi), "Oh! Come with Me to Portugal" (Ratsi, Patsi, Kissie), "The Purity Brigade" (Violet), "I Do, So There!" (Violet), "Grogan's Fancy Ball" (Blinky Bill), "On the Beach at Narragansett" (Ichabod),

"For the Twentieth Time, We'll Drink" (chorus), "At ze Naughty Folies-Bergère" (Violet), Finale Act 2: "For in the Field." Some alternative and interpolated songs included: "You and I" (Ichabod), "Good Old Glory," "We'll Dance in the Moonlight," "A Simple Little Girl," "A Nice Young Man," "Dinah, de Moon Am Shinin," "Don't You Know? I'm a Philosopher" [ex-"Conundrums"] (by Charles Osborne/William Gould) (Ichabod)

Even though the Casino Theatre made another good try with a similarly Gaiety-ish piece called *The Casino Girl* (1900), *The Belle of New York* remained an isolated international success for the Broadway musical theater of the turn-of-the-century years. Its chief attraction had been its novelty, and that same "novelty" didn't draw twice. It would be another two decades yet before America would truly leap onto the international musical stage; and by then that stage would have a very different sound to it.

If America and England had proved to be not quite ready, in 1896, to receive a well-built musical comedy such as *Lost, Strayed and Stolen*, Europe certainly was. Because, along with the English musical comedies, and that tiny handful of pretty Parisian opérettes headed by *La Poupée*, the most successful musicals on the European stage of the 1890s were the vaude-ville-opérettes (the "vaudeville" part was soon dropped from the description) which, in the wake of *Niniche, Lili,* and their kind, now proliferated on the French stage. In many ways, these pieces were the most satisfying musical plays yet to have made their way to the stage—certainly for anyone who wanted a musical made up from a proper play-like book and a score which was, if not an essential part of that book, at least thoroughly in keeping with it. The vaudevilles-opérettes were, indeed, finely constructed and written farcical plays, plays which could have existed equally well as first-class comedies without their musical part, but they were decorated with a bright, bristling, and never over-expansive musical part which, like the li-bretti, always leaned firmly towards the comical rather than anything reeking of the romantic or sentimental. This was musical comedy in the full meaning of each of the two parts of the expression.

One of the most successful of the earlier successors to the Variétés/Judic series was the 1886 *Joséphine vendue par ses soeurs*, a hilarious turning upside down of the biblical story of Joseph and his multicolored topcoat with the sexes reversed, which actually—and not unfairly—called itself an opéra-bouffe. Authors Paul Ferrier and Fabrice Carré (1856–1921) confected a delight-ful comic tale in which Joséphine was a budding opera starlet, favored above all her sisters by their voluminous concièrge mamma. The girls get their annoying sister signed up by a yearning Egyptian pasha for what she thinks is his Opera House and is, of course, something more like his harem. Mamma and the soprano's passionately adoring baritone set off to the rescue, and Mamma soon takes control. A farcical libretto, full of cleverly plotted ups and downs, was ac-companied by a lively score featuring moments of mock-operatic romance and despair for the operatic lovers, and spicy, soubretty ones for youngest sister Benjamine and the firmly anti-French Egyptian she finally subdues. That score was the work of Victor Roger (1853–1903), and it was he who would go on to illustrate some of the finest vaudeville-opérettes of the following decade, with his neat, tuneful, catchy, but never soaringly sentimental melodies.

In 1890, Roger provided the music for Maurice Desvallières (1857–1926) and Antony Mars's (1861–1915) comical perversion of another biblical tale into present-day Paris, *Les Douze femmes de Japhet*. Japhet of the twelve wives was, in their rewrite, a Mormon, and the motor for the plot was his twelfth wife, a little Parisienne who turns out to have had a momentous past during which she was the faithless wife of none other than the wealthy and now woman-hating uncle on whom Japhet has founded all his hopes for the future. Two years later, the same composer followed up with the music for Mars's most successful collaboration with Hippolyte Raymond (1844–1895), *Les Vingt-huit jours de Clairette*. There were no biblical strains in this one; it was a bristling military vaudeville depicting the fortunes and misfortunes of a rapier-wielding wife who innocently follows her husband to his military service camp and is taken, in turn, for a cadet and for her own husband's mistress, and gets mixed up in some high and some not-so-high farce through two hours of music and merriment. In 1897 Roger combined with Maurice Ordonneau (1854–1916) on a tale of multiple disguises and mix-ups in a private home that gets taken for *L'Auberge du tohu-bohu*, and then he went on, later that same year, to set to music what was probably the outstanding single example of the new-style vaudeville, a nearly naughty tale of Parisian nightlife called *Les Fêtards*. A plethora of comical characters—from a penniless silly-ass Frenchman with a vast title who is pursuing a horsy American with a vast fortune, to a bulging duenna with memories of the days when she was a petite circus dancer and the plaything of a King or three—were combined in a plethora of hilarious subplots around a merry but moral main story which more than kept up the reputation of the contemporary French stage for intricate and wildly farcical-humorous playwriting.

LES FÊTARDS, an opérette in 3 acts by Antony Mars and Maurice Hennequin. Music by Victor Roger. Produced at the Théâtre du Palais-Royal, Paris, 28 October 1897.

Characters: Ernest III d'Illyrie, Le Marquis de Châtellerault, Le Duc Jehan de Beaugency La Marquise Edith de Châtellearault, Théa, Madame Maréchal, Le Comte de Trénitz, Pontbichet, Eugène, Angèle, Fred, John, Jollivet, Pontgiraud, Le Doyen des abonnées, Sarah, Paméla, Carmen, &c.

Plot: Edith, an American Quaker heiress who is deeply into evangelism, good works, and larynx-to-instep nighties, has married a French nobleman. He, who has no time for tracts or wincyette, sneaks off to Paris and pays court to a little dancer whenever he can get away from this unbendingly proper wife. But Edith discovers what is happening, and herself heads for Paris. She goes to see Théa, the dancer, in her dressing room and, without divulging her identity, asks for her advice. The dancer is sorry for the bewildered woman and attempts to explain to her that she needs a rather different attitude to life and wifeliness if she wishes to hold her husband's attention. While Théa is on stage, Edith tests out some of her newly learned precepts by trying on the girl's clothes and make-up, and she is in full regalia when the randy King of Illyria arrives, ready to lay siege to the famous Théa. With Théa's collusion and then some agile fibs and plots, Edith gets to become "Théa" for a night of partying during which she manages both to keep the King from scoring his point with her, and to stop her husband from getting near to the real Théa. When the night and its morning-after revelations are done, the chastened Marquis heads back home with a rather different wife.

Songs: "Voilà l'heure où suivant l'usage" (chorus), "Je suis marquis de Châtellerault" (Marquis, Duc), "Nous avons tous en ce bas monde" (Edith), "C'est aussi la première fois" (Marquis, Edith), "La p'tit" Théa" (Le Roi), "Mère Maréchal, ton art sans égal" (dancers), "La beauté, la jeunesse ont un rêve éphémère" (Mme Maréchal), "Bravo Théa" (chorus), "Ah! messieurs, c'est vraiment un beau soir de gala" (Théa), "C'est par la coquett'rie" (Théa, Edith), "Si le révérend me voyait" (Edith), "En contemplant votre personne" (Le Roi), Finale Act 2/1: "Le ballet vient de finir" /"J'arrive d'un pays lointain" (Le Roi), "O Dieu malin" (Théa), "Je n'avais pas de parapluie" (Mme Maréchal), "J'ai pris le rapide pour Paris" (Edith), "Regardez d'abord ma coiffure" (Edith, Marquis, Duc), "Grégoire, Grégoire" (Mme Maréchal), Finale Act 3: "Bien que je sois Américaine."

Les Fêtards had a remarkable career, going out from France to become a huge hit in its German version, and all over again in a George Edwardes English remake (with English music) as *Kitty Grey*, but—if it was undoubtedly the most widely popular of its kind and times—it was far from the only such piece to score on all sorts of fronts. The comic history of *La Demoiselle du téléphone*, who kept track of her boyfriend's movements through her switchboard before going out in a series of disguises to curtail his excesses, the hilarious history surrounding the will of *L'Oncle Célestin*, the brother-sister swap of identities that was *Toto*, and such comical pieces as the misadventures of *Miss Helyett* (who fell over a cliff and was rescued by someone who saw what only a husband should see) or those, more colorful, of the victim of *L'Enlèvement de la Toledad*, were other finely written comic pieces which traveled to several countries and languages other than their own, assuring that the substantial musical comedy was well represented in all languages during the fin-de-siècle years. And eventually, a few years on from *Lost, Strayed or Stolen*, the theaters of the English-speaking countries started to take notice. Before too long, the little plots of the early Gaiety musicals would start to give way to musical comedies with a real, solid backbone of plot.

SOME NOTABLE MUSICALS 1890–1899

1890   DER ARME JONATHAN [Penniless Jonathan] (Karl Millöcker/Hugo Wittmann, Julius Bauer) Theater an der Wien, Vienna, 4 January

LA BASOCHE [The student king] (André Messager/Albert Carré) Opéra-Comique, Paris, 30 May

ROBIN HOOD (Reginald De Koven/Harry B. Smith) Opera House, Chicago, 9 June

CARMEN UP-TO-DATA (Meyer Lutz/George R. Sims, Henry Pettitt) Gaiety Theatre, London, 4 October

MISS HELYETT (Edmond Audran/Maxime Boucheron) Théâtre des Bouffes-Parisiens, Paris, 12 November

LES DOUZE FEMMES DE JAPHET [Japhet's twelve wives] (Victor Roger/Antony Mars, Maurice Desvallières) Théâtre de la Renaissance, Paris, 16 December

1891   DER VOGELHÄNDLER [The birdseller] (Karl Zeller/Moritz West, Ludwig Held) Theater an der Wien, Vienna, 10 January

L'ONCLE CÉLESTIN [Uncle Célestin] (Edmond Audran/Maurice Ordonneau, Henri Kéroul) Théâtre des Menus-Plaisirs, Paris, 24 March

LA DEMOISELLE DU TÉLÉPHONE [The telephone girl] (Gaston Serpette/Antony Mars, Maurice Desvallières) Théâtre des Nouveautés, Paris, 2 May

WANG (Woolson Morse/J. Cheever Goodwin) Broadway Theatre, New York, 4 May

THE NAUTCH GIRL (Edward Solomon/Frank Desprez/George Dance) Savoy Theatre, London, 30 June

A TRIP TO CHINATOWN (Comp. & arr. Percy Gaunt/Charles Hoyt) Madison Square Theatre, New York, 9 November

1892   LES VINGT-HUIT JOURS DE CLAIRETTE [Clairette does military service] (Victor Roger/Antony Mars, Hippolyte Raymond) Théâtre des Folies-Dramatiques, Paris, 3 May

TOTO (Antoine Banès/Paul Bilhaud, Albert Barré) Théâtre des Menus-Plaisirs, Paris, 10 June

IN TOWN (Frank Osmond Carr/Adrian Ross, James Leader [i.e., James Tanner]) Prince of Wales Theatre, London, 15 October

A SZULTÁN [The sultan] (György Verö) Népszinház, Budapest, 19 October

1893   MOROCCO BOUND (Frank Osmond Carr/Adrian Ross/Arthur Branscombe) Shaftesbury Theatre, London, 13 April

THE LADY SLAVEY (John Crook/George Dance) Theatre Royal, Northampton, 4 September

LITTLE CHRISTOPHER COLUMBUS (Ivan Caryll/George R. Sims, Cecil Raleigh) Lyric Theatre, London, 10 October

A GAIETY GIRL (Sidney Jones/Harry Greenbank/Owen Hall) Prince of Wales Theatre, London, 14 October

COUSIN-COUSINE [Boy cousin, girl cousin] (Gaston Serpette/Maurice Ordonneau, Henri Kéroul) Théâtre des Folies-Dramatiques, Paris, 23 December

1894   DER OBERSTEIGER [The mine foreman] (Karl Zeller/Moritz West, Ludwig Held) Theater an der Wien, Vienna, 6 January

THE GAY PARISIENNE (Ernest Vousden, then Ivan Caryll/George Dance) Theatre Royal, Northampton, 1 October

ROB ROY (Reginald De Koven/Harry B. Smith) Herald Square Theatre, New York, 29 October

L'ENLÈVEMENT DE LA TOLEDAD [The rape of La Toledad] (Edmond Audran/ Fabrice Carré) Théâtre des Bouffes-Parisiens, Paris, 17 November

THE SHOP GIRL (Ivan Caryll/Adrian Ross/Henry J. W. Dam) Gaiety Theatre, London, 24 November

1895   AN ARTIST'S MODEL (Sidney Jones/Harry Greenbank/Owen Hall) Daly's Theatre, London, 2 February

GENTLEMAN JOE (Walter Slaughter/Basil Hood) Prince of Wales Theatre, London, 2 March

THE NEW BARMAID (John Crook/Frederick Bowyer, William Edwards Sprange) Opera House, Southport, 1 July

THE WIZARD OF THE NILE (Victor Herbert/Harry B. Smith) Casino Theatre, New York, 4 November

1896 SHAMUS O'BRIEN (Charles Villiers Stanford/George H. Jessop) Opera Comique, London, 2 March

EL CAPITAN (John Philip Sousa/Tom Frost/Charles Klein) Broadway Theatre, New York, 20 April

THE GEISHA (Sidney Jones/Harry Greenbank/Owen Hall) Daly's Theatre, London, 25 April

MY GIRL (F. Osmond Carr/Adrian Ross/James T. Tanner) Gaiety Theatre, London, 13 July

LOST, STRAYED OR STOLEN (Woolson Morse/J. Cheever Goodwin) Fifth Avenue Theatre, New York, 21 September

LA POUPÉE [The doll] (Edmond Audran/Maurice Ordonneau) Théâtre de la Gaîté, Paris, 21 October

LE PAPA DE FRANCINE [Francine's daddy] (Louis Varney/Victor de Cottens, Paul Gavault) Théâtre Cluny, Paris, 5 November

THE CIRCUS GIRL (Ivan Caryll, Lionel Monckton/Adrian Ross, Harry Greenbank/ James Tanner, Walter Palings) Gaiety Theatre, London, 5 December

1897 L'AUBERGE DU TOHU-BOHU [The topsy-turvey tavern] (Victor Roger/Maurice Ordonneau) Théâtre des Folies-Dramatiques, Paris, 10 February

THE SERENADE (Victor Herbert/Harry B. Smith) Knickerbocker Theatre, New York, 16 March

THE DANDY FIFTH (Clarence C. Corri/George R. Sims) Prince of Wales Theatre, Birmingham, 11 April

VENUS AUF ERDEN [Venus on earth] (Paul Lincke/Heinrich Bolten-Bäckers) Apollo-theater, Berlin, 6 June

THE BELLE OF NEW YORK (Gustave Kerker/Charles M. S. McLellan) Casino Theatre, New York, 28 September

LES FÊTARDS [The good-time guys] (Victor Roger/Antony Mars, Maurice Hennequin) Palais-Royal, Paris, 28 October

LES P'TITES MICHU [The little Michu girls] (André Messager/Georges Duval, Albert Vanloo) Théâtre des Bouffes-Parisiens, Paris, 16 November

LA REVOLTOSA [The revolting girl] (Ruperto Chapí/Guillermo Fernández Shaw, José Lope da Silva) Teatro Apolo, Madrid, 25 November

1898 DER OPERNBALL [The opera ball] (Richard Heuberger/Victor Léon, Heinrich von Waldberg) Theater an der Wien, Vienna, 5 January

A RUNAWAY GIRL (Ivan Caryll, Lionel Monckton/Aubrey Hopwood, Harry Greenbank/ James Tanner, Seymour Hicks, Harry Nicholls) Gaiety Theatre, London, 21 May

A GREEK SLAVE (Sidney Jones/Harry Greenbank, Adrian Ross/Owen Hall) Daly's Theatre, London, 8 June

THE FORTUNE TELLER (Victor Herbert/Harry B. Smith) Wallack's Theatre, New York, 26 September

VÉRONIQUE (André Messager/Georges Duval, Albert Vanloo) Théâtre des Bouffes-Parisiens, Paris, 10 December

1899 FRAU LUNA [Madam Moon] (Paul Lincke/Heinrich Bolten-Bäckers) Apollotheater, Berlin, 1 May

DIE LANDSTREICHER [The tramps] (Carl Michael Ziehrer/Leopold Krenn, Carl Lindau) Venedig in Wien, Vienna, 29 July

A CHINESE HONEYMOON (Howard Talbot/George Dance) Theatre Royal, Hanley, 16 October

SAN TOY (Sidney Jones/Harry Greenbank, Adrian Ross/Edward A. Morton) Daly's Theatre, London 21 October

WIENER BLUT [Viennese ancestry] (Johann Strauss pasticcio, arr. Adolf Müller II/Victor Léon, Leo Stein) Carltheater, Vienna, 26 October

FLORODORA (Leslie Stuart/Ernest Boyd-Jones, Paul Rubens/Owen Hall) Lyric Theatre, London, 11 November

THE ROSE OF PERSIA (Arthur Sullivan/Basil Hood) Savoy Theatre, London, 29 November

LES SALTIMBANQUES [The fairground-folk] (Louis Ganne/Maurice Ordonneau) Théâtre de la Gaîté, Paris, 30 December

*A*t the turn of the century, the world of the musical theater was bubbling along healthily, but it was existing very largely, insofar as its biggest hits were concerned, on a diet of English musical comedy—the Gaiety kind and the Daly's kind. Both the French- and German-language theaters were in temporary decline. In France the best days of the vaudeville style of opérette had now passed, while in Central Europe no theater composers had yet come forward to replace Suppé, Millöcker, Strauss, and Zeller, but both Paris and Vienna were still turning out a regular supply of works to usually rather limited success on their home stages, and both would again and before very long rise to the fore, the one rather more quickly than the other. As for the American stage, although it had now produced several home-sized successes and one international hit, it was still searching for its own way among a mixture of cheerfully lowbrow entertainments, rather stiffly imitative and/or old-fashioned costume comic operas, and home-made versions of the English styles of musicals. But it, too, would soon begin to turn out shows of a different and more substantial type, shows that would lead to the first blossoming of the American musical in the 1910s, and ultimately to its resounding épanouissement on the international stage in the 1920s.

There were two notable developments in the musical theater in the years between the turn of the century and the Great War, two developments that would help promote a significant change in the kinds of entertainments that held the top of the market in the first decades of the new century. One of these developments was in the area of the libretto, and the other in that of music. The all-conquering English musical theater had got along, in recent years, on merrily minimal libretti. At the Gaiety, the barest bones of a plot were used to hold the comedy and songs and dances of the evening together, while at Daly's, although the story of the piece was more romantic and even dramatic, it was rarely adventurous or particularly clever. In neither case would the book of the show ever have stood up as a piece of theater without its all-important songs and dances. But, little by little, in the first years of the 1900s, English libretti started to become rather more ambitious. They started, in fact, to become altogether more like those for those vaudeville-opérettes which had just celebrated their heyday on the French stage. English musical comedy, on both sides of the Atlantic, began to get itself a backbone of a kind it had never had before.

The second, musical, event was all Viennese. The outside world had happily taken to its heart the merry music of the Austrian theater composers of the nineteenth century, but the success won by Suppé, Millöcker, and Strauss would be quite eclipsed by the vast vogue for Central European music and musicals that was set off in the first years of the twentieth century. What has become known as "Viennese operetta" (even though an amount of it came from elsewhere, and the word "operetta" has been denatured in the English language into now meaning only romantic musical theater) flooded the world's stages for more than two decades, as the new tidal wave of Central European composers—Lehár, Fall, Straus, Eysler, Kálmán, Jacobi, Gilbert, and others—established themselves as the biggest international stars of this particular era of the musical stage.

Neither of these developments, of course, took place overnight, and neither meant that the present kinds of popular shows simply came to an end. Shows with happily skimpy books continued to come out of London, Chicago, New York, and other English-language theaters as the musical-with-a-backbone began, ever so slowly, to make itself a place on English stages, and it took a good half-dozen years, during which the Central European stages produced many a flop alongside their burgeoning successes, before the "Viennese" musical swept to triumph all round the world.

The English-language stage of the earliest years of the century turned out some first-magnitude hits: George Edwardes and his Gaiety Theatre mounted *The Messenger Boy* in 1900, *The Toreador* in 1901, and then, following the demolition of the original Gaiety, shifted to their new home (again called the Gaiety) on the Aldwych and opened there, in 1903, with *The Orchid*. More of the same—more of the enormously popular same. At Daly's, Lionel Monckton took over as chief composer and turned out *A Country Girl* (1902), a piece thoroughly in the Daly's mode even if it was set in period England rather than the picturesque East, and it made an equally big success. Leslie Stuart and Owen Hall followed up *Florodora* with a fantasy called *The Silver Slipper*, Paul Rubens wrote words and music for a blowaway piece of fluff called *Three Little Maids*, which had even less substance to it than any other musical in town but which nevertheless hit popularity, Seymour Hicks starred in a modern version of the Cinderella story called *The Catch of the Season*, and Gaiety-style pieces such as *The Earl and the Girl* and *The School Girl*, produced in other theaters by other managers, added to the gaiety of the nations through long runs, even longer tours, and productions all round the world. On the other side of the Atlantic, too, amid Americanized versions of the produce of the British stage, there were further, home-made hits—the clonish *The Casino Girl*, a brace of the fairy-tale spectaculars (a genre which seems to survive through all ages and eras while everything around it changes), *The Wizard of Oz* and *Babes in Toyland*, and—much more interesting and individual than any of these—a sparky brand of musical play that came first out of Chicago, and which mixed just a little of the craziness of opéra-bouffe into its tales of exaggerated Americans in strange and comical situations and weird foreign places. *The Burgomaster, The Sultan of Sulu,*

The Prince of Pilsen, The Yankee Consul, The Sho-Gun, and *The Red Mill* were all pieces with a bright étincelle of comical individuality about their free-swinging stories, and that spark helped make the most successful of them, Gustave Luders (1865–1913) and Frank Pixley's (1867–1919) *The Prince of Pilsen*—a hilarious piece about a Cincinnati brewer on holiday in Nice who is mistaken for a European prince, illustrated by an attractive mixture of ex-European and new-American music—into the most wholly satisfying American musical to have yet been put on the stage, as it gamboled from Boston to New York to London, Paris, and Sydney.

While all this lively, loose-jointed kind of musical theater was cleaning up right round the world, however, the plot was thickening. The use of a coherent, even intricate, comic plot of integral theatrical value was, of course, not something brand new in the musical theater. As we have seen, the French had been doing it for many years in the various eras of the vaudeville, and the Possen of the German stage had always leaned heavily on their perhaps less complex but certainly playworthy texts, rather than on their musical decoration. Similarly, the idea of basing a musical on an existing text was nothing new. The Austrian stage's wholesale pillaging of French sources in the nineteenth century, from *Die Fledermaus* to *Der Opernball*, was the most sizeable example, but the English-language stage had not shied away from inter-continental borrowing either. It had, however, borrowed pre-used opéra-comique libretti rather more often than plays, and such pieces as *Erminie*, which had used a foreign text as their inspiration, had usually treated their aging source material in a pretty cavalier fashion. What was not usual in the English theater was the taking of a well-made comedy and its reshaping as a musical comedy.

There had, of course, been some attempts. Broadway, with its staunch background of both French and German theater, and a long record of remusicking foreign hits (for copyright rather than artistic reasons), had dipped into the French comic theater for the libretto to *Lost, Strayed or Stolen* and the German with a remake of a German musical comedy, *Im Himmelshof*, as *Hodge, Podge and Co.*, and had also produced its own remake of *Les Fêtards*, *The Rounders*, with rather less success than Edwardes's British version as *Kitty Grey*. That same *Kitty Grey* was undoubtedly London's most important example of the French-to-English genre until 1902, when Edwardes produced *The Girl from Kay's*. *The Girl from Kay's* had all the cards on its side: it was produced by London's top musical producer, written by London's top librettist, Owen Hall, here firing on all cylinders with his slicingly smart dialogue and society swipes, and much of its music was by the British theater's most attractive composer of light theater music, Ivan Caryll. And it had a plot. The plot that it had was actually pinched, and only when Léon Gandillot, the author of the Parisian comedy from which it had been pilfered, was set wise by a magazine article and sued, did Hall and Edwardes come clean . . . and come up with the cash and a credit. Needless to say, the sexy subtleties of the Parisian farce underwent some English overhauling, and by the time the story of a wild-oat sowing Frenchman, torn between the mistress of his youthful years and the girl he has now dutifully to wed, reached the stage in London (where it was and is, of course, unheard of for a young man to have had sex before marriage), it was altogether less "dangerous." It had also been infiltrated by a character which was much more to British tastes than the equivalent which Gandillot created: a rich and un-educated American called Mr Hoggenheimer. "Piggy" Hoggenheimer was an uncultured boor, clumsily and hilariously out of place in the upper-class purlieus of Park Lane, but he was also a bit of a sweetheart and, as created by comedian Willie Edouin, who had also been the star of *Florodora*, "Piggy" became one of the big attractions of the show. The music of *The Girl from Kay's*, too, underwent a bit of infiltration. As he did at the Gaiety, the French-trained Caryll composed a set of numbers which were made, French vaudeville style, to belong to the musical's story and characters. But the way things were in the musical theater at this time decreed that a musical comedy needed to have those additional songs which gave variety (and which brought producers and artists plugging money from publishers), and so the shorter-than-usual score for *The Girl from Kay's* got its extras—extras that included several in situ songs, but also involved an incidental shopgirl singing a coon song and the deeply irrele-vant tale of what went on between "Matilda and the Builder."

THE GIRL FROM KAY'S, a musical comedy in 3 acts by Owen Hall, based on *La Mariée recalcitrante* by Léon Gandillot. Lyrics by Adrian Ross and Claude Aveling. Music by Ivan Caryll, Cecil Cook, and others. Produced at the Apollo Theatre, London, 15 November 1902.

Characters: Norah Chalmers, Mrs Chalmers, Mr Chalmers, Winnie Harborough, Max Hoggen-heimer, Harry Gordon, Ellen, Nancy Lowley, Hilda French, Mary Methuen, Hon. Percy Fitzthistle, Theodore Quench QC, Jane, Joseph, &c.

Plot: Norah Chalmers has just been married to the lad-about-town Harry Gordon, so she gets all choked up when she catches him kissing the girl who has brought her new hat from Kay's stores. It is quite a chaste kiss—a kind of good-luck and goodbye affair from an ex-girlfriend—but Norah doesn't see it like that, and she retaliates with woman's time-honored weapon, the "recalcitrance" of the play's original title. No honeymooning for Harry. Two acts of amorous adventures in a honey-moon hotel, where the honeymooners are sleeping in separate rooms, and which is populated by shopgirls, bridesmaids, Norah's relations, and all sorts of other folk including an interfering Ameri-can millionaire, eventually bring events to a happy end, and Winnie from Kay's gets the biggest prize of all: she is safely tied up to the fabulously wealthy Mr Hoggenheimer of Park Lane.

Songs: Opening Chorus: "We're the Bright and Bridal Bevy" (by Cook), "As I Came Up the Aisle" (by Bernard Rolt) (Norah, bridesmaids), "We've Come for You Ladies" (by Cook) (chorus), "The Bonnet Shop" (Winnie), "Relations" (Harry), Finale Act 1: "Now We See the Carriage" (by Meyer Lutz), "Sunday at Flacton-on-Sea" (by Cook) (chorus), "Semi-detached" (Harry, Norah), "Goody, Goody Girls" (Mary), "Customers at Kay's" (Winnie), "Bob and Me" (by Howard Talbot) (Ellen), "Papa" (by Lionel Monckton/Ross) (Norah), "Smiling Sambo" (by Talbot) (Nancy), "I Don't Care" (by Paul Rubens) (Harry), Finale Act 2: "He Has Gone His Ways" (by Cook), Valse, "Make It Up" (Winnie, Harry), "Love at the Door" (Mary), "A High Old Time" (by A. D. Cam-meyer) (Harry), "Mrs Hoggenheimer" (Winnie), Finale Act 3: "She'll Marry Hoggenheimer." Addi-tional and alternative numbers included: "Glass, Glass" (by Paul Rubens) (Fitzthistle), "My Birth-day Party" (quartet), "Matilda and the Builder" (by Ernest Bucalossi/J. Hickory Wood) (Harry).

THE STAGE SOUVENIR.

"Marriage" not a bad arrangement:
If I give her anything too, it'll
belong to me just the same"

"MAX HOGGENHEIMER."
Mr. WILLIE EDOUIN.

22

The Girl from Kay's:
"Rude? I'm not rude,
I'm rich." American
millionaire "Piggy"
Hoggenheimer blun-
dered his endearing
way to a final curtain
. . . where it was he
who got the girl of
the title!

The Girl from Kay's had a fine West End career,
but it found its greatest success in America, where
after a splendid first run it went on to a lengthy road
life, not just one but two locally made musequels,
and a full-scale remake.

French plays would gradually become the fa-
vorite raw material for musical comedy libretti, but
there was no huge rush to follow *The Girl from
Kay's* with more of the same, in spite of its success.
Berlin got a successful musical called *Madame
Sherry*, which boasted a Parisian text by the skillful
Maurice Ordonneau, and Edwardes followed up
his first "French" hit with a splendid musicalization
of the Sardou comedy *Madame Sans-Gêne*, composed by Caryll alone this time and entitled *The
Duchess of Dantzic*. Then he went on to bring
"French" musical comedy to the Gaiety. A year after the hit Parisian comedy *Coquin de printemps*
had been musicalized for Vienna as *Frühlingsluft*,
Edwardes had it re-musicalized by Caryll as *The
Spring Chicken*. In both cases the result was a frank
and far-flung hit. The new kind of musical play was
definitely catching on.

And so it continued, through the next decade or
so, with authors looking more and more often to the
comic theater for their libretto-material, and very
often with success. Sometimes, too, they looked not just to the French stage but to the English.
Top librettist-lyricist Basil Hood (1864–1917) attempted to make a musical comedy out of the
Romeo and Juliet story, but his producer got cold feet and *The Belle of Mayfair* finally turned out
to be just another merry—though decidedly successful—musical comedy with mild Shake-
spearean echoes; Robert Courtneidge announced that his musical *The Dairymaids* was based on
another piece of Shakespeare, *Measure for Measure*, though one would have had to take a mi-
croscope to the low jinks of this most low comical of British musicals of the period to find it, but
then he went on to turn out an excellent musical stage version of Fielding's *Tom Jones*.

Several other shows of the period even went so far as to use original texts made in the "vaudevillesque" or "French" manner. Owen Hall followed up *The Girl from Kay's* with the jolly, comical tale of *Sergeant Brue*, another triumph for actor Edouin as the copper who sets up a robbery so that he can nab the criminal and win himself promotion, while Paul Rubens, hitherto

known for his tuneful but often rather tasteless songs and for such thoroughly twee tales as *Three Little Maids*, came up with a delicious piece of thorough-going musical comedy called *Mr. Popple (of Ippleton)*. This charming musical tale of a "country mouse" chappie who gets embroiled in the extra-marital-beds naughtiness of the big city was so very vaudevillesque that it was hard to believe that Rubens hadn't borrowed it from somewhere, but, wherever he got it from, the result was an excellent musical comedy. America's German-theater megastar Adolf Philipp (1864–1936), on the other hand, took quite the opposite tack when he produced the saucy *Alma, wo wohnst du?* He claimed that his show was based on a Parisian vaudeville, but in fact the multi-talented Philipp had written, composed, produced, and starred in it himself!

Pieces like *Alma*, which went on from its original, off-Broadway, German-language production to become one of the most successful Broadway musicals of its season, had probably alerted American writers to the possibilities of a fine, comic play-worthy libretto in musical comedy, but when the keystone Broadway musical comedy came, it came from, and thanks to, no less a person than Ivan Caryll. After his many years with George Edwardes, Ivan Caryll had left the Gaiety, left Britain, and moved to New York. There, he teamed up with *Belle of New York* librettist McLellan, and between them they turned out a series of top-notch musical comedies firmly based on up-to-date Parisian comedies. The second of their collaborations was the outstanding one. Caryll had got hold of—among a bundle of others—the rights to the Marcel Guillemaud/Georges Berr comedy *Le Satyre*, a thoroughly sexy story whose title referred to a mysterious fellow who leaps politely upon ladies in the Paris woods and . . . embraces them. McLellan made it into suitable stuff for American ears, Caryll set it with a sparkling score of the sweepingly bright-hearted sort of music he wrote best (and which the limited vocal talents of the Gaiety folk had often prevented his writing) and the result was *The Pink Lady*. *The Pink Lady* was a model musical comedy. Its text was a finely made network of comical and comical-romantic plotting, and if the conventions of the time meant that McLellan's contribution occasionally had to hide its French frankness under rather obvious euphemisms, and his lyrics were often fairly functional rather than spicily imaginative, the gaiety of the original piece was never lost. And Caryll's score—limited to just a dozen numbers, plus openings and finales, and thus never threatening to swamp the show's book—was delicious stuff. Solos—including two pieces, The Kiss Waltz (aka "Beautiful Lady') and "By the Saskatchewan," which would become first-class hits—duos, and some finely made concerted music all came together with a decidedly more substantial and structured book than was usual to make up a really satisfying musical play.

THE PINK LADY, a musical comedy in 3 acts by C. M. S. McLellan, based on *Le Satyre* by Marcel Guillemaud and Georges Berr. Music by Ivan Caryll. Produced at the New Amsterdam Theatre, New York, 13 March 1911.

Characters: Philippe Dondidier, Madame Dondidier, Claudine, Angèle, Lucien Garidel, Benevol, Bébé Guingolph, Désirée, Maurice d'Uzac, La Comtesse de Montanvert, Serpolette Pochet, Pochet, Crapote, Dr Majou, Pan, &c.

Plot: Lucien Garidel has come to the Joli Coucou restaurant in the Bois de Compiègne for a last little lunch (etc.) with his mistress, the demi-mondaine Claudine, before getting wed to his Angèle. But Angèle has chosen to lunch that same day at that same restaurant, so Lucien has to pass Claudine off as the wife of the little antiques dealer Dondidier. Suddenly there is an alarm. The Countess de Montanvert has been "got" by the famous "satyr." Heaven's sake, she's been kissed! And the Countess is sure she knows who did it. She accuses Dondidier, and the police get on his track. Now Dondidier suddenly finds himself a celebrity, adored by the whole feminine neighborhood who threaten to scratch out the eyes of the entire Parisian police force if they lay a finger on their dear little satyr. And as Dondidier discovers a new spring in his middle-aged step, the little cloud which hung momentarily over the young to-be-weds floats gently away.

Songs: "Here's a Lady" (chorus), "Bring Along the Camera" (Benevol), "I'm Single for Six Weeks More" (Lucien), "Love Is Divine" (Angèle, Maurice), "By the Saskatchewan" (Bébé, Désirée), "In a French Girl's Heart" (Claudine), Finale Act 1: "The Game I Hunt I Never Miss," "O Fortunate Man Who Has Taste and Gold" (chorus), The Intriguers: "My Name's Garidel, Hers, Claudine" (Lucien, Claudine, Dondidier, Crapote), "Donny Didn't, Donny Did" (ensemble), The Kiss Waltz: "I Have Kisses in Plenty" (Claudine), "Hide and Seek" (Angèle, Dondidier), "The Right to Love" (Claudine, Lucien, Angèle, Claudine), Finale Act 2: "Again a Cry," Chorus & Parisian Two-Step, "The Hudson Belle" (dance), "I Like It" (Dondidier), "My Beautiful Lady" (Claudine, Angèle), Finale Act 3: "Flow, River, Flow."

The Pink Lady was followed by a second hit from the same team, *Oh! Oh! Delphine*, and a hugely successful version of the French comedy *Les Dragées d'Hercule* made over by librettist Otto Hauerbach (1873–1963) and composer Rudolf Friml (1879–1972) and entitled *High Jinks*, before London—whose best effort at a "French" musical comedy since *The Spring Chicken* had been the Gaiety's 1911 show *Peggy*—climbed firmly onto the rocket to the newest musical comedy moon and trotted out a whole series of international triumphs made to the same pattern: *Tonight's the Night* , *Theodore & Co.*, *Yes, Uncle!*, a remake of Ivan Caryll's Broadway piece *The Girl Behind the Gun* as the triumphant *Kissing Time*, and *A Night Out*. This series of ex-French musicalized comedies were to become some of the outstandingly popular musicals of their time, but writers realized that even if much of the best comic stage-writing was to be found on the Paris stage, that didn't mean that all of it was, and—a few lengths behind the galloping "French" musical—a number of shows began to appear that, rather than bits of Shakespeare or Fielding, had taken modern plays from nearer at home as their sources. Broadway's *The Red Widow*, which made a musical comedy out of Colonel Savage's melodramatic novel and play *His Official Wife*, was an early winner, a London musicalization of Pinero's famous *The Magistrate* as *The Boy* turned out to be one of the West End's longest running musicals in a long time and set off a fashion for Pinero-with-music which lasted a number of years, Jerome K. Jerome's *Fanny and the Servant Problem* made up into a delightful musical as *The Rainbow Girl*, and—most successful of all—the Broadway comedy *The Aviator* got a musical going-over as the international hit musical comedy *Going Up*. It was an impressive list, and, casting a retrospective eye down its contents, it can be seen that a very large number of the major musical comedy successes of the first two decades of this century on the English-language stage were, indeed, musicals whose credits carried the words "based on."

But, while one section of the English musical comedy was getting itself this splendidly enjoyable new bit of backbone, there were plenty of other shows crowding onto the stage which preferred to follow other and more established paths. Even though George Edwardes ventured into "French" musical comedy with such Gaiety shows as *The Spring Chicken* and *Peggy*, the good old Gaiety strain of musicals still carried happily on, both at that theater and at others all around London. Pieces such as *The Girls of Gottenberg, Havana, Our Miss Gibbs,* and *The Sunshine Girl* (which were actually interleaved between *The Spring Chicken* and *Peggy* at the Gaiety), and the pretty Paul Rubens piece about *Miss Hook of Holland* and the two Dutch pretenders for her little Dutch hand, occasionally featured a smidgin more libretto than had previously been the case, but the accent was, as ever, very much more on the merriment of their comic scenes and situations, and on their songs and dances, than on their "play" part. None of which stopped the best of them from becoming decided hits.

Similarly, on the other side of the Atlantic, alongside the extravagantly comical musicals of the *Sho-Gun* type and another interesting and up-to-date set of Chicago musicals of which the wholly here-and-now musical play *The Time, the Place and the Girl* was the outstanding example, the tradition of Harrigan and of Hoyt was carried on, and carried on to excellent effect, by another versatile writer-player-producer. The lively, unpretentious George M. Cohan (1878–1942) launched a series of jolly, tuneful musical comedies—pieces which dipped merrily into melodrama and domestic romance with equal ease—which kept the genuinely American musical play happily to the fore through the decades up to the war. Such shows as *Little Johnny Jones* and *45 Minutes from Broadway*, and the simple, catchy, thoroughly vernacular songs that they included ("Give My Regards to Broadway," the one about Mary being a grand old name, &c.), did not find an audience beyond America, but at home they toured the country with great popularity for seasons on end as Cohan—writer, performer, and producer—established himself as one of the outstanding personalities of the American theatrical scene of his times.

During the turn-of-the-century years, the more romantic strain of English musical play had found its best representation in the Daly's musicals, with their classic mixture of the sentimental, the colorful, and the comical in both story and music, but by the middle of the century's first decade, the product at Daly's theater had gone rather sour. A weak piece called *The Cingalee*, produced there in 1906, heralded the end of the era which had peaked with *The Geisha* a decade earlier, as Edwardes switched to importing musicals instead of commissioning them for the theater that had not long since been the cradle of the best romantic musicals in the English language. But the romantic musical play was still a popular part of the public's theatergoing preferences, and it did not go away. Or not for long.

The Savoy Theatre tradition of English opéra-bouffe had faded out after *The Gondoliers* and *The Nautch Girl*. Sullivan and his new partner, the same Basil Hood who had tried to musicalize *Romeo and Juliet*, turned out an excellent musical version of the *Arabian Nights* Abu Hassan story as *The Rose of Persia*, and Hood went on to team with another fine composer, Edward German (1862–1936), on the last Savoy show, the tongue-in-cheek Olde Englishe *Merrie England*, but neither of these—though equipped with fine libretti and a rich mixture of romantic and comic music—succeeded in setting up anything approaching the kind of run that even the second or third level of musical comedies was achieving. When producer William Greet (1851–1914) bought out the Carte family's interests in the theater, he soon switched the popular members of the Savoy's company to playing musical comedy instead of comic opera.

When Courtneidge produced German's fine musical version of *Tom Jones*, with its soaring soprano music and vigorous English ballads, the reaction was similar: praise and a disappointing run. Producers were better off putting out musical comedy—so they did. Or else they turned out pieces that hedged their bets by going half-and-half. George Edwardes produced a half-Gaiety/half-Daly's musical about *The Quaker Girl* who salvaged some compromising letters for a French politician and won a reprieve for her Bonapartist girlfriend to the accompaniment of a pretty and not very romantic score by Lionel Monckton, at his new third base, the Adelphi Theatre, and Courtneidge mounted the show which, no small thanks to its more substantial nature, turned out to be the most wholly successful English musical of its decade, the fantastical musical play called *The Arcadians*. *The Arcadians* skipped merrily through two acts of jolly doings in naughty London town for the benefit of a group of fairy-tale folk who have flown in to bring a message of truth and beauty to the debauched citizens of Britain. It gave its writers plenty of opportunities to poke fun at contemporary foibles and fads, and its composers—Talbot of *A Chinese Honeymoon* fame and the ubiquitous Monckton—an enviable chance to write both up-to-date tunes for the up-to-date Brits and some lovely lyrical lines for the fairy folk.

THE ARCADIANS, a fantastic musical play in 3 acts by Alexander M. Thompson and Mark Ambient. Lyrics by Arthur Wimperis. Music by Howard Talbot and Lionel Monckton. Produced at the Shaftesbury Theatre, London, 28 April 1909.

Characters: James Smith/Simplicitas, Jack Meadows, Peter Doody, Mrs Smith, Eileen Kavanagh, Sombra, Chrysea, Astrophel, Strephon, Bobbie, Sir George Paddock, Percy Marsh, Reggie, Sir Timothy Ryan, Harry Desmond, Time, Lady Barclay, Hon. Maud Barclay, Marion, Beatrice, Amaryllis, Daphne, Dryope, &c.

Plot: Caterer and amateur aviator James Smith crashes his plane in Arcadia, and is rescued by the pure and perfect locals, a race to whom unworthy thoughts and deeds are all unknown. Horrified at Smith's thoughtless fibbing, they dunk him manfully in the Well of Truth, remake him as the virtuous "Simplicitas," and then set off in a proselytizing party to London, to bring enlightenment and truth and beauty to its perverted inhabitants. They arrive at Askwood race track, and their costume and their magical talents provoke a raging curiosity as they unwittingly interfere in both the romances and the races that are in progress. Simplicitas soon takes advantage of his new position as

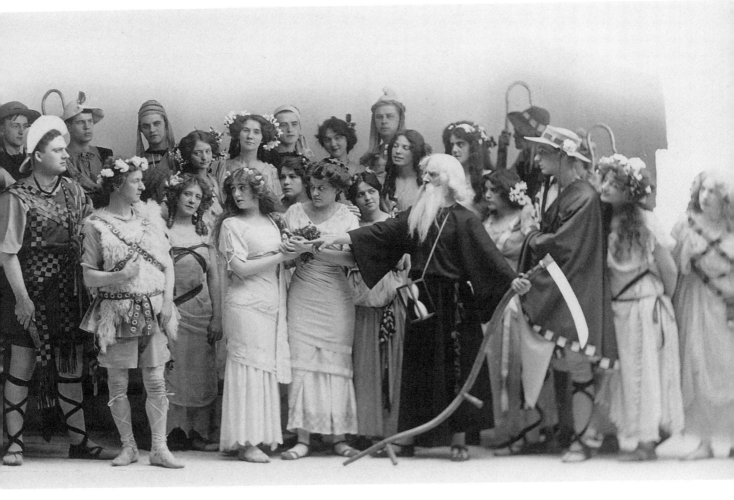

the adored curiosity of the town and opens an Arcadian Restaurant, but before long the real Arcadians have had enough. London is incurable. So they go home, leaving the city and the now rehumanized James Smith to their deserts.

Songs: "Arcadians Are We" (chorus), "I Quite Forgot Arcadia" (Time), "The Joy of Life" (Sombra, Chrysea, Astrophel, Strephon), "Look What Hovers Above Us" (chorus), "The Pipes of Pan" (Sombra), "All a Lie!" (ensemble), "Sweet Simplicitas" (Simplicitas), Finale Act 1: "To All and Each," "That's All Over" (chorus), "Back Your Fancy" (Bobbie), "The Girl with the Brogue" (Eileen), "This Is Really Altogether Too Provoking" (chorus), "Arcady Is Ever Young" (Sombra), "Somewhere" (Simplicitas, Mrs Smith), "Charming Weather" (Jack, Eileen), "Fickle Fortune" (Jack), Finale Act 2: "The Horses Are Out," "Plant Your Posies" (chorus), "I Like London" (Chrysea), "My Motter" (Doody), "Half Past Two" (Jack, Eileen), "Cheer for Simplicitas" (chorus), "All Down Piccadilly" (Simplicitas), "Truth Is So Beautiful" (quintet), "My Heart Flies Homing" (Sombra), Finale Act 3: "All Down Piccadilly." Alternative and additional numbers included: "Bring Me a Rose" (Eileen), "Light Is my Heart" (Sombra), "Come Back to Arcady" (Sombra), "Whoppers"

The Arcadians: "I quite forgot Arcadia." Time explains to the inhabitants of Arcadia how, thanks to his forgetfulness, they missed out on the last couple of dozen centuries.

(Simplicitas), "The Only Girl Alive" (Jack), "Have a Bit on with Me" (Bobbie), "I'll Be a Sister to You" (Chrysea), "Love Will Win" (Jack), "The Two-Step" (Chrysea, Bobbie), "Little George Washington" (trio).

In 1908, however, the year before *The Arcadians* came to the stage, the romantic musical again staked its place in the West End with its biggest success since Daly's days. *King of Cadonia* was a full-scale Ruritanian saga—a piece about a mid-European queen, obliged to wed for reasons of state, and the anti-monarchist noble with whom she falls in love. Its music was by no less a musician than the hero of Daly's himself, Sidney Jones, and its libretto was the work of a young man called Freddie Lonsdale (1881–1954). Lonsdale would remain the outstanding librettist to the British romantic musical—scoring enormous hits with the banditland musical *The Maid of the Mountains* (music: Harold Fraser-Simson) and the adaptation to the musical stage of Booth Tarkington's *Monsieur Beaucaire* (music: André Messager), before switching to the comic theater and making himself a place there as one of the English stage's favorite writers of highish-society comedy.

In the America of the 1900s, the full-blooded romantic musical put in much more regular appearances than it did in Britain, with new scores bearing the names of *Robin Hood*'s Reginald De Koven or the English expatriate musician Julian Edwards (1855–1910) appearing on the bills season after season. Both musicians wrote in a resolutely "classical" style, turning out scores which, in spite of the occasional attempt at an up-to-date formula or song-style, mostly had a distinct and sometimes rather stiff air of bygone years about them. And although each found occasional success—and lavish praise from those critics who longed for the return of the correctest form of old-style comic opera in preference to the flibbertigibbet musical comedy—neither succeeded in producing a piece which would either travel or endure. Altogether more successful than either De Koven or Edwards, however, was Victor Herbert. The composer of *The Fortune Teller* and *The Serenade* proved himself distinctly more versatile than his colleagues, as he spread himself from one end of the 1900s musical-theater spectrum to the other, supplying the music for the songs-and-scenery fairy-tale show *Babes in Toyland* on the one hand, and for such lively low jinks as the Yankees-abroad vehicle for comedy stars Montgomery and Stone, *The Red Mill*, at the other. Nor did he abandon the romantic musical, and, in fact, he scored his most memorable successes with two pieces written to feature singers who had previously made an international career in the less demanding corners of the world of opera. In 1905 he set to music a frothy if conventional little tale about a little French shopgirl, *Mlle Modiste*, who like all good comic-opera shopgirls ends up as a diva, as a vehicle for Fritzi Scheff, and in 1911 he produced what has (with a little help from the musical cinema) turned out to be his most enduring musical of all, the deep-South story of the runaway Countess (impersonated by Emma Trentini) who was *Naughty Marietta*. *Naughty Marietta* was a little unusual in that it set its romantic-operatic story in a fairly recognizable America—or, at the very least, a kind of "Ruritania" that was altogether nearer to home than usual. Previously, a romantic musical had almost always been set in some colorful and idealized part of Europe and, not coincidentally, had also copied European styles of writing. But, coming after such pieces as the 1902 *The Mocking Bird*—also set in historical Louisiana—and *When Johnny Comes Marching Home*, a Julian Edwards/Stan Stange show which actually took the Civil War as its background and plot-motor, this new American romantic musical confirmed the rising confidence in things American that had begun, at last, to grow in the American musical theater. The year after, *Naughty Marietta* was followed up by another successful romantic musical play with an operatic heroine (the same Signora Trentini) and this time with a contemporary American setting. The music may have been, yet again, by a new American—Prague-born Rudolf Friml—but *The Firefly* had nothing Central European about it. And in just two years, the American stage had produced its two most effective romantic musicals to date.

NAUGHTY MARIETTA, a musical comedy in 2 acts by Rida Johnson Young. Music by Victor Herbert. Produced at the New York Theatre, New York, 7 November 1910.

Characters: Captain Richard Warrington, Simon O'Hara, Lieutenant Governor Grandet, Étienne Grandet, Marietta d'Altena, Adah, Lizette, Sir Harry Blake, Rudolfo, Florenze, &c.

Plot: To avoid an unwanted marriage, Countess Marietta d'Altena runs away from France, disguised as a casket girl, on a bride-ship to the colony of New Orleans. She has sworn that she will wed only the man who can complete the unfinished song which runs in her head. In America, however, her identity is discovered by Étienne Grandet, the son of the colony's temporary governor and a villain who has been plundering the local villages as the piratical Bras Priqué. He determines to marry this potentially profitable daughter of France, and cruelly dumps Adah, his quadroon mistress, in furtherance of his aims. Adah has her revenge by betraying Grandet's double identity to the apparently woman-proof backwoods ranger, Dick Warrington, and before the curtain falls "Captain Dick" has both routed the pirate and completed Marietta's song.

Songs: Opening Chorus (ensemble), Mysterious Melody (Fanchon), "Tramp, Tramp, Tramp" (Dick, Simon, &c.), "Taisez-Vous" (chorus), "Song from the Fountain" (Marietta), "It Never, Never Can Be Love" (Dick), "If I Were Anybody Else But Me" (Simon, Lizette), "'Neath the Southern Moon" (Adah), Italian Street Song: "Zing, Zing" (Marietta, chorus), Finale Act 1, Dance of the Marionettes: "Turn Like Dat-a Pierrette" (Marietta, Rudolfo), "You Marry a Marionette" (Étienne), "New Orleans, Jeunesse dorée" (chorus) , "The Loves of New Orleans" (chorus), "'The Sweet By-and-By" (Lizette), "Live for Today" (Marietta, Adah, Dick, Étienne, chorus), "I'm Falling in Love with Someone" (Dick), "It's Pretty Soft for Simon" (Simon), Finale Act 2: "Ah! Sweet Mystery of Life" (Dick, Marietta).

The innovations in the English-language musical had, in the 1900s, been largely in the area of libretto. The musical part of those musicals, more often than not, had been the work of the same men—Caryll, Jones, Monckton, Stuart, and Rubens in Britain, and Herbert, De Koven, and Edwards in America, to whom were now added Luders, Cohan, and others more ephemeral—who had already been to the fore before the turn of the century. But very soon, that would all change, for the next important novelty in the English musical theater—and ultimately the whole world's musical theater—would be on the musical front.

ENTER THE WIDOW

In the meanwhile, however, a new musical voice had already come to the fore, and was sweeping, if not all, then a very great deal of musical stages clean. It was the voice of the new epoch of Central European musicals, of the "Viennese operetta," and it arrived almost in tandem with the turn of the century.

With the disappearance of almost all of the star musicians and writers of the Central European musical theater of the nineteenth century, the last years of the old century had seen new hits thin on the boards of the Viennese, Budapest, and Berlin stages. Carl Michael Ziehrer (1843–1922), Paul Lincke (1866–1946), György Verö (1857–1941), Richard Heuberger (1850–1914), and their libretto-writing fellows, who had won what successes there were in those years, were clearly not going to launch a whole new era of musical-theater successes unaided—the take-overs were awaited keenly. And, little by little, they came. But when they came, they brought with them a different kind of musical theater, and a different kind of music: simpler, more jaunty, freer in some ways than the music of the old masters. And that music was teamed with light-hearted libretti or didn't lumber around in remakes of ancient French comic opera texts but used sprightly Central European stories set, very often, in contemporary times. New music, new stories . . . that they would have a breath of fresh air about them was inevitable. But they ended up having more than just that.

The first gust of this fresh, twentieth-century air came in 1901, with the production of the extremely light and bright *Das süsse Mädel* at the Carltheater. Written by two prolific adapters and writers of the 1890s musical stage, Alexander Landesberg (1848–1916) and Leo Stein (1861–1921), and dealing with a couple of youngsters due to wed each other who both have other preferences (and stick to them!), the musical was the first full-length work of the composer Heinrich Reinhardt (1865–1922). Reinhardt's score was quite unlike anything the Vienna Operette stage was used to. It was light, bright and tuneful, and full of the simplest of waltzing and country rhythms and themes which it had no qualms about repeating and reprising over and over and over again, till those easy, catchy tunes had well and truly caught. The critics sniffed at it as insubstantial, the public loved it, and *Das süsse Mädel* became the first hit of the new Viennese century. It was swiftly followed by others. Berlin brought out a merry "French" musical comedy about the high jinks surrounding the setting up—for the benefit of a wealthy uncle who thinks he's been supporting his bachelor nephew's family—of a phoney *Madame Sherry*, and its equally lightweight music bore the signature of the almost neophyte Hugo Felix (?1866–1934). Then, three weeks later, the Theater an der Wien premièred the maiden work of

Die lustige Witwe: The very original widow. Mizzi Günther and Louis Treumann, the Viennese creators of the roles of Hanna and Danilo.

yet another composing freshman. *Wiener Frauen* had a fair run, but its composer, the young Franz Lehár (1870–1948), scored the biggest success of the new century to date just four weeks later when his second show was mounted at the opposition Carltheater. *Der Rastelbinder*, a characterful, Viennese tale, constructed by Victor Léon on the same lines as *Das süsse Mädel*, told of a youthful betrothal finally set aside (as in Reinhardt's piece) to let young love have its own way. It featured a big, show-stealing rôle of an old Jewish onion seller for the house's chief light comedian, Louis Treumann, and he, and the merry, lilting music which the young Hungarian composer provided as accompaniment, went far in making the show one of the musical-theater triumphs of its era.

Only a few weeks more down the line, yet another first-up composer of the new generation saw his first musical produced in Vienna and, this time, it was the Theater an der Wien—rather outpointed by the Carltheater in recent months—that had the hit. It was a hit as big as *Der Rastelbinder*. The show was *Bruder Straubinger*, its text was by Ignaz Schnitzer (1839–1921)—

the Hungarian journalist who'd adapted the text for Strauss's *Zigeunerbaron*—and Moritz West of *Der Vogelhändler*, and the composer was Edmund Eysler (1874–1949). The story was a piece of eighteenth-century Rhineland foolery about a young soldier who loses his identity papers and has to masquerade for most of the night as a grandfather. The rôle was a gift for Viennese mega-star Alexander Girardi, and the extraordinarily melodious Eysler provided him with the biggest song-hit to come out of the Operette world in years, a big and beautiful waltz asserting "Küssen ist keine Sünd"—kissing's no crime. And the new names just kept coming: 1904 saw another Hungarian, Heinrich Berté (1857–1924), make his début with *Der neue Bürgermeister*, Pepi Hellmesberger (1855–1907) produce his most popular piece, *Das Veilchenmädel*, and the un-tried Oscar Straus (1870–1954) come up with—of all things—a merry burlesque of the Volsung sagas in *Die lustigen Nibelungen*, while 1905 introduced Leo Ascher (1880–1942) with the suc-cessful, American-set *Vergeltsgott* and Leo Fall (1873–1925) with the mythological and unsuc-cessful *Der Rebell*. The starters were all at the gate—and four or five years previously it would have been a brave man who could have predicted the size of the field. Now it remained to be seen who would be the musicians to confirm their early promise, who would turn this budding new era of musical theater into a success, and, above all, who would be the composer to launch the keystone show that would carry the new-style Operette to the rest of the world.

It was, of course, Franz Lehár. And the show was the most successful of all those remade French comedies of the early part of the twentieth century, the reincarnation of Meilhac's *L'Attaché d'ambassade* as *Die lustige Witwe*—a lady better known to English listeners under Adrian Ross's English title, *The Merry Widow*.

DIE LUSTIGE WITWE, an Operette in 3 acts by Victor Léon and Leo Stein, based on *L'Attaché d'ambassade* by Henri Meilhac. Music by Franz Lehár. Produced at the Theater an der Wien, Vienna, 30 December 1905.

Characters: Baron Mirko Zeta, Valencienne, Graf Danilo Danilowitsch, Hanna Glawari, Camille de Rosillon, Vicomte Cascada, Raoul de St Brioche, Bogdanowitsch, Sylviane, Kromow, Olga, Pritschitsch, Praskowia, Njegus, Lolo, Dodo, Jou-Jou, Clo-Clo, Margot, Frou-Frou, &c.

Plot: The Pontevedrian government is worried sick. The incredibly rich banker Glawari has died, leaving his fortune to his young wife of just a few days, and she is now being avidly courted by half of masculine Paris. Pontevedro cannot afford to have the Glawari millions go out of the country, so a dutiful and handsome young Pontevedrian is ordered to go out and woo, win, and wed Madame Glawari and her money. Danilo Danilowitsch, the man chosen for this patriotic duty, was—unfortu-nately—the man who was left on the shelf when it was arranged that Hanna was to wed Glawari, and he's naturally very touchy where she is concerned. He also still loves her. When it seems that Hanna has been compromising herself with a tenorious Frenchman, the rewarmed Danilo angrily throws in his mission, but Hanna is innocent of any dalliance. She was only protecting a married friend. She has every intention of marrying Danilo, and by the end of the evening she has wooed him and his tender ego to her side.

Songs: "Verehrteste Damen und Herren" (Cascada, Zeta, &c.), "Ich bin eine anständige Frau"

(Valencienne, Camille), "Bitte, meine Herr'n" (Hanna), "O Vaterland, du machst bei Tag"/"Da geh' ich zu Maxim" (Danilo), "Ja was? Ein traute Zimmerlein" (Valencienne, Camille), Finale Act 1: "Damenwahl!"/"O kommet doch, o kommt, Ihr Ballsirenen," "Ich bitte, hier jetzt zu verweilen"/"Es lebt' eine Vilja" (Hanna), "Dummer, dummer Reitersmann" (Hanna, Danilo), "Ja, das Studium der Weiber ist schwer" (Danilo, Zeta, Cascada, St Brioche, Njegus, &c.), "Meine Freund, vernunft!" (Valencienne, Camille), "Wie eine Rosenknospe" (Camille), "Sieh dort den kleinen Pavillon" (Valencienne, Camille), Finale Act 2: "Ha! Ha! Ha!"/"Ein flotter Ehestand muss ein" (Hanna)/"Es waren zwei Königskinder" (Danilo), "Ja, wir sind es die Grisetten" (Valencienne, grisettes), "Lippen schweigen" (Danilo, Hanna), Finale Act 3.

Die lustige Witwe was an enormous success in Vienna, and it went forth from Austria to become an enormous success all round the world, establishing the modern "Viennese Operette" as the new musical-theater craze in the years before the Great War. However, although—like the musical comedy hits of the English theater of the 1910s—it was based on lively piece of French comedy writing, and although it was illustrated with sparkling, fresh, dance-rhythmed music of the merriest kind, *Die lustige Witwe* was never to be perceived as the same type of musical comedy as *The Spring Chicken*, *The Pink Lady*, *High Jinks*, *Kissing Time*, and the rest of their species. For its French comedy was not a wickedly farcical modern one, but—like the one that had served for the book of *Die Fledermaus*—one that was more than half a century old, and for all that its two central characters were light-comedy lovers with light-hearted melodies to sing, rather that the swooning, dueting Prince and Princess of the most romantic of musicals, the result was not an up-to-date comedy musical. In sum, the period Parisian *Die lustige Witwe* was not seen as the successor to the Gaiety musical play, but to the Daly's one. And when George Edwardes launched the piece (titivated with a few additions and alterations, which included a distinct lowering of the comedy of chief comedian Baron Zeta, and the boosting of the girlie element) on London, at the beginning of its cavalcade around the English-singing world, it was precisely at the home of *The Geisha* and *A Greek Slave* that he mounted his *Merry Widow*. In the years that followed, as the flow of merry European musicals to nations and stages beyond grew to a vast, variegated volume, many pieces that were thoroughly up-to-date in their comedy and their deliciously dancing music would successfully join the more romantic musicals on the export trail: but somehow that romantic image remained attached to the Continental musical, and the word "operetta" began to get twisted, in the English language, into applying only to the period, the sentimental, the romantic, and the musically lush among musical plays.

Of course, the Operettic produce of the prewar decade in Europe was not all in that vein, and the hits that followed *Die lustige Witwe* onto the stage in Vienna, Budapest, and Berlin—and very often moved on from there to many another stage—covered all areas and styles of musical theater. The *Witwe*'s co-librettist, Stein, combined with Karl Lindau (1853–1934) and with Eysler on a Posse-like piece called *Künstlerblut* in which the slightly aging Girardi pulled off a tour de force as an aging theater star obliged to give up his soubrette to a younger man, Ziehrer turned out a book of tunes for what his authors called a "vaudeville-Operette" in *Ein tolles Mädel*, Georg Jarno supplied the popular actress Hansi Niese with some fine songs to sing in the rôle of *Die Försterchristl*, the country lass who warms the heart of the Emperor himself, and Oscar Straus composed the music for a delicious fantasy (with a song for a dragon!) called *Hugdietrichs Brautfahrt* and then for the thoroughly romantic *Ein Walzertraum*. *Ein Walzertraum* followed the feelings of a Viennese officer who, married to a foreign princess, finds himself unable to cope with his wife's position and his own homesickness. The little Viennese musician with whom he almost has a fling teaches his wife how to keep her husband home and happy. Straus provided a flowing, lilting, thoroughly light-hearted and Viennese-y score, touched with just a whiff of pretty sentiment, as an accompaniment to this tale—a score very different from the merry, sparky music with which Caryll would illustrate virtually the same story as the Parisian musical comedy *S.A.R.* the following year—and *Ein Walzertraum* was Vienna's biggest success in the years immediately following the launch of *Die lustige Witwe*.

However, if *Ein Walzertraum* and Straus hit the hardest at home in the wake of *Die lustige Witwe*, other shows and other musicians proved to be more popularly successful when the produce of the Central European stage began to flood stages further afield. Leo Fall, Germany's Jean Gilbert (1879–1942), and the Hungarians Imre Kálmán (1882–1953) and Viktor Jacobi (1883–1921) were to share the brightest of the limelight with Lehár on the international scene, and they shared it thanks to a range of musicals which went from the most chic of made-over Parisian comedies to the most thoroughly lavish of romantic costume musicals.

Leo Fall had failed with his first musical, *Der Rebell*, in 1905, and that failure had cleared the Theater an der Wien stage for the hurried production of *Die lustige Witwe*. But he would soon compensate for that first miss with not one but three outsized hits in just two seasons. In July 1907, the theater at Mannheim brought out his *Der fidele Bauer*—a Victor Léon story of the small-town lad made good who weds into a social family and then becomes ashamed of the peasant father who sacrificed everything for him. It was a piece of a flavor as far from the brittle Parisianisms of Léon's *Die lustige Witwe* as could be: thoroughly local, colored with the atmosphere of the Upper Austrian countryside, and with a score of music that rippled with waltzing, marching melody such as had rarely if ever been heard on the musical stage. Then, four months later, the Theater an der Wien produced Fall's *Die Dollarprinzessin*. This time he had set a book which chronicled the up-and-down romance between an American businesswoman and a poor but proud émigré nobleman, and his show began with a chorus of lady office typists who sang their song to the clacking accompaniment of their machines. Then, at the end of the following year, after the peasanty musical and the up-to-date New Yorkish one, Fall set another Léon book—one which, although its action took place in Amsterdam, was palpably made in imitation of French comedy—under the title *Die geschiedene Frau*. And this one was perhaps the biggest hit of all.

DIE GESCHIEDENE FRAU, a musikalische Schwank in 3 acts by Victor Léon. Music by Leo Fall. Produced at the Carltheater, Vienna, 23 December 1908.

Characters: Karel van Lysseweghe, Jana van Lysseweghe, Pieter te Bakkensijl, Gonda van der Loo, Rechsanwalt de Leije, Judge Lucas von Deesteldonck, Scrop, Willem Krouwevleit, Martje Krouwevleit, Ruitersplat, Dender, Professor Tonger, Professor Wiesum, &c.

Plot: Die geschiedene Frau—the divorcée—of the title is Jana van Lysseweghe, and she is getting divorced because she has been told that her husband had a quickie with an over-exuberant "actress" in a sleeping car during an overnight train trip. Now the whole thing is getting settled in court, before a judge who seems to have decided where the guilt lies even before he starts. She's miserable, and he's miserable, but the judge says he did it, so by the end of the first act the divorce is pronounced and Karel dutifully proposes to make as honest a woman as is possible of the co-respondent, Miss Gonda van der Loo. But after two further acts of pretences, blackmail and almost-mismatches, things get straightened and sorted out. Karel—who actually didn't do it—and Jana get back together again, while Miss van der Loo agrees to become the wife of the determinedly pursuing judge!

Songs: "Die wen'gen Worte nur" (Jana, Judge), "O jemine, o jemine" (chorus, Karel, Judge), "O Echestand, o Echestand, wie schön bist du!" (Willem, Martje, Karel, Jana, Judge), "O Schlafcoupé, ach Schlafcoupé" (Gonda), Finale Act I: "Nun, Jana, sprich, was soll es mit uns beiden?"/"Freie Liebe!" (Gonda), "Sir Roger, Sir Roger"(Willem, Martje, chorus), "Gonda, liebe kleine Gonda" (Karel, Gonda), "Kind, du kannst tanzen!" (Karel), Zärtlichkeitsterzett: "Kinder, ihr kommt mir so sonderbar vor" (Pieter, Karel, Jana), "Ich und du, Müllers Kuh" (Gonda &c.), Finale Act 2: "Sir Roger, dem zu Ehren man diesen Tanz bennant" (Jana &c.), Kirmesstanzlied: "Mahndach, Dinsdach, Wunsdach" (Willem, Martje, chorus), "Puppenspiel, Puppenspiel" (Jana), "Man steigt nach!" (Gonda, Scrop), Finale Act 3: "Warum? Warum?"/"Du, ach du, bist wieder mein"

After *Die geschiedene Frau*, which confirmed him around the world as perhaps the very hottest show composer of his time, Fall went on to supply the prewar stage with even more varieties of lively musical shows: from the from-the-French sex-tale of *Das Puppenmädel* to the romantische Operette *Die schöne Risette*, with its fairy-tale story of royal lovemaking, the seductive period tale of the French policeman Fouché and his band of feminine spies known as *Die Sirene*, and the antique baby-mix-up comicalities of the lovely *Der liebe Augustin*, before launching into a period of colorfully romantic and romantic-comic period pieces in the war and postwar years which would bring him even further success, and the Central European stage several of its outstanding musicals of the era.

Imre Kálmán made his first successes in his native Hungary, but before long he moved his base to the city which now acted as the principal showcase for international buyers of musical plays—Vienna. He shifted with a major hit, for his operett *Tatárjárás*, produced in early 1908 in Budapest, was taken up a year later by Karczag of the Theater an der Wien. Produced at the Viennese theater under the title *Ein Herbstmanöver*, this lively tale of love during an army exercise, with its inexorably melodious score, became Karczag's biggest hit in the three years since *Die lustige Witwe*. A second of Kálmán's Budapest pieces became an even more thoroughly international hit. The 1910 énekes színjáték (play with songs) *Az obsitos*, a piece about a soldier who impersonates his war-dead friend to spare a mother's heartbreak, got topical remakes in no fewer than four major centers (on both sides of the combat!) when the war came. Kálmán soon added to his hit total with his Viennese musicals, and the first big success to come from among them was *Der Zigeunerprimás*, a musical featuring Girardi as an Hungarian gipsy violinist whose career and hopes for a young wife are both put in the shade by his own son. Kálmán utilized Hungarian and gipsy tones in his music, mixing them with the more usual Viennese ones to provide a dashing and occasionally touching score, and the musical was a fine success in Vienna before traveling to Broadway where, under the title *Sari*, it proved itself as one of the most popular of all Viennese works on the American stage.

Kálmán's compatriot and contemporary Viktor Jacobi did not go to Vienna. For the first and most productive decade of his career, he stayed home in Hungary, and his outstanding works were given their premières in Budapest. His earliest writing for the musical stage was, under the influence of Hungary's most famous musical—the 1904 fairytale play *János vitéz*—spent mostly in composing scores for fantasies and fairy plays. However, aware that such pieces were not going to be bought by the smart and lucrative producers of the English-language theater-world, in 1911 he switched tack and wrote a Wildish-Western musical, set on the American West Coast, availing itself of the old marriage-market plot so famously used in the opera *Martha*, and invested with all those lashings of low comedy which so appealed to English and American audiences. *Leányvásár*—the girl market—proved that the combination was fairly attractive to the home market as well, but Jacobi's aim proved straight. *The Marriage Market* was picked up by George Edwardes, invested with even more low comedy and a few songs from some British hardy annual songwriters, and the resulting piece staged with considerable success at Daly's Theatre. But Jacobi had better to follow. Three years later, he turned out *Szibill*, a romantic musical play about an opera singer trying to save her deserter lover from the law who, at the crucial moment, is mistaken for a Grand Duchess—and finds that the Grand Duke in question is not at all averse to letting her continue right to the end of the charade. The rôle of the singer, Szibill, was gratified with a scoreful of lushly singable music, the jolly folk of the piece who played out their parts alongside the central love story were given some magnificently rhythmic and Puszta-flavored dance numbers, and *Szibill* turned out to be the most appreciable romantic musical yet to have come out of Budapest. Its overseas progress was rather held up by the war, but eventually it confirmed its hometown success in a whole run of foreign productions.

The Berlin musical theater had, over the years, contributed but little in the way of notable shows to the international stage. There had been Dellinger's *Don Cesar*, and Paul Lincke's little musical spectaculars had won a showing in Central Europe, but all in all the score-sheet was pretty empty. However, in the years before the war, for the first time the German stage found itself in the limelight, as it turned out a whole series of jolly musical comedies which would go round the world. The musician whose name went with the large proportion of these shows was Jean Gilbert—not a Frenchman, but a German taking a fashionably French nom de plume (which he hastily changed back when war broke out)—and between 1909, when his first big hit,

Polnische Wirtschaft, was brought out in Cottbus, and the outbreak of war, he forged himself an international reputation little inferior to those of Fall and Lehár.

Gilbert's pieces, the earliest of which were labeled "Posse" rather than "Operette," were indeed comical plays decorated with musical numbers, and those comical plays were the work of some of Berlin's most successful theater-writers of the moment: Jean Kren (1862–1922) and Alfred Schönfeld (1859–1916), whose Thalia-Theater presented a whole end-to-end run of their and Gilbert's musicals, and Georg Okonkowski (1863–1926) and Kurt Kraatz (1856–1925), who together had supplied the text for *Polnische Wirtschaft*. It was Okonkowski who came up with the text for the show that would make Gilbert's international reputation, and that text was—like so many of the best contemporary shows in so many other countries—a remake of a popular French play, Mars and Desvallières' *Fils à Papa*. The musical version took a wink at the Bible with its title: *Die keusche Susanne*—chaste Susannah.

DIE KEUSCHE SUSANNE, a Posse (Operette) in 3 acts by Georg Okonkowski, based on *Fils à Papa* by Antony Mars and Maurice Desvallières. Music by Jean Gilbert. Produced at the Wilhelm Theater, Magdeburg, 26 February 1910.

Characters: Baron Conrad des Aubrais, Delphine des Aubrais, Jacqueline, Hubert, Lieutenant René Boislurette, Pomarel, Susanne Pomarel, Charency, Rose Charency, Alexis, Mariette, &c.

Plot: Mme Pomarel has won an award as an exemplar of virtuous living in her hometown, but when she's in Paris, and her husband isn't looking, she enjoys a flirtatious night on the town. Last time round, she had a little fling with the womanizing Lt Boislurette. Now the Pomarels are back in town again, to see their equally super-respectable friends, the geneticist des Aubrais and his family. Daughter Jacqueline has a young man these days—and its Boislurette! That night, the Aubrais house gradually empties as Papa, son, daughter, Boislurette, and Mme Pomarel all sneak quietly out for a night at the Moulin-Rouge. Amid the dancing and the champagne, the farcical complexities wind up to an almighty peak, until Charency, a jealous, moral-crusading colleague of des Aubrais, leads in the police, only to find that the mysterious woman to whom the Baron is dancing so close is . . . Mme Charency! The next day, all the gallivanting is swept worriedly under the mat, and while the three wayward spouses ponder whether home isn't less exhausting, the junior members of the des Aubrais family get ready to prove their father's theory of heredity: they've taken to the night life with a vengeance.

Songs: "Liebe Baronin, wie fühlen welch' Glück"/"Ja solch ein Mädchen in der Jugend" (Delphine, Jacqueline, chorus), "Er kommt, er kommt, empfanget in voller Zeremonie" (Delphine, Jacqueline, Aubrais, chorus), "Ist es denn wahr, was alle sagen?" (Jacqueline, René), "Wir sind ein zärtlich Ehepaar" (Pomarel, Susanne), "Das ist Paris, dein Parfüm und dein Duft" (Susanne, René, Hubert), Finale Act 1: "Welch' hohe Ehr"/"Das ist Madame Tugendpreis," "Es lebe der Tanz, das Glutelixir" (ensemble), "Zum erstenmal im Separé" (Hubert), "Doch immer muss du artig sein" (Susanne, Hubert), "Wenn die Füssen sie heben" (René), "Ha, Jacqueline was kommst du her?"/"Wenn der Vater mit dem Sohne" (Susanne, Jacqueline, Rose, René, Hubert, Aubrais), Finale Act 2: "Eine Verlobung wird hier gefeiert"/"Trink wenn du allein bist," "Singe, mein Schatz, wie die Lerche, juchhe!" (Jacqueline, Hubert), "Komm, du mein kleines Hahnenmännchen," Schlussgesang: "Wenn der Vater mit dem Sohne."

After *Die keusche Susanne*, Gilbert turned out a remarkable row of successful Berlin musical comedies which were quickly snapped up by other producers in other cities, the English-language theaters at their head: the "French" musicals *Autoliebchen* and *Die moderne Eva*, *Puppchen*, and two pieces titled and written with an eye to the latest crazes, *Die Tango-prinzessin* and *Die Kino-Königin*. The newly fashionable topic of the cinema was, indeed, the topic for two almost simultaneous musicals, for the rival Berliner Theater and their songwriter Walter Kollo (1878–1940) beat the tryout of the Metropoltheater's *Die Kino-Königin* to the stage by just a few weeeks with their movieland musical *Filmzauber*, and the two shows eventually went around the world in opposition to each other. However, the international career of the Berlin musical comedy was cut short just a few years after it had begun. Germany went to war with its best customers, and its best customers put up the shutters. It would be a few years before the export of Berlin musicals to Britain, in particular, would restart, and although Gilbert managed to gather back some lost ground and score several more international successes, what had looked like becoming—in the early 1910s—a veritable era of German musical comedies on the world's stages fizzled frustratingly away in a kind of theatrical coitus interruptus.

The success of *Die lustige Witwe* ensured that the name of Franz Lehár became the best-known, world-wide, of any of his compatriots and colleagues in the musical theater. Yet Lehár's career in the years following his 1905 megahit did not go wholly smoothly, and in the 1910s composers such as Fall and Eysler did more consistently well than he with their new works. However, in the decade before the war, Lehár did turn out two further pieces that went on to fine international careers. One was another bright, Parisian tale of romance, the story about *Der Graf von Luxemburg* and his marriage for money which turns to real love. The other was much darker, richer, and more lush in its textual and musical colorings, for *Zigeunerliebe* was an unusually passionate piece, set in the composer's native Hungary, with a heroine who has to make a choice between a passionate and probably painful love-life as the paramour of a romantic gipsy or a comfortable and conventional married existence. Both shows have survived into the modern repertoire.

If Oscar Straus's big Vienna hit *Ein Walzertraum* did less well in some foreign countries than it did at home, the composer more than made up for this with the international career of another, more wholly comical Operette which had actually had only a mediocre run in Vienna. *Der tapfere Soldat* was—for once—not a "French" Operette, but an "English" one, its libretto being based on G. B. Shaw's play *Arms and the Man*. What became known in English as *The Chocolate Soldier* turned out to be one of the best-loved of all Viennese Operetten of the pre-war years, second only to *The Merry Widow* in America and Britain, just as *Ein Walzertraum* was second only to the same piece at home, and English-singing sopranos of several decades poured out their straight-faced hearts to "My Hero" in Stan Stange's version of the heroine's humorously over-the-top arietta.

Although the young composers who had scored the first big pre-*Witwe* successes did not score quite as brilliantly on the international stage as Fall, Kálmán, Lehár, Gilbert, Jacobi, or Straus, they did not by any means fade away. Reinhardt turned out several further successful pieces for Vienna, topped by a piece of pretty romantic nonsense called *Die Sprudelfee* which had a fine success in America as *The Spring Maid*, and Eysler racked up a vast list of musical comedies, full of the most ineffably tuneful of Viennese melody, which—inexplicably—got very little in the way of a showing outside Central Europe. After the triple-header of thoroughly Austrian musicals—*Pufferl*, *Die Schützenliesel*, and *Künstlerblut*—with which he followed up his first big success, he turned out an end-to-end run of musical plays which filled the Wiener Bürgertheater between 1910 and the war: the Altwiener Stück *Der unsterbliche Lump*, the story of the jilted man who became the misogynistic *Der Frauenfresser*, the adventures of the inattentive husband and his novelist wife who pictured their marriage in her "fictional" *Der lachende Ehemann*, and the tale of the expatriate Viennese who tries to pick up his old life during *Ein Tag im Paradies*. And each and every one was decorated with the most singable of songs.

But if Eysler's music did not travel, there were plenty of others whose music did. These years saw the melodies and the dancing rhythms of the Viennese stage sweep the world, and on the back of that music the whole spectrum of the new wave of Central European Operette—from the most comical, farcical pieces, both "French" and original, to the most thoroughly and richly romantic—went forth to occupy a considerable proportion of that world's musical stage.

SOME NOTABLE MUSICALS 1900–1914

1900 THE MESSENGER BOY (Ivan Caryll, Lionel Monckton/Adrian Ross, Percy Greenbank/Alfred Murray, James Tanner) Gaiety Theatre, London, 3 February
THE CASINO GIRL (Ludwig Englander/Harry B. Smith) Casino Theatre, New York, 19 March
THE BURGOMASTER (Gustave Luders/Frank Pixley) Dearborn Theatre, Chicago, 17 June
KITTY GREY (Howard Talbot, Augustus Barratt, et al./Adrian Ross/J. Smyth Piggott) Theatre Royal, Bristol, 27 August

1901 LES TRAVAUX D'HERCULE [The labors of Hercules] (Claude Terrasse/Robert de Flers, Gaston de Caillavet) Théâtre des Bouffes-Parisiens, Paris, 7 March
THE SILVER SLIPPER (Leslie Stuart/W. H. Risque/Owen Hall) Lyric Theatre, London, 1 June
THE TOREADOR (Ivan Caryll, Lionel Monckton/Percy Greenbank, Adrian Ross/Harry Nicholls, James Tanner) Gaiety Theatre, London, 17 June
DAS SÜSSE MÄDEL [The sweet lass] (Heinrich Reinhardt/Leo Stein, Alexander Landesberg) Carltheater, Vienna, 25 September
BLUEBELL IN FAIRYLAND (Walter Slaughter/Aubrey Hopwood, Charles H. Taylor/Seymour Hicks) Vaudeville Theatre, London, 18 December

1902   A COUNTRY GIRL (Lionel Monckton/Adrian Ross/James Tanner) Daly's Theatre, London, 18 January

THE SULTAN OF SULU (Alfred Wathall/George Ade) Studebaker Theatre, Chicago, 11 March

MERRIE ENGLAND (Edward German/Basil Hood) Savoy Theatre, London, 2 April

THREE LITTLE MAIDS (Paul Rubens, Howard Talbot/Percy Greenbank) Apollo Theatre, London, 20 May

MADAME SHERRY (Hugo Felix/Benno Jacobsen) Centraltheater, Berlin, 1 November

THE GIRL FROM KAY'S (Ivan Caryll, Cecil Cook/Owen Hall) Apollo Theatre, London, 15 November

DER RASTELBINDER (Franz Lehár/Victor Léon) Carltheater, Vienna, 20 December

1903   THE WIZARD OF OZ (Alfred Baldwin Sloane, Paul Tietjens/Glen MacDonough/Frank Baum) Majestic Theatre, New York, 20 January

BRUDER STRAUBINGER (Edmund Eysler/Ignaz Schnitzer, Moritz West) Theater an der Wien, Vienna, 20 February

LE SIRE DE VERGY [The Lord of Vergy] (Claude Terrasse/Robert de Flers, Gaston de Caillavet) Théâtre des Variétés, Paris, 16 April

FRÜHLINGSLUFT [Spring air] (Josef Strauss pasticcio, arr. Ernst Reiterer/Carl Lindau, Julius Wilhelm) Venedig in Wien, Vienna, 9 May

THE PRINCE OF PILSEN (Gustave Luders/Frank Pixley) Tremont Theatre, Boston, May

THE SCHOOL GIRL (Leslie Stuart/Charles H. Taylor/Henry Hamilton, Paul Potter) Prince of Wales Theatre, London, 9 May

BABES IN TOYLAND (Victor Herbert/Glen MacDonough) Majestic Theatre, New York, 13 October

THE DUCHESS OF DANTZIC (Ivan Caryll/Henry Hamilton) Lyric Theatre, London, 17 October

THE ORCHID (Ivan Caryll, Lionel Monckton/Percy Greenbank, Adrian Ross/James Tanner) Gaiety Theatre, London, 28 October

THE EARL AND THE GIRL (Ivan Caryll/Percy Greenbank/Seymour Hicks) Adelphi Theatre, London, 10 December

1904   THE YANKEE CONSUL (Alfred Robyn/Henry Blossom) Chicago, then Broadway Theatre, New York, 22 February 1904

THE SHO-GUN (Gustave Luders/George Ade) Studebaker Theatre, Chicago, 4 April

SERGEANT BRUE (Liza Lehmann/Owen Hall) Strand Theatre, London, 14 June

THE CATCH OF THE SEASON (Herbert Haines, Evelyn Baker/Charles H. Taylor/Cosmo Hamilton, Seymour Hicks) Vaudeville Theatre, London, 9 September

M DE LA PALISSE [Monsieur de la Palisse] (Claude Terrasse/Robert de Flers, Gaston de Caillavet) Théâtre des Variétés, Paris, 2 November

LITTLE JOHNNY JONES (George M. Cohan) Liberty Theatre, New York, 7 November

DIE LUSTIGEN NIBELUNGEN [The jolly Niebelungs] (Oscar Straus/Rideamus) Carltheater, Vienna, 12 November

IT HAPPENED IN NORDLAND (Victor Herbert/Glen MacDonough) Lew Fields Theatre, New York, 5 December

1905   MR POPPLE (OF IPPLETON) (Paul Rubens) Apollo Theatre, London, 17 March

THE SPRING CHICKEN (Ivan Caryll, Lionel Monckton/Adrian Ross, Percy Greenbank/George Grossmith) Gaiety Theatre, London, 30 May

DIE SCHÜTZENLIESEL [Shooting-Liesel] (Edmund Eysler/Leo Stein, Carl Lindau) Carltheater, Vienna, 7 October

MLLE MODISTE (Victor Herbert/Henry Blossom) Knickerbocker Theatre, New York, 25 December

DIE LUSTIGE WITWE [The merry widow] (Franz Lehár/Leo Stein, Victor Léon) Theater an der Wien, Vienna, 30 December

1906   FORTY-FIVE MINUTES FROM BROADWAY (George M. Cohan) New Amsterdam Theatre, New York, 1 January

HUGDIETRICHS BRAUTFAHRT [Hugdietrich's bridal journey] (Oscar Straus/Rideamus) Carltheater, Vienna, 10 March

PARIS, OU LE BON JUGE [Paris, or A good judge] (Claude Terrasse/Robert de Flers, Gaston de Caillavet) Théâtre des Capucines, Paris, 18 March

THE BELLE OF MAYFAIR (Leslie Stuart/Basil Hood, C. H. E. Brookfield) Vaudeville Theatre, London, 11 April

THE DAIRYMAIDS (Paul Rubens, Frank E. Tours/Arthur Wimperis/Robert Courtneidge, Alexander M. Thompson) Apollo Theatre, London, 14 April

HANS LE JOUEUR DE FLÛTE [Hans, the flute player] (Louis Ganne/Maurice Vaucaire, Georges Mitchell) Monte Carlo, 14 April

THE GIRL BEHIND THE COUNTER (Howard Talbot/Arthur Anderson/Leedham Bantock) Wyndham's Theatre, London, 21 April

THE TIME, THE PLACE AND THE GIRL (Joe Howard/Frank Adams, Will M. Hough) La Salle Theatre, Chicago, 20 August

THE RED MILL (Victor Herbert/Henry Blossom) Knickerbocker Theatre, New York, 24 September

KÜNSTLERBLUT [Artistic blood] (Edmund Eysler/Carl Lindau, Leo Stein) Carltheater, Vienna, 20 October

1907   MISS HOOK OF HOLLAND (Paul Rubens/Austen Hurgon) Prince of Wales Theatre, London, 31 January

EIN WALZERTRAUM [A waltz-dream](Oscar Straus/Felix Dörmann, Leopold Jacobson) Carltheater, Vienna, 2 March

SON P'TIT FRÈRE [Her little brother] (Charles Cuvillier/André Barde) Théâtre des Capucines, Paris, 10 April

TOM JONES (Edward German/Charles H. Taylor/Alexander M. Thompson, Robert Courtneidge) Apollo Theatre, London, 17 April

THE GIRLS OF GOTTENBERG (Ivan Caryll, Lionel Monckton/Adrian Ross/George Grossmith, L. E. Berman) Gaiety Theatre, London, 15 May

DER FIDELE BAUER [The jolly peasant] (Leo Fall/Victor Léon) Mannheim, 25 July

DIE DOLLARPRINZESSIN [The dollar-princess] (Leo Fall/Arthur M. Willner, Fritz Grünbaum) Theater an der Wien, Vienna, 2 November

DIE FÖRSTERCHRISTL [Forest-Christl] (Georg Jarno/Bernhard Buchbinder) Theater in der Josefstadt, Vienna, 17 December

1908   TATÁRJÁRÁS [Autumn maneuvers] (Imre Kálmán/Károly Bakonyi) Vígszinház, Budapest, 22 February

HAVANA (Leslie Stuart/Adrian Ross/George Grossmith, Graham Hill) Gaiety Theatre, London, 25 April

KING OF CADONIA (Sidney Jones/Adrian Ross/Frederic Lonsdale) Prince of Wales Theatre, London, 3 September

S.A.R. (Ivan Caryll/Léon Xanrof, Jules Chancel) Théâtre des Bouffes-Parisiens, Paris, 11 November

BUB ODER MÄDEL? [Boy or girl?] (Bruno Granichstädten/Felix Dörmann, Adolf Altmann) Johann Strauss-Theater, Vienna, 13 November

DER TAPFERE SOLDAT [The brave soldier] (Oscar Straus/Rudolf Bernauer, Leopold Jacobson) Theater an der Wien, Vienna, 14 November

DIE GESCHIEDENE FRAU [The divorcée] (Leo Fall/Victor Léon) Carltheater, Vienna, 23 December

1909   OUR MISS GIBBS (Ivan Caryll, Lionel Monckton/Adrian Ross, Percy Greenbank/James Tanner, et al.) Gaiety Theatre, London, 23 January

DIE SPRUDELFEE [The spa-fairy] (Heinrich Reinhardt/Arthur M. Willner, Julius Wilhelm) Raimundtheater, Vienna, 23 January

AFGAR, ou Les Loisirs andalous [Afgar, or What the Andalusians do in their spare time] (Charles Cuvillier/André Barde, Michel Carré fils) Théâtre des Capucines, Paris, 10 April

THE ARCADIANS (Howard Talbot, Lionel Monckton/Arthur Wimperis/Alexander M. Thompson, Mark Ambient) Shaftesbury Theatre, London, 28 April

DER GRAF VON LUXEMBURG [The Count of Luxemburg] (Franz Lehár/Arthur M. Willner, Robert Bodanzky) Theater an der Wien, Vienna, 12 November

POLNISCHE WIRTSCHAFT [Polish husbandry] (Jean Gilbert/Alfred Schönfeld/Georg Okonkowski, Kurt Kraatz) Stadttheater, Cottbus, 26 December

1910   ZIGEUNERLIEBE [Gipsy love] (Franz Lehár/Arthur M. Willner, Robert Bodanzky) Carltheater, Vienna, 8 January

THE BALKAN PRINCESS (Paul Rubens/Arthur Wimperis/Frederic Lonsdale) Prince of Wales Theatre, London, 19 February

DIE KEUSCHE SUSANNE [Chaste Susannah] (Jean Gilbert/Alfred Schönfeld/Georg Okonkowski) Wilhelm-Theater, Magdeburg, 26 February

PEGGY (Leslie Stuart/C. H. Bovill/George Grossmith) Gaiety Theatre, London, 4 March

AZ OBSITOS [The soldier] (Imre Kálmán/Károly Bakonyi) Vígszinház, Budapest, 16 March

ALMA, WO WOHNST DU? [Alma, where do you live?] (Adolf Philipp) Wintergarten "zum schwarzen Adler," New York, 25 October

DAS PUPPENMÄDEL [The doll-girl] (Leo Fall/Leo Stein, Alfred M Willner) Carltheater, Vienna, 4 November

THE QUAKER GIRL (Lionel Monckton/Adrian Ross, Percy Greenbank/James Tanner) Adelphi Theatre, London, 5 November

NAUGHTY MARIETTA (Victor Herbert/Rida Johnson Young) New York Theatre, New York, 7 November

DIE SCHÖNE RISETTE [Pretty Risette] (Leo Fall/Arthur M. Willner, Robert Bodanzky) Theater an der Wien, Vienna, 19 November

1911   DIE MODERNE EVA (Jean Gilbert/Georg Okonkowski, Alfred Schönfeld) Neues Operetten-Theater, Berlin, 18 October

THE RED WIDOW (Charles Gebest/Channing Pollock, Rennold Wolf) Astor Theatre, New York, 6 November

THE PINK LADY (Ivan Caryll/Charles M. S. McLellan) New Amsterdam Theatre, New York, 10 November

LEÁNYVÁSÁR [The girl-market] (Viktor Jacobi/Ferenc Martos, Miksa Bródy) Király Színház, Budapest, 14 November

ALT-WIEN [Old Vienna] (Josef Lanner pasticcio, arr. Emil Stern/Gustav Kadelburg, Julius Wilhelm) Carltheater, Vienna, 23 December

1912   DER LILA DOMINO [The purple mask] (Charles Cuvillier/Emmerich von Gatti, Béla Jenbach) Stadttheater, Leipzig, 3 February

DER LIEBE AUGUSTIN [Dear Augustin] (Leo Fall/Rudolf Bernauer, Ernst Welisch) Neues Theater, Berlin, 3 February

THE SUNSHINE GIRL (Paul Rubens/Arthur Wimperis/Cecil Raleigh) Gaiety Theatre, London, 24 February

AUTOLIEBCHEN [Motorcar-love] (Jean Gilbert/Alfred Schönfeld/Jean Kren) Thalia-Theater, Berlin, 16 March

OH! OH! DELPHINE (Ivan Caryll/Charles M. S. McLellan) Knickerbocker Theatre, New York, 30 September

DER ZIGEUNERPRIMÁS [The gipsy fiddler] (Imre Kálmán/Fritz Grünbaum, Julius Wilhelm) Johann Strauss-Theater, Vienna, 11 October

FILMZAUBER [Cinema-magic] (Walter Kollo/Rudolf Schanzer, Rudolf Bernauer) Berliner Theater, Berlin, 19 October

THE FIREFLY (Rudolf Friml/Otto Harbach) Lyric Theatre, New York, 2 December

PUPPCHEN [Dolly] (Jean Gilbert/Alfred Schönfeld/Jean Kren, Kurt Kraatz) Thalia-Theater, Berlin, 10 December

1913   DIE KINO-KÖNIGIN [The cinema queen] (Jean Gilbert/Georg Okonkowski, Julius Freund) Metropoltheater, Berlin, 8 March

DER LACHENDE EHEMANN [The laughing husband] (Edmund Eysler/Julius Brammer, Alfred Grünwald) Wiener Bürgertheater, Vienna, 19 March

THE PEARL GIRL (Howard Talbot, Hugo Felix/Basil Hood) Shaftesbury Theatre, London, 25 September

DIE TANGOPRINZESSIN (Jean Gilbert/Alfred Schönfeld/Jean Kren, Kurt Kraatz) Thalia-Theater, Berlin, 4 October

WIE EINST IM MAI [Once upon a time, in May] (Walter Kollo, Willi Bredschneider/Rudolf Bernauer, Rudolf Schanzer) Berliner Theatre, Berlin, 4 October

THE GIRL FROM UTAH (Sidney Jones, Paul Rubens/Adrian Ross, Percy Greenbank/James Tanner) Adelphi Theatre, London, 18 October

POLENBLUT [Polish ancestry] (Oskar Nedbal/Leo Stein) Carltheater, Vienna, 25 October

THE LITTLE CAFÉ (Ivan Caryll/Charles M. S. McLellan) New Amsterdam Theatre, New York, 10 November

HIGH JINKS (Rudolf Friml/Otto Harbach/Leo Ditrichstein) Lyric Theatre, New York, 10 December

FLUP . . . ! (Josef Szulc/Gaston Dumestre) Théâtre de l'Alhambra, Brussels, 19 December

EIN TAG IM PARADIES [A day at the "Paradise"] (Edmund Eysler/Leo Stein, Béla Jenbach) Wiener Bürgertheater, Vienna, 23 December

1914   SZIBILL [Sybil] (Viktor Jacobi/Ferenc Martos, Miksa Bródy) Király Színház, Budapest, 27 February

CHIN-CHIN (Ivan Caryll/James O'Dea/R. H. Burnside, Anne Caldwell) Globe Theatre, New York, 20 October

RUND UM DIE LIEBE [A voyage around love] (Oscar Straus/Robert Bodanzky, Friedrich Thelen) Johann Strauss-Theater, Vienna, 9 November

TONIGHT'S THE NIGHT (Paul Rubens/Percy Greenbank/Fred Thompson) Shubert Theatre, New York, 24 December

FIRST CATCH YOUR FRENCH PLAY . . .

Some of the many musicals of the last years of the nineteenth and the early twentieth centuries that owed their libretti to the French comic stage

1895	KIS FÍU	Bébé (A. Hennequin, de Najac)
1896	LOST, STRAYED OR STOLEN	Le Baptême du petit Oscar (Grangé, Bernard)
1896	BUM-BUM	La Cigale (Meilhac, Halévy)
1897	DAS ROTHE PARAPLUIE	Le Voyage de Corbillon (Mars)
1897	DER COGNAC-KÖNIG	La Frontière de Savoie (Scribe, Bayard)
1897	HÁROM LÉGYOTT	Les Dominos roses (A. Hennequin, Delacour)
1898	KATZE UND MAUS	La Bataille de dames (Scribe)
1898	DER OPERNBALL	Les Dominos roses (A. Hennequin, Delacour)
1899	IHRE EXCELLENZ	Niniche (A. Hennequin, Millaud)
1899	THE ROUNDERS	Les Fêtards (Mars, M. Hennequin)
1899	PAPA'S WIFE	Mam'zelle Nitouche/La Femme à Papa (Millaud, Meilhac)
1899	FRÄULEIN PRÄSIDENT	Nelly Rosier (Bilhaud, M. Hennequin)
1900	THE CADET GIRL	Les Demoiselles de St Cyriens (Gavault, de Cottens)
1900	DER SECHS-UHR ZUG	Décoré (Meilhac)
1900	DIE STIEFMAMA	La Femme à Papa (Millaud, A. Hennequin)
1901	KITTY GREY	Les Fêtards (Mars, M. Hennequin)
1901	DIE DEBUTANTIN	Le Mari de la débutante (Meilhac, Halévy)
1901	THE PRIMA DONNA	La Siège de Grenade (Chivot, Duru)
1901	AUCH SO EINE!	Maison Tamponin (Blum, Toché)
1901	DIE PRIMA DONNA	Le Mari de la débutante (Meilhac, Halévy)
1902	DAS GEWISS ETWAS	unidentified
1902	DIE DAME AUS TROUVILLE	La Turlutaine de Marjolin (Péricaud, Soulié, Darantière)
1902	WIENER FRAUEN	unidentified
1902	THE GIRL FROM KAY'S	La Mariée recalcitrante (Gandillot)
1902	MADAME SHERRY	Madame Sherry (Ordonneau, Burani)
1903	THE DUCHESS OF DANTZIC	Madame Sans-Gêne (Sardou)

1903	THE OFFICE BOY	Le Jockey malgré lui (Ordonneau, Gavault)
1903	FRÜHLINGSLUFT	Coquin de printemps (Jaime, Duval)
1904	BEFEHL DES KAISERS	Ordre de l'Empereur (Ferrier)
1904	A SZALMAÖZVEGY	Les Vacances du mariage (M. Hennequin, Valabrègue)
1904	KAM'RAD LEHMANN	unidentified (Chivot, Duru)
1905	THE SPRING CHICKEN	Coquin de printemps (Jaime, Duval)
1905	DIE LUSTIGE WITWE	L'Attaché d'ambassade (Meilhac)
1906	SEE-SEE	La Troisième lune (Ferrier, de Grésac)
1906	GYÖNGYYÉLET	Tire-au-flanc! (Mouëzy-Eón, Sylvane)
1906	LES MERVEILLEUSES	Les Merveilleuses (Sardou)
1907	MADAME TROUBADOUR	La Petite Marquise (Meilhac, Halévy)
1907	IHR SECHS-UHR ONKEL	unidentified (Kéroul, Barré)
1907	THE HOYDEN	La Soeur (T. Bernard)
1907	FRAU LEBEDAME	Divorçons (Sardou, E. de Najac)
1908	MARY'S LAMB	Madame Mongodin (Blum, Toché)
1908	S.A.R.	Le Prince Consort (Xanrof, Chancel)
1908	THE ANTELOPE	Le Cabinet Piperlin (Burani, Raymond)
1909	DIDI	La Marquise (Sardou)
1910	DIE KEUSCHE SUSANNE	Fils à Papa (Mars, Desvallières)
1910	DAS PUPPENMÄDEL	Miquette et sa mère (de Flers, de Caillavet)
1911	DIE MODERNE EVA	Place aux femmes (M. Hennequin, Valabrègue)
1911	PEGGY	L'Amorçage (Xanrof, Guérin)
1911	THE PINK LADY	Le Satyre (Guillemaud, Berr)
1911	DAS MÄDEL AUS MONTMARTRE	La Dame de Chez Maxim (Feydeau)
1911	GRI-GRI	Gri-Gri (Chancel, Henriot)
1911	AZ EZRED APJA	Le Papa du régiment (Mouëzy-Eón, J. Durieux)
1912	OH! OH! DELPHINE	La Grimpette (Guillemaud, Berr)
1912	TANTALIZING TOMMY	La Petite Chocolatière (Gavault)
1912	THE KISS CALL	Un Coup de téléphone (Berr, Gavault)
1912	ALL FOR THE LADIES	Aimé des femmes (M. Hennequin, Mitchell)
1912	THE MAN FROM COOK'S	Un Voyage Cook (Ordonneau)
1912	AUTOLIEBCHEN	Dix minutes d'auto (Berr, Decourcelle)
1912	EIN KITZLICHE GESCHICHT	Une affair scandaleuse (Gavault, Ordonneau)
1912	EXCEEDING THE SPEED LIMIT	unidentified (Mars)
1913	HIGH JINKS	Les Dragées d'Hercule (M. Hennequin, Bilhaud)
1913	THE LITTLE CAFÉ	Le Petit Café (T. Bernard)
1913	OH, I SAY!	Une nuit de noces (Kéroul, Barré)
1913	FINOM FAMILIA	unidentified (T. Bernard)
1913	ANGST VOR DER EHE	Le Colombier (M. Hennequin, Veber)
1914	PAPA'S DARLING	Le Fils surnaturel (Vaucaire, Grenet Dancourt)
1914	LOUTE	Loute (P. Veber)
1914	LÉNI NENI	Le Portrait de ma tante (Barré, Kéroul)

1914	DIE NACHTPRINZESSIN	La Duchesse des Folies-Bergère (Feydeau)
1915	TONIGHT'S THE NIGHT	Les Dominos roses (A. Hennequin, Delacour)
1916	THEODORE & CO.	Théodore et cie. (Gavault, Nancey, Armont)
1917	THE GRASS WIDOW	Le Péril jaune (Bisson, St Albin)
1917	YES, UNCLE	Le Truc du Brésilien (Armont, Nancey)
1918	TELLING THE TALE	Une nuit de noces (Kéroul, Barré)
1918	THE GIRL BEHIND THE GUN	Madame et son fileul (Veber, M. Hennequin)
1918	THE CANARY	Le Coffre-fort vivant (Berr, L. Verneuil)
1918	SEE YOU LATER	Loute (P. Veber)
1919	APPLE BLOSSOMS	Un Mariage sur Louis XV (Dumas)
1919	OH, DON'T, DOLLY!	Bébé (A. Hennequin, de Najac)
1919	THE GIRL FOR THE BOY	La Petite Chocolatière (Gavault)
1920	A NIGHT OUT	L'Hôtel du Libre Échange (Desvallières, Feydeau)
1920	THE NIGHT BOAT	Le Contrôleur de wagons-lits (Bisson)
1920	HONEYDEW	Les Surprises du divorce (Bisson)
1921	LITTLE MISS RAFFLES	Souris d'hôtel (Armont, Gerbidon)
1921	KIKI	Le Zèbre (Armont, Nancey)
1922	THE BLUE KITTEN	Le Chasseur de Chez Maxim (Mirande, Quinson)
1922	THE BLUSHING BRIDE	unidentified
1922	THE FRENCH DOLL	Jeunes filles de palaces (Armont, Gerbidon)
1922	ORANGE BLOSSOMS	La Passerelle (de Croisset, de Grésac)
1923	LA PRESIDENTESSA	La Présidente (M. Hennequin, Veber)
1924	IL CONTROLORE DEI WAGONI LETTI	Le Contrôleur de wagons-lits (Bisson)
1925	A NAUGHTY CINDERELLA	Pouche (Falk, Peter)
1925	DER LETZTE KUSS	Un fil à la patte (Feydeau)
1925	LA DAMA DI MONTMARTRA	La Dame de Chez Maxim (Feydeau)
1925	AZ ÁRTLATLAN ÖZVEGY	Mademoiselle Josette, ma femme (Gavault, Charvay)
1926	OH, PLEASE!	La Présidente (M. Hennequin, Veber)
1926	OH, KAY!	La Présidente (M. Hennequin, Veber)
1926	IN DER JOHANNISNACHT	La Belle Aventure (de Flers, de Caillavet, Rey)
1922	PRIMAROSA	Primerose (de Flers, de Caillavet)
1927	LOVELY LADY	Déjeuner de soleil (Birabeau)
1927	THE MADCAP	Le Fruit vert (Gignoux, Théry)
1928	A KISS IN A TAXI	Le Monsieur de cinq heures (Veber, M. Hennequin)
1928	CRI-CRI	Madame Sans-Gêne (Moreau, Sardou)
1929	BOOM BOOM	Mademoiselle ma mère (Verneuil)
1930	MEINE SCHWESTER UND ICH	Ma soeur et moi (Berr, Verneuil)
1932	EINE FRAU, DIE WEISS, WAS SIE WILL	Le Fauteuil (Verneuil)
1933	BEZAUBERNDES FRÄULEIN	La Petite Chocolatière (Gavault)

6 THOSE
MAGNIFICENT
MADCAP
YEARS

he next important change in the flavor and style of the musical theater and its entertainments started to become evident around about the time that the world went to war. While the Central European Operette continued to flourish gaily, supplying as much of the world as was still willing to listen to "enemy" music with most of the best of its classically proportioned romantic and romantic/comic musicals, the newly book-sophisticated musical comedies of the other two main traditions—the French- and English-language ones—began to undergo a musical face-lift.

The music of the "popular" style of musical theater had, through the years, very largely reflected the popular music of its period in its scores: the favorite melodies of today and yesterday, the latest trend in popular song—from the parlor ballad to the tyrolienne to the coon song via a whole series of other longer or, often, short-lived fashions—and, of course, the preferred dance rhythms of the day: lancers, quadrilles, marches, waltzes, polkas, barn dances, plus whatever happened to be the most recent craze in exotic, comic, or novelty dances. In the early twentieth century, the public passion for the music of the dance took on new proportions and, as the world was flooded with a variegated range of jaunty new rhythms and easy-to-do dance-styles with which to fill its burgeoning range of ever-more-popular dance-halls, the whole character of popular dance and popular music took on a new look. During the first quarter of the new century, subtitles such as the two-step, the shimmy, the boston, the tango, the fox-trot, the one-step, and the java began to appear on sheet-music-covers alongside those of the eternally popular waltz and march, and the words "ragtime" and "jazz" came sassing out of America to lend their flavor to this latest fashion in popular music. And pretty soon, all this merry, foot-swiveling, syncopated melody made its way into the musical theater.

One of the results of this change in taste and style was that a different group of music-writers eventually became the musicians à la mode of the musical theater. Composers such as Sidney Jones, Lionel Monckton, and Leslie Stuart in England, Victor Herbert in America, and André Messager in France found themselves no longer in the swim as writers for the popular end of the musical theater. For that area of the theater no longer needed or wanted "composers," even ones with a proven hand for the writing of a takeaway number. It needed and wanted "songwriters"—songwriters whose melody-manufacturing men were in tune and in time with

Some of the most popular of the dances that invaded the music and musical-theater of the early twentieth century . . .

THE TWO-STEP: A parading routine for a pair of dancers, performed to direct, rhythmic music which was introduced to ballrooms at the turn of the century, the two-step was one of the most popular early examples of the new easy-to-do dances of the modern era.

THE SHIMMY: A vigorous, solo dance routine of a would-be sexy variety, involving a lot of eneregetic body-wobbling and performed to jazzy music with a marked rhythm. First promoted as such in the earliest years of the new century, it would develop later into such patent dances as the Charleston of the 1920s.

THE BOSTON: A simple 3/4 routine (valse Boston) which took the "walking" steps as seen in such dances as the two-step and interbred them with the traditional waltz. It was—alongside the two-step—one of the earliest of such dances to become popular.

THE TANGO: A 2/4 dance routine mixing seductively gliding steps with dramatically rhythmic ones which was popularized in South America in the late nineteenth century and then, in a more sophisticated form, in the Paris of the early 1900s. The Parisian "maxixe" made its way swiftly into the musical theater—being seen as early as 1905, danced by Gabrielle Ray and Dorothy Craske, in George Edwardes's London production of *Lady Madcap*, and as a sextet in his *The Spring Chicken*—before the tango went on to become progressively more exaggerated and, ultimately, in later decades, almost a burlesque of its original self.

THE ONE-STEP: A simple, walking routine, related to the cake-walk, and performed by a couple to a jaunty, soft ragtime piece of lightly syncopated dance music. Popularized in America in the 1910s, it was frequently embroidered upon to make up the speciality dances which proliferated in the years that followed.

THE FOX-TROT: A mixture of trotting and gliding steps, performed to music of the one-step variety, developed in America in the early 1910s. Under the influence of the fashion for performance dances, the fox-trot later dropped its more comical "trot" aspect in favor of the more elegant gliding portion of its movement, and in the 1920s the "slow fox-trot" became a romantic favorite.

---

the new music and the new dance rhythms. And so, effectively, musical comedy swapped its score of "music" for a score of "songs." The kind of concerted music which had so long been a feature of the musical comedy stage began to go into a steady decline from which it would never recover, composers such as Jones and Monckton shook their heads and went into voluntary retirement, and even though a number of their contemporaries tried their hand at new-style musical comedy (in Messager's case, even with some success), they almost invariably found they were out of their depth in such unfamiliar waters. Now it was the turn of writers whose natural habitat was the popular song market—and who had previously heard their work played on the musical stage only as interpolated songs stuck more or less incongruously into one of the composer's shows—to take their place at the footlights.

Almost in parallel, during the 1910s, both the French- and English-language stages developed a tradition of songwriter's musical comedies and, in the 1920s, as that pair of traditions blossomed, the one alongside the other, with an exceptional vigor, the world of the musical theater found itself in what was its veritable Golden Age. All three of its principal areas—the French-, the English-, and the German-speaking—were simultaneously producing a regular stream of outstanding musical plays. It was Nirvana. But it was the last time it would ever happen.

The French musical theater had got pretty much becalmed since the 1890s. There had been an attempt at a revival of the opéra-bouffe tradition when librettists Robert de Flers (1872–1927) and Gaston de Caillavet (1870–1915) authored a series of fine bouffe libretti which were musically set by Claude Terrasse (1867–1923) (*Les Travaux d'Hercule, Le Sire de Vergy, M de la Palisse, Paris, ou Le Bon Juge*), but those shows proved to have a real appeal only to a specialist and mostly sophisticated audience, and failed to become international hits. There were isolated successful attempts at fairy-tale opérette with such pieces as Ganne's merrily marching *Hans, le joueur de flûte*, or with thoroughly French musicalized comedy, as when Ivan Caryll made one of his periodic returns to his French base and wrote the score to an adaptation of the hit play *Le Prince Consort (S.A.R.)*, but undoubtedly the most interesting event in the French musical theater of this time was the production of a much smaller piece than any of these. It was called *Son p'tit frère*, it was described as an "opérette légère," it was mounted at the little 200-seat Théâtre des Capucines, and it sported a cast of just nine performers. Its text was the latest variation on the good old classical Grecian high jinks—so often to be found at important junctures in musical-theater history—but here the high jinks were of the most Parisian variety. Which meant, of course, that the whole thing was based on sex.

Son p'tit frère was the story of a slightly sagging ancient Athenian courtesan who inveigles an innocent and luscious young lad from out of town into living-in with her on the pretext that she is his long-lost sister. She's altogether delighted when it becomes necessary to admit she lied. The libretto of André Barde (1874–1945), glittering with up-to-date French humor and sporting both a lot of delicious wit and some howling Ancient Franco-Greek word-twisting, was illustrated by an ultra-light score written by Charles Cuvillier (1877–1955) and accompanied (for such was the Capucines' budget) by just a piano. Their bristling, intimately scaled little musical was a splendid small-house success which found itself a fine afterlife at home and a fair one abroad. But, for all its success, *Son p'tit frère* was only a precursor, and although Cuvillier later went on to win international success with his rather more normally sized *Der lila Domino*, the merry *La Reine joyeuse*, and Barde's even more thoroughly sexual harem tale *Afgar, ou Les Loisirs andalous*, it was not he—or even his brilliant librettist—who would turn out the show that would send the jazz-age French musical comedy into orbit.

That show didn't come until a decade later, and its authors were another sparky young writer of comedy and comical lyrics, Albert Willemetz (1887–1964) (co-credited with Fabien Sollar), and the popular songwriter Henri Christiné (1867–1941). Once again, *Phi-Phi* was dubbed "opérette légère," once again it was created for a tiny house—the 210-seat, underground wartime venue called the Théâtre de l'Abri—once again it sported a minimal cast, of just six principals, eight chorines, and two dancers, and, even if it managed a small orchestra instead of a single piano, it was still a distinctly small-scale enterprise. However, l'Abri was run by manager Gustave Quinson (?1867–1943), who was also supremo of the Bouffes-Parisiens, and when the Bouffes went unexpectedly dark, he transferred the production of his new musical out of its little house and into the old home of Offenbach and *Orphée aux enfers*. And there, in a theater more than four times the size of the one it had been built for, the jazz-age equivalent of *Orphée* found an even bigger success than its illustrious predecessor had done.

PHI-PHI, an opérette légère in 3 acts by Albert Willemetz and Fabien Sollar. Music by Henri Christiné. Produced at the Théâtre des Bouffes-Parisiens, Paris, 12 November 1918.

Characters: Phi-Phi, Madame Phi-Phi, Aspasie, Périclès, Le Pirée, Ardimédon, les petites modèles.

Plot: Since none of his house models has the qualities required, sculptor Phidias (Phi-Phi to his intimates) has been looking outside the atelier for a model for the character of "virtue" in his new statue, and one day he brings home this innocent little lass called Aspasie, whom he has picked up walking the streets of ancient Athens. Being a very Parisian Ancient Greek, he clearly intends to do more than just sculpt her. Simultaneously, the virtuous Mme Phi-Phi is tracked home from the supermarket by a randy young Princeling against whom—after he has been hired to impersonate "love" in the statue—she defends her honor valiantly for almost half an act. Then Périclès, tyrant of Athens, puts in an appearance. He actually pays for the statue and, of course, as the history books tell us, he also helps himself to Aspasie. The curtain comes down on a good old traditional Parisian ménage à cinq: husband, wife, his mistress, her lover, and the mistress's wealthy provider. Happy ending all round. Ah, civilization!

Songs: "Nous sommes les petites modèles" (models), "C'est une gamine charmante" (Phidias), "Maître, lorsqu'on a vingt ans" (Aspasie), "Je connais toutes les historiettes" (Aspasie), "Vertu, Verturon, Verturonette" (Phidias), "J'sortais des portes de Trézène" (Mme Phidias, Phidias, Ardimédon, le Pirée), Finale Act 1: "Pour l'amour," "Ptolomée sera-t-il vainqueur?" (models), "Ah! cher monsieur" (Aspasie), "Non, s'il faut que je vous explique" (Aspasie), Prière à Pallas (Mme Phidias), "Tout tombe" (Ardimédon), Ballet, "Ah! tais-toi" (Mme Phidias, Ardimédon), Finale Act 2: "Le procédé vraiment nouveau," Duo des souvenirs (Mme Phidias, Ardimédon), "Bien chapeautée" (Aspasie), Chanson des petits païens (Phidias), "Pour être heureux, que faut-il?" (Phidias, Mme Phidias, Ardimédon, Aspasie, Périclès), Finale Act 3: "Aspasie, et moi Périclès."

The success of *Phi-Phi*, with its deliciously bright libretto and its dazzling score of light, laughing, modern music—swoopingly swooning tongue-in-cheek waltz music, jaunty comic songs, and a selection of topical and point numbers—only grew larger as the festivities in postwar France rose to their peak. This jazz-age musical comedy became the "victory musical" par excellence, and when the incredulous Quinson tried to downgrade it to another, smaller house after the first part of its run (to allow him to produce Broadway's *The Pink Lady* at the Bouffes!), he swiftly saw his error and brought the musical of its era back to its original home. There it continued on till it had topped a total of more than 1,000 representations—an absolutely huge run for the Paris theater of the time.

Needless to say, this enormous hit provoked a follow-up, and, as the romantic opérette with its big orchestra, numerous chorus, and extravagant staging was pushed palely away into a tiny corner, Quinson and other Parisian producers began to fill the stages of the city's more modestly proportioned theaters with a series of similar musical comedies, superbly crafted comical plays with words and songwords that demanded to be listened to (and which could actually be heard over the now lightweight accompaniment), where cleverly made ensembles replaced sub-operatic choruses, and where the story, its action, and its songs were the thing, rather than the scenery, the frocks, or a ballet of forty nubile almost-in-time-with-each-other demoiselles. The "musical comedy" had thoroughly arrived at adulthood, and this series of shows proved to be the singing, dancing, side-splitting joy of the French theater of the 1920s. Unfortunately, they weren't able to bring too much side-splitting joy to audiences further afield. Of the other main musical-theatrical centers only Budapest welcomed the French musicals of the twenties with the same enthusiasm as their home country. Elsewhere they were more often than not judged quite simply unproduceable. Not to mention untranslatable. And when, occasionally, an overseas producer was tempted into putting one on the stage, it arrived there so badly botched that there was no chance of success. Why? Well, the problem of these années folles shows was not that they weren't good—there was no question that they were brilliant, arguably the most brilliant set of comical musical plays the world had or has ever seen—it was, quite simply, their subject matter. Each and every one of these musical comedies found the very largest part of its comedy in things sexual. The plots circulated entirely round things sexual. The songs were little masterpieces of quadruple entendre or sexual wit. Even the music seemed to be in sympathy. And, of course, to foreigners—even the theoretically "liberated" foreigners of the 1920s—this was unthinkable. Sex displayed and spoken of in such a way on the stage was dangerous enough, but sex as funny? A ménage à cinq, with everyone happily participating, funny? Good heavens, no. It was . . . why, it was indecent.

Christiné, Willemetz, and producer Quinson, all of whom would remain key figures in the musical comedy world throughout the années folles, naturally followed up their big success with more of the same, and *Phi-Phi* was succeeded at the Bouffes-Parisiens by *Dédé*. There was no Ancient Greece about *Dédé*. This time Willemetz moved full-square into present-day Paris for his libretto, and Urban, the creator of the title-rôle of *Phi-Phi*, again played the title-rôle as a modern young man desperately angling for an affair with a married lady he has met and danced with at a tango tea. So that they can meet without arousing any suspicion, he buys the shoe-shop she patronizes. Amid a perfect skein of passes, counter-passes, and just the occasional well-handled pass, we learn that Odette is in fact the wife of the previous shop-owner, and she has targeted Dédé as a mug buyer for her husband's failing business. But Odette has principles and she feels she really has to give the poor fellow some return for his money. Only it doesn't quite turn out like that, because Dédé has this dapper, womanizing, oozy-charming friend . . . and a disastrously devoted shop manageress. Once again Christiné's score rippled with melody and dancing rhythms—the fox-trot and the shimmy crooned out by Maurice

Chevalier in the rôle of best-friend Robert, or the tango as seductively danced by Urban and Maguy Warna as Odette—and once again the result was a first-class hit.

Quinson, however, having a number of theaters under his control—either as manager or "godfather"—was not going to rely on just two men to supply him with this new kind of exorbitantly money-making musical theater, and his first step towards establishing himself a stable of writers was to hire the songwriter Maurice Yvain (1891–1965) to set a text by the comic playwright Yves Mirande (1875–1957) for the Théâtre Daunou, run by his lady friend Jane Renouardt. Everyone got lucky. Yvain began his theatrical career setting one of the best and brightest books his skillful librettist ever wrote, Mirande and lyricist Willemetz (credited separately for the songwords in this show, for what seems to be the first time in the French theater) got a score no whit less memorable and of-the-moment than those Christiné had produced, with fox-trot, one-step, shimmy, and waltz all fashionably to the fore, and Quinson got, in *Ta bouche*, another very big hit.

TA BOUCHE, an opérette in 3 acts by Yves Mirande. Lyrics by Albert Willemetz. Music by Maurice Yvain. Produced at the Théâtre Daunou, Paris, 1 April 1922.

Characters: Monsieur Pas de Vis, Bastien Pas de Vis, La Comtesse, Eva, Mélanie, Jean, Marguerite, Mag, Margot.

Plot: Bastien and Eva are more-or-less-effectively engaged and have been busy happily rehearsing the intimacies of their wedding night when his father and her mother discover that each other's pretences are hollow: both families are fake-wealthy and both are here at this fashionable-ish resort trying to catch a wealthy mate for their children. Eva and Bastien are indignantly torn apart, and their attempts at keeping in touch are zealously destroyed by their parents. The boy is sadly married off to a plain but wealthy woman, the girl gives herself over to teasingly collecting jewelry from moneyed gentlemen. But then, years on, they meet up at the seaside again and the old bell rings. After it has finished ringing, in a room at a seedy hotel, Eva finds she's come out with the wrong cloak. It belongs to Bastien's wife. Mme Pas de Vis is right there, ringing bells with someone else! Bastien is mortified, shocked, stunned. Cuckolded by a woman with a face like a sausage roll?! It takes Eva until the next summer to track the devastated fellow down. He is, of course, divorced and thus alimonedly rich, she is rich, and now, two summers, two acts, and goodness knows how many years on, they are free not only to rehearse their marriage but carry it richly out.

Songs: "Souffrez au lever du rideau" (Marguerite, Mag, Margot), "Ta bouche" (Eva, Bastien), "Voilà comment est Jean" (Comtesse, Pas de Vis), "Le Petit Amant" (Bastien), Duo des Terres et des Coupons (Comtesse, Pas de Vis), "Si tu savais, maman" (Eva, Comtesse), "Quand on veut plaire aux demoiselles" (Pas de Vis), Finale Act 1: "Le temps devient frisqué," "Non, non, jamais les hommes" (Eva), "De mon temps" (Comtesse), "Ça, c'est une chose" (Bastien), "Machinalement" (Bastien), "Puisqu'un heureux hasard" (Comtesse, Pas de Vis, Mélanie, Jean), Valse du Volupté: "La seconde étreinte" (Eva, Bastien), Finale Act 2: "C'est inouï comme il fait chaud," Duetto des Domestiques (Mélanie, Jean), "Nous ne disons jamais de mal de personne" (Mag, Marguerite), "Quand on a du sens" (Pas de Vis, Comtesse), "Pour toi" (Eva), "Au milieu de notre entretien" (Mélanie, Jean), "Comment pourrions nous fair'" (Comtesse, Mélanie, Pas de Vis, Jean), Finale Act 3: "Heureux, oui nous le sommes."

Pas sur la bouche: The marriage of Gilberte Valandray and her husband seems unshakably happy. But this is the jazz age . . . so look out!

The success of *Ta bouche* prompted Quinson to hire the same team to turn out his new musical for the Bouffes-Parisiens, and the boom continued. *Là-haut* didn't have quite the same wittily farcical construction and dialogue that the earlier piece had had, for it was made to measure for two stars of the music-hall world, Maurice Chevalier (who had been very popular in *Dédé*) and the jolly, plump little Dranem. Chevalier played a car-crash victim, allowed by the heavenly powers that be to go back to earth to say goodbye to his wife. Dranem was the guardian angel who goes with him, and who has blushingly to oversee what his charge's idea of saying goodbye entails. Yvain supplied the men with songs suggestively crooning and come-onnishly fox-trotting for the one, and sparkily foolish and characterful for the other, and even Chevalier's walk-out (when Dranem proved the main attraction) didn't detract from the pulling-power of a lively musical which added one more notch to Quinson's moneybelt. And while Yvain held the stage at the Bouffes-Parisiens, down at the Daunou could be seen the latest Christiné show, a delicious, light-hearted piece of up-to-date comic theater called *Madame*.

The next to join Quinson's "stable" was none other than André Barde—nearly twenty years on from *Son p'tit frère*, but still as fresh as ever. For his first Quinson musical, he was teamed with Yvain, and the resultant show, *Pas sur la bouche*, was mounted at the Théâtre des Nouveautés.

Yet again, the result was a hit of the first degree, and Barde and Yvain went on to collaborate on eight more musical comedies over the next decade. None, however, in spite of such lively successes as *Un bon garçon* or *Oh! Papa . . .* , came within a street of their first big success.

PAS SUR LA BOUCHE, an opérette in 3 acts by André Barde. Music by Maurice Yvain. Produced at the Théâtre des Nouveautés, Paris, 17 February 1925.

Characters: Gilberte Valandray, Georges Valandray, Eric Thomson, Mlle Poumaillac, Huguette Verberie, Charley, Faradel, Madame Foin, &c.

Plot: The socially busy wife of Parisian metallurgist Valandray is sighed after by a selection of hopefully mistress-seeking young men, but—on metallurgical principles—her husband is supremely assured as to her fidelity: scientifically surely the man who first puts the "mark" on a woman has her "sealed" to him for life. On account of these same principles, however, he becomes distinctly concerned when it seems that Gilberte had in fact been previously married, before she met him. To an American. Indeed, to an American with whom Valandray is currently doing business and who is a guest in their home. He is actually right. Gilberte was, for a while, Mrs Eric Thomson, but she has no more intention of succumbing to her ex-husband's newly aroused interest than to her horde of young hopefuls. Events rise to farcical heights in a series of comings and goings at a hopeful little garçonnière on the Quai Malaquais, and when it finally seems that the marriage-mangling truth must come out, Gilberte's highly colored maiden aunt comes to the rescue. She claims that she was the Mlle Poumaillac who was once Mrs Thomson and, to prove it, she kisses her "ex-husband" plumb on the lips. Knowing his own susceptibilities, Thomson has lived all his adult life by the rule "pas sur la bouche," and the kiss devastates him into Mlle Poumaillac's arms for a passionate happy ending. What Valandray doesn't know will never hurt him.

Songs: "Quand une maîtress' de maison" (girls), "Je l'aime mieux autrement" (Huguette, Faradel), "Ce qu'on dit et ce qu'on pense" (Mlle Poumaillac), "Comme j'aimerais mon mari" (Gilberte), "Je suis venu te dire bonjour" (Valandray), "C'est de la réclame" (Charley), "Pic et pic et colégram" (Charley, Huguette), "Rien qu'un baiser"/"La Péruvienne" (Gilberte), Finale Act 1: "Il faudrait"/"C'est un petit dîner," "J'ai le hoquet" (Faradel), "Je me suis laissé embouteiller" (Valandray), "Quand on n'a pas ce que l'on aime" (Mlle Poumaillac), "Soirs de Méxique" (Gilberte, Charley), "Ça, c'est gentil" (Huguette, Charley), "Il suffit d'un rien" (Gilberte, Valandray), "Pas sur la bouche" (Thomson, girls), "Je suis le numéro un" (Thomson, Valandray, Gilberte, Mlle Poumaillac), Finale Act 2: "Sur le Quai Malaquais"/"Je suis une Poumaillac" (Mlle Poumaillac), "Mon bon!" (Valandray), "Est-ce bien ça?" (Huguette), "Par le trou" (Mme Foin), "Bonjour, bonsoir" (Gilberte, Charley), "O Sam!" (Mlle Poumaillac, Thomson), Finale Act 3: "Dites-vous quand vous serez partis."

Quinson and his "stable" were not, of course, the only men working in the now red-hot field of musical comedy. The success of *Phi-Phi* and the confirmation of that success by the half dozen big hits that followed it meant that more than half the theater managers in Paris wanted a new musical comedy for their houses. The less than half that didn't, of course, were those whose theaters were too big to hold an example of what was an essentially intimate kind of show, and where the occasional essay at a modern musical comedy had proven to be a mistake. The 200-seat Capucines and the 900-place Bouffe-Parisiens were fine, but already in a house like the Apollo—the Parisian home of *La Veuve joyeuse*—with its 1,200 capacity, the small cast, small orchestra, and limited scenic and spangle content that were an integral part of the best of musical comedy were ill at ease. But, even given these limitations, the France of the early twenties turned out something like thirty or forty new musicals per year, and Yvain and Christiné, the undisputed stars of the genre, couldn't write the songs for them all.

The first music man to have a show hotfoot it to public notice amid the end-to-end Yvain and Christiné shows at the Bouffes-Parisiens was Raoul Moretti (1893–1954), a prolific young composer of songs and dance music. He was teamed with Willemetz (and the artist Cami) on what they called an "opérette bouffe," a comical send-up of the famous tale of the Burghers of Calais, produced with Dranem and *Phi-Phi* heroine Alice Cocéa at the head of a strong Bouffes cast, and entitled provocatively *En chemyse*. It provoked, all right. The mayor of Calais petitioned the government to put a stop to a show which made fun of his great, patriotic fourteenth-century townsmen, and *En chemyse* disappeared from the Bouffes stage! But Moretti had not too many months to wait for a long-running success. When the Bouffes-Parisiens reopened after the summer break it was with another of his shows, *Troublez-moi*, written to a more up-to-date and farcically comic libretto by Mirande. Dranem was again the star, as a comic little nouveau riche ready to marry off his daughter to the taxman's son in return for "protection," and the score—songs and ensembles in the mode of the moment—lifted Moretti up to the top theatrical shelf. He would go on to find further success with Mirande and Willemetz on the light-hearted *Trois jeunes filles . . . nues!* (they weren't, but they went on the stage which was almost as bad), with Barde on a lively piece of comedy which cast the comic Milton as a lift boy who inherits money and goes into Parisian society as *Comte Obligado*, and, as late as 1932—when the genre was beginning to wither slightly—with one of the most successful latter-day musical comedies, *Un soir de réveillon*, written to a book by proven comedy writers Armont and Gerbidon.

Moretti was a young newcomer when he found success, but Josef Szulc waited a long time for his consecration. The Polish-born Szulc (1875–1956) had struggled for years to get his work a showing before his *Flup . . . !*, a comical piece about a railway porter who stands in for an aristocrat in colonial Ceylon, was produced in Belgium in 1913. Five years before *Phi-Phi*, it featured Urban as its leading man. Szulc had a musical version of Pierre Veber's hit comedy *Loute* produced in Marseille and saw *Flup . . . !* reach Lyon and *Loute* played in America before, finally, in 1920, he got his break on the Paris stage. And having arrived there, he stayed, for he had at least one musical on show in that city for most of the 1920s—as well as a good deal of the 1930s. The songwriter provided the score for pieces at the Daunou—notably the distinctly successful *Le Petit Choc* (libretto by revue expert P.-L. Flers)—and later for the Bouffes-Parisiens (*Flossie*, another success), and even for the vast Théâtre du Châtelet (*Sidonie Panache*), but the bulk of his shows were made for the smaller houses of the city, and particularly the Capucines, where he scored a fine pair of hits with *Quand on est trois* and *Mannequins* in 1925.

The successful singer-songwriter Gaston Gabaroche (1884–1961), Raoul Mercier (d 1973), and other musicians of the dance-halls, nightclubs, and music-halls likewise had their hour or hours of success in the world of musical comedy, but the genre of the moment also attracted writers from other and more lofty areas. Often they failed in their attempts at popular writing or, more especially, in writing for the intimate theater, with its special and demanding criteria, but just occasionally they hit the bullseye, and then the result could be remarkable. The shining case in point was *L'Amour masqué*, the work of the playwright Sacha Guitry (1885–1957) and of the seventy-year-old composer Messager, who had made his mark nearly thirty years back down the track with *Véronique* and *Les p'tites Michu* and had most recently turned out a veritable old-style light opera on the *Monsieur Beaucaire* story, mounted in England before being brought to France with considerable success. Guitry broke many of the modern musical comedy rules. Certainly his story was in every way based on sex, but it was sex in the age of elegance, sex in (and out of) period costume, and written not in the up-to-date dialogue that Barde, Mirande, and Willemetz purveyed so effectively, but in exquisite prose—lyrical, charming, and witty in turn. Messager's elegantly well-made version of what was almost the music of the moment (including a comical tango for Urban as an improbable Baron) was a perfect accompaniment to Guitry's superior "comédie en trois actes et en vers libre" and with Guitry himself, and his wife, the superb singing actress Yvonne Printemps, in its central rôles, *L'Amour masqué* turned out a triumph.

L'AMOUR MASQUÉ, a comédie musicale in free verse in 3 acts by Sacha Guitry. Music by André Messager. Produced at the Théâtre Édouard VII, Paris, 15 February 1923.

Characters: Elle, Lui, Le Maharadjah, Le Baron d'Agnot, the Interpreter, Two Servants, Maître d'Hôtel, Valet de Pied, &c.

Plot: Elle, twenty years old, quite ravishing and blissfully happy, is successfully set up with two extravagantly wealthy protectors, a Maharadjah and a Baron, but she has fallen passionately in love with a photograph of an unknown young man which she has stolen from her photographer's studio. An elegant greying gentleman who unmistakably resembles the photo comes to her home to investigate, and she makes him promise to bring his son that night to the masked ball. While her two masked servants effectively distract the attentions of two proprietorial noblemen, romance blossoms, and it is not until the morning after that Elle discovers that Lui is no one's son, but the elegant gentleman himself, a few years down the line from his day in front of the photographer's camera.

Songs: "Veuillez accepter quelques roses" (Servants), "J'ai vingt ans" (Elle), "J'ai deux amants" (Elle), Tango chanté: "Valentine a perdu la tête" (Baron), "Kar toum belafft" (Mahadjah, Interpreter, Elle), "Mon rêve" ["Tout l'histoire en quatre mots"] (Elle), reprise "J'ai vingt ans" (Elle), "Depuis l'histoire de la pomme" (Elle, Servants), "Fête charmante" (guests), "Entre mes bras" (Elle, Lui), "J' n'aim' pas les bonnes" (Baron), Chant Birman: "Lalla vabim ostogénine" (Maharadjah), "Le Koutchiska" (Interpreter), Couplets de charme: "Elle est charmante" (Elle), "Ah! quelle nuit!" (Lui), "Le Maharadjah me disait" (Interpreter, Servants, Elle), "Ah! quelle nuit!" (Baron), "En un seul mot" (Elle), "Excellente combinaison" (1st Servant, Interpreter), reprise "J'ai deux amants" (Elle).

Messager went on, after *L'Amour masqué*, to compose the score for two thoroughly modern musicals, both in tandem with no less a librettist than Albert Willemetz. *Passionnément* (with Maurice Hennequin), a piece about an American wife whose jealous, pleasure-cruising husband disguises her as an old woman, and her inevitable fall to a sexy young Frenchman, and the sea-going bit of musical bunks that was *Coups de roulis* both found some considerable success, and both have lasted into the modern repertoire, but Messager's scores showed just a little less of the "folie" of the années folles than the best works of Yvain, Christiné, and Szulc, and his collaboration with Guitry remains the outstanding feature of his "modern" period.

The great age of French musical comedy continued right through that picturesque postwar period known, for its deliriously up-to-date excesses, as les années folles, and it came to an end only as they merged into the very much less picturesque and distinctly down-in-the-mouth 1930s. Then, with the world no longer in that same rejoicing mood in which it had been a dozen years earlier, the flaming, foolish fun and the dizzy dancing had to stop, and the witty and unselfconsciously sexy comedy musical found itself replaced as the main kind of musical-theater entertainment of the French stage by the romantic opérette à grand spectacle: big, lush productions mounted for long runs in big, lush theaters—the type of musical theater that always seems to surface and flourish in hard or unhappy times. It was a form diametrically different from the one that had prospered over the last decade and a half, and one which would never produce the splendid, imaginative kind of listen-to-the-words pieces that the 1920s had so merrily lavished on its public. Now, in rather less-gay-than-before Paris, it was time to look at your musical rather than to listen to it.

THE JAZZ AGE IN ENGLISH

The English-language theater went through almost the same curve as the French had done during this prolific period. It started the war years, of course, in a distinctly more healthy state than its Gallic counterpart, but it too found a peak during the mid-twenties, bursting forth with a group of musical plays that would travel the world, and win vast popularity, only to fold itself away into supplying a less appetizing, and again more look-than-listen, set of shows for hometown entertainment in the thirties.

Now, however, in contrast to the past umpteen decades, the bulk of what was best in the English musical theater was no longer coming out of London. London had come to the end of an era, an end that was almost symbolically marked by the death of George Edwardes in 1915. The Gaiety musical which he had created and so successfully purveyed over nearly twenty years was also a thing of the past, replaced by the new comedy-with-a-backbone musical play. As for the Daly's musical, which he himself had abolished in favor of *The Merry Widow* and its successors, it would come back briefly during the wartime years, when such picturesque and romantic shows were the required entertainment, but it too was almost done. The spectacular remake of the Ali Baba story as *Chu Chin Chow* and the latest in the line of comic-opera banditland musicals, *The Maid of the Mountains*, filled London houses for long runs during the war years and established themselves as fondly remembered and revivable favorites, and the comedy musical reached its British peak with such wartime hits as *Tonight's the Night*, *Theodore & Co.*, *The Boy*, *Who's Hooper?*, *Yes, Uncle!*, *Kissing Time*, and *A Night Out* between 1915 and 1920, but in the 1920s virtually all the best and most successful musical plays that were seen on the London stage were imports.

But not all were translations. Far from it. For the American stage, during these years, at last found its feet, and found them with a vengeance. After the advance scouting party that had made the trip out of America and into the theaters of rest of the world some twenty years earlier in the form of *The Belle of New York*, the full-scale invasion of the world's stages by the made-in-America musical play was now to take place.

These new musicals were, like the French successors to *Son p'tit frère*, the lightest and brightest of musical comedies, and again like the postwar French pieces they used the new kind of popular music—the work of the popular songwriter or "Tin Pan Alley" tunesmith—as their scores. Some of them, too, were designed for New York's smallest theaters—though Broadway's very smallest was already half as big again as the Capucines or l'Abri, and its standard "small" house some three times larger. And some of them combined a light comic-romantic and dancing story with the spectacle of the romantic musical and the glitz of the variety or revue stage. But all these musicals were, in fact, even given such similarities or parallels, actually very different in character from their European counterparts.

First, of course, there was the subject-matter and the tone. The sexual shenanigans which were the heart of so many of the French shows were a non-starter for American authors. It was marriage and how to get it (preferably with money, good looks, and a nice croony voice attached) rather than sex and how to get it (with no strings necessarily attached) that made up the center of the stories of a large part of postwar and 1920s musical comedies. If a show such as the 1915 *So Long, Letty* based itself on a tale of wife-swapping, it was wife-swapping not because of a bit of mutual, on-the-side lust, but wife-swapping because each husband thinks he might be better suited by the personality of his pal's wife. If the married hero of *No, No, Nanette* sets up charge accounts for three young sirens at expensive stores, it's not because he is into mistresses in triplicate, but because he likes seeing pretty girls smile. It was all as innocuous as could be. This meant, of course, that the comedy of these musical comedies was of a different brand from that of the French plays. The farcical, sex-based imbroglios of the Gallic musicals were usually replaced by a set of rather less complex hurdles which would lead light-comedy leading man and ingénue to an unencumbered, and usually moneyed, connubial final curtain, and often a large amount of the essential comedy of the piece fell—in good old Gaiety style—into the hands of a principal and lowish-to-very-low comedian, who was tacked into this romantic little plot and onto the top of the playbill. The lyrics to the songs, of course, reflected these differences as well.

The music too was different. As on the Continent, the evening still delivered a regular flow of fox-trots and one-steps and shimmies and waltzes, but—in the country where so many of these rhythms and song-styles had developed—they were written with an altogether different hand: simpler and more direct, built to catch the ear and the tapping part of the foot with their jaunty tunes, and often, like the old interpolated numbers, barely attached to the story in which they were displayed. In fact, here a songwriter frequently could (and frequently did) take an all-purpose "pop" song out of one show and plonk it right into another. In the same vein, the numbers in these shows were laid out and orchestrated—often by someone other than their composer—with arrangements which might make them into popular songs, whereas, even when Yvain, for example, used jazz musicians in his bands, the lay-out and orchestration of the French scores were inevitably "opérettic." And popular songs these new American show songs indeed became—the favorite songs of the Broadway musicals of these years were frequently among the favorite songs of their era, fullstop. Both in America and abroad. Needless to say, under such conditions, ensemble writing, a feature of the works of Christiné, Yvain, and their kind, all but disappeared: a finale of an act more often than not consisted of a unison reprise of one of its most pluggable songs rather than a piece of concerted music. On the Broadway of the twenties, people didn't sing too often in close harmony—but they danced in close harmony. And they danced—and sang—to the most do-it-yourselfably between-the-eyes tunes and rhythms ever to hit the stage. And the rest of the world couldn't wait to join in.

It was a moment or two, however, before quite the whole world did. During the war years, the American stage and the British stage continued pretty much in tandem, turning out an on-going series of well-built, play-based musical comedies, a number of which went out from America, in the footsteps of *The Pink Lady* and *High Jinks*, to be seen further afield, some with more and some with less success. The sparky, wife-swapping *So Long, Letty*, a Los Angeles play remade as a musical with songs by producer-to-be Earl Carroll (?1892–1948), exported with great success to the flourishing theaters of Australia after its coast-to-coast triumph in America, and Ivan Caryll's "French" musical *The Girl Behind the Gun* (renamed *Kissing Time*) was a veritable triumph at both ends of the English-speaking world. But the biggest success of the 1914–18 period went to a musical with songs written not by a member of the "old guard" such as Caryll, but to one of the new men—one of the "songwriters" who were now starting to take over the musical comedy theater in America.

Going Up was based on a play rather less successful than the originals of *The Pink Lady*, *High Jinks*, and *Kissing Time*, and unlike them—and like *So Long, Letty*—it was not a piece of French comic theater, but a local one. This was a trend that would continue and grow over the years to come, but *Going Up* was the biggest success of the kind to date. The libretto was the combined work of the play's original author and of the same man who had so successfully put

together the adaptations which served as libretti to Broadway's versions of *Madame Sherry* and *High Jinks*, Otto Harbach (ex-Hauerbach), and he also supplied the words for the delightfully catchy melodies provided as a score by Louis Hirsch (1881–1924). Hirsch, a songwriter who had come up through Tin Pan Alley, into the theater, via the interpolated-number game and a period providing revue material and songs with which to botch the Shubert brothers' productions of Continental shows, had been responsible for giving London its most effective introduction to the up-to-date transatlantic style of dance and dance-music between 1912 and 1914 with a series of the virtual variety shows that were these days billed as "revue" (*Hullo, Ragtime!, Hullo Tango, Come Over Here, Honeymoon Express*). But *Going Up*—with its curious dance "The Tickle Toe" and its gently lilting "If You Look in Her Eyes"—gave him his biggest success of all.

Going Up: Years before the musical stage got invaded by helicopters, the aeronauts had already flown in. The only trouble is this fellow doesn't know how to drive an airplane, and for the love of this pretty girl, he's going to!

GOING UP, a musical comedy in 3 acts by James Montgomery and Otto Harbach, based on Montgomery's play *The Aviator*. Lyrics by Otto Harbach. Music by Louis Hirsch. Produced at the Liberty Theatre, New York, 25 December 1917.

Characters: F. H. Douglas, Mrs Douglas, Grace Douglas, Jules Gaillard, Madeleine Manners, Hopkinson Brown, Robert Street, James Brooks, Sam Robinson, John Gordon, Miss Zonne, Louis, &c.

Plot: Robert Street has written a best-seller about flying called *Going Up*, but he's never actually been in a plane, so when the champion aviator, Gaillard, challenges him to an aerial contest with the girl they both love as the prize, Street has to get down to some hurried conning. When the contest takes place, Street stays up the longer and wins . . . because his lessons hadn't got as far as teaching him how to come down.

Songs: "Hello! Hello!" (Miss Zonne &c.), "I'll Bet You" (John Gordon), "I Want a Boy (who's determined to do what I say)" (Madeleine, Hoppy), "If You Look in Her Eyes" (Madeleine, Grace), "Going Up" (Gaillard &c.), Finale Act 1: reprise "Going Up," "The Touch of a Woman's Hand" (Grace), "Down! Up!" (Street, Brown, Brooks, Robinson), "Do It for Me" (Hoppy, Madeleine), "Everybody Ought to Know How to Do the Tickle-Toe" (Grace), "Kiss Me" (Grace, Gaillard), reprise "When You Look in Her Eyes" (Grace, Street), Finale Act 2: reprises "Hip Hooray! See the Crowds Appearing" (chorus), "There's a Brand New Hero" (Hoppy, Madeleine, &c.), "Here's to the Two of You" (Grace), reprise "Going Up" (chorus), Finale Act 3: reprises "Going Up"/"Tickle Toe."

In spite of its "play" backbone, *Going Up* was not produced as a small-house musical. It was mounted by George Cohan and his partner Sam Harris at the 1,200-plus seater Liberty (where there was plenty of room for a sizeable chorus to dance the "Tickle Toe" en masse and the airplanes to hurtle spectacularly across the sky), and went on from there to make a smash at the London Gaiety Theatre—outrunning such modern winners as *Tonight's the Night* and *Theodore & Co.*, and becoming the biggest hit that house had seen since the heyday of George Edwardes—and another in Australia, where it joined the handful of musical comedies from both sides of the Atlantic (*High Jinks, Kissing Time, A Night Out, So Long, Letty, Tonight's the Night*) which were the down-under blockbusters of their time.

The small-scale Broadway musical did co-exist with the middle-to-larger-scale musical comedy of the *So Long, Letty* and *Going Up* kind, and Hirsch later ventured briefly in that direction, but it was another songwriter, another and much more experienced veteran of the interpolated song habit, who became the favorite musician for such intimate pieces in the early 1910s: Jerome Kern (1885–1945). Kern had spent almost a decade providing single numbers or handfuls of songs as additional material for shows both in Britain and in America. Initially, the shows in question had been musical comedies of the Gaiety type, loose-limbed and loosely constructed and capable of taking in almost any song on any of the standard topics and sentiments without too much problem, and put-into-shows Kern numbers such as "How'd You Like to Spoon with Me?" or "They Didn't Believe Me" became popular favorites. However, since the arrival of the all-conquering European Operette on American shores, the songwriter's west-of-the-Atlantic ditties had been sandwiched much less congruously between slices of Fall, Straus, Ziehrer, Heuberger, Gilbert, Eysler, and Jacobi. In 1912 Kern ventured for the first time with a complete set of show songs of his own, and thereafter he turned out a veritable stream of musical comedies for the American stage. In the manner of the time, a good number of these were made-over comedies—versions of a piece by *Naughty Marietta* author Rida Johnson Young, of the French farce *Une nuit de noces*, a revamped and remusicked edition of the charming London show *Mr Popple (of Ippleton)*, a musicalized version of the American play *Over Night*— and a small handful of them were presented not on the stage of such standard-sized houses as the George M. Cohan, the Casino, or the Knickerbocker, but at a little 299-seater called the Princess Theatre on West 39th and Broadway.

Nobody Home (the remake of *Mr Popple*) did fairly, and the musicalized *Over Night (Very Good Eddie)* did decidedly well, before the little series came to a peak in 1917 with one of the jolliest musical comedies of its era, the merrily farcical *Oh, Boy!*, and then faded away after the rather routine *Oh, Lady! Lady!!* These last two pieces, and a third—a remake of the George Ade schooldays comedy *The College Widow* as the sweetly ingenuous *Leave It to Jane*, which had been intended for the Princess but ultimately played a larger and more lucrative house— were the work of a prolific trio of writers: the Anglo-American librettist and adapter Guy Bolton, English novelist and lyricist "Plum" Wodehouse, and Kern. Their little spate together of two and a half successes and two and a half flops—even though what success *Oh, Boy!* and *Leave It to Jane* had was limited solely to America—would, years later, win them a surprising sort of three-headed cult status, and the phrase "the Princess Theatre musicals"—a group whose two and a half successes had totted up audience figures a fraction of the size of other shows around town—would be strangely referred to as if they had some kind of significance. However, significant or not, *Oh, Boy!* was still a cracking piece of musical comedy, and even if it failed to appeal to the world in general in the way that its fellow 1917er *Going Up* had done, it joined with that piece in confirming the new healthiness of the Broadway musical comedy.

OH BOY!, a musical comedy in 2 acts by Guy Bolton and P. G. Wodehouse. Music by Jerome Kern. Produced at the Princess Theatre, New York, 20 February 1917.

Characters: Jim Marvin, Lou Ellen Carter, George Budd, Jackie Simpson, Judge Carter, Mrs Carter, Miss Penelope Budd, Briggs, Constable Simms, Jane Packard, Polly Andrus, &c.

Plot: George and Lou Ellen have been secretly married—secretly, because her parents wouldn't approve of him, and his money source of a Quaker aunt thinks he's far too young. But their wedding night develops into a farce. George's flat is invaded by a loud partying pal and his tail of girls, Lou Ellen is forced for pretence's sake to go back to her family home, and then a runaway criminal, pursued by the police, climbs through the window. Jackie's "crime" is that, during a kind of ruckus provoked by a naughty old gentleman at a rather lively club, she bopped an interfering policeman in the eye. Before the night is out, Jackie has posed as the new Mrs Budd, and as the Quaker aunt, but— helped by the fact that the naughty old gentleman at the lively club has turned out to be Lou Ellen's theoretically severe papa, she also helps things to a happy ending in which she is rewarded (though some would call it the opposite) with the eternal devotion of George's loud and partying pal.

Songs: "Let's Make a Night of It" (ensemble), "You Never Knew about Me" (George, Lou Ellen), "A Packet of Seeds" (Jim, Jane, Polly, &c.), "An Old-Fashioned Wife" (Lou Ellen), "A Pal Like You" (Jackie, Jim), "I'll Just Dream about You" (George), "Till the Clouds Roll By" (George,

Jackie), "A Little Bit of Ribbon" (Jane), "The First Day in May" (Jackie, Jim, George), "Koo-la-loo" (Jim &c.), Dance (featured dance duo), "Rolled into One (Jackie), "Oh, Daddy, Please" (George, Lou Ellen, Judge), "Nesting Time in Flatbush" (Jackie, Jim), "Words Are Not Needed" (Lou Ellen), "Flubby Dub the Caveman" (Jackie, Jim, George), Finale Act 2. Additional and alternative songs included "Wedding Bells."

Although the Princess Theatre venture lasted only four years, the small-scale musical play—with its limited settings, limited cast (though, unlike Paris, Broadway stopped short of renouncing the chorus girl), and limited musical backup—didn't disappear with it. In fact, it went onwards and upwards, and in 1919 it was one of Broadway's other small houses, the 700-odd-place Vanderbilt Theatre under producer Carle Carleton, which turned out the international hit that the Princess hadn't managed to produce. The show was called *Irene*, and it was a musical version of an unsuccessful comedy written three years earlier by *Going Up*'s James Montgomery (1882–1966), equipped with songs composed by Harry Tierney (1890–1965)—whose major Broadway credit to date was a half-dozen interpolated songs for a Shubert brothers' botch of an imported musical comedy that had once been by Leo Ascher—and Tin Pan Alley lyricist Joseph McCarthy (1885–1943), who had made his Broadway bow with the songwords for the last show (also by Montgomery) at the Vanderbilt. *Irene*, with its Cinderella-style story of a poor but pure and pretty lassie who wins herself the American equivalent of a (well-heeled) fairy prince, was a fine example of the sentimental musical comedy which would become the most popular kind of Broadway musical play over the years to come, but its appeal and success went far beyond Broadway. This pretty little tale, with its light-as-a-leaf songs and its charming dances, carried on after a two-year stint in New York not only to capture Britain and Australia, but even to penetrate deep into the Continent. Even Budapest took time off from its enjoyment of French musical comedy to make the acquaintance of *A tündérek cséldje*, or "the fairy-like servant girl, a spectacular American operett" (!), at the little Lujza Blaha Színház while the original still ran on in America.

IRENE, a musical comedy in 2 acts by James Montgomery, based on his play *Irene O'Dare*. Lyrics by Joseph McCarthy. Music by Harry Tierney. Produced at the Vanderbilt Theatre, New York, 18 November 1919.

Characters: Irene O'Dare, Mrs O'Dare, Jane Gilmour, Helen Cheston, Donald Marshall, Mrs Marshall, Madame Lucy, J. P. Bowden, Robert Harrison, Lawrence Hadley, Eleanor Worth, Mrs Cheston, &c.

Plot: A little Irish–New Yorkish shopgirl called Irene O'Dare gets sent out on a professional mission to the mansion of the sighworthily wealthy Marshall family, and there she catches the eye of the young gentleman of the house. In spite of her mother's Irish conviction that there's an ulterior motive of the most ruinous kind lurking behind young Donald's actions, Irene accepts his offer to help her get on in the world, and happily assumes the place as a model with a friendly couturier called Madame Lucy that he finds her. Madame Lucy (who is, to mother's alarm, a man) sends

Irene to model his gowns at a great ball in Long Island. She causes a winsomely glamorous, all-singing and all-dancing sensation, and, of course, it is only the space of an act before Donald is offering to make an Irish-American Princess out of the little shopgirl.

Songs: Opening (ensemble), "Hobbies" (Eleanor &c.), "Alice Blue Gown" (Irene), "Castle of Dreams" (Eleanor &c.), "The Talk of the Town" (Lucy, Jane, Helen), "To Be Worthy of You" (Irene &c.), Finale Act 1, Opening Act 2, "We're Getting Away with It" (Lucy, Donald, Robert, Jane, Helen), "Irene" (Irene), "To Love You" (Bowden, Irene), "Sky Rocket" (Irene), "(The) Last Part of Every Party" (Jane, Helen, &c.), "There's Something in the Air" (ensemble), Finale Act 2.

The Vanderbilt went on turning out delightful smallish-scale musical comedies for a number of years, and the little house scored another hit with a second show which would follow *Irene* not only to Britain and Australia but also into Central Europe. For *Little Jessie James*, however, author Harlan Thompson (1890–1966) put aside the sentimental, Cinderella-style story that was central to *Irene* and her ilk, and went instead for a rip-roaring piece of farcical musical comedy which centered round a retractable bed. It was as near to the knuckle and to the French style as it was possible to be in the age and place, and, since songwriter Harry Archer (1888–1960) supplied an up-to-date, dancing score topped by a veritable international hit song ("I Love You") to go with all the high-spirited high jinks, success was assured. Archer and Thompson followed *Little Jessie James* with several other happy little comedy musicals before the Vanderbilt series followed the Princess one into the past, leaving Broadway to concentrate thereafter mostly on larger and more lavishly staged entertainments.

Jerome Kern—following his little detour into the intimate theater—had already set off down the same track, and that track had swiftly led him to his own first world-sized hit. It was the newest example of the Cinderella brand of musical. After *Irene*, and after Hirsch's like-minded and happily lilting *Mary*, Guy Bolton took his turn at the type of tale of the time and turned out the story of *Sally*. It wasn't a very complicated story. A little blonde restaurant dishwasher with yearnings to be a dancer stands in for a flamboyant and notorious Continental ballerina at a party and ends up with a starring part in *The Ziegfeld Follies* and, of course, the standard handsome American fairy prince. As a piece of stage writing, it was far from *Little Jessie James* or its own author's *Oh, Boy!* in quality, but it fulfilled its purpose of displaying its dancing star, Marilyn(n) Miller, in a virtual variety-musical mélange of dance and song, and its chief low comedian in some cheerfully low comedy, to excellent effect. The songs in question were the work of Kern and expatriate British lyricist Clifford Grey (1887–1941), and they included one which would become a long-lived favorite. As *Sally* made herself loved through long runs in America, in Britain, and in Australia, "Look for the Silver Lining" became established as the latest standard to add to the already bulging Jerome Kern songbook.

In the couple of years following the production of *Sally*, several other Broadway musicals went out to further-flung parts of the world in the wake of their initial success on home ground. Hirsch followed up with *The O'Brien Girl,* which made a decided hit in Australia, and George

No, No, Nanette: The ladies of the piece both take their turn at fits of the "Where-Has-My-Hubby-Gone Blues." But it's all just a little bit of not-really-naughty-at-all misunderstanding.

M. Cohan made a successful shot at a Cinderella musical with the tale of *Little Nellie Kelly*, while Kern turned out *Good Morning, Dearie* and Bolton teamed with his *Very Good Eddie* partner, Philip Bartholomae (1880–1947), on an odd throwback of a piece called *Tangerine*, which, in turn-of-the-century style, dumped some quarreling Americans on a crazy tropical island to the accompaniment of some songs by hack writers Carlo and Sanders. Then, in 1924, came the big one: the keystone show which—more than *Going Up* had done, more than *Irene* had done—would establish the jazz-age American musical throughout the world. It was called *No, No, Nanette*.

NO, NO, NANETTE, a musical comedy in 3 acts by Frank Mandel and Otto Harbach, based on *My Lady Friends* by Mandel and Emil Nyitray (and *Oh! James* by May Edgington). Lyrics by Otto Harbach and Irving Caesar. Music by Vincent Youmans. Produced at the Harris Theatre, Chicago, 7 May 1924.

Characters: Jimmy Smith, Sue Smith, Nanette, Billy Early, Lucille Early, Tom Trainor, Winnie, Betty, Flora, Pauline, &c.

Plot: Sue Smith, wife of wealthy Jimmy, is extremely careful with his money so, rather than let it bank up and go moldy, Jimmy gets his kicks spending it on a trio of cute little vampires. But the time comes when the cute little vampires threaten to become an embarrassment, and Jimmy has to get his lawyer pal Billy amicably to terminate their cute little arrangements. Billy assembles the girls at Atlantic City for the termination but, unfortunately, Jimmy and his niece Nanette are weekending at Atlantic City at the same time. Then Billy's suspicious wife Lucille and an unbelieving Sue turn up to find out what's going on, and things get to look a lot worse than they really are before they start getting better. But since no one actually did anything they oughtn't, the little sea-breeze that has momentarily ruffled a brace of devoted marriages soon blows itself out.

Songs: "How Do You Do?" ["Flappers Are We"] (chorus, Pauline), "The Call of the Sea" (Billy), "Too Many Rings Around Rosie" (Lucille), "I'm Waiting for You" (Nanette, Tom), "I Want to Be Happy" (Jimmy, Nanette), "No, No, Nanette" (Nanette), Finale Act 1: "It's Always No, No, No," "The Deep Blue Sea" (Nanette), "My Doctor" (Pauline), "Fight over Me" (Jimmy, Winnie, Betty), "Tea for Two" (Nanette, Tom), "You Can Dance with Any Girl" (Lucille, Billy), reprise "I Want to Be Happy" (Jimmy, Billy, Winnie, Betty, Flora), Finale Act 2: "Society's Excited," "Hello, Hello, Telephone Girlie" (Billy, Betty, Winnie, Flora), Where-Has-My-Hubby-Gone Blues: "Who's the Who?" (Lucille), "Pay Day Pauline" (Pauline), Finale Act 3. Alternative and added songs include "Take a Little One-Step" (by Youmans/Zelda Sears) (Billy, Nanette), "I've Confessed to the Breeze" (Tom, Nanette).

No, No, Nanette was a fine example of an American jazz-age musical comedy. Its book was light, lively, and well constructed on the bones of the successful modern comedy that was its original, it was up-to-date in its style, its sometimes verging-on-the-slangy dialogue, and its characters, and it was just sufficiently "naughty" with its suggestion that there actually did exist a clean-living American husband (the play's original had been British!) who might sneak off to the seaside for an adulterous weekend with a floozie, without being naughty enough actually to have such a thing happen. It was wholly pleasant and amusing, and it kept that tone of smiling merriment throughout the evening, undamaged by the seeming falling apart of each and every couple in the cast. For Mandel and his co-writers were careful to let us know in advance what the characters don't know—nothing untoward has happened: it's all a matter of a good old musical comedy misunderstanding.

The comedy part of this particular musical was also nicely modern. *No, No, Nanette*'s only concession to the old-days passion for low comedy was the inclusion of a stock comedy maid, equipped with two incidental comedy songs (which were cut when the show was exported). There was no equivalent of the jokey, clowning, deposed low-comedy Grand Duke who helped the little dishwasher to stardom in *Sally*, no equivalent of the extravagantly fake French dressmaker who had launched *Irene* towards her rich husband. The characters of *No, No, Nanette* were part of a play—a very flimsy, innocuous play, but a four-cornered play for all that—and they were simply modern New Yorkers written and played as such. And such nice people to spend an evening with.

The music of the show was, similarly, splendidly in the modern mode. Songwriter Vincent Youmans (1898–1946) matched his numbers to the style and weight of the story delightfully, and turned out a bookful of catchily rhythmic melodies which would become long-term favorites: Tom and Nanette's loping little dream of "Tea for Two," Jimmy's ingenuously good-hearted "I Want to Be Happy" with its assertion "but I won't be happy till I've made you happy too," Lucille's song-and-dance warning to her mate that "You Can Dance with Any Girl at All (as long as you come home to me)" or, in one of the show's few slower moments, her bluesical view of a faithless husband in "Who's the Who?" Nanette—the repressed lass who wants to raise a little jazz-age hell before she settles down to married life—revolted in prettily soprano tones at always being told "No, No, Nanette," and the chorus responded, but, in the modern way, concerted music was at a minimum, even though the score did feature a constructed second-act finale which took the action through to the end rather than being just a couple of unison reprises of the most pluggable numbers of the act.

However, what made the numbers of *No, No, Nanette* and its kind so very attractive to theatergoers was their danceability. It was nothing new for a show to break or end almost every song with a dance—even way back in burlesque days a breakdown or a cellarflap had been tacked into or onto most numbers—but it was new for those dances to be dances of the rhythmic modernity and choreographic expertise that the world was now being shown in these postwar years. Exhibitions of elegant one-to-one dancing, specialty dances (including the durable, not to say inextinguishable, tap-dance) which were more than a mere solo novelty like the old-time skipping-rope dance or the graceful skirt-dance, platoons of chorines who no longer just stepped and/or kicked and performed two or three very basic steps in the guise of "ballet," but (as much as the stage space would allow) actually danced. Everybody danced. From the moment Billy and the chorus got the proceedings moving, singing and dancing a routine about the seaside all round a city drawing room, through Tom and Nanette's little one-to-one pieces together, via such moments as the "challenge" dance in which two of the cuties respond to Jimmy's invitation to "Fight over Me," the chorus's performance of "Hello, Hello, Telephone Girlie," Lucille's One-Step, and Billy and Nanette's Two-Step, the show rarely stopped dancing for long. Dancing to the rhythms of the 1920s, with both grace and style as well as unbounded energy.

It was this dance element which proved to be *Nanette*'s most overwhelming attraction when the show went abroad, and, indeed, as it traveled—first to Britain and then all across the European continent—this piece of dancing-and-laughter musical comedy became a veritable showcase for modern American dance music and modern choreography. Since American musicals had been sighted only rarely in the theaters of Europe up to the time of *Nanette*'s arrival, the show caused a sensation with its style and its novelty, establishing the Broadway jazz-age musical right across the world, and making itself an indelible place in the history of the musical theater.

And so the dancing musical comedy became a feature of the age, as dancing stars such as *Sally*'s Marilyn(n) Miller—who scored again in a messy but tuneful more-of-the-same follow-up as *Sunny*—or the skillful brother and sister team of Adele and Fred Astaire, who exported a series of musicals (*For Goodness' Sake, Lady, Be Good!, Funny Face*) from Broadway to London for tidy runs, appeared top-billed on Broadway marquees.

Over the few years following the keystone success of *No, No, Nanette*, a fine flow of up-to-date musical comedies followed their most famous sister out of America and around the world, musical comedies equipped with modern melodies credited to a variety of modern songsmiths. Alongside Hirsch, Youmans, and Kern, alongside Harry Tierney and Harry Archer, there appeared on the playbills of the world such names as Con Conrad (1891–1938), George Gershwin (1898–1937), the all-said-in-one-breath team of De Sylva, Brown, and Henderson—Buddy De Sylva (1895–1950), Lew Brown (1893–1958), and Ray Henderson (1896–1970)—and Richard Rodgers (1902–1979) and his songwriting partner Lorenz Hart (1895–1943). And above those names were such titles as *Mercenary Mary, Lady, Be Good !, Sunny, Kitty's Kisses, Oh, Kay!, Hit the Deck, Good News*, and *A Connecticut Yankee*.

The years—with a little bit of help from a few folk who for one reason or another have had an interest in making one songwriter or another fashionable and profitable, and also from the musical cinema—have dealt strangely with the shows of this period, their writers and songwriters and their reputations. As a result, some of the internationally most successful musicals of the American 1920s have, three-quarters of a century down the line, been shoved into virtual oblivion, while others—less thoroughly popular in their own time—survive, alongside *No, No, Nanette*, as the representatives of the first great age of the American musical stage. *Little Jessie James*, the most widely seen of the period's intimate musicals, is one such casualty, but an even more glaring one is the work of vaudevillian and songwriter Con Conrad.

The German-American Conrad (real name, Conrad Dober) did everything he should to be remembered. He turned out some top-notch singles ("Ma, He's Makin' Eyes at Me," "Margie," "Singin' the Blues"), provided the songs for three Broadway successes in three years in a very short but sweet stage career, and then headed for Hollywood, where he promptly won movieland's first ever "best song" Oscar for his song "The Continental." And he died young—aged just 47. But even that didn't make him durably fashionable. In the 1920s, however, Conrad flew high, and two of his small set of stage shows went out from Broadway to become major international hits— probably the two most outstanding musical comedy hits, in fact, to have come out of America in the post-*Nanette* years. And the greatest of these was *Mercenary Mary*.

Mercenary Mary was built well and truly on the *Nanette* model. It was even based on another play co-written by *His Lady Friends* author Emil Nyitray, one which had much of the same flavor as the nearly-naughty *Nanette*, and it employed Irving Caesar—who had had such success with his songwords for *Nanette*'s "I Want to Be Happy" and "Tea for Two"—as its lyricist. The show had only an average Broadway run, but—like *The Belle of New York*'s—that initial record proved to be a fallacious one. *Mercenary Mary* went on to London, where it promptly outran every other U.S. musical comedy of its era, bar the unchallengeable *Nanette*, to Australia, to Paris, and finally to Budapest where it did even better, establishing itself quite simply as the most successful American musical of all time on Hungarian soil, even over and above the monolithic *Nanette*.

MERCENARY MARY, a musical comedy in 3 acts by Isabel Leighton and William B. Friedlander, based on *What's Your Wife Doing?* by Herbert Hall Winslow and Emil Nyitray. Lyrics by Irving Caesar. Music by Con Conrad and William B. Friedlander. Produced at the Longacre Theatre, New York, 13 April 1925.

Characters: Jerry, Norah, Mary Skinner, Chris Skinner, Grandpa Skinner, Edith Somers, Patrick O'Brien, Lyman Webster, Judge Somers, June, Bellamy Shepard, &c.

Plot: Chris and Mary have to decided to get divorced. Only temporarily, but long enough for Chris's rich grandpa (who disapproves of her) to rewrite his will in Chris's favor. The "other man" in the divorce will be penniless Jerry, Mary's old flame, and his reward will be a share in the pickings. Sufficient of a share to allow him to come up to the financial standards demanded by the rich and suspicious uncle of his sweetheart, June. Things start to go wrong when grandpa is late for the little scene of dissension-leading-to-divorce that has been arranged for his benefit. Mary gets nervously tipsy, then takes Jerry's amorous acting for real revived romance, and trouble looms. It looms for a whole other act before the obligatory happy ending.

Songs: "Over a Garden Wall" (Jerry, Edith, &c.), "Just You and I and the Baby" (Patrick, Norah), "Charleston Mad" (June), "Honey, I'm in Love (with you)" (Jerry, Edith), "They Still Look Good" (Grandpa), "Tomorrow" (June, Lyman), Dance (Norah, Patrick), "Come Along" (ensemble), "Mercenary Mary" (Mary), Finale Act 1, Dance (Norah), "Beautiful Baby" (Jerry), "(I want to be a) Chaste Woman" (Mary, Jerry), "Cherchez la femme" (Norah, Patrick, &c.), "Everything's Going to Be All Right" (Jerry, June), Dance specialities (ladies' chorus), Finale Act 2.

Conrad's second show successfully to cross the seas sailed under slightly confusing colors. Herbert Clayton and Jack Waller, the producers of the hit London versions of *No, No, Nanette* and *Mercenary Mary*, purchased the rather more intimate and neatly farcical *Kitty's Kisses* as a follow-up to their two super-sized successes, but on the same trip they also purchased another musical, a piece equipped with numbers by a couple of rising songwriters called Richard Rodgers and Lorenz Hart, and once back in London they settled down to a bit of good old-fashioned botching. They decided not to produce the Rodgers and Hart piece, but they winkled some of the best numbers out of its musical part, and stuck them instead into *Kitty's Kisses'* merry story of understandings and misunderstandings in a hotel room. As a result, the show that was mounted in London was a kind of a hybrid, with a score part Conrad and friends, part Rodgers and friend. And, confusingly—given that it was mostly *Kitty's Kisses*—it was billed under the more attractive title of the rejected show: *The Girl Friend.* *The Girl Friend* which wasn't *The Girl Friend* was, however, a singular success. Singular enough, in fact, that, while both its originals went no further than America in their original shape, Waller and Clayton's bastardized version of *Kitty's Kisses* went on to become a hit in Australia and other English-dancing centers, and also went on to be played on the Continent.

So, the biggest tally of individual hits in this era went to Harbach and Montgomery among the textwriters, and to Youmans, Hirsch, Conrad, Tierney, and the comparatively veteran Kern as songwriters, but oddly enough none of this group of musicians went on to run up the kind of list of subsequent successes that their forerunners, or indeed the French songwriters, had done. Youmans had a second fine success with a sea-going saga called *Hit the Deck*, Hirsch had some song-hits but less theatrical long life out of the pretty, Cinderella-ry *Mary* and a home-town winner in the delightful *The Rainbow Girl*, and Tierney hit the only other real bullseye of his career with a romantic South American-banditland musical called *Rio Rita*, which was a very far cry indeed from *Irene* and the other winning musical comedies of this era in character. Kern chalked up several successes on home ground with pieces such as *The Night Boat* and *Good Morning, Dearie*, but *Sally* and to a lesser degree *Sunny* remained his only international references until he, too, switched to the romantic musical.

There were, however, other writers and musicians who—alongside these megahit-makers—turned out many a musical which won a definite, if more measured, success both at home and abroad, and at the head of that list came songwriter George Gershwin, normally teamed with his lyric-writing brother Ira, and the highly successful threesome of popular-songsmiths De Sylva, Brown, and Henderson.

Between 1924 and 1927, the Gershwin brothers turned out no fewer than five variegated musical comedies which would be seen all around the English-dancing world. Two of them, *Lady, Be Good!* and *Funny Face*, were made to the measure of the dapper dance-and-comedy duo the Astaires, and each found a fine ration of success as performed by the most elegant pair of American dance stars of their era. When the Astaires were not around to play and dance the rôles that had been tailored for them, the shows went altogether less well, so although both musicals put up fine runs on Broadway and the West End they didn't get much further. A third, the story of a little variety performer known as *Tip-Toes* and her two acts of ups-and-downs on the way to wealth, social position, and an American fairy prince, was a vehicle for the delicious dancing soubrette Queenie Smith, but at the other end of the scale there was *Oh, Kay!*—a firmly book musical based on the Parisian hit comedy *La Présidente*, with a light comedy actress who barely danced at all starring in a clever, farcical intrigue. The featured dance routines were still there, but they and their exponent were simply glued into the action as à la mode decoration to a fine piece of musical comedy.

The texts for this set of shows ranged from expert (as in *Oh, Kay!*) to almost non-existent (as in, for example, the altogether less structured *Tell Me More*), and this was one fact which undoubtedly helped the former to survive into later years as a revivable prospect while the latter faded forgettably away. The other fact, of course, was the songs. Gershwin already had popular song hits ranging from "Swanee" and "Stairway to Paradise" to the exciting, pianistic "Rhapsody in Blue" to his credit before scoring his first stage success, but numbers such as "Fascinatin' Rhythm," "Lady, Be Good!," "Kickin' the Clouds Away," "That Certain Feeling," "Someone to Watch over Me," "Clap Yo' Hands," "Do, Do, Do," and "S'Wonderful"—numbers from the energetically rhythmic to the gently lolloping, but all moving merrily along in the dance-tinted idioms of the moment—added materially to his hit-list, as the five musicals made their way to the edge of the English world, and just occasionally beyond. For Paris saw its local "Nanette," Loulou Hégoburu, as Tip-Toes.

In what would turn out to be a hopeless search for another *No, No, Nanette*, Paris also got a glimpse of a De Sylva, Brown, and Henderson musical. The individual pop songs of what was probably the most popular songwriting team in the English-speaking world had been liberally displayed in Parisian variety houses, so it was no surprise to see their first attempt at a stage musical go from Broadway to Britain and then to Paris—not to mention Australia and Budapest. *Good News* was college musical, a tale of schooldays sweethearting whose plot hung on the efforts of footballing hero Tom to get good enough grades to be allowed to play in the Big Game. It was what hung on the plot, however, which was all important: the series of high-energy dances, zingy numbers, or wide-eyed teenage love songs performed by the youngsters who made up the cast—the cakewalky-cum-Charlestonny "Varsity Drag," "The Best Things in Life Are Free," "Good News," "Lucky in Love." *Good News* was a full-sized hit on Broadway, but oddly enough it failed to catch on in its British, French, and Australian productions, and it was left to Budapest to give what it called "Schoolboy Love" its best transatlantic reception, a reception which, however, didn't come near to that won there by *Mercenary Mary*. De Sylva, Brown, and Henderson went on to secure a series of good Broadway runs with a series of comical musicals—*Manhattan Mary, Hold Everything!, Follow Thru, Flying High*—which were long on lively numbers and routines but getting almost as short on book as the old Gaiety shows. Both *Hold Everything!* and *Follow Thru* were seen abroad but, by and large, the pick of the eminently detachable songs from the shows—pieces such as "You're the Cream in My Coffee" and "Button up Your Overcoat"—traveled and lasted very much better than the shows which existed to display them.

The overwhelming fashion of these years for anything that sang and danced with an American accent meant that a number of American songwriters wrote not only for the home stage but also for, in particular, the London theater. Kern—an old habitué of the London stage—provided the West End's Winter Garden Theatre with two "American" shows (*The Cabaret Girl, The Beauty Prize*), then Gershwin—who had already musicked a couple of London revues—took over and stuck together a score of half-used and half-new numbers to illustrate the English story of *Primrose*. And in 1927 the rising team of Rodgers and Hart took a turn at a London musical. *Lido Lady* wasn't a very wonderful show. It was sort of cluttered together as a vehicle for the popular comedy team of Jack Hulbert and Cicely Courtneidge and it, too, sported a patchwork score of proven and new numbers, one which didn't always do its songwriters much credit. But *Lido Lady* ran for eight months (259 performances) in London, it was exported to Australia and to Paris, and, with *A Connecticut Yankee* and *Heads Up* failing emphatically away from home, *Peggy-Ann* failing less emphatically, and *The Girl Friend* being eviscerated for the benefit of *Kitty's Kisses*, it actually ended up being the most successful of its writers' works outside America.

In America, however, the pair did rather better. Between 1926 and 1931, when they temporarily abandoned Broadway for Hollywood, the songwriters illustrated a dozen musical comedies. *A Connecticut Yankee*, a musical version of a comical Mark Twain story which yet again utilized the favorite musical-comedy idea of a quarter-of-a-century earlier—an American plonked down in strange, foreign places—proved to be the best liked among them, but a remake of the favorite old dream-sequence show *Tillie's Nightmare* as *Peggy-Ann* and the original version of *The Girl Friend* also had fine runs. But, as with so many contemporary shows, it was the songs that came out of those shows (or that were stuck into them) which proved to be the enduring element. In an era when American songs were the rage from one end of the world to the other, pieces such as "The Blue Room," "Mountain Greenery," "You Took Advantage of Me," "My Heart Stood Still," and "With a Song in My Heart" established themselves via performance out of the show and on the newly talking cinema screen in a way, and in areas, that the shows themselves never did.

There were other American musical comedies, too, which won varying degrees of success on Broadway and around America but which failed to travel in the way that the most widely popular pieces did. Some—like a series of very personal pieces for the exuberantly eccentric comedy team the Marx Brothers, or a jolly old-fashioned jaunt called *Shuffle Along*, which was played by a cast of black singers and dancers—were quite simply too closely attached to the performers for whom they had been created to be reproducible elsewhere, while others just failed to catch the imagination of producers further abroad—notably in a London which was still very much the gateway to and from Europe. However, London was far from infallible in its choices, and it was noticeable that Australia—always in these years an interesting "judge" of English-language theater—picked up a good number of these American musical comedies which weren't played in London, and sometimes did very well with them. The outstanding example was the Los Angeles musical *So Long, Letty*, which became a perennial favorite down under, but pieces such as the shipboard Friml/Harbach *You're in Love*, with its above-the-orchestra sleepwalking scene, Hirsch's Cinderella-ry *The O'Brien Girl*, or, one notch down, the cowboys-and-comics musical *Whoopee* and Cohan's T*he Rise of Rosie O'Reilly* also did well on colonial stages.

However, during the 1920s the American stage was doing more than turning out virtually all that was the most enjoyable in the way of English musical comedy. In spite of the fact that Broadway had relied for many years on Continental sources for its romantic musicals, and that the most successful practitioners of the genre up to that time—Herbert and Friml—had latterly turned their attentions very largely to trying to write à la mode musical comedy, the home-made romantic musical, which had hardly known a hit since Friml's *The Firefly* in 1912, was to rise during the 1920s to its most successful heights.

The spur to this slightly surprising development was the vast success won by some recently imported, Continental musicals, and, in particular, by the American remake of the Viennese

THE INTERNATIONAL HIT PARADE OF AMERICAN MUSICAL COMEDIES OF 1910–1930

The list is arranged in the order of the length of the shows' original London runs. The original Broadway run figures are given in brackets, and other contemporary main center productions are noted after the London figure. Aust= Australia, Hun=Hungary, Fr=France, Aut=Austria, Ger=Germany.

No, No, Nanette (Youmans/Caesar/Harbach, Mandel) [321]	665 /Aust, Fr, Aut, Ger
Going Up (Hirsch/Montgomery, Harbach) [351]	574/Aust
Mercenary Mary (Conrad, Friedlander/Caesar/Leighton, Friedlander) [136]	446/Aust, Fr, Hun
Kitty's Kisses (as The Girlfriend) (Conrad/Harbach, Bartholomae) [170]	421/Aust, Hun
Irene (Tierney/McCarthy/Montgomery) [670]	399/Aust, Hun
Sally (Kern/ Grey/Bolton) [570]	387/Aust
High Jinks (Friml/Harbach) [217]	383/Aust
Sunny (Kern/Harbach, Hammerstein) [517]	363/Aust
Lady, Be Good! (G. Gershwin/I. Gershwin/F. Thompson, Bolton) [329]	326/Aust
Hit the Deck (Youmans/Grey, Robin/Fields) [352]	277/Aust, Fr
Little Nellie Kelly (Cohan) [274]	265/Aust
Funny Face (G. Gershwin/I. Gershwin/F. Thompson, Gerard Smith) [244]	263/Aust
Tell Me More (G. Gershwin/I. Gershwin, De Sylva/Wells, F. Thompson) [100]	263/Aust
Oh, Kay! (G. Gershwin/I. Gershwin/Wodehouse, Bolton) [256]	214
Sons o' Guns (Swanstrom, B. Davis, Coots/F. Thompson et al.) [297]	211/Aust
Queen High (Gensler/De Sylva/Schwab) [378]	198/Aust
Little Jessie James (as Lucky Break, 1934) (Archer/H. Thompson) [393]	198/Aust, Ger, Hun
Poppy (S. Jones/D. Donnelly) [344]	188
Tip Toes (G. Gershwin/I. Gershwin/F. Thompson, Bolton) [192]	182/Aust, Fr
Oh! Oh! Delphine (Caryll/McLellan) [258]	174/Aust
Hold Everything (Brown, Henderson, De Sylva, McGowan) [413]	173
His Little Widows (Schroeder/Johnson Young, Duncan) [72]	172/Aust
Oh, Boy! (as Oh, Joy!) (Kern/Wodehouse/Bolton) [475]	167/Aust
Kid Boots (Tierney/McCarthy/Harbach, McGuire) [482]	163/Aust
Follow Thru (Brown, Henderson, De Sylva, Schwab) [401]	148/Aust
The Blue Kitten (Friml/Harbach, Duncan) [140]	140
Peggy-Ann (Rodgers/Hart/Fields) [354]	134
Good News (Brown, Henderson, De Sylva, Schwab) [551]	132/Fr, Hun
The Pink Lady (Caryll/McLellan) [312]	124*/Aust, Fr, Hun
The Five o'Clock Girl (Ruby, Kalmar/Bolton, F. Thompson) [278]	122
Katinka (Friml/Harbach, B. Davis) [220]	108/Aust
The Only Girl (Herbert/Blossom) [240]	107
Mary (Hirsch/Harbach, Mandel) [219]	90/Aust
Topsy and Eva (R. Duncan, V. Duncan/Cushing) [165]	89
Marjolaine (Felix/Hooker/Cushing) [136]	67
The Little Whopper (Friml/Harbach, Dudley) [224]	53/Aust

Very Good Eddie (Kern/Bartholomae, Bolton) [342]   48/Aust
A Connecticut Yankee (Rodgers/Hart/Fields) [421]   43
Happy Go Lucky (Johnstone/Cook/Vernon) [52]   37
Castles in the Air (Wenrich/Peck) [162]   28/Aust
Sometime (Friml/Johnson Young) [283]   28
Heads Up (Rodgers/Hart/McGowan) [144]   20
The Cocoanuts (Berlin/Jackson) [375]   16
Angel Face (Herbert/R. B. Smith/H. B. Smith) [57]   13

* played by a visiting unit company

Other Broadway musicals comedies produced in Australia, but not in the UK: *So Long, Letty, Canary Cottage, You're in Love, The Red Widow, Three Twins, Oh, Lady! Lady!!, Tangerine, Leave It to Jane, The O'Brien Girl, Good Morning, Dearie, Betty Lee, The Rise of Rosie O'Reilly, Listen Lester, Whoopee*

show *Das Dreimäderlhaus*. This super-sentimental story of heartbroken love illustrated by a score of homogenized Schubert music had, under the title *Blossom Time*, triumphed all over the country as one of the most genuinely popular musicals of all time. The romantic musical—lush, lavish, and large in story, in staging, and in music—had proven that it could be a best-seller in postwar America, so it was judged a propitious time to produce more such pieces, alongside the slick and snazzy musical comedies. But these shows didn't have to come from the Continent. America had its own "Continental" composers, and they were about to prove that they could turn out hits that were as big even as *Blossom Time*.

The two composers who were responsible for the scores of those shows which would make the mid-1920s the heyday of the American romantic musical were both from Europe. Rudolf Friml came from Prague, Sigmund Romberg (1887–1951) from Hungary. But both of them had been many years in America, and both were thoroughly experienced in working for the Broadway musical stage. Friml, of course, already had a fine track-record with pieces ranging from *The Firefly*, with its ex-operatic leading lady, to the enormously successful *High Jinks* to his credit. Romberg, on the other hand, had been a musical pieceworker for the Shubert brothers, supplying a stream of those additional numbers which were used to botch the scores of Continental shows, making them less "Continental" for what was supposed to be local tastes. Among his Americanizations had been *Das Dreimäderlhaus-Blossom Time*. Both these men hit paydirt with homegrown musicals in the year 1924. Friml set to music what looked suspiciously like an adaptation of the Broadway play *Tiger Rose*, while Romberg musicked a version of the successful German play *Alt Heidelberg*, and—as *Rose Marie* and *The Student Prince*—their shows rocketed the homegrown romantic musical to the very top of the heap.

Rose Marie: "Totem-tom-tom!" Wanda, the dancing murderess, leads a vast troupe of chorines in the spectacular highlight of the most successful romantic musical to come out of 1920s Broadway.

ROSE MARIE, a musical play in 2 acts by Oscar Hammerstein II and Otto Harbach. Music by Rudolf Friml and Herbert Stothart. Produced at the Imperial Theatre, New York, 2 September 1924.

Characters: Émile La Flamme, Rose Marie La Flamme, Hard-Boiled Herman, Jim Kenyon, Sergeant Malone, Lady Jane, Edward Hawley, Blackeagle, Wanda, Ethel Brander, &c.

Plot: The Canadian Rockies trapper Émile La Flamme wants his sister, Rose Marie, to wed the well-off city man Edward Hawley, but she refuses. She is in love with the miner, Jim Kenyon. Hawley has Jim accused of the murder of the Indian Blackeagle, with whom Kenyon had a mining claim dispute, and while the accused man flees from the Mounties, Émile takes Rose Marie down from the mountains to the city, where Hawley can more easily convince her of the desirability of a comfortably-off life. But when Wanda, once Hawley's and later the Indian's mistress, hears that the two are to be wed, she confesses. She murdered her drunken concubine in defence of the man she loves—Hawley. The Mounties have their woman, and Rose Marie can return to the mountains where the man she loves is waiting for her.

Songs: "Vive la Canadienne" (chorus), "Hard-Boiled Herman" (Herman), "Rose Marie" (Jim, Malone), "Lak Jeem" (Rose Marie), "The Mounties" (Malone), Indian Love Call: "When I'm Calling You" (Rose Marie, Jim), "Pretty Things" (Rose Marie), Eccentric Dance (Herman, girls), "Why Shouldn't We?" (Herman, Jane), "Totem-tom-tom" (Wanda &c.), Finale Act 1: "Well, It's Time to Get Ready," reprise "Pretty Things" (chorus), "Only a Kiss" (Malone, Jane, Herman), Finaletto: "I Love Him" (Rose Marie &c.), "The Minuet of the Minute" (Rose Marie, Herman), Wanda Waltz, "One Man Woman" (Jane), "The Door[way] of My Dreams" (Rose Marie), Bridal Finale: "Come, Rose Marie," Finale Act 2: "Dear Place, Where Once I Thought."

THE STUDENT PRINCE, a musical play in 4 (latterly 2) acts by Dorothy Donnelly, based on *Alt-Heidelberg* by Wilhelm Meyer-Förster and its American adaptation *Old Heidelberg* by Rudolf Bleichman. Music by Sigmund Romberg. Produced at Jolson Theatre, New York, 2 December 1924.

Characters: Prince Karl-Franz, Dr Engel, Count von Mark, Lutz, Hubert, Josef Ruder, Gretchen, Kathie, Toni, Detlef, von Asterberg, Lucas, Princess Margaret, Grand Duchess Anastasia, Captain Tarnitz.

Plot: Karl-Franz of Karlsberg comes to Heidelberg to attend the local University and takes lodging, along with his tutor and his valet, at Ruder's "Inn of the Three Golden Apples." For Karl-Franz this is the opportunity long dreamed of to lead a normal young man's life rather than one constricted by the demands of the Karlsberg court, and he is soon taking advantage of his new freedom by falling duet-fully in love with Ruder's niece, Kathie. But before he has had time to taste life to the full, he is recalled to Karlsberg. His grandfather, the king, is dying. Karl-Franz will soon succeed to the throne, and already he is expected to make a state marriage with the Princess Margaret. He cannot resist the throne, but for years he resists the marriage. Finally he goes to Heidelberg once more, to find Kathie, but Margaret has got there first, and all has been explained. Kathie knows that Karl-Franz must fulfil the duty his rank imposes on him, and so when the two do meet again it is only to say "goodbye."

Songs: "By Our Bearing So Sedate" (chorus), "Golden Days" (Engel, Prince), "To the Inn We're Marching" (students), Drinking Song: "Drink, Drink, Drink" (students) "I'm Coming at Your Call" (Kathie), "Come Boys, Let's All Be Gay Boys" (Kathie), "In Heidelberg Fair" (ensemble), "Gaudeamus igitur" (students), reprise "Golden Days" (Engel), "Deep in My Heart" (Kathie, Prince), "Come Sir, Will You Join Our Noble Saxon Corps?" (Detlef, Asterberg, Lucas), Serenade: "Overhead the Moon Is Beaming" (Prince), "The Carnival of Springtime," "Student Life" (Prince, Detlef, Asterberg, Lucas), "Come, Your Time Is Short," "Thoughts Will Come to Me" (Prince, Engel), "Just We Two" (Margaret, Tarnitz), Finale Act 3: "What Memories" (Prince), reprise student songs and "Deep in My Heart."

The two shows were, in fact, quite different in style. *Rose Marie* was built on the classic romantic lines of a Daly's Theatre or European musical with, on the one side, a soprano heroine and a robustly singing baritone hero pursuing a temporarily blighted romance, on the other a little comic and his lively soubrette running their lives and love lives in parallel, and a villain of deepest dye to keep the lovers apart until the final curtain. It was perhaps unusual for the principal danseuse of the entertainment to be the evening's murderer (and to go straight from that murder to lead a spectacular ballet), but otherwise *Rose Marie* was laid out in the most traditional pattern of the English-language romantic musical stage. It was, however, a show in the line of such pieces as *The Mocking Bird*, *When Johnny Comes Marching Home*, and *Naughty Marietta* and, while choosing a colorful and romantic setting for its action, it nevertheless chose that setting not among the crowned heads and long-lost gipsy princesses of a Ruritanian Europe but in a reasonably recognizable version of a part of the Americas—the Canadian Rocky Mountains. A Rocky Mountains inhabited by a large troupe of red-coated mounties and by a vast troupe of dancing squawlets.

The music of the piece, too, was in the traditional style. The soprano and her baritone cornered the large part of it, both in lyrical solo and in lyrical duet, the soubret characters had some lightsome comedy pieces as contrast, and there were some spectacular set pieces for the spectacular folk: the mounties rendering a virile occupational chorus or the squawlets, crammed elbow-to-elbow all across the stage and with their dancing murderess at their head, performing what proved to be the picturesque highlight of the piece, the driving massed dance called "Totem-tom-tom."

The Student Prince followed a different Continental idiom. The play from which it was drawn took place in the favorite operettic setting of an imaginary European court, but its characters did not fall quite so neatly into the traditional mold. Of course, there was still a vibrantly voiced leading man and a slightly coloratura soprano with whom he joined in a richly swelling love duet before the end of the first act, and there were still the comedy folk—the Prince's puffed-up valet and the servants of his Heidelberg lodgings—but the first act was given over very largely to the students of Heidelberg University and their welcome to their new fellow-student, and to a great deal of youthful masculine music. It was the students who, with the young lovers, musically dominated a score in which there was little place for the conventional light comedy and soubret numbers which were normally interleaved with a romantic musical's romantic musical moments, and there was no pause in the action for such spectacular set-piece displays of dance as *Rose Marie*'s dancing-murderess ballet.

Romberg's European background made him an ideal illustrator of the old *Alt-Heidelberg* story, with its "unhappy" (like *Das Dreimäderlhaus*) ending, and *The Student Prince* emerged as a much more "European" musical than *Rose Marie*, both more dramatic (in spite of the other piece's murder) and darker in coloring, as well as musically more masculine.

It was perhaps this difference in flavor which led the two keystone pieces of the new wave of American romantic musicals to have distinctly different lives. Both had long and hugely successful runs on Broadway and splendid subsequent careers at home, but one went round the world, establishing itself as the most successful romantic musical in Broadway history, while the other got altogether less international exposure and, when it did, won an altogether much more mitigated response.

It was the more novel, more spectacular *Rose Marie* which was the big winner. It went from Broadway to London in the usual fashion, and triumphed both there and in the other English-speaking corners of the world, but then it went across the Channel to create an unparalleled sensation in Paris and eventually to make its way to such venues as Berlin and Budapest. *The Student Prince*, on the other hand, did not succeed in London or make a mark in Europe and, like several other shows, found its main international fame—and its songs their most enduring currency—in the English-speaking world only as a result of a subsequent movie version. Between them, however, the two pieces thoroughly launched the home-made romantic musical on a Broadway already full of musical comedy riches and made-over Continental hits,

The Desert Song:
Rudolf Valentino
meets Elinor Glyn.
This most gloriously
romantic musical
owed much more to
Hollywood than to
the Moroccan wars
which its authors
vowed were their in-
spiration.

and, between them, their two composers—Friml and Romberg—would, over the handful of
years that followed, turn out a group of shows which would become the very large part of the
backbone repertoire of the American romantic musical stage.

Friml followed up *Rose Marie* with a pair of pieces in the *Student Prince* vein—period costume musicals whose action took place in a courtly European setting. *The Vagabond King* was
a musicalization of a Justin Huntly McCarthy play which put the historical French poet
François Villon into the "king for a day" situation which had done duty for many remakes of
the Abu Hassan story, and *The Three Musketeers* was a new musical version of the swashbuckling Dumas tale of D'Artagnan, his jolly rapier-wielding comrades-in-arms, and the guilty
love-affair of the Queen of France. Both yielded some rousing masculine music ("The Song of

the Vagabonds," "Song of the Musketeers," "My Sword"), both gave the opportunity for some colorful stage display, and both had a fine success throughout America without following *Rose Marie* to epic success overseas.

While Friml followed the way and the flavor of Romberg's big hit with his other two principal successes, Romberg switched to a manner altogether more like that of *Rose Marie* in his next two outstanding works. For the first of them, he also switched to *Rose Marie*'s librettists, Oscar Hammerstein and Otto Harbach, and—working with *No, No, Nanette*'s Frank Mandel—the team came up with one of the very best books of this particular era of romantic musical plays in the deliciously tongue-in-sheik "Rudolf Valentino meets Elinor Glyn" romance of *The Desert Song*. Like *Rose Marie*, *The Desert Song* featured a standard little-comic-and-soubrette team of fun-makers in tandem with its romantic tale of love and terrorism in the Riff Mountains, like *Rose Marie* it featured a dancing villainess (though this one didn't actually kill anyone), and like *Rose Marie* it chose a colorful but less conventional subject and setting than the Ruritanian romances of the European costume dramas of *The Student Prince* or *The Vagabond King*. This tale took place in those North African deserts which had proven such a stirring background to Rudolf Valentino's screenic lovemaking.

THE DESERT SONG, a musical play in 3 acts by Otto Harbach, Oscar Hammerstein II, and Frank Mandel. Lyrics by Harbach and Hammerstein. Music by Sigmund Romberg. Produced at the Casino Theatre, New York, 30 November 1926.

Characters: General Birabeau, Pierre Birabeau, Paul Fontaine, Margot Bonvalet, Azuri, Bennie Kidd, Susan, Clementina, Sid el Kar, Ali Ben Ali, Hadji, Hassi, Nindar, Neri, Lieutenant La Vergne, Sergeant de Boussac, &c.

Plot: Pierre Birabeau, the apparently foolish son of the French Governor of Morocco, leads a double life for, behind his "foolishness," he is actually the mysterious masked "Red Shadow" who leads the marauding Riffs of the area in their armed struggle against their colonial masters. His pretence of stupidity, however, means that he is at a disadvantage when it comes to wooing his beloved Margot, who seems to be ready to wed Paul Fontaine, the captain of the French troops against whom the "Red Shadow" fights. But Pierre learns that Margot really has dreams of Hollywooden romance, and so, dashingly dressed in his masked disguise, he descends on Government House and carries her off to the moonlit desert. When the Governor comes to rescue her, Pierre is unable to draw his sword against his own father and, by this "cowardice," forfeits his position at the head of the Arab band. But he is able to return home bearing the costume of the "Red Shadow" and the news that he has killed the outlaw. And only his father—and just maybe his new wife—will ever know the truth.

Songs: Feasting Song: "High on a Hill" (Sid el Kar, Riffs), Riff Song: "Ho!" (Pierre, Sid el Kar, Riffs), "Margot" (Pierre), "I'll Be a Buoyant Girl" (Susan), "Why Did We Marry Soldiers?" (chorus), French Military Marching Song (Margot &c.), "Romance" (Margot), "Then You Will Know" (Pierre, Margot), "I Want a Kiss" (Paul, Pierre, Margot), "It" (Bennie, Susan), "The Desert Song" (Pierre, Margot), Finale Act 1: "My Little Castagnette" (Clementina, chorus), Song of the Brass Key (Clementina), "One Good Man Gone Wrong" (Bennie, Clementina), Eastern and Western Love:

["Let Love Go" (Ali Ben Ali), "One Flower Grows Alone in Your Garden" (Sid el Kar), "One Alone" (Pierre)], Sabre Song (Margot), Finaletto (Margot, Birabeau, Pierre), "Farewell" (Riffs), "All Hail to the General" (chorus), Azuri's Dance, Finale Act 2. Additional and alternative numbers include "Let's Have a Love Affair" (Bennie, Susan).

The Desert Song was a vast success both in America and all around the English-speaking world, and it also made more inroads into other languages and countries than any other piece of its kind except the all-conquering *Rose Marie*, with its principal songs—from the super-romantic title song immortalizing "Blue heaven and you and I, and sand kissing a moonlit sky . . ." to the driving, masculine song of the Riffs and Margot's vocal fireworks in praise of what she thinks is "Romance"—becoming longtime favorites.

Romberg turned out some of his finest work in *The Desert Song*, notably in the triptych of songs—basso, baritone, and tenor—contrasting Eastern and Western attitudes to women and to love, and he was to provide more and equally splendid music in the same vein for the next piece which Hammerstein and Mandel (with Lawrence Schwab this time as the third team-member) authored for him. *The New Moon* was—like an earlier success in *Naughty Marietta*—set in that most old-worldly romantic corner of the as-yet-not-United States of America, French Louisiana, and, again like Mrs Young's piece, it told the tale of a runaway. This time the runaway was a man, Robert Misson, fleeing the Parisian law for having killed a royal rapist. When he is recaptured, he pirates the ship returning him to France and sails to an island where he sets up a putative "republic." He is saved from retribution by the fall of the French monarchy. Needless to say, there was a lady in the affair as well, but Romberg once again proved his particular skill in writing for the male voice in a score which included such show-song classics as "Stout-Hearted Men," "Lover, Come Back to Me," and "Softly, As in a Morning Sunrise," and the show went on to follow its predecessors to international success on the stage and the singing screen.

If Friml and Romberg (who scored a further success—in France—with the vast dance-and-scenery spectacle that was *Nina Rosa*) dominated the English romantic music theater from a musical point of view, there was no doubt as to who dominated it from a textual point of view. Oscar Hammerstein II had had a hand in the libretto and lyrics of each of *Rose Marie*, *The Desert Song*, and *The New Moon* as well as in several romantic pieces musically illustrated by composers more accustomed to providing songs and dances for musical comedy: Vincent Youmans's *Wildflower*, George Gershwin's *The Song of the Flame* (each songwriter paired with the same utilitarian Herbert Stothart who had written the less memorable portions of *Rose Marie*), and Jerome Kern's *Show Boat*, for which he provided both the stage adaptation of Edna Ferber's sentimental period novel and the songwords.

Show Boat has become, in the last decades of the twentieth century, the great survivor of this era of romantic musical plays. Something about it has earned it the right to be favored and fashionable over and above all its contemporaries in a modern musical-theater world which largely overlooks the outstanding works of this most outstanding period of its existence. However, at the time when it first appeared on the stage, it met with a fine but scarcely extravagant reaction and compiled a fine but by no means extravagant record. Nothing to compare with *Rose Marie*, or even with *The Desert Song* and *The Student Prince*, none of which wins the same consideration as *Show Boat* does in this day and age.

Show Boat continued the trend towards home-country settings for musicals both comic and romantic, and—in spite of being based on an extant novel—it continued firmly in the way of that romantic musical tradition which had been exemplified in Hammerstein's other great pieces of recent years. There was soprano and baritone romance on the one hand—the devil-may-care riverboat gambler and the showboat owner's daughter—soubret comedy and song and dance as supplied by a couple of the showboat's singing-and-dancing employees on the other, and some fine, old-fashioned, stand-up comedy from the heroine's jolly papa. Rather than spectacular dance routines or student harmonies, the "extras" on this occasion included some Negro-flavored numbers for the showboat's maid and the Mississippi riverside workers, a fine rôle—equipped with stand-up solos—for the singer who played the showboat's leading lady, and the interpolation (into the score of Broadway's most popular interpolator of earlier years) of several numbers culled from the hits of the period in which the show was set.

SHOW BOAT, a musical play in 2 acts by Oscar Hammerstein II, based on the novel by Edna Ferber. Lyrics by Hammerstein. Music by Jerome Kern. Produced at the Ziegfeld Theatre, New York, 27 December 1927.

Characters: Cap'n Andy Hawkes, Parthy Ann Hawkes, Magnolia Hawkes, Gaylord Ravenal, Julie la Verne, Steve Baker, Frank Schultz, Ellie May Chipley, Joe, Queenie, Pete, Windy, Rubberface, &c.

Plot: When Julie, a Mississippi showboat's mulatto leading lady, and her husband are threatened with arrest for miscegenation and have to quit their jobs, Magnolia, the young daughter of the boat's owner, and a personable gambler called Ravenal take over their parts in extremis. They fall in love, marry, and leave the river, but the unreliability of Ravenal's "profession" means that their life together suffers some violent ups and downs. And, at the bottom of one "down," he leaves her. Thanks to an act of abnegation by the tender-hearted Julie, Magnolia finds work as a club singer. She works her way up to Broadway stardom, and in her greying years is brought back together with her husband on the same riverbank where they first met, so many years before.

Songs: "Cotton Blossom" (chorus), Parade and Ballyhoo (Andy &c.), "Where's the Mate for Me?" (Ravenal), "Make Believe" (Ravenal, Magnolia), "Ol' Man River" (Joe), "Can't Help Lovin' Dat Man" (Julie, Queenie, Magnolia, Joe, Windy), "Life on the Wicked Stage" (Ellie May), "Till Good Luck Comes My Way" (Ravenal), "Misery" (chorus), "I Might Fall Back on You" (Ellie May, Frank), "C'mon Folks" (Queenie), "You Are Love" (Ravenal, Magnolia), The Wedding, At the Fair (chorus), Speciality Dances, "In Dahomey" (chorus), "Why Do I Love You?" (Ravenal, Magnolia), "Bill" (lyric by P. G. Wodehouse & Hammerstein) (Julie), reprise "Can't Help Lovin' Dat Man" (Magnolia), Apache Dance, reprise "Make Believe," "Goodbye My Lady Love" (by Joe Howard)

(Frank, Ellie May), "After the Ball" (by Charles K. Harris) (Magnolia), reprise "Ol' Man River" (Joe), "Hey, Feller" (Queenie), reprise "You Are Love" (Ravenal), reprise "Why Do I Love You?" (Kim), Dance specialities and impersonations, Finale Act 2. Alternative and additional numbers include: "Dance Away the Night," "Nobody Else But Me," &c.

This picturesque and sometimes un-obvious tale—even if it had yet another little lady magically making it, *Sally*-fashion, from poverty to Broadway stardom—combined with a delightfully diverse score featuring such soon-to-be-favorites as the romantic "Make Believe," the riverside work song "Ol' Man River," the lament "Can't Help Lovin' Dat Man," and the cabaret torch song "Bill," the borrowed songs and a colorful selection of World's Fair entertainment, to help make *Show Boat* one of the most successful musicals of its time. And the most successful 1920s Broadway musical of later times.

Although it was America which produced almost all of the best in the way of English musical theater during the 1920s, the London stage was still introducing regular new musicals to its own public. Many were little better than imitations of foreign shows—American or Continental—while others were simple star-vehicles or attempts to prolong or repeat past successes and recipes, and the music that many of these pieces sported was very often a poor imitation of transatlantic styles or ordered from transatlantic songwriters of well below the first level. Such, indeed, was the fashion for American music and musicians that one producer, who had hired a group of local songwriters to provide the score for his new show, hid their identities under an umbrella name which purported to be that of a new American songwriter. However, this era on the London stage did turn out a tiny handful of winning shows, including one highly successful romantic musical and one delightfully light-hearted comical musical.

The romantic piece got its inspiration not from America, but from the Continent. And not from the modern Continental musical, but from the ancient *Die Fledermaus. Bitter-Sweet* was as much of a surprise as *Show Boat* had been. Whereas the American romantic musical had sprung from the pen of a man wholly known to date as the composer of sprightly, dance-rhythmic songs and popular ballads, the British one came—words, lyrics and music—from the hands of one best known for some of the wittiest and cleverest revues and comedies of his time: Noël Coward. *Bitter-Sweet* was no more like those revues and comedies than it was like the merry Frenchified musical comedy of *Die Fledermaus*, but neither again was it built in the classic mode of a *Geisha* or a *Rose Marie*. There was no baritone leading man to deliver stirring singing, there were no soubrettes, and there was no spectacular ballet or other divertissement. *Bitter-Sweet* was the work of a playwright: a simple, sentimental, and even slight period tale of personal tragedy, illustrated with a series of songs for the woman to whom it all happened, and with some mostly bright incidental moments for a number of supporting characters—a Viennese cabaret singer, a baritonic soldier, a quartet of effete English aristocrats, and an elegant bunch of Austrian ladies of the evening—and equipped with few of the conventional features of the modern romantic musical. *Bitter-Sweet* had a huge success in London, easily outrunning all but *Rose Marie* of its transatlantic sisters in its initial run before going on to further successes around the country, but it found only limited favor beyond British shores and never established itself in the international light-operatic repertoire as it might have been expected to.

BITTER-SWEET, an operette in 3 acts by Noël Coward. Produced at His Majesty's Theatre, London, 12 July 1929.

Characters: Sarah, Marchioness of Shayne (Sari Linden), Carl Linden, Manon (La Crevette), Captain August Lutte, Dolly Chamberlain, Lord Henry Jekyll, Vincent Howard, Herr Schlick, Lieutenant Tranitsch, Lotte, Freda, Gussi, Hansi, Hugh Devon, &c.

Plot: The Marchioness of Shayne tells the story of her life. She was to have married a safely social young man, but instead she ran away with her handsome Austrian music master. After they were married, he worked as a conductor in a Viennese café and, to make ends meet, Sari took work there too, as a dancing partner, saving for the day when they might buy their own little establishment. Then one day a lustful soldier tried to force Sari to sex, and Carl was killed trying to protect her. Sari went on to become a successful singer, and ultimately to wed the kindly Marquis of Shayne. She has lived on, but her heart died the night that Carl Linden died.

Songs: "The Call of Life" (Sarah), "If You Could Only Come with Me" (Carl), "I'll See You Again" (Sarah), "What Is Love?" (Sarah), "The Last Dance" (chorus), Finale Act I: "Eeny Meeny Miny Mo"/"I Love You"/Footmen Quartette/reprise "The Call of Life," "Life in the Morning" (chorus), "Ladies of the Town" (Lotte, Freda, Gussi, Hansi), "If Love Were All" (Manon), "Little Café" (Sarah, Carl), "We Wish to Order Wine" (chorus), "Tokay" (Lutte), "Bonne Nuit, Merci"/"Kiss Me Before You Go Away" (Manon), "Ta-ra-ra-boom-de-ay" (chorus), "Alas, the Time Is Past" (wives), "We All Wore a Green Carnation" (quartet), "Zigeuner" (Sarah), reprise "I'll See You Again" (Sarah).

The West End winner of the 1920s on the musical comedy front was a Cinderella musical—but not a sentimental poor-girl-gets-American-fairy-prince piece like those which had been the rage on Broadway a few years earlier. The Cinderella of this show was a fellow, his "prince" was an American heiress, his ugly sisters were a pair of up-to-date and wholly masculine slickers, and the rest of the tone of the show was in keeping. The songs for *Mr Cinders* were ordered from Chappell publishers on the any-American-songwriter-will-do principle, and what the producer got was a little bundle of cut-offs from flop shows by America's most frequently flopped show-writer, Richard Myers. That little bundle was, however, topped by a good half-score by local man Vivian Ellis, and these songs proved to be a group that were as delightfully light-footed and charmful as anything around. The heroine's instruction to "Spread a Little Happiness" became an enduring standard, and *Mr Cinders* itself became a delightful comedy-and-songs hit.

AN INTERNATIONAL HIT PARADE OF ENGLISH ROMANTIC MUSICALS OF THE 1920s.

The "top ten" contemporary winners among those romantic musicals written in the English language during the 1920s. The figures given here are for the show's initial runs in New York, London, and Paris.

	US	UK	FR
Rose Marie (Friml, Stothart/Hammerstein, Harbach)	581	851	1,250
(also played in Australia, Hungary, Germany, et al. and filmed* in America)			
The Desert Song (Romberg/Hammerstein, Harbach, Mandel)	471	432	210
(also played in Australia and filmed in America)			
Bitter-Sweet (Coward)	159	697	(?)
(also played in Australia and Hungary, and filmed in Britain)			
The Student Prince (Romberg/Donnelly)	608	96	x
(also played in Australia and Germany, and filmed in America)			
Show Boat (Kern/Hammerstein)	575	350	115
(also played in Australia and filmed in America)			
The Vagabond King (Friml/Hooker, Post)	511	480	x
(also played in Australia and filmed in America)			
The New Moon (Romberg/Hammerstein, Mandel, Schwab)	509	148	237
(also played in Australia and filmed in America)			
Nina Rosa (Romberg/Caesar/Harbach)	137	111	710
Rio Rita (Tierney/McCarthy/Thompson, Bolton)	494	59	x
(also played in Australia and filmed in America)			
The Three Musketeers (Friml/Wodehouse, Grey/MacGuire)	318	240	x

*Film versions of 1920s musicals ranged widely in their degree of fidelity to the original stage show.

OPERETTE FOR ALL

While the French- and English-singing stages were flooding the world with some of the best and brightest musicals of the twentieth—or any other—century, the Central European theater was more than holding its own. Between the war and the end of the 1920s, Austria, Germany, and Hungary continued to turn out a veritable tidal wave of splendid new musical plays, as the masters of the prewar Operette carried right on producing pieces with every bit as much appeal as those they had written and composed during the first great days of the twentieth-century Operette.

The war years themselves saw the production of three of the very biggest and best such pieces. While the conflict raged, and while the folk on the other side of the battle and the English Channel gorged their musical-theater selves on the spectacular oriental splendors of *Chu Chin Chow*, the banditland ones of *The Maid of the Mountains*, or the merriest of stout-backed musical comedies, Vienna's theaters introduced Emmerich Kálmán's *Die Csárdás-fürstin*, Leo Fall's *Die Rose von Stambul*, and the biggest and most international hit ever to have come out of Vienna, the sentimental Schubert story of *Das Dreimäderlhaus*. But these three remarkable hits were not alone: in the same year that the two last named pieces were given their

Das Dreimäderlhaus: "Haiderl und Hederl und Hannerl Tschöll . . ." The three little maids of the show's title.

first productions, Edmund Eysler's Viennese *Hanni geht's tanzen,* Leo Ascher's Berlin hit *Der Soldat der Marie,* and Albert Szirmai's Hungarian's success *Mágnás Miska* all made their bow as well. And so it went on. The Central European stage was buzzing.

Das Dreimäderlhaus was a typical wartime piece. It boasted a comfy, sentimental story about the good old days when people weren't busy killing each other (and which, of course, would come right on back just as soon as the war was won), full of reminders of the simple happinesses and charming ways of yesteryear, the whole topped off with a score of fine and fondly remembered music. The story was a love story—one of the loved-and-lost variety—and it was attached to the character of no less a personality than Franz Schubert, the famous and romantically short-lived Viennese composer. The score was made up of a series of arrangements of his melodies.

DAS DREIMÄDERLHAUS, a Singspiel in 3 acts by Arthur Maria Willner and Heinz Reichert, based on the novel *Schwammerl* by Rudolf H. Bartsch. Music taken from the works of Franz

Schubert, selected and arranged by Heinrich Berté. Produced at the Raimundtheater, Vienna, 15 January 1916.

Characters: Franz Schubert, Baron Franz Schober, Moriz von Schwind, Kupelwieser, Christian Tschöll, Fr. Marie Tschöll, Hannerl, Haiderl, Hederl, Demoiselle Lucia Grisi, Johann Michael Vogl, Count Scharntorff, Andreas Bruneder, Ferdinand Binder, Nowotny, &c.

Plot: Two of Franz Schubert's circle of jolly Viennese-about-town are courting the daughters of the court glazier Tschöll and, because of this, Schubert meets the third daughter, Hannerl. She takes singing lessons from him and, shyly, the two fall in love. But the actress Grisi fancies that her current flame, the poet Franz Schober, has been showing an interest in Hannerl, and she jealously warns the girl off the "philandering Franz." Hannerl mistakes her meaning and her man. Then Schubert asks Schober to sing a song he has written. It is a love song expressing to Hannerl the feelings the composer cannot bring himself to speak. But the girl, who has been turned away from Schubert by Grisi's insinuations, believes that the sentiments are Schober's. She agrees to marry him. Schubert is left alone with only his music for comfort.

Songs: "Fesch und schneidig, allweil g'mütlich" (musicians), "Haiderl und Hederl und Hannerl Tschöll" (Haiderl, Hederl, Hannerl), "Horch, horch die Lerch' im Ätherblau" (Schober, Vogl, Schwind, Kupelwieser), "Unter einem Fliederbaum" (Vogl, Schwind, Schubert, Kupelwieser, Schober), "Was Schön'res konnt's sein als ein Wiener Lied?" (Hannerl, Schubert), Finale Act 1: "Unter einem Fliederbaum"/"Steht in Wien wo auf der Bastei ein Haus" (Hannerl), "Zu jeder Zeit" (Schubert), "Wer's Mäderl freit" (Schober, Bruneder, Binder, Hannerl, Haiderl, Hederl), "Sei g'scheit, wer wird denn schmollen?" (Schober, Grisi), "Was uns dies Blümchen verschafft" (Hannerl, Schubert), "Was ist über's Leberl krochen?"/"Mädel sei nicht dumm" (Schober, Hannerl), "Geh, Alte, schau" (Tschöll), Finale Act 2: "Ich schnitt' es gern in alle Rinden ein," "Nicht klagen" (Schubert), "Tritt ein Jüngling in die Ehe" (Schober, Hannerl), Finale Act 3: "Es soll der Frühling mir künden" (Schubert).

Das Dreimäderlhaus had a truly remarkable, world-wide success. It ran for over 1,100 performances in Vienna, topped the 1,000 mark in its first Berlin run (at a time when such runs were extraordinary), and proved a first-class hit in Budapest, before going on to the rest of the world and to a whole series of remakes which, if anything, made it even more sentimental (but also less well made) than before. Paris swapped the rather unprepossessing original title for the more appropriate *Chanson d'amour* for a fine first run which was followed by four revivals in just thirteen years, America welcomed *Blossom Time* (in a version by the soon-to-be writers of *The Student Prince*, poor Schubert actually died at the final curtain, to a chorus of angel voices!) with the kind of reception no such piece had received in living memory, and London went crazy for *Lilac Time* through more than six hundred nights of a version which, like the American one, revamped Berté's arrangements, but unlike its transatlantic equivalent stopped short of the angel voices and the dying composer. Their national versions wore a groove round both America's and Britain's touring circuits for many years.

In spite of the fact that they were infinitely more original in every way than it was, and superbly tuneful to boot, the other two great wartime Operetten didn't find the same world-wide success as did *Das Dreimäderlhaus.* But then, again, nothing did. However, Kálmán's show did establish itself all around Europe, becoming one of the most favored Viennese pieces of all in the French theater, and missing out—thanks to some rather hamfisted adapting in its British and American versions, which insisted respectively that the heroine was *The Gipsy Princess* or *The Riviera Girl*—only on the English-language market. The composer's music for *Die Csárdásfürstin* was among his most charming and effective, ranging tunefully and with Hungarian-accented flair through a series of sweeping lyrical duets for the soprano heroine and tenor hero and some rhythmic and light-hearted numbers for a pair of Viennese roués. If its libretto, by Leo Stein of *Die lustige Witwe* fame and Béla Jenbach, was a pretty see-through affair—yet another tale about the aristocrat and the lady of the theater—its cabaret and palace settings nevertheless provided the opportunity for plenty of attractive scenes and numbers of all varieties.

DIE CSÁRDÁSFÜRSTIN, an Operette in 3 acts by Leo Stein and Béla Jenbach. Music by Emmerich Kálmán. Produced at the Johann Strauss-Theater, Vienna, 17 November 1915.

Characters: Leopold Maria, Fürst von und zu Lippert-Weylersheim, Fürstin Anhilde, Edwin Ronald, Komtesse Stasi, Graf Boni Káncsiánu, Sylva Varescu, Feri von Kerekes, General von Rohnsdorff, Eugen von Rohnsdorff, Botschafter MacGrave, &c.

Plot: Edwin Ronald, son of the Fürst Leopold, has gone through a form of betrothal with the singer Sylva Varescu, but his parents unilaterally announce his engagement to their niece, Stasi. Boni, a jolly little aristocrat-about-town, brings Sylva to the ball at the princely palace at which Edwin's engagement is announced, but the young man refuses to go along with his parents' wishes and announces to all that he will wed Sylva. It takes another act of comings and goings before Edwin and Sylva, and Boni and Stasi, are paired tidily off.

Songs: "Heia! Heia! In den Bergen ist mein Heimatland!" (Sylva), "Die Mädis, die Mädis, die Mädis vom Chantant" (Boni, Feri), "Mädchen gibt es wunderfeine" (Edwin, Sylva), "Ganz ohne Weiber geht die Chose nicht" (Boni), "O jag' dem Glück nicht nach auf meilenfernen Wegen" (Sylva), Finale Act 1: "Die Mädis vom Chantant," &c., Schwalbenduett: "Machen wir's den Schwalben nach" (Edwin, Stasi), "Weisst du es noch?" (Edwin, Sylva), "Hurra! Hurra! Man lebt ja nur einmal" (Stasi, Sylva, Edwin, Boni), "Mädel, guck!" (Boni, Stasi), "Tausend kleine Engel singen" (Edwin, Sylva), Finale Act 2: "Verehrte, liebe Gäste," "Jaj, mamám, Bruderherz" (Feri, Sylva, Boni), reprise "Ganz ohne Weiber geht die Chose nicht" (Boni, Edwin), reprise "Mädel, guck!" (Stasi, Boni), Schlussgesang: reprise "Tausend kleine Engel singen."

Das Dreimäderlhaus went round the world, *Die Csárdásfürstin* got about halfway, but *Die Rose von Stambul*—of the three probably the most musically luscious, the most textually original and comical, and easily the most modern in its subject matter—didn't make it out of Central Europe. Not successfully, anyhow. At home, however, it was a megahit. Produced at the Theater an der Wien, the original home of *Die lustige Witwe*, it proved to be that house's biggest success in the ten years and many, many more Operette productions since their landmark musical. Like *The Desert Song*, *Die Rose von Stambul* took that long favorite musical-theater venue of the mystic Orient for its setting—but not the Orient of the Arabian Nights: a much more up-to-date Orient with no genies or forty thieves anywhere about. Kondja Gül, the "rose of Stambul" of the title, is a Pascha's daughter—but not a Pascha's daughter like the Sáffi of *Der Zigeunerbaron* or the heroine of a *Chu Chin Chow*. She is the very model of a modern Pascha's daughter, educated in Europe, and therefore of a mood to rebel against the wearing of the veil and her father's intention to marry her off, Eastern-style, to his minister's son. This conflict between the old Eastern values and those of modern Europe ran through both the romantic plot and its particularly successful comic counterpart, giving it decidedly more of a backbone than many of its contemporaries around the world.

However, although Brammer and Grünwald's libretto was a fine one, it was the music which was the real joy of *Die Rose von Stambul*. Since *Der liebe Augustin in* 1912, Leo Fall hadn't really turned up a full-scale hit, but the composer of so many triumphant successes of the 1900s still had plenty of winning notes in his inkwell. And here he poured them out lavishly, in a handful of soaring romantic tenor and soprano pieces (including two complete, full-scale duo finales) which were in quite a different vein from the lively measures of such pieces as *Der fidele Bauer* and *Die geschiedene Frau* and which were, quite simply, some of the loveliest and most singable Operette melodies Vienna had ever heard.

DIE ROSE VON STAMBUL, an Operette in 3 acts by Julius Brammer and Alfred Grünwald. Music by Leo Fall. Produced at the Theater an der Wien, Vienna, 2 December 1916.

Characters: Exzellenz Kemal Pascha, Kondja Gül, Midili Hanum, Achmed Bey, Müller senior, Fridolin Müller, Désirée, Lydia Kooks, Black, Sadi, Bul-Bul, Djamileh, &c.

Plot: During her years studying in Europe, Kondja Gül has developed a great admiration for the works of the poet André Lery, whose works express support for the "liberation" of Eastern women. Now he has written to her. But she has no chance for the romance that seems to threaten: she must marry her father's choice, his minister's son, Achmed Bey. So marry she does, but on condition. She will not be wholly his until he has wooed and won her, European-style. And so, while the comical little Fridolin from Hamburg and Midili from the Pascha's harem float merrily into marriage, Kondja and Achmed ride rockily through their first three days as man and wife. But all comes right in the Honeymoon Hotel where Fridolin and Midili have been celebrating their wedding, for Achmed Bey and André Lery are one and the same person and "the rose of Stambul" has in fact been wed to the man who would have been her own choice.

Songs: "Wonnig mögen deine Träume sein" (Bul-Bul), "Als ich noch ein wildes, kleines, Sonnenbraunes Mädel war" (Kondja), "Die Mädchen aus dem Abendland" (Midili, Kondja), "'s ist alles im Leben Bestimmung" (Midili, Fridolin), "O Rose von Stambul" (Achmed), Finale Act 1: "Kennen Sie das alte schöne wundersame Keramlied" (Kondja, Achmed), "Bald naht die Stunde der holdesten Feier" (chorus), "Ihr stillen, süssen Frau'n" (Achmed), "Fridolin, ach wie dein Schnurrbart sticht" (Midili, Fridolin), "Sie kommt" (ensemble), "Das ist das Glück nach der Mode" (Kondja, Achmed), "Ich bin, ich bin die Lilly vom Ballett" (Fridolin), "Es duften Moschus und Myrrhen" (ensemble), "Ein Walzer muss es sein" (Kondja, Achmed), Finale Act 2: "Dem Glücklichen schlägt keine Stunde" (Achmed, Kondja), Schnucki-Duett: "Geh', sag doch Schnucki

After the war was over, the Operette continued to blossom in a harvest of both comical musicals and lushly romantic ones. Many were written in the prewar style but, soon, many others appeared which followed the newest fashions both musically and textually. And to the celebrated musical names of the prewar and wartime years—Kálmán, Lehár, Eysler, Fall, Gilbert, Szirmai, Straus—there would eventually be added new ones: men such as the singer-songwriter-turned-composer Bruno Granichstädten (1879–1944) and the Hungarian Pál Ábrahám (1892–1960), with jazzy new tones to put alongside the more traditional styles of Austro-Hungarian music.

The first big hit of the postwar years came not from Vienna but from the flourishing Berlin theater, where Jean Gilbert's *Die Frau im Hermelin* was mounted in August of 1919. Gilbert, whose career on the international stage had taken off with such éclat in the few years before the war, had seen his prospects shattered by the conflict. The channel through which his works had made their way from Central Europe to the rest of the world had been Britain and, with the declaration of war, "enemy" music was swiftly swept from the London stage. For the duration of the years of combat, only von Gatti and Jenbach's *Der lila Domino*—with a score by the French Cuvillier—had been played long and loud on a London stage which a few years earlier had been ringing with Germanic

Die Rose von Stambul: "Lily vom Ballett . . ." Fridolin gets himself dolled up in feminine garb so as to get inside the Pascha's harem and see his sweetheart.

musicals. The return of the Operette to the English stage began with the London production of the previously tried-out *Szibill* and the disappointing local version of *Die Csárdásfürstin*, and then came what adapter Freddie Lonsdale—he of *King of Cadonia* and *Maid of the Mountains* fame—called *The Lady of the Rose*. Gilbert's prewar pieces had been out and out musical comedies, light-hearted pieces of foolery with takeawayable "Schlager" or "hit songs" woven into their action, but *Die Frau im Hermelin* was nothing of the kind. Its story was a romantic, period wartime one (Verona in 1810, to be precise) with more than a touch of *Madame Favart* about it. Its heroine was a local countess who, while her husband hides in his own home in the guise of a servant, has to fight for her virtue against the Colonel of the invading forces. Gilbert supplied some delightful waltzing, polka-ing music as an accompaniment and the show became a huge hit, going on from Berlin to Budapest and Vienna, and effectively re-establishing the German musical on the British stage with a run of more than 500 nights at Daly's Theatre. It then went on to America, where it fell into the hands of the Shubert brothers, which meant that by the time it got to the stage, although it had reverted to something more like its original title as *The Lady in Ermine*, its book had been given a silly and saccharine rewrite and its score plugged full of interpolated songs. But it still managed to survive for more than 200 nights.

The prolific Gilbert followed up this hit with an explosion of new musical plays of all kinds: during the 1920s he composed the scores for no fewer than twenty full-sized Operetten which were premièred in Berlin, Vienna, Hamburg, Dresden, and even London and New York, pieces that ranged from the six-handed musical comedy *Dorine und der Zufall* to the romantic *Katja, die Tänzerin* with its glamorous Monte Carlo love-story of a deposed princess-turned-dancer and the prince who deposed her, and its merrily almost-up-to-date dance music. *Katja* proved again that what the rest of the world wanted from Central Europe was not its musical comedies but its romantic musicals. While *Dorine* did well only in middle Europe, *Katja* went forth to find as great a success in Britain as *The Lady of the Rose* had done—only *Lilac Time* of the Operetten of this era outran the Gilbert pair on the London stage—a good career further afield, and a couple of screen versions.

Central Europe and its musical-writers—who knew where the greatest profits to their purses lay—were not slow to get the message, and in the 1920s the largest number of the Operetten which came out of Austria, Germany, and Hungary were pieces built on the standard romantic-comic Operette lines. Not all of them caught on on a wider scale, but many were given a mounting in the English- and sometimes the French-singing theater, and in spite of the fact that, particularly in America, they were often torn to bits and remade to what were considered to be local tastes, a percentage succeeded in establishing themselves as world-wide hits in the same way that *Die Frau im Hermelin* and *Katja, die Tänzerin* had done.

The composer who switched most dramatically and obviously from the comedy musical to the romantic one was Franz Lehár. In 1920, the composer of *Die lustige Witwe* turned out a merrily waltzing, marching, mazurka-ing Operette called *Die blaue Mazur*, written to the umpteenth libretto about the bride who won't connube on her wedding night and has to be wooed and won by her husband. It entertained Vienna for a top-notch 333 performances, but it failed to take off in its English and French productions. A textually fragile, visually spectacular piece which used a rehash of the score of his 1916 piece *Der Sterngucker* as its music, put together by the Italian theatrical jobber Carlo Lombardo and advisedly subtitled as a "Revue-Operette," also scored a light-hearted Viennese success, under the title *Libellentanz*, before, in 1924, the little French sex comedy which had for its heroine a girlie called *Cloclo* closed down the "comic" part of Lehár's career. From now on there would be no more comedy musicals from him, either of the old, costume comedy variety of *Die lustige Witwe* or *Der Graf von Luxemburg*, or even of the more up-to-date variety. Romance would rule.

Lehár had, of course, already ventured into the romantic on more than one occasion, the most notable example being the passionate *Zigeunerliebe* of 1910, and the most recent a kind of Operettic *Carmen* piece about a lovelorn Frenchman and a Spanish gipsy called *Frasquita* and a romance about a Viennese girl and a Chinese Prince entitled *Die gelbe Jacke*, both of which had had good if not exceptional runs at home. Now, however, in 1925 he launched himself headlong into what would be a series of six romantic Operetten, musicals which mixed a story of tortured and/or torrid romance that almost inevitably ended in separation or unhappiness with a score of soaring light operatic music. In these Operetten, the romantic characters and their music thoroughly outweighed, and sometimes even virtually submerged, their light comedy song-and-dance soubret counterparts. Big emotions, big singing, and a certain amount of amorously inspired gloom were their trademarks.

The show which set this series in motion was *Paganini*, a conventional period romance written by composer-author Paul Knepler around the much-dramatized character of the celebrated violinist and that of the married and rather royal Anna Elisa of Lucca and Piombino. While her husband is off chatting up a singer, Anna Elisa begins a passionate but doomed affair with the violinist. And when the Princess is recalled to her royal duties, Paganini, like *Das Dreimäderlhaus*'s Schubert, gives himself over to his greatest love—his music. Unlike Berté, Lehár didn't turn to the works of Paganini for his music, but composed instead a full-blooded Operettic score in which the tenor rôle of the violinist—created by actor-turned-Heldentenor Carl Clewing—was pre-eminent. It produced one number—the merry assertion that "Gern hab' ich die Frau'n geküsst" (better known to English-speaking listeners as "Girls Were Made to Love and Kiss")—which became a world-wide takeaway hit, but much of the score was in an altogether less light-hearted spirit and the predominant coloring of *Paganini* was one of deepest romance.

The show found mostly only limited runs as it went on from Vienna to Berlin, Budapest, Paris, and London, but it—and, so it is said, the performance given of its title-rôle in the Berlin production by the tenor Richard Tauber—encouraged Lehár to continue with more works in the same vein. For the second romantic-unhappy-ending Operette of his 1920s series he plunged wholeheartedly into the realm of the gloomy and the tenorious with an adaptation of a Polish play about a Russian princeling, *Der Zarewitsch*. The heir to the Russian throne isn't interested in girls. Only in boys. This is not good for the future of the dynasty, so the politicians go to work on his susceptibilities. They dress up a dancing girl as an athletic lad and send her along to introduce him to straight sex. The two fall in love, but then the politicians have to pull them apart so that their Czar-to-be can be paired off with a more aristocratically suitable wife and heir-producing mother. *Der Zarewitsch* was even more cloudy in coloring than *Paganini* had been, for its hero spent almost the whole night being miserable, whether about having to have something to do with a girl, or later at not being able to do it with the one he wanted. It was also even more tenorious (although the dancing girl actually got the plum number of the score), but it was not notably more successful. Good rather than grand runs in Berlin and Vienna led to a flop in France and nothing in an English-language theater which was obviously more interested in its own unhappy Princeling—the Karl-Franz of *The Student Prince*—than this one.

The third of Lehár's new Operetten was *Friederike*. This time Tauber got to impersonate the poet Goethe, and his unhappy ending had him leaving his village sweetheart to go off to become a famous bachelor poet in a court where married poets were not hired. He also got to sing the next of Lehár's tenor bon-bons—"O Mädchen, mein Mädchen." *Friederike* went through a similar round to the other two. It did well enough at home, and it made it to Broadway and to London, but it caused no great stir in either place.

Lehár had never been chary of reusing music, and even plots and characters, from his earlier and less successful shows, but for his next two Tauber-vehicles he actually made over two of his reasonably well-liked musicals of recent years. *Endlich allein*, a more smiling piece of theater which had an incognito Prince and Princess falling in love while holed up up a mountain in a snowstorm, was remade as *Schön ist die Welt*, but the more successful exercise—and indeed, the big success of this Lehár series of Operetten—was the rewrite of *Die gelbe Jacke*. Tenorized with such solos as "Dein ist mein ganzes Herz," fitted out with a nice, new-fashioned unhappy ending, and retitled *Das Land des Lächelns*, it became a full-scale Central European hit.

DAS LAND DES LÄCHELNS, a romantische Operette in 3 acts by Ludwig Herzer and Fritz Löhner-Beda, based on the libretto *Die gelbe Jacke* by Victor Léon. Music by Franz Lehár. Produced at the Metropoltheater, Berlin, 10 October 1929.

Characters: Prince Sou-Chong, Lisa, Mi, Graf Gustl von Pottenstein, Graf Ferdinand Lichtenfels, Tschang, Lori, Fu-Li, Exzellenz Harbegg, Obereunuch, Fini, Franzi, Vally, Toni, &c.

Plot: A young Viennese widow marries a Chinese prince, but when the pair return to the East she finds that she cannot cope with the Eastern way of life and, above all, the fact that local law insists that the Prince also take a Chinese wife. Although she is as much in love with her husband as ever, Lisa returns to Vienna. But Sou-Chong's sister, the little Princess Mi, who has enviously witnessed the freedoms that Western women enjoy and who has become fond of the jolly hussar, Gustl, has to stay behind. East is East.

Songs: "Hoch soll sie leben!" (chorus), "Ich danke für die Huldigung"/"Gern, gern wär' ich verliebt" (Lisa), "Freunderl, mach' dir nix draus" (Gustl, Lisa), "Immer nur lächeln" (Sou Chong), "Bei einem Tee à deux" (Lisa, Sou Chong), "Von Apfelblüten einen Kranz" (Sou Chong), Finale Act 1: "Wir sind allein," "Dschinthien wuomen ju chon ma goa can" (chorus), "Wer hat die Liebe uns ins Herz gesenkt" (Lisa, Sou Chong), "Im Salon zur blau'n Pagode" (Mi), "Meine Liebe, deine Liebe" (Gustl, Mi), "Dein ist mein ganzes Herz" (Sou Chong), "Ich möcht wieder einmal die Heimat seh'n" (Lisa), Finale Act 2: "Mit welchem Recht?"/"Dein war mein ganzes Herz," "Märchen vom Glück" (chorus), "Zig zig zig zig ih!" (Gustl, Mi), "Wie rasch verwelkte doch!" (Mi), Finale Act 3: "Diesselbe Sonne"/"Liebes Schwesterlein"/"Immer nur lächeln."

The other most prolific provider of Operetten to the world's stages during these years was Emmerich (ex-Imre) Kálmán. In the years after the war, and his big success with *Die Csárdás-*

fürstin, Kálmán continued with a run of successful pieces for the Vienna theater. A piece called *Die Faschingsfee*—a rebooked edition of one of his early Hungarian shows—was followed initially by the tale of the princess who pretends to be *Das Hollandweibchen*, and then by the three most appreciable of Kálmán's postwar works. The first of these was *Die Bajadere*, a piece written to a text by top librettists Brammer and Grünwald and telling the story of an Indian prince's efforts to win and woo a Parisian prima donna. It was made memorable, however, not so much by its fairly standard romantic plot but by a particularly sparky parallel comic one about a lass with two men who always finds herself irresistibly drawn to whichever of them she isn't currently married to, and by a score which included both some of the composer's loveliest melody and also some splendidly merry dances, a set which ranged from the fox-trot and the boston to the waltz and—less expectedly—the good old-fashioned Ländler and the can-can!

Die Bajadere had a generally fine career, but it was Kálmán's next piece which proved to be his most successful of all. For *Gräfin Mariza*, Brammer and Grünwald switched from Paris back to the composer's native Hungary as the setting for what was little more than a standard tale of aristocratic love. No fashionable (and already becoming clichéd) unhappy ending here, just a simple story of love and pride and money of the kind that had been popular ever since *Die lustige Witwe* . . . and before. But the composer immersed himself happily in the Hungarian tones which he purveyed so superbly, and gave the tale (which was, like that of *Die Bajadere*, neatly lightened with some less romantic characters) a musical illustration which—from the hero's sizzling gipsy solo to the loping little seduction song of a gently comical outbacks Baron—was one of the highlights of his stage career. *Gräfin Mariza* became a major hit in home territory, and went out to become one of Kálmán's most widely successful works, particularly in America.

GRÄFIN MARIZA, an Operette in 3 acts by Julius Brammer and Alfred Grünwald. Music by Emmerich Kálmán. Produced at the Theater an der Wien, Vienna, 28 February 1924.

Characters: Gräfin Mariza, Fürst Moritz Dragomir Popolescu, Baron Koloman Zsupán, Graf Tassilo Endrödy-Wittemburg, Lisa, Karl Stephan Liebenberg, Fürstin Bozena Cuddenstein zu Chlumetz, Penizek, Borko, Manja, Tschekko, &c.

Plot: Tired of being courted by every good-timer and gold-digger in Vienna, the overly eligible Gräfin Mariza announces a fictitious engagement to a Baron Zsupán, and disappears from town to her estates in Hungary. But then a real Zsupán turns up at the gate, all ready and willing to wed. By the end of the evening, after the regulation amount of ups and down and misunderstandings, Mariza has found true love with her impoverished but proudly aristocratic estate manager, and jolly little Zsupán has been merrily redirected towards the same gentleman's sweet soubrette of a sister.

Songs: "War einmal ein reicher Prasser" (Manja), Kinderlied: "Wir singen dir, wir bringen dir" (Tassilo, children), "Grüss mir dir süssen, die reizenden Frauen" (Tassilo), "Lustige Zigeunerweisen" (chorus)/"Höre ich Zigeunergeigen" (Mariza), "Sonnenschein, hüll' dich ein" (Tassilo, Lisa), "Komm mit nach Varasdin" (Zsupán, Mariza), Finale Act 1: "Komm Csigán" (Tassilo)/ "Geigen schaller, Lichter blitzen"/"Eh ein kurzer Mond ins Land mag entfliehn," "Herr Verwalter, bitte sehr" (Lisa, Mariza, &c.), "Ich möchte träumen von dir" (Lisa, Zsupán), "Genug ich will mit Geschäften mich nicht ennuyieren"/"Einmal möcht' ich wieder tanzen" (Tassilo, Mariza), "Winkt im Gläse der Tokaier" (Populescu, Mariza, Zsupán), "Sag' ja, mein Lieb, sag' ja" (Tassilo, Mariza), "Behüt dich Gott!" (Zsupán, Lisa), Finale Act 2: "Hei! Mariza! Hei! Mariza!"/"Siebzig, Achtzig, Hunderttausend!"/"Auch ich war einst ein reicher Csardaskavalier!" (Tassilo), reprise "Ich möchte träumen" (Zsupán), "Braunes Mädel von der Puszta" (Populescu, Zsupán, Mariza), reprise "Komm mit nach Varasdin" (Zsupán, Lisa), "Ob's der Liebe Herrgott war" (Tassilo), Schlussgesang: "Sag' ja!" (Tassilo).

Kálmán followed up *Gräfin Mariza* with another sparkling success in the same vein. This time the impoverished aristocrat was a circus star, and the proud lady whom he courts and weds in disguise, *Bettelstudent*-fashion, as an instrument of the revenge of a scorned and powerful man, was the unwitting instrument of his poverty. The parallel light comedians were a little circus performer and the funny little son of a wealthy German. Although the ingredients were well-used ones, the show came out as a delightful and easily digestible bit of romantic-comic entertainment, and *Die Zirkusprinzessin* has remained in the repertoire in Central Europe to this day. It was, however, to be the composer's last real hit. He visited America and—as Jacobi had done before him, and with only the same half-success—provided Broadway with a home-made "Viennese" musical in the form of the swashbuckling *Golden Dawn*, then, back at base, set two very different Brammer/Grünwald texts with only some success. One, *Die Herzogin von Chicago*, confronted an old-world prince and a brash, rich and up-to-date Chicago heiress, and combined music representative of each of its protagonists in its score in a manner which was found only partly comfortable. The other, *Das Veilchen von Montmartre*, was a staggeringly old-fashioned bit of love-in-a-merry-starving-Montmartre-garret nonsense which brought real personalities of the historical artistic world to the stage in an underpowered sort of Operettic *La Bohème*. It was a pale piece, which had none of the Hungarian virility of the composer's best shows, from *Tatárjárás* to *Gräfin Mariza*. Over the last twenty-three years of his career the composer brought only three new works to the stage (a fourth was produced posthumously), and, even though they showed that his gift for melody was unimpaired, neither the history of the *Kaiserin Josephine*, nor an operetticized version of the Mayerling story manufactured for Broadway under the girlie title of *Marinka*, nor an awkward *Oklahoma!*-clone piece of cowboyland romance called *Arizona Lady* left much of a mark.

The other successful composers of the prewar and wartime years also ranged some big hits alongside the postwar works of Kálmán and Lehár, and the biggest of them actually totted up a more important international success than any of the nowadays better remembered or better plugged works of those two men. *Madame Pompadour* was the last great hit to come from probably the greatest hit-smith of them all, Leo Fall. In 1922, just three years before his death, and fifteen years on from *Der fidele Bauer* and *Die Dollarprinzessin*, fourteen after *Die geschiedene Frau*, a decade down the line from *Der liebe Augustin*, and six years after the huge success of *Die Rose von Stambul*, Fall turned out the music for a merrily farcical Operette which bent not a whit towards the blossoming fashion for Angst-ridden tenor-soprano romance and fashionably unhappy endings. The heroine of Schanzer and Welisch's libretto—a libretto made to measure for Germany's biggest musical-theater star, the sparklingly un-Angstish Fritzi Massary—was a Madame Pompadour who is out for a bit of a fling on the side while her King is out of town. The rôle and the show glittered with the liveliest kind of farcical fun, Fall's music glittered with all the brilliance of his greatest works, and all that glittering added up to a first-class Operettic evening in the theater. *Madame Pompadour* conquered Berlin and Vienna in the person of Massary, Budapest in the hands of that city's top operettic star, Sári Fedák, and London, as impersonated by Evelyn Laye, while the Dutch soprano Beppi de Vries fronted a fine Australian production. Even France welcomed the show, with Raymonde Vécart as its star, and only America, where a Charles Dillingham production struck star casting and re-re-casting problems on the road, failed to turn the show into a hit.

MADAME POMPADOUR, an Operette in 3 acts by Rudolf Schanzer and Ernst Welisch. Music by Leo Fall. Produced at the Berliner Theatre, Berlin, 9 September 1922.

Characters: Marquise de Pompadour, King Louis XV, René comte d'Estrades, Joseph Calicot, Belotte, Madeleine, Maurepas, Poulard, Prunier, Collin, Boucher, Tourelle, &c.

Plot: While the satirical poet Calicot is performing his new song at one of Paris's bohemian taverns, he is watched both by his old friend René d'Estrades, up from the country for a weekend off the marital leash, and by a pretty lady who is both the subject of his rash song and, before long, the recipient of René's amorous advances. She is the king's mistress, la Marquise de Pompadour. The two men both find themselves arrested for sedition, but Pompadour "sentences" René to be her personal bodyguard and Calicot to write a play for her. She is all prepared to enjoy her new young bodyguard, when she discovers that he is the husband of her half-sister. Then the King—alerted by his police-chief—returns, finds René in Pompadour's boudoir, and flings him in prison. But the man is her sister's husband! King and police-chief both look silly, and the over-ready René is stunned. As the Marquise swans on to a new adventure, he returns chastenedly to his wife.

Songs: "Die Pom-Pom-Pompadour" (Calicot, chorus), "Der brave Bürger lebt in Frieden" (René), "Heut' könnt einer sein Glück bei mir marchen" (Pompadour, Belotte), "Ein intimes Souper" (René, Pompadour), "Liebe lehrt die Esel tanzen" (Belotte, Calicot), Finale Act 1: "Laridi, laridon, laridallallera," "Bemeisternd unsere Ungeduld" (chorus), "Ich bin dein Untertan" (René, Pompadour), "Wozu hast du denn die Augen?" (Pompadour, Madeleine, Belotte), "Madame Pompadour" (René), "Josef, ach Josef" (Pompadour, Calicot), Finale Act 2: "Wo ist Madame?," "Wenn die Kirschen wieder reifen" (Calicot, Belotte), "Dem König geht's in meinem Schachspiel meistens kläglich" (Pompadour).

Oscar Straus—continually on the scene since his big success with *Ein Walzertraum* in 1907—was another who supplied the European stage with a liberal helping of Operette scores in the years after the war: two in 1919 and no fewer than a dozen during the 1920s. The majority of those that were successful found their success, as his very long-running 1914 piece *Rund um die Liebe* had done, mainly at home—the sweetly rural tale of the *Dorfmusikanten*, the village virtuoso, and his hometown girl, the French-comical piece in which the telephone-girl *Riquette* is hired as a fake mistress to cover a gentleman's more culpable affair, the equally French but sort-of-historical story of *Teresina* and the aristocratic husband the Napoleonic law gives to her, and an on-the-bandwagon piece which centered round the world's newest Ruritania, *Hochzeit in Hollywood*—but only one of his shows proved to have a wider appeal. *Der letzte Walzer* was a romantic musical, but, like *Madame Pompadour*, it was a made-for-Massary musical, and the central rôle—a woman who, like a kind of Operettic Tosca, outwits the powerful man who has condemned her lover to death in order to have her for himself—was one which ran the gamut from passion to comedy with the kind of dashing espièglerie that was the star's forte. The rôle of Vera Lisaweta, with its drama, its pathos, its flirting, its triumph, and with numbers to match each and every mood, was a singing actress's delight, and after Massary had finished purveying it to Berlin audiences, Broadway's Eleanor Painter, Vienna's Betty Fischer, London's José Collins, and a whole pleiad of others all got their money's worth out of it and its rich range of music.

Another of the men who had helped the twentieth-century Operette to take off, and who had since run up an extensive list of hometown hits without ever finding that one big international winner that might make his name more widely fashionable, was Edmund Eysler. With the scores for no fewer than twenty-five full-length and several more one-act Operetten already to his credit by 1920, this most thoroughly Viennese of Viennese composers added another fourteen in the decade that followed, a group that was topped by a singular success with an olde-Vienna Operette called *Die gold'ne Meisterin*, produced at the Theater an der Wien in 1927. The score which Eysler provided for this work was an outstanding one, thoroughly in the prewar idiom and simply glistening with melody, but whether it was just that fashion had moved on, or that the rest of the world couldn't get up an interest in the story of a goldsmith's wife with social pretensions who falls in love with one of her own workers, the show didn't follow up its Viennese success with overseas productions, and Eysler never did get the kind of international exposure he deserved.

Even though many of Hungary's most outstanding composers had abandoned their homeland for the richer pickings to be found in Vienna, Berlin, or the United States, the musical theater in Budapest still flourished, and still turned out its quota of hits—including one which became decidedly international. *Alexandra* had a score by Albert Szirmai, who had posted up such a happy wartime triumph with *Mágnás Miska*, and a libretto by Ferenc Martos, author of some of Hungary's very best libretti. It was a well-made piece, with a stout story in which a sea captain temporarily marries the Russian Grand Duchess who is his royal master's fiancée in order to help her escape from the Revolution. No prizes for guessing the ending. Szirmai's score of sometimes interestingly inventive but always soaring waltz music for his lovers, and lighter, Hungarian-marked dance numbers and marches for the supporting characters, combined with Martos's merry work to make up a fine musical which would end up touring the world. It toured the world, however, in rather battered shape, for what the British and Americans called *Princess Charming* was one of the era's worst sufferers from the inelegant practice of remaking Continental musicals for their English versions. Martos and Szirmai's work was evidently considered too original and substantial for London and Broadway audiences, so in its English producers' hands its book was sliced up, conventionalized, and invaded by a clownish low comedian, and its shapely score was decorated with some simple dancing ditties and comic songs by local writers. And it succeeded.

The more straightforwardly comical musical—as opposed to those whose comic part was subordinate to a romantic central plot—did still exist on the Central European stage, but few such pieces were among the long-runners of the era, few of them transferred to other countries, and when they did they were inclined to be subjected to the same kind of musical and textual abuse that *Alexandra* had suffered. An example of this was the Vienna hit *Der Tanz ins Glück*. Robert Bodanzky and Bruno Hardt-Warden concocted a piece of comical nonsense about a hairdresser masquerading as a count in order to win the hand of a hatmaker's daughter, a "count" whose impersonation is uncovered thanks to the clumsiness of the music-hall attendant he has hired to be his "valet." The one-step and the fox-trot featured in Robert Stolz's score alongside Viennesey songs and marches, and the piece won a fine hometown run before going abroad. There, if anything, it suffered more severely than *Alexandra* had done, but in precisely the same way. The valet's rôle was hugely expanded, the original songs were replaced almost entirely with a mixture of "pop" songs in the unsophisticated style of the old pasticcio shows, and speciality acts and dance routines were shoveled into the proceedings until the whole entertainment resembled less a musical comedy than one of the heterogeneous variety shows which at the time were glorified under the name of "revue." And it still did all right.

Alongside the larger-scale romantic Operetten, there was yet a little corner reserved on the Central European stage for the more intimate musical, and Berlin was responsible for launching one of the most attractive of these—the charming little *Das Vetter aus Dingsda*. A cast of nine, no chorus, one set, and a time-span of just twenty-four hours: everything about the show was intimate, and its little love-story about a Dutch lassie who moons over a dream-lover for so long that she almost misses real love when it comes along was of similar proportions. The young Eduard Künneke (1885–1953) supplied a suitably intimate score, which neatly mixed the fox-trot, the tango, and the boston into its elsewhere plaintive and pretty music, and the piece turned out to be a hit which traveled widely. Künneke went on to find other successes with ever larger pieces, but *Das Vetter aus Dingsda* remains his most durable credit.

"Viennesed" versions of the fox-trot, the tango, the boston, and the one-step were by now an integral part of the musical language of up-to-date Central Europe. Only Operetten such as the olde-Austrian *Die gold'ne Meisterin* could and did wholly ignore the now not-so-newest trend in dance music. But the American popular music world, which had been responsible for developing so many of those forms, had well and truly moved on since those early dancing days, and a part of its pop music—the kind that was now being used to botch the Continental musicals imported into America and Britain—was, these days, often music of a more aggressively "go-ey" nature. And this music and these songs were being called "jazz." It was, of course, not what we today would class as jazz—classic jazz, with its inherently improvisatory nature—but rather a kind of song-style developed from the sounds and rhythms of jazz in the same way that the previous decade had manufactured songs from the sounds and rhythms of ragtime and of the dances of Europe. Smoothed down, made over, made easy, and generally commercialized, "jazz" was the mood music of the moment.

Europe was not slow to pick up on the latest American fashion, and the jazz song was soon avidly listened to and then avidly copied all around the old Continent. And eventually it began to find its way into shows, there to cohabit without too much discomfort with the more traditional music of the European stage. The most successful exponent of this kind of potpourri of old sounds and new in the European theater of the 1920s was Bruno Granichstädten, and the musical with which he made his biggest hit was *Der Orlow*. The show was, not unreasonably, set in America, and the plot concerned the battle between a sprightly local car magnate and one of his workers for the hand and heart of a beautiful ballerina. When we learn that the carworker is in fact a deposed Russian Grand Duke and that he has smuggled out of Europe a diamond of fabulous worth (the "Orlow" of the title), we are in no doubt as to how things are going to end. The songs of the piece ran through shimmy, boston, tango, and fox-trot time, as well as more romantic rhythms when the hero and his dancer got together, and even ventured into 12/8 meter for one piece, but Granichstädten's orchestration made his "American" pieces sound rather different to those to which Central Europe had now become accustomed. Portions of the music were scored for "jazz band": alto and tenor sax, two trombones, banjo, piano, and drums. Not a fiddle in sight.

Der Orlow, with its up-to-date novelties as a major attraction, was a huge Viennese hit, and it ran for over 650 performances on its production at the Theater an der Wien. However, not surprisingly, it did not travel with the same felicity. America and Britain did not really need to import their "jazzy" musicals from the Continent. The London production was a brief flop, and America's producers—who were still snapping up the rights to large handfuls of European musicals in the wake of *Blossom Time*—didn't even bother with this one.

Like the rest of the world, it also didn't bother much with another, German, musical which came out at the end of the decade. Not to start with, anyhow. London's Lyric Theatre in Hammersmith had recently mounted a newly tidied-up version of the eighteenth-century classic *The Beggar's Opera* with enormous success, and this success had resulted both in a brief new fashion for revivals of elderly musicals and also in a bandwagon-jumping bit of copycatting by other theatrical hopefuls out to make some cash on the back of a very out-of-copyright work. Austria turned out a new *Beggar's Opera* remake called *Der Liebling von London*, and then Germany— copying the copycat—turned out *Die Dreigroschenoper*. Elisabeth Hauptmann and Bertolt

Brecht's version of Gay's once incisively comic text was a hectoringly melodramatic one, direct and scathing, with no thought or care for light and shade, Kurt Weill's music echoed it in a series of jazzy, edgy, dark-toned songs, and the show was produced—with an Operettic leading man, and in a colorfully spectacular style which must have been meant to burlesque the Operette stage in the same way the original show had burlesqued the Italian opera—at Berlin's Theater am Schiffbauerdamm. It went on to other centers thereafter, but it won only an indifferent to awful reception outside Central Europe, and it was not until several decades later, when its simplistic, grand-guignolesque theatricality became à la mode, that the piece began to become first a favorite and then almost a cult. Since the 1950s, on the wings of the modern fashion for the work of Weill and of the politically extravagant Brecht, most particularly among intellectuals, students, and the managers of subsidized theaters, *Die Dreigroschenoper* has won a vast number of productions, establishing itself ahead of any and every show to have come out of the German musical theater as its most often-played representative on the late twentieth-century stage, while its songs—topped by the nasal, eerie Morität (best known to English speakers as "Mack the Knife")—have become regularly performed favorites in largely the same milieus.

DIE DREIGROSCHENOPER, Stück mit Musik in a prelude and 8 scenes, based on *The Beggar's Opera* by John Gay. Translated by Elisabeth Hauptmann. German adaptation by Bertolt Brecht. Music by Kurt Weill. Produced at the Theater am Schiffbauerdamm, Berlin, 31 August 1928.

Characters: Jonathan Jeremiah Peachum, Frau Peachum, Polly Peachum, Macheath, Brown, Lucy, Trauerweidenwalter, Hakenfingerjakob, Münzmatthias, Sägerobert, Ede, Jimmy, Filch, Spelunkenjenny, Dolly, Molly, Betty, Dixie, Reverend Kimball, Smith, Beggar, &c.

Plot: See The Beggar's Opera.

Songs: Morität: "Und der Haifisch, der hat Zähne" (Street Singer), Morgenchoral: "Wach' auf, du verrotteter Christ" (Peachum), "Anstatt Dass" (Peachum, Mrs Peachum), Hochzeitslied: "Bill Lawgen und Mary Syer" (three thieves, Street Singer), Seeräuberjenny: "Meine Herrn heut sehn Sie mich Gläser aufwaschen" (Jenny), Kanonen-Song: "John war darunter und Jim war dabei" (Brown, Macheath), Liebeslied: "Siehst du den Mond über Soho" (Polly, Macheath), Barbarasong: "Einst glaubte ich" (Polly), Finale Act 1: "Was ich möchte, ist es viel?," Abschiedslied: "Er kommt nicht wieder" (Polly), "Die Liebe dauert oder dauert nicht" (Macheath), Ballade von der sexuellen Hörigkeit: "Da ist nun einer schon der Satan selber" (Mrs Peachum), Zuhälterballade: "In einer Zeit" (Jenny, Macheath), Ballade vom angenehmen Leben: "Da preist man uns das Leben grosser Geister" (Macheath), Eifersuchtsduo: "Komm heraus, du Schönheit von Soho" (Lucy, Polly), Finale Act 2: "Ihr Herrn, die ihr uns lernt," Lied von der Unzulänglichkeit meschlichens Strebens: "Der Mensch lebt durch den Kopf" (Peachum), Salomonsong: "Ihr saht den weisen Salomon" (Jenny), Ruf aus den Grabe: "Nun hört die Stimme, die um Mitlied ruft" (Macheath), Grabschrift: "Ihr Menschenbrüder, die ihr nach uns lebt" (Macheath), Finale Act 3: "Horch! Horch! Horch!"

The Central European 1920s produced a phalanx of fine musicals of all kinds to set alongside the dazzling musical comedies of the French theater, and the triumphant two-part output of its American counterpart. Among them, the three centers furnished the stages of the world with a variety of entertainments like no other era before it and no other after it, for never again would the three principal theaters of the world—the French, the English, and the German—flourish simultaneously and provide the world with such an array of musical theater. In just a few years the boom would be over, but, in the meantime, the musical-theater world had never had it so good.

SOME NOTABLE MUSICALS 1915–1929

1915   ADDIO, GIOVINEZZA [Goodbye to youth] (Guiseppe Pietri/Camasio, Oxilia) Politeama Goldoni, Livorno, 20 January
BETTY (Paul Rubens/Adrian Ross/Frederic Lonsdale, Gladys Unger) Daly's Theatre, London, 24 April
SO LONG, LETTY (Earl Carroll/Oliver Morosco, Elmer Harris) Morosco Theatre, Los Angeles, 3 July
DIE KAISERIN [The empress] (Leo Fall/Julius Brammer, Alfred Grünwald) Metropol-theater, Berlin, 16 October
DIE CSÁRDÁSFÜRSTIN [The csárdás-countess] (Emmerich Kálmán/Leo Stein, Béla Jenbach) Johann Strauss-Theater, Vienna, 17 November
KATINKA (Rudolf Friml/Otto Harbach) 44th Street Theatre, New York, 23 December
VERY GOOD EDDIE (Jerome Kern/Schuyler Green/Philip Bartholomae, Guy Bolton) Princess Theatre, New York, 23 December

1916   DAS DREIMÄDERLHAUS [The house of the three girls] (Franz Schubert, arr. Heinrich Berté/Arthur M. Willner, Heinz Reichert) Raimundtheater, Vienna, 15 January
MÁGNÁS MISKA [Miska, the magnate] (Albert Szirmai/Károly Bakonyi) Király Színház, Budapest, 2 February
CHU CHIN CHOW (Frederic Norton/Oscar Asche) His Majesty's Theatre, London, 31 August
DER SOLDAT DER MARIE [Marie's soldier] (Leo Ascher/Alfred Schönfeld, Bernhard Buchbinder, Jean Kren) Neues Operettenhaus, Berlin, 2 September
THEODORE & CO. (Ivor Novello, Jerome Kern/Clifford Grey, Adrian Ross/George Grossmith, H. M. Harwood) Gaiety Theatre, London, 19 September
HANNI GEHT'S TANZEN [Hanni goes dancing] (Edmund Eysler/Robert Bodanzky) Apollotheater, Vienna, 7 November
DIE ROSE VON STAMBUL [The rose of Stambul] (Leo Fall/Julius Brammer, Alfred Grünwald) Theater an der Wien, Vienna, 2 December

1917   THE MAID OF THE MOUNTAINS (Harold Fraser-Simson/Frederic Lonsdale) Daly's Theatre, London, 10 February
OH, BOY! (Jerome Kern/P. G. Wodehouse/Guy Bolton) Princess Theatre, New York, 20 February
THE BETTER 'OLE (Herman Darewski et al./James Hurd/Bruce Bairnsfather, Arthur Eliot) Oxford Theatre, London, 4 August

DAS SCHWARZWALDMÄDEL [The girl from the Black Forest] (Leon Jessel/August Neidhart) Komische Oper, Berlin, 25 August

LEAVE IT TO JANE (Jerome Kern/Guy Bolton, P. G. Wodehouse) Longacre Theatre, New York, 28 August

THE BOY (Howard Talbot, Lionel Monckton/Adrian Ross, Percy Greenbank/Fred Thompson) Adelphi Theatre, London, 14 September

DREI ALTE SCHACHTELN [Three old maids] (Walter Kollo/Rideamus, Herman Haller) Theater am Nollendorfplatz, Berlin, 6 October

YES, UNCLE! (Nat Ayer/Clifford Grey/Austen Hurgon, George Arthurs) Prince of Wales Theatre, London, 29 December

1918   A PACSIRTA [The lark] (Franz Lehár/Ferenc Martos) Király Színház, Budapest, 1 January

THE RAINBOW GIRL (Louis Hirsch/Rennold Wolf) New Amsterdam Theatre, New York, 1 April

THE GIRL BEHIND THE GUN (also known as KISSING TIME) (Ivan Caryll/P. G. Wodehouse, Guy Bolton) New Amsterdam Theatre, New York, 16 September

LA REINE JOYEUSE [The merry queen] (revised version) (Charles Cuvillier/André Barde) Théâtre Apollo, Paris, 1 November

PHI-PHI (Henri Christiné/Albert Willemetz, Fabien Sollar) Théâtre des Bouffes-Parisiens, Paris, 12 November

GOING UP (Louis Hirsch/Otto Harbach) Liberty Theatre, New York, 25 December

1919   MONSIEUR BEAUCAIRE (André Messager/Adrian Ross/Frederic Lonsdale) Prince's Theatre, London, 19 April

DIE FRAU IM HERMELIN [The lady in ermine] (Jean Gilbert/Ernst Welisch, Rudolf Schanzer) Theater des Westens, Berlin, 23 August

WHO'S HOOPER? (Ivor Novello, Howard Talbot/Clifford Grey/Fred Thompson) Adelphi Theatre, London, 13 September

IRENE (Harry Tierney/Joseph McCarthy/James Montgomery) Vanderbilt Theatre, New York, 18 November

1920   DAS HOLLANDWEIBCHEN [The Dutch lady] (Emmerich Kálmán/Leo Stein, Béla Jenbach) Johann Strauss-Theater, Vienna, 30 January

THE NIGHT BOAT (Jerome Kern/Anne Caldwell) Liberty Theatre, New York, 2 February

DER LETZTE WALZER [The last waltz] (Oscar Straus/Julius Brammer, Alfred Grünwald) Berliner Theater, Berlin, 12 February

DIE BLAUE MAZUR [The blue mazurka] (Franz Lehár/Leo Stein, Béla Jenbach) Theater an der Wien, Vienna, 28 May

A NIGHT OUT (Willie Redstone/Clifford Grey/George Grossmith, Arthur Miller) Winter Garden Theatre, London, 19 September

MARY (Louis Hirsch/Otto Harbach, Frank Mandel) Knickerbocker Theatre, New York, 18 October

L'ACQUA CHETA [Still waters] (Guiseppe Pietri/Angelo Nessi/Agusto Novelli) Teatro Nationale, Rome, 27 November

SALLY (Jerome Kern/Clifford Grey/Guy Bolton) New Amsterdam Theatre, New York, 21 December

DER TANZ INS GLÜCK [The dance towards happiness] (Robert Stolz/Robert Bodanzky, Bruno Hardt-Warden) Raimundtheater, Vienna, 23 December

1921 DAS VETTER AUS DINGSDA [The cousin from Thingummyjig] (Eduard Künneke/Rideamus, Hermann Haller) Theater am Nollendorfplatz, Berlin, 15 April

SHUFFLE ALONG (Eubie Blake/Flournoy Miller, Aubrey Lyles) 63rd Street Theatre, New York, 23 May

TANGERINE (Monte Carlo, Alma Sanders/Philip Bartholomae, Guy Bolton) Casino Theatre, New York, 9 August

THE O'BRIEN GIRL (Louis Hirsch/Frank Mandel, Otto Harbach) Liberty Theatre, New York, 3 October

GOOD MORNING, DEARIE (Jerome Kern/Anne Caldwell) Globe Theatre, New York, 1 November

DÉDÉ (Henri Christiné/Albert Willemetz) Théâtre des Bouffes-Parisiens, Paris, 10 November

DIE BAJADERE (Emmerich Kálmán/Julius Brammer, Alfred Grünwald) Carltheater, Vienna, 23 December

1922 TA BOUCHE [Your lips] (Maurice Yvain/Albert Willemetz/Yves Mirande [Gustave Quinson]) Théâtre Daunou, Paris, 1 April

FRASQUITA (Franz Lehár/Arthur M. Willner, Heinz Reichert) Theater an der Wien, Vienna, 12 May

MADAME POMPADOUR (Leo Fall/Rudolf Schanzer, Ernst Welisch) Berliner Theater, Berlin, 9 September

LITTLE NELLIE KELLY (George M. Cohan) Liberty Theatre, New York, 13 November

1923 KATJA, DIE TÄNZERIN [Katja the dancing-girl] (Jean Gilbert/Rudolf Österreicher, Leopold Jacobson) Johann Strauss-Theater, Vienna, 5 January

WILDFLOWER (Rudolf Friml, Herbert Stothart/Oscar Hammerstein II, Otto Harbach) Casino Theatre, New York, 7 February

JE T'VEUX [I want ya!] (René Mercier, Fred Pearly, Gaston Gabaroche, Albert Valsien/Battaille-Henri/Wilned, Marcel Grandjean) Théâtre Marigny, Paris, 12 February

L'AMOUR MASQUÉ [Cupid in a Mask] (André Messager/Sacha Guitry) Théâtre Édouard VII, Paris, 15 February

LÀ-HAUT [Up there] (Maurice Yvain/Yves Mirande [Gustave Quinson]) Théâtre des Bouffes-Parisiens, Paris, 31 March

CIBOULETTE (Reynaldo Hahn/Robert de Flers, Francis de Croisset) Théâtre des Variétés, Paris, 7 April

LE PETIT CHOC [The little "collision"] (Josef Szulc/P.-L. Flers) Théâtre Daunou, Paris, 25 May

LITTLE JESSIE JAMES (Harry Archer/Harlan Thompson) Longacre Theatre, New York, 15 August

MADAME (Henri Christiné/Albert Willemetz) Théâtre Daunou, Paris, 14 December

1924 GRÄFIN MARIZA [Countess Mariza] (Emmerich Kálmán/Julius Brammer, Alfred Grünwald) Theater an der Wien, Vienna, 28 February

GOSSE DE RICHE [Little rich girl] (Maurice Yvain/Jacques Bousquet, Henri Falk) Théâtre Daunou, Paris, 2 May

NO, NO, NANETTE (Vincent Youmans/Irving Caesar, Frank Mandel, Otto Harbach) Harris Theatre, Chicago, 7 May

ROSE MARIE (Rudolf Friml, Herbert Stothart/Oscar Hammerstein II, Otto Harbach) Imperial Theatre, New York, 2 September

TROUBLEZ-MOI [Get under my skin . . .] (Raoul Moretti/Yves Mirande) Théâtre des Bouffes-Parisiens, Paris, 17 September

LADY, BE GOOD! (George Gershwin/Ira Gershwin/Guy Bolton, Fred Thompson) Liberty Theatre, New York, 1 December

THE STUDENT PRINCE (Sigmund Romberg/Dorothy Donnelly) Jolson Theatre, New York, 2 December

1925 RIQUETTE (Oscar Straus/Ernst Welisch, Rudolf Schanzer) Deutsches Künstlertheater, Berlin, 17 January

PAS SUR LA BOUCHE [Not on the lips] (Maurice Yvain/André Barde) Théâtre des Nouveautés, Paris, 17 February

DER ORLOW (Bruno Granichstädten/Ernst Marischka) Theater an der Wien, Vienna, 3 April

MERCENARY MARY (Con Conrad, William B. Friedlander/Irving Caesar/Isabel Leighton) Longacre Theatre, New York, 13 April

QUAND ON EST TROIS [When there are three of us] (Josef Szulc/Pierre Veber, Serge Veber, Albert Willemetz) Théâtre des Capucines, Paris, 20 April

P.L.M. [Railway] (Henri Christiné/Rip) Théâtre des Bouffes-Parisiens, Paris, 21 April

THE VAGABOND KING (Rudolf Friml/W. H. Post, Brian Hooker) Casino Theatre, New York, 21 September

SUNNY (Jerome Kern/Oscar Hammerstein II, Otto Harbach) New Amsterdam Theatre, New York, 22 September

MANNEQUINS (Josef Szulc/Jacques Bousquet, Henri Falk) Théâtre des Capucines, Paris, 30 October

PAGANINI (Franz Lehár/Paul Knepler, Béla Jenbach) Johann Strauss-Theater, Vienna, 30 October

ALEXANDRA (Albert Szirmai/Ferenc Martos) Király Színház, Budapest, 25 November

TROIS JEUNES FILLES . . . NUES! [Three girls – stripped!] (Raoul Moretti/Yves Mirande, Albert Willemetz) Théâtre des Bouffes-Parisiens, Paris, 3 December

CIN-CI-LÀ (Virgilio Ranzato/Carlo Lombardo) Teatro dal Verme, Milan, 18 December

TIP-TOES (George Gershwin/Ira Gershwin/Fred Thompson, Guy Bolton) Liberty Theatre, New York, 28 December

1926 PASSIONNÉMENT [With passion] (André Messager/Albert Willemetz, Maurice Hennequin) Théâtre de la Michodière, Paris, 15 January

DIE ZIRKUSPRINZESSIN [The circus princess] (Emmerich Kálmán/Julius Brammer, Alfred Grünwald) Theater an der Wien, Vienna, 26 March

KITTY'S KISSES (Con Conrad/Gus Kahn/Otto Harbach, Philip Bartholomae) Playhouse Theatre, New York, 6 May

OH, KAY! (George Gershwin/Ira Gershwin/Guy Bolton, P. G. Wodehouse) Imperial Theatre, New York, 8 November

UN BON GARÇON [A good waiter] (Maurice Yvain/André Barde) Théâtre des Nouveautés, Paris, 13 November

THE DESERT SONG (Sigmund Romberg/Oscar Hammerstein II, Otto Harbach, Frank
Mandel) Casino Theatre, New York, 30 November

J'AIME [I'm in love] (Henri Christiné/Albert Willemetz, Saint-Granier) Théâtre des
Bouffes-Parisiens, Paris, 22 December

1927   RIO RITA (Harry Tierney/Joseph McCarthy/Fred Thompson, Guy Bolton) Ziegfeld
Theatre, New York, 2 February

DER ZAREWITSCH [Son of the czar] (Franz Lehár/ Béla Jenbach, Heinz Reichert)
Deutsches Künstlertheater, Berlin, 21 February

HIT THE DECK (Vincent Youmans/Leo Robin, Clifford Grey/Herbert Fields) Belasco
Theatre, New York, 25 April

LADY LUCK (Jack Strachey, H. B. Hedley/Desmond Carter/Firth Shephard) Carlton
Theatre, London, 27 April

GOOD NEWS (Ray Henderson/B. G. De Sylva, Lew Brown/Laurence Schwab) 46th Street
Theatre, New York, 6 September

DIE GOLD'NE MEISTERIN [The lady goldsmith] (Edmund Eysler/Julius Brammer,
Alfred Grünwald) Theater an der Wien, Vienna, 13 September

LULU (Georges van Parys, Philippe Parès/Serge Veber) Théâtre Daunou, Paris,
14 September

A CONNECTICUT YANKEE (Richard Rodgers/Lorenz Hart/Herbert Fields) Vanderbilt
Theatre, New York, 3 November

FUNNY FACE (George Gershwin/Ira Gershwin/Fred Thompson, Paul Gerard Smith)
Alvin Theatre, New York, 22 November

COMTE OBLIGADO (Raoul Moretti/André Barde) Théâtre des Nouveautés, Paris,
16 December

SHOW BOAT (Jerome Kern/Oscar Hammerstein II) Ziegfeld Theatre, New York,
27 December

1928   YES (Maurice Yvain/Albert Willemetz/René Pujol, Pierre Souvaine) Théâtre des Capucines,
Paris, 26 January

THE THREE MUSKETEERS (Rudolf Friml/P. G. Wodehouse, Clifford Grey/W. A.
McGuire) Lyric Theater, New York, 13 March

SO THIS IS LOVE ("Hal Brody"/Desmond Carter/Stanley Lupino, Arthur Rigby) Winter
Garden Theatre, London, 25 April

DIE DREIGROSCHENOPER [The threepenny opera] (Kurt Weill/Elisabeth Hauptmann, Bertolt Brecht) Theater am Schiffbauerdamm, Berlin, 31 August

CASANOVA (Johann Strauss, arr. Ralph Benatzky/Ernst Welisch, Rudolf Schanzer) Grosses
Schauspielhaus, Berlin, 1 September

THE NEW MOON (Sigmund Romberg/Frank Mandel, Oscar Hammerstein II) Imperial
Theatre, New York, 19 September

MR CINDERS (Vivian Ellis, Richard Myers/Leo Robin, Clifford Grey, Greatrex Newman)
Opera House, Blackpool, 25 September

COUPS DE ROULIS [Wavy waters] (André Messager/Albert Willemetz) Théâtre Marigny, Paris, 29 September

FRIEDERIKE (Franz Lehár/Ludwig Herzer, Fritz Löhner-Beda) Deutsches Künstler-theater, Berlin, 4 October

WHOOPEE (Walter Donaldson/Gus Kahn/William A. McGuire) New Amsterdam Theatre, New York, 4 December

1929 LOVE LIES ("Hal Brody"/Desmond Carter/Stanley Lupino, Arthur Rigby) Gaiety Theatre, London, 20 March

BITTER-SWEET (Noël Coward) His Majesty's Theatre, London, 12 July

ARTHUR (Henri Christiné/André Barde) Théâtre Daunou, Paris, 4 September

DAS LAND DES LÄCHELNS [The land of smiles] (Franz Lehár/Ludwig Herzer, Fritz Löhner-Beda) Metropoltheater, Berlin, 10 October

THE WHITE HOU

*T*he years since the war had been the most prolific and productive in the history of the international musical stage and, although it was inevitable that such a bonanza should come to an end, that it should have come to an end quite so emphatically and quite so generally was a bit of a shocker. Of course, social circumstances didn't help. The economic depression which hit the world in the early 1930s had an obvious effect both on theater-going and on theatrical production. All around the world, the lavish levels of productions of new musicals that had been attained in the thriving twenties tumbled, and attendance figures tumbled as well. The theater was no longer—and was never going to be again—the vigorous institution it had been in the couple of decades up to that time when the first clammy intimations of the hard years of the 1930s began to appear in people's pockets.

The three traditions which had prospered, the one alongside the other, in the 1920s foundered almost together, but they foundered in different ways and with different degrees of severity. Undoubtedly the hardest hit of the three was the Central European musical theater, which suffered devastatingly from the political correction and ethnic cleansing imposed in these years by the Hitler régime. A vast proportion of the most important creative personnel of the Operette world were, at first, prevented from working in their profession, then ultimately forced to flee, initially from Germany, and later from Austria and Hungary as well, and the Operette, which was already coming to a crisis point where its star composers—many of them on the scene now for some thirty years—were reaching the latter part of their careers without too many obvious heirs in sight, found itself bled of virtually all its most effective writers. The result was even more severe than might have been expected, for the musical-theater tradition of Central Europe—desperately wounded—quite simply collapsed into a coma from which even now, more than half a century on, it still shows but small signs of awakening.

At the dawn of the 1930s, however, there was still hope. Although Lehár was tailing off and out with his last vehicles for the tenorious Tauber—the less gloomy than usual *Schön ist die Welt* and, in 1934, the wilfully sub-operatic and less than successful *Giuditta*—although Kálmán, Eysler, Gilbert, Straus, and their contemporaries were now turning out the tag-end of their long lists of works, mostly Operetten which were without the éclat or effect of their early ones, although Szirmai—following the unhappy Jacobi—had abandoned Europe for the to-be-unfulfilled promises of America, and although Granichstädten, Stolz, and others had turned most of their attentions to the blossoming fashion for musical film, there were still a handful of newer men around who seemed capable of keeping the ship afloat. There was Eduard Künneke, who scored a second success with a jolly, colorful, up-to-date musical comedy called *Glückliche Reise* — a piece far away in flavor and style from the charming *Das Vetter aus Dingsda* which would remain his chief credit; there was Ralph Benatzky, the musical director of the Berlin Grosses Schauspièlhaus, who had had success in musicking both small-scale shows and vast spectaculars such as the *Casanova* mounted at his home theater; and there was Pál Ábrahám.

Ábrahám was a Hungarian, classically trained and with a keen penchant for the sounds and rhythms of modern popular music. His name made its first appearance on a musical playbill in 1928 as the "composer" of a show score which included numbers by half a dozen Tin Pan Alley songwriters as well as his own material. He followed that up with a fine Budapest hit, the musicalization of a popular Hungarian play as *Az utolsó Verebély lány*, before relocating to what were at that stage still the more profitable purlieus of Berlin. There, in the next three years, he brought to the stage the up-to-date scores — a merry mélange of traditional Operette melodies and jazzy American-flavored pieces — for three musicals. Those three musicals would be the last peak of the Operette before it began its descent into Hell.

Viktória was actually written in Hungarian and first staged in Budapest, but it was subsequently taken up in nearly all the main centers — first Leipzig, then Berlin, London, Paris, and Sydney, not to mention film-land. Only Broadway passed, and it was left to the enterprising theater in St Louis — which introduced a number of fine (and often less cavalierly rewritten) foreign works to America in these years — to give the musical its transatlantic première. The show was a classic mixture of the romantic and the soubret, the main triangular romance which was at the heart of the piece being seconded by another, sweeter romance between the heroine's brother and his little Japanese bride and by a lively bit of song-and-dance sweethearting for the hero's batman and a fake French maid. However, the music that illustrated it did not have the same flavor as Lehár's music to the sometimes not dissimilar *Das Land des Lächelns*. Ábrahám had achieved the most successful interbreeding of the traditional and the modern to be found in the Central European musical theater, and his score — fitted to a thoroughly international cast of characters — included a variety of musical pieces that went from traditional Hungarian and Russian to American cabaret and to a droll little piece that was supposed to be Franco-Japanese.

VIKTÓRIA, an Operette in a prologue and 3 acts by Imre Földes. Lyrics by Imre Harmath. Music by Pál Ábrahám. Produced at the Király Színház, Budapest, 21 February 1930.

Characters: John Cunlight, Viktória Cunlight, Graf Ferry Hegedüs, O Lia San, Riquette, Stefan Koltay, Janczi, Béla Pörkölty, Tokeramo Pagani, James, Japanese Oberbonze, Kamakuri o Miki, Russian Officer, a Cossack, &c.

Plot: Hussar captain Stefan Koltay and his batman Janczi escape from a Siberian death-camp and find their way to Tokyo. There Koltay encounters Viktória, the woman who had pledged to wed him before he went off to war. Thinking him dead, she at last agreed to marry John Cunlight, the American ambassador to Japan. Cunlight is transferred to St Petersburg, and Koltay, refusing to renounce Viktória, goes there with them, but when the ambassador sees his wife's terror at Koltay's expressed intention to hand himself back to the Russians, he realizes that she still loves him. A year later, back in their Hungarian hometown, the two are finally brought together by a husband who loves his wife well enough to give her up.

Songs: "An des Baikals Strand" (chorus), "Nur ein Mädel gibt es auf der Welt" (Koltay), "Glück und Freude heut' im Haus" (chorus), "Rote Orchideen" (Viktória), "Pardon, Madame" (Viktória, Cunlight), "Heut wird er mein!" (Lia), "Meine Mama war aus Yokohama" (Lia, Ferry), Finale Act 1: "Haho! Haho! Schöne Braut"/reprise "Nur ein Mädel gibt es auf der Welt" (Viktória), "Wir singen beide: Do do do Dodo!" (Ferry, Riquette), "Du warst der Stern meiner Nacht" (Viktória, Koltay), "Mausi, süss warst du heute Nacht" (Ferry, Lia), "Reich mir zum Abschied noch einmal die Hände" (Viktória, Koltay), "Honved-Banda" (Janczi, Riquette), Finale Act 2: "Hei! Hei! Wolgamädel tanz' mit mir!"/"Schöne Petrowna," "Winzerfest, Weinlesefest!" (Pörkelty, chorus), "Nur ein Ungarn, gibt es auf der Welt" (Viktória), "Ja so ein Mädel, ein ungarisches Mädel" (Janczi, Riquette), Finale Act 3: "Winzerfest, Weinlesefest!"

Viktória was followed up by a second piece with a similar flavor, but one which gave itself over more frankly to its American side. *Die Blume von Hawaii* was set on the Pacific island of the title, and its characters included both the guitar-twanging locals and the American governor of the island, his staff, and his family. The plot actually centered around the efforts of a patriotic front to restore the deposed Princess of Hawaii to the throne of her fathers, but that plot had to share space—of course—with a love story. Another three-cornered one, as in *Viktória*. The pretendants for the Princess's hand are a local Prince who had been her childhood sweetheart and an American captain of marines, and as in the earlier show it is the old, same-nation lover who gets her and the brave American who renounces his claims (but this time gets her virtual double as a consolation prize!). However, much of the joy of *Die Blume von Hawaii* came from its supporting characters: the jazzing governor's daughter and her attaché sweetheart and, most of all, the American blackface cabaret singer Jim Boy, whose musical moments— jauntily displayed alongside the soaringly lyrical love-songs and duets given to the romantic threesome—sported such titles as "Wir singen zur Jazzband im Folies-Bergère," "Bin nur ein Jonny," and "My Golden Baby." *Die Blume von Hawaii* did not win the same international exposure that *Viktória* had done, perhaps for the same reasons that *Der Orlow* had failed to export effectively, but in Central Europe it has remained a popular favorite and a part of the revivable repertoire up to this day.

Ábrahám's third show went back to the old continent for its setting, with a story of the marital misunderstandings that go on in the South of France during a *Ball im Savoy* . Once again, the mixture of romance, comedy, and a truly international potpourri of musical styles combined to make the piece a hit, and Ábrahám seemed launched as Central Europe's new star of the musical theater. But it was not to be. Soon the Jewish composer was on the run from Berlin, first to Vienna and ultimately to America, and, although he kept on writing for a while, and had several shows staged with a certain amount of success during the rest of the 1930s, his career and health both soon wasted away.

The two biggest international hits to come out of Central Europe in these last lively years of the heyday of the Operette were actually not the work of Ábrahám. Neither were they pieces with the up-to-date musical-play character of his three hit shows. Both were, in essence, big, spectacular pieces: lavishly staged good-old-daisical shows of the "wartime" variety. One was yet another of the many so-and-so-and-his-music musicals that had followed relentlessly on, through a list of composers from Offenbach to Chopin, behind the success of *Das Dreimäderl-haus*. This time it was the oh-so-obvious Strauss family who got the treatment, and Johann II whose putative love-life and struggles against his father's determination to keep him from a musical career were set to pasteurised versions of their music in a four-hour long biomusical. *Walzer aus Wien* went out from its initial success in Vienna to become *Waltzes from Vienna*, *Valses de Vienne*, *The Great Waltz*, and a long-running success in a series of grossly lavish productions across the world.

The other megahit of this time was no less spectacular in its production values, but it boasted a far livelier libretto and a delightful selection of distinctly more modern pieces of music. *Im weissen Rössl* was a musicalization of a favorite old German comedy about a bunch of city folk holidaying at an inn in the Salzkammergut, and it found its fun in the working out of the complex chain of romances that involves nearly all of them. Its music was largely the work of house composer Benatzky, but he interpolated into his score a number of individual pieces by other composers: Granichstädten, Stolz, Hans Frankowski, Anton Paulik, and others were all represented in the joyously fluid score that illustrated the merry goings-on "Im weissen Rössl am Wolfgangsee." The show was produced at Berlin's Grosses Schauspielhaus—a theater which specialized in enormous, lavish scenic productions to the extent that the "concept" or the staging of the show very often took precedence over its content. It was not a theater for a sophisticated audience, but it provided plenty of attractions for an audience which went to look rather than listen. With *Im weissen Rössl*, however, the theater dropped all the lavish romantic period decoration that had characterized such pieces as *Casanova* and *Die drei Musketieren*, it dropped the overdose of spangles and shimmy-steps that were a feature of their revusical productions and their murderously overstaged and messed about revivals of classic musicals, and instead house-director and choreographer Erik Charell turned out a show that was a sweet, bright and charming piece of thoroughly German/Austrian musical theater. Of course, Charell and the Schauspielhaus weren't going to change their spots overnight. *Im weissen Rössl* still boasted real rain, a practical train, a selection of live animals, and all the other accoutrements of the spectacular stage, and it still sported the house's vast squadron of dancers who invaded the stage at the slightest excuse, or none, with massed and extraneous dance routines—but here, instead of being just so much jaw-dropping lavishness, the cows and the train and the rain went to make up a real

Im weissen Rössl: The bulging playbill for Vienna's production of this huge spectacular lists the attractions of a piece that survived not just because of its mega-production, but because at its heart lay a delightful comedy story and characters.

stage picture, and instead of the now clichéd steps of the popular chorus dances of the era, the dancers performed stage versions of the Ländler and the Schuhplattler. Though Charell and Benatzky still managed to squeeze a jazz band into the proceedings. The result of this change of air was remarkable. *Im weissen Rössl* turned out to be the biggest musical-theater hit that the Grosses Schauspielhaus had ever had and the biggest musical-theater hit that Berlin and Germany had ever had, and—as *White Horse Inn, L'Auberge du Cheval Blanc, A fehér Lö,* and so forth—it went on from there to become internationally the most successful and often-played musical that Germany had ever produced.

IM WEISSEN RÖSSL, a Singspiel in 3 acts by Hans Müller, based on the play by Oskar Blumenthal and Gustav Kadelburg. Lyrics by Robert Gilbert and others. Music by Ralph Benatzky and others. Produced at the Grosses Schauspielhaus, Berlin, 8 November 1930.

Characters: Josepha Vogelhuber, Leopold Brandmayer, Wilhelm Giesecke, Franz, Gustl, Der Kaiser, Ottilie, Dr Otto Siedler, Sigismund Sülzheimer, Dr Hinzelmann, Klärchen, Der Bürgermeister von St Wolfgang, Kathi, Johann, Martin, &c.

Plot: Josepha, landlady of the Zum weisses Rössl inn at St Wolfgang, has put aside the best room in her hotel for the lawyer Dr Siedler, who is coming this week for his annual holiday. Her adoring head waiter, Leopold, knows that she's got her eye on Siedler, and he makes sure the plum room goes instead to the irascible underwear manufacturer Giesecke. When Siedler arrives, Josepha indignantly restores his room to him, but the lawyer has now met Giesecke's daughter, and soon Leopold is diligently and with forethought promoting a romance between the pair. Giesecke is determined that his daughter shall make a business match with the son of his competitor, but when that bald and unbeautiful young man arrives he quickly strikes up a love-match with a stuttering little lassie called Klärchen instead. And Leopold, who has finally gone too far in interfering in his employer's affairs, is sacked. But then an even more important visitor arrives: the Emperor Franz Josef himself. A little royal-fatherly advice, and Josepha's eyes are opened. Siedler is not for her. She will marry the devoted Leopold and they will run the Zum weisses Rössl together.

Songs: "Hallo! Wirtschaft! Frühstuck! Frühstuck!" (chorus), "Aber meine Herrschaften! Nur hübsch gemütlich" (Leopold), "Es muss was Wunderbares sein" (Leopold), "Das ist der Zauber der Saison" (chorus), "Im weissen Rössl am Wolfgangsee" (Josepha), "Eine Kuh, so wie du, ist das Schönste auf der Welt" (chorus), "Die ganze Welt ist himmelblau" (by Robert Stolz) (Siedler, Ottilie), Finale Act 1: reprises "Es muss was Wunderbares sein"/"Im weissen Rössl am Wolfgangsee"/"Wenn es hier mal richtig regnet," "Alle schönen guten Gaben" (chorus), "Zuschau'n kann I net" (by Bruno Granichstädten) (Leopold), "Es ist wohl nicht das letzte Mal" (Siedler, Ottilie) "In Salzkammergut" (Josepha), "Was kann der Sigismund dafür" (by Robert Gilbert) (Sigismund), "Wie tauchen dann zusammen munter" (chorus), "Und als der Herrgott Mai gemacht" (Sigismund, Klärchen), Finale Act 2: "Rechtes Bein und linkes Bein," "Leise, leise, leise, leise" (chorus), "'s ist einmal im Leben so" (Kaiser), "Mein Liebeslied muss ein Walzer sein" (Ottilie, Siedler), Finale Act 3: reprise "Mein Liebeslied muss ein Walzer sein." Additional and alternative numbers included: "Erst wann's aus wird sein" (by Hans Frankowski), "Miska und Will" (chorus), "Ischl" (by Anton Paulik/Karl Farkas) (chorus), Quodlibet (by Paulik/Farkas), "Ich hab' es fünfzigmal geschworen" (by Granichstädten/Farkas).

Im weissen Rössl, *Walzer aus Wien*, *Viktória*, and an inventive "Spiel in Nachtleben" (a tale of nightlife) called *Die Wunder-Bar*, which set its effective and dramatic tale of amorous intrigue in a working nightclub and transformed the auditorium into that club, all came out in 1930. *Die Blume von Hawaii* appeared in 1931—a year which saw the production of a very backward-looking Berlin hit in the shape of a remake of the *Dubarry* story with a pasticcio of Millöcker music as its score—and Künneke's *Glückliche Reise* in 1932. *Ball im Savoy*, a stage version of Stolz's successful film *Zwei Herzen in dreivierteltakt*, and Oscar Straus's last vehicle for Massary, the charming and successful *Eine Frau, die weiss, was sie will*, were premièred in 1933, and Lehár's last musical, *Giuditta*, in 1934. And that was it. Then came the dark. The best that the Central European stage could come up with in the decade that followed were Fred Raymond's pretty but unexceptional little tale of a *Saison im Salzburg* (with a plot that centered around a kind of sticky waffle!) and yet another twentieth-century nineteenth-century musical decorated with the music of the Strauss family. *Drei Walzer*, however, had the great advantage over its predecessors in that it was musically arranged by a masterly hand of Oscar Straus, and was not pinned to one of those soupy so-and-so-and-his-music libretti, but to a pretty tale of period Vienna. Only, this show was produced in Switzerland, and in the atmosphere of the time, it did not make its way to Berlin, Vienna, or Budapest.

If the Central European musical quite simply faded away—going from full-strength prosperity to virtual extinction in just a handful of years—the French stage did little better. The first years of the 1930s saw the last of the true musical comedies of the années folles dance their merry way across a Parisian stage literally invaded by a plethora of lavishly produced shows imported from Vienna, Berlin, Budapest, New York, and London. *Friederike*, *Die Csárdásfürstin*, *Madame Pompadour*, *The Desert Song*, *The New Moon*, *Bitter-Sweet*, *Gräfin Mariza*, *Hit the*

Deck, Das Land des Lächelns, Nina Rosa, Im weissen Rössl, Frasquita, Valses de Vienne, Viktória, Die Blume von Hawaii, the Hungarian *Öfelsége frakkja*, and even Romberg and Benatzky musicals actually made to order for Paris, all took to the French stage in just the first three years of the decade, and the local writers, who had so dominated the scene with their brilliant musical plays only a few years earlier, could put up barely a handful of still sprightly and piquant musical comedies alongside them. And so the inevitable happened. Since it was opérette à grand spectacle and music made to its measure that drew the crowds nowadays, rather than the witty words and dancing tunes of a decade earlier, the men who had fabricated the hits of the twenties shifted their pen into their other hand and started to write musicals along those lines.

The results were not wholly unsuccessful. Not from a commercial point of view. Josef Szulc did splendidly with the North African tale of *Sidonie Panache*, a piece of which the highlight was not its words or its music but an on-stage cavalry charge; Maurice Yvain supplied the scores for *Au soleil du Mexique* and two other pieces for the vast stage of the Théâtre du Châtelet; and Christiné teamed with Tiarko Richepin on two other spectaculars for the same house. And the public came to look, and intermittently to listen, through considerable runs.

Alongside these megamusicals, the French stage did, however, turn out a handful of more realistically sized shows. A funny Caribbean piece called *Toi c'est moi* with a score composed by the Cuban "inventor" of the rhumba, Moïse Simon, a sentimental wartime piece called *La Cocarde de Mimi-Pinson*, a vehicle for the film-star Fernandel as the military-buffoonish *Ignace*, and a merry series of Marseillaise shows written by and starring the actor Alibert all did well enough on home stages, but the French musical theater of the middle and later 1930s produced only one show which proved to be both enduringly successful and exportable—and it was hardly a French show at all. *Trois Valses* was nothing more or less than a French adaptation of the same *Drei Walzer* which had been mounted earlier in Zürich. In spite of its failure to travel eastwards, it had—thanks to the friendship between Oscar Straus and Yvonne Printemps—come to Paris, made over as a vehicle for France's most celebrated singing actress. *Trois Valses* wasn't quite *Drei Walzer*. It had been remade to give maximum opportunities to its star—who got to sing Johann Strauss I melodies in act 1, Johann Strauss II tunes in act 2, and up-to-date numbers by Oscar Straus in the last act—as well as sufficient acting moments for her partner, Pierre Fresnay, to earn his co-star billing while yet hardly singing at all. The remake proved an enormous success, and the show—which might otherwise have ended with its Zürich run—went on to London, to Broadway, to endless revivals on the French stage and ultimately to the screen in a French film version which is one of the cinematic classics of its time.

TROIS VALSES, an opérette in 3 acts and 11 tableaux by Léopold Marchand and Albert Willemetz, based on the libretto by Paul Knepler and Armin Robinson. Music written and arranged by Oscar Straus, using the melodies of Johann Strauss I and Johann Strauss II. Produced in this version at the Théâtre des Bouffes-Parisiens, Paris, 22 April 1937.

Characters: Fanny Grandpré/Yvette Grandpré/Irène, Octave de Chalency/Philippe de Chalency/ Gérard de Chalency, Brunner père/Dulaurier/Le Producteur, Brunner fils, Beltramini/Cyprien de Chalency-Croixville/L'Auteur/Le Metteur en scène, Saint-Prix/Le Compositeur, La Douarière de Chalency/Mme Jules, Le Président de Chalency, Le Colonel de Chalency, Le Maréchal de Chalency/L'Amant/L'Assistant, Le Commandant Sosthène de Chalency, Florent, Céleste/Mlle Raphaëlson, Mme Castelli/Capitaine des Grenadiers, Le Peintre/Le Directeur/Founicola, Le Régisseur, &c.

Plot: 1867: the danseuse Fanny Grandpré is in love with the aristocratic Octave de Chalency, but she leaves him and goes abroad rather than have him marry her and lose his place in society and his commission in the army. 1900: Fanny's daughter, Yvette, is a star of the Parisian opérette. She meets the handsome Philippe de Chalency and the two fall in love, but once again their romance is balked. 1937: Yvette's daughter Irène is a film-star, hired to make a film about her grandmother's life and love. The part of Octave has proven difficult to cast, and in the end has been given to a neophyte who is nevertheless perfect in the rôle. He ought to be, for he is Philippe's son, Gérard de Chalency. And this time love has its way.

Songs: "C'est la saison d'amour" (Fanny), Duo des deux Brunner (Brunner père, Brunner fils), "Nous arrivons, que nous veut-on?" (Sextet), Le Conseil de famille (La Douarière, Le Président, Le Colonel, Le Maréchal, Le Commandant, Cyprien), "Te souvient-il?" (Fanny), "C'est l'amour" (ensemble), "Je t'aime" (Yvette), "Quand sur la pièce" (ensemble), "Oui, je t'aime, ô Paris" (Yvette), "Chez Maxim's au petit matin" (Yvette, Philippe), Couplets de l'habilleuse (Mme Jules), Quattour polyglotte (Producteur, Assistant, Founicola, Mlle Raphaëlson), Finale Act 2, "C'est le destin, peut-être" (Irène), Duo de la synchronisation (Assistant, Irène), "Comme autrefois" (Brunner), "Je ne suis pas ce que l'on pense" (Irène), Finale Act 3.

Unlike the Central European musical theater, its French equivalent did not go under terminally in the 1930s. It had still a little life left to it, and in the 1940s it would again come alive for a while before, in its turn, succumbing utterly a couple of decades later.

The English-language theater during these years sank altogether less low than its French and German partners. Both Broadway and London managed to keep themselves theatrically afloat through the Depression, turning out a series of musicals for their own entertainment which, nevertheless, did not very often—as the musicals of the previous era had done—go on to find a wider audience.

As in the 1920s—though now less markedly—it was the American stage which contributed most of those shows which proved widely popular in English-singing theaters. They were not, by and large, either shows which had the zingy modernity of the Broadway musicals of the twenties, or ones which had the glamorously escapist appeal and rolling music of the same era's romantic pieces, but they nevertheless managed to fill quite a few theaters for quite a few performances, and—often with the aid of the newly popular musical film—they made into long-living standards a goodly number of the songs that were played in them.

That newly popular musical film, however, didn't do Broadway a lot of favors. The dollars and the opportunities to be mined working in the cinema industry persuaded quite a few of the songwriting stars of the 1920s to devote themselves to this alternative form of song- and money-making, and, at one time or another in the last years of the twenties and the first half of the thirties, most of the men who had made the music for the Broadway musical of the jazz age trotted across the continent to Hollywood. Some found success there and stayed, others found little, or else found themselves ill-suited by the life- and work-styles of the film world, and returned—with more or with much less success—to the theater. But, for whatever reason—and in some cases it was just a case of a career that died—a large proportion of the men whose names had so merrily decorated Broadway's bills during the boom years since the end of the war were no longer to be found to the theatrical fore in the 1930s. Youmans—Mr *No, No, Nanette* himself—Rudolf Friml, Sigmund Romberg (who turned out five more romantic musicals but without his former far-flung success), Harry Tierney, and Harry Archer all faded away in failure, Conrad and the De Sylva, Brown, and Henderson team devoted themselves to filmland, and if Rodgers and Hart found little success out west and returned fairly soon to Broadway, Jerome Kern spent several years writing productively for the screen rather than for the stage, and turned out only one more Broadway musical after his return to the theater. As for George Gershwin, he moved on both to the cinema and to a different field of theatrical endeavor with his folk opera *Porgy and Bess* before his premature death in 1937.

Before Kern's departure for filmland and Gershwin's for the folk opera, however, both supplied the theater with a handful of 1930s musicals. In the wake of *Show Boat*, Kern devoted himself to the romantic musical rather than the musical comedy, and in the first years of the thirties he turned out three such pieces set to libretti which were either conventionally "Continental" or which turned back to the good old Americans-in-romantic-places formula. The romantic places nowadays were not extravagantly colorful oriental islands, but rather present-day Paris and Brussels. Americans-in-Paris shows would become quite as much a cliché over the years to come as the other kind had been around the beginning of the new century.

Music in the Air was sort of Sacher-Torte Operette. And like all Sacher-Torte which are made anywhere but Vienna, it wasn't the real thing and it showed. Oscar Hammerstein II turned out an imitation Viennese book, full of the clichés of the Continental Operette—the tempestuous diva and her composer lover, the little village lassie who almost becomes a star but goes home instead to her village sweetheart—which Kern set with a score that was mostly anything but Viennese in flavor. Numbers such as "I've Told Every Little Star" and "The Song Is You" and a pretty production, however, did enough to give *Music in the Air* a fair Broadway run and an almost fair London one. In Australia, it bombed catastrophically.

The other two pieces were similarly handicapped by weak libretti, this time written by the other champion book-writer of the past years, Otto Harbach. *The Cat and the Fiddle* was a Belgian-based love-story featuring a serious Continental composer and an American popular song-writer (she sticks her songs in his serious-to-pretentious musical scena and makes it into a hit), and *Roberta* was a romantic-plus-comic piece set around a Parisian dressmaking concern. A footballing hero and the assistant modiste of the business he inherits provided the love-story, and she—of course—turned out to be (oh no!!) a Princess. Songs such as the first show's "She Didn't Say 'Yes'" and the second's "Smoke Gets in Your Eyes" and "Yesterdays" showed that Kern was still turning out some of the best songs on Broadway, and, not surprisingly, those numbers survived very much better than the creaky shows did. After a series of films in the mid-1930s, Kern returned to Broadway one last time in 1939 with *Very Warm for May*, which added "All the Things You Are" to his list of show-song hits.

The Gershwin brothers did altogether better with their book-writers. Their 1930 musical *Girl Crazy*—libretto by a third favorite of former years, Guy Bolton, and John McGowan—was a merry bit of wildish-West nonsense which dumped its high-living New Yorkish hero down not in the up-to-date Ruritania of Paris, but in the middle of the much more fun-filled American nowheres. Of course, he still found a girl there. And she sang "But Not for Me" and "Embraceable You." Alongside these romantic ballads, the score to the show also included pieces both atmospheric ("Cactus Time in Arizona," "I'm Bidin' My Time"), lively ("I Got Rhythm"), and comic ("Boy, What Love Has Done to Me"), all of which helped the cheerful *Girl Crazy* to tot up the best Broadway record of any Gershwin show bar the Astaire-ful *Lady, Be Good!*

In spite of this success, the Gershwins changed direction dramatically for their next piece. *Of Thee I Sing* was, quite simply, an American opéra-bouffe. It was also a piece of deliciously extravagant burlesque writing such as the Broadway stage had never spawned before. The text for the musical was the work of George S. Kaufman and Morrie Ryskind, both of whom had had a hand (as writer, and as rewriter) in an earlier Gershwin musical called *Strike up the Band* (1927, 1930). *Strike up the Band*—which drew its fun from a preposterously surreal tale of international political goings-on not too far distant in flavor from that of *La Grande-Duchesse de Gérolstein*—had, in fact, gone halfway along the "bouffe" path which *Of Thee I Sing* was so successfully to take, but it had succeeded only slightly better in its remake than in its aborted initial version, and its title-song—meant as a parody—had suffered the fate of such other mock-patriotic pieces as W. S. Gilbert's "When Britain Really Ruled the Waves" and ended up being taken at its face value.

There was no chance at all of anyone taking *Of Thee I Sing* at face value. It was written with true bouffe flair, its characters were deliciously over-the-top and to-the-point, and its story of one ordinary everyday American President's acquisition of both a bed in the White House and a muffin-baking wife was witty, pointed, and yet never vicious. Kaufman and Ryskind's portrait of the Vice President, chosen by lot and whose name and function no one can ever remember—until he is called on to deputize for his principal—was a special success. Gershwin used a whole different musical artillery for his score to this piece, capturing the spirit of burlesque splendidly in pieces ranging from a campaign song in praise of love to a dramatic first-act finale in which the President's rejected would-be spouse descends on the White House with all the storming power of Katisha in *The Mikado*. The result was a musical which had a fine Broad-

Of Thee I Sing: "Love is sweeping the country . . ." An American presidential election is won by a candidate running on a ticket of "Love." Alas, it was only a fantasy.

way run, won itself a Pulitzer Prize, and made itself a special spot in the sun in the history of the Broadway stage.

OF THEE I SING, a musical comedy in 2 acts and 11 scenes by George S. Kaufman and Morrie Ryskind. Lyrics by Ira Gershwin. Music by George Gershwin. Produced at the Music Box Theatre, New York, 26 December 1931.

Characters: Louis Lippman, Francis X. Gilhooley, Matthew Arnold Fulton, Senator Robert E. Lyons, Senator Carver Jones, Alexander Throttlebottom, John P. Wintergreen, Diana Devereaux, Mary Turner, Miss Benson, Vladimir Vidovitch, Yussef Yussevitch, The Chief Justice, The French Ambassador, Nora, senate clerk, Maid, Guide, &c.

Plot: John Wintergreen has been nominated for President, with whatshisname as his running mate, and the boys of the Committee are setting out his campaign plan. An Ordinary American tells them that what Ordinary Americans care about most (apart from money, of course) is Love, so Wintergreen goes to the hustings on a program of Love. Since he is a bachelor, without even a steady girl, the boys organize a competition to find a Mrs President, and the winner is the voluptuous southern belter Diana Devereaux. But, meanwhile, John has found his own girl, secretary Mary Turner, a girl who mightn't be voluptuous but who can—hurrah!—cook corn muffins. John puts his foot down, weds his Mary, and wins his election, but then the jilted Miss Devereaux threatens to cause an international incident, and it looks as if—for the safety of the nation—the President may have to be impeached. But fate is on the side of John and Mary. Mary is pregnant. So while John and Mary settle down to rule their subjects and their baby with a loving hand, Miss Devereaux has instead to make do with the hand of the man who constitutionally stands in for the President when he is for some reason unable to fulfill a duty. The Vice President. Whatshisname.

Songs: "Wintergreen for President" (chorus), "Who Is the Lucky Girl To Be?" (Jenkins, chorus) "The Dimple on My Knee" (Diana, Jenkins, chorus), "Because, Because" (Diana, Jenkins, chorus), Finaletto: "As the Chairman of the Committee"/"How Beautiful"/"Never Was There a Girl So Fair"/"Some Girls Can Bake a Pie" (John), "Love Is Sweeping the Country" (Jenkins, Miss Benson, &c.), "Of Thee I Sing" (John, Mary, &c.), Finale Act 1: Entrance of Supreme Court Justices (Supreme Court Justices)/"[Here's] a Kiss for Cinderella" (John), "I Was the Most Beautiful Blossom" (Diana), reprise "Some Girls Can Bake a Pie," "Hello, Good Morning" (Jenkins, Miss Benson, secretaries), "Who Cares?" (John, Mary, reporters), Finaletto: "Garçon, s'il vous plaît" (French Soldiers)/Entrance of the French Ambassador (French Ambassador &c.)/"The Illegitimate Daughter" (French Ambassador), reprise "Because, Because" (Diana), "We'll Impeach Him"/reprise "Who Cares?" (John, Mary), "The [Senatorial] Roll Call" (Throttlebottom), Finaletto: Impeachment Proceeding/reprise "Garçon, s'il vous plaît"/reprise "The Illegitimate Daughter"/"Jilted" (Diana)/"Who Could Ask for Anything More?"/"I'm About to Be a Mother" (Mary), "Posterity [Is Just Around the Corner]" (John)/"Trumpeter, Blow Your Horn," Finale Act 2: "On That Matter No One Budges."

The most persistently prolific of those Broadway writers of the twenties who carried on through into the 1930s were undoubtedly the songwriting team of Richard Rodgers and Lorenz Hart. To their dozen musicals of the previous decade they added, in spite of more than a three-year break in the early part of the decade when they devoted themselves to Hollywood, another nine in the 1930s, and then three more between 1940 and 1942, when their last, and longest-running, new musical of all was mounted—a round two dozen shows in a little over two decades. The second dozen were a really mixed bunch—a piece of made-to-measure comedy material for star comic Ed Wynn (*Simple Simon*), a comedy set in the world of the already outmoded silent movies (*America's Sweetheart*), a circus super-spectacular (*Jumbo*), a dance-and-romance show juxtaposing modern dance and ballet (*On Your Toes*), a kiddie let's-put-on-a-show show (*Babes in Arms*), a revusical piece in the vein—but not of the quality—of *Strike Up the Band* and *Of Thee I Sing* (*I'd Rather Be Right*), a Hungarian fantasy (*I Married an Angel*), a new helping of souped-up Shakespeare (*The Boys from Syracuse*), a college musical (*Too Many Girls*), an old-fashioned bit of marriage-marketing (*Higher and Higher*), a slice-of-lowlife musical play (*Pal Joey*), and an Ancient Greek or Roman (it couldn't quite make up its mind which) spooflet called *By Jupiter*.

The subjects may have been different, but the songs were not. The songwriting style of Rodgers and Hart, well established now after their many years in partnership, featured in each and every show in all its public-pleasing glory. It was an agreeable, middle-of-the-road style—neither aggressively jazzy or Tin Pan Alleyish, nor even remotely "operettic," with music that curled itself tunefully round lyrics which, at their best, were neatly colloquial, amusing, and apparently effortless. Their songs were made to be popular, and, from *Simple Simon*'s lamenting "Ten Cents a Dance," through *Jumbo*'s announcement of "The Most Beautiful Girl in the World," *On Your Toes*'s dream of a place where "There's a Small Hotel," and *Babes in Arms*'s veritable bagful of enduring hits—"The Lady Is a Tramp," "Where or When," "My Funny Valentine," "Johnny One-Note"—to the winners from *The Boys from Syracuse* ("Falling in Love with Love," "This Can't Be Love"), *Too Many Girls* ("I Didn't Know What Time It Was"), and *Pal Joey* ("Bewitched"), that is exactly what they became.

The shows themselves found mostly only fair fortunes. *Simple Simon* and *America's Sweetheart* each notched up just 135 performances on Broadway, but most of the post-Hollywood shows—those produced between 1935 and 1942—compiled satisfactory runs of some 200 or 300 nights in New York, with *Higher and Higher* being the one notable flop, and *By Jupiter* topping the poll with a Broadway life of 427 performances. Overseas, however, showed very limited interest. Britain, which had not given Rodgers and Hart's 1920s shows much stageroom, tried *On Your Toes*, but booted it out of the West End after only a short run, and *By Jupiter*, which was shut down before reaching the West End, and Australia staged only *I Married an Angel*, which turned out to be one of the biggest disasters in Australian show-business history. Yet, soon after, both countries gave a joyous welcome to another Broadway success, a high-spirited, low-comical piece of old-style musical comedy called *Follow the Girls*, which gave book credits to veterans Guy Bolton and Fred Thompson, and had songs by the unconsidered Phil Charig. It lasted 882 nights on Broadway, 572 in London, and clocked up a fine four months' stay in Sydney!

However, the songs of Rodgers and Hart remained well loved all round the English-speaking world, and in later years several of their shows got a second chance. A *Connecticut Yankee* was revised and revived, a small-scale production of *The Boys from Syracuse* resulted in its winning further-afield showings in the 1960s, and *On Your Toes* was given two major revivals, the second of which established it—more than half a century on—for a successful London run and productions round the world. However, the big winner on this second-chance system was *Pal Joey*. On its original production, John O'Hara's tale of a cocky, medallion-man club performer and the sex-seeking society dame who enjoys him—at a price—during the length of an act and a bit drew a lot of nose-twitchy opinions. But a revival, in 1952, found folk now more able to take its slice-of-sleazy-life story. Now it seemed "adult" rather than "sordid." *Pal Joey* got the London showing it had missed first time round, and went on from there to become far and away the most appreciated of Rodgers and Hart's works in the later years of the twentieth century.

PAL JOEY, a musical in 2 acts by John O'Hara, based on his own short stories. Lyrics by Lorenz Hart. Music by Richard Rodgers. Produced at the Ethel Barrymore Theatre, New York, 25 December 1940.

Characters: Joey Evans, Mike Spears, Gladys Bumps, Vera Prentiss Simpson, Melba Snyder, Ludlow Lowell, Linda English, Louis, &c.

Plot: Joey Evans works in clubs, as an MC-cum-song-and-dance man, and he also works the old line with any girl who comes within reach. Even one like Linda English, who is clearly a nice girl. But he finds himself on the other end of the fishing line when he is himself picked up by the wealthy socialite Vera Simpson. She clothes him, feeds him, houses him, bankrolls, him and buys him a night-club of his own. Then a couple of other folk from the club decide there is money in this for them, too. They will blackmail the Simpsons over this affair. But Vera's been here before. It only takes a handful of friendly phone calls and the blackmailers are nabbed. And Joey's back where he started. Club closed, bank-account closed, door closed. And yet still putting on the big talk and the side.

Songs: "Chicago [A Great Big Town]" (girls), "You Mustn't Kick It Around" (Joey, girls), "I Could Write a Book" (Joey, Linda), reprise "Chicago" (Joey, girls), "That Terrific Rainbow" (girls), "What Is a Man?" (Vera), "Happy Hunting Horn" (Joey), "Bewitched [Bothered and Bewildered]" (Vera), "Pal Joey" (Joey), Dance: "Joey Looks into the Future," "The Flower Garden of My Heart" (Louis & girls), "Zip" (Melba), "Plant You Now, Dig You Later" (Gladys, girls), "[In Our Little] Den of Iniquity" (Vera, Joey), "Do It the Hard Way" (Joey), "Take Him" (Vera, Linda), reprise "Bewitched" (Vera).

If the Broadway works of Rodgers and Hart failed to export, the same certainly could not be said for those of the other most prominent show-songwriter of the 1930s. The bulk of those American musical shows which did travel the English world in the thirties, and in the early forties, had numbers by Cole Porter (1891–1964).

Porter had been around for a dozen years, writing songs for revues or for interpolation in musical plays on both sides of the Atlantic, while leading a high society life in a selection of the world's costlier pleasure spots. However, from the late 1920s he began to take his theater work rather more seriously, and in 1928 he presented Broadway with his first musical-play score since his just-out-of-college days: a baker's half-dozen of songs—including the (then) mildly suggestive "Let's Do It"—as musical illustration for *Paris*, the latest show mounted for the benefit of Broadway's most popular French star, Irene Bordoni, by her producer-writer husband, E. Ray Goetz. He followed up this piece with two others for Goetz: a Gaiety-style show called *Fifty Million Frenchmen* ("You Do Something to Me," "You've Got That Thing") and the less successful *The New Yorkers* ("Love for Sale"), before scoring his first international success.

Gay Divorce was notable for two things: it was Fred Astaire's last appearance on the musical-comedy stage, and it introduced the song "Night and Day," a number which would end up in one of the very top spots in the Cole Porter register of enduring songs. *Gay Divorce* had a fairly routine libretto—Astaire played a lovelorn chappie who substitutes his sexy self for the professional co-respondent designed to help the object of his affections win a divorce from her encumbrant husband—but the star, appearing this one and only time without his now retired sister, danced and sang the show to success on Broadway and in Britain, just as he had *For Goodness Sake*, *Lady, Be Good!*, and *Funny Face*. In Australia, without Astaire, things went rather less well.

Another star vehicle, an adaptation of the tale of a *Nymph Errant* in pursuit of the loss of her virginity, written for the British star of *Oh, Kay!*, Gertrude Lawrence, was a failure, but in 1934 Porter combined with a coven of librettists on a really happy musical, the piece which would end up as the lasting musical-theater memorial to the Broadway thirties. It had a coven of librettists for the simple reason that, with the book completed, the sets ordered, and the songs written, rewritten, and dug out of his bottom, middle, and upper drawers by the unwasteful Porter, the producer decided he didn't like the show's sea-going story. Director Howard Lindsay (1888–1968) and Russel Crouse (1893–1966) were seconded to do something about it, and they transformed Bolton and Wodehouse's unloved *Bon Voyage* into a different sea-going piece, with a title which reeked more of the jazzical twenties than it did of the struggling-for-amusement thirties: *Anything Goes*.

ANYTHING GOES, a musical comedy in 2 acts by Guy Bolton and P. G. Wodehouse, revised by Howard Lindsay and Russel Crouse. Lyrics and music by Cole Porter. Produced at the Alvin Theatre, New York, 21 November 1934.

Characters: Billy Crocker, Elisha Whitney, Reno Sweeney, Sir Evelyn Oakleigh, Hope Harcourt, Mrs Wadsworth T. Harcourt, Moon-Face Mooney, Bonnie Latour, Bishop Dobson, Ching, Ling, The Purser, William Oakleigh, Mrs Wentworth, &c.

Plot: Billy Crocker stows away on a liner heading for England in order to pay court to the girl he loves, in spite of the fact she is heading Blightywards in order to marry a baronet. With the help of a petty criminal with a ticket to spare, an adoring and chummy cabaret-singer-cum-evangelist, and a succession of disguises, he avoids detection for a while, but when he is discovered it is assumed he is the passenger whose berth he has borrowed: Public Enemy Number One. He is temporarily lion-ized but, since his beloved Hope doesn't join in the admiration, he admits the truth. He spends the rest of the transit in the brig but, with a little help from his friends, he manages to stop Hope making her marriage of business convenience in time for a happy ending.

Songs: "I Get a Kick Out of You" (Reno, Billy), "Bon Voyage"/"There's No Cure Like Travel" (chorus), "All Through the Night" (Billy, Hope), "There'll Always Be a Lady Fair" (quartet), "Where Are the Men?" (Bonnie), "You're the Top" (Reno, Billy), "Anything Goes" (Reno &c.), "Public Enemy Number One" (chorus), "Blow, Gabriel, Blow" (Reno), "Be Like the Bluebird" (Moon-Face), reprise "All Through the Night" (Hope, Billy), "Buddie, Beware" (Reno), "The Gypsy in Me" (Hope), Finale: "Anything Goes." Additional number: reprise "I Get a Kick Out of You" (Reno).

Porter's most important hit to date saw the songwriter in fine and typical form, and along-side numbers slinky, raunchy, and swooningly amorous, plus a belting revivalist song which (in the same phrase used as the title to Edward Eliscu's *The Little Racketeer* song of a couple of seasons earlier) encouraged "Blow, Gabriel," the score featured several of the very particular style of song which would become the composer's trademark—catalog songs whose lyrics listed a long line of topical, imaginative, and very often celebrity-named comparisons with whatso-ever happened to be the topic of the song. "I Get a Kick Out of You," for example, mentioned all the things that the duettists don't get a kick out of—from cocaine to airplane rides to cham-pagne—before summing up in each case with its friendly conclusion, "You're the Top" ran off a catalogue of other things that were also "the top"—the Louvre, the Coliseum, Napoleon brandy—and with which the other half of this mutual admiration society was apparently con-sidered the par, while "Anything Goes" detailed a gory list of things, from short skirts to slangy speech, that mightn't have passed social muster once but which in this easygoing day and age now do. It was a species of song to which Porter would return again and again, eventually to the point of exhaustion, but the best of the series have remained, like the catalog songs of W. S. Gilbert, both long-time favorites (in spite of the fact that some of their catalog items are in-comprehensible to audiences half a century and more on) and interesting examples of topical songwriting in a period when that popular Victorian habit had rather faded away.

Anything Goes had a fine Broadway run, a good London one, and a disappointing one in Aus-tralia, but it did not stop its career there. In later years, it was one of the few 1930s musicals to be given revivals and, its score stuffed with Porter songs taken from other shows as additions or replacements to the originals (a bit of botching which mattered less than it might have, as Porter's songs—and those of most of his contemporaries—were pretty movable items, suffi-ciently little attached to the show they happened to end up in to be readily switchable), it es-tablished itself as the quintessential musical of its period. A major revival, mounted in 1987, at a time when the carefree, comedy musical with easy-to-sing songs had all but disappeared from the musical theater, handily outran the original production.

Porter followed up *Anything Goes* with several shows whose favorite songs traveled even if their shows didn't—the rather too in-jokey *Jubilee* ("Begin the Beguine," "Just One of Those Things"), a fresh vehicle for the Reno Sweeney of *Anything Goes*, Ethel Merman, called *Red, Hot and Blue* ("It's De-lovely," "Down in the Depths"), and another for the same show's male stars, Victor Moore and William Gaxton, *Leave It to Me!* ("My Heart Belongs to Daddy," "Most Gentlemen Don't Like Love")—but by the end of the 1930s the songwriter was riding high on a series of brightly colored musical plays which each totted up a fine run on Broadway before being exported across the Atlantic and—in one case—the Pacific. *Dubarry Was a Lady* (408 performances on Broadway, 178 in London) was a piece in which Miss Merman featured as a cabaret singer dreamed back into ancient France by an adoring swain, *Panama Hattie* (501 and 308 ditto) featured the same star as another performer, this time with a kid to get round before she can wed the kid's papa, *Let's Face It* (547 and 348) was a farcical musical which sent some neglected wives out on a revengeful gigolo-spree, and *Something for the Boys* (422 and 92), a set-in-the-here-and-now musical, was given over to Miss Merman's efforts to cheer up the boys in uniform (with the help of a set of radio-receiving teeth), and the four among them made up a quartet of happy wartime hits which added a further handful of items to the Porter popular song lists—"Friendship," "Make It Another Old Fashioned, Please," "Let's Not Talk About Love."

This tiny handful of exportable musicals was scarcely enough to feed the whole of the English-language theater, but, in spite of the large decrease in product coming in from abroad, 1930s London proved to have more than enough home-made material to fill those theaters which had not been given over to that picturesque and enormously popular kind of show known as "revue."

During the 1930s, London remained resolutely attached to the dance-and-laughter type of musical. Sometimes with the dance taking precedence, other times with the comedy to the fore. But the two elements—the laughter and the dance—were the staples of the era's musical theater in Britain. Such comic performers as Laddie Cliff, Stanley Lupino, Bobby Howes, Leslie Henson, Fred Emney, Richard Hearne, Cicely Courtneidge, and the dance teams of Jack Buchanan and Elsie Randolph, Roy Royston and Louise Browne, and Cyril Ritchard and Madge Elliott were the stars of the period through series of shows made to their measure.

Laddie Cliff (1891–1937) had been the moving force behind the first group of musicals to get up steam in a London theater which had been largely dominated by European and American shows during the 1920s. The little bespectacled dancer and comedian—who quadrupled as performer, producer, director, and choreographer—launched what would turn out to be a series of musicals in the late 1920s, and he found his first success with a remusicked version of the American musical *His Little Widows*, with songs by local lads H. B. Hedley and Jack Strachey (and a couple of second-hand Rodgers and Hart numbers interpolated). *Lady Luck* starred Henson, the Ritchard/Elliott team, and Cliff and his dancing wife Phyllis Monkman, and it ran at the new Carlton Theatre for 324 performances. Cliff followed this first hit by starring Bobby

Howes in a weird musical melodrama (with time out for dances) called *The Yellow Mask*, but in 1928 he returned to the *Lady Luck* formula with another dance-and-laughter piece called *So This Is Love*. This time, Cliff shared the comedy with Stanley Lupino and the dancing with the elegant Ritchard and Miss Elliott, and the songs were credited to a fictitious American called "Hal Brody"—which was mostly Messrs Hedley and Strachey again. The piece was staged at the Winter Garden, for many years now the home of an unbroken string of shows by transatlantic songwriters (*Sally*, *The Cabaret Girl*, *The Beauty Prize*, *Primrose*, *Tell Me More*, *Kid Boots*, *Tip Toes*, *The Vagabond King*), and it proved a decided hit.

Cliff promptly followed up with more of the same—comical, modern stories decorated with the lightest of musical numbers, the majority of which were meant to be danced to. *So This Is Love* was followed by *Love Lies*, *The Love Race*, and *The Millionaire Kid*, and Cliff even made an attempt to set up a second company which could hold the fort, now based at the Gaiety Theatre, in town, while he took his A company out touring. *Darling, I Love You* and *Blue Roses* with comedian George Clarke as their chief attraction didn't attract, and the B Company was soon abandoned. But Cliff gathered his forces and his fortunes, and he was soon back, to score two further successes with the farcical, dancing *Sporting Love* and *Over She Goes*, each decorated musically by the popular musician Billy Mayerl. Both were London successes, both were filmed, both went to the provinces for tidy tours, and the last of the set even appeared on the Australian stage. But in 1937 Laddie Cliff died, aged forty-six, and the flourishing musical comedy business which he had set up faded away.

Jack Buchanan was another star of the British 1930s who mixed performing, directing, choreographing, and producing, and with equivalent success. In the twenties, Buchanan had starred himself in several shows—including the comical *Battling Butler* (which won the unlikely distinction in those years of also making a hit on Broadway) and the circussy *Boodle*—before beginning the dance-and-laughter partnership with Elsie Randolph which would give him his most successful time in the theater. The light-footed, wisecracking pair were first seen as a star team in the 1928 musical *That's a Good Girl*, and in the 1930s they went on to feature in *Stand Up and Sing*, *Mr Whittington*, and *This'll Make You Whistle* before ending their time together in the wartime *It's Time to Dance*.

Although they relied, like Cliff's shows, on fun and on dancing, the Buchanan-Randolph musicals were essentially different in character to, in particular, the little dancer's later pieces. In Cliff's shows, the cheerful, knock-about comedy which featured Lupino and Cliff came at the heart of the matter, and, particularly after the departure of Ritchard and Miss Elliott from the company, the juveniles with their pretty dancing and featherweight songs took a secondary place. In a Buchanan musical, it was the light leading-man comedy and his elegant and sometimes elegantly comic dance routines which were the centerpiece of the entertainment.

Quite the opposite was true of a third successful series of musicals, of which comedian Leslie Henson was the central star. Since *Lady Luck*, Henson had mixed imported musical comedy

(*Funny Face, Follow Through,* the London version of *Little Jessie James*) and straight comedy, as well as appearing in a merry musical made up from a German libretto and some American songs and called—not unsuitably—*Nice Goings On.* But in 1935 he moved to the Gaiety Theatre, and there began a series of enjoyably humorous musical comedies which would fill the house—and many a provincial theater—until the war. Henson, the huge, monocled comedian Fred Emney, and the acrobatic, dancing Richard Hearne provided the fun, and the suave juvenile Roy Royston and American danseuse Louise Browne assured the pretty dancing and the romance in a series of shows—whose libretti were credited to the experienced Guy Bolton and Fred Thompson and the newer-come Douglas Furber—which balanced comedy progressively more extravagant than that of the Cliff shows with light-hearted romancing and useful but unmemorable songs in fine proportions and won *Seeing Stars, Swing Along, Going Greek,* and *Running Riot* end-to-end success.

Comedy was also the crux of a fourth set of shows, a set which was constructed around the little hero of *The Yellow Mask,* Bobby Howes. Howes had gone on from his musical melodrama to confirm his new-found stardom in perhaps the most wholly satisfying London musical of the period, the up-to-date reverse-Cinderella tale of *Mr Cinders,* and now producer Jack Waller featured him in a run of musicalized comedies, with just a handful of songs mostly written by Waller and his musical amanuensis Joe Tunbridge: *For the Love of Mike,* a version of the fine play *Nothing But the Truth* made over as *Tell Her the Truth,* and a remake of *Ambrose Applejohn's Adventures* called *He Wanted Adventure.* The three gave Howes some three years of employment, and a hit song in "Got a Date with an Angel," but producer and star topped all three when Howes teamed up again with his *Mr Cinders* co-star, Binnie Hale, in the sweetly comical *Yes, Madam?* A story about a couple of little sweethearts posing as servants in order to fulfill the conditions of a musical comedy will gave the stars a series of comical situations through which to gallop, Waller and Tunbridge supplied a score of charming and comical songs, and the show topped 300 nights in London before going on to other centers. Howes found further success with *Please, Teacher!* and then in 1937 he was teamed with comedienne Cicely Courtneidge in *Hide and Seek.* The chemistry didn't quite come off, but Howes came out of the experience with the song of his career: Vivian Ellis's "She's My Lovely."

If her double act with Howes was less than a full-sized success, Miss Courtneidge was soon to make up for it. During the decade since her husband, Jack Hulbert, had had *Lido Lady* put together as a vehicle for her, Cicely Courtneidge had been seen largely on film and in revue, but after her return in *Hide and Seek* she again devoted herself to the musical-comedy stage, and she and Hulbert struck the target immediately with the comical spy-story *Under Your Hat.* Like the early Howes shows, this one had only a handful of songs as its musical part, but, unlike those very play-based texts, this one was largely a series of sketches, allowing the two stars to get into as many fixes and disguises as possible on their way to rescuing that all-important piece of stolen machinery from the nasty foreign spy. The series carried on into the 1940s, with the wartime *Full*

Swing, *Something in the Air*, and *Under the Counter* confirming the success of *Under Your Hat* and the drawing power of London's favorite auntie-comedienne.

Many of these star-stamped shows notched up West-End runs of 200, 300, or even 500 nights, but the grandest total of all was scored by a musical which lasted for no fewer than 1,646 performances in the West End. The figure is, in fact, a rather deceptive one (as "long-run" figures are, for a variety of reasons, always apt to be). *Me and My Girl* was a wartime show, and one which played twice nightly—or, during the height of the war, twice daily—thus totting up its long run in doubly quick time. However, even without those run-inducing circumstances, there is no doubt that it was a big, big success. Like those other shows of the era, it was a star vehicle for a favorite comedian-producer: Lupino Lane. Lane had previously been seen in another comedy with a handful of songs called *Twenty to One*, a racing tale which cast him as a cheeky little cockney chappie by the name of Bill Snibson. *Twenty to One* had been a fine success, and Lane decided to order a second Bill Snibson musical to follow. In fact, the new Bill Snibson musical had absolutely nothing to do with the old one except in that Lane played the same kind of cheeky-cockney character, and he was once again called Bill Snibson.

Like the Howes musicals and the Cicely Courtneidge shows, *Me and My Girl* was mostly comedy and only slightly musical. In fact, when the show opened at London's Victoria Palace, after some fairly hectic chopping of the songs and the script and diverse other makings and remakings on the road to town, it sported just eight numbers: a Gilbert-and-Sullivanish patter song for a supporting character playing a lawyer, a number apiece for the ingénue and the soubrette, a duo for Lane with each of them, two choruses, and a thumping, repetitious dance routine which gloried in the title of "The Lambeth Walk." But, out of the eight, two proved hits: the title duo between our hero and his girl and that thumping, repetitious dance routine. Diligently worked up into a dance craze, and then an easy-to-sing, home-sweet-homeish marching song for the wartime British troops in Europe, it engraved itself into the public consciousness with a lasting effect that few numbers of its era achieved.

Me and My Girl repeated the performance given by *Chu Chin Chow* and *The Maid of the Mountains*, by *Das Dreimäderlhaus* and *Die Rose von Stambul* in the first war. It supplied happy, good-old-days entertainment for a public desperately in need of such entertainment, and it supplied it better than any other show in town. Lane repeated his musical several times thereafter, and was eventually succeeded as Bill by his son, but *Me and My Girl* limited its success to Britain for half a century. It was only in later years when, with the score brought up to conventional 1980s size by the addition of extra songs written by Noel Gay for the show's amateur version, and a few of his "pop" songs, *Me and My Girl* Mark II was launched. Much in the same way that *Anything Goes* had topped its first-time-round lifespan in a revival half a century down the line, *Me and My Girl* scored a multi-year run in London, and then went out from there to Broadway, to Europe, and to corners of the world undreamed of at the time of its creation, establishing itself rather late in the day as the world's most successful 1930s musical.

ME AND MY GIRL, a musical comedy in 2 acts by L. Arthur Rose and Douglas Furber. Music by Noel Gay. Produced at the Victoria Palace, London, 16 December 1937.

Characters: Bill Snibson, Sally Smith, Hon. Gerald Bolingbroke, Lady Jacqueline Carstone, The Duchess of Dene, Sir John Tremayne, Herbert Parchester, Lord and Lady Battersby, Lord Jasper Tring, Charles, Mrs Brown, Cook, Bob Barking, &c.

Plot: It is discovered that cockney Bill Snibson is the heir to an earldom, and he is whisked away from his comfy East End home and his girl, Sally, to Hareford House, where the Duchess of Dene and Sir John Tremayne are to decide whether he is a fit and proper person to be elevated to the peerage. Becoming fit and proper is a heck of trial, especially when the nubile Lady Jacqueline dumps her upper-crusty fiancé and starts making heavy passes at little Bill. But the big hitch in Bill's progress is Sally. The idea of another Earl of Hareford making the sort of misalliance that resulted in Bill in the first place is too much for the Duchess, but Bill has no intention of giving Sally up. By the final curtain, of course, Bill has got them all sorted out. He's not only turned out fit and proper, but he's got his girl as well.

Songs: "A Weekend at Hareford" (chorus), "Thinking of No One But Me" (Jacquie), "The Family Solicitor" (Parchester), A Domestic Discussion: "An English Gentleman" (servants), "I Would If I Could" (Jacquie, Bill), "Me and My Girl" (Bill, Sally), "The Lambeth Walk" (chorus), "Take It on the Chin" (Sally), Finale. Interpolated numbers included: "We're Going to Hang Out the Washing on the Siegfried Line" (by Jimmy Kennedy and Michael Carr).

If I've dealt with the shows of the British 1930s here under their stars rather than, as previously, under their writers or songwriters, it's because during the 1930s songwriting in Britain was at rather a low ebb. The fashion for anything at all that was American resulted in not just the importation of shows and songs by some of the best American songwriters, but also the importation of a number of very much less adept transatlantic musicians whose efforts at composing for the London stage did not produce anything remotely near the quality of the songs of their more talented countrymen. Alongside them, H. B. Hedley, Jack Strachey, Billy Mayerl, Noel Gay, Joe Waller, and others turned out some jolly songs, some pretty songs, and some songs which caught for a little while, songs that were not always imitative, but mostly just good enough to become dance band fodder for a nonce after their shows had closed, before vanishing for eternity. "Got a Date with an Angel" and "She's My Lovely" were exceptions rather than the rule. And so was the composer of that last song.

Vivian Ellis, who had been responsible for London's biggest native musical comedy hit of the 1920s with *Mr Cinders*, wrote the songs for a dozen musicals and a number of revues during the 1930s, contributing to *Stand up and Sing* and supplying all the songs for *Hide and Seek, Running Riot, Under Your Hat,* and another musical-comedy success, *Jill Darling,* a nimble bit of nonsense about a prohibitionist MP who gets drunk and who is replaced on the hustings by his double, and in which one of Ellis's successful songs, "I'm on a See-Saw," was introduced. In the face of the overwhelming trends of the time, Ellis's songs maintained a pleasant elegant ease which made the best of them the best of their time and place, and it was no surprise when he went on to compose the score for an altogether more substantial piece of musical theater which would be London's most important home-made musical hit of the 1940s.

There was, of course, more substantial musical theater going on in the 1930s as well. The romantic musical had not been wholly abandoned amid the craze for dance-and-laughter shows, and, indeed, the decade was to see the birth of the most important series of romantic musicals to have come out of the London theater since the heyday of Daly's Theatre.

The success of *Bitter-Sweet* naturally encouraged Noël Coward to venture further into the romantic theater, and during the 1930s he turned out two more pieces on similar lines: one for each of the Continent's two greatest stars of the musical stage. *Conversation Piece* starred Yvonne Printemps. Coward the author wrote her a rôle in which she could slip into French as often as possible (for she spoke no English) as an alluring little French lass who is set up in Brighton by a penniless aristocratic adventurer in the hope that she will catch a rich husband who will support them both. She attracts all sorts of people, right up to the Prince Regent, but she falls in love with her fellow adventurer. Coward the musician supplied his star with some delightful music—the solo "I'll Follow My Secret Heart" being the favorite—and contrasted these romantic pieces, as he had done in *Bitter-Sweet*, with some of the crisply witty numbers which were his speciality—"There's Always Something Fishy About the French," "Regency Rakes." Coward the director replaced the leading man with Coward the actor during rehearsals. The result was a fair success, but *Conversation Piece* did not succeed in establishing itself as it might have. But it did do much better than the Fritzi Massary vehicle, *Operette*, a rather awkward piece set in the Victorian theater and echoing the first act of *Trois Valses* rather resoundingly, which failed completely.

However, if Coward did not succeed in turning out another romantic musical which could equal *Bitter-Sweet* in success, another multi-talented man of the British stage did. Ivor Novello had, like Coward, made his early mark in the theater writing songs in the popular vein, and in the years between 1916 and 1924 his name had appeared on the bills of five musicals, including such successes as *Theodore & Co.* (with Kern) and *Who's Hooper?* (with Howard Talbot), as well as a number of revues. Then, after a decade away from the musical theater, during which he favored his work as a playwright, a film actor, and a stage actor, he returned with a wholly different kind of musical. *Glamorous Night* was made to measure and to order for the Theatre Royal, Drury Lane. That theater, which had prospered so gloriously in the 1920s with its end-to-end productions of the great romantic musicals of the Broadway stage, had gone through a very up and down history since. Coward's patriotic pageant *Cavalcade*, which had taken splendid advantage of the theater's potential and reputation for spectacle, had been a success, Robert Stolz's *Wild Violets (Wenn die kleinen Veilchen blühen)* had managed a fair run, but *Ball im Savoy*, Englished for the occasion by no less a man than Oscar Hammerstein II, had done poorly, and *The Three Sisters*, an "English" musical ordered from Jerome Kern, was a total flop. "The Lane" was in a decided spot. So Novello invented *Glamorous Night* to fit the bill:

spectacular, glamorous, big in every way, and with himself—a big star—in the leading rôle. Since Novello could not sing, playing the leading part in a large-house musical could have been a small problem, but the author-star was unfazed. In *Glamorous Night* it is the women—from the prima donna to a wholly irrelevant stowaway on the escaping liner—who get most of the score to sing.

GLAMOROUS NIGHT, a musical play in 2 acts by Ivor Novello. Lyrics by Christopher Hassall. Music by Novello. Produced at the Theatre Royal, Drury Lane, London, 2 May 1935.

Characters: Militza Hájos, Anthony Allen, King Stefan of Krasnia, Baron Lydyeff, Phoebe, Cleo Wellington, The Queen, Lorenti, The Purser, Nico, Phyllis, &c.

Plot: The republican Baron Lydyeff is attempting to force the King of Krasnia to abdicate, but the King's mistress, the opera singer Militza Hájos, keeps his resolve firm. One night, an attempt is made to shoot the diva in the opera house, but the marksman's aim is turned by a young British tourist who is in the audience. Militza has to flee, and she chooses the ship on which the young Anthony Allen had come to Krasnia. The villains sink the ship, but the two struggle ashore and, as they make their way back to the Krasnian capital, their feelings for each other grow. Anthony shoots down Lydyeff, just as he is about to win over the weakening King, but there is to be no happy ending. Militza cannot leave her uncertain monarch to govern their country alone. She must stay at his side, where she is needed, while Anthony returns to England on his own.

Songs: "Her Majesty Militza" (chorus), "Fold Your Wings" (Militza, Lorenti), "Shine Through My Dreams" (Lorenti), "Glamorous Night" (The Queen, Militza, Lorenti), Rumba and Skating Waltz, "Shanty Town" (Cleo), Gipsy Wedding, March of the Gipsies, The Singing Waltz, "When the Gipsy Played" (Militza). Additional number: "The Girl I Knew" (Cleo).

Glamorous Night was built to use all the facilities of the spectacular stage—the shipwreck which ended the first act was a memorable piece of stagework—but it did not, for all that, neglect the basics. Novello's libretto was a well-built one, and his songs, virtually all of which were presented either as part of an operetta within the show or as part of a ball or concert, were lushly melodious pieces in the most lavish vein of the romantic stage. They were also pieces which would remain favorites for half a century with sopranos from one end of the British empire to the other.

Novello followed up *Glamorous Night* with three further spectacular musicals for Drury Lane. *Careless Rapture* and *Crest of the Wave* did well enough—though less well than the first show had done—but in 1939 he turned out one which topped them all. *The Dancing Years* was set in Austria, but not in the chocolate-box Austria of too many ersatz Operetten. At the dawn of the new conflict, it was set in wartime Vienna, during the previous war. However, it was inspired by, and even partly based on, something that was very much actuality—the repression of music by Jewish composers in the Germany of the 1930s. Novello played the composer who was at the center of this story, and Mary Ellis, the star of *Glamorous Night*, was once again his diva. *The Dancing Years* was stopped short in its run by the war—Drury Lane became the headquarters of the troops' entertainment association—but in spite of being turfed out of town to

Glamorous Night: "Her Majesty Militza . . ."
The show was written to show off the resources
of the Theatre Royal, Drury Lane—including
a chorus of two hundred.

tour it managed to return when circumstances were more favorable, and it eventually totted up 1,156 West End performances before going on to become one of the classics of the English romantic stage.

THE DANCING YEARS, a musical play in 3 acts by Ivor Novello. Lyrics by Christopher Hassall. Music by Novello. Produced at the Theatre Royal, Drury Lane, London, 23 March 1939.

Characters: Rudi Kleber, Grete Schoner, Maria Ziegler, Hattie Watney, Franzel, Prince Charles Metterling, Cäcilie Kurt, Otto Breitkopf, Countess Lotte, Ceruti, &c.

Plot: The poor composer Rudi Kleber finds his life changed when the diva Maria Ziegler stops for breakfast at the inn where he lives and hears him play his music. To the despair of his landlady's adoring little niece, Grete, Rudi is whisked off to the city to write Maria's new Operette. It is not long before the two become lovers, but Rudi cannot ask Maria to marry him. Before he left, he made little Grete a promise: he would never marry anyone without giving her the chance to turn him down first. Rudi sticks to his foolish promise, and when Grete finally comes back from school in England he duly pops the question. The answer from the now grown-up girl is, of course, "no," but Maria has overheard the proposal, left the house, and fled to her old lover, the Prince Metterling. She becomes Princess Metterling and bears the child that she knows is Rudi's, but when war strikes Vienna she is able to help the man she loved and loves escape from the invading forces.

Songs: Dawn Prelude, "Uniform" (Franzel), "Waltz of My Heart" (Maria), "The Wings of Sleep" (Maria, Fr. Kurt), "Lorelei"/"My Life Belongs to You" (Maria, Fr. Kurt, Ceruti), "I Can Give You the Starlight" (Maria), "My Dearest Dear" (Maria, Rudi), "Primrose" (Grete), reprise "My Dearest Dear," "In Praise of Love" (chorus), Leap Year Waltz, reprise "My Dearest Dear."

Although his show songs became long-sung favorites, the musicals of Ivor Novello were never given Broadway or Continental productions, nor did they export very much elsewhere. However, there was one romantic musical of the period which did. *Balalaika* was an unashamed rip-off of Novello, masterminded by radio potentate Eric Maschwitz (1901–1969). It had started life as a spectacular piece called *The Gay Hussar*, written by Maschwitz and his radio colleague George Posford (1906–1976), which had lumped its great trucks of scenery round the provinces in 1933 without making it to the West End, but after the success of *Glamorous Night* Maschwitz took up his old piece, rebuilt it on lines as similar as possible to Novello's, hired as many of Novello's creative staff as he could, and remounted his musical in the West End as *Balalaika*.

The love story of a Russian ballerina—daughter of a Russian revolutionary—and a Russian nobleman, torn apart when the Revolution strikes, but finally reunited in free Paris, was not unlike that of Maschwitz and Posford's radio-musical-turned-film *Goodnight Vienna*, and like that piece it lent itself to a glamorous production. The most effective scene was a triple stage showing a ballet in progress on the stage of the Maryinsky Theatre, the audience where the ballerina's father makes an attempt on the life of the Czar, and the theater's backstage. The score included new numbers by the German expatriate Bernhard Grün (1901–1972) and some arrangements of Russian traditional music, but it was Posford who scored the hit with his baritone ballad "At the Balalaika." *Balalaika* had a run of 570 performances in the West End, went on to been seen in Australia and in a highly successful Parisian production, and became the first British musical to be made into a Hollywood musical—even though little of its music apart from Posford's central song survived to the screen.

So, the anticlimactic thirties did produce some good and successful musical theater, even if little of it was musical theater of an enduring kind. There were still enough appreciable new shows being produced, for example, to allow Australia—that uncommon yardstick of the musical stage—to fill its theaters. It is perhaps interesting to look at just what shows Australia—sitting unchauvinistically on the other side of the globe, turning out little or no original work of its own, and with the produce of the whole world to pick and choose from—did choose in these years.

Between the beginning of 1930 and the end of 1939, there were 38 musicals given their first performance in Australia. Fifteen of them were from Britain (*Love Lies, Mr Cinders, The Love Race, So This Is Love, Blue Roses, Bitter-Sweet, Turned Up, Hold My Hand, Nice Goings On, Jill Darling, Yes, Madam?, Swing Along, Balalaika, Over She Goes,* and *Under Your Hat*); twelve came from America (*Follow Through, The New Moon, Sons o' Guns, Dearest Enemy, Funny Face, Top Hole, Music in the Air, Listen Lester, Gay Divorce, Roberta, Anything Goes,* and *I Married an Angel*), and eight were imported from Central Europe (*Walzer aus Wien, Die Dubarry, Im weissen Rössl, Eine Frau, die weiss, was sie will, Viktória, Ball im Savoy,* the elderly *Die Csárdásfürstin,* and *Wenn die kleinen Veilchen blühen*), while three were pieces with a local connection. From France there came none.

This was not a position which would last for long. The next 38 musicals to come out in Australia would take not ten, but 22 years. And of that 38 no fewer than 26 came from Broadway; ten were from Britain, while Europe was represented by just *Irma la douce* and by a souped-up remake of *Die Fledermaus*. But this was scarcely surprising. For in the 1940s the Broadway musical theater once again became as powerful and as productive as it had been in the 1920s, and this time there was no Central European Operette and no French musical comedy to share the busiest stages of the world. The product of the English-language musical theater had them all to itself, and the bulk of that musical theater—and the best—would come from America. Just forty years on from that time when the tardily blooming American stage had had to rely on imported musicals for most of the best of its entertainment it would establish itself wholeheartedly as the center of the musical-theater universe.

SOME NOTABLE MUSICALS 1930–1940

1930   DIE WUNDER-BAR (Robert Katscher/Geza Herczeg, Karl Farkas) Wiener Kammerspiele, Vienna, 17 February

VIKTÓRIA (Pál Ábrahám/Imre Földes, Imre Harmath) Király Színház, Budapest, 21 February

MEINE SCHWESTER UND ICH [My sister and I] (Ralph Benatzky/Robert Blum) Komödienhaus, Berlin, 29 March

WALZER AUS WIEN (Johann Strauss I and II, arr. Julius Bittner and/or Erich Korngold/A. M. Willner, Heinz Reichert, Ernst Marischka) Wiener Stadttheater, Vienna, 30 October

IM WEISSEN RÖSSL [At the "White Horse'] (Ralph Benatzky et al./Robert Gilbert/Hans Müller) Grosses Schauspielhaus, Berlin, 8 November

GIRL CRAZY (George Gershwin/Ira Gershwin/Guy Bolton, Jack McGowan) Alvin Theatre, New York, 14 November

SCHÖN IST DIE WELT [The world is beautiful] (Franz Lehár/Arthur M. Willner, Robert Bodanzky) Metropoltheater, Berlin, 3 December

1931   DIE BLUME VON HAWAII [The flower of Hawaii] (Pál Ábrahám/Imre Földes, adapted by Alfred Grünwald, Fritz Löhner-Beda) Stadttheater, Leipzig, 24 July

ENCORE CINQUANTE CENTIMES [Fifty centimes more] (Henri Christiné, Maurice Yvain/André Barde) Théâtre des Nouveautés, Paris, 17 September

THE CAT AND THE FIDDLE (Jerome Kern/Otto Harbach) Globe Theatre, New York, 15 October

AU PAYS DE SOLEIL [In the land of sunshine] (Vincent Scotto/René Sarvil/Henri Alibert) Moulin de la chanson, Paris, 22 October

OF THEE I SING (George Gershwin/Ira Gershwin/George S. Kaufman, Morrie Ryskind) Music Box Theatre, New York, 26 December

1932   UN SOIR DE RÉVEILLON [One new year's eve] (Raoul Moretti/Paul Armont, Marcel Gerbidon, Georges Boyer) Théâtre des Bouffes-Parisiens, Paris, n.d.

MUSIC IN THE AIR (Jerome Kern/Oscar Hammerstein II) Alvin Theatre, New York, 8 November

GLÜCKLICHE REISE [Have a good trip] (Eduard Künneke/Kurt Schwabach/Max Bertuch) Kurfürstendamm-Theater, Berlin, 23 November

GAY DIVORCE (Cole Porter/Dwight Taylor) Ethel Barrymore Theatre, New York, 29 November

1933   MR WHITTINGTON (John W. Green, Joseph Tunbridge, Jack Waller/Clifford Grey, Greatrex Newman, Douglas Furber) London Hippodrome, London, 1 February

OH! PAPA . . . (Maurice Yvain/André Barde) Théâtre des Nouveautés, Paris, 2 February

EINE FRAU, DIE WEISS, WAS SIE WILL [A woman, who knows what she wants] (Oscar Straus/Alfred Grünwald) Metropoltheater, Berlin, 1 September

TROIS DE LA MARINE [Three sailor boys] (Vincent Scotto/René Sarvil/Henri Alibert) Nouvel-Ambigu, Paris, 20 December

BALL IM SAVOY [A ball at the Savoy] (Pál Ábrahám/Alfred Grünwald, Fritz Löhner-Beda) Grosses Schauspielhaus, Berlin, 23 December

1934 GIUDITTA (Franz Lehár/Paul Knepler, Fritz Löhner-Beda) Staatsoper, Vienna, 20 January
CONVERSATION PIECE (Noël Coward) His Majesty's Theatre, London, 16 February
TOI C'EST MOI [You, that's me] (Moïse Simons/Bertal-Maubon, Chamfleury/Henri Duvernois, [Albert Willemetz, André Mouëzy-Éon]) Théâtre des Bouffes-Parisiens, Paris, 19 September
YES, MADAM? (Jack Waller, Joseph Tunbridge/Bert Lee, R. P. Weston, K. R. G. Browne) London Hippodrome, London, 27 September
ANYTHING GOES (Cole Porter/adapted by Russel Crouse, Howard Lindsay) Alvin Theatre, New York, 21 November
JILL DARLING (Vivian Ellis/Desmond Carter, Marriott Edgar) Saville Theatre, London, 19 December

1935 SPORTING LOVE (Billy Mayerl/Desmond Carter, Frank Eyton/Stanley Lupino, Arthur Rigby, Arty Ash) Gaiety Theatre, London, 31 March
GLAMOROUS NIGHT (Ivor Novello/Christopher Hassall) Theatre Royal, Drury Lane, London, 2 May
DREI WALZER [Three waltzes] (comp. & arr.Oscar Straus/Paul Knepler, Armin Robinson) Stadttheater, Zürich, 5 October
UN DE LA CANEBIÈRE [A chap from the Canebière] (Vincent Scotto/Raymond Vincy, René Sarvil) Théâtre des Célestins, Lyon, 10 November
TWENTY TO ONE (Billy Mayerl/Frank Eyton/Arthur Rose) London Coliseum, London, 12 November

1936 IGNACE (Roger Dumas/Jean Manse) Théâtre de la Porte Saint-Martin, Paris, 4 February
ON YOUR TOES (Richard Rodgers/Lorenz Hart/George Abbott) Imperial Theatre, New York, 11 April
BALALAIKA (George Posford, Bernhard Grün/Eric Maschwitz) His Majesty's Theatre, London, 22 December

1937 BABES IN ARMS (Richard Rodgers/Lorenz Hart) Shubert Theatre, New York, 14 April
TROIS VALSES (comp. & arr. Oscar Straus/Léopold Marchand, Albert Willemetz) Théâtre des Bouffes-Parisiens, Paris, 22 April
ME AND MY GIRL (Noel Gay/Douglas Furber/Arthur Rose) Victoria Palace, London, 16 December

1938 LEAVE IT TO ME! (Cole Porter/Sam Spewack, Bella Spewack) Imperial Theatre, New York, 9 November
THE BOYS FROM SYRACUSE (Richard Rodgers/Lorenz Hart/George Abbott) Alvin Theatre, New York, 23 November
UNDER YOUR HAT (Vivian Ellis/Archie Menzies, Arthur Macrae, Jack Hulbert) Palace Theatre, London, 24 November

1939 THE DANCING YEARS (Ivor Novello/Christopher Hassall) Theatre Royal, Drury Lane, London, 23 March

DUBARRY WAS A LADY (Cole Porter/Herbert Fields, B. G. De Sylva) 46th Street Theatre, New York, 6 December

1940   PANAMA HATTIE (Cole Porter/Herbert Fields, B. G. De Sylva) 46th Street Theatre, New York, 30 October

PAL JOEY (Richard Rodgers/Lorenz Hart/John O'Hara) Ethel Barrymore Theatre, New York, 25 December

$\mathcal{T}$he years of the Great War, not to mention the Franco-Prussian one, had been the occasion for the musical theater to get a fine fillip. On each occasion, the musical had come out of a war-filled period with a thrivingly theatrical bang, ready to launch itself into a period of full-blown flourishing and prosperity. Whether it was that the general economic situation had been stimulated by the world's wartime activities, whether it was that people at war needed musical-theater entertainments to forget the horrors going on outside the theater, or—in the days afterwards—to celebrate victory, armed conflict certainly seemed to be good for the musical stage, and the 1939–45 war was no exception to this apparent rule. Both on the English- and the French-language stage, the years immediately following the end of the war saw the musical theater take on a new lease of life. However, this time round, neither tradition reacted as it had at the end of the First World War. In 1918, the public had wanted musical comedy: farcical, funny, and (in the French case) sexy comedies set with light-footed, dance-rhythmic songs. Musicals that were the essence of unloosed gaiety. After the second war, both went for something distinctly different: a return to the classical tenets of the Daly's Theatre style of musical, that mixture of the romantically lyrical and the soubrettily light-comic which had flourished on the Continent right up till the destruction of the Central European Operette establishment, and which had been exemplified on the English-language stage, during the same period, by such pieces as *Rose Marie*, *The Desert Song*, and *Show Boat*.

It was, in fact, one of the authors of those three last-named pieces, the librettist and lyricist Oscar Hammerstein II, who was again the author of the biggest musical-theater winner of the wartime years. After his great successes of the 1920s, Hammerstein had thoroughly languished in the 1930s. His output had totalled no fewer than ten musicals, of which only the turgid Amerikaner-Strudel *Music in the Air* had put up any kind of a showing, anywhere. His last effort had been a full-scale romantic piece set in the now rather clichéd purlieus of period New Orleans and featuring the thousand-and-umpteenth little heroine of musical theater who becomes a prima donna, amid other worn-out variations on worn-out themes. *Sunny River* had been illustrated by a score composed by the now declining Sigmund Romberg, and it seemed that the librettist's star was going in the same direction. Down. But then Hammerstein struck up a new partnership: one which would send him inexorably back up to the heights he had inhabited in his first heyday.

Like Hammerstein, songwriter Richard Rodgers had had a long and successful career in the musical theater. In collaboration with his partner of always, lyricist Lorenz Hart, he had turned out a succession of nearly thirty shows for the English-language stage, a list which had included several hit musicals and even more hit songs. But, although that list had included a multicolored variety of shows, none, since their very early love-in-the-war piece, *Dearest Enemy* (1923), could have been described as a romantic musical. Now, with Hart sidelined by an ever-more-unreliable life- and work-style, Rodgers paired up with Hammerstein. The composer of so many neatly attractive theater songs yoked up in harness with the king of the romantic musical stage of the 1920s. And it worked.

The first show that Rodgers and Hammerstein wrote together was a full-scale musical version of an ingenuous little musical "folk play" called *Green Grow the Lilacs*. The play—illustrated by such songs as "Git Along, Little Dogies," "Goodbye Old Paint," "Sam Hall," "The Little Brass Wagon," "Custer's Last Charge," "Skip to My Lou," "Way Out in Idyho," and "Oh, Bury Me Not on the Lone Prairie"—had originally been mounted by the Theatre Guild—an organization founded with rather more lofty ideals than the production of such sweetly naive pieces of period Americana—and had run for a couple of months. Now, a dozen years down the line, with wartime making such innocently good-old-daisical pieces once more thoroughly à la mode, the guild had their little play made over as a proper, original musical, and they called it *Oklahoma!*

OKLAHOMA!, a musical play in 2 acts by Oscar Hammerstein II, based on the musical folk play *Green Grow the Lilacs* by Lynn Riggs. Music by Richard Rodgers. Produced at the St James Theatre, New York, 31 March 1943.

Characters: Aunt Eller Murphy, Curly McClain, Laurey Williams, Will Parker, Ado Annie Carnes, Andrew Carnes, Ali Hakim, Gertie Cummings, Jud Fry, &c.

Plot: Laurey Williams is counting on farmhand Curly McClain asking her to be his partner at the box social over at the Skidmore place but, when he does, she plays hard to get and, when that little scene doesn't end quite as she'd expected, she ends up spitedly partnering the darkly dour Jud Fry instead. But Jud is no chocolate box cowboy. At the dance, he starts to come on heavy. Curly comes to the rescue, and—when the baddie has been bested—the little affair ends with a wedding. But it doesn't end there. The sullen Jud turns up at the wedding and draws a knife on the bridegroom. There is a struggle, and Jud falls on his own knife. As the evening ends, the young couple are preparing to start their new married life together amid the celebrations for the brand new state of Oklahoma.

Songs: "Oh, What a Beautiful Mornin'" (Curly), "The Surrey with the Fringe on Top" (Curly), "Kansas City" (Will), "I Cain't Say 'No'" (Annie), "Many a New Day" (Laurey), "It's a Scandal, It's a Outrage" (Ali, ensemble), "People Will Say We're in Love" (Laurey, Curly), "Pore Jud Is Daid" (Curly, Jud), "Lonely Room" (Jud), "Out of My Dreams" (Laurey), Ballet: "Laurey Makes Up Her Mind," "The Farmer and the Cowman" (chorus), "All er Nuthin'" (Will, Annie), "Oklahoma!" (Curly, company).

Oklahoma!: "That shiny little surrey with the fringe on the top." Curly tempts Laurey with thoughts of a night out in style—country style.

Hammerstein filled out the spinal and romantic Laurey-loves-Curly story with a rather more substantial comic part than the original play had possessed. The play's soubrette, Ado Annie Carnes, was given a pair of chaps on whom to lavish her attentions—Will Parker, the earnest young farmhand who wants to marry her, but who is only going to be allowed to do so by Annie's father once he's saved up $50, and the traveling Jewish peddler who calls himself Ali Hakim. Ali isn't after marriage, it's Annie's congenital inability to say "no" that interests him. In fact, the idea of getting stuck with her—or with any one girl—isn't on his schedule at all. As for Annie, she is able to concentrate only on whichever chap happens to be nearest at any given time. Will has great difficulty in not spending his money as soon as he's got it, and Ali, in his turn, has to concentrate on keeping clear of Annie's Pa, who is determined that the dallying peddler should make his daughter an honest woman, while at the same time promoting the candidacy of Will—to the extent of virtually bankrolling him—for the post of husband. The merry antics of the three characters made up one of Hammerstein's most successful comic subplots of all time. In fact, in some ways, the subplot was better built than the main plot, for Jud's return and death and the summary ending which followed it seemed curiously tacked on to the tiny little main story. But no one seemed to mind that too much.

The songs which the pair turned out as illustration for their show didn't attempt to ape the cowboy songs of the original, but neither did they launch into the traditionally lush and ringingly vocal styles of the normal romantic period musical. The music for the romantic characters—the baritonic Curly and his soprano Laurey—were appealingly simple: his opening carol of rural happiness "Oh, What a Beautiful Mornin'" and his lilting description of "The Surrey with the Fringe on Top" in which he is offering to take his partner to the ball, her pouting assertion that "Many a New Day" will dawn before she lets a boy get her down, and above all their delicately teasing little duo detailing all the things they mustn't do in case "People Will Say We're in Love." Curly also got to lead off the evening's finale—a kind of rollingly rich-voiced western patriotic song in praise of the new state of "Oklahoma!"

The comic songs were equally as successful. Hammerstein was clearly much more at ease writing amusing lyrics for these Amerirural soubrets than he was at supplying songwords for cutesy French demoiselles and other such transoceanic characters. Annie and Will were given some charming pieces, songs whose words sounded as natural as they did amusing—her soon-to-be-famous declaration of nearly nymphomania, "I Cain't Say 'No,'" his period-topical description of the wondrous things to be seen in the big city of "Kansas City," and his foot-down insistence that she limit her practical expressions of loving to just him in "All er Nuthin'" were a highly successful trio of comedy songs.

Another feature of *Oklahoma!* was its dance routines. Instead of using just simple country dances—like the second-act opening confronting "The Farmer and the Cowman"—to illustrate this simple country show, choreographer Agnes de Mille took a wander back into the world of the balletic style of musical-theater dance, a world which had been somewhat (if not precisely wholly) neglected among the fashions for one-to-one dancing, speciality numbers, and platooned choruses in the between-the-wars years. Miss de Mille inserted a Dream Ballet at the climax of the first act, a dance scene in which the confused and already worried Laurey, after a whiff of some kind of salts, goes into a daydream in which she is balletically battled over by Curly and Jud, and that scene proved to be one of the show's most popular features.

Oklahoma! pleased by its ingenuousness and its naturalness, by its tuneful and amusing songs with their mostly easily colloquial lyrics, by its merry hoe-down and its melodramatic ballet, and by its gay insouciance and total triviality in a period where insouciance was at a premium and triviality was a luxury. It pleased so much that it went on to become the biggest musical-theater success that Broadway had ever seen, staying on at the St James Theatre for no fewer than 2,212 performances before—when the war was done—going forth to been seen in Britain and in Australia with similar success.

The war years saw several other successful musicals produced—the last of the Rodgers and Hart collaborations, *Pal Joey* and *By Jupiter*, Cole Porter's *Panama Hattie*, his musicalized comedy *Let's Face It* and *Something for the Boys*, and the merrily old-fashioned *Follow the Girls* among them. But there were also some names newer to musical-theater honors among the winners.

Over the years, a number of the stars and also some of the lesser lights of the Continental musical stage had left Europe to try their luck in the lucrative lands abroad. The political and social upheavals of the 1930s accentuated that flow enormously, and musicians such as Ábrahám, Granichstädten, Gilbert, Katscher, Szirmai, Stolz, Ascher, Hans May, and Bernhard Grün and librettists Gustav Beer, Rudolf Bernauer, and Alfred Grünwald all made their way to Britain and/or to America, where they attempted to continue their work in the musical theater. But, like Kálmán and Jacobi in earlier years, not one of them—even when they could get their shows mounted—managed to turn out a musical which could be accounted a success. But one émigré from the German-dominated countries of those years did actually succeed in briefly becoming part of the Broadway establishment, and that was the composer of *Die Dreigroschenoper*, Kurt Weill.

Weill began the overseas part of his career with a series of failures, when he allowed his music to be overwhelmed by, or used simply as the pendant to, libretti with a message. But when he gave up the preaching and proselytizing business for the entertainment business, his fortunes changed. During the war years, Weill composed the scores to two successful shows, two pieces which took favorite musical-theater ideas of yesteryear, dressed them up in today's clothes, and turned them into a couple of thoroughly enjoyable modern musicals.

The first of the pair was *Lady in the Dark*. Moss Hart's libretto for this show—which, for all that it based itself on an age-old convention, was by no means a conventional musical play— dipped into the fashionable world of psychiatry for its subject-matter. Its heroine undergoes a course of analysis with the aim of finding out why that thing called true happiness is escaping her. The series of dreams that she relates to the psychiatrist who is supposed to be going to set her right made up the musical part of the show: three long sung-through scenas or dream sequences. What made these dream sequences different from those of Victorian days, when such a "dream" was normally used to allow the introduction of things glamorous, scenic, or balletic, was that—even though they didn't wholly shun the just-for-show spectacular element— Weill and Ira Gershwin's musical memories were both meaningful and apparently incoherent with all the incoherence of real dreams. But these unconventional musical sections did also hold a handful of more conventional, extractable songs, and the history of "Jenny," the girl whose determination to be determined was her downfall, the rattlingly nonsensical list of composers' names that was "Tschaikowsky," and the longingly melodied "My Ship," the song that was the key to the heroine's hang-up, all proved to be happily extractable portions of a score not really written in portions.

LADY IN THE DARK, a musical play in 2 acts by Moss Hart. Lyrics by Ira Gershwin. Music by Kurt Weill. Produced at the Alvin Theatre, New York, 23 January 1941.

Characters: Liza Elliott, Dr Brooks, Miss Foster, Maggie Grant, Alison du Bois, Russell Paxton, Charley Johnson, Randy Curtis, Kendall Nesbitt, Ben Butler, Miss Stevens, &c.

Plot: Smart, severely dressed Liza Elliott seems to have everything. Ten years of successful career at the head of *Allure* magazine, more years of a well-heeled, devoted if married lover. Yet she suffers depressions and nightmares. What is wrong? What is she lacking? Bit by bit she delves into her past and her personality, and finally it comes out. She hides behind her smartness, her boss-lady image, her severe clothes, because—since childhood—the woman who runs a magazine telling other women how to be conventionally beautiful has had this inferiority complex about her own looks. And, so, she has attracted men who have been attracted by that boss-lady image, and not by the Liza that Liza would like to have been. When the curtain falls she seems to have found her femininity and a more relaxed attitude to life.

Songs: "O, Fabulous One in Your Ivory Tower"/"The World's Inamorata"/"Only One Life to Live"/"Girl of the Moment"/"It Looks Like Liza," "Mapleton High Chorale"/"This Is New"/"The Princess of Pure Delight"/"This Woman at the Altar," "The Greatest Show on Earth"/"Ladies and Gentlemen"/"Dance of the Tumblers"/"Order in the Arena"/"I'm the Attorney"/"He Gave Her the Best Years of His Life"/"Tschaikowsky" (Ringmaster)/"Jenny" (Liza), "My Ship" (Liza).

The second successful Weill musical was one that was much more straightforward in construction. *One Touch of Venus* was a fantastical musical based on a half-century-old novel, *The Tinted Venus*, written by the popular British novelist "F. Anstey," whose similarly fantastical *The Brass Bottle* had already been adapted to the musical stage. The adaptation was done by the patented humorists S. J. Perelman and Ogden Nash. *One Touch of Venus* was, not unexpectedly then, a thorough-going musical comedy, and one which held to the regular musical-comedy forms. Although it had a glamorous leading lady—an Anatolian statue of Venus (not tinted in this version) which, in good old-fashioned *Schöne Galathee* style, has come to life—that lady was a creature of comedy, the gentleman with whom she became involved in up-to-date New York was a funny little barber called Rodney Hatch, and the handsome, wealthy man who became concerned in sufficiently heartfelt fashion to sing beautiful ballads to her was never taken seriously. Sing as soulfully, ruefully as he might, one did not feel sorry for the charming Mr Savory; one merely smiled at his amorous foolishness in the knowledge that he was far better off without the love of this crazy creature from fantasyland.

This time, Weill provided regular songs as musical illustration. They were songs which had little of the sound or style of his tinny and sometimes fingernails-up-the-blackboard pieces for *Die Dreigroschenoper,* and none of the power of the music he had composed for his dramatic German work *Der Silbersee*, but which were by no means just a pale copy of the Broadway music of the 1930s. The best of them combined a sufficient tang of his earlier style with some lushly romantic melodies, and songs such as Savory's "West Wind," Venus's admission "I'm a Stranger Here Myself," or "Speak Low" became takeaway successes. The songwriters interspersed their ballads with some nifty comic material—Rodney coming to the conclusion that "The Trouble with Women" is men, or his ghastly fiancée and her mother relating their trip "Way Out West in Jersey"—and the show's score came out as one of classical shape and proportions. Modern classical shape and proportions, that is, for since *One Touch of Venus* hit Broadway just seven months after *Oklahoma!*, it also featured a sizeable dose of ballet scenas. Ballet scenas façon Agnes de Mille (sometimes staged by Miss de Mille herself, or else by someone else in imitation of Miss de Mille) were to become an almost inescapable feature of musicals in the years after *Oklahoma!* This show had two, a routine showing New York taking its "Forty Minutes for Lunch" and a quasi-dream sequence in which Rodney described the sweet suburban life that Venus can expect when she becomes his wife ("Venus in Ozone Heights"), a depiction which shocks the goddess back to unreality, and makes her hurriedly renounce New York and this world.

Both *Lady in the Dark* and *One Touch of Venus* were well received on Broadway, but neither succeeded in attracting any attention at all further afield, and it was not until a generation later, when Weill and his works had become the subject of a well-maintained world-wide cult, that both pieces began getting fresh and far-off productions.

One of the most successful wartime pieces was actually a piece about the war. Perhaps that is putting it a bit strongly: let's just say that the characters were involved in a little bit of action that was somewhere on the fringe of the war, one of those wars so beloved of the stage and the screen where everyone gets into uniform and has a jolly, comical time and no one ever kills anyone else or gets killed themselves. *Follow the Girls* had so little construction that it was very nearly a concert or variety show, but its tiny plot about a burlesque artiste sent to run a military canteen at that ever-so-front-line venue of Great Neck, Long Island, served as the frame for a series of sketchy comic scenes and lively numbers in a nicely unadventurous vein. There mightn't have been too much to the show, but it proved to be happy wartime entertainment, and it went through long runs in America, in Britain, and in Australia.

It was, however, possible to put the war on the musical stage in rather more realistic terms, and—very much nearer to the center of the action—that did actually happen. The musical called *The Lisbon Story* was definitely not a musical comedy: if anything it was a tragedy with incidental musical interludes. And it was a most unusual piece to find on the stage in wartime when, as past experiences had shown, the last thing the public wants to see and hear is a dramatic and deadly story about the war in progress. But *The Lisbon Story* was the exception. It was an odd concoction, a sort of a dramatic Ivor Novello–style show with heroic purposes, and it was made up of a Harry Purcell libretto that seemed like the script for a wartime patriotic film, a selection of songs for its leading lady (in the rôle of a Parisian prima donna) and for a series of supporting characters, and some sizeable set-piece ballets. Not de Mille–style scenas, but a dramatic ballet-within-an-opérette-within-the-show, and a Portuguese festival sequence in which choreographer Wendy Toye combined musical-theater dance and regular ballet to great effect. *The Lisbon Story* caused some raised eyebrows. Its dramatic story, in which the prima donna, after agreeing to the German commandant's request to return very visibly to the Paris stage only so she can help an important scientist escape, is ultimately shot dead by him, on the stage where she is performing a ballet representing the rape of Innocence by Evil, was not like anything previously seen on the musical stage, and the dances—with a pair of celebrated Polish ballet-dancers featured—were the most substantial to have been seen in the regular musical theater in memory. As for Harry Parr Davies's songs, they included a couple of successful singles with infallible wartime titles—"Someday We Shall Meet Again" and "We Must Never Say Goodbye"—and one enduring hit. A hit which had nothing to do with anything. To cover a scene change, a group of Portuguese fishermen carôled out the liltingly tacked-in tale of "Pedro the Fisherman" and the song went on to become one of Britain's most popular show-songs of its era. *The Lisbon Story* played for over five hundred nights in wartime London, in a run interrupted by bombing raids, before going on to tour and ultimately to be made into a film.

Much more typical wartime entertainment was the Broadway hit *Song of Norway*, a piece that was built on precisely the same premise and precisely the same foundations as the biggest hit of the previous war, *Das Dreimäderlhaus*. Like its famous forerunner, it took as its libretto a fictional love-story which was tacked on to the name and character of a famous composer and, again like the Operettic Schubert-story, it took as its musical score a made-over version of some of the composer's melodies. The composer chosen for such treatment on this occasion was Edvard Grieg, and the story he was pinned on to had him gallivanting glamorously off around the world with an operatic diva who is promising him the earth and a few stars as well, before the death of his best hometown pal draws him back to his hometown girl and to a less showy path to music and to fame. As in *Das Dreimäderlhaus*, the keystone song was a bit of untouched original music—Grieg's famous "I Love You"—but the bulk of the score was made up of adapted melodies, and they were adapted for voices of considerable scope and caliber. Lavishly scored, lavishly staged, and lavishly sung, *Song of Norway* scored a decided hit. Grieg joined Schubert and the Strausses (*Walzer aus Wien*) at the top of the hit list of composers whose lives and music had been musical-theaterized with success, and Robert Wright and George Forrest, who had organized the musical side of the show, marked themselves out as the modern masters of the pasticcio genre with a score which was every bit the equal of Berté's, and altogether superior to the emulsified Strauss of *Walzer aus Wien*. Unlike most of its contemporaries, this thoroughly picturesque and thoroughly singable show traveled as well. Its 840 performances on Broadway were followed by 526 in London and a fine production in Australia, and 25 years on, it even made it to the Valhalla of the Cinerama screen.

The third success of 1944, alongside *Song of Norway* and *Follow the Girls*, was a piece that was made on a much less extravagant scale than this. *On the Town* was built to the old revusical format—a series of songs and scenes tacked on to a wisp of a plot which existed only for their benefit. It was a perfectly agreeable little plot of the day-in-town variety, but it was very little, and, rather than any kind of well-worked-out intrigue, it was the delicious set of characters who inhabited it, the comical ups and downs that they experienced as they all chased through the urbs and suburbs of New York in pursuit of the evening's balletic ingénue, and the cheeky songs and the of-the-moment dance scenes that they stopped on their chasing way to perform, which were the nitty gritty of the evening's entertainment.

On the Town was written by a team of newcomers to the musical theater, all of whom would go on to have remarkable careers. Adolph Green (b 1915) and Betty Comden (b 1915), performers and writers with a little revue group, wrote the book and lyrics, the young Leonard Bernstein (1918–1990), on the brink of what would be an outstanding career in classical music, provided the score, a score which included a grand dollop of that exceptional dance music which would become one of his most magnificent musical-theater achievements, and Jerome Robbins, formerly of the ballet, staged the dance portion of piece. The result was a little, light-hearted musical comedy of a delicious freshness and unpretentiousness, which scored a decided hit.

ON THE TOWN, a musical in 2 acts by Betty Comden and Adolph Green, based on the ballet *Fancy Free*. Music and additional lyrics by Leonard Bernstein. Produced at the Adelphi Theatre, New York, 28 December 1944.

Characters: Chip Offenbloch, Gabey, Ozzie, Ivy Smith, Brünnhilde Esterházy, Claire de Loon, Judge Pitkin W. Bridgework, Lucy Schmeeler, Madam Dilly, &c.

Plot: Sea-going Chip, Gabey, and Ozzie get off their ship for a first-ever day in New York and set out in search of girls. But Gabey gets smitten with a picture of a girl he sees on the subway, so the other lads selflessly agree to help him track down his ideal sweetheart. Chip gets sidelined by an aggressively eager lady cab-driver, and Ozzie ends up in the embraces of an impulsive and engaged student of anthropology, but Gabey finds his girl all on his own—only to lose her. So the evening is spent chasing some more, and the friends have only just found Ivy—who is not the classy dame Gabey thought, but a Coney Island cooch dancer— when it's time to go back to the ship.

Songs: "I Feel Like I'm Not Out of Bed Yet" (chorus), "New York, New York" (Chip, Gabey, Ozzie), Dance: "Miss Turnstiles," "Come Up to My Place" (Hildy, Chip), "[I Get] Carried Away" (Claire, Ozzie), "Lonely Town" (Gabey), Dance: "Lonely Town," "Do-do-re-do" (Ivy, Mme Dilly), "I Can Cook, Too" (Hildy), "Lucky to Be Me" (Gabey), Times Square Ballet, "So Long, Baby" (chorus), "I'm Blue" (nightclub singer), "Ya Got Me" (Hildy), "I Understand" (Pitkin), Imaginary Coney Island Ballet [Playground of the Rich], "Some Other Time" (Claire, Hildy, Ozzie, Chip), Dance: Real Coney Island, reprise "New York, New York."

The examples that were set by and in *Oklahoma!* had—not unnaturally, given the size of its success—been quickly followed. It wasn't just the dance scene craze that caught on. Other writers actually made full-scale attempts to clone themselves an *Oklahoma!* in more or less colorable detail, but they did so mostly without sufficient talent and mostly without success. It was left to Rodgers and Hammerstein to be the successors to themselves, and in 1945 they came up with a second winning piece of musical theater written in the same romantic vein as the first. *Carousel* was a musical remake of another of the Theatre Guild's old productions, but one with rather more in the way of references than Riggs's little folk play had had. *Liliom* had been, and still was, an international hit, a play written by the Hungarian playwright Ferenc Molnár which had gone out from its original production in Budapest to score memorable success in all sorts of countries and all sorts of languages. In the same way that *One Touch of Venus* had been transferred from its original English setting to a New York one, now *Liliom* was transported from its original Hungary to be set on the coast of New England. Gone were the days when it was necessary for a musical, and particularly a romantic musical, to be set in the far-off purlieus of Ruritania or an imaginative island somewhere in the southern Pacific. But Hammerstein made more alterations than just this bit of resituating to Molnár's play. The play was a slightly bitter, dour one, with occasional tones—and a central character—which resembled somewhat those of *Pal Joey*, but Hammerstein's musical version softened down and sweetened up those tones, making the heroine into a pretty ingénue and the hero into a lusty baritonic lad rather than the vagabond and lout of the original, and the curious, fantastical ending (not without overtones of that of *The Beggar's Opera*) was also altered, allowing the evening to finish on a note of hope rather than of disappointment.

The songs which Rodgers and Hammerstein provided for this slightly sweetened slice-of-life story were often in the vein of their *Oklahoma!* ones, but some were influenced by the fact that *Carousel* had a different flavor and delved into its people to a different degree of depth from that of the insouciant little story of the girl who flirts her way into a nasty spot in a haybarn. When *Carousel*'s Julie Jordan sings her beautiful love song "What's the Use of Wond'rin'?," with its philosophy of I'll love him, right or wrong, she and her song have layers of feeling to them that a Laurey Williams could never achieve. However, at other times the similarities between the two shows were more noticeable: the duo "If I Loved You," for example, was a colorable successor to "People Will Say We're in Love." But there were no comic soubret numbers this time round, for *Carousel* had none of the comic characters which had given such life to the earlier show. The secondary rôles, in this musical, belonged to a gentle couple—a mill girl and a fisherman, who wouldn't have known what nymphomania meant, and who duetted together of their future married life in the sweet words of William Hutchinson's old song "When the Children Are Asleep."

The score of *Carousel* featured two pieces in particular, however, which would be and remain standouts. One of these was a big baritonic Soliloquy for the leading man, and it was the authors' chief weapon in trying to turn Molnár's layaboutish Liliom into their misguided but likeable or even loveable Billy Bigelow. Learning that his wife is pregnant, Billy finds himself transformed at the thought of fatherhood. It will change everything, including his ill-behaved ways. He thinks of his life with a son or a daughter and comes up with the philosophy that "you can have fun with a son but you have to be a father to a girl." His wife doesn't come into the song a lot, though. The second number was another piece which emphasized the changes

Hammerstein had made to the play's emphases: it was a song for a supporting character, a rousingly religious piece in which a round-voiced mezzo-soprano soared forth the maxim that "You'll Never Walk Alone" while you walk with God. Rodgers and Hammerstein—perhaps wisely—never again attempted a soliloquy of the kind they gave to Billy Bigelow, but this big lady's song for a big lady's voice would become a regular in their musicals in the years that followed, and the little group of like-voiced numbers that eventuated have remained some of their best-loved show-songs.

CAROUSEL, a musical play in 2 acts by Oscar Hammerstein II, based on *Liliom* by Ferenc Molnár. Music by Richard Rodgers. Produced at the Majestic Theatre, New York, 19 April 1945.

Characters: Julie Jordan, Billy Bigelow, Carrie Pipperidge, Enoch Snow, Nettie Fowler, Mrs Mullin, Jigger Craigin, Heavenly Friend, Starkeeper, David Bascombe, Louise, &c.

Plot: The carnival barker Billy Bigelow marries the mill girl Julie Jordan, but since a married man is no draw to a carnival carousel he loses his job. He is unable to find work and the young couple's situation goes from bad to worse. Then Julie discovers she is pregnant. Now Billy knows that they must have money, and so he agrees to take part in a robbery. The hit goes wrong, and, rather than face a life in jail, Billy commits suicide. At the gates of Heaven his spirit is turned back, and he returns to earth to try to earn himself a slice of worthiness. But Billy's attempts to approach his fifteen-year-old daughter go just as wrong as every tender thing in his life did, and he can only stand and watch as his wife and child go into the future with hope in their hearts.

Songs: Carousel Waltz, "You're a Queer One, Julie Jordan" (Carrie, Julie), "Mister Snow" (Carrie), "If I Loved You" (Julie, Billy), "June Is Bustin' Out All Over" (Nettie &c.), June Dance, "When the Children Are Asleep" (Snow, Carrie), "Blow High, Blow Low" (Jigger &c.), Hornpipe Dance, Soliloquy ["My Boy Bill"] (Billy), Finale Act 1: reprise "June Is Bustin' Out All Over," "A Real Nice Clambake" (ensemble), "Geraniums in the Winder" (Enoch), "Stonecutters Cut It on Stone" (Jigger &c.), "What's the Use of Wond'rin'?" (Julie), "You'll Never Walk Alone" (Nettie), "The Highest Judge of All" (Billy), Ballet: "Billy Makes a Journey," reprise "You'll Never Walk Alone."

Carousel followed the path established by *Oklahoma!* from New York to London, but it didn't find the same success as its predecessor. Partly, no doubt, because it didn't arrive on the same wave of Victory as the earlier show had done, but partly also because its more somber colorings had a lesser appeal. In fact, those same somber colorings were, in spite of the vast success of *Oklahoma!* in Australia, responsible for the show's not even being picked up down under. The songs, however, went everywhere and, particularly after a well-made and faithful film version was issued, they became firm favorites. Given its sources, *Carousel* might have been expected to find the same kind of rehabilitation in later years that *Pal Joey* and *Die Dreigroschenoper* have enjoyed, but a major revival in the 1990s was a disappointment and the show lives on mainly in its outstanding numbers.

If *Carousel* confirmed the vogue for the newest wave of romantic musicals, there was nevertheless still space on the stage for the more old-fashioned kind. The reception won by the 1944

Song of Norway had proven this, and the following year Ivor Novello's latest London piece thoroughly confirmed it. *Perchance to Dream* was not a Drury Lane show, and it did not feature the shipwreck or train crash that was obligatory for a made-for-the-Lane musical. However, in other respects, it was built on much the same lines as *Glamorous Night* and *The Dancing Years* had been, as a colorful piece of romance matching Novello as non-singing leading man with one soprano leading lady, one soubrette juvenile lady, and one boomingly contralto duenna. This particular piece was one of the through-the-generations shows that had become popular with musicals such as *Wie einst im Mai* (and its U.S. rewrite as *Maytime*) and *Trois Valses*, and it gave Novello and his ladies the chance to appear in a variety of rôles and a variety of period costumes. The ladies also, of course, once again got the virtual totality of the songs, and in this score Novello turned out some of his most enduring pieces—the soprano declaration that "Love Is My Reason for Living," the hurtling contralto description of "Highwayman Love," and the parlor duet for the two women which would become Novello's best-known show-song, "We'll Gather Lilacs." *Perchance to Dream* was a triumph in London, totting up 1,022 performances in the West End before going to the provinces and to South Africa. But that was it. Like the rest of Novello's works, it saw only its music go on to popularity on a wider scale.

PERCHANCE TO DREAM, a musical play in 3 acts by Ivor Novello. Produced at the London Hippodrome, London, 21 April 1945.

Characters: Sir Graham Rodney/Valentine Fayre/Bay, Melinda/Melanie/Melody, Lydia Lyddington/Veronica/Iris, Ernestine Flavell/Mrs Bridport, The Vicar/Mazelli, Sir Amyas Wendell, Lady Charlotte Fayre, William Fayre/Bill, Lord Failsham, Edgar Pell, Susan Pell/Miss Rose, Miss Alice Connors, &c.

Plot: The action takes place at house called Huntersmoon. In 1818 it is inhabited by the noble Graham Rodney, who keeps gay company there while secretly riding at night as a highwayman. When he meets and falls in love with his cousin Melinda, he vows to return to the straight and narrow, but he rides just one last time, to fulfill a wager, and is killed. In 1845 the master of Huntersmoon is the choirmaster Valentine Fayre. He weds Veronica, the illegitimate daughter of Rodney and his mistress, but when her schoolfriend Melanie visits the lightning of love strikes. On the day before he is to perform for royalty at Windsor, Veronica goes up to town, and Melanie flings herself at Valentine. He cannot resist. But when Veronica returns, it is with the news that she is pregnant. Melanie's moment is over, and she kills herself. In 1945 the house is still in the same family. And this time round pays for all. Bay, the grandson of Valentine and Veronica, and his Melody—who resembles strangely Melinda and Melanie—will be wed, and the unhappy ghosts of the house laid to rest.

Songs: "When Gentlemen Get Together" (chorus), "Love Is My Reason for Living" (Lydia), "The Path My Lady Walks" (Mazelli), "A Lady Went to Market Fair" (quintet), "The Night That I Curtsied to the King" (Melinda), "Highwayman Love" (Ernestine) Ballet: "The Triumphs of Spring," "Autumn Lullaby" (chorus), "A Woman's Heart" (Veronica), "We'll Gather Lilacs" (Veronica, Mrs Bridport), "The Victorian Wedding," "The Glo-Glo" (Melanie), reprise "We'll Gather Lilacs," "Poor Lonely Mortals" (ensemble).

Novello's musicals racked up some of the most impressive runs among the shows on view in wartime London, but the comedy musical—a brand which inherently clocks up less extensive totals than the romantic spectacular—was far from put in the shade. *Under the Counter*, the latest in the series of musical comedies which had re-established Cicely Courtneidge on the stage in her persona as everybody's favorite funny auntie, was produced on a comparative shoestring and with due attention to wartime economies. It also took those economies as a part of its topic, in a lively piece of fluffy star-centered comedy which featured Miss Courtneidge as a British comedienne in wartime, interfering in black-marketeering and getting into governmental string-pulling—all on account of Love, of course. The show was economic in its songs too: there were only five of them and, in the Novello fashion, they were given as songs from a show being rehearsed within the show. *Under the Counter* proved to be happy wartime entertainment, clocked up 665 West End showings, and was even exported to Broadway. Broadway, however, didn't want to have anything to do with imports from Blighty at this stage in time, so Miss Courtneidge waddled off to Australia and played there for a year instead.

The classically proportioned romantic musical which proved so popular on the English-speaking stage in the early 1940s—from *Oklahoma!* and *Song of Norway* to *Carousel* and *Perchance to Dream*—also proved itself to be the mode, and to the mood of the moment, in the French theater. Since the fading of the musical comedy tradition of the 1920s, the French theater had stumbled along on a series of glitzy and unmemorable spectaculars, shows where the costumes and the cavalry charges were more important than the words and music, even though those words and that music were often written by men who had proven themselves exceptional artists in the musical-comedy field. But in 1945 France got its own *Oklahoma!*

La Belle de Cadix was a romantic musical play which was built on absolutely classic lines. A richly singing hero and a soprano heroine supported by soubrette, soubret, and second comedian for the lighter moments, and a mildly threatening villain for the mildly threatening ones (a line-up identical to that of *Oklahoma!*), all made their romantic and/or comic way through a pair of plots and a lot of songs amid the colorful scenery of southern Spain, the south of France, and the movie-making world—settings every bit as picturesque as the wildish, period out-western venues of its American counterpart.

Written by Raymond Vincy (d. 1968), a lyricist and librettist who had had a hand in the smilingly naive but thoroughly endearing series of song-overflowing Marseillaise opérettes put out before the war, *La Belle de Cadix* was equipped with tunes by a young songwriter making his first appearance in the musical theater. Francis Lopez (1916–1995) would go on to become a feature of the Parisian stage for a couple of decades, a fixture there for half a century, and an embarrassment to it for nearly the last half of that time. But in 1945 he was full of fresh, half-Hispanic music and lively melodies, and those from *La Belle de Cadix* launched him onto the hit list in no mean manner.

La Belle de Cadix actually wasn't mounted on one of Paris's megastages. It was written to order and to measure for the middle-sized Gaîté-Montparnasse as a hurried replacement for a variety show which had fallen out. It was mounted on a restricted budget—restricted, in fact, to such an extent that the star tenor, a dapperly dark young fellow called Luis Mariano who had once been an art student, also designed the scenery. But *La Belle de Cadix* turned out to be a greater hit by far than any of the big-house pieces. Vincy's merry, well-constructed tale, featuring—like *Oklahoma!* again—a particularly successful comic triangle alongside its romantic plot and people, and Lopez's primary-colored songs, lively, nostalgic, sweepingly sentimental, and delivered by Mariano in a popular tenor voice that would make him the dreamboat on which a million housewives yearned to sail, combined in a show which, as *Oklahoma!* had done in the English-speaking world, gave a fresh boost to the classic romantic musical, and indeed to the musical theater in general, throughout France. And its songs—"La Belle de Cadix," "Le Coeur des femmes," "Rendez-vous sous la lune"—became the show-song hits of their era. *La Belle de Cadix* would be followed by a decade of shows, many of them by Vincy and Lopez, many of them built devotedly to the same format, which would give the French theater back at least some of the élan it had had in the twenties and lost in the thirties, in what would prove to be its last real flourish of the twentieth century.

LA BELLE DE CADIX, an opérette in 2 acts by Raymond Vincy and Marc-Cab. Lyrics by Maurice Vandair. Music by Francis Lopez. Produced at the Gaîté-Montparnasse, Paris, 24 December 1945.

Characters: Carlos Médina, Dany Clair, Manillon, Maria-Luisa, Ramirès, Cécilia Hampton, Pépa, Le Roi gitan, Juanito, Perrucha, &c.

Plot: Film-star Carlos Médina goes on location to Cadiz. As his film goes into production, the cast is completed by a number of locals, among them the ambitious guitarist Ramirès and his fiancée Maria-Luisa, who is to play Carlos's gipsy bride. But the little assistant director Manillon entrusts the local lassie he is busy chasing with the casting of the Gipsy King who performs that gipsy wedding. Pépa brings a real gipsy king and, when the scene is done, Carlos and Maria-Luisa are wed for real. Carlos, who is heavily engaged to an American heiress, is appalled, but he cannot get divorced until he is well away from the susceptible gipsies of Cadiz. By the time that happens, of course, he has fallen in love.

Songs: "Au Palm Beach la vie est belle" (chorus), "Chanter pour vous" (Carlos), "Pour savoir s'arranger" (Manillon), "Désir" (Carlos), "Les Sentiers de la montagne" (Maria-Luisa), "Pour toi, Pépita" (Manillon, Pépa), "La Fiesta Bohémienne" (Carlos), "Je revois le clocher du village" (Carlos), "Rendez-vous sous la lune" (Maria-Luisa, Carlos), "La Belle de Cadix" (Carlos), Flamenco, "C'est un rêve" (Maria-Luisa), Finale Act 1: "Ma belle de Cadix, unissons-nous," "Ô ma gitane, dis-moi gi" (Manillon, Pépa), "Maria-Luisa" (Carlos), "Le Coeur des femmes" (Ramirès), "Mon muchacho" (Pépa), "Une nuit à Grenade" (Carlos), Finale Act 2: reprise "La Belle de Cadix"/"Dans les bois des oiseaux."

La Belle de Cadix was France's "victory musical," in the same way that *Phi-Phi* had been in the years following the Great War, and in the same way that *Oklahoma!* and *Annie Get Your Gun* were wherever English was sung. But whereas *La Belle de Cadix* had the victory scene pretty much to itself, until it was joined by the second—and even more satisfying—piece from the Vincy-Lopez team in late 1947, *Oklahoma!* had to share the honors of the postwar communiqué, and it too shared them most particularly with a show that had come out two years in its wake. It was a musical which did not follow the nouveau-romantic style of *Oklahoma!*, did not feature its traditional layout or partake of its dance scenas, but, rather, looked back to the shows of the prewar days with their lusty comical heroines and their good-humored tales. There was, of course, a good reason for this. *Annie Get Your Gun* was constructed to star the lady who had been the central feature of so many of those prewar musicals, the amiably brash Ethel Merman, who was anything but a romantic soprano. She was squarely in the fine old tradition of what earlier days had called coon-shouters, that band of chesty wallopers who, with ladies like the ebullient May Irwin at their head, had been the joy of Broadway in the early part of the century. To cast outback Annie with such a star was eminently more suitable than having a lusty western sharpshooter who trilled high B flats like Puccini's *La fanciulla del West*. There was, however, a concession to the old-new style in the leading man: Annie's partner was as thoroughgoing a baritone as Rodgers's Curly McClain or Billy Bigelow.

Herbert and Dorothy Fields's romanticization of the lives of the real-life crackshots Annie Oakley and Frank Butler was originally to have had songs by Jerome Kern, but Kern died before the score was written and, instead, the commission went to Irving Berlin (1888–1989). Known as the writer of innumerable popular songs and a swatch of well-liked revues rather than for his hitherto small contribution to the book-musical theater, Berlin promptly proved that he could do theatrically as well as anyone when he wanted to by turning out a bookful of songs romantic, comic, pointed, and rousing which would go on to become classics of the English musical theater—"My Defences Are Down," "Anything You Can Do, I Can Do Better," "You Can't Get a Man with a Gun," "They Say It's Wonderful," "Doin' What Comes Natur'lly," "There's No Business Like Show Business."

Annie Get Your Gun played for 1,147 performances in its first run on Broadway. If that was short of *Oklahoma!*'s record-breaking total, the later show nevertheless put up just as good, in fact—all round—rather better, a showing on the international scene. In England, where it opened just five weeks after its competitor, in the West End's largest capacity theater, the London Coliseum, *Annie Get Your Gun* was performed for nearly three years to bursting houses. It closed in May 1950, five months before *Oklahoma!*, which had played out the tag end of its run in the unloved Stoll Theatre after passing the bulk of its three and a half London years at the Theatre Royal, Drury Lane—the West End's second largest regular playhouse! However, if *Oklahoma!* had an infinitesimal edge in London, *Annie Get Your Gun* triumphed in Australia,

where it was seen for a year in Sydney and nearly as long in Melbourne, totting up in the process runs of a kind that that country had never seen before. And then the show went into Europe, first of all to France—where it was retitled *Annie du Far-West*, and eventually, in the years after the fashion for the produce of the Anglophone stage had once again caught in on the Continent, to Germany and to Austria.

Annie Get Your Gun: "I'm an Indian too!" Annie Oakley gets inducted into Chief Sitting Bull's tribe as an honorary squaw.

ANNIE GET YOUR GUN, a musical comedy in 2 acts by Herbert and Dorothy Fields. Music and lyrics by Irving Berlin. Produced at the Imperial Theatre, New York, 16 May 1946.

Characters: Annie Oakley, Dolly Tate, Winnie Tate, Frank Butler, Charlie Davenport, Colonel William F. Cody (Buffalo Bill), Chief Sitting Bull, Foster Wilson, Mac, Major Gordon Lillie (Pawnee Bill), Tommy Keeler, Wild Horse Ceremonial Dancer, &c.

Plot: When outback girl Annie Oakley beats professional show sharpshooter Frank Butler in a match, show boss Buffalo Bill is quick to sign her up. To calm Frank's susceptibilities, she is rated only as an assistant, but she's thrilled, and she's even more thrilled when it seems that Frank might have susceptibilities of another order as well. But then, one day, she is persuaded to perform a wildly spectacular trick in the show. It comes off well, too well, and Frank's amour propre is so dented that he quits Buffalo Bill and goes off with a rival entertainment. Bill and Annie take their show to Europe, where Annie is lionized by the rich and famous and returns home with a chestful of gold and jeweled trophies—but no cash. A merger with Frank's equally strapped group seems in order, and an Anne-Frank merger seems on the cards as well, but that old amour propre gets in the road again and it's only when Annie finally realizes that you can get a man with a gun . . . if you use that gun to miss the target . . . that a happy and thoroughly merged ending heaves over the horizon.

Songs: "Buffalo Bill" (chorus), "I'm a Bad, Bad Man" (Frank), "Doin' What Comes Natur'lly" (Annie), "The Girl That I Marry" (Frank), "You Can't Get a Man with a Gun" (Annie), "[There's No Business Like] Show Business" (Charlie, Buffalo Bill, Frank), "They Say It's Wonderful" (Frank, Annie), "Moonshine Lullaby" (Annie), "I'll Share it All with You" (Winnie, Tommy), Ballyhoo, "My Defenses Are Down" (Frank), "I'm an Indian Too" (Annie), Adoption Dance, reprise "You Can't Get a Man with a Gun" (Annie), "[I Got] Lost in His Arms" (Annie), "Who Do You Love, I Hope?" (Winnie, Tommy), "[I Got the] Sun in the Morning" (Annie), reprise "They Say It's Wonderful" (Frank, Annie), "Anything You Can Do" (Frank, Annie). Additional number: "An Old-Fashioned Wedding" (Annie, Frank).

Annie Get Your Gun and *Oklahoma!*, both enormously successful, have remained the best-remembered and best-loved musicals of their era, but in London they had to put up with competition from a third piece which was, for a while, just as successful as they. *Bless the Bride* opened at the Adelphi Theatre—like Drury Lane, once a home of the spectacular melodrama, and also one of the city's larger houses—just four days before *Oklahoma!* hit town. It, too, was a romantic musical play, but one with a rather different style about it. Alan P. Herbert's pretty, sentimental, and gently funny book was not shaped on classic lines. Rather than writing a modern-day Daly's Theatre musical, he turned out a libretto that might have once been counted opéra-comique. No jolly soubrets here, no villain, everything in this tale was centered on little Miss Lucy Willow from England, a Home Counties ingénue who falls in love with a traveling French actor. Like the heroine of *Bitter-Sweet*, she runs away with her handsome foreigner to Europe, but unlike Coward's Sarah she isn't left alone there to live out a doomed and tragic romance. Lucy's whole and hellishly English family go gallivanting after her. Rather than using this event as the starting point for a cavalcade through some of Europe's prettier places, as an old Gaiety show might have done, and as musicals had been doing right up until the war, *Bless the Bride* stayed firmly in France and beamed firmly in for a whole act on the romance between Lucy and her Pierre, and on the antics of the Willow family, forced to set foot in abhorrently foreign parts, and finding themselves Englishly incapable of coping with all those funny foreign people who have the cheek not to be able to speak English. Unlike the more genuinely romantic *Bitter-Sweet*, too, *Bless the Bride* had a happy ending. Its soprano and its tenor

Bless the Bride: Original stars Lisbeth Webb, Georges Guetary, and Betty Paul pose for a portrait.

got to have their final curtain clinch. However, Herbert—an admired humorist whose theater work could, nevertheless, be distinctly ponderous—lightened his last act with one little touch of winning originality in the character of Thomas Trout. Thoroughly everday Thomas was to have married Lucy before she ran away, and when she runs back, and she thinks her Frenchman has been killed in the war, she finally agrees to wed him after all. But then Pierre comes back, and Thomas, who has been waiting all his life to do something, anything, exceptional, gets his chance. In spite of the plighted troth, he gives up the girl he loves to the man she loves. The scene and the half-humorous song in which he did so was one of those little cold-shudder moments that you don't often get in musicals, but "My Big Moment" wasn't the sort of song that was going to be among the hits of the show. The hits were all for the stars, the soprano and the tenor duetting together in "This Is My Lovely Day," he rhapsodising over "A Table for Two" and letting rip with the merry tale of "Ma Belle Marguerite," and the pair joining with the mezzo of the cast in the waltzing trio "I Was Never Kissed Before" were all musical moments which became takeaway hits. And the music? All this deliciously light-handed operettic music was the work of none other than Vivian Ellis, the London stage's most appreciable writer of dance-musicked songs for the 1920s and 1930s stage. Like Kern, like Rodgers, he had moved across from the musical comedy to the romantic musical and there he, like they, turned out his most enduring work.

Bless the Bride rendered no quarter at all to the two huge imported hits through 1947 and 1948, but whether it might have gone on to equal their vast runs can never be known, for producer C. B. Cochran—in what was undoubtedly the biggest mistake of his career—took the show off. Why? Because he had made his money and he was tired of maintaining the same show through month after month of sameness. He wanted to put on Herbert and Ellis's new show. So *Bless the Bride* was pulled after 839 performances, and *Tough at the Top* came into the

Adelphi instead. It flopped. *Bless the Bride* had a fine subsequent career in Britain, but that was it. America, decidedly uninterested in the West End these days, and the other English venues ignored the show in favor of the more red-blooded produce of the Broadway stage, and *Bless the Bride*'s big moment remained its first run.

BLESS THE BRIDE, a musical show in 2 acts by A. P. Herbert. Music by Vivian Ellis. Produced at the Adelphi Theatre, London, 26 April 1947.

Characters: Lucy Veracity Willow, Augustus Willow, Albert Willow, Mary Willow, Harriet Willow, Alice Charity Willow, Hon. Thomas Trout, Cousin George, Pierre Fontaine, Suzanne Valdis, Nanny, Monsieur Robert, &c.

Plot: Lucy Veracity Willow, of Mayfield, Sussex, is to be wed to the Hon. Thomas Trout. But then she meets the French actor Pierre Fontaine and within two whacks of a croquet ball they are smooching in the shrubbery. The next day, while the family waits at the church, Lucy heads not for her wedding but for France. The romantic idyll the two had hoped for is soon ripped apart. First of all the family arrives in outraged English pursuit, and then war is announced. Pierre dons uniform and goes off to fight France's latest foe, while Lucy goes sadly back to Mayfield. The news comes that Pierre is dead, and Lucy reluctantly agrees to take up the interrupted wedding where she broke it off, but the news is false. Now Pierre's jealous companion Suzanne repents her lie, and she brings a battered but living Pierre across to Sussex in time for a happy ending.

Songs: "Croquet" (chorus), "Too Good to Be True" (Thomas, Lucy), "Any Man But Thomas T" (Lucy), "En Angleterre les demoiselles" (Suzanne), "Oh, What Will Mother Say?" (Augustus, Mary, Lucy, &c.), "I Was Never Kissed Before" (Lucy, Pierre, Suzanne), "Where Is The Times?" (Augustus &c.), "Marry Me" (Albert, Harriet), "The Silent Heart" (Lucy), "Ma Belle Marguerite" (Pierre), "God Bless the Family" (ensemble), "Ducky" (Nanny), "Bless the Bride" (chorus), "Bobbing" (chorus), "Mon pauvre petit Pierre" (Suzanne, Lucy, Pierre), "The Englishman" (Mary, Augustus, Thomas, George), "Un consommé" (Frontenac, Martel, &c.), "A Table for Two" (Pierre), "This Is My Lovely Day" (Pierre, Lucy), "The Fish" (ensemble), "This Man Could Never Be a Spy" (Lucy, Suzanne, &c.), "To France" (Pierre), reprise "This Is My Lovely Day" (Lucy), "Twenty-One Candles" (the Misses Willow), "Here's a Kiss for One-and-Twenty" (the Misses Willow), "My Big Moment" (Thomas), "Summer" (Lucy), reprise "This Is My Lovely Day" (Pierre, Lucy).

In the last years before the turn of the 1950s, while *Annie Get Your Gun*, *Oklahoma!*, and *Bless the Bride* held the center of attention in the West End, a number of other successful musicals were introduced to the London stage. They were, however, by and large, musicals with a flavor of the avant-guerre to them—and they were, by and large, musical comedies. Leslie Henson starred in a latter-day dance-and-laughter piece called *Bob's Your Uncle* through 363 showings, Fred Emney featured for 666 performances in a broadly musical-comic piece called *Blue for a Boy*, which had been adapted from a play by the same German authors who had supplied the basis for the successful *Nice Goings On*, and Cicely Courtneidge starred first as *Her Excellency*—an ambassador to South American parts who gets herself into all sorts of pickles, amorous and political—through 252 performances and then as a vivacious actress who finds her home is being used by a smuggling ring in *Gay's the Word* for no fewer than 504 performances. The musicians credited for the songs displayed in this set of winners were, respectively, Noel Gay of *Me and My Girl*, Harry Parr Davies, the young composer of *The Lisbon Story*, the American songwriter Manning Sherwin, who had supplied some discreet tunes for several West End shows of the thirties, and Ivor Novello, returning to the musical-comedy arena where he started his career one last time.

Gay's the Word was Novello's last musical, for he died just weeks after its production, while still performing in the last of those romantic musicals, the songs of which have survived as his only remembered legacy to the stage. *King's Rhapsody* was certainly one of the best of the Novello musicals, and it undoubtedly gave its author and composer his best—if not necessarily his showiest—rôle of any in the series as an unwillingly crowned and even more unwillingly wed Ruritanian Prince. In *King's Rhapsody* we were not a million miles from *The Student Prince* and its ilk, or from the good old *King of Cadonia* of forty years earlier, but Novello's story and characters allowed a touch more light and shade than was to be found in the cheerfully simple tale of *Alt-Heidelberg*. As for the score, it produced the usual romantic Novello bonbons, a chocolate-boxful of tunes topped by the soprano's waltzing "Someday My Heart Will Awake," and *King's Rhapsody* ran through 839 performances, in what might have been a much longer run had it not been cut short by its star's demise.

KING'S RHAPSODY, a musical romance in 3 acts by Ivor Novello. Produced at the Palace Theatre, London, 15 September 1949.

Characters: Nikki, Princess Cristiane, Queen Elena of Murania, King Peter of Nordland, Marta Karillos, Countess Vera Lemainken, Vanescu, Princess Kirsten, Princess Hulda, Count Egon Stanieff, Madame Koska, &c.

Plot: Nikki of Murania is living in exile in Paris with his mistress, the actress Marta Karillos, when he is recalled home to succeed to the throne, and to wed his mother's chosen bride, the young Cristiane of Nordland. Nikki refuses to meet Cristiane, but he is not above seducing a maidservant one drunken night. Only it isn't a maidservant, it's the lonely Cristiane. The young Queen soon becomes beloved by the whole country, but it takes time for Nikki to overcome his fears of being managed by the women in his life and effectively to take his place as King. He takes it only to promote legislation which will reduce the crown to a figurehead. When he is defeated by his country's self-preserving politicians, he is forced to abdicate and he returns to exile, leaving Cristiane to rule Murania until their son is old enough to become King.

Songs: "Greetings" (chorus), "Someday My Heart Will Awake" (Cristiane), "Fly Home, Little Heart" (Vera), "Mountain Dove" (Cristiane), "If This Were Love" (Cristiane), "The Mayor of Perpignan" (Marta), "The Gates of Paradise" (Cristiane, Vera, Egon), "Take Your Girl" (Vera, chorus), "When the Violin Began to Play" (Cristiane), "Ave Maria" (chorus), reprise "Someday My Heart Will Awake" (Cristiane).

In contrast to London, the Broadway of the later 1940s welcomed a considerable number of new writers who would quickly make their presence felt, and among the first to establish themselves at the top of the polls were the team of Alan Jay Lerner (1918–1986) (words) and Fritz Loewe (?1904–1988) (music). Lerner and Loewe followed the same path that Rodgers and Hammerstein had taken, and they found their first memorable success with a romantic musical built squarely on the classical format. *Brigadoon* was, actually, yet another Americans-in-strange-places musical, and in some ways it might even have been considered another "dream" musical, but—whether one or both of these—it was essentially a romantic musical concocted with an ineffable and otherworldly kind of charm which made it probably the most thoroughly romantic of all the romantic pieces of its era. The setting of its story was Scotland, but not period Scotland, or merrie Scotland, or even modern-day Scotland—it was a mixture of all three. For, like Mark Twain's Yankee who ended up in the court of King Arthur, or the washroom attendant who zipped himself back to the age of Madame Dubarry, the young pair of American tourists who were the central chaps of this tale got time-warped. They walked out of an everyday twentieth-century Scottish forest and into what they eventually discover is the eighteenth century. It took them a while to notice that there were no mod cons and that the funny way the locals talked wasn't just good old Scottish quaintness and behind-the-timesness. But it took them no time at all to get around the local lassies. The baritone, of course, falls for the soprano, and his light-comic friend, by musical-theater law, finds himself being debagged by the soubrette. Lerner made a delightful libretto from this tale and its situations, and the German-born Loewe turned out a set of tartan-tinted tunes which gave off not even a whiff of the Continent and its traditions. Pieces such as the sweetly tenorious "Come to Me, Bend to Me" and the yearningly soprano "Waitin' for my Dearie" or the lovely "The Heather on the Hill," the Scottish-dancing "I'll Go Home with Bonnie Jean" and the slightly more conventional baritone solo "It's Almost Like Being in Love" were teamed with a couple of sparky comic songs for the man-chasing soubrette in an immensely appealing score. Since this was the age of the inescapable dance scena, *Brigadoon* was also rather heavily laden with dances, choreographed by the dance-maker of the moment, Agnes de Mille. A dramatic choreographed chase worked well, and a sword dance and some other highlandish dancing gave the expected Scottish coloring, but the insertion of a long, danced, action-stopping funeral sequence gave evidence of a trend towards choreographic overload which would go on to become an unbalancing feature in some musicals in the years to come. *Brigadoon*, however, more than succeeded in keeping its balance, and it followed *Oklahoma!* and *Annie Get Your Gun* both to splendid runs all around the English-speaking world and to the cinema screen.

BRIGADOON, a musical play in 2 acts by Alan Jay Lerner. Music by Frederick Loewe. Produced at the Ziegfeld Theatre, New York, 13 March 1947.

Characters: Tommy Albright, Jeff Douglas, Andrew MacLaren, Jean MacLaren, Fiona

MacLaren, Charlie Dalrymple, Meg Brockie, Archie Beaton, Harry Beaton, Mr Lundie, Angus MacGuffie, Sandy Dean, Jane Ashton, &c.

Plot: While out hunting in the Highlands, Tommy and Jeff come upon the village of Brigadoon. Brigadoon appears on earth only once every hundred years for, in the eighteenth century, when it was threatened with invasion, the local minister prayed to God for help, and the village was miraculously snatched away out of this world for all but one day a century. So, in two hundred years only two days have passed since "the miracle." Tommy is soon romancing pretty Fiona, and Jeff is soon being swarmed over by saucy Meg, but trouble is quick to come. At the wedding of Fiona's sister Jean and her young Charlie, the girl's rejected suitor threatens to leave the village. If he does Brigadoon will be thrown forever into darkness. As he is chased towards the boundaries, he falls and is killed. The village is saved. When Brigadoon's day on earth is done, the boys leave, but back in New York Tommy finds he cannot forget Fiona. He returns to Scotland, and such is the power of his love that the village half-reappears, allowing him to leave this world for Brigadoon, Fiona, and all eternity.

Songs: "Once in the Highlands" (chorus), "Brigadoon" (chorus), "Down in MacConnachy Square" (chorus), "Waitin' for My Dearie" (Fiona), "I'll Go Home with Bonnie Jean" (Charlie), "The Heather on the Hill" (Fiona, Tommy), "The Love of My Life" (Meg), "Jeannie's Packin' Up" (chorus), "Come to Me, Bend to Me" (Charlie), "Almost Like Being in Love" (Tommy), Wedding Dance, Sword Dance, The Chase (ensemble), "There But for You, Go I" (Tommy), "My Mother's Weddin' Day" (Meg), Funeral Dance, "From This Day On" (Tommy), reprise "Brigadoon."

A large load of dance was also a feature of a more comical musical, *High Button Shoes*, but this was not surprising as the show's staging was the work of Jerome Robbins, the choreographer-turned-director who had been responsible for the delightfully ingenuous high jinks of *On the Town*. *High Button Shoes* was ingenuous in a different kind of way—it was a little tale of period American small-town skulduggery, with ingenuously small-town characters who sang such prettily ingenuous Jule Styne/Sammy Cahn songs as "Papa, Won't You Dance with Me?" and "I Still Get Jealous." Robbins's dances ran from the tango to a Bathing Beauty Ballet, a story piece staged in the slapstick style of a Mack Sennett Keystone Kops movie which proved the highlight of the evening's entertainment. *High Button Shoes* proved decidedly popular on Broadway and later put up a respectable run in London before being put away. Songwriter Styne (1905–1994), however, would become a Broadway regular, turning out a long list of shows over a long list of years and, every now and then, turning out the songs for a show—such as the merry 1949 musical-theater adaptation of the celebrated Anita Loos novella *Gentlemen Prefer Blondes*, with its famous assertion that "Diamonds Are a Girl's Best Friend"—which proved a winner.

If Styne's career-long percentage rate of enduring hits to flops and demi-flops was less than satisfying, that of Frank Loesser (1910–1969) was quite simply staggeringly great. During his lifetime Loesser wrote the songs for six musicals, and if one gave out pre-Broadway, and a second failed there, the other four were—in varying degrees from hit to super-hit—all winners.

The first among these was actually a fairly unsatisfying piece. George Abbott (1887–1995), the director-cum-author who had worked in either or both capacities with Rodgers and Hart on so many of their 1930s musicals, adapted the famous farce *Charley's Aunt* as the libretto for a musical. Only, in adapting Brandon Thomas's superbly crafted and shaped piece of work, he uncrafted and misshaped it. In order to create a big star-vehicle rôle at the center of his musical, he quite simply combined the two principal male rôles of the original play: two rôles which originally shared a great deal of interplay and separate but parallel plotlines. The result was a libretto banal in the extreme. Loesser, with a dozen years of extremely popular songwriting to his credit, set the resulting book with songs as his musical-theater début. Pieces such as the lovingly pseudo-English "My Darling, My Darling" or the jauntily pseudo-English "Once in Love with Amy" stood alongside the altogether un-English "The New Ashmolean Marching Society and Students Conservatory Band" in a score which gave little hint of what its writer could do. But, misconceived, misshapen, and under par or not, *Where's Charley?* succeeded. It had good runs on Broadway and in Britain, and only in Australia did it go down the drain, following *Music in the Air* and *I Married an Angel* on to the list of biggest imported disasters of the antipodean century.

Two years later, however, Loesser turned out a musical of a wholly different color and caliber. *Guys and Dolls* was a show based on some stories by Damon Runyon, the author of a comical set of very individually flavored pieces set among the fairly lowlife folk of the New York City heartstreets. Once again, the show had book troubles, but on this occasion it had them only before the musical made its way to the stage, and it was another Broadway neophyte—another neophyte who would have a fine career in the musical theater—who was responsible for finally remaking the book of *Guys and Dolls* as it ultimately appeared on the stage. Abe Burrows (1910–1985) captured the essence of Runyon's characters and their gloriously quirky ways and ways of expression in a text which used characters and plot elements from several of Runyon's stories, and Loesser provided those characters with a characterful set of songs which fitted them like a good pair of tight jeans. The baritonic hero, the gambling Sky Masterson, cruised out a description of his compatibility with the small hours of the morning ("My Time of Day"), rattled the dice with a rousing call to "Luck Be a Lady" and duetted in the best baritone-soprano fashion with his soprano Sarah that "I've Never Been in Love Before," while she got tipsy on rum to the twinkling inanities of "If I Were a Bell" or plotted marital policies with the eternally affianced and never-wedded Adelaide in "Marry the Man Today" (and change his ways tomorrow), but it was that same and delightfully original Adelaide—the two-bit night-club singer whose allergies have run riot every time during the fourteen years that her wedding has been postponed—who drew some of the score's most outstanding moments. She bleeped out a couple of ditsy night-club songs ("A Bushel and a Peck," "Take Back Your Mink"), hacked away at her recalcitrant man and his haversackful of bad habits ("Sue Me") and poured out her woes to the accompaniment of more post-nasal drip than any girl should have to put up with in the uniquely funny soliloquy known as Adelaide's Lament.

Guys and Dolls was like nothing seen on Broadway for years . . . probably not since Harrigan had celebrated the below-average New Yorker in his happy nineteenth-century shows. But, unlike Harrigan's shows, *Guys and Dolls* and its thoroughly New Yorkish team of characters had an appeal that was not limited just to America. The show had superb runs both in America and in Britain, establishing itself at the top of a career which would finally bring it a reputation as one of the very greatest—if not, quite simply, the greatest without any kind of qualification—musical to have come out of the greatest years of the Broadway musical theater. Australia, however, must have been scared off by the *Where's Charley?* flop. It hosted *Song of Norway* and *Brigadoon*, but passed on *Guys and Dolls*. For the meanwhile.

Guys and Dolls: "I love you, a bushel and a peck, you bet ya purty neck I do . . . !" Ever-loving Adelaide and her Hot-Box girls go to work.

GUYS AND DOLLS, a musical fable of Broadway in 2 acts based on a story and characters by Damon Runyon. Book by Abe Burrows and Jo Swerling. Lyrics and music by Frank Loesser. Produced at the 46th Street Theatre, New York, 24 November 1950.

Characters: Miss Adelaide, Nathan Detroit, Nicely-Nicely Johnson, Sarah Brown, Sky Masterson, Arvide Abernathy, Benny Southstreet, Rusty Charlie, Big Jule, Harry the Horse, Angie the Ox, General Matilda B. Cartwright, Lieutenant Brannigan, &c.

Plot: Nathan Detroit needs some stake money to set up his illegal crap game, so he makes what he thinks is a sure-fire bet with the big gambler Sky Masterson. Masterson has to get the holy-roller girl Sarah Brown to go with him on a day-trip date to Havana! But Sky promises Sarah a dozen genuine sinners to fill her terminally ailing mission on the day her General comes for a check-up, so Sarah goes. Then Sky sets to work to get his sinners: he rolls dice with them not for cash but for their "marker." The losers are obliged to put in an appearance at the mission. As for Sky, he simply loses his heart. The reformed gambler marries Sarah and ends up banging the bass drum in the mission band. The probably less reformed Nathan also gets hooked by his extra-long-term fiancée, the nightclubby Miss Adelaide.

Songs: Fugue for Tinhorns ("I Got a Horse Right Here") (guys), "Follow the Fold" (Sarah &c.), "The Oldest Established Permanent Floating Crap Game in New York" (Nathan &c.), "I'll Know" (Sarah, Sky), "A Bushel and a Peck" (Miss Adelaide), Adelaide's Lament: "The Average Unmarried Female" (Adelaide), "Guys and Dolls" (guys), Dance: Havana, "If I Were a Bell" (Sarah), "My Time of Day" (Sky), "I've Never Been in Love Before" (Sarah, Sky), "Take Back Your Mink" (Miss Adelaide), "More I Cannot Wish You" (Arvide), Crapshooters' Dance, "Luck Be a Lady" (Sky), "Sue Me" (Nathan, Adelaide), "Sit Down, You're Rockin' the Boat" (Nicely-Nicely), "Marry the Man Today" (Adelaide, Sarah), reprise "Guys and Dolls."

It was not *Guys and Dolls*, however, any more than it was *Oklahoma!*, *Annie Get Your Gun*, or *Brigadoon* which proved to be the landmark show which took the English-language musical back into the theaters of Europe where *The Mikado*, *The Geisha*, *No, No, Nanette*, and *Rose Marie* had prospered in their turn but where, in more recent years, the produce of London and of Broadway had been less frequently and less successfully seen. The show that achieved that breakthrough—or break-back, to be more accurate—was not by one of the new young wolves of the Broadway scene, but by one of its getting-on-for-elder statesman. Like such other stars of the musical comedy past as Kern, Novello, and Ellis, Cole Porter now switched away

from the "songwriter's show" to a kind of musical play which could almost be considered a romantic musical, and which was, in any case, certainly built on the most classic of principles. Its leading man was as robust a lyric baritone as could be wished, its soprano leading lady verged on the operatic, and there was a jolly pair of dancing soubrets to lend their support in a lighthearted parallel plot which was neatly dovetailed into the romantic one. A romantic one which, nevertheless, and in spite of all the lush singing, was far from being conventionally "romantic" and, indeed, smacked altogether more of the comical. The romantic setting of *Kiss Me, Kate* was that good old standby, the theater, and, at one stage removed, the period musical comedy that was played within it. The title of the show was actually the title of that show-within-the-show, the performance of pieces from which took up a sizeable chunk of the evening: the try-out of a Broadway musical reduction of Shakespeare's *The Taming of the Shrew*. But it was what went on during the performance of this unlikely piece of sung-and-danced Shakespeare which provided the fun in Sam and Bella Spewack's clever libretto.

The songs fell into two groups—the cod-Bard pieces which were supposed to be part of the musical-inside-the-musical, and those which belonged to the characters of Spewack and Porter's show. The first were a merry lot—Petruchio disarmingly admitting "I've Come to Wive It Wealthily in Padua" and rolling off a catalogue of the faults that the wife in question could have if only she were rich, Kate spitting out "I Hate Men," or Bianca fleet-footedly sharing out her favors among "Tom, Dick or Harry"—but it was from the second group that the real favorites came: the stars' reminiscences of youthful touring days in a tatty operetta company ("Wunderbar"), the soubrette's perky assertion that she is "Always True to You in My Fashion"—which listed all the temptations she couldn't be expected to resist—and the show's one real love song, the rollingly seductive "So in Love." Remarkably, given Porter's past record of movable parts, almost every song seemed custom-made for its place in the show, and only a revusical front-cloth piece for a couple of low comedians, which insisted in a barrage of punishing Shakespearianisms that you should "Brush up Your Shakespeare" as an aid to sexual gratification, was patently tacked in. There was even a concerted finale. And no ballet scena—the dance highlight of the night was a heat-slowed routine in the stage-door alley which languorously opened the second act ("Too Darn Hot").

Kiss Me, Kate scored a first-class success throughout the English world—this time Australia joined in whole-heartedly—but then it went further. After going on stage in London in 1951, and Australia in 1952, in 1955 the show made an appearance at Frankfurt's Städtische Bühnen and from there, slowly but surely, it made its way through Central Europe, establishing itself as a classic of the European musical stage which has been revived there regularly up to this day, but also opening the door into Europe for some of the other most appreciable musicals of the contemporary English-singing stage. From *Kiss Me, Kate* onwards, a regular flow of musical plays made its way from the stages of America and Great Britain into Europe with a vigour never before known, and if some of the outstanding writers and shows of the extra-European continents never succeeded in gaining a foothold there (the works of Rodgers and Hammerstein being a notable example), others found both major success and a permanent place in the repertoire. But *Kiss Me, Kate* got there first.

KISS ME, KATE, musical comedy in 2 acts by Sam and Bella Spewack based on *The Taming of the Shrew* by William Shakespeare. Lyrics and music by Cole Porter. Produced at the New Century Theatre, New York, 30 December 1948.

Characters: Fred Graham [Petruchio], Harry Trevor [Baptista], Lois Lane [Bianca], Lilli Vanessi [Katharine], Bill Calhoun [Lucentio], Hattie, Ralph, Harrison Howell, First Gangster, Second Gangster, "Gremio," "Hortensio," Paul, Stage Doorman, &c.

Plot: Fred Graham is co-starring with his ex-wife, Lilli Vanessi, in the musical *Kiss Me, Kate*. She's engaged to a wealthy politician, and he's making heavy moves towards the show's soubrette, Lois, but it's clear the old spark is still aglow. Lois's boyfriend Bill lights the touchpaper of trouble when he signs a gambling IOU in Fred's name, and a couple of heavies move in to put the squeeze on the show's star on opening night. However, they turn out to have their uses, for when Lilli throws a deep-hurt tantrum at discovering Fred's intentions towards Lois and threatens to walk out, the "boys" force her to continue rather than see the box-office have to return "their" money to the public. By the time the evening is over, happy endings have had time to work themselves out all round.

Songs: "Another Op'nin', Another Show" (Hattie, chorus), "Why Can't You Behave?" (Lois), "Wunderbar" (Fred, Lilli), "So in Love" (Lilli), "We Open in Venice" (ensemble), "Tom, Dick or Harry" (Bianca, Hortensio, Lucentio, Gremio), Rose Dance, "I've Come to Wive It Wealthily in Padua" (Petruchio), "I Hate Men" (Katharine), "Were Thine That Special Face" (Petruchio), "I Sing of Love" (Bianca, Lucentio, solos, and chorus), Tarantella, Finale Act I: "Kiss Me, Kate," "Too Darn Hot" (Paul), "Where Is the Life That Late I Led" (Petruchio), "Always True to You in My Fashion" (Lois), "Bianca" (Bill &c.), reprise "So in Love" (Fred), "Brush up Your Shakespeare" (Gangsters), Pavane, "I Am Ashamed That Women Are So Simple" (Katharine), Finale Act 2: "Kiss Me, Kate"

Rodgers and Hammerstein had confirmed the success of *Oklahoma!* with the success of *Carousel*, and they confirmed it all over again with their third hit musical of the 1940s, *South Pacific*. Like *Guys and Dolls*, *South Pacific* was based on characters and incidents taken from a collection of like-flavored short stories. But the James Michener stories which were the starting point for *South Pacific* were not like Runyon's comical New Yorkeries, for they were as dramatic as they were comic. They were set in the islands of the south Pacific but, again, they could not have been less like the curious old Americans-in-weird-places stories that had served for so many musicals around the turn of the century—the south Pacific of these tales was a real and contemporary one, and the show was set during the war not long ended.

The line-up of players in *South Pacific* differed from those of both *Oklahoma!* and *Carousel*, but there was a good reason for this and for the deviation from the usual spectrum of characters on view at the heart of a romantic musical play. Both of this show's star rôles were written to order for specific artists, the celebrated operatic basso Ezio Pinza and the popular soubrette

Mary Martin, who acted and sang out a musical-theatrically unconventional and dramatic wartime love story about an aging Frenchman and a perky American nurse. Alongside their story there ran a second tale in which the same subject was looked at—the triumph of love over differences of age and of race, over all kind of prejudices and dissimilarities. But while the first romance had a happy end, the second—between the show's juvenile man, in the rôle of an American lieutenant, and a little island girl—climaxed in tragedy with the young man's death in action before he could carry out his resolve to fly in the face of the accepted and leave America for the islands and his girl.

Given this dramatic and casting layout, the show featured a score rather different in character from those of the two previous hits. Here, the romantic singing was virtually all for the men—the Frenchman rolling out some of the most beautiful basso love-music in musical-theater history in the long-breathed "This Nearly Was Mine" and "Some Enchanted Evening," and the young lieutenant hymning his native sweetheart as "Younger Than Springtime" in a longing light baritone—while the star soubrette sparked out a series of bouncy pieces in contrast. At Miss Martin's insistence there were no duets for the star couple—wisely, she was not going to attempt to harmonize with the twenty-vocal-gunned star of the Metropolitan Opera—but, more oddly, there were none for the juvenile pair either. The score for *South Pacific* had no successor to "People Will Say We're in Love" and "If I Loved You." One thing which remained stable from the *Carousel* layout, however, was the big lady's song for the big lady's voice. "You'll Never Walk Alone" very definitely did have a follow-up. Here, the lady in question was the lit-

South Pacific: Fraternization on a wartime Pacific island. The nursing staff go out for a healthy jog, and what do they meet? A bunch of servicemen who are all agreed that "There is nothing like a dame."

tle, wizened, war-profiteering islander known as Bloody Mary. Mary was played largely for comedy, sharing the traditional low comedy moments of the play with a klutzy GI called Billis, but the song with which she made her mark was a thoroughly romantic one: a soaring soprano piece in praise of the local island known as "Bali H'ai" which—given that the heroine's music was all soubrettery—was the lyrical highlight of the feminine part of the show's music.

South Pacific was a more complete musical than either *Oklahoma!* or *Carousel*. Although its libretto, with its "would-you-let-your-daughter-marry-a-black-man" theme and its oafish low comedy, has perhaps aged less well than theirs have, it was better shaped and more significant than the first named, and less softened-up and sweetened-down than the second. As for its score: its lyric music saw Rodgers at his most full-bloodedly romantic, while the lighter numbers included several which became soubrette favorites. And, together, they made up a very superior piece of musical theater which took the English-speaking theaters of the world by storm before going on to become a memorable Hollywood musical movie.

SOUTH PACIFIC, a musical in 2 acts by Oscar Hammerstein II and Joshua Logan based on *Tales of the South Pacific* by James Michener. Lyrics by Oscar Hammerstein II. Music by Richard Rodgers. Produced at the Majestic Theatre, New York, 7 April 1949.

Characters: Ensign Nellie Forbush, Émile de Becque, Bloody Mary, Liat, Luther Billis, Stewpot, Lieutenant Joe Cable, Ngana, Jerome, Captain George Brackett, Commander William Harbison, Lieutenant Buzz Adams, Professor, &c.

Plot: Middle-aged Frenchman Émile de Becque has lived all his life in the Pacific since fleeing his homeland as a young man after being involved in a killing. When the war brings American troops to his island he falls in love with the nurse, Nellie Forbush. She returns his feelings, but she cannot get over his past—not the killing, but his relationship with an island woman and the two children born of that liaison. Another small-town American, Joe Cable, engineered into a meeting with the beautiful islander Liat by her greedy and ambitious mother, Bloody Mary, is in a similar position. His love for the girl is checkmated by an upbringing in which he has been taught to consider that any feeling between them would be almost unnatural. When Joe and Émile go on a dangerous mission to a neighboring island, things become clearer. Nellie realizes how foolish she is to consider anything but the man and their love, and when de Becque returns, safe and sound, it is to find a happy ending. But Joe Cable, who had similarly decided to give up small-town America for the islands and for Liat, does not return. For the younger pair there is no happy ending.

Songs: "Dites-moi" (Jerome, Ngana), "A Cockeyed Optimist" (Nellie), Twin Soliloquies: "Wonder How It Feels" (Émile, Nellie), "Some Enchanted Evening" (Émile), "Bloody Mary" (chorus), "There Is Nothin' Like a Dame" (chorus), "Bali H'ai" (Mary), "I'm Gonna Wash That Man Right Out of My Hair" (Nellie), "A Wonderful Guy" (Nellie), "Younger Than Springtime" (Joe), "This Is How It Feels" (Émile, Nellie), Soft Shoe Dance, "Happy Talk" (Mary), "Honey Bun" (Nellie), "You've Got to Be Carefully Taught" (Joe), "This Nearly Was Mine" (Émile), Finale Act 2: reprises "Dites-moi" and "Some Enchanted Evening."

SOME NOTABLE MUSICALS 1941–1950

1941   LADY IN THE DARK (Kurt Weill/Ira Gershwin/Moss Hart) Alvin Theatre, New York, 21 January

LET'S FACE IT (Cole Porter/Herbert Fields, Dorothy Fields) Imperial Theatre, New York, 29 October

GET A LOAD OF THIS (Manning Sherwin/Val Guest/James Hadley Chase) London Hippodrome, London, 19 November

1942   BY JUPITER (Richard Rodgers/Lorenz Hart) Shubert Theatre, New York, 2 June

1943   SOMETHING FOR THE BOYS (Cole Porter/Herbert Fields, Dorothy Fields) Alvin Theatre, New York, 7 January

OKLAHOMA! (Richard Rodgers/Oscar Hammerstein II) St James Theatre, New York, 31 March

THE LISBON STORY (Harry Parr Davies/Harold Purcell) London Hippodrome, London, 17 June

ONE TOUCH OF VENUS (Kurt Weill/Ogden Nash/S. J. Perelman) Imperial Theatre, New York, 7 October

1944   FOLLOW THE GIRLS (Phil Charig/Dan Shapiro, Milton Pascal/Fred Thompson, Guy Bolton) Century Theatre, New York, 8 April

SONG OF NORWAY (Edvard Grieg pasticcio, arr. Robert Wright, George Forrest/Milton Lazarus) Imperial Theatre, New York, 21 August

ON THE TOWN (Leonard Bernstein/Adolph Green, Betty Comden) Adelphi Theatre, New York, 28 December

1945   CAROUSEL (Richard Rodgers/Oscar Hammerstein II) Majestic Theatre, New York, 19 April

PERCHANCE TO DREAM (Ivor Novello) London Hippodrome, London, 21 April

UNDER THE COUNTER (Manning Sherwin/Harold Purcell/Arthur Macrae) Phoenix Theatre, London, 22 November

LA BELLE DE CADIX [The belle of Cadiz] (Francis Lopez/Raymond Vincy) Casino Gaîté-Montparnasse, Paris, 24 December

1946   ANNIE GET YOUR GUN (Irving Berlin/Dorothy Fields, Herbert Fields) Imperial Theatre, New York, 16 May

CHANSON GITANE [Gipsy song] (Maurice Yvain/André Mouëzy-Éon, Louis Poterat) Théâtre de la Gaîté-Lyrique, Paris, 13 December

1947   FINIAN'S RAINBOW [Burton Lane/E. Y. Harburg, Fred Saidy] 46th Street Theatre, New York, 10 January

BRIGADOON (Frederick Loewe/Alan J. Lerner) Ziegfeld Theatre, New York, 13 March

BLESS THE BRIDE (Vivian Ellis/A. P. Herbert) Adelphi Theatre, London, 26 April

HIGH BUTTON SHOES (Jule Styne/Sammy Cahn/Stephen Longstreet) New Century Theatre, New York, 9 October

ANDALOUSIE (Francis Lopez/Albert Willemetz/Raymond Vincy) Théâtre de la Gaîté-Lyrique, Paris, 25 October

1948   VIOLETTES IMPÉRIALES [Imperial violets] (Vincent Scotto/Paul Achard, René Jeanne, Henri Varna) Théâtre Mogador, Paris, 31 January

QUATRE JOURS À PARIS [Four days in Paris] (Francis Lopez/Raymond Vincy) Théâtre Bobino, Paris, 28 February

WHERE'S CHARLEY? (Frank Loesser/George Abbott) St James Theatre, New York, 11 October

KISS ME, KATE (Cole Porter/Bella Spewack, Sam Spewack) New Century Theatre, New York, 30 December

1949   SOUTH PACIFIC (Richard Rodgers/Oscar Hammerstein II, Joshua Logan) Majestic Theatre, New York, 7 April

KING'S RHAPSODY (Ivor Novello/Christopher Hassall) Palace Theatre, London, 15 September

GENTLEMEN PREFER BLONDES (Jule Styne/Leo Robin/Anita Loos, Joseph Fields) Ziegfeld Theatre, New York, 8 December

1950   GAY'S THE WORD (Ivor Novello/Alan Melville) Saville Theatre, London, 16 February

CALL ME MADAM (Irving Berlin/Howard Lindsay, Russel Crouse) Imperial Theatre, New York, 12 October

GUYS AND DOLLS (Frank Loesser/Jo Swerling, Abe Burrows) 46th Street Theatre, New York, 24 November

BLUE FOR A BOY (Harry Parr Davies/Harold Purcell/Austin Melford) His Majesty's Theatre, London, 30 November

Many of the Operetten produced in Central Europe 1914–1940 were exported widely around the rest of the world. It wasn't, however, always those shows that had been the most successful at home that traveled to best effect and, in the shadow of the two most thoroughly international blockbusters of the time, *Das Dreimäderlhaus* and *Im weissen Rössl*, major Central European hits such as *Der Orlow* and *Die Rose von Stambul* failed to export while pieces such as *Der lila Domino* and *Die Frau im Hermelin*, which had originally had more modest careers, proved—for various reasons—to be full-scale hits abroad. Other musicals, such as *Das Land des Lächelns* or *Die Dreigroschenoper*, initially unsuccessful on the English-language stage, had to wait for later changes in fashion or fortune before becoming popular. The following list, based on the contemporary runs achieved by Operetten of this period in New York and/or London, is arranged to give a necessarily approximate "hit parade" of the musical theater exported from Austria, Germany, and Hungary in that quarter of a century when those countries supplied such an important amount of the world's musical-theater entertainments.

Operetten were produced in Austria unless otherwise shown. [G] = Germany, [H] = Hungary, [S] = Switzerland, [HOL]= Netherlands, [IT]= Italy. Where a Viennese theatre name only is shown rather than a figure, it is either because I haven't been able to get precise data on the length of run from that theater's records, or because the show was played in repertoire season(s) only. An asterisk after a performance's total shows that it was not actually checked out or counted up by me, but has been taken on trust from other sources. "Fr" (France) and "Aust" (Australia) note productions of the musical in question in those other two principal musical-theater areas of the time. CT = closed in tryout, x = not produced in this country.

	AUT	UK	USA	
Das Dreimäderlhaus [Lilac Time, Blossom Time]	1,100+	626	319	Fr, Aust
Im weissen Rössl [G] [White Horse Inn]	693	651	223	Fr, Aust
Walzer aus Wien [The Great Waltz, Waltzes from Vienna]	Stadt	607	298	Fr
Die Frau im Hermelin [G]				
[The Lady of the Rose, The Lady in Ermine]	141	514	232	Aust
Katja die Tänzerin [Katja, the Dancer]	207	501	112	Aust
Der lila Domino [G] [The Lilac Domino]	x	747	110	Aust
Madame Pompadour [G]	209	491	80	Fr, Aus
Az obsitos [H] [Her Soldier Boy]	82	372	204	
Szibill [H] [Sybil]	Stadt	347	168	Aust
Die Dubarry [G] [The Dubarry]	35	397	87	Fr, Aust
Der letzte Walzer [G] [The Last Waltz]	255	280	199	Fr
Der Tanz ins Glück [Whirled into Happiness, Sky High]	200	244	220	Aust
Alexandra [H] [Princess Charming]	77	362	56	Aust
Gräfin Mariza [Countess Mariza]	396	68	321	Fr
Ein Tag im Paradies [The Blue Paradise]	220	x	360	
Drei Walzer [S] [Three Waltzes]	x	122	189	Fr
Die Csárdásfürstin [The Gipsy Princess, The Riviera Girl]	533	212	78	Fr, Aust
Das Vetter aus Dingsda [G] [The Cousin from Nowhere]	72	105	181	Aust
Filmzauber [G] [The Girl on the Film]	8	232	56	Aust
Die Wunder-Bar [Wonder Bar]	Kamm	210	76	
Wenn die kleinen Veilchen blühen [HOL] [Wild Violets]	x	291	StLouis	Aust
Casanova [G]	Volksop	329	x	Aust
Die Kino-Königin [G]				
[The Cinema Star, The Queen of the Movies]	286	109	106	Aust
Zsuzsi kisasszony [H] [Miss Springtime]	x	x	230	
Die Zirkusprinzessin [The Circus Princess]	344	x	192	

Title				
Eine Frau, die weiss, was sie will [G] [Mother of Pearl]	36	181	x	Aust
Endlich allein [Alone at Last]	116	x	177	
Meine Schwester und ich [G] [Meet my Sister]	Kom	167	8	
Der Apachen [The Apache]	Apollo	166	CT	
Lady Hamilton [S] [Song of the Sea]	x	156	x	
Der Zigeunerprimas [Sari]	180	x	151	
Friederike [G]	205	110	84	
Viktória [H] [Victoria and Her Hussar]	121	100	StLouis	Fr, Aust
Das Land des Lächelns [G] [The Land of Smiles]	101	71	CT	Fr, Aust
Der lachende Ehemann [The Laughing Husband]	201	78	48	
Ball im Savoy [G] [Ball at the Savoy]	Scala	148	x	
Die blaue Mazur [The Blue Mazurka]	333	140	x	Fr
Chopin [H] [White Lilacs]	x	x	136	
Offenbach [H] [The Love Song]	Stadt	x	135	
Libellentanz [IT] [The Three Graces]	Stadt	121	x	Fr
Mädi [G] [The Blue Train]	72	116	x	
Polenblut [G] [The Peasant Girl]	250	x	111	
Die Perlen der Kleopatra [Cleopatra]	61	110	x	
Die Rose von Stambul [The Rose of Stambul]	480	x	103	
Drei arme kleine Mädels [G] [Three Little Girls]	?	x	103	
Cloclo	62	95	x	
Riquette [G] [Naughty Riquette]	Raim	CT	88	
Die Bajadere [The Yankee Princess]	406	x	80	
Musik in Mai [Music in May]	Raim	x	80	
Sterne, die wieder leuchtet [G] [Springtime of Youth]	x	x	68	
Die schöne Schwedin [The Girl from Brazil]	51	x	61	
Paganini [G]	138	59	x	Fr
Die moderne Eva [G]	6	x	56	
Das Veilchen vom Montmartre [Kiss in Spring]	109	49	CT	Fr
Die Dame in Rot [G] [The Lady in Red]	x	x	48	
Der Orlow [Hearts and Diamonds]	650	46	x	Fr
Frasquita	195	36	CT	Fr
Wenn Liebe erwacht [G] [Love's Awakening]	x	35	x	
Farsangi lakodalom [H] [Love Adrift]	Hofop	21	x	
Frühling im Herbst [G] [Holka Polka]	x	x	21	
Drei alte Schachteln [G] [Phoebe of Quality Street]	JohS	x	16	
Die schöne Unbekannte [My Lady's Glove]	103	x	16	
Hotel Stadt Lemberg [G] [Marching By]	58*	x	12	
Die Dreigroschenoper [G] [The Threepenny Opera]	'3mths'	x	12	Fr
Der Sterngucker [The Stargazer]	79+60	x	8	
Die Tanzgräfin [G] [The Dancing Duchess]	204	x	CT	
Wenn zwei sich Lieben [Lieutenant Gus]	110	x	CT	
Venus in Seide [S] [Venus in Silk]	x	CT	CT	

Such remakes as the Broadway rewritings of *Das Weib im Purpur* [167 performances in Vienna] as *The Red Robe*, *Was tut man nicht alles aus Liebe* as *Follow Me*, or the hit Berlin show *Wie einst im Mai* as the long-running *Maytime* [492 Broadway performances] are not included here, as their rewriting was so extensive as to leave the resulting shows textually or musically unrecognizable in relation to their originals.

By the dawn of the 1950s, America had thoroughly taken over the position previously held in turn by France, by Britain, and by Austria as the epicenter of the world's musical theater—as the creative source from which the bulk of the shows that entertained musical-theatergoers around the world flowed. That world had, however, changed somewhat in character and in scope. In Central Europe, the level of inspiration among writers and composers seemed to have fallen right off the bottom of the barometer, and in France, equally, the musical theater no longer flourished with the kind of vivacity that had been its pride throughout the previous hundred years. Not just new musical theater, but musical theater fullstop. Increasingly, those European theaters which had through the years rivaled one another with their productions of the latest in musical-theater entertainment, both home-made and brought from abroad, new and old, now gave themselves over to other kinds of entertainment, or else quite simply floundered into unviability. And this was a situation which was going to get worse—much worse—before, decades down the line, the musical stage in Europe would start to show just a tiny twitch of reinvigoration. In the years after the war, it was the English-speaking musical theater which held total sway, it was English-speaking countries where "musicals," as they were now called, flourished as the most popular form of theatrical entertainment, and the very great bulk of the musicals on which those theaters and those countries flourished were the product of a booming Broadway which, in its turn, was now flourishing with a vigor that had never been greater, and which was made to appear even greater yet by the virtual vacuum in which it existed. There was no doubt about it—as far as musicals were concerned, during the next twenty years or so it was Broadway just about all the way.

The men and women who turned out the shows that would be the great attractions of the next decade were very largely the same people who had been responsible for the hits of the 1940s. Rodgers and Hammerstein added two further outstanding hits to the three they had notched up in the previous decade in *The King and I* and *The Sound of Music*, before Hammerstein's death in 1960; Wright and Forrest topped the success of the pasticcio *Song of Norway* with one even greater in the splendidly satisfying pasticcio musical version of the splendid old play *Kismet*; Lerner and Loewe went on from *Brigadoon* to further success with *Paint Your*

Wagon and *Camelot* and to total triumph with *My Fair Lady*; Frank Loesser followed up *Guys and Dolls* with the warm and wonderful *The Most Happy Fella* and the comical *How to Succeed in Business Without Really Trying*; Comden, Green, and Bernstein contributed *Wonderful Town* as a team before going on, each, to further successes with other partners; and Irving Berlin provided the songs for another jolly piece of breezy musical comedy in *Call Me Madam*. So many shows, so many hits that traveled from New York to London and to Sydney with lavish success, and which made themselves the great events of an entire era of musical theater. Those other countries and cities that didn't choose to share in its joys were surely the losers.

This group of happy hits was not, however, a series of shows all born and bred in the same image, or even in the same lineage. Among them, there was a delightful variety to be found—but a variety which was no longer on the "classic" lines of past years. The division of earlier days between the romantic musical and the musical comedy was not now as definite as it had been, and both textually and musically the shows of these days often trod a middle path, with romance and fun mingling happily together, rather than being divided off into separate areas as they had been in the kind of show which posited a romantic, lyrically singing hero and heroine on the one hand, and a supporting pair of soubrets and or a low comedian, equipped with "pop" songs and dance material, on the other.

The musical of the 1950s demanded, first of all, a strong narrative—a story with a beginning and a middle and an end, in which subplots and peripheral or irrelevant incidents and characters were kept to a minimum. There was rarely place in a musical these days for a pasted-in person who was included in the show merely to allow him to do his singing, dancing, or stand-up comical thing. Many libretti were—as in the best days of the farcical musical comedy—happily based on existing plays or books, and since the classic line-up of voices and characters—romantic and comic—was no longer any sort of an obligation, there was greater freedom left to the authors to develop a solid and dramatically sensible text, a text of which the lyrical portion more and more made up an integral part. There was as little place for the irrelevant number of the "interpolated" kind that had flourished in the early part of the century in the score of a modern musical as there was for the irrelevant performer. The new kind of musical play was very much of a whole, and even the decorative bits—songs, dances, and humorous scenes—were expected to contribute to that whole. The music of the modern musical was, similarly, a blend of that used in the two extremes of the older styles of show. Most of the composers for this era of shows had a background in popular songwriting, but often in their show-writing they stretched themselves and their musical talent into a wider range of musical styles, and several songwriters whose original habitat had been on or near to Tin Pan Alley went on to produce some very considerable lyric and romantic musical writing in their stage works. Frank Loesser, for example, who in earlier days had been responsible for "A Slow Boat to China" and "Baby It's Cold Outside," went on to compose the vibrant love music for *The Most Happy Fella*. This wholeness, this coherency, in the musical theater was of course not something that was new—the librettists of Hervé and Offenbach had already worked in a similarly tightly organized fashion—but after an era when Broadway and the musical theater in general had seen so many of the loose-limbed kind of songwriters' shows, with their movable and detachable songs, and so many romantic musicals, with their classic but now rather clichéd love-story/low-comedy layout, the thorough-going musical play, worthy of that name, was a species of entertainment much appreciated.

Richard Rodgers and Oscar Hammerstein II actually supplied five musicals to the Broadway stage during the 1950s, but of them only the first and the last proved to be hits on the scale and of the value of their three successes of the forties. Three attempts at writing musicals with contemporary American settings—a wan little theatrical love-story called *Me and Juliet*, a curiously uninteresting lowish-life piece called *Pipe Dream*, and the altogether more felicitous but scarcely enthusiasm-provoking *Flower Drum Song*, with its small story of amours and marriage among the San Francisco Chinese community—did less well than the two full-bloodedly romantic pieces with which they opened and closed the decade.

The King and I was a musical based on the memoirs of Anna Leonowens, a canny Victorian Englishwoman who had spent some time as governess to the children of the perfectly "civilized" King of Siam (he was, after all, a subscriber to the *New York Evening Post*) and then lived off the story of her exotic experiences for the rest of her life ("Mrs Leonowens, late Governess of the Royal Family of Siam, will appear at the YMCA Hall 20 November 1874. Admission 50 cents"). Since the rôle of Anna was constructed expressly for the comedy actress Gertrude Lawrence, Hammerstein told this romanticized version of her story—in which the prettily proselytizing lady's attempts to divert the King from his "savage" ancestral ways to those of righteously hoop-skirted Victorian England were highlighted—with a sufficiently light touch, but the romantic and lyric elements that had been a feature of their biggest successes were not neglected. While Miss Lawrence was given charmingly light comic moments and lightweight music suitable to her talents, and the non-singing Yul Brynner, cast in what had been intended as a robust baritone rôle as the King, was also excused both a heavy vocal load and an unhistoric love affair (but offered the hint of an attraction towards his co-star), the three most important supporting characters, each an integral part of the show's well-made story (if not of the real Mrs Leonowens's life), were given the serious love-stories and the lyrical singing of the entertainment. The result was a well-made musical in which a range of sentiments and musical styles, and some attractive Eastern settings and costumes, were combined with the utmost success, and both the show and its songs—from the jaunty little "I Whistle a Happy Tune" and the tender "Hello, Young Lovers" (which sweetened up Mrs Leonowens's character in the same way their Soliloquy had done for Billy Bigelow) to the stirringly beautiful latest of the team's big lady's songs—the "Something Wonderful" intoned by the King's adoring head wife—and the full-bloodedly tenor/soprano duos "We Kiss in a Shadow" and "I Have Dreamed"—became long-time favorites.

THE KING AND I, a musical in 2 acts by Oscar Hammerstein II, based on the novel *Anna and the King of Siam* by Margaret Landon. Music by Richard Rodgers. Produced at the St James Theatre, New York, 29 March 1951.

Characters: Anna Leonowens, The King, Lady Thiang, Tuptim, Lun Tha, Prince Chulalongkorn, Louis, The Kralahome, Sir Edward Ramsey, Captain Orton, &c.

Plot: Widowed Anna Leonowens takes up a position as governess to the children of the King of Siam and immediately starts to impose her Victorian-English ideas of right and wrong not only on the children but on the whole of the royal household, including the all-powerful King. He, with ambitions towards being accepted and approved of by the powerful and "civilized" British, allows her a long leash, but they clash when, with Anna's connivance, one of the royal concubines attempts to run away with her lover. The King orders the man's execution, the girl kills herself, and the Englishwoman brands her royal employer a savage and quits. Before she can depart from Bangkok, however, the King dies and Anna remains. She will help his young son make Siam into a country as civilized as Britain.

Songs: Arrival at Bangkok, "I Whistle a Happy Tune" (Anna), "My Lord and Master" (Tuptim), "Hello, Young Lovers" (Anna), March of the Royal Siamese Children, "Children Sing, Priests Chant" (chorus), "A Puzzlement" (King), "The Royal Bangkok Academy" (Anna, children), "Getting to Know You" (Anna), "We Kiss in a Shadow" (Lun Tha, Tuptim), "Shall I Tell You What I Think of You?" (Anna), "Something Wonderful" (Thiang), Finale Act 1: Prayer to Buddha, "Western People Funny" (Lady Thiang, wives), "I Have Dreamed" (Lun Tha, Tuptim), Ballet: The Small House of Uncle Thomas (Tuptim), Song of the King (King), "Shall We Dance?" (Anna, King).

Romantic subjects and settings proved once again to be the collaborators' most effective recipe for success when they plumped for another tale of far-off and picturesque places in what was to be their last show together. *The Sound of Music* had a story which was based on the true history of a family group of singers who had fled Austria at the German invasion some twenty years earlier. Its heroine, Maria Rainer—a fledgling nun assigned to extra-conventual work as a governess—did better than Mrs Leonowens. Sent, like her predecessor, to educate the children of an aristocrat, she was allowed (in perfect accordance with historical fact) not only to lead her little charges and their father to living in accordance with her philosophy of life, but also to win the consummation of a full-blown romance and marriage with her employer. This progression from reasonably dutiful nunlet to winsome wife, interrupted by an up-and-down romance on his part and some considerable heart-searching on hers, was the backbone of the story of the show which, when the wedding was done, then concentrated on its protagonists' resistance to the invasion and their flight to freedom.

The musical line-up of *The Sound of Music* was again different from that of the earlier shows, and, as in the case of *The King and I*, that difference was caused by casting considerations. The show, and the rôle of Maria, was expressly constructed as a vehicle for Mary Martin, the soubrette star of *South Pacific*, and the songs were duly written to her measure. This time, however, she had no blossoming basso as a partner—the rôle of her aristocratic hero was as vocally underwritten as that of Anna Leonowens's King—and, equally, she had no lyrically robust juveniles, like those of *The King and I*, to contend with. The score of *The Sound of Music* was written almost wholly for the benefit of Maria. Almost—for Rodgers and Hammerstein did not forgo their big lady's song, and the one which they wrote here, for the actress playing the part of the Mother Superior of Maria's abbey, turned out to be perhaps the most popular of all: the soaring homily "Climb Every Mountain." The substantial singing of the show's score did, in fact, fall entirely to the sub-operatic inmates of the abbey, and the all-female choruses and ensembles performed by the nuns provided a useful contrast to the pretty ditties sung by Maria for and with the children of the piece. Two slightly more acrid pieces for the two slightly more acrid principal characters who impinged on the action helped the balance as well, although they were rather submerged under the welter of soprano singing—weighty, lightweighty, and juvenile—which was the body of the show's score.

The Sound of Music won some brickbats from the critics for its sweetness-and-light ingenuousness, but the public's reaction was unmitigatedly pro. The show turned out to be an enormous success on Broadway, proved to be the most successful and long-running Broadway musical ever played on the West End stage up to its time, and then went on to a wider consecration, largely thanks to a particularly outstanding film version. The unforgettable performance of Julie Andrews as the screen Maria, playing out her story before some dazzling photography of the Austrian Salzkammergut, turned the filmed *The Sound of Music* into the most popular filmed stage musical in history, and helped ingrain its favorite songs deep into popular memory.

THE SOUND OF MUSIC, a musical in 2 acts by Howard Lindsay and Russel Crouse, based on the memoir "The Trapp Family Singers" by Maria Augusta Trapp. Lyrics by Oscar Hammerstein II. Music by Richard Rodgers. Produced at the Lunt-Fontanne Theatre, New York, 16 November 1959.

Characters: Maria Rainer, Captain Georg von Trapp, Mother Abbess, Sister Berthe, Sister Margaretta, Sister Sophia, Frau Schmidt, Franz, Rolf Gruber, Elsa Schräder, Max Detweiler, Herr Zeller, Liesl, Friedrich, Louisa, Kurt, Marta, Gretl, Brigitta, &c.

Plot: The Mother Abbess of Nonnberg Abbey finds the sincere but exuberant Maria Rainer not wholly suited to life in a convent and so she sends her back into the outside world to look after the seven children of the widowed Captain von Trapp. Maria finds the young von Trapps a sad group, with an often absent father who has no idea of how to cope with children, and utterly lacking in family love and friendship. Maria quickly wins her charges over, but unwittingly also wins their father. Horrified, she flees back to the convent, but the Abbess sends her back to face life, the children, and von Trapp. Soon, the worldly Viennese woman who was to have been the second Baroness von Trapp departs, defeated, and Georg and Maria are wed. However, since von Trapp refuses to partake of the régime being set up by the invading Germans, the family is obliged to flee Austria. With the help of the nuns, they pass over the Alps of Maria's childhood to safety abroad.

Songs: Preludium ("Dixit Dominus") (nuns), "The Sound of Music" (Maria), "Maria" (Abbess, Margaretta, Berthe, Sophia), "My Favorite Things" (Maria), "Do-Re-Mi" (Maria), "Sixteen Going on Seventeen" (Rolf, Liesl), "The Lonely Goatherd" (Maria), "How Can Love Survive?" (Max, Elsa), reprise "The Sound of Music" (children), Ländler, "So Long, Farewell" (children), "Climb Every

Mountain" (Abbess), "No Way to Stop It" (Elsa, Max, Georg), "An Ordinary Couple" (Maria, Georg), Processional ("Maria") (nuns), reprise "Do-Re-Mi" (Trapp family singers), "Edelweiss" (Georg), reprise "So Long, Farewell" (Trapp family singers), reprise "Climb Every Mountain."

Between 1950 and 1960, Lerner and Loewe turned out only three musicals, but they notched up an altogether better average of success than Rodgers and Hammerstein did—three stage successes, of varying dimensions, which made up into three movie musicals of rather less note, however, than the celluloid *The King and I* and *The Sound of Music*—and they also pulled out the Big Plum: the show from that decade that was, above all others, to be the megahit of the world's musical stage. That show was *My Fair Lady*.

My Fair Lady was, like so many of the best-made musicals, an adaptation of an already successful stage play. Of course, to make up into an effective modern musical, the stage play in question normally had to have certain qualifications. Firstly, it had to have enough "fat" on it to be able to be slimmed by the 30 or 40 percent necessary to leave sufficient time for the songs and the dances without damaging the playwright's original plot or characterizations. Then again, it had to be written in good, clear, middle-of-the-road prose and dialogue. Nothing too cerebral, too witty, too demanding of hard brainwork from its audience. And it needed to feature recognizable, likable, easy-to-get-on-with characters equipped with sentiments and, usually, romances of the same flavor. All of these requisites made the works of the English playwright George Bernard Shaw—much to his indignation—ideal libretto fodder, a fact which had been already proven a half-century earlier by the success of the musicalization of his *Arms and the Man* as *Der tapfere Soldat (The Chocolate Soldier)*.

The central characters of Shaw's *Pygmalion* were a modern variation of those of the statue-come-to-life story of Greek mythology. Professor Henry Higgins didn't invigorate a statue, though, in the way that so many successful musical-theater men and women had done through the years, from *Die schöne Galathee* and *Adonis* up to *One Touch of Venus*; he transformed a distinctly live young woman into an altogether different young woman by the simple expedient of changing her speech. When, under Higgins's tetchy tuition, Eliza Doolittle swaps her tortured East End vowels for the crystalline clipped English of the educated classes, she finds herself both accepted as a lady, and also gradually becoming a lady, with a lady's senses and sensibilities. Lerner's libretticized version of the play, which slimmed the original expertly, followed the example given by Hammerstein in *The King and I* by adding a new romantic touch to the story, a touch which would have undoubtedly rendered the fortunately defunct Shaw furious. The relationship between Higgins and Eliza was given overtones of attraction and romance, and the musical ended not with the play's slightly sour practicality, but with an undertaste of cherubs, tulle, and pink fire.

The rôle of Eliza Doolittle was a fine example of what was becoming the classic leading lady's rôle in the modern musical theater. It was a rôle of a strongly defined character which was

My Fair Lady: "Look at her, a prisoner of the gutter, condemned by every syllable she utters . . ." Professor Higgins makes acquaintance with the sprawling vowels of Miss Eliza Doolittle.

neither the classic romantic ingénue—a Rose Marie or a Laurey Williams, equipped with soprano solos and love duets—nor a regulation soubrette, a lass who bounced through the evening providing the light comic relief to the more intense romancing and performing songs and dances to measure, nor yet that favorite creation of the American stage, the brash, coonshouting dame, as epitomized by such stars as May Irwin and Ethel Merman. This leading lady had her characterful moments, her bright moments, her romantic moments in turn. She was sometimes one and sometimes another of the standard types of yesteryear, but at her best she was a well-drawn character whose individualities were all her own, and in Eliza Doolittle, Lerner, with a little help from Mr Shaw and from musician Loewe, created a fine example of the type. Eliza began the evening as a yowling, thick-headed cockney who dreamed impossibly of home comforts in "Wouldn't It Be Loverly?" or battered away at her teacher with all the power of the biggest belter in town in "Just You Wait," and by the end of the act—with her vowels all nicely repackaged—she was soaring out her latest bit of dreaming in the soprano strains of "I Could Have Danced All Night." The two faces of Eliza were neatly represented by the two different musical styles—when the "proper" Eliza renounced her newfound dignity in her later attacks on Higgins ("Without You") or her fisheyed admirer Eynsford-Hill ("Show Me"), and returned to her aggressive, fishwifely personality of the opening scenes, the musical strains turned back from the lyrical to the between-the-eyes. If with an improved vowel system.

My Fair Lady also followed *The King and I* in having a hardly-singing male lead. The rôle of

Higgins was certainly not denuded of numbers—pieces like the briskly bigoted "Why Can't the English?" or "A Hymn to Him" or the amazedly romantic "I've Grown Accustomed to Her Face" were splendid songs—but their vocal lines made little demand on the actor, and they were performed by the musical's original Higgins, British non-singing actor Rex Harrison, in an easy-going kind of Sprechgesang which gained a singular new vogue thanks to his performance. The more traditional, low-comedy part of Eliza's boozy, wordful cockney father was equipped with a couple of pieces in turn-of-the-century music-hall style, and the only lyric moment of the male part of the score was a wide-eyed serenade for the foolish Eynsford-Hill, getting his kicks just from wandering up and down on "The Street Where You Live." That song and the other more sentimental pieces of the score—"I Could Have Danced All Night" and "I've Grown Accustomed to Her Face"—turned out, as so often was and is the case, to be among the most enduring highlights of a score which was particularly rich in enduring highlights.

My Fair Lady followed up super-sized success on Broadway, in Britain, and round the English-speaking world by moving out beyond the confines of that world. It not only followed *Kiss Me, Kate* into Europe—challenging its predecessor as the most successful foreign musical to have been introduced on to European ground since the turn of the century—but it also made its way to countries and to stages where the modern musical theater had hitherto made little mark, and even on such grounds it triumphed, becoming the most successful musical of its era from one end of the globe to the other.

MY FAIR LADY, a musical in 2 acts by Alan Jay Lerner, based on *Pygmalion* by George Bernard Shaw. Music by Frederick Loewe. Produced at the Mark Hellinger Theatre, New York, 15 March 1956.

Characters: Henry Higgins, Eliza Doolittle, Colonel Pickering, Mrs Pearce, Mrs Eynsford-Hill, Freddy Eynsford-Hill, Clara Eynsford-Hill, Alfred P. Doolittle, Mrs Higgins, Zoltan Karpathy, Harry, Jamie, Queen of Transylvania, &c.

Plot: Dialectician Henry Higgins bets his colleague Pickering that he can pass off a cockney girl as a duchess at a society ball simply by educating her in the proper kind of speech. Covent Garden flower-girl Eliza Doolittle is the guinea pig. She moves in with Higgins, Pickering, and their housekeeper, and is put through a hard régime of learning which causes more than one blow-up on either side. A first essay into society at the Ascot races turns to disaster when the content of Eliza's conversation proves not on a par with her new vowels, but when the night of the ball comes she triumphs. Then what? The bet is over, but the new Eliza cannot fit back into her old world and has no other place in her new one except with Higgins. And Higgins has—it seems—no feelings. Or does he?

Songs: "Why Can't the English?" (Higgins), "Wouldn't It Be Lovely?" (Eliza, cockneys), "With a Little Bit o' Luck" (Alfie), "I'm an Ordinary Man" (Higgins), "Just You Wait" (Eliza), "The Rain in Spain" (Eliza, Higgins, Pickering), "I Could Have Danced All Night" (Eliza &c.), Ascot Gavotte (chorus), "On the Street Where You Live" (Freddy), The Embassy Waltz, "You Did It" (Pickering &c.), "Show Me" (Eliza), "Get Me to the Church on Time" (Alfie), A Hymn to Him: "Why Can't a Woman" (Higgins), "Without You" (Eliza), "I've Grown Accustomed to Her Face" (Higgins).

Lerner and Loewe's other two musicals of the 1950s might not have reached the parts of the world that *My Fair Lady* did, but both had more than a little to recommend them. Both, like *My Fair Lady* were period pieces, but they chose decidedly diverse periods as their settings. The first of the two, *Paint Your Wagon*, which was brought out in 1951, was set in the new favorite among American venues, the west of earlier and rougher days, the west of the cinema's hugely popular brand of deodorized violence films, the cowboy genre. *Paint Your Wagon*, an original script and not an adaptation of a book, play, or screenplay, neatly avoided the clichés of the bang-bang-and-bang movie, in a book that had some fine, masculine moments in it, some wry humor, and some unexaggeratedly real-ish glances at the old west, as well as the inevitable handful of cowboy clichés. Its story of one man's gold-town, its rise and its inevitable and painful fall, was paired with the mostly unsugary love story of his daughter and a young Mexican goldhunter, and also with a score of nicely virile numbers: the campfire ballad "They Call the Wind Maria," the loping signature of the outbacks man, "Wand'rin' Star," the gentle lovesong to a lost love, "I Still See Elisa," and the lively goldrush ensemble "I'm on My Way" were fine features of a musical which—much more than most Broadway pieces of its time—put the accent on the male rather than the female. *Paint Your Wagon* turned out to be one of the best of Broadway's out-west musicals, and Loewe's songs—which had no more flavor of his German origins and education than his "English" music for *My Fair Lady* —lasted long as baritone show-song favorites.

For *Camelot*, the pair returned to England as a setting, but this time it was thoroughly olde England, for the musical was based on T. H. White's whimsically human retelling of the Arthurian legend, *The Once and Future King*. Arthur and the Knights of the Round Table, traditionally depicted (except by Chivot and Duru!) as mail-clad heroes of about one and a half dimensions, had been given warmth and personality in White's charmingly cockeyed retelling of their tale, and much of this charm survived into the stage musical that was made from his book. *My Fair Lady* star Julie Andrews played a petulant Guenevere to the boyish Arthur of Richard Burton in a gently effective retelling of the history of the King's strivings to establish the rule of good in ancient England before ultimately being undone by evil magic and evil men. The musical part of the show was as full of good things as all Loewe's scores, ranging from the sweetly unserious moments of the queen's "The Simple Joys of Maidenhood" and "Take Me to the Fair," or the King's realistic "I Wonder What the King Is Doing Tonight," to the tender "I Loved You Once in Silence," and to some rousingly baritone moments ("If Ever I Would Leave You") for the actor playing the painfully perfect Sir Lancelot du Lac. The warmly personal aspect of Lerner's *Camelot* was all but submerged in a physical production which rated among the most splendid and lavish on record, but that physical production undoubtedly did as much as the show as written, and its authors' track record, to ensure the success of a musical which has endured as a revivable prospect through the decades.

The mixture of romantic splendor and humor that characterized *Camelot* was also a feature of Wright and Forrest's merry oriental successor to *Song of Norway*, the vivacious *Kismet*, but the musical part of this remake of Eddie Knoblock's successful and clever comedy did not follow the modern Broadway style as practiced by Rodgers and by Loewe. The score of *Kismet* was wholeheartedly and full-bloodedly romantic in character, and it was made over from considerable music of classic value—as the music of *Song of Norway* had been—for full-blooded lyrical voices of scope and quality. It was also made over with a skill and to an effect that quite simply put all the pasticcii and pasticcio-makers of the past decades in the shade.

The libretto of *Kismet* was a tried and true piece of Arabian-Nightsery, a comical story about a roguish street-poet, Hajj, who accidentally finds himself credited with magical powers and made the favorite of a wicked wazir who is plotting to make his young Caliph into a cipher for his own power. The rôle of Hajj was written for a rich-voiced baritone, while the young Caliph and his elusive beloved—the poet's daughter, no less—inherited the tenor and soprano music, and some juicy contralto moments fell to the luscious wife of the evening's villain in a score made up from themes from, and arrangements of, the works of the Russian composer Alexsandr Borodin, which ranged from soaring solos to richly written ensembles, and which gave its vocalists opportunities for expansive singing such as few other shows of the time did. The deeply colored music, the highly colored production values, and the multi-colored combination of romance and humor drawn from Knoblock's top-notch tale made *Kismet* a musical apart in a period when the usual Broadway fare tended to be much more musically "popular," but the musical itself was nevertheless a first-class hit, and one which has, like its most popular songs— the romantic "A Stranger in Paradise" and "This Is My Beloved," the beautiful "The Olive Tree" and the lovely, lascivious "Not Since Nineveh"—survived the test of time triumphantly.

KISMET, a musical Arabian Night in 2 acts by Charles Lederer and Luther Davis, based on the play of the same title by Edward Knoblock. Lyrics by Robert Wright and George Forrest. Music selected and arranged from the works of Alexsandr Borodin by Wright and Forrest. Produced at the Ziegfeld Theatre, New York, 3 December 1953.

Characters: Hajj, Marsinah, the Caliph of Baghdad, the Wazir, Lalume, Omar, Jawan, Chief Policeman, the Princesses of Ababu, Princess Samaris, Princess Zubbedeyah, Widow Yussef, Imam, &c.

Plot: The poor but wily poet Hajj catches the attention of the wicked Wazir who suspects him of having magic powers, and counts on his sorcerial aid to force the local Caliph to wed a useful foreign princess. But, at the same time, that same Caliph falls in love with a girl encountered by chance, and that girl—though neither he nor her father knows it—is none other than Hajj's daughter, Marsinah. As the Wazir searches vainly for his monarch's lost love, circumstances pile one upon the other the evidence of Hajj's "powers" and the villain is amazed when it seems that the man he regards as his private magician has brought Marsinah to his own harem. Indeed he has, but he had thought to secrete her there for safety. Thinking his beloved is a wife of the Wazir, the Caliph gives in to the proposed marriage of state, but Hajj discovers the truth of what is going on, and with the help of the Wazir's susceptible wife, disposes of his nasty plotting patron and brings events to a happy end.

Songs: "The Sands of Time" (Imam, muezzins), "Rhymes Have I" (Hajj, Marsinah), "Fate"

(Hajj), Bazaar of the Caravans (Bangleman &c.), Ababu Dance I, "Not Since Nineveh" (Lalume), "Baubles, Bangles and Beads" (Bangleman, Marsinah), "A Stranger in Paradise" (Marsinah, Caliph), "He's in Love" (Policemen), "Gesticulate" (Hajj), Finale Act 1: reprise "Fate," "Night of My Nights" (Caliph), reprise "A Stranger in Paradise" (Marsinah), "Was I Wazir?" (Wazir), "Rahadlakum" (Lalume, Hajj, Ayah), "And This Is My Beloved" (Lalume, Hajj, Caliph, Marsinah), "The Olive Tree" (Hajj), "Zubbediya" (Ayah &c.), Samaris' Dance, Ababu Dance II, Finale Act 2: "Play on the Cymbal."

If *Kismet* relied on the richest of romantic music for its score, the strains of popular music were—in contrast—very evident in a piece which came from right at the other end of the musical-theater see-saw, the second musical to come from the *On the Town* team of Comden, Green, and Bernstein. After their revusically constructed début piece, the trio turned towards a more vertebrate kind of show second time around and turned out a delightful musical comedy version of another thoroughly I-Love-New-Yorkish piece, the hit play *My Sister Eileen*, under the I-Love-New-Yorkish title of *Wonderful Town*. Comden, Green, and *My Sister Eileen* were all as far away in character and style as could be from the romantically foreign, period-piece musicals with which Rodgers and Hammerstein, Lerner and Loewe, and Wright and Forrest triumphed during the 1950s. The play and the libretto fabricated from it were a modern piece of the lightest of comedy with an up-to-date, here-and-now setting, the love-stories that were galloped through and over during its two hours and a bit of light-heartedness had barely a deep thought to them, the endearingly foolish and recognizably real characters were never for a second to be taken seriously, and every moment of the libretto and the lyrics was devoted to pure and simple musical comedy of the most attractive sort—the same sort that had been so liberally on display in *On the Town*. Bernstein illustrated his colleagues' lively songwords with the same kind of vibrantly lively music as he had provided for the earlier show—turning out such winners as the homesick duo of two sisters from "Ohio" who were the piece's central characters, and the lilting admission to being just "A Little Bit in Love"—and, once again, also contributed some superior dance music for the dance moments of a show which bubbled frequently into dance, and the sum total was an up-to-date musical comedy which thoroughly deserved the description and its fine Broadway run.

After *Wonderful Town*, the team split up and writers and composer went their separate ways, but both went towards further successes in the musical theater, with shows that—like their first two—were thoroughly here and now in character. Comden and Green scored a success with the book and lyrics for the merry tale of an answerphone girl who gets mixed up in a romance with one of her customers in *Bells Are Ringing* to the strains of songs with music by Jule Styne ("The Party's Over," "Just in Time"), while Bernstein left the realms of New Yorkish comedy and moved on instead to something that resembled much more a New Yorkish tragedy in the contemporary American remake of the Romeo and Juliet story as *West Side Story*.

West Side Story was a musical that was essentially youthful. But it was youthful with a difference. There had been many musicals about school-age children before—the pretty collegiate tales of *Leave It to Jane* and *Good News* or the cutesy *Babes in Arms* had all featured juvenile protagonists, and Rodgers and Hammerstein quite simply invaded the stage with embraceable tots in the 1950s in *The King and I* and *The Sound of Music*—but none of the under-age principals of these shows was anything like those of *West Side Story*. These children—just teens or truly teens—had nothing at all of the collegiate or the cutesy about them; they were children of the street, immigrant kids battling other immigrant kids for their bit of turf, just as the Skidmores and the Mulligans had done in the plays of Ned Harrigan in the nineteenth century. But Harrigan's characters had been adults and their ridiculously self-important antics had been displayed for laughs: the boys and girls of Arthur Laurents's slice-of-life libretto to *West Side Story* were pubescent youngsters, and their foolish cock-of-the-walk games were played and displayed as deadly serious. Deadly and death-dealing, for Laurents (b 1918) followed the outlines of Shakespeare's tragedy with the kind of fidelity that Basil Hood had not been permitted in *The Belle of Mayfair,* and at the end of the evening the three principal boys of this sad story all lay dead on the streets of New York.

Bernstein's music for *West Side Story* echoed and illustrated this vibrant young subject and story, with its dark drama and its youthfully exaggerated sentiments and spirits, remarkably. Maria, the young Juliet of the piece, carolled out an "I Feel Pretty" which was more heartfeltly ingénue than ingénue, Tony—her Romeo—soared out the praises of "Maria" in a number which was more rapturous than rapturous, and the two dreamed together in "One Hand, One Heart" of a place "Somewhere" where they might be happy together, away from the conflicts and artificial hatreds of their corner of the world with a hopeful innocence that was all the more affecting in that it could be seen and heard to be hopeless. And when the sung part of the score rose to its peak, in the dramatic and sentimental duo between a Maria whose love leads her to help Tony escape after he has murdered her brother, and that brother's girl, Anita, and the girl's exaggeratedly youthful sentiment ("I Have a Love") was contrasted textually and musically with the more pragmatic and clear-seeing feelings of perhaps the only almost grown-up young person in the story ("A Boy Like That"), the effect was stunning.

The sung part of the score of *West Side Story* was, however, only one part. The other was the dance music. *West Side Story* was choreographed and directed by the same man who had been responsible for staging Bernstein's maiden work, *On the Town,* Jerome Robbins, and the show was laid out in the same dance-strong manner. Here, however, the dance was not bottled up in a selection of set-piece scenas: it permeated the entire show. Half the time that the young folk in this show moved, they danced, and they danced with an aggressiveness and élan that was filled with the energy of their age and their character. For those dance sections, Bernstein provided music that was equally bursting with aggressiveness and élan, dance music that was a million miles away from the posed music of Laurey's dream ballet in *Oklahoma!* or *Brigadoon*'s funeral scene, and which was unchallengeably the most remarkable such music to have been heard on the musical-theater stage.

West Side Story: The larking about that goes down at Doc's looks pretty harmless. But when the Jets start taking themselves and their kids' games too seriously, it's time for tragedy.

West Side Story was an original, and like so many originals—no matter what their quality— it did not at first win the kudos and popularity it might have. The show had a fine Broadway run—though not one which approached the totals set up by the more approachable and "easy" *My Fair Lady* and its ilk—but it was unable to find a producer in Britain until Bernstein's publishers took things in hand and sponsored a British version themselves. As it happened, Britain actually proved more appreciative than Broadway had been, but a wider career for the show and its music blossomed only after a particularly well-made 1961 film version hit the world's screens. Forty years on, *West Side Story* is now accepted as one of the great classics of the twentieth-century musical stage.

WEST SIDE STORY, a musical in 2 acts by Arthur Laurents, based on Shakespeare's *Romeo and Juliet*. Lyrics by Stephen Sondheim. Music by Leonard Bernstein. Produced at the Winter Garden Theatre, New York, 26 September 1957.

Characters: Riff, Tony, Bernardo, Maria, Anita, Chino, Doc, Officer Krupke, Action, A-rab, Baby John, Snowboy, Big Deal, Diesel, Gee-Tar, Mouthpiece, Tiger, Graziella, Velma, Minnie, Clarice, Pauline, Anybodys, Pepe, Indio, Luis, Anxious, Nibbles, Juano, Toro, Moose, Rosalia, Consuelo, Teresita, Francisca, Estella, Margarita, Lieutenant Schrank, Glad Hand, &c.

Plot: The "Jets" and the Puerto Rican "Sharks" are two groups of juveniles who play at war games in the streets of New York's west side. Trouble stirs when Maria, the sister of Bernardo, the big boss of the Sharks, and Tony, a former leader of the Jets, fall in love. Bernardo provokes a "rumble" with the aim of getting Tony, but the boys' childish test of strength turns to drama when a knife makes its appearance at what should have been a "manly" fist fight. Bernardo stabs Riff, Tony's friend, to death and Tony, in his turn, cuts down the Puerto Rican. For love of Maria, Anita, Bernardo's girl, agrees to help Tony escape the law, but the mistrust between the Jets and the Sharks is such that Tony's friends refuse to believe in her sincerity, and as a result tragedy strikes again— Tony is shot down in the street by a revengeful Puerto Rican.

Songs: Prologue, "The Jet Song" (Riff, Jets), "Something's Coming" (Tony), The Dance at the Gym, "Maria" (Tony), "Tonight" (Tony, Maria), "America" (Anita, Rosalia, girls), "Cool" (Riff, Jets), "One Hand, One Heart" (Tony, Maria), reprise "Tonight" (Tony, Maria, Anita, Riff, Bernardo), The Rumble, "I Feel Pretty" (Maria), Ballet including "Somewhere" (a girl), "Gee, Officer Krupke" (Jets), "A Boy Like That" (Anita), "I Have a Love" (Maria), Taunting scene, Finale Act 2: "Hold My Hand."

Between the production of *Wonderful Town* and that of *West Side Story*, Bernstein supplied one further score to Broadway, and suffered an unaccustomed flop. The musical in question was another adventurous venture—an attempt to turn Voltaire's vast, picaresque satiro-philosophical novel *Candide* into a musical. Unfortunately, the text-writers approached their task with rather more earnestness than flair, and in spite of a score full of brilliant burlesque fireworks, the show went under. However, *Candide* eventually accomplished what very few failed shows have ever succeeded in accomplishing: nearly two decades down the line it was revised, revived—succeeded and survived. The revisions made by librettist Hugh Wheeler and lyricist Stephen Sondheim effectively turned the show into the type of piece that the music had been written to fit: a joyous slice of opéra-bouffe extravagance which made its satirical and philosophical points through laughter and burlesque rather than through dogmatism. *Candide* went on to become a much-admired favorite, revived regularly (though sometimes in further fiddled-with versions, which mostly risked dragging it back towards its original earnestness), if mostly under subsidized circumstances, while the heroine's extravagantly coloratura lament "Glitter and Be Gay," a masterly burlesque of the operatic jewel song, established itself as a fixture in the soprano repertoire.

The adventurous form and content of pieces like *West Side Story* and *Candide* were, however, the exception rather than the rule in the 1950s, and the bulk of Broadway's musical plays dealt with more straightforward subjects. Abe Burrows, the librettist of *Guys and Dolls*, followed that triumph, three years later, with another fine success, but *Can-Can* was a piece which scarcely boasted the individuality of his first big hit. As its title suggested, this one was a gay Paree musical, a piece which pasted a conventional pair of love-stories, one romantic, one soubretty, on to a background of a real event—the banning of the chahut or can-can in nineteenth-century Paris—and on to the time-honored, clichéd, all-merry-in-Montmartre image of the French capital. Burrows's considerable skills as a writer and a humorist were employed on this already much-musicalized subject (Hungary, Austria, and Spain had all produced musicals on the subject soon after the event) with some success, and Cole Porter supplied a set of songs variously French-onion-soupy ("I Love Paris," "C'est magnifique"), sparky ("Live and Let Live," "Never Give Anything Away") and sincere ("Allez-vous en") which proved happily extractable. The dance element of the show was also considerable, with a scene at the Quat'z Arts Ball providing the occasion for a Garden of Eden Ballet featuring the young Gwen Verdon, soon to be one of Broadway's outstanding musical-theater stars, at its center. The combination of fun, glamour, onion soup, and Miss Verdon proved a decidedly catching one, and *Can-Can* had a good career without echoing the larger success of Porter's *Kiss Me, Kate* or of the librettist's *Guys and Dolls*.

Laurents and Sondheim themselves also went rather more conventional after their triumph with *West Side Story* when they turned out a musical that was also based on fact, if rather more recent fact. *Gypsy* was a gotta-make-it-good-in-showbiz musical, based on the memoirs of burlesque peeler Gypsy Rose Lee, and following the rise of that lady up that much-musical-theatrically-trod old road from mousy, mama-ridden childhood to superstardom. However, the spotlight in *Gypsy* wasn't on Gypsy, it was on the mama—for the rôle of mama was created expressly for end-of-career megastar Ethel Merman, a decade down the road from her outstanding success with *Annie Get Your Gun*. She was equipped with a set of Sondheim/Styne songs from which the optimistic "Everything's Coming Up Roses" emerged to make its way into a hundred club acts and holiday-camp performances, but among which the most momentous was the star's final scene, known as Rose's Turn, in which, alone on a post-show stage, the frustrated stage mother strutted the stuff she'd never had a chance to show.

Laurents and Sondheim had done shakingly well in *West Side Story* at establishing a nervy, exciting, dramatic feel, in a sinewy piece peopled by a set of characters who wanted to be tough but were only vulnerable children under it all, and a vibrant realness which seemed both modern and immediate. Such a dramatic feel was, undoubtedly, less suited to the essentially undramatic climb of one little performer of yesteryear up the scree slope to striptease-success, to the accompaniment of the elephantine encouragements of her obsessed mother, but some of that nervy toughness nevertheless came through in this retelling of a conventional showbizzy tale, with a result that *Gypsy*—and most particularly its central character—came out as a slick, hard-plastic piece and person. It was a style and a flavor that had and has its fans, and—after only a fair career first time round—the hard, glittery *Gypsy* with its mega-mama central rôle has, a couple of decades down the line, become a favorite with a particular group of musical-theater enthusiasts.

Hard and glittery was, however, not yet a generally popular style on Broadway, and Frank Loesser's follow-up to *Guys and Dolls* was characterized by a style and feeling wholly the opposite. *The Most Happy Fella* was as warm and winning a piece of musical theater as had ever hit the stage, its characters were as real, unstagey and attractive as could be, and the songs that they sang—which, like the libretto, were the work of the multi-talented Loesser—tumbled from a cornucopia of all the most likable styles. The show's story was based on Sydney Howard's romantic play *They Knew What They Wanted*, a piece about a penpal bride who discovers that her groom is not the handsome youth whose picture has been sent to her, but his aging Italian winegrower employer. The play watched Amy go through anger and misplaced passion to a real love for the kind and loving man who had been afraid to tell her the truth, as she nursed him back to health after an accident, and it was well into the second act before the evening's love duet, "My Heart Is So Full of You," blossomed forth at the climax of the show's score. Loesser's score was a remarkable one and quite unlike those for *Where's Charley?* and *Guys and Dolls* with their very specific characteristics. The rôle of Tony was written for an operatic baritone voice, that of Amy for a true, clear Broadway soprano of the modern kind, and the ensemble of the show was given some full-blooded, sing-outable music which must have made every vocalist among them content. The musical followed classic lines by pairing the lovers and their lyric music with a pair of light comic performers—a city waitress and a farmhand—who ran a lively romance in parallel, and lively songs such as "Big D," "Oh, My Feet," and "Standing on the Corner (watching all the girls go by)" contrasted in approved fashion with the lyrical part of the evening in a very long, but richly satisfying piece of musical theater.

This kind of winning warmth was also evident in one of the few outstanding 1950s musicals which came from the pen of men—or, in this case, just one man—wholly new to the Broadway musical-theater scene. The man was Meredith Willson (1902–1984), flautist, songwriter, and radio personality, and the show was called *The Music Man*. It was perhaps no coincidence that one of the chief movers behind *The Music Man* was none other than that other ex-film man Frank Loesser. It was he who persuaded Willson to persist with attempts at making his memories of his Iowa childhood into a musical. It took a good many years, but the result paid for all: *The Music Man*—even if it has not made as much noise as some other musicals of its era—remains one of the most delightful works to have come out of the heyday of the Broadway musical stage.

The "music man" of the title was a slightly shysterish traveling salesman whose ability to sling a pitch does him proud until he comes to a town in good old stubborn-necked Iowa where his art can't sustain him through a stay stretched too long for sentimental reasons. The show paired a slightly-singing leading man with a sweetly-singing leading lady who was given music in the same happily straight and unwooffy Broadway soprano vein of the time as *The Most Happy Fella*'s Amy, but *The Music Man* had no soubrets, just some barely singing supporting comedy players, and the rest of the score was devoted largely to ensemble music: the ever-quarreling members of the School Board were melded into a barber-shop quartet by the harmonizing hero of the piece, the ladies took up Classical dance instead of pickalittling gossip, the youngsters (for the show had its young folk, as well as a particularly effective tot count) were led into more lively dancing, and the whole town rang to one of the most popular marches ever to have come out of the musical theater in the rousing "Seventy Six Trombones."

THE MUSIC MAN, a musical comedy in 2 acts by Meredith Willson, based on a story by Willson and Franklin Lacy. Produced at the Majestic Theatre, New York, 19 December 1957.

Characters: "Professor" Harold Hill, Marcellus Washburn, Marian Paroo, Mrs Paroo, Winthrop Paroo, Mayor Shinn, Mrs Eulalie Shinn, Zaneeta Shinn, Tommy Djilas, Charlie Cowell, Ewart Dunlap, Oliver, Hix, Jacey Squires, Olin Britt, Amaryllis, Alma Hix, Maud Dunlop, Ethel Toffelmeier, Mrs Squires, &c.

Plot: Harold Hill travels in musical instruments, and by the time they are delivered to his country customers, and they realize they're no use if they can't play them, he's long gone from town. Part of his pitch is to sell music as a cure from the ills of the modern world, so in River City he leads off his pitch by attacking the new pool hall. It's owned by the mayor. Soon he has the vengeful mayor and the school board all anxious to see his "professorial" credentials. He wins an unlikely ally in the local librarian, Marian Paroo, who sees what a shiny trumpet can do for her shy, stuttering little brother, as gradually he brings the warring, bickering folk of the city to contentment through music and humanity. But he falls in love with Marian, stays too long, and his phoney credentials are finally debunked by the mayor. Only, Harold Hill has brought such goodwill to River City and its folks that they insist that he should be allowed his happy ending.

Songs: "Rock Island" (Charlie Cowell, salesmen), "Iowa Stubborn" (chorus), "Trouble" (Harold), Piano Lesson (Marian, Mrs Paroo), "Goodnight, My Someone" (Marian), "Seventy-Six Trombones" (Harold &c.), "Sincere" (School Board), "The Sadder-But-Wiser Girl" (Harold, Marcellus), "Pick-a-Little, Talk-a-Little" (Ladies)/"Goodnight, Ladies" (School Board), "Marian the Librarian" (Harold), "My White Knight" (Marian), "The Wells Fargo Wagon" (Winthrop &c.), "It's You" (School Board), "Shipoopi" (Marcellus), "Lida Rose" (School Board)/"Will I Ever Tell You?" (Marian), "Gary, Indiana" (Winthrop), "Till There Was You" (Marian, Harold), Finale Act 2.

The other songwriting "newcomers" of this period who made the brightest mark on the musical-theater scene were a team: Jerry Ross (1926–1955) and Richard Adler (b 1921). The team wrote just two musicals, in two consecutive years. Both were Broadway hits, both launched a brace of songs which are still heard today, both traveled successfully to other English-speaking stages, both made up into successful Hollywood films, both have been brought back in revival, but they had no successors, for Ross died at a very young age, and Adler never again found the same success with other partners. The two pieces were *The Pajama Game* and *Damn Yankees*, two pieces each based on modern comic novels, each set in the America of the here and now, but of somewhat different flavor, in their libretti, at least.

The Pajama Game was the story of a union versus employers stand-off. The most forward representative of the union in the Sleep-Tite pajama factory is a hard-boiled little female who rejoices in the name of Babe, the longstop for the management is a soft-in-the-head superintendent called Sid who falls for her use of unfair weapons. Today, he could have had her up for some variety of sexual harassment in the office. Anyway, he turns coat for the love of this determinedly ambitious dollybird and helps her win what she at least thinks is a victory by robbing his own boss's safe. If the libretto—put together by George Abbott and Richard Bissell, author of the original novel—and its central characters were fairly distasteful, Ross and Adler decorated it with a winning selection of easy-to-sing songs—the hero's baritonic "Hey, There (you with the stars in your eyes)," Babe's bristling but lilting denial, "I'm Not at All in Love," and a couple of pieces for the secretary, Gladys, the dancing star of a piece in which dance was heavily featured: her description of the passion-pit "Hernando's Hideaway" and a number tacked in as entertainment at a union meeting (!) in which she oozed across the stage with a pair of chaps to the seductive "Steam Heat."

Damn Yankees had an altogether different feel, perhaps because it was about altogether more likable people. Abbott, working again with the original novelist, turned out a thoroughly warming and amusing story about a fanatical baseball fan who sells his soul to the devil in order to be transformed into a run-slamming young ball player who will help his team win the pennant. The trouble is, the devil—out of pure devilish meanness—has no intention of letting him do so; he's going to let him down at the last moment when it's already too late for him to do anything about being thoroughly damned. With a bit of help from the devil's mantrap assistant, the undulating Lola, Joe manages to win out on both fronts and get safely back to his wondering wife. Once again, the musical was illustrated by some really likable songs—the underdog baseball team trying to rely on "Heart" (in glorious harmony) to win them a match and Lola's comeonnish glorification of her own irresistibility, "Whatever Lola Wants," being the big winners—and the show too was a winner.

During the 1950s, the more spacious musical houses of London were very largely devoted to playing the West End versions of these big Broadway hits, but the fountain of creativity did not by any means dry up in Britain, and—following what would be the largest large-house success for a homegrown show in some years in the *Brewster's Millions* musical *Zip Goes a Million* (Palace Theatre, 1951), a number of delightful and successful musicals written on a smaller scale made their appearance. Most of these had their origins in the country's so-called "club" and "repertory" theaters—the former being small, private fringe theaters in the London area, the latter provincial houses which did not, in fact, play a genuine "repertory" of shows in the manner of the French and German and subsidized houses, but simply ran a series of plays with more or less the same company through an annual season. Neither type of house—though both were rel-

atively recent creations—had the habit of producing musicals, particularly original musicals. But in the 1950s that changed, and since the first musical to issue forth from each kind of house proved to be the biggest winner of all, this new kind of mini-musical soon became all the rage.

The Players' Theatre—an institution housed under a railway arch in central London which played—and plays—as its principal entertainment programs based on Victorian and Edwardian music-hall material, made the breakthrough when it mounted a little 1920s-style musical written by a young man called Sandy Wilson (b 1924) as one part of its 1953 program. *The Boy Friend* willingly took as its inspiration *No, No, Nanette* and its happy, dancing sisters, but it in no way burlesqued the tradition of three decades earlier. The show was not a parody but a "new 1920s musical." It was all there: the rich little heroine in desperate search of true unmoneyed love, the Lord's son who wants to be loved for himself, their incognito meeting alongside the sunny plages of the South of France, and the disastrous moment when he disappears, leaving her to believe her idyll has been a false one. There was the ineffably French madame of the finishing school who discovers her old wartime paramour in the person of our heroine's father, a naughty off-the-leash English aristocrat of too many summers with an eye for the girls, a bouncy dancing soubrette to bother the boys and to dance duos with a sizzlingly stepping American lad, and—of course—girls, girls, girls. *The Boy Friend* missed not one twenties trick, and it packaged up all the charms that had made the success of its kind of musical in a book and a set of songs and dances which were as delightful and as charming as any that had appeared in the real 1920s. The entire population of the finishing school chorused the praises of "The Boy Friend," our heroine and her beau dreamed "I Could Be Happy with You" and of "A Room in Bloomsbury," Madame vamped out the "You-Don't-Want-to-Play-with-Me Blues" and chided "Fancy Forgetting," the soubrette asserted "Safety in Numbers" where men are concerned, and challenge-danced with her American to "Won't You Charleston with Me?" and the old beau got saucy with a boopdedooping schoolgirl in "It's Never Too Late to Fall in Love" in a score where nearly every number was earmarked for the standards list. The show was a fine success in its little auditorium and it was duly enlarged, restaged, and, by stages, made its way to the West End, to Broadway (the only English musical produced there in the fifties), and ultimately all round the world, becoming a veritable phenomenon of the musical theater.

THE BOY FRIEND, a new musical comedy of the 1920s by Sandy Wilson. Produced in its original one-act version at the Players' Theatre, London, 14 April 1953, and in its enlarged two-act version 18 October 1953. Produced at Wyndham's Theatre, London, 14 January 1954.

Characters: Polly Browne, Percival Browne, Madame Dubonnet, Tony, Lord Brockhurst, Lady Brockhurst, Bobby van Husen, Maisie, Dulcie, Nancy, Fay, Marcel, Pierre, Alphonse, Hortense, Pepe, Lolita, &c.

Plot: Ever-so-rich little Polly Browne will not be going to the Côte d'azur Carnival Ball, for she does not have a boyfriend. Each postulant has always been turned away as a fortune hunter. But then, on the very eve of the affair, she meets a messenger boy who thinks she's nothing but a secretary, and soon they are dreaming together of a sweet unmoneyed existence à deux. After the ball. Alas, Tony disappears and poor little Pierrette is left alone under the fairylights, without her Pierrot. But he has not really run away. It's just that his parents turned up in town, and since he was indeed no messenger boy, but a little lordling out in disguise in search of true love, he ran away rather than be discovered. So Polly and Tony will have their happy ending, even if it is in rather more than the one room in Bloomsbury they had promised each other.

Songs: "Perfect Young Ladies" (Hortense &c.), "The Boy Friend" (Polly, girls), "Won't You Charleston with Me?" (Maisie, Bobby), "Fancy Forgetting" (Mme Dubonnet), "I Could Be Happy with You" (Polly, Tony), "Sur la plage" (ensemble), "A Room in Bloomsbury" (Polly, Tony), "It's Nicer in Nice" (Hortense &c.), "The You Don't Want to Play with Me Blues" (Mme Dubonnet), "Safety in Numbers" (Maisie), "The Riviera" (chorus), "It's Never Too Late to Fall in Love" (Lord Brockhurst, Dulcie), Carnival Tango, "Poor Little Pierrette" (Mme Dubonnet &c.).

Hot on the heels of the original production of *The Boy Friend* the provincial repertory theater produced its first musical-theater hit. In the same way that the repertoire theaters of the Continent (and, occasionally, of England) had done in the nineteenth century, the Bristol Old Vic company produced a lighthearted, revusical piece of comic and musical entertainment as a kind of end-of-term jollification after the productions of the "proper" plays of the season were done. Their first attempt was a Bristol-themed collection of sketches and songs written by three company members and called *Christmas in King Street* (the company's theater was situated in that street), their second was a slightly more vertebrate piece, also with a light local flavouring, which was called *Salad Days*. *Salad Days* was constructed and composed by the Old Vic's Dorothy Reynolds and Julian Slade with the aim of giving each of the company's members the opportunity to show off talents that the year's list of plays hadn't exploited—the pretty soprano voice of one, the mime talents of another—in what was nothing more strenuous than an amusing evening of gaiety and unagressive charm.

The items were, this time, strung on to a plot—even if it was a plot which weighed about as much as those of the least hardworking Gaiety musicals had done. Two graduating students of Bristol University set out to take the first steps into life, a life which will be crowned by marriage for her and a career for him. Their pursuit of that pair of ultimates led them through a series of scenes both comical and occasionally fantastical which almost always managed to be at least a little bit relevant. The comic highlight of the piece was a sketch-scene in which the heroine's mother chatted crazedly and incessantly down the telephone while being womanhandled by a batty beautician, managing—no matter into what position she was twisted by her torturer—to keep the phone to both ear and mouth, and the flow of chatter uninterrupted. Another scene featured a preposterous dress model, blinded and hamstrung by "fashionable" clothes, teetering on the brink of the footlights and disaster. The songs were as simple as could be—only the ingénue was given anything but the most short-ranged numbers—but they made a virtue of simplicity, and the pretty "I Sit in the Sun," in which the lass looks over the prospect of a summer of sorting out a suitable husband, the lively "We're Looking for a Piano," and a tacked-on comedy nightclub number about "Cleopatra" all became favorites.

Salad Days proved quite a phenomenon. This ingenuous little piece was brought from Bristol to the West End, a West End dominated by the big musicals from Broadway, and it not only triumphed there but quite simply outran each and every one of its big-theater competitors, totting up what was at that time the longest run—2283 performances—ever achieved by a musical on the London stage. One critic surmised that its vast success was due to a public reaction against the "hard-boiled" nature of the ubiquitous American shows with their brash American characters—a search for something sweeter and lighter, less aggressive and aggressing to the ears—yet the Broadway musicals that had preceded *Salad Days* and *The Boy Friend* into the West End over the past decade were scarcely as "hard-boiled" as some that were to come, and it seems the comment may have been inspired by the recent opening in London of *Pal Joey*. There was, however, no quarreling with the figures and the result: *Salad Days* ran in the London theater nearly ten times as long as *Pal Joey*, it went on to be produced all around Britain and the colonies, and it was revived on several occasions for briefer runs, establishing itself as a thoroughgoing hit. It did not, however, follow *The Boy Friend* to Broadway, where it would undoubtedly have been found altogether too quaintly "English," whimsical and . . . soft-boiled.

SALAD DAYS, a musical entertainment in 2 acts by Dorothy Reynolds and Julian Slade. Music by Julian Slade. Produced at the Theatre Royal, Bristol. Produced at the Vaudeville Theatre, London, 5 August 1954.

Characters: Jane, Timothy, Mr Dawes, Mrs Dawes, Aunt Prue, Lady Raeburn, Sir Clamsby Williams, P. C. Boot, Troppo, Asphinxia, Police Inspector, Augustine Williams, Heloise, Ambrose, Fosdyke, Nigel Danvers, Fiona, Manager of the Night Club, Zebediah Dawes, Electrode, Rowena, &c.

Plot: Freshly graduated Jane and Timothy have parents who have purposes in life for them. Like all nice little University graduates, she must marry and he must get a job. So while Jane's mother starts the husband hunt, Timothy does the round of useful uncles who might give him a job. But the job he takes in the meanwhile is an odd one: he and Jane are confided the care of an old piano by an odd kind of tramp, and it turns out that the piano makes people dance. In all sorts of unlikely and undignified places. The piano gets them into umpteen fixes, but by the time the evening ends the youngsters have reached their (parents') goals: they have married each other and, since the tramp turns out to be a long-lost uncle of Timothy's, he has got his job.

Songs: "Things That Are Done by a Don" (dons), "We Said We Wouldn't Look Back" (Timothy, Jane), "Find Yourself Something to Do" (Mr Dawes, Mrs Dawes, Aunt Prue), "I Sit in the Sun" (Jane), "Oh, Look at Me, I'm Dancing" (Jane, Timothy), Bishop's Dance, reprise "Oh, Look at Me, I'm Dancing" (ensemble), "Hush-Hush" (Clamsby, Fosdyke, Timothy), "Out of Breath" (ensemble), "Cleopatra" (Manager of the Nightclub), "Sand in My Eyes" (Asphinxia), "It's Easy to Sing a Simple Song" (Timothy, Jane, Nigel, then Fiona), "We're Looking for a Piano" (ensemble), "The Time of My Life" (Jane), Saucer Song (Jane, Timothy, Uncle Zed), "We Don't Understand Our Children" (Lady Raeburn, Mrs Dawes), reprise "Oh, Look at Me, I'm Dancing" (ensemble), reprise "We Said We Wouldn't Look Back" (Jane, Timothy).

The Boy Friend and *Salad Days* naturally inspired more efforts on like lines—a fine and funny burlesque of the 1910s musical called *Chrysanthemum* (which got—unofficially—reincarnated on the screen as *Thoroughly Modern Millie*), a lively piece called *Grab Me a Gondola* that took in high-jinks at the Venice Film Festival, et al.—and by the later 1950s the London theater was turning out some fine musical shows, though still mostly shows on a limited scale. Two of the very finest of these appeared in 1958, but—for some reason—both were given considerably less than their due as far as runs were concerned.

During the 1950s there had begun a fashion—more among the purveyors of musicals than among audiences—for West End pieces that fancied themselves as "realistic," "adult" musicals, pieces whose preferred setting was the ever-so-adult streets of Soho or the East End of London, where every *News of the World* reader knew that naughty, lowlife things were supposed to go on. Mostly these were pretty amateurish shows, but among all the cod cockneyisms and jolly knees-uppish songs there appeared one fine and sinewy musical play. *Expresso Bongo* was a musical based on a newspaper novella written by Wolf Mankowitz, a novella which used as its starting point and inspiration the recent rise to fame of Britain's first rock 'n' roll star, the East End cockney Tommy Steele. In the musical, the star was called "Bongo" Herbert, but it was not on him that the main light shined. The star and central character of *Expresso Bongo* was the actor playing Johnny, the small-time agent who created "Bongo," and the story followed his efforts to get the boy and himself up from the coffee bars of Soho to the big time, with its recording contracts and television appearances. Of course, no sooner does Bongo start to look like a sizeable money-maker than the vultures and the vamps arrive, Johnny loses his rising star to a more powerful agency and to a showy actress with a taste for young flesh, and as the show ends he is preparing to start over with another young performer. The songs for *Expresso Bongo* were the work of David Heneker (b 1906), Julian More (b 1928) (of *Grab Me a Gondola*), and Monty Norman (b 1938), and they ranged from some acid parodies of contemporary pop music to songs ranging from the torchy ("Time") to the revusically comical ("We Bought It") in a score which backed up its libretto forcibly. The show—with actor Paul Scofield starred as Johnny—did only fairly well: its 315 London performances were followed by a film (with different music and the young Cliff Richard as Bongo) and a production in Budapest, but that record was still much better than that put up by the other remarkable show of the year, Sandy Wilson's *Valmouth*.

Valmouth belonged to diametrically the opposite end of the theatrical spectrum from *Expresso Bongo*. If the one piece was roughly "realistic," the other was utterly and exquisitely artificial. Wilson brocaded together a remarkable libretto—a text far distant in character from that of the ingenuous *Boy Friend* in every possible way—from the very specially flavored novellas of Ronald Firbank: arcane, greenly glistening tales of exotic vices and extravagances, peopled by such characters as the centenarian nymphomaniac Lady Parvula Panzoust, the masochistically superreligious Mrs Hurstpierpoint and the vast, unfathomable black masseuse Mrs. Yajnavalkya. He set this violently high-colored tale with a clear, crisp, clever, and musically unpretentious set of songs which highlighted its perversities perfectly, and the result was a show which pleased a few mightily but which proved to have little appeal for the public at large. *Valmouth* remains to this day one of those musicals prized by a few, occasionally revived, but never likely to win the wide appreciation of "easier" pieces.

The biggest success of the later 1950s was, indeed, a piece with much more obvious charms. It was, again, a small piece, and it was one that flirted with the current fashion for the lowlife in musical theater, but it flirted with it with a smile rather than with the effortful heartiness of most West End efforts. For *Irma la douce*, even if it came to the English stage courtesy of Messrs Heneker, More, and Norman, was not their original work. It had its origins on the French stage, and it was the first French musical to be successfully exported westwards for something like half a century. A charmingly comical, happily fantastical little piece, illustrated by a scoreful of songs by Edith Piaf's preferred songwriter, Marguerite Monnot (1909–1961), *Irma la douce* won much of its appeal from the brand of "argot" or street-slang in which author Alexandre Breffort (d 1971) had written the dialogue spoken by the pimps and doxies of his Parisian under-the-sheets-world. For his heroine, Irma, was a whore—the favorite sort of whore of fiction and the stage, the sweet and happy lassie of integral innocence who just happens to earn her bread screwing paying customers—and the show's story took place in the "milieu," the world inhabited by those who make their living from prostitution. Charmingly.

Irma la douce was a distinct Parisian success, but its prospects further abroad seemed rather hamstrung by its dialogue. How to translate Breffort's racily off-beat language? It would be like trying to translate the Runyonisms of *Guys and Dolls* into French. Fortunately, the authors of *Expresso Bongo* managed to find just the right tone of voice for the occasion, and *Irma la douce* went on to become an international hit in its English version, scoring fine runs on the West End and Broadway, as well as going on to productions in all sorts of other countries and languages and establishing the collaborators' versions of the show's top numbers as successful singles ("Avec les anges" as "Our Language of Love," "Dis-donc").

IRMA LA DOUCE, a musical play in 2 acts by Alexandre Breffort, based on his story of the same title. Music by Marguerite Monnot. Produced at the Théâtre Gramont, Paris, 12 November 1956.

Characters: Irma la Douce, Nestor le Fripé, Bob le Hotu, Polyte le Mou, Jojo les Yeux Sales, Roberto les Diams, Frangipane, Dudu la Syntaxe, Persil le Noir, Bébért le Méthode, Police Inspector, Monsieur Bougne, Le Président, L'Avocat de Nestor, &c.

Plot: A University law student called Nestor who is doing a study of "le mileu" gets involved with a little "poule" called Irma. But Nestor isn't very sophisticated: he gets all hot under the waistband when Irma goes out to earn their daily brioche, and so he works out a system whereby Irma can still think she's supporting him, but he really has her all to himself. He disguises himself as a rich, bearded customer called Oscar, and pays Irma for her exclusive custom. She brings the money back to him and the next day, etc., etc. Only, of course, he has to get a job on the side to finance all this double-crossing. Eventually the schedule, both schedules, prove too exhausting and so Nestor kills Oscar off—and gets arrested for murder! Convicted and exiled to Devil's Island, he hears that Irma is pregnant, so he escapes, paddles across the Atlantic Ocean to Paris, and is greeted as . . . Oscar! It's the beard! But coping with a reincarnated man is beyond Parisian bureaucracy, so Nestor and Irma have their happy ending, with twins—one for each father.

Songs: "Because" (Bob), "Polyte-le-Mou" (Mecs), "Me v'là, te v'là" (Irma, Nestor), "Avec les anges" (Irma, Nestor), "Elle a du chien" (Clients), "Ah! Dis-donc, dis-donc" (Irma), "To Be or Not to Be" (Mecs), "La Cave à Irma" (Nestor), "Je cherche qui" (Irma), "L'Aventure est morte" (Nestor), "C'est dur de croire qu'il n'est plus là" (Irma), "Irma la douce" (Irma), "Y'a que Paris pour ça" (ensemble), "Hardi, joli gondolier" (ensemble), "Il a raison" (ensemble), "Il est né le môme à Irma" (ensemble).

Among other small to middle-sized West End musicals of the time, Heneker and Norman combined with Mankowitz again on a further successful medium-sized musical in *Make Me an Offer*—a convincing East End piece set in the world of the street marketeers—and the young songwriter Lionel Bart (b 1930) won both a song hit with the title number to the otherwise amateurish *Fings Ain't Wot They Used t'Be* and a show hit in his collaboration with Laurie Johnson on the score to the rumbustious piece of Fielding-to-music called *Lock Up Your Daughters*

("When Does the Ravishing Begin," "On a Sunny Sunday Morning," "I'll Be There"). Produced to open the new Mermaid Theatre, this piece of restoration sex comedy decorated with particularly lively numbers set off a temporary fashion for "bawdy" musicals which was mostly an improvement on the fashion for "realistic" ones, but which spawned very little in the way of further successes.

London, however, did not by any means have the monopoly on smaller-sized shows, and, in fact, technically the biggest survivor of all among the more intimate shows of these years was—and is—a show launched in America. *The Fantasticks*—first tried out at Barnard College Summer Theatre in 1959, and produced in a 150-seat theater off-Broadway in 1960—is actually still running in New York, almost forty years down the line, surviving as a sweetly gentle little reminder of the more attractive face of the mostly rather more effortful 1960s. The show's text is a version of Edmond Rostand's *Les Romanesques*, and it tells the story of two youngsters whose romantic ideas have to be pandered to, whose exaggerated ideas have to be lived out, before they can settle down to enjoy their adult life. The tale was illustrated with some gently attractive numbers, from which the lazily romantic "Try to Remember" proved the takeaway hit, the piece was staged in a sparsely simple and stylized way, and the little show turned out a small-theater hit which went on—thanks to its small running costs—to become a statistical phenomenon in the musical theater. Produced around the world in many small houses for small runs, it did not, however, establish itself in anything like the same way away from its little New York home.

Another small-scale piece which found a statistically less notable fate than *The Fantasticks*, but which survives rather less datedly several decades down the line, was the fairytale burlesque *Once Upon a Mattress*. This nifty little retelling of the Hans Christian Andersen story of the Princess and the Pea was written with a good helping of low comic flair and some jolly wit, and illustrated with some lively numbers composed by Mary—daughter of Richard—Rodgers. But, in spite of a good first run in America, the little musical didn't catch on abroad and it never established itself as the seasonal regular that it might have been expected to become.

SOME NOTABLE MUSICALS 1951–1959

1951   THE KING AND I (Richard Rodgers/Oscar Hammerstein II) St James Theatre, New York, 29 March
A TREE GROWS IN BROOKLYN (Arthur Schwartz/Dorothy Fields) Alvin Theatre, New York, 19 April
ZIP GOES A MILLION (George Posford/Eric Maschwitz) Palace Theatre, London, 20 October
PAINT YOUR WAGON (Frederick Loewe/Alan J. Lerner) Shubert Theatre, New York, 12 November

LE CHANTEUR DE MEXICO [The singer from Mexico] (Francis Lopez/Henri Wernert/Raymond Vincy, Félix Gandéra) Théâtre du Châtelet, Paris, 15 December

1952 LOVE FROM JUDY (Hugh Martin/Timothy Gray/Eric Maschwitz) Saville Theatre, London, 25 September

LA ROUTE FLEURIE [The flowery road] (Francis Lopez/Raymond Vincy) Théâtre de l'ABC, Paris, 19 December

1953 WONDERFUL TOWN (Leonard Bernstein/Betty Comden, Adolph Green) Winter Garden Theatre, New York, 25 February

THE BOY FRIEND (Sandy Wilson) Players' Theatre, London, 14 April

CAN-CAN (Cole Porter/Abe Burrows) Shubert Theatre, New York, 7 May

KISMET (Borodin pasticcio, arr. Robert Wright and George Forrest/Charles Lederer, Luther Davis) Ziegfeld Theatre, New York, 3 December

1954 À LA JAMAÏQUE [Off to Jamaica] (Francis Lopez/Raymond Vincy) Théâtre de la Porte Saint-Martin, Paris, 24 January

THE PAJAMA GAME (Richard Adler, Jerry Ross/George Abbott, Richard Bissell) St James Theatre, New York, 13 May

SALAD DAYS (Julian Slade/Dorothy Reynolds) Vaudeville Theatre, London, 5 August

1955 DAMN YANKEES (Richard Adler/Jerry Ross/George Abbott, Douglass Wallop) 46th Street Theatre, New York, 5 May

MÉDITERRANÉE (Francis Lopez/Raymond Vincy) Théâtre du Châtelet, Paris, 17 December

1956 CHRYSANTHEMUM (Robb Stewart/Neville Phillips, Robin Chancellor) New Lindsay Theatre Club, London, 14 March

MY FAIR LADY (Frederick Loewe/Alan Jay Lerner) Mark Hellinger Theatre, New York, 15 March

THE MOST HAPPY FELLA (Frank Loesser) Imperial Theatre, New York, 3 May

IRMA LA DOUCE (Marguerite Monnot/Alexandre Breffort) Théâtre Gramont, Paris, 12 November

BELLS ARE RINGING (Jule Styne/Betty Comden, Adolph Green) Shubert Theatre, New York, 29 November

CANDIDE (Leonard Bernstein/Richard Wilbur et al./Lillian Hellman [replaced subsequently by new libretto by Hugh Wheeler]) Martin Beck Theatre, New York, 1 December

GRAB ME A GONDOLA (James Gilbert/Julian More) Lyric Theatre, London, 26 December

1957 WEST·SIDE STORY (Leonard Bernstein/Stephen Sondheim/Arthur Laurents) Winter Garden Theatre, New York, 26 September

THE MUSIC MAN (Meredith Willson) Majestic Theatre, New York, 19 December

1958 EXPRESSO BONGO (David Heneker, Julian More, Monty Norman/Wolf Mankowitz) Saville Theatre, London, 23 April

VALMOUTH (Sandy Wilson) Lyric Theatre, Hammersmith, London, 2 October

1959 ONCE UPON A MATTRESS (Mary Rodgers/Marshall Barer, Jay Thompson, Dean Fuller) Phoenix Theatre, New York, 11 May

GYPSY (Jule Styne/Stephen Sondheim/Arthur Laurents) Broadway Theatre, New York, 21 May

LOCK UP YOUR DAUGHTERS (Laurie Johnson/Lionel Bart/Bernard Miles) Mermaid Theatre, London, 28 May

MAKE ME AN OFFER (David Heneker, Monty Norman/Wolf Mankowitz) Theatre Royal, Stratford East, London, 17 October

THE SOUND OF MUSIC (Richard Rodgers/Oscar Hammerstein II/Russel Crouse, Howard Lindsay) Lunt-Fontanne Theatre, New York, 16 November

*I*n the 1960s, the English-language musical theater continued to dominate the scene with all the strength and brilliance that it had shown in the 1950s, and a number of new musicals which would challenge even the outstanding hits of the earlier decade made their first appearance on the stages of Broadway and of Britain. Several of these were new works by folk who had already contributed successfully to the musical stage in the 1950s or even earlier, but an encouraging number were the work of writers new to the arena. It seemed that—with all this new blood around—the musical as it was being written in the 1950s and 1960s was going to continue healthily on in its happily established vein for a good many years to come. And that in spite of a notable change in the nature of popular music with the advent, in the mid-1950s, of the style known as "rock 'n' roll."

Popular music had always, through the years, been the source of the musical language of at least one important section of the stage musical play. So, was the kind of show music to which the world had become accustomed over recent years now going to be replaced by this heavily rhythmic, unsophisticatedly lyricked kind of popular song which, as far back as 1956, had already surfaced in an isolated number in the British show *Grab Me a Gondola*, and which, as early as 1958, had been used as subject-matter for the musical stage in *Expresso Bongo?* The first successful musical show of the 1960s indicated, perhaps, what the musical theater's answer would be: like *Expresso Bongo*, *Bye Bye Birdie* was about the pop music business, but its team of young writers did not use rock music as their score—only, like the earlier show, as their subject. For the moment, at least, the musical stage was going to stick with the kind of songwriting it knew.

The Rodgers and Hammerstein partnership which had been such a flagship to the musical stage of the 1940s and the 1950s had been ended by the death of Oscar Hammerstein, and although Rodgers continued intermittently to turn out musicals through the next two decades, he never again found the success of those years. He was, however, a touch unlucky. In the 1960s he wrote the scores for two shows, and on the second of these he allied himself with the top textwriting talent around—librettist Arthur Laurents and lyricist Stephen Sondheim—to turn Laurents's play *The Time of the Cuckoo* into a musical. The resulting show, *Do I Hear a Waltz?*, was a splendid musical play in which both songwriters turned out some memorable material, but, when it started its townwards run, it was not a conventional musical of its times. Nobody danced, for example. But, instead of daring to be different, the creative team took fright, hurried conventionalizing remakes were done, and the show reached Broadway in a less than settled state which led it to failure. Rodgers would never get as close to a winner again.

The Lerner and Loewe team, too, was on its last legs. After the success of *Camelot*, Fritz Loewe retired from the stage into real, imagined, or useful ill-health. Like Rodgers, Lerner continued without his partner, for nearly three decades, right up to his death, and like Rodgers he never again found the same success in spite of boosting his works with his own very sizeable personal fortune. Loewe survived his collaborator by a couple of years, but wrote no more stage musicals.

Frank Loesser and Abe Burrows did, however, have one more hit to deliver before they also disappeared from the scene, Loesser to a premature death in 1969 and Burrows to other high-flying activities which brought him back to the musical stage only rarely. That one hit was a particularly high-spirited and happy one. *How to Succeed in Business Without Really Trying* took the up-to-date and eminently burlesqueable topic of Big Business as its setting and the moving force in its story, and the transformation into a libretto of the Shepherd Mead novel which was the show's source was a piece of work as skillful as Burrows's *Guys and Dolls* book. Loesser captured the gaily tongue-in-cheek, contemporary idiom of the tale and its characters in his songs and the result was one of the finest and funniest musical comedies to have come to the boards since the war.

HOW TO SUCCEED IN BUSINESS WITHOUT REALLY TRYING, a musical in 2 acts by Abe Burrows, Jack Weinstock, and Willie Gilbert, based on the book of the same name by Shepherd Mead. Songs by Frank Loesser. Produced at the 46th Street Theatre, New York, 14 October 1961.

Characters: J. Pierrepont Finch, J. B. Biggley, Rosemary Pilkington, Mr Bratt, Mr Gatch, Mr Jenkins, Mr Tackaberry, Mr Peterson, Smitty, Miss Jones, Bud Frump, Mr Twimble, Hedy la Rue, Miss Krumholtz, Wally Womper, Mr Ovington, &c.

Plot: Window-cleaner "Ponty" Finch has ambitions to rise and, with a little booklet entitled "How to Succeed in Business Without Really Trying" as his bible, he manipulates his way rung by rung up the corporate ladder at World Wide Wickets—beginning in the mailroom, and by the interval making it to Vice President in Charge of Advertising, with the devoted Rosemary Pilkington at his side in the posts of secretary and fiancée. Perils and jealousies are inevitably encountered, and the most perilous and jealous of them is the boss's nephew-by-marriage, Bud Frump. Frump's maneuverings lead Ponty into proposing a disastrous TV advertising gimmick which ends in the big boss being caught in a scarlet-faced spot with a pneumatic employee, but when the even-bigger boss turns up somehow Ponty emerges whiter-than-white, heading for the chairman's position that his book had promised him right from page one.

Songs: "How to" (Ponty), "Happy to Keep His Dinner Warm" (Rosemary, Smitty), "Coffee Break" (Frump, Smitty, ensemble), "The Company Way" (Ponty, Twimble, Frump, &c.), "A Secretary Is Not a Toy" (Mr Bratt), "Been a Long Day" (Smitty, Ponty, Rosemary), "Grand Old Ivy" (Ponty, Biggley), "Paris Original" (Rosemary, Smitty, Miss Jones, &c.), "Rosemary" (Ponty, Rosemary, Frump), Finale Act 1, "Cinderella, Darling" (Smitty, Rosemary, &c.), "Love from a Heart of Gold" (Biggley, Hedy), "I Believe in You" (Ponty), "The Yo Ho Ho" (ensemble), "Brotherhood of Man" (Ponty, Miss Jones, Mr Womper, &c.), Finale: reprise "The Company Way."

Jule Styne, who'd notched up a pair of successes in the fifties to add to the pair of successes he'd turned out in the forties, did a little less well in the sixties. From a half-dozen new shows, he managed only one real hit. That hit was, however, with a very great deal of help from its leading lady, to give him not only a show success and a film success, but also a very considerable set of song successes. *Funny Girl* was a biomusical based on the love-life, and fragments of the career, of the American comedienne Fanny Brice, and the star was impersonated by the young Barbra Streisand. She delivered the torchy "Don't Rain on My Parade" and the sixtiesish hymn to "People (who need people)" with a power and passion that lifted them right up the hit parades and into the repertoires of a hundred nightclub and cruise-ship performers. *Funny Girl* was, however, a show with more to it than just a powerhouse central performance. Its star got to be endearingly funny as well as wrenchingly torchy, and pieces such as "I'm the Greatest Star" and "Cornet Man" allowed her to run the other bits of the gamut in a rôle which had everything. *Funny Girl* with Streisand triumphed on Broadway, on the hit parades, and on the cinema screen, but when the star was obliged to quit the cast in London, the show folded quickly. *Funny Girl* without Streisand was never to have the same attraction as *Funny Girl* with Streisand, but fortunately that film version enshrining one of Broadway's outstanding performances of recent decades remains around for the enjoyment of later generations.

Some of the men who had been responsible for London's turn-of-the-decade hits also continued on into the 1960s with notable success, and at their head were two versatile writer-songwriters, Lionel Bart and David Heneker. The first to strike at the dawn of the new decade was Bart, whose best credit to date had been as lyricist for the successful *Lock Up Your Daughters*. Next time round, he went solo on the musicalization of another piece of period classic writing — a rather better-known one this time than Fielding's *Rape Upon Rape* — and the result was a musical version of Charles Dickens's turgid tearjerker *Oliver Twist*. By the time Bart had finished with it, *Oliver!* was certainly not turgid, and there was an awful lot of jollity intermingled with the teary bits. The villainous thiefmaster Fagin, the grim undertaker Sowerberry (a thoroughly burlesquey name!) and his wife, who are the child's first employers, and the pompous and pitiless beadle who turns him from the workhouse all became figures of fun on the musical stage, while the parish waifs and the apprentice juvenile thieves of Dickens's story were turned into musical-theater tots who kicked up their heels to a jolly cockney tune. But, among these moments of dulcified Dickens, Bart kept a strong dramatic thread running with the story of the brutal thief Bill Sikes and his doxie Nancy, and what had always been the climactic scene in dramatic adaptations of *Oliver Twist* in the nineteenth century — Sikes's murder of Nancy, and his subsequent flight across the roofs of London before falling to his own death — was retained in all its drama.

The score of the show reflected this mixture of sweet and strong. The little boys knees-upped to "Consider Yourself" or chorused longingly of "Food, Glorious Food," Oliver wondered winsomely "Where Is Love?," Nancy pounded out a pair of stage-cockney pub songs, and Fagin amiably pattered out stealing-instructions and warped philosophy in turn, but when the show showed its other face, and Nancy lit the touch paper on the despairing love song "As Long as He Needs Me," the piece moved into a different dimension.

The mixture of sweet and strong proved to be precisely to the taste of the times. More *The Sound of Music* rather than more *Expresso Bongo* was what was required by contemporary audiences. And, as mounted by the *Lock Up Your Daughters* team of director Peter Coe and architect-designer Sean Kenny on a multi-purpose set which allowed the many scenes of the show to be galloped through without endless hiatus, *Oliver!* proved to fit the bill precisely. It was a mighty success, going on from its original record-breaking run in London (2,618 performances) to success as the longest-running British musical of all time in America, and thence to Australia and even, ultimately, further afield.

OLIVER!, a musical in 2 acts by Lionel Bart, based on the novel *Oliver Twist* by Charles Dickens. Produced at the New Theatre, London, 30 June 1960.

Characters: Oliver Twist, Mr Bumble, Mrs Corney, Mr Sowerberry, Mrs Sowerberry, Charlotte, Noah Claypole, Fagin, The Artful Dodger, Bill Sikes, Nancy, Bet, Mr Brownlow, Mr Grimwig, Mrs Bedwin, Old Sally, &c.

Plot: Orphan Oliver is turned out of the parish workhouse for asking for extra food and, after an unhappy time as apprentice to an undertaker, he falls in with a band of London street-thieves masterminded by one Fagin. On his first pocket-picking mission he gets nabbed, but he is taken in by his kindly victim, the gentle Mr Brownlow. The thief Bill Sikes and his unwilling girl, Nancy, kidnap the boy before he can give their gang away and take him back to Fagin's den, but Nancy secretly arranges to restore him to Brownlow. She is caught in the act by Sikes, who murders her but then, attempting to escape with the boy, falls to his death from the city rooftops. While Oliver—who is none other than Brownlow's long-lost grandson—is restored to wealth and happiness, Fagin sets out to find opportunities elsewhere, and other folk to rob.

Songs: "Food, Glorious Food!" (Boys), "Oliver!" (Bumble, Mrs Corney, &c.), "I Shall Scream" (Bumble, Mrs Corney), "Boy for Sale" (Bumble), "That's Your Funeral" (Sowerberry, Mrs Sowerberry), "Where Is Love?" (Oliver), "Consider Yourself" (Dodger &c.), "You've Got to Pick a Pocket or Two" (Fagin), "It's a Fine Life" (Nancy), "I'd Do Anything" (Nancy, Bet, Dodger, Oliver), "Be Back Soon" (Fagin &c.), "Oom-pah-pah" (Nancy, Bet), "My Name" (Sikes), "As Long as He Needs Me" (Nancy), "Who Will Buy?" (Oliver &c.), "Reviewing the Situation" (Fagin).

Bart went on to write another fine musical, a Liverpudlian piece called *Maggie May*, which had not an ounce of sweetness with which to dilute its toughness but which proved a success on home ground without winning equivalent favor further afield, followed by a Cohans and Kellys tale of racial conflict told against an extremely scenic panorama of East End London during the *Blitz*, before sombering sadly out of the musical theater after an all too short career.

Half a Sixpence: "If I had money to burn . . ." Artie Kipps's dream has come true. Mr Chitterlow shows him the "something-to-his-advantage" announcement in the newspaper.

A short career was certainly not the lot of David Heneker. Having come to the fore with *Expresso Bongo* in 1958, when already over fifty years of age, he did not say farewell to the West End until he was seventy-eight years old, more than quarter of a century later. It was, however, in the 1950s and the 1960s that he found his biggest success, and it was in 1963 that he composed the show and the songs for which he is best remembered. Like *Oliver!*, *Half a Sixpence* was a musical based on a piece of classic literature: H. G. Wells's story of the dangers of unaccustomed wealth, *Kipps*. The show was constructed as a vehicle for the same star for whom Bart had originally intended *Oliver!* (until it was pointed out to him that Master Twist was a child) and who had been the inspiration for *Expresso Bongo*, the rock singer turned stage performer Tommy Steele. As Kipps, Steele was cast as a cheeky little chappie not far distant from Lupino Lane's characters of the 1930s and 1940s, and Heneker supplied him with a set of songs—topped by a yearning, charmful title-song and a rousingly music-hally interlude called "Flash, Bang,

Wallop!"—which would become standards. The show—which sported no tots in its cast, had a tart little leading lassie and indulged several tons less in cuteness than *Oliver!*—and its star (who was not above indulging in a bit of grown-up cuteness when he thought it would work) triumphed in London, on Broadway, and on the cinema screen, and *Half a Sixpence* went down as one of the classic musicals of its period.

HALF A SIXPENCE, a musical in 2 acts by Beverley Cross, based on the novel *Kipps* by H. G. Wells. Music and lyrics by David Heneker. Produced at the Cambridge Theatre, London, 21 March 1963.

Characters: Artie Kipps, Ann Pornick, Chitterlow, Mrs Walsingham, Helen Walsingham, Young Walsingham, Sid Pornick, Buggins, Pearce, Flo Bates, Mr Shalford, Mrs Botting, &c.

Plot: Artie Kipps is working in a draper's shop when he learns he has inherited a fortune. The money brings him the attentions of folk who'd never wanted to know him before, among whom are the poor but proud Walsingham family. The mother gives him social ambitions, the daughter asks him to dine, and the son takes charge of Artie's "business affairs." Soon Artie is proposing to Helen Walsingham instead of his long-time sweetheart, the Walsinghams' maid Ann. But Kipps can't live up to the pretensions of his new "family" and he soon realizes he's been a fool. He marries Ann and is planning a rich life for them when the news comes that young Walsingham has lost all the money. Artie reins in his ambitions, comes back to earth, and settles down happily to run a bookshop. When news comes that a forgotten investment has won him a second fortune, he turns it down.

Songs: "All in the Cause of Economy" (Apprentices), "Half a Sixpence" (Artie, Ann), "Money to Burn" (Artie &c.), "The Oak and the Ash" (Helen), "I'm Not Talking to You" (Ann), "A Proper Gentleman" (ensemble), "She's Too Far Above Me" (Artie), "If the Rain's Got to Fall" (Artie &c.), "The Old Military Canal" (ensemble), "The One Who's Run Away" (Artie, Chitterlow), "Long Ago" (Ann), "Flash, Bang, Wallop!" (Artie), "I Know What I Am" (Ann), "I'll Build a Palace for My Girl" (Artie)/"I Only Want a Little House" (Ann). Alternative number: "The Party's on the House."

Like Bart, Heneker went on to further success, scoring largely with his contribution to the up-to-date Cinderella musical *Charlie Girl*—a piece which collected itself a West End run to challenge the very best and most popular musical shows—but, in later years, his precise and elegant songmaking proved less à la mode, and he failed to find again the prominence he had known in his first decade in the musical theater.

The first of the new names to make a mark on the musical stage of the sixties were the team of Michael Stewart (1929–1987) (libretto), Lee Adams (b 1924) (lyrics), and Charles Strouse (b 1928) (music), who collaborated on the making of the bright, youthful, and thoroughly up-beat *Bye Bye Birdie*. Stewart's libretto was full of fun. Just as *Expresso Bongo* had done, the piece centered not on the Birdie of the title—an up-and-coming pop singer of an Elvis-Presleyish shade—but on his agent. However, the hero of *Bye Bye Birdie* was no tattily realistic and down-beat trier: Albert Peterson was a bright little goer, with an aurally aggressive Jewish mother and a fed-up secretary-cum-girlfriend, who wasn't designed to be played by a Paul Scofield but by song-and-dancing comedian Dick van Dyke. The show's story followed the disasters that occur when Birdie gets drafted and Albert sets up a big TV-ed occasion to mark his departure for duty. It all goes so wrong that the evening ends with Albert giving up the pop business and going off with his relieved Rosie to become a respectable schoolteacher. During the course of the events, he also got to deliver the desperately upbeat "Put on a Happy Face" alongside Birdie's pre-army cry for a night out, "I've Got a Lot of Living to Do," and a disabused piece for the older generation bemoaning modern "Kids," in a score which was as lively as its libretto.

Bye Bye Birdie got a good international showing, but Strouse and Adams took time to come up with another hit on the same scale. Stewart, however, did not. He launched straight into a career as one of Broadway's most successful librettists, confirming the success of *Bye Bye Birdie* the very next year with a remake of the pretty tale of *Lili* as the libretto to a charming musical called *Carnival*. On this occasion, he was teamed with songwriter Bob Merrill (b 1921), the writer of a sackful of 1950s novelty numbers, from "Sparrow in a Treetop" and "Belle, Belle, My Liberty Belle" to "How Much Is That Doggie in the Window?" and "Where Will the Dimple Be?," who had turned to the musical stage with some success when he supplied the songs for two shows based on the plays of Eugene O'Neill, *New Girl in Town* (1957) and *Take Me Along* (1959). *Lili* was more obvious musical-theater material than O'Neill—a charming and sentimental love-story about an orphan girl and a misanthropic, crippled puppeteer who can express his feelings to her only through the mouths of his dolls, played out in front of a colorfully circussy background. Merrill supplied a matchingly charming score, topped by the latest variation on the "Love Makes the World Go Round" theme, and the show had a good Broadway run. It failed, however, further afield. Merrill went on to provide the lyrics to Jule Styne's tunes for *Funny Girl*, but then faded disappointingly away into a series of unsuccessful and/or mediocre shows. Stewart, however, continued onwards and upwards, and with his third Broadway show he scored the kind of success that comes only rarely.

Hello, Dolly! was a musical based on an American rewrite of a classic Austrian musical comedy hit, Johann Nestroy's *Einen Jux will er sich machen*, the story of a couple of lads out on the big town and the adventures that befall them. It was a theme which had already proven highly successful in the American musical theater in the nineteenth-century musical *A Trip to Chinatown*, but *Hello, Dolly!* was an altogether more substantial and structured piece of writing than the joyous old farce comedy. Thanks to a Thornton Wilder remake of the original play as *The Matchmaker*, however, the focus of the piece was now different: the central character was now the lady in the affair, the lady that the title said Hello to. The principal plotline followed her efforts to make a wealthy match for herself with a resisting customer who had originally been intended as a husband for a less-than-delighted client, but the boys still went out on the town, and one of them came home with the pretty milliner from whom Mrs Levi had taken over the rich, aging Mr. Vandergelder.

The songs for *Hello, Dolly!* were the work of another newish man in town. Jerry Herman (b 1933) had made his first appearance as a musical-theater songwriter on Broadway not long after Stewart had arrived on the scene, and his 1961 show *Milk and Honey*, a friendly musical about middle-aged love, with an Israeli setting and some attractive songs, had been welcomed with a fine run of 543 performances. *Hello, Dolly!* would make that total look tiny. Herman's score was one of smilingly straightforward and catchy tunes, songs happily upbeat in sentiment, in feeling, and in melody. The little Irish milliner sighed sweetly over her prospects of romance in "Ribbons Down My Back," the two lads on a spree enthused "Put on Your Sunday Clothes" and went parading innocently with their girls with what they hoped might be "Elegance," while the star (equipped with a usefully slightly singing partner, which allowed her that much extra musical space) belted out her determination to get the most out of life "Before the Parade Passes By." But the song which sealed the songwriter's fame and the show's megasuccess was its title number. The climactic scene of the show takes place at the Harmonia Gardens Restaurant, a place where the late Mr Ephraim Levi used to take his wife, and where she was obviously a great favorite. Tonight, in her pursuit of Mr Vandergelder, she returns there, and what happens? Service is suspended while the whole personnel of the Harmonia Gardens goes into a vast routine, chorusing "Hello, Dolly!" as they whirl their old friend about in a kind of welcome that was surely never accorded to any non-paying customer in any New York restaurant in history. "Hello, Dolly!" became such a hit—with a little help from a gravelly, idiosyncratic cover version by Louis Armstrong—that it even inspired the ultimate accolade of a Broadway plagiarism suit. If the song was a megahit, however, so was the show. *Hello, Dolly!* quite simply appropriated for itself the Broadway long-run record, with a first run of 2,844 performances during which a nova of sometimes rather aging stars were seen in the rôle originated by Carol Channing.

Oddly enough, although it traveled more widely than almost any recent musical, the show went rather less well overseas than it had on Broadway. It didn't actually fail in Britain, but it had to be recast with vibrant local favorite Dora Bryan to keep it going for a respectable run, and London revivals have indeed failed, while even a dazzling performance by Belgian star Annie Cordy in a French version couldn't lift the show to Parisian triumph. Australia and German-speaking countries were more welcoming, but a film version, with Barbra Streisand starred as a very believable, conveniently aged, and less vastly out-front Dolly, found less favor than the original had done. At the time of writing, *Hello, Dolly!* is back on Broadway with its original star in place, thirty years on. But since London's last revival featured female impersonator Danny La Rue in its star rôle, this one won't be the most unlikely *Dolly* yet.

HELLO, DOLLY!, a musical in 2 acts by Michael Stewart, based on *The Matchmaker* by Thornton Wilder. Music and lyrics by Jerry Herman. Produced at the St James Theatre, New York, 16 January 1964.

Characters: Mrs Dolly Gallagher Levi, Horace Vandergelder, Cornelius Hackl, Barnaby Tucker, Irene Molloy, Minnie Fay, Ermengarde, Ambrose Kemper, Ernestina Money, Judge, &c.

Plot: The matchmaker Dolly Gallagher Levi has decided to remarry for the good of her middle

Hello, Dolly!: Out-of-town lads Cornelius and Barnaby are more interested in saying "Hello" to ladies a little younger. Here they put on their best manners to impress the pretty milliner Irene Molloy.

and declining years, and she decides that her victim shall be the wealthy Horace Vandergelder whom she had originally earmarked for the little would-be-ex-milliner Irene Molloy. Horace goes to New York for the day to march in a parade and look over Mrs Molloy, and it takes only that one day for Dolly to divert him in the direction she has planned. In the meanwhile, Vandergelder's employees, Cornelius and Barnaby, who have profited from their boss's absence from his store to sneak a day off, have sweethearted up with Irene and her assistant, Minnie Fay. They take the girls to the swank Harmonia Gardens, the very place Dolly chooses for her dinner-time move-in on her unwilling prey, and the whole lot of them get mixed up together in a truly farcical situation which ends with the entire party being dragged off to a surreal kind of law court, before they all go home to Yonkers to the lives Dolly has arranged for them. Hers, of course, will be as Mrs Vandergelder.

Songs: "Call on Dolly" (ensemble), "I Put My Hand In" (Dolly), "It Takes a Woman" (Horace), "Put on Your Sunday Clothes" (Cornelius, Barnaby), "Ribbons Down My Back" (Irene), "Motherhood" (Dolly &c.), "Dancing" (Dolly, Cornelius, &c.), "Before the Parade Passes By" (Dolly), "Elegance" (Cornelius, Barnaby, Irene, Minnie Fay), The Waiters' Galop, "Hello, Dolly!" (Dolly &c.), Polka Contest, "It Only Takes a Moment" (Cornelius), "Goodbye, Dearie" (Dolly), reprise "Hello, Dolly!" Additional and alternative numbers included: "World Take Me Back" (Dolly), "Love, Look in My Window" (Dolly).

Herman followed up the success of *Hello, Dolly!* with another "grande dame" musical—a show featuring a glossy, out-front, no-longer-juvenile leading lady as its overwhelming star—when he transformed Patrick Dennis's already stage- and screen-experienced *Auntie Mame* into a musical comedy star. The madcap *Mame* (who was spared the exclamation point), as impersonated by Angela Lansbury, went through a selection of the hilarious antics which had already made her such a favorite on page, stage, and screen, as she brought up her orphaned nephew in the most unconventional way—but with a pretty fair final result—to the accompaniment of a lively set of songs among which the massed and repeated welcome of the entire American South (clad in hunting pinks, no less!) to "Mame" stood out as the natural successor to "Hello, Dolly!" Mame and her actressy pal Vera tried unconvincingly to convince each other that they were "Bosom Buddies," Mame got momentarily and retrospectively responsible as she wondered what she'd do with the little lad "If He Walked into My Life Today," and her very plain secretary related in song what happened when she took her employer's advice and dipped into Living with a capital L (Gooch's Song). The result was a full-sized Broadway hit. *Mame* also had a respectable run on the London stage with Ginger Rogers as its star, and, if it didn't follow its elder sister into Europe, it nevertheless turned out to be a first-class favorite in South America, where it still gets regular showings thirty years on.

Around the same time that Stewart and Herman entered the musical theater, another writer who was to make himself a very significant place on that same scene also made his first appearance on a Broadway bill. Songwriter Cy Coleman (b 1929) had a career as a jazz pianist and a handful of winning popular songs to his name when he first popped up in the musical theater as the composer of the songs to *Wildcat*, a bouncy little tale of love among the oil-wells which had been constructed to feature comedienne Lucille Ball in its starring rôle. Coleman's songs—with lyrics written by Carolyn Leigh (1926–1981)—were suitably written in the upbeat, straightforward style of the moment, and Miss Ball struck a gusher with the most upbeat and straightforward of them all, the lively invitation "Hey, Look Me Over."

Coleman was soon to prove, however, that there was much more than this kind of simple "holiday-camp" style of song to his palette, for his second collaboration with Miss Leigh, and with the rising young playwright Neil Simon (b 1927), was a show of altogether more sophistication than *Wildcat* had been. *Little Me* was a musical version of another Patrick Dennis novel, another Patrick Dennis novel featuring a thoroughly memorable grande dame at its center—but one with a different air to her from the more famous Auntie Mame. Simon caught that difference precisely. *Little Me*, the story of the fabulous life of bazooka-breasted little Belle Poitrine from the wrong side of the tracks, and of her lifelong search for the wealth, culture, and social position that will allow her to wed the rich boy she loves, was told in a bubbling burlesque tone that brought the book's pages to the stage perfectly, and Coleman and Leigh's laughingly clever set of songs illustrated the story with an admirable comical aptness. Belle belted out her ambition to get off of "The Other Side of the Tracks," and resisted the advances of an insistent beau who tried song-and-dancingly to persuade her "I've Got Your Number," the entire American army in Europe sighed for the home comforts that could be supplied by "A Real Live Girl," and the music swelled into a burlesque "I Love You" every time hero and heroine touched. *Little Me* was not, however, in spite of all temptations, a grande-dame musical. Nothing so simple. The top of the bill went not to Belle but to the comedian—Sid Caesar in the original production—who played all (well, most) of the men in her life. Caesar cavorted as the beloved and deeply perfect Noble Egglestone, as the mean old Mr Pinchley who provides Belle with her first exit from Poverty, as the French vocalist Val du Val whom she marries, and as the Prince of Ruritanian Rosenzweig who helps her with her social position, in what was the comedy rôle of the epoch. Broadway, however, showed only limited enthusiasm for *Little Me*: it clearly preferred its Patrick Dennis ladies to be grandes dames, for Belle Poitrine got less of a welcome than the more out-front Auntie Mame. London, on the other hand, gave the two ladies and their shows something like equal attention, and later confirmed its amiable attitude to burlesque Belle when the show was given its first West End revival.

Coleman followed up *Little Me* in 1966 with another musical built around a sizeable female star. Simon was again the librettist, and the show was a musicalized version of an Italian screenplay about a luckless whore in search of true love. She wasn't a real whore by the time she got to Broadway, though, just a lovably wide-eyed dance-hall hostess with weaknesses. For *Sweet Charity*, Coleman teamed up with the doyenne of Broadway's lyricists, Dorothy Fields, and between them they turned out a score of sassy and sentimental songs which caught the flavor of their story with the same adeptness as the musician had shown in his *Little Me* numbers: a coven of dance-hall hostesses giving the come-on to any "Big Spender" who might have wandered in, a schlock-religion messiah propounding his gospel of "The Rhythm of Life," and the heroine's going hopefully up "If My Friends Could See Me Now" and coming hopefully down "Where Am I Going?" Gwen Verdon starred as the Charity of the title on Broadway, and *Sweet Charity* was launched on a career which took it into a whole array of countries and languages, and to the musical screen, over the years that followed.

SWEET CHARITY, a musical in 2 acts by Neil Simon, based on the screenplay *The Nights of Cabiria* by Federico Fellini, Tullio Pinelli, and Ennio Flaiano. Lyrics by Dorothy Fields. Music by Cy Coleman. Produced at the Palace Theatre, New York, 29 January 1966.

Characters: Charity Hope Valentine, Helene, Nickie, Carmen, Vittorio Vidal, Ursala, Herman, Oscar Lindquist, Daddy Johann Sebastian Brubeck, &c.

Plot: Unlucky-in-love dance-hall girl Charity, dumped by her latest man, finds her next adventures in unlikely places. She is picked up by a film-star wanting to spite his mistress and ends up stuck in his bedroom cupboard overnight while the pair make up their quarrel. Then she gets involved with Oscar, a claustrophobic tax accountant whom she meets in a stuck lift, and who is into alternative religion. And he's serious. This is it. Charity can start dreaming of curtain materials and babies' bootees. But Oscar keeps seriously thinking of all those men in Charity's past and in the end it gets to him. So, just like all the rest, he wiggles out, and sweet Charity is left just to go on hoping that maybe the next man will be the right man.

Songs: "You Should See Yourself" (Charity), The Rescue, "Big Spender" (Helene, Nickie, &c.), Charity's Soliloquy (Charity), "Rich Man's Frug," "If My Friends Could See Me Now" (Charity), "Too Many Tomorrows" (Vidal), "There's Gotta Be Something Better Than This" (Charity, Helene, Nickie, &c.), Charity's Theme, "I'm the Bravest Individual" (Charity, Oscar), "The Rhythm of Life" (Brubeck &c.), "Baby, Dream Your Dream" (Helene, Nickie, &c.), "Sweet Charity" (Oscar &c.), "Where Am I Going?" (Charity), "I'm a Brass Band" (Charity), "I Love to Cry at Weddings" (Herman). Additional and alternative numbers included remusicked versions of "Sweet Charity" and "I'm the Bravest Individual."

The Broadway long-run record established by *Hello, Dolly!* was a short-lived one. Only months after Stewart and Herman's musical had notched up its statistical victory, it was out-pointed by another new musical by another newish team of writers: librettist Joseph Stein (b 1912), lyricist Sheldon Harnick (b 1924), and composer Jerry Bock (b 1928). Stein had done quite well with a pair of mid-1950s musicals—*Plain and Fancy* and the made-for-Sammy-Davis-Jr *Mr Wonderful*—before the trio got together on the songwriters' first Broadway musical: an unsuccessful piece about the world of musclemen called *The Body Beautiful*. Stein then had a go at the seemingly needless task of turning O'Casey's *Juno and the Paycock* and Eugene O'Neill's *Ah! Wilderness* into musicals, before teaming up again with his *Body Beautiful* partners—who had, meanwhile, rolled out three further shows, of varying value, with other librettists (the jolly politician musical *Fiorello!*, the umpteenth jolly whores show *Tenderloin*, and the pretty little Hungarian tale of *She Loves Me*)—on the show that would shoot them into the musical-theater stratosphere.

Fiddler on the Roof was an unusual piece to find on the Broadway of the 1960s. It was a musical which had neither the zingy humor nor the glamour and grandes dames of its most successful contemporaries: where they were a vibrant red and green, or glittering lamé and tinsel, this musical was a deep brown. Put together from a set of short stories of pre-Soviet Russian Jewish life, it had for its "hero" a lovable but unexceptional little country milkman, and the central part of the show's action showed us the various stages of his wondering incomprehension as the traditional family values by which he has lived his life crumble away around him. It should have been sad, it should have been shameful, but it wasn't. For Tevye, the milkman, was a character in a million: his great quality was understanding, or, when understanding was lacking, acceptance. Acceptance of the will of God, and an almost Candide-like belief in the goodness of God and of the world in spite of everything he sees. Add a dash of pragmatism, and a good deal of love—and it was pretty clear to see that Tevye was no ordinary musical comedy hero.

Fiddler on the Roof: The traditional life of the village of Anatevka is falling apart around Tevye the milkman and Golde, his wife.

Bock and Harnick wove into the story of Tevye, his wife, their daughters, and their neighbors in the little village of Anatevka a set of songs which were gently colored with the flavor of their time and place, and of the Jewish people. Like the story and its characters, they were an endearing lot: Tevye ruefully demanding of God why life couldn't have been made just a little easier for him in the rumbling "If I Were a Rich Man," the village tailor Motel bursting out with happiness at winning his longed-for bride in "Miracle of Miracles," the milkman and his wife looking over life in "Sunrise, Sunset" or joining in what must be one of the oddest and yet most real love duets in all musical theater. "Do You Love Me?," Tevye suddenly demands of his wife. After twenty-five years of an arranged marriage, he suddenly needs to know, to hear the words said, and she—roughly and redly—finally manages to get round to saying them. The solo numbers, mostly unshowy and gentle in character, were supported by and contrasted with some rousing ensemble music ("To Life," "Anatevka," "Tradition") which—like the people of Anatevka—provided a colorful background to the story, and by some lively, rhythmic folkdance-style music. But in *Fiddler on the Roof* there was little dancing, save at the wedding feast of Tzeitel and Motel, and even there—since the story took place in a time and a place where women were not permitted to dance—it was almost entirely restricted to the men of the cast. But that did not prevent a version of the traditional bottle dance from becoming one of the highlights of the show.

If *Fiddler on the Roof* was unusual in its character and in its style, it also proved unusual in its effect. The show not only triumphed on Broadway, knocking off the freshly set long-run record established by *Hello, Dolly!* before it was even cool, but it went on to a career in the rest of the world which far outshone that of its immediate rival, and indeed almost any other musical of the postwar era. Everywhere that *Fiddler on the Roof* went—round the English-speaking world and right through Europe, just for starters—it became a hit, and it remains established today as both one of the twentieth century's outstanding musicals and a piece as unique in its way as *West Side Story*.

FIDDLER ON THE ROOF, a musical in 2 acts by Joseph Stein, based on the stories of Sholom Aleichem. Lyrics by Sheldon Harnick. Music by Jerry Bock. Produced at the Imperial Theatre, New York, 22 September 1964.

Characters: Tevye, Golde, Tzeitel, Hodel, Chava, Shprintze, Bielke, Motel Kamzoil, Perchik, Lazar Wolf, Mendel, Yente, Grandma Tzeitel, Fruma-Sarah, Fyedka, Avram, Shandel, The Fiddler, &c.

Plot: Tevye, the milkman of the little Russian village of Anatevka, works hard and brings up his five daughters in accordance with the holy book. Soon the first of them will be married, and Tevye is concerned that they shall have good husbands. But Tzeitel will not marry the well-off butcher to whom her father has betrothed her, and—rather than see her unhappy—he shamefacedly breaks off the match and lets her marry her sweetheart, Motel, the tailor. The second daughter leaves home to wed a rabble-rousing "student," and the third goes furthest of all and weds outside the Jewish faith. And then, as the traditions of centuries begin to tumble down around the folk of Anatevka, the pogroms begin. Tevye, Golde, and what remains of their family set out for a new life in a new land, where they will continue to lead their lives according to the holy book and pray that God will watch over them and theirs.

Songs: Prologue/"Tradition" (Tevye, ensemble), "Matchmaker, Matchmaker" (Tzeitel, Hodel, Chava), "If I Were a Rich Man" (Tevye), Sabbath Prayer (Tevye, Golde, &c.), "To Life" (Tevye, ensemble), "Miracle of Miracles" (Motel), Tevye's Dream (Tevye, Golde, Fruma-Sarah, Grandma Tzeitel, &c.), "Sunrise, Sunset" (Tevye, Golde), Bottle Dance, Wedding Dance, "Now I Have Everything" (Perchik, Hodel), "Do You Love Me?" (Tevye, Golde), "I Just Heard" (ensemble), "Far from the Home I Love" (Hodel, Tevye), "Anatevka" (ensemble), Epilogue.

Bock and Harnick did not, sadly, follow up their outstanding hit in the same way that Coleman and Herman did. They turned from the warm realism of *Fiddler on the Roof* to sometimes brittle and campy humor in a set of three one-act musicals called *The Apple Tree*, then tried to repeat their winning formula with another period Jewish piece in a musical about *The*

Rothschilds, before Bock withdrew from the arena. And, as in so many similar cases, the remaining songwriting partner found little success in what new collaborations he essayed in the field. Stein, however, did go on to further hits, and he did it in harness with yet another exciting new team of young writers who had made their first appearance on Broadway only in the mid-1960s, and who had very quickly found considerable success.

John Kander (b 1927) and Fred Ebb (b 1932) made their first contribution to the Broadway stage, as a team, in 1965, with a rather naive little piece called *Flora, the Red Menace*. But the following year they turned out an altogether more substantial piece of work when they provided the songs for Joe Masteroff's encapsulation of the Berlin stories of Christopher Isherwood, and of John van Druten's successful play drawn therefrom, as *Cabaret*. *Cabaret* dealt with the same period of world history as *The Sound of Music* had done, but it dealt with it in a very different way. A way as different as the difference between the Baroness Maria von Trapp and Christopher Isherwood. And, whereas *The Sound of Music* had been set in Austria, *Cabaret* was set in Berlin, in the 1930s, as National Socialism started breeding the conditions that would lead to war. Like *Fiddler on the Roof*, the show dealt with the problems of ordinary Jewish people faced with racial envy and hatred, but *Cabaret* was no more like *Fiddler on the Roof* than it was like *The Sound of Music*. The former was wholly real, the latter wholly romantic, while *Cabaret* combined and contrasted an esoteric setting and characters with real events and real people in a way that made the real people even more real and the grotesques even more grotesque. The story of a plain and desperately ordinary English girl, trying to lead what she thinks is a gloriously decadent life in the nightspots of Berlin, and that of a plain and desperately ordinary German housewife who finds devotion late in life and has to give it up because of other people's prejudices, were set in front of a series of scenes played in a garish Berlin cabaret house, with an epicene and leering master of ceremonies, an orchestra and chorus of galumphingly German girls, and an audience of weary would-be-decadents, and each part of the show had its own music. In the cabaret, there was an oily "Willkommen," a bit of tatty troilism ("Three Ladies"), a bit of topical anti-Jewishness ("If You Could See Her Through My Eyes"), and a bit of stirring Nazism ("Tomorrow Belongs to Me"), alongside which Sally's coyly English plea "Don't Tell Mama" had all the ghastliness of little-girl sex; in real life Sally and the young writer with whom she shacks up shared quieter moments, and the gentle romance between their landlady and the greying Jewish fruit dealer who is her lodger progressed in gentle numbers. The juxtaposition of the two elements was a difficult one, but it came off well enough for *Cabaret* to run up a good record on Broadway, and fair ones elsewhere.

However, *Cabaret* was to have an unusual life. After its first runs were done, it was made into a film. The film made some heavy alterations to the libretto, with the landlady and her fruit man being thinned down and almost out, and instead some younger and prettier people brought in to represent the Jewish Problem, but the major change came in the rôle of the English girl, Sally Bowles. She was no longer portrayed as a not-very-capable little no one who thinks she's someone (a characterization which had been something of a problem, given that Sally was at least the show's equal leading lady), but played by Liza Minnelli as a touching and foolish girl, albeit one whose talents as a singer were from another world. The tremulously come-onnish "Don't Tell Mama" was replaced by some stingingly singable numbers, and this Sally Bowles's performance of "Mein Herr" and "Money, Money, Money" on the cabaret stage, and the reachingly longing "Maybe This Time" in the real-life moments of the film, lifted the rôle into another dimension. It also helped the film to enormous success, and, as a result, *Cabaret* the musical started being revived. With this new, starry kind of Sally Bowles at its center—and many a Minnelli wannabe eager to fling herself into an imitation of the film's star—*Cabaret* was quite a different show. Not a more coherent one, necessarily, but certainly a more showy one. And certainly a decidedly popular one.

CABARET, a musical in 2 acts by Joe Masteroff, based on the Berlin stories of Christopher Isherwood, and the play *I Am a Camera* taken therefrom by John van Druten. Lyrics by Fred Ebb. Music by John Kander. Produced at the Broadhurst Theatre, New York, 20 November 1966.

Characters: Master of Ceremonies, Clifford Bradshaw, Sally Bowles, Fräulein Schneider, Herr Schultz, Fräulein Kost, Ernst Ludwig, &c.

Plot: American writer Cliff Bradshaw comes to Berlin and boards at the lodging house run by Frln Schneider. There he meets a strange, dying-to-be-decadent English girl called Sally Bowles who is performing in a local cabaret, and soon they are sharing room and life. Cliff works very little, but he earns keep-money by couriering for a pupil until he discovers that what he is carrying is money for the Nazi party. When he refuses to continue, he is beaten up. Further evidence of the uncomfortable situation in Berlin comes when Frln Schneider gets engaged to her Jewish lodger, Herr Schultz, and they attract some anti-Jewish demonstration. Cliff decides to leave Berlin, Frln Schneider cannot, so she must give up her hope of marriage, Sally could—but she won't. She cannot see the truth, any more than she can see that she is anything but the shockingly unusual person she wants so very much to be. And then, as the harsh voice of the cabaret MC repeats the welcome with which he opened proceedings, it begins to get very dark.

Songs: "Willkommen" (MC), "So Who Cares?" (Frln Schneider), "Don't Tell Mama" (Sally), Telephone Song (ensemble), "Perfectly Marvelous" (Cliff, Sally), "Two Ladies" (MC, ladies), The Pineapple ["It Couldn't Please Me More"] (Frln Schneider), "Tomorrow Belongs to Me" (waiters), "Why Should I Wake Up?" (Cliff), The Money Song (MC), "Married" (Frln Schneider), "Meeskite" (Herr Schultz), reprise "Tomorrow Belongs to Me," "If You Could See Her Through My Eyes" (MC), "What Would You Do?" (Frln Schneider), "Cabaret" (Sally), reprise "Willkommen," reprise "Cabaret." Additional and alternative numbers included: "Maybe This Time" (Sally), "Mein Herr" (Sally), "Money, Money, Money" (MC, Sally), "Don't Go," "I Don't Care Much."

The film of *Cabaret* and its greater theatrical success were still in the future when Kander and Ebb provided Broadway with their next scores—a warm little Canadian story called *The Happy Time* which was a distinct contrast to the earlier show—and then a further contrast again—a collaboration with Stein on a red-blooded version of the famously filmed Greek tale of *Zorba*. *Zorba* was on a tough wicket—after all, probably the most famous thing about the film was Mikos Theodorakis's zithery "Zorba's Dance," and here was a musical version of the show which would, of course, have to do without that ubiquitous piece of music. But Kander and Ebb met the challenge triumphantly, turning out a score which had nothing to it of the stand-up performance material of *Cabaret*'s most appreciated scenes, but which—in musical segments which sometimes barely resembled conventional songs—illustrated splendidly the tough and tender story of the roughnecked Greek and the sweet aging cocotte who becomes his mistress. The lady's death scene, in which she sings wanderingly of her childhood memories and her lost beauty ("Happy Birthday"), was a wonderfully moving piece of writing, and the screeching descent of the plundering village women on her home the moment she has died, a thing of real horror. *Zorba* had a fair success on Broadway—though it was far from as successful there as *Cabaret*—and even though the rest of the English world generally failed to pick up on it, Central Europe did. There, the red blood was evidently appreciated, and *Zorba* became one of the best-liked musicals of its period, in preference to *Cabaret*.

The two writers who had looked like the most oncoming men of the musical theater in the 1950s—Arthur Laurents and Stephen Sondheim—did rather less well in the 1960s. Laurents turned out just three libretti: a glum grande-dame parable called *Anyone Can Whistle*, which was a quick flop, the unlucky *Do I Hear a Waltz?*, and an amazingly awkward mixture of show-bizz and simplistic isms called *Hallelujah, Baby!*, which it seemed hard to credit as the work of the author of *West Side Story*, before disappearing from the bookwriting scene for nearly a quarter of a century. His lyricist on the first two of these musicals was again his *West Side Story* partner Sondheim, but Sondheim found altogether more success when he joined with another superior librettist, Larry Gelbart (b 1923), on a small-scale show which saw him make his Broadway début as a composer.

A *Funny Thing Happened on the Way to the Forum* took another trip to that notoriously successful setting for musical plays—classical antiquity—but, this time, not just for the frocks and fun to be found there. This show actually took the form of the classical Roman comedy, its traditional stock characters and motifs, and built a modern musical play on and around them. The paterfamilias (father), the servus (slave), the miles (soldier), and the senex (old man), and all the other character-types who peopled each of the plays of Plautus and Terence, were introduced in a splendidly complex comic tale which could, indeed, have come straight from the pen of one or other of the Roman masters, and—as a bonus—those characters were supplied with a bundle of lively modern songs on topics both ancient and eternal. The juvenile lady cooed with all the ingenuousness of a Gilbertian heroine that her only talent was being "Lovely," father and son summarized each other's sexual potential—or lack of it—in a liltingly wordful "Impossible," Ancient Roman lust came thoroughly to the fore in the slavering assertion that "Everybody Ought to Have a Maid" for the extra-curricular advantages she brings, and the swaggering, baritonic soldier waxed suboperatic as the drama rose to its explodable height, in a set of jolly, lightweighted, and lighthearted songs that echoed the merriment of the show's story and dialogue delightfully. *A Funny Thing Happened on the Way to the Forum* was a first-rate success both at home and abroad—even though foreign adapters had some trouble adapting the music-hall-joke title.

A FUNNY THING HAPPENED ON THE WAY TO THE FORUM, a musical in 2 acts by Larry Gelbart and Burt Shevelove, based on the works of Plautus. Music and lyrics by Stephen Sondheim. Produced at the Alvin Theatre, New York, 8 May 1962.

Characters: Senex, Domina, Hero, Pseudolus, Hysterium, Erronius, Philia, Marcus Lycus, Miles Gloriosus, Tinitinnabula, Panacea, Geminae, Vibrata, Gymnasia, the Proteans.

Plot: The slave Pseudolus is out to earn his freedom by securing for his young master the exorbitantly pretty girl he has spied in the window of a nearby slave-seller. Unfortunately, she's already been sold to a military captain, but Pseudolus doesn't let that stop him. A few imaginative lies and a bit of imaginative finagling, and Philia is out of the shop and into the house. And then the fun begins, as lusting father, suspicious mother, lovestruck son, string-pulling slave, and demanding military captain get caught up in a farrago of farcical situations which are sorted out only when it is discovered that the soldier and the virgin he has bought are actually brother and sister, the long-lost children of a driveling old neighbor who has been mumbling about being a subplot since way back in Act 1.

Songs: "Comedy Tonight" (Pseudolus &c.), "Love, I Hear" (Hero), "Free" (Pseudolus, Hero), The House of Marcus Lycus, "Lovely" (Philia, Hero), "Pretty Little Picture" (Pseudolus, Hero, Philia), "Everybody Ought to Have a Maid" (Senex, Pseudolus, Hero, Lycus), "I'm Calm" (Hysterium), "Impossible" (Senex, Hero), "Bring Me My Bride" (Miles Gloriosus, Pseudolus, &c.), "That Dirty Old Man" (Domina), "That'll Show Him" (Philia), reprise "Lovely" (Pseudolus, Hysterium), Funeral Sequence and Dance (Miles Gloriosus, Pseudolus, &c.), reprise "Comedy Tonight" (ensemble). **Additional and alternative numbers:** "Farewell" (Domina), The Echo Song (Hero, Philia).

A Funny Thing Happened on the Way to the Forum had a good international career, but nothing like the one that was won by the 1965 musical *Man of La Mancha*. *Man of La Mancha* was the umpteenth musical stage show to be written around the Don Quixote story, and it was written by 1960s people in a 1960s manner. But the writers and their director were, apparently, not so confident of their material, for they took the option long favored by nervous stagewriters and "framed" their tale. That is to say, they made it a play within a play, thus removing their characters one step from reality and from the need to be dramatically convincing as people. In *Man of La Mancha* we were shown the part of the traditional tale of the daydreaming Quixote and his faithful servant Sancho Panza that led him to his "fair Dulcinea" before he is brought forcibly back to reality and the bosom of his grasping family, but we were shown it as played out (for not wholly convincing reasons) by the author Cervantes and his servant while in prison, awaiting a summons before the Inquisition. The songs of Joe Darion and Mitch Leigh (b 1928) illustrated the play within the play effectively, and two of them proved takeaway hits: a stirring title-song announcing Cervantes' assumption of the character of Quixote, and—above all—the evening's theme song, Quixote's emotional description of his Quest: "The Impossible Dream."

Man of La Mancha was a major Broadway hit and, even though it failed when taken to Britain, it went on to become a sizeable success in Australia, to be liberally produced around Europe, and to be made into a Hollywood film. Its creators, however, never succeeded in coming up with a second show of anything like the same attractions.

MAN OF LA MANCHA, a musical by Dale Wasserman, based on his television play *I, Don Quixote* and on *Don Quixote* by Manuel de Cervantes y Saavedra. Lyrics by Joe Darion. Music by Mitch Leigh. Produced at the ANTA Washington Square Theatre, New York, 22 November 1965.

Characters: Don Quixote [Cervantes], Sancho Panza [Manservant], Aldonza, Innkeeper [Governor], Dr Carrasco [Duke], Padre, Antonia, Housekeeper, Barber, Pedro, Maria, &c.

Plot: The imprisoned Cervantes relates the story of Alonso Quijana, who called himself Don Quixote of La Mancha and went out into the world as a knight errant to right its wrongs. As he sets out on his quest, Quixote stops at an inn on the road to Toboso—which he conceives to be a castle—in order to have the master dub him a knight, and there he meets up with the serving wench Aldonza. In spite of her insistence that he look at her as she really is, and in spite of the brutal mockery of the muleteers who use the inn, he takes her as his lady and treats her with other-worldly chivalry. But Quijana-"Quixote" is not allowed to continue his quest for long. The old man's family comes after him, anxious that he and his money should not escape them, and his son-in-law—whom Quixote sees as his enemy, the Great Enchanter—forces him to look at his own reflection. The dream is broken, Quixote fades, and Quijana returns home. But as he dies, with his faithful servant and the now believing Aldonza at his side, Quijana becomes Quixote again, for one last glimpse at the "impossible dream."

Songs: "Man of La Mancha" (Quixote, Sancho), "It's All the Same" (Aldonza), "Dulcinea" (Quixote), "I'm Only Thinking of Him" (Padre, Housekeeper, Antonia), "I Really Like Him" (Sancho, Aldonza), "What Do You Want of Me?" (Aldonza), "Little Bird" (muleteers), Barber's Song (Barber), The Golden Helmet of Mambrino, "To Each His Dulcinea" (Padre), The Quest: "The Impossible Dream" (Quixote), The Combat, The Dubbing, The Abduction, Moorish Dance, Aldonza (Aldonza), The Knight of the Mirrors, "A Little Gossip" (Sancho), reprise "Dulcinea," reprise "The Impossible Dream," reprise "Man of La Mancha," The Psalm, reprise "The Impossible Dream."

Alongside the outstanding hits of the 1960s, the decade also saw many other fine and/or successful musicals produced. Actor and pop singer Anthony Newley (b 1931) scored a hit with a very small-scale musical written in collaboration with Leslie Bricusse (b 1931) and entitled *Stop the World—I Want to Get Off*, a virtual one-man show which followed the not very nice character, impersonated by Newley, through life, its vicissitudes, and its women to the accompaniment of a group of songs which proved to be distinctly to the taste of the times. The torchy "Once in a Lifetime" and "What Kind of Fool Am I" became nightclub standards, and the little show (which originally cost just £2,000 to mount) became an oft-produced favorite with small houses and big-part-seeking stars.

Another unlikely show which won a considerable success was a version of Chaucer's *Canterbury Tales*, a selection of the tales told in the aged poem set with a handful of bouncy, simple, forgettable songs. At a time when the abolition of censorship on the British stage was looming nigh but hadn't quite made it, *Canterbury Tales* provided a respectable way of getting sex onto the stage. Because it was based on a classic piece of Eng. Lit.—as *Lock Up Your Daughters* had been—it counted as "bawdy" rather than censorable—though goodness knows what the censor's reaction would have been to an original musical, set in modern times, which showed a chap getting a poker shoved up his backside.

Popular songwriter Burt Bacharach turned to the musical theater to supply the music for *Promises, Promises*, a merry musical-comedy version of the screenplay *The Apartment* which spread its charms around the world with considerable success, and sent "I'll Never Fall in Love Again" into the hit parades; Sherman Edwards masterminded perhaps the most unlikely hit of all in *1776*, a fetching and surprisingly dramatically effective musical retelling of the circumstances surrounding the signing of the Declaration of Independence; a tiny little off-Broadway piece called *Dames at Sea* burlesqued the film musicals of the 1930s with an adorable cheek, and another, not much larger, brought the famous characters of Charles Schultz's *Peanuts* comic strip to the slightly singing stage in *You're a Good Man, Charlie Brown*; but the two other notable shows of the era were pieces which belonged to areas of the musical-theater genre which were set apart.

The romantic musical play had undergone such changes over the past decade or so that it could almost have been considered to have extinguished itself. Although period romanticism was on show in pieces like the one-step-removed *Man of La Mancha*, a show such as *Fiddler on the Roof* replaced real romanticism with something that more resembled a slightly romantic reality. The days of the frankly romantic "operetta," with its soprano heroine and its baritone hero, or with those fine, free-singing creations of the 1940s and 1950s, the Broadway soprano and her Broadway baritone, seemed to have disappeared. There had been Julie Andrews in *Camelot*—but her rôle had been light comedy rather than real romance—and there had been Anna Maria Alberghetti in *Carnival* (no quibbling on the sopranoishness there) in what was next to a child's rôle, but the very largest proportion of musical leading ladies of the time were the up-to-date descendants of the coon-shouting girls, stars whose singing voice lived in their chest rather than in their head. The men, too, had had their vocal moments—Richard Kiley's singing of Don Quixote being a supreme example—but by and large the richly light operatic singing that had been so long a feature of the musical stage seemed to be dying away. But in 1964 came evidence that the romantic musical play was indeed alive and that it could still flourish in the most brilliant fashion. It was evidence which came, though, by accident.

An American amateur singer and legal person wrote a romantic musical that was based on

Robert and Elizabeth: "Woman and man were made for each other . . ." In the garden at Wimpole Street, Robert Browning encourages Elizabeth Barrett back to health.

the highly successful play *The Barretts of Wimpole Street*. He touted it around Broadway without success, then touted it to Britain and got a bite—from a film company. The film company didn't seem to realize that screen rights in the original property would prevent their filming its musical version, but they weren't wholly silly. They insisted that the musical be tried out in the theater first, and they handed it on to a young producer. He wasn't going to say "no," but he knew immediately that the show he'd been handed was a horror. So he called in a rewriter. The rewriter insisted on the employment of a certain director, and she in turn brought along a young Australian composer to mend the insufficiencies in the show's score. He mended, she mended, they all mended with such vivacity, that by the time the show got to the stage it was quite simply all their own work. It was also an enormous success.

The libretto to *Robert and Elizabeth* was a splendidly slimmed version of the famous play, and the score was the most remarkable piece of romantic musical-theater writing to have been seen on the musical stage in years. Its most remarkable feature was the music written for the rôle of the poet Elizabeth Barrett, the central figure of the original play, and here introduced by the Australian soprano June Bronhill, the most outstanding light opera performer of her generation. The rôle and its music were written to measure for Miss Bronhill and they used every ounce and every extreme that her voice had to offer, powering up to high D natural in the dramatic monologues and songs which were the heart of her part as Elizabeth fought against the mysterious illness that had her couch-tied (Soliloquy, "Want to Be Well," "The World Outside"), struggled against her tyrannical, too-loving father, hurling out her justification of the right of "Woman and Man" to love, or jubilated over refound health ("The Real Thing") and at-last found love ("I Know Now"). The vocal and dramatic bravura of the rôle of Elizabeth was backed up by some contrastingly effective music for the two men of the play—warmly energetic baritone songs for Browning and dramatic Sprechgesang for Barrett—and some moments of charm and humor for the younger members of the tyrannized Barrett family ("The Girls That Boys Dream About," "Pass the Eau de Cologne," "Hate Me Please") in a score which boasted classic proportions but distinctly adventurous limits.

Robert and Elizabeth ran for nearly 1,000 performances in London, and went on from there to most other corners of the English-speaking world where a consummate dramatic actress with a solid top D could be found, but it never reached Broadway. The American gentleman, horribly miffed at the insult that had been proffered to his writing abilities, used his connection with the law effectively to block the show's entrance to New York, and the American producer who had bought the rights to present it there had to fight for twenty years to establish that he did in fact have the right. But, by then, the momentum had rather gone, and so *Robert and Elizabeth* never got closer to Broadway than New Jersey.

ROBERT AND ELIZABETH, a musical in 2 acts by Ronald Millar, based on *The Barretts of Wimpole Street* by Rudolf Besier. Music by Ron Grainer. Produced at the Lyric Theatre, London, 20 October 1964.

Characters: Edward Moulton-Barrett, Elizabeth Barrett, Robert Browning, Henrietta, Arabel, George, Alfred, Henry, Charles, Septimus, Octavius, Bella Hedley, Captain Surtees Cook, Doctor Chambers, Wilson, Mr Macready, Evans, &c.

Plot: Elizabeth Barrett has been bedridden since the accident which killed her brother, watched over by her sternly Victorian father with a concern and expressions of love which border on the incestuous. In her invalid state, she has begun to write poetry, and her verse has attracted the attention of the successful poet Robert Browning. When he bursts into her life, full of vigor and love, she finds the strength to leave her bed and walk, but her father jealously crushes her newfound confidence and makes plans to take his family away from London and the threat represented by Browning. But, encouraged by Browning and by her brothers and sisters, Elizabeth finally succeeds in getting out of the house long enough for her and Browning to be married. As the pair leave for their honeymoon under the sunny skies of Italy, Edward Moulton-Barrett is left standing defeated and wretched on Vauxhall Station.

Songs: "Here on the Corner of Wimpole Street" (ensemble), "The Family Moulton-Barrett" (family), "The World Outside" (Elizabeth), "The Moon in My Pocket" (Browning), "I Said Love" (Browning, Elizabeth), "Want to Be Well" (Elizabeth), "Love and Duty" (family), "You Only to Love Me" (Henrietta), "The Real Thing" (Elizabeth &c.), "In a Simple Way" (Robert, Elizabeth), "I Know Now" (Robert, Elizabeth), Soliloquy (Elizabeth), "Pass the Eau de Cologne" (family), "What's Natural" (Bella), "I'm the Master Here" (Barrett), "Escape Me Never" (Browning), "Hate Me, Please" (Henrietta, Cook), "Under a Spell" (Browning), "The Girls That Boys Dream About" (family, Wilson), "What the World Calls Love" (Barrett), "Woman and Man" (Elizabeth), "Frustration" (Browning). Additional number: "Long Ago I Loved You" (Browning).

There could scarcely have been a piece more different from *Robert and Elizabeth* than *Hair*. Where the one was carefully and craftsmanly constructed on the bones of a classic play, the other was tacked together—on an almost invisible backbone—from a host of movable and replaceable pieces; where the one was a period romantic piece with a beginning, a middle, and an end, central characters of depth, and other such classic unities, the other was a shapeless mass of modernity peopled by characters whose lack of depth was their main characteristic; where the one was illustrated with a dazzling, limit-reaching array of that kind of music which was the traditional decoration of the romantic musical, the other displayed a selection of the recent kinds of "pop" music which had moved in to squeeze out the rather more energetic and shapely rock 'n' roll of the 1950s; where the one had as its aim simultaneously to move and to entertain, the other was first and foremost meant—and meant with devastating earnestness—to shock. Because, of course, there's good money in shock.

With all the earnestness that characterized the 1960s and the strivingly modern youth of that era, *Hair* was subtitled "an American tribal love-rock musical." The tribal bit got into the description because the characters who took part in the entertainment were shown as being members together of a "tribe," a kind of low-energy, hedonistic group with not much on its communal mind except free love (i.e., sex), free drugs, and free anything else. In the course of what passed for the action of the evening, the tribe did their best to be offensive to the starchily painted adults of the cast-list, as well as, of course, to the deliciously waiting-to-be-offended audience, displaying as much anti-social action and delivering as many naughty words (the quota was significantly increased between the tryout and Broadway) and songwords as possible, while periodically sneering at religion and anything else that might be a serious consideration for anyone else. And even proffering a snitch of striptease as a curtain to the first act. Anything, just anything, that might grab a gobbet of aghastly attention.

The songs that were attached to this text were written by its authors, Rado and Ragni, and by Galt MacDermot (b 1928), a Canadian musician who'd been around for a while on the fringes of the popular music world. Some of them were simply vehicles for the naughty words—titles like "Hashish," "Colored Spade," "Sodomy," and "Prisoners in Niggertown" (all part of the additions) were calculated attention-grabbers—but others, such as the little love-story song "Frank Mills," had more to them. It was the number "Aquarius," however, which won the most notice, going on to become a kind of anthem for that part of the 1960s generation which was into caftans and flower-power and the kind of half-baked mysticism and astrology that went with them, with a second number which had also been part of the original score, "Good Morning, Starshine," running it a close second.

Hair was certainly different. Determinedly different. Determinedly aimed at the younger generation, the middle-aging caftanners, and also anyone who might be nicely shocked. And, oddly enough, it was the last category which did the show proudest, helping significantly to make it into the enormous hit that it became. Middle-aged, middle-class matrons went mad for the "American tribal love-rock musical." *Hair* went on to have extended runs on Broadway, in Britain, and in Australia, and even Europe opened itself up to be happily offended by the fashionable new show. There was no "why?" about it—*Hair* was quite simply a very big hit. And, against all logic, it stayed around. Three decades later, when the petals had well and truly fallen off the flower-power movement, when the show's naughty words were no longer naughty to anyone, when nudity had become an everynight occurrence in the theater, when the trendy astrology of "Aquarius" no longer rang bells with anyone but a handful of geriatric hippies, *Hair* was still to be found trundling round the theaters and halls of Europe, with all its aged "shockers" preserved determinedly, as in aspic.

Hair was, however, a novelty hit, a one-off. It had no real successors, and the shows that attempted to follow its various manners did not stay around long. Similarly, pop music of the kind that it featured did not become a regular feature of the musical theater. Change of such a kind was not for just yet. But it would not be long.

HAIR, an American tribal love-rock musical by Gerome Ragni and James Rado. Music by Galt MacDermot. Produced at the Public (Anspacher) Theatre, New York, 17 October 1967, and in a revised version at the Biltmore Theatre, New York, 29 April 1968. *Characters*: Claude, Berger, Woof, Hud, Jeannie, Crissie, Dionne, Angela, Mom, Dad, &c.

Plot: The tribe are into a kind of hedonism. Doing what they want, having what they want, paying for nothing, being responsible for nothing, and being loved for it. They take pills and fuck each other and grow their hair long as a kind of tribal membership badge and make posters and say things like "groovy" and have more hang-ups that you can imagine. Then Claude gets called up for the army. He'll be going to Vietnam. His long hair cut off, he leaves the tribe and starts his journey into real, adult life.

Songs included: "Aquarius" (solo & ensemble), "Donna" (Berger), "Hashish" (ensemble), "Manchester, England" (Claude), "Colored Spade" (Hud), "Sodomy" (Woof), "I'm Black" (Hud, Woof, Berger, Claude)/"Ain't Got No" (Woof, Hud, Dionne), "I Got Life" (Claude), "Air" (Jeannie, Crissie, Dionne), "Initials" (ensemble), "Going Down" (Berger), "Hair" (Berger, Claude), "My Conviction," "Don't Put It Down" (Berger), "Frank Mills" (Crissie), "Be-In" (ensemble),

"Hare Krishna" (ensemble), "Where Do I Go?" (Claude), "The Electric Blues," "Easy to Be Hard" (Sheila), "White Boys"/"Black Boys" (girls), "Walking in Space" (ensemble), "Three-Five-Zero-Zero"/"What a Piece of Work Is Man" (ensemble), "Good Morning, Starshine" (Berger, Claude, Sheila, Dionne), "The Bed" (ensemble), "Exanaplanetooch" (Claude). Additional and alternative songs included: "I Believe in Love," "Hung," "Don't Put It Down," "Abie Baby," "Prisoners in Niggertown," "Dead End," "Let the Sun Shine In."

SOME NOTABLE MUSICALS 1960–1969

1960   BYE BYE BIRDIE (Charles Strouse/Lee Adams/Michael Stewart) Martin Beck Theatre, New York, 14 April

THE FANTASTICKS (Tom Jones/Harvey Schmidt) Sullivan Street Playhouse, New York, 3 May

OLIVER! (Lionel Bart) New Theatre, London, 30 June

CAMELOT (Frederick Loewe/Alan Jay Lerner) Majestic Theatre, New York, 3 December

1961   CARNIVAL (Bob Merrill/Michael Stewart) Imperial Theatre, New York, 13 April

STOP THE WORLD—I WANT TO GET OFF (Anthony Newley/Leslie Bricusse) Queen's Theatre, London, 20 July

HOW TO SUCCEED IN BUSINESS WITHOUT REALLY TRYING (Frank Loesser/Abe Burrows, Jack Weinstock, Willie Gilbert) 46th Street Theatre, New York, 14 October

1962   A FUNNY THING HAPPENED ON THE WAY TO THE FORUM (Stephen Sondheim/Larry Gelbart, Burt Shevelove) Alvin Theatre, New York, 8 May

LITTLE ME (Cy Coleman/Caroline Leigh/Neil Simon) Lunt-Fontanne Theatre, New York, 17 November

1963   HALF A SIXPENCE (David Heneker/Beverley Cross) Cambridge Theatre, London, 21 March

1964   HELLO, DOLLY! (Jerry Herman/Michael Stewart) St James Theatre, New York, 16 January

FUNNY GIRL (Jule Styne/Bob Merrill/Isobel Lennart) Winter Garden Theatre, New York, 26 March

FIDDLER ON THE ROOF (Jerry Bock/Sheldon Harnick/Joseph Stein) Imperial Theatre, New York, 22 September

ROBERT AND ELIZABETH (Ron Grainer/Ronald Millar) Lyric Theatre, London, 20 October 1965

MAN OF LA MANCHA (Mitch Leigh/Jo Darion/Dale Wasserman) ANTA Washington Square Theatre, New York, 22 November

CHARLIE GIRL (David Heneker, John Taylor/Hugh and Margaret Williams, Ray Cooney) Adelphi Theatre, London, 15 December

1966   SWEET CHARITY (Cy Coleman/Dorothy Fields/Neil Simon) Palace Theatre, New York, 29 January

MAME (Jerry Herman/Jerome Lawrence, Robert E. Lee) Winter Garden Theatre, New York, 24 May

CABARET (John Kander/Fred Ebb/Joe Masteroff) Broadhurst Theatre, New York, 20 November

1967   HAIR (Galt MacDermot/Gerome Ragni, James Rado) Anspacher Theatre, New York, 17 October

1968   JOSEPH AND THE AMAZING TECHNICOLOR DREAMCOAT (Andrew Lloyd Webber/Tim Rice) Colet Court School, London, 1 March

CANTERBURY TALES (John Hawkins, Richard Hill, Nevill Coghill, Martin Starkie) Phoenix Theatre, London, 21 March

ZORBA (John Kander/Fred Ebb/Joseph Stein) Imperial Theatre, New York, 17 November

PROMISES, PROMISES (Burt Bacharach/Hal David/Neil Simon) Shubert Theatre, New York, 1 December

DAMES AT SEA (Jim Wise/Robin Miller, George Haimsohn) Bouwerie Lane Theatre, New York, 20 December

1969   1776 (Sherman Edwards/Peter Stone) 46th Street Theatre, New York, 16 March

AMERICAN MUSICALS IN THE WEST END 1945–1970

In the quarter of a century after the Second World War, the Broadway musical dominated the musical stages of the world, and most particularly the English-singing stages of the world. This list (which takes no heed of such imponderables as theater sizes, forced runs, star pregnancy, &c.) shows the statistical "order of preference" in which the American-written musicals of Broadway's boom years were received in the other main musical-theater center of the time, London. An asterisk indicates that the show was also given a contemporary production in Australia (and of London's top 27, only two—including *Guys and Dolls!*—failed to make the trip Down Under).

The Sound of Music	2,386*
My Fair Lady	2,281*
Fiddler on the Roof	2,030*
Annie Get Your Gun	1,304*
West Side Story	1,039*
The King and I	946*
Hello, Dolly!	794*
South Pacific	792*
A Funny Thing Happened	762*
Brigadoon	685*
Kismet	648*
The Pajama Game	578*
Promises, Promises	570*
Carousel	566*
Guys and Dolls	545
Song of Norway	526*
How to Succeed in Business	520*
Camelot	518*
Call Me Madam	486*
Sweet Charity	484*
Paint Your Wagon	477*

Flower Drum Song	464
Mame	443*
Where's Charley?	404*
Kiss Me, Kate	400*
The Music Man	395*
Can-Can	375*
Little Me	334
Fanny	333
Cabaret	316
Plain and Fancy	315
High Button Shoes	293
The Most Happy Fella	288*
Wish You Were Here	281
Bells Are Ringing	270*
Bye Bye Birdie	268*
Damn Yankees	258*
Man of La Mancha	253*
Pal Joey	245
Gentlemen Prefer Blondes	223
Wonderful Town	205
She Loves Me	189
Do Re Mi	170
1776	168*
No Strings	135
Dames at Sea	127*
Golden Boy	118
You're a Good Man, Charlie Brown	116*
I Do! I Do!	116*
Funny Girl	109*
The Boys from Syracuse	100
High Spirits	93*
Your Own Thing	65*
Isabel's a Jezebel	61
Candide	60*
Fiorello!	56
Finian's Rainbow	55*
On the Town	53
The Fantasticks	44*

Little Mary Sunshine	44*
Belle Starr	40
Once Upon a Mattress	38*
Carnival	36*
The Wayward Way	36
Cindy	29
The Man with a Load of Mischief	26
Lute Song	24
All in Love	22
Simply Heavenly	16
The Love Doctor	16
The Dancing Heiress	15
Pocahontas	12
The Crystal Heart	7

Also produced in Australia: *Wildcat, Fade Out—Fade In*, plus the French *Irma la douce* and the London musicals *Zip Goes a Million, The Boy Friend, Salad Days, Grab Me a Gondola, Lock Up Your Daughters, Oliver!, Free as Air, Sail Away* (a British musical, but first produced in America), *Stop the World—I Want to Get Off, Instant Marriage, Robert and Elizabeth, Half a Sixpence, The Canterbury Tales, Charlie Girl*. The only shows that made the opposite voyage, West End–Broadway, during the same period were *The Boy Friend, Oliver!, Half a Sixpence, Stop the World—I Want to Get Off*, and France's *Irma la douce*, although both *Salad Days* and *Valmouth* were seen off-Broadway, *The Canterbury Tales* and *Lock Up Your Daughters* were given tryouts, and *Robert and Elizabeth* was produced away from New York.

$\mathcal{I}$n the quarter of a century that had passed since the Second World War, and in which the English-language stage had operated as far and away the most important producer of new musical plays, a multi-colored variety of musicals had made themselves a place in the sun and in the more or less permanent repertoire. There had been merry modern comedy with pieces such as *How to Succeed in Business Without Really Trying*, merry ancient comedy with shows of the *A Funny Thing Happened on the Way to the Forum* and *The Boy Friend* variety, witty burlesque comedy of the *Little Me* and *Candide* kind, romantic comedy of all colors from *The Music Man* to *Sweet Charity* to *Fiddler on the Roof*, offbeat comedy from *Guys and Dolls* to *Valmouth*, as well as fantasy, adaptations of classic literature, classically built love-cum-comedy pieces, grande-dame musicals, and a whole range of more dramatic shows, from *Carousel* and *South Pacific* to the song-and-dance drama of *West Side Story*, the downbeat *Expresso Bongo*, and the black and green nastiness of *Cabaret*. All these shows, however, whatever their differences of shade and story, shared several things in common. First, they stuck firmly to the songs-and-scenes layout that had for so many years been standard in the musical theater. The story of the piece progressed throught its forward-going stages, punctuated and illuminated by musical numbers which mostly had some relevance to the story or its characters—a factor which had now become regarded, by theorists in particular, as virtually a must, and in any case as something devoutly desirable. Even dances were required to do at least something of a job, rather than being the purely decorative items that they had been of yore. As for the musical part of the entertainment, "songs" really did describe it most aptly. Even in the more romantic pieces—even in such musically ambitious pieces as *Robert and Elizabeth*—genuine ensemble work (as opposed to slightly harmonized choruses and duos) and such musical montages as the operatically shaped concerted finale of earlier years were rarities. A musical score consisted very largely of "numbers," supported—in some cases—by a goodly dose of dance music which was often not just rearrangements of tunes from elsewhere in the musical, but custom-made orchestral music of some ambition.

Various efforts were made to vary the standard shapes and styles of the musical, even during these peak years of its postwar prime, and some such experiments found a degree of success. The attempts to establish a "Broadway opera" form, characterized by such exciting shows as the heavily dramatic and sung-through *The Consul* and *Street Scene*, foundered when the shows—in spite of their qualities—proved commercially unviable, but—like the "folk opera" *Porgy and Bess*—a handful were well enough thought of later to find themselves revivals, under subsidized conditions, in opera houses strapped for attractive and approachable modern pieces for their repertoires. At the other end of the scale came the altogether more commercial display that was *Hair*, with its minimal structure, its effortful obscenities, its glimpse of nudity, its sackful of 1960s isms, and its swathe of poppishly musicked songs. *Hair* proved to have much more purse-pillaging mileage in it, but it also proved to be a novelty hit, one which spawned no successful successors, and the pop music of the 1960s turned out to have no more of an effective place in the musical theater than the rock 'n' roll of the 1950s had had.

At the turn of the decade, however, Broadway saw the production of a show which did successfully depart from the standard musical-theater norms, and departed from them successfully enough that it was both to turn out itself to be one of the most popular musicals the world had seen, and equally to establish a whole alternative fashion in musical-theater writing and composition.

Jesus Christ Superstar was an unlikely piece from a number of points of view. To start with, its subject—the last days of the life, and the death, of Jesus Christ—wasn't exactly the kind of stuff that musicals were normally made of. But that was almost an incidental. It was the show's form and tone which made it so startlingly different. Its writers called their show a "rock opera," and it was as good an expression as any to describe what they had created. "Rock"—like "jazz" and "ragtime" in earlier days—had become a term rather broader in its meaning than it had originally been: it no longer referred just to the jolly, rhythmic rock 'n' roll style of music which had been launched as the most up-to-date thing in "pop" music in the 1950s, but covered a more general (though, for its time, fairly heavily aggressive) style of youthfully oriented and driving music. As for "opera," well, the significance of that word here was simply that the score for the show was musically continuous. *Jesus Christ Superstar* was a sung-through work in which the succeeding pieces of dialogue and the set-pieces—songs and ensembles—were all set to music in the manner of a classical opera. It was a manner which the show's creators—writer Tim Rice (b 1944) and composer Andrew Lloyd Webber (b 1948)—had already used to good effect in their first staged work, a happy little "cantata" retelling the biblical story of *Joseph and the Amazing Technicolor Dreamcoat*, which had been written for performance by a group of London schoolboys.

This introduction of the cantata form into the musical theater was not something wholly new, for almost exactly a hundred years before the appearance on the stage of *Joseph* and of *Superstar*, that very same form had had a brief flourishing in Britain. But not in the theater—in the music-halls. Forbidden by law to produce anything that might be described as a "stage play," music-hall owners had instead produced "cantatas" (some with famous composing names attached to them): dramatic tales told in a series of sung numbers, without any illegal dialogue or action or production values. In the latter days of this trend, one such little piece had made it into the theater, and had been given a full and highly successful stage production: Gilbert and Sullivan's *Trial by Jury*. Since then, however, the genre had been fairly theatrically disused, and such sung-through shows which had appeared on the English-language stage had mostly been ones which had some kind of operatic ambition and weight.

In *Jesus Christ Superstar*, the writers expanded both the notion of the sung-through "cantata" form—taking it from what had in *Joseph* originally been a fifteen-minute scena, full of schoolboyish fun and easy-to-sing musical parody, up to the proportions of a full-length musical play, mostly dramatic in nature, with vocal lines that reached into the parts of the stave that few other recent musicals had been able to reach—and the textual and musical flavor of the earlier piece.

Rice's words were not quite like anything else that had existed up till now in the musical theater. They were thoroughly colloquial, with the colloquialness—and with a grown-uppish version of the sense of humor—of the boys for whom *Joseph* had been originally written. They came at their subject, be it serious or be it humorous, from a delightfully fresh angle, which sometimes made the past fifty years of thoroughly crafted theatrical lyric-writing seem quite simply old hat, even artificial. And, like all the very best of song words, they seemed to come out effortlessly.

The music composed by Lloyd Webber for *Superstar* was altogether more substantial than that which he had written for *Joseph*. In *Superstar*, he delivered a brand of music which—for all that it was called "rock"—had rather more substance to it than the melodies of the usual pop chart song. The urgent and forceful nature of the rock idiom was there, but the bones that lay under the surface of the score were of a more thoroughly classical shape. Just as the jazz and ragtime idioms had been adapted for song and, eventually, for show music, here was the rock idiom being modified into a theatrically acceptable and dramatically effective style of music by being cross-bred with the solid tenets of a more regular style of theater music.

The voices that were chosen to sing the music indicated the direction in which the composer was heading. The show's two principal rôles—Jesus and Judas—were written to be performed by what is now known as a "pop tenor": a voice which used the method of vocal production of a rock vocalist, with its scorched colorings and searing use of chest voice, on music of a range and scale that had nothing to do with what was heard on the hit parades. It was highly demanding music, requiring considerable vocal strength, range, and stamina, and, particularly in the early years of this new style of musical-theater writing, artists with the ability to perform the music and the rôles for which it was written were extremely difficult to find. But—just as had happened when opéra-bouffe had hit the English-speaking world, and had found that world unequipped with artists educated with the combination of talents needed for its performance—the pool of players quickly grew, and those with potential for such performances quickly became more adept at singing and playing in the new style.

For the moment, this "new style" concerned only the male voices. Even though *Superstar* allowed a little more space for female singing than the all-male *Joseph* had done, the writers did not give their only female principal—the singer playing Mary Magdalene—the same kind of searingly wide-ranging singing. Her rôle in the text was that of a pacifier, and her music was written in a pure, warm, and gentle country vein which contrasted happily with the violent vocal lines given to the two central men.

Alongside the pop tenor and country voices, however, *Superstar* sported several other voice styles. The parts of the two principal Pharisee priests were written at the very extremes of the male vocal range—one scraping deep black notes from several lines and spaces below the bass stave, another twittering horribly above the treble stave in a hectic counter-tenor in a novel and effective piece of part writing—while Pontius Pilate was written for a regular baritone and the chorus music of the show demanded trained voices at both ends of its harmonies. Only the part of Herod, who appeared briefly with a cruel little comedy number which rather resembled a vaudeville turn, was wholly lacking in vocal values.

In yet another unorthodox move, *Jesus Christ Superstar* was heard as a gramophone recording before it was brought to the stage. This actually wasn't done on purpose: it was done because the only person who could be found to put trust in this unlikely musical was a recording executive at MCA records. So the company put out an expensive double-disc recording of the entire score of the unproduced *Jesus Christ Superstar*. The executive got the sack for spending so much of his company's money on flying such an unlikely kite, but the record not only caught the attention that the show had failed to win on paper, it ended up topping the American LP lists on no fewer than four occasions, and generally causing quite a stir. When the stirring was done, and the piece had been performed as a concert cantata in several countries, and after the odd contractual up and the odd contractual down had been gone through, the record company allied with a stage producer, and *Jesus Christ Superstar* was finally brought to the stage in 1971. Because the recording had been such a success in America, that first theatrical production was seen on Broadway. Because *Hair* had been so successful, the director of *Hair* was let loose on the show. The result was a gimmicky 1960ish sort of production which only half convinced, and which totted up a good rather than a remarkable run. However, other productions were already scheduled, notably an Australian one which turned out to be a memorable success, and by the time *Superstar* was mounted in the West End it had been realized that neither the story nor Rice and Lloyd Webber's rock opera version of it was in need of gimmicky staging. London's production of *Superstar* was an effective bit of straightforwardly dramatic theater which succeeded to such effect that, before its initial run was done, it had become the latest holder of the London long-run record.

JESUS CHRIST SUPERSTAR, a rock opera in 2 acts by Tim Rice. Music by Andrew Lloyd Webber. Produced at the Mark Hellinger Theatre, New York, 12 October 1971.

Characters: Jesus of Nazareth, Judas Iscariot, Mary Magdalene, Caiaphas, Annas, Pontius Pilate, King Herod, Simon Zealotes, Peter, Maid by the Fire, Priests, &c.

Plot: Judas Iscariot is a worried man. The humanitarian and religious crusade of which he is a part is being endangered by the growth of an enormous, hysterical personality cult surrounding his

Jesus Christ Superstar: John 19:41.

leader, Jesus of Nazareth. Jesus is being hailed as a Messiah, a king, and some of his followers are behaving like fanatics. Soon the Roman rulers of Judaea will hear of the stir he is creating, and there will be trouble. So Judas goes to the Priests. It is in their interest to quiet this troublemaker too, so, with the help of Judas, Jesus is arrested as he prays alone in the Gardens of Gethsemane. He is brought before the Governor, Pilate, and then before King Herod, both of whom refuse to judge him, but in the face of an angry populace and a prisoner who will not defend himself, Pilate finally gives in. Jesus is crucified, and Judas—understanding that his part in this affair has been simply one of a puppet on God's strings—commits a tortured suicide. And the turning of Jesus of Nazareth into an all-time Superstar is on its way.

Songs: "Heaven on Their Minds" (Judas), "What's the Buzz" (chorus), "Strange Thing, Mystifying" (Judas), "Everything's All Right" (Mary), "This Jesus Must Die" (Priests), "Hosanna" (chorus), "Simon Zealotes" (Simon Zealotes), "Poor Jerusalem" (Jesus), Pilate's Dream (Pilate), The Temple (Jesus &c.), "I Don't Know How to Love Him" (Mary), "Damned for All Time" (Judas), "Blood Money" (Judas), The Last Supper: "Look at All My Trials and Tribulations" (Apostles), Gethsemane: "I Only Want to Say" (Jesus), The Arrest, Peter's Denial (Peter), Herod's Song: "Try It and See" (Herod), "Could We Start Again, Please?" (Mary, Peter), Judas's Death (Judas), Trial before Pilate and The 39 Lashes (Pilate &c.), "Superstar" (Judas &c.), The Crucifixion, John 19:41.

The triumph of *Jesus Christ Superstar* did not result in a rush to the world's stages of new musicals written in imitation of Rice and Lloyd Webber's work (although biblical subjects became briefly the rage), and since the authors themselves turned out only increasingly expanded versions of *Joseph*, and a soon-shelved companion piece to it called *Jacob's Journey*, in the years immediately following their first big hit, the songs-and-scenes musical remained the norm throughout the 1970s.

The early part of the decade was, in fact, rather disappointing. Many of the writers who had made Broadway bristle with good things in the 1950s and the 1960s now withdrew or faded from the scene, and others failed to come up with shows equal to their earlier successes. Comden and Green (book) and Adams and Strouse (songs) got nearish to success with the latest grande-dame musical, *Applause*, a song-and-dance remake of the cult film *All about Eve* in which the slightly-singing Lauren Bacall took the rôle made famous on the screen by Bette Davis, and Frank Loesser—with a little help from Beverley Cross and Tommy Steele—won a posthumous success when his much-loved film score for *Hans Christian Andersen* ("Thumbelina," "Wonderful Copenhagen," "The King's New Clothes," &c.) was used as the basis for a stage musical. But pieces such as Stewart and Coleman's *Seesaw*, Stewart and Herman's *Mack and Mabel*, Lerner's mega-grande-dame piece about *Coco*, with Katharine Hepburn starring as Mlle Chanel, Rodgers's attempt at musicalizing *Flowering Cherry* as *Two by Two*, or—what should have been a sure-fire hit—a dispiritingly tamely musicalized version of the hilarious screenplay (yet another one) *Some Like It Hot* under the title *Sugar*: all failed to hit the mark convincingly, and left at best a song or two behind them.

Fortunately, however, there were some new writers at hand to fill some of the gap left by the men and women of experience, but there was also one among the heroes of the earlier decades who proved himself to be thoroughly on form in the first years of the 1970s: Stephen Sondheim. If Sondheim had had a rather less productive than expected 1960s, he more than compensated for that between 1970 and 1973, turning out the songs—lyrics and music—for three substantial shows, as well as contributing to the triumphant remake of the 1950s show *Candide*, which staged its resurrection during this same period.

The first of the three pieces to appear was *Company*, an individual and interesting piece of musical theater which did not follow the normal shape of a musical play. It was, certainly, made up of songs and of scenes, but those songs and scenes did not follow a story in a linear fashion through its various stages from a beginning to an end. Instead, librettist George Furth (b 1932) presented a series of sketches of New Yorkish married life, threaded not onto a plotline but around a character. That unifying character was Bobby, a friend to each of the couples, who was seen visiting each pair in turn and watching them display themselves and their foibles in comic sketches and comic songs. Those sketches and songs were interleaved with episodes and people from his own private and staunchly unmarried life.

This kind of structure, in which each individual scene was a presentation of a character or characters, was an ideal one for displaying the kind of sophisticated and witty character songs at which Sondheim has proved himself the modern master, and the score for *Company* duly introduced a bundle of clever, attractive, and enduring numbers: the cynical assertion that it's "The Little Things You Do Together" that make for a happy marriage, the frantic pre-wedding jitters of a later-in-life bride who suddenly, but temporarily, decides she is not "Getting Married Today," the post-coital duo in which a one-night-stand air hostess gets ready to fly off to "Barcelona" while Bobby pretends to try to persuade her—with too much success—to stay, the waspish drunken hymn of a waspish drunken dame to "The Ladies Who Lunch," and the frustrated, babbling assertion of three of our hero's regular bedmates that "You Could Drive a Person Crazy" by not being serious about Relationships with a capital R.

Company had good runs in both America and Britain, and found itself a firm niche in the revivable repertoire thanks not only to its eminently performable songs and tart, up-to-date New Yorkish talk, but also because its array of rôles, each of which had its moment in song or scene, was notably appealing to actors and to producing groups. Outside the English language, however, it found fewer takers.

COMPANY, a musical in 2 acts by George Furth. Music and lyrics by Stephen Sondheim. Produced at the Alvin Theatre, New York, 26 April 1970.

Characters: Robert, Sarah, Harry, Susan, Peter, Jenny, David, Amy, Paul, Joanne, Larry, Marta, Kathy, April.

Plot: A group of Robert's good friends have gathered at his New York apartment to spring a surprise 35th birthday party on him. There is a birthday cake with candles on it, which he is expected to blow out and make a wish. But the good friends would happily make that wish for him: that he should be married, like them. We see Robert visiting dieting Sarah and alcohol-almost-free Harry, we see him with Ivy League Peter and southern-belle Susan who are getting divorced, we see him with strivingly modern David and conservative Jenny who only—of course—tries marijuana to please her modern husband, with Paul and Amy who are getting married after years of living together, and with long-suffering Larry and embarrassing Joanne, and we see him hoeing his own row with air-hostess April, kooky Marta, and out-of-town Kathy. And all the time there is talk of marriage, the idea that married life is normal life, floating in the air. Robert doesn't show up for the party, so all the good friends go home, leaving him to be unmarried a bit longer. But, given the pressures and the friends, how much longer?

Songs: "Company" (Robert &c.), "The Little Things You Do Together" (Joanne &c.), "Sorry-Grateful" (Robert, Harry, David, Larry), "You Could Drive a Person Crazy" (Kathy, April, Marta), "Have I Got a Girl for You" (Larry, David, Peter, Paul), "Someone Is Waiting" (Robert), "Another Hundred People" (Marta), "Getting Married Today" (Amy, Paul, Jenny), "Side by Side by Side" (Robert &c.), "What Would We Do without You?" (Robert &c.), "Poor Baby" (Sarah, Susan, Jenny, Amy, Joanne), "Tick Tock" (music by David Shire), "Barcelona" (Robert, April), "The Ladies Who Lunch" (Joanne), "Being Alive" (Robert), Finale (ensemble). Additional number: "Marry Me a Little" (Bobby).

The same format that was used in *Company* was followed again in *Follies*, which appeared the year after. Once again the libretto—this time the work of James Goldman—was less than linear, once again the characters of the piece were a group of folk gathered together for a party, and once again the evening was spent almost entirely examining the insides of the people in question, who were presented in sketch-scene and in song, up until the moment when the entertainment was rounded off. The people of *Follies* were rather different from those of *Company*, however. Whereas the earlier group of folk had been average middle-class, middle-income, middle-to-lowish-intelligence New Yorkers of no particular distinction, the characters of *Follies* were a bunch of showbizzy extroverts—a bunch of one-time revue dancers and singers brought back together for a reunion, umpteen years on. The main similarity between them and their predecessors was that—self-centered, self-dramatizing, exasperating, and ultimately tiresome—most of them were a pretty difficult bunch to like or to sympathize with.

The linking element in *Follies* was not one person, but a group of four. Two married couples who had been a togethersome quartet in the days when the wives were Follies girls and the boys stage-door Johnnies, and who are now standardly miserable with their lives and their spouses and all ready to cause a little bit of trouble for one another with a little bit of revelation of a little bit of ancient infidelity. And when the entertainment is over, all that's happened is that they've all made each other a little bit more unhappy than they already were. But in the meantime there has been a multi-colored parade of musical numbers. The numbers of *Follies*, which were, of course, much more showy than those of *Company*, were mostly presented as new-old show songs. Some were performed as such by the aging artistes: a pretty pair of dance-and-song sweethearts tripping to the delicate rhythms of "Rain on the Roof," a Continental soprano, behind whose wobbly voice of today can be heard the pure sound of her youth ("One More Kiss"), a far-too-French song for a doubtless phoney French performer ("Ah! Paris"), a squawked-out soubrette song by a now voiceless grandmother ("Broadway Baby"), or a whole routine, half-remembered, performed by the alumni of the chorus ("Who's That Woman?"). One series of numbers, introduced by a no-longer-young revue tenor ("Loveland"), featured the four principals, and their younger selves, in a sequence in which their feelings were expressed in the exaggerated styles of the stage—an over-the-top torch song for the miserable Sally, a clownish "God-Why-Don't-You-Love-Me Blues" for her made-miserable husband, and so forth. Alongside these pieces of performance-within-a-performance material, there was also a handful of here-and-now songs, of which an aged vocalist grinding out a hymn to survival, "I'm Still Here," was to become a virtual grande-dame anthem.

Follies didn't have the same kind of success as *Company*, although it was exhumed, rewritten, and performed in several countries beyond America in later years, but a number of its songs became nightclub favorites, usually—as has so often happened with parody material—performed straight rather than with the hint of knowing exaggeration they held in the show itself.

For his third show of the early 1970s, Sondheim teamed with a third fine playwright, Hugh Wheeler (1912–1987), and this time he abandoned the largely plotless "party" format of the previous two shows and returned to the straightforward musical play with a beginning, a middle, and an end all in their usual places. The libretto for *A Little Night Music* was, like so many pieces of recent years, developed from a screenplay, and it was a screenplay of certain quality: Ingmar Bergman's 1955 Swedish *Smiles of a Summer Night*. The music with which the composer illustrated it was of equal quality, and altogether more ambitious than that which he had written for the wittily worded modern songs featured in the two previous musicals. The sophisticated, rueful comedy of *A Little Night Music* was accompanied by a score of waltzing music of all shapes and styles—solo and ensemble—which ranged from the beautiful to the raunchy and which was at every turn an effective partner to the story and the characters. Some numbers were, indeed, "items" which summed up a character in much the same way that the *Company* and *Follies* songs had done—an aged dame grouching over the debased status of "Liaisons" with the great and the crowned in modern times, a merry maidservant taking an enjoyable serving of sex secure in the knowledge that when she's had her fun she'll settle down and marry "The Miller's Son"—but the majority were worked tightly into the fabric of the play, and the most appreciable moments came in ensemble. One of these was a triple-melodied piece in which the middle-aged man who has wed a child bride is anxious to make love "Now," while she shies away promising only "Soon," and downstairs his pubescent son saws at his cello, frustrated out of his trousers at always being told "Later." The girlish soprano of the young woman, the hectic tenor of the boy, and the rumpled baritone of the husband and father combined their thoughts and their tunes in a trio of enormous effectiveness. No less effective was a rollicking little story piece in which everyone prepares to take "A Weekend in the Country." It is a weekend which is going to be decisive in all their lives, a weekend which will set the wandering souls of the story on the right paths, but half of them have a horror of going. By the time the number has ended and the first-act curtain prepares to fall, they have all sealed their fate: they are indeed going.

The wry comedy of the tale was reflected in numbers such as the duo ("You Must Meet My Wife") in which our hero admits to his horrified ex-mistress that his new wife is still a virgin, in the twin soliloquies ("It Would Have Been Wonderful") in which he and the lady's boilingly jealous current bedmate review their unsatisfactory amorous situations, and in the piece in which he and the mistress, with whom he is soon to be reconciled, start to see more clearly the foolishness of their ways ("Send in the Clowns"). This last number proved—with a little help from a Frank Sinatra recording—to be the somewhat surprising takeaway tune of a show in whose sung section the leading lady otherwise took an uncharacteristically minor part.

Elegantly staged, on a particularly atmospheric set, *A Little Night Music* did elegantly. It did not achieve the extended run won by other more out-front shows, but it duly went through a long list of productions, all around the world, and has remained firmly in the revivable repertoire with the well-merited ticket of "classic" all over it.

A LITTLE NIGHT MUSIC, a musical comedy in 2 acts by Hugh Wheeler, suggested by the screenplay *Smiles of a Summer Night* by Ingmar Bergman. Music and lyrics by Stephen Sondheim. Produced at the Shubert Theatre, New York, 25 February 1973.

Characters: Desirée Armfeldt, Fredrik Egerman, Anne Egerman, Henrik Egerman, Madame Armfeldt, Fredrika Armfeldt, Count Carl-Magnus Malcolm, Countess Charlotte Malcolm, Petra, Quintet [Mr Linquist, Mrs Nordstrom, Mrs Anderssen, Mr Erlansson, Mrs Segstrom], &c.

Plot: Lawyer Fredrik Egerman has married the very young Anne but, in deference to his bride's childish qualms, has as yet not consummated the marriage. So, when his former mistress, actress Desirée Armfeldt, comes to town he is only too anxious and pleased to renew acquaintance, in spite of the peril represented by her current man, an explosively virile young hussar. Desirée is pleased too, and she invites the Egermans to her mother's place in the country. When the hussar hears of this he turns up too, with his wife in tow. When the weekend and its packet of conflicting passions are over, the waltz among the ill-matched partners has moved them on: young Anne has run away with Fredrik's son Henrik, Desirée and Fredrik have given up trying to prolong their youth in relationships with the young and have settled into what will be a comfortable middle-age together, while the hussar has—temporarily at least—gone back to his wife.

Songs: Overture and Night Waltz (quintet), "Now" (Fredrik), "Later" (Henrik), "Soon" (Anne), "The Glamorous Life" (ensemble), "Remember?" (quintet), "You Must Meet My Wife" (Fredrik, Desirée), "Liaisons" (Mme Armfeldt), "In Praise of Women" (Carl-Magnus), "Every Day a Little Death" (Charlotte, Anne), "A Weekend in the Country" (ensemble), "The Sun Won't Set" (quintet), "It Would Have Been Wonderful" (Fredrik, Carl-Magnus), "Perpetual Anticipation" (Mrs Nordstrom, Mrs Anderssen, Mrs Segstrom), "Send in the Clowns" (Desirée), "The Miller's Son" (Petra), reprise "Send in the Clowns" and Night Waltz (Fredrik, Desirée).

In spite of its eminent success, Sondheim did not ever return to the warm, witty, and sophisticated style with which he had so notably succeeded in *A Little Night Music*. Beginning with his next show, he and his authors began purposefully to distance themselves from the mainstream of popular musical theater, turning out a run of pieces in which warmth, wit, and above all accessibility were all firmly denied. The result of this deliberately élitist orientation was to mortgage any kind of success on the commercial stage and with a general public: the idiosyncratic set of musicals to which Stephen Sondheim has contributed scores since 1976 have not been successful on a commercial basis, but they have found a fervent following among the minority at whom they are aimed, and—as the Sondheim legend has grown to considerable proportions—they have also, no matter what their record on the commercial stage, found a welcoming home in the subsidized theaters of the world.

The composer and lyricist contributed to two more musicals in the 1970s. In 1976—in an era when America was suffering from a good deal of conscience over its involvement in Vietnam—he wrote the score to a deliberately slow-paced, pageant-like show which presented in an Oriental manner, and from an Oriental viewpoint, the story of the "invasion" of pure and unspoiled Japan by the horrid Commodore Perry, and its subsequent opening up to the influences of crassly commercial America. The show included some moments in which the lyricist's skill with words could be appreciated, others where the songwords suffered from an opaqueness which in a less obviously sincere context might have seemed pretentious, and the oriental-flavored music given to the all-male cast lacked both the melody and appeal of the waltz tunes of *A Little Night Music*. *Pacific Overtures* was a short-lived failure.

The second piece, produced in 1979, was on altogether different lines. *Sweeney Todd* was a musical melodrama, a grand guignolesque version of the famous old *String of Pearls* story about the murdering London barber whose victims were made into the filling for his accomplice's meat pies. A vaguely lefty version of the old play, adapted by Chris Bond, had been recently produced with some success in Britain, and it was on this that Wheeler based his libretto, a libretto which rationalized the old story quite believably (while making Todd the hard-done-by hero of the affair rather than the murdering villain) and which didn't shrink from one drop of the blood-spurting melodrama, of a kind nowadays usually reserved for the cinema, that the story involved. Sondheim set the grisly tale with a darkly glooming score that burst intermittently out of its blackish tones into a grimly ferocious humor, for a blackly baritone Todd, a raucously semi-singing Mrs Lovett, a pair of sweet-toned juveniles, and some steely voiced villains—basso and tenor. Todd thundered out his revengeful "Epiphany" and wooed his enemy, the Judge, into his deadly barber's chair singing horribly of "Pretty Women," Mrs Lovett hawked "The Worst Pies in London" in corncrake tones and hideously cooed the parlor song "By the Sea" as she attempted to flirt with her partner in crime, while the juvenile man serenaded his "Johanna" in more conventional style, and, in a rare moment of relief from the highly colored action, devoted little Tobias promised Mrs Lovett "no one's gonna hurt you."

Sweeney Todd was produced in extravagantly spectacular fashion, with a meaningful olde English factory looming over the action and a vast pipe organ pasted onto the proscenium arch, but it managed only a fair run on Broadway and flopped completely in London. However, it was subsequently reproduced in England in a shrunken version which brought the piece down to the original small-house proportions of Bond's play, and, helped by the same rise in Sondheim's stocks which has led to others of his less-than-winning works being brought back to the stage, this much more immediate carve-'em-up-two-feet-from-your-nose version, with the story and music taking precedence over scenery and "message," has in more recent years won itself a good deal of the popularity the large-stage version missed out on first time round.

SWEENEY TODD, the Demon Barber of Fleet Street, a musical thriller in 2 acts by Hugh Wheeler, based on a play by Chris Bond. Music and lyrics by Stephen Sondheim. Produced at the Uris Theatre, New York, 1 March 1979.

Characters: Sweeney Todd, Anthony Hope, Mrs Lovett, Judge Turpin, Johanna, A Beggar Woman, The Beadle, Tobias Ragg, Pirelli, Jonas Fogg, &c.

Plot: Once upon a time a powerful judge took a fancy to the pretty, foolish wife of a Fleet Street barber. He had the husband transported for a fake crime, raped the wife, and kept their little daughter Johanna as his own. Fifteen years on the barber, Todd, returns to England, primed for revenge. He sets up in his old practice and, with the connivance of the pie-shop woman Mrs Lovett, goes about attracting the Judge to what will be a last shave at his shop. To keep his identity secret until he can succeed in his aims, he murders the charlatan Pirelli, and cuts up his corpse to become the meat for Mrs Lovett's pies. There will be many corpses more, as Todd takes out his hatred of mankind in indifferent murders, and Mrs Lovett's trade blossoms. Todd's young friend Anthony falls in love with Johanna, but the Judge immures her in an asylum until she can be forced to become his own wife. Anthony helps the girl to escape, and Todd lures the Judge to his shop with the promise that the runaways can be found there. Then begins a ghastly carnage in which Todd murders the Judge, Mrs Lovett, and his own unrecognized wife, before being himself done to death by his accomplice's devoted, crazed shopboy.

Songs: "The Ballad of Sweeney Todd" (Todd &c.), "No Place Like London" (Todd, Anthony, Beggar Woman), "The Barber and His Wife" (Todd), "The Worst Pies in London" (Mrs Lovett), "Poor Thing" (Mrs Lovett), "My Friends" (Todd, Mrs Lovett), "The Ballad of Sweeney Todd" part 2, "Green Finch and Linnet Bird" (Johanna), "Ah, Miss!" (Anthony, Johanna, Beggar Woman), "Johanna" (Anthony), "Pirelli's Miracle Elixir" (Pirelli, Tobias, Todd, Mrs Lovett), The Contest (Pirelli), "The Ballad of Sweeney Todd" part 3, "Wait" (Mrs Lovett), "The Ballad of Sweeney Todd" part 4, "Kiss Me" (Anthony, Johanna), "Ladies in Their Sensitivities" (Beadle, Judge), "Pretty Women" (Todd, Judge, Anthony), "Epiphany" (Todd, Mrs Lovett), "A Little Priest" (Todd, Mrs Lovett), "God, That's Good" (chorus), reprise "Johanna" (Anthony, Beggar Woman, Todd, Johanna), "City on Fire" (Beggar Woman), "By the Sea" (Todd, Mrs Lovett), Wigmaker Sequence (Todd, Anthony), "The Ballad of Sweeney Todd" part 5, The Letter (Todd &c.), "Not While I'm Around" (Tobias, Mrs Lovett), Parlor Songs (Beadle, Mrs Lovett, Tobias), reprise "City on Fire," Final Sequence, reprise "The Ballad of Sweeney Todd."

The other most successful new musicals of the first years of the 1970s came from new writers, or writers newly come to the musical-theater field. None of these men were to stay long, or to establish themselves in the way that the writing stars of the previous era had done, but they left behind a handful of shows among which several have proved to be perennials.

The first to appear was the songwriting team of Gary Geld (b 1935) and Peter Udell (b 1934), whose previous success had come with such popular numbers of the 1960s as "Ain't Gonna Wash for a Week," "Sealed with a Kiss," and "Ginny Come Lately." They proved that there was more substance to their talent than simple songwriting for simple voices when they turned out the score for a 1970s adaptation of the Ossie Davis play *Purlie Victorious*, a vigorous, energetic score of considerable vocal demands which turned the agreeably comical tale of con and counter-con into a thoroughly uplifting musical. The *Purlie* of the piece was a preacher from the cotton-picking plains of Georgia, and the story concerned itself with his efforts to raise enough cash to buy the local Big Bethel Chapel as a venue for his preaching—preaching which seems to consist of some rather woolly ideas expressed in some rather 1960s words, notably that most severely overworked and unqualified one, "freedom." His means of raising the wind are, however, a touch unorthodox: in fact, they're downright fraudulent. They are also decidedly funny. Purlie has his little Lutiebelle impersonate a girl for whom the nasty Ol' Cap'n Cotchipee holds some money in trust. She blows the impersonation, but the Ol' Cap'n is double-crossed instead by his own son, Charlie, drops dead at the treason, and Purlie gets his chapel.

The show's score was a vibrant mixture of the gospelly and the folksy which got off to a stunning start in the opening scene with the rousing, scalding gospel funeral of the villain of the piece ("Walk Him up the Stairs"), and peaked in a sizzling pair of wide-ranged songs for Lutiebelle, one in adoration of "Purlie" and the other rejoicing "I Got Love." The folk element came by a comical showing in Charlie's continuing (and ultimately successful) attempts to write a made-to-measure folk song. *Purlie* had a fine run on Broadway but, perhaps handicapped by the fact that the necessary black casting was more difficult to achieve adequately in other centers, it did not get itself produced further afield.

The same fate befell Geld and Udell's second musical, a musicalization of the 1965 James Stewart film *Shenandoah*. It seemed that—in an era which apparently favored novelty shows—the straightforward romantic musical play was no longer loved. Even one which purveyed the fashionable antiwar sentiments of this show. The sentimental, charming *Shenandoah* was greeted by the sophisticates and critics—much as *The Sound of Music* had been a decade and a half earlier—with barely concealed sneers: it was old-fashioned. And it was, of course. It was splendidly old-fashioned: full of heart-tugging moments and simple country charm, and (almost going too far) with a couple of kiddies (one black, one white) strongly featured. The music was in a country vein, ranging from some richly baritonic soliloquies for the star of the show, John Cullum, cast here as the mind-my-own-business farmer who refuses to get involved in the Civil War, to a dainty two-girl duet ("We Make a Beautiful Pair") and a touching tenor solo for a broken young soldier, making his way back from the war to "The Only Home I Know." The public liked it—but producers elsewhere didn't come running. A run of over a thousand Broadway nights did not lead to any productions further afield. Geld and Udell wrote the songs for one more show, and Udell then teamed with composer Gary Sherman on two more, but none was successful: their moment at the front of the stage was limited to the early and mid-1970s.

The same could be said for the very young songwriter Stephen Schwartz (b 1948), but—unlike Geld and Udell—Schwartz did have the pleasure of seeing his successful musicals go on from their first productions, in the earliest 1970s, to get extremely wide showings, all round the world. The first of them, *Godspell*, was very definitely a novelty item—a collection of biblical tales and parables put together as a college exercise by John Michael Tebelak, decorated with some jolly little sort-of-biblical Schwartz songs ("Day by Day," "Turn Back O Man," "We Beseech Thee"), and played and staged in a style which took a whole range of contemporary school-age preoccupations and attitudes as their inspiration. The cast of ten young people larked around in a mixture of clown costume and casual clothes, faces comically painted, bouncing their way with an eager youthful innocence through versions of incidents and items from the gospels of Matthew, Mark, Luke, and John and other parts of the Old and New Testaments that were told and sung in a mixture of modern-speak and St James version English. And the audience was given a glass of wine at the interval. Ingenuous in the extreme, a veritable antidote, with its uncomplicatedly moral and religious flavor and friendly high spirits, to that other monster "modern" success, *Hair*, *Godspell* became a surprise hit. Indeed, a huge hit. It became a feature of the off-Broadway scene for more than five years before finally shifting up to Broadway itself to finish its run. And while that run continued, the musical was shown in all corners of the world, establishing itself for frequent revivals right through the seventies and even into the eighties, and winning many, many fond partisans.

The success of *Godspell* helped win a Broadway production for *Pippin*, a piece which Schwartz had written as a teenager and which was now given a thorough remake and a major expansion under the tutelage of experienced director-choreographer Bob Fosse (1927–1987). *Pippin* was a more conventional book musical than *Godspell*. It had a story which had a beginning and an end—the search of Charlemagne's son Pippin for "himself"—but that story was carefully "framed," in the same way that that of *Man of La Mancha* had been. A band of white-faced *Godspell*y players introduced the history of the young Prince who (like the young hero of *The Fantasticks*) goes out into the world—a very 1960s version of the world—and experiences its dangers and its promises before finally settling down. His voyage of discovery was punctuated by some songs which were a mite more substantial than the *Godspell* ones, and two of them— the Leading Player's introductory "Magic to Do" and Pippin's longing for his own personal "Corner of the Sky"—became takeaway favorites. An attractive production and a famous advertising campaign which made novel use of television as a selling medium helped *Pippin* to almost two thousand nights on Broadway. Elsewhere, however, it proved not to have the same appeal as in America, and its very strong flavor of an era whose earnest posturings seem in retrospect to have been mildly ridiculous has not helped it to have the ongoing life of the earlier show.

Schwartz had his third long-running success in three shows produced when he supplied some incidental songs for *The Magic Show*, a musical which existed almost entirely to allow magician Doug Hemming to show off his amazing talents as an illusionist, but when he ventured into the conventional musical theater with a musical remake of the famous French film *La Femme du boulanger* the songwriter faced failure, and, in spite of several later returns to the musical theater, he never recaptured the winning streak that had been his in the 1970s.

Jim Jacobs and Warren Casey had only one musical-theater hit, but it was one of the very biggest of all. Biggest in success, that is, for like *Godspell* and *Hair*, their *Grease* came from the off-Broadway theater, the smaller-house, out-of-the-mainstream area of the New York theater which was, at that time, the usual home for anything that was not what was considered conventionally "Broadway" in size, shape, and color. Unlike *Godspell* and *Hair*, however, *Grease* was not striving to be youthfully modern. Quite the contrary. It was, quite simply, the latest in the series of good-old-days musicals. But these good old days were pretty near to hand: indeed, they were in the memory of almost everyone, for they were only just out of sight, back beyond the stirred-up sixties—and already provoking nostalgia. *Grease* was a show in the *Boy Friend* vein (it even used the same "new '50s musical" styling that the earlier show had), a loving, tongue-in-cheek remembrance of the 1950s, those bright and busting years before the onset of all the angst, isms, and attitudes that the would-be world-changers of the 1960s had shoved so liberally down the planet's communal throat. The story was a sweetly innocent little one of teenaged dreams and pains, the songs—schooldays disaster songs, a girl-group number, pieces croony and open-eyedly lovestruck, and a shower of period dances—were happy reflections of the numbers of the young days of rock 'n' roll, and the show was a record-breaking hit. For *Grease* moved swiftly from off-Broadway to Broadway and, by the time it eventually closed, it had outrun *Fiddler on the Roof* and all the other musicals of previous years and appropriated itself for a little while the title of the Great White Way's longest-running musical.

Curiously, though, the rest of the world didn't pick up on *Grease* in the same way that it had on that other bit of friendly, innocent entertainment that was *Godspell*. Not to start with, anyway. But in 1978 a film version of the show was made, and that film version—with John Travolta and Olivia Newton-John in its lead rôles and the show's original score topped up with two chart-rocketers ("You're the One That I Want," "Hopelessly Devoted to You") and some genuine bits of 1950s music—became a world-wide box-office sensation, and in its wake the stage show staged a comeback. The real comeback, however, didn't happen until the 1990s. By then, the 1950s were starting to look less like the good old days and more like Paradise lost, and nostalgia was rife in a musical theater which was weighed down with compilations of aging pop tunes glued to a romanticized version of a writer's or performer's story in the old so-and-so-and-his-songs style, and with heavily scenic, star-name revivals of old shows. *Grease* was given the new

stars-and-spectacle treatment, and the little musical which had been such a big hit became a big musical which looked like being a big hit all over again, as the show installed itself happily both in one of the West End's largest auditoriums and back on a Broadway from which it didn't seem to have been very long away.

Grease: A glimpse of the fifties, when the world was young and so were we. Oh, dear, did we really look like that?

GREASE, a new '50s rock 'n' roll musical by Jim Jacobs and Warren Casey. Produced at the Eden Theatre, New York, 14 February 1972, and at the Broadhurst Theatre, 7 June 1972.

Characters: Danny Zuko, Sandy Dumbrowski, Betty Rizzo, Marty, Jan, Doody, Roger, Kenickie, Sonny, Frenchy, Vince Fontaine, Johnny Casino, Cha-Cha di Gregorio, Teen Angel, Miss Lynch, Patty Simcox, Eugene Florczyk.

Plot: Sandy and Danny met at the beach during the summer and they got sweetly friendly, but when school starts up again, and new-girl Sandy meets Danny again, she finds him disappointingly off-hand. But that's because his pals are watching and Danny has to keep up his high-school Romeo image. She also has to suffer the ridicule of Rizzo, the tough-talking leader of the girls' gang, over her chocolate-box looks and refined ways. Hurt feelings lead her to stay at home while Danny goes to the school dance with Rizzo, but Rizzo is soon back with her own boyfriend, and Danny has got as far as taking Sandy to the drive-in movies. Then Rizzo misses a period, and when Sandy tries to sympathize she gets taken to pieces for her pains: Rizzo would rather be her unpretentious self than a Sandra-Dee doll like Sandy any day. That does it. It's a case of conform or die. Next time we see Sandy she's undergone a transformation: leather jacket, bouffant hair-do, hoop earrings, cigarette, gum, and more attitude than a lamppost. Since Rizzo's period came on after all, everyone can have a happy ending. Especially Danny.

Songs: "Alma Mater" (Patty, Eugene, Miss Lynch, &c.), "Summer Nights" (Sandy, Danny, &c.), "Those Magic Changes" (Doody &c.), "Freddy, My Love" (Marty, Jan, Frenchy, Rizzo), "Greased Lightnin'" (Kenickie &c.), "Mooning" (Roger, Jan), "Look at Me, I'm Sandra Dee" (Rizzo), "We Go Together" (ensemble), "Shakin' at the High-School Hop" (ensemble), "It's Raining on Prom Night" (Sandy), "Born to Hand-Jive" (Johnny Casino), "Beauty School Dropout" (Teen Angel, Frenchy, &c.), "Alone at a Drive-in Movie" (Danny &c.), "Rock 'n' Roll Party Queen" (Doody, Roger) , "There Are Worse Things I Could Do" (Rizzo), reprise "Look at Me, I'm Sandra Dee" (Sandy), "All Choked Up" (Danny, Sandy, &c.), reprise "We Go Together" (ensemble). Additional and alternative numbers included: "Hopelessly Devoted to You" and "You're the One That I Want" (both by John Farrar).

Another small-sized novelty show which turned itself into a recurring event, and even something of a cult, started its life in an upstairs room (they hadn't yet been dignified with the nowadays name of studio theater) at London's Royal Court Theatre the year after *Grease* had first been seen on the stage. It was another piece (and there were quite a few, mostly less successful, around this time) which leaped joyfully into previously taboo areas for its subject-matter and its staging, but it presented its variations on the sexual theme and delivered its of-the-period message of "don't dream it, be it" with such a cheerful, tongue-in-cheek innocence that it was impossible to take even the shadow of offense. *The Rocky Horror Show* was a tiny, nine-handed piece which imitated as it spoofed the sci-fi-with-sex world of the cinema. A couple of toothpaste-white young Americans encounter an omnisexual creature from outerspace who is shacked up in a Transylvanian castle in the middle of the American countryside (you'd have thought that would have put them on their guard, wouldn't you?) constructing a hunky human male for his own personal pleasure(s), and both boyish Brad and ingenue Janet get thoroughly introduced to the highways and byways of sex before they make their escape. You were clearly being encouraged to think that their experience of a little bit of outerspatial sex would lead them to a fuller and more fulfilled/fulfilling (sex) life in their married-to-each-other future.

The musical numbers that decorated the little story were as tiny and as incidental as could be, but an introductory piece promising a "Science Fiction—Double Feature," parodies of rock 'n' roll and of the novelty dance craze ("The Time Warp"), a breathy invitation to "Touch-a Touch-a Touch-a Touch Me," and the hero's presentation of himself as a "Sweet Transvestite from Transsexual, Transylvania" provided a merrily toe-tapping accompaniment to the goings on, and the original production of *The Rocky Horror Show* ended up becoming a 1970s favorite, running through 2,358 performances in a series of clapped-out cinemas in Chelsea before playing out its last days in a West End theater. Australia went mad for the piece, and though an effort to take it to Broadway foundered, *The Rocky Horror Show* was to have its moment in America. A film version was made, flopped, and disappeared, but years later it resurfaced as a cult item in late-night campus cinemas. A whole ritual grew up around the film, ritual involving chanted responses to the dialogue, the throwing of rice at a wedding scene—and, later, more potentially dangerous items such as (why??) frozen peas!—and the clicking on of cigarette lighters at dark moments in the plot. Elsewhere, where the film did not get shown, the rituals were transferred to revivals of the stage show, and so *The Rocky Horror Show* became less a musical and more an interactive game, touring around Britain in particular with its ever-increasing band of devotees in pursuit. More devotees meant more revivals, and the show became a feature of the British road in the later 1980s. It even tried its hand back in the West End on a couple of occasions, and it continues to flourish as a particularly curious example of do-some-of-it-yourself musical theater.

THE ROCKY HORROR SHOW, a rock musical by Richard O'Brien. Produced at the Theatre Upstairs at the Royal Court Theatre, London, 19 June 1973.

Characters: Frank'n'furter, Brad Majors, Janet Weiss, Usherette/Magenta, Narrator, Riff-Raff, Columbia, Rocky, Eddie/Dr Evrett Scott.

Plot: Brad and Janet get benighted in the American countryside and take shelter at the castle where Frank'n'furter—a husky fellow who sports fishnet tights and a suspender belt—lives with his hunchbacked butler and a couple of curious, nymphomaniacal women called Magenta and Columbia. Frank has just created Rocky, a perfect if somewhat naive and dense specimen of manhood, for his private enjoyment, but that night he enjoys Brad and Janet in turn—until news comes that Rocky has escaped from the laboratory. Frank and Brad both have hysterics when it turns out he has found his way to the newly liberated Janet. Now Brad and Janet's tutor Dr Scott turns up. He is a government agent and he knows that the Frank'n'furter household are really—gasp—outerspatial aliens. Frank turns his libido-livening machines on the earthlings, but his pleasure at watching their performance is cut short when the butler turns up in a very different guise. He has taken over. Gunning down Frank and Columbia, he departs with Magenta for outerspace, leaving the humans to go back to everyday American life, enriched—it is hoped—by their contact with the sweet transvestite from Transsexual, Transylvania.

Songs: "Science Fiction—Double Feature" (Usherette), "Dammit, Janet" (Brad, Janet), "Over at the Frankenstein Place" (Brad, Janet, Riff-Raff, &c.), "Sweet Transvestite" (Frank, Brad, &c.), "Time Warp" (Riff-Raff, Magenta, Columbia, Narrator), "The Sword of Damocles" (Rocky), Charles Atlas Song (Frank), "Whatever Happened to Saturday Night?" (Eddie), "Touch-a Touch-a Touch-a Touch Me" (Janet, Rocky), "Once in a While" (Brad), "Eddie's Teddy" (Dr Scott), "Planet-Shmanet-Janet" (Frank &c.), "Rose Tint My World" (company), "I'm Going Home" (Frank), "Super Heroes" (Brad, Janet, Narrator), reprise "Science Fiction—Double Feature" (Usherette, company).

Among the novelty shows, "party" shows, and screenplays-into-musicals of the early 1970s, there were still a handful of successful musicals produced which followed the tried and triumphant tradition of the musicalized play. *Purlie* was one, of course, *Raisin*, a musical remake of Lorraine Hansberry's *A Raisin in the Sun*, which had a good Broadway run from 1973, was another, and there was a contemporary remake of *Two Gentlemen of Verona* (1971), with Galt MacDermot music, which had a go at reaching all the places *Hair* had reached but didn't reach them for nearly as long. Perhaps the most enjoyable, however, was a musical based on Keith Waterhouse and Willis Hall's highly successful Yorkshire play about the dreamaday lad who was called *Billy Liar*. In spite of its rural north-of-England setting and its prosaic characters, *Billy Liar* lent itself perfectly to transmutation into a large-stage musical, for it was the latest in that line of "dream" musicals which stretched from the Victorian *A Dream of Whitaker's Almanac* to *Zigeunerliebe* to *Tillie's Nightmare* to *A Connecticut Yankee* to *Lady in the Dark*. The stage of London's Theatre Royal, Drury Lane, was filled with the colorful product of the self-deluding imaginings of Billy Fisher's brain as he daydreamed himself president of his own private land of Ambrosia, a match-winning football player, or a famous rock star, but in between the glittering scenes of dreamed life the all-too-real daily life of the real Billy Fisher in Stradhoughton, Yorks, went inexorably forward, and Billy became more and more enmeshed in the troubles his fantasizing and the everyday lies he has told to all and sundry had created for him. The show introduced Michael Crawford to the musical stage in the rôle of Billy, dreaming in John Barry and Don Black's songs that "Some of Us Belong to the Stars" and musing "I Missed the Last Rainbow," and featured Elaine Paige as rough-as-guts Rita, the garage attendant who is one of two girls to whom Billy has theoretically committed himself. Those two girls shared one of the evening's best comic numbers, "Any Minute Now," as they both waited for Billy to turn up for a promised date with very different attitudes. *Billy* played for over nine hundred performances in the vastness of the Theatre Royal, and was later seen on the Continent and in South America, but another complication over rights prevented it being seen in the USA.

1975 was a good year on Broadway. It saw *Shenandoah* introduced to the stage, and it saw a high octane rewrite of the old *Wizard of Oz* story called *The Wiz*, with an all-black cast of jazzy-voiced vocalists and apparently jointless dancers, and some leapingly characterful numbers (the yellow-brick road replacement "Ease on Down the Road," the cowardly tale of the "Mean Ole Lion," the bad witch's tantrummy "[Don't Nobody Bring Me] No Bad News"), that would tot up no fewer than 1,672 Broadway performances without, similarly, making good elsewhere. It also saw the welcome return to the top of Kander and Ebb, who, following *Cabaret*, *The Happy Time*, and *Zorba*, had popped in a flop with a 1971 remake of the British comedy *Breath of Spring* under the opaque title of *70, Girls, 70*. This time round, they picked a very American play as their source—the half-century-old satirical comedy *Chicago*—and in harness with director-choreographer Bob Fosse they turned it into what they called a "musical vaudeville." The "satirical" bit of Maurine Watkins's play had been its attitude to the law and the press, both of which were presented as at the best manipulable and at the worst corrupt, and the authors of the musical kept that attitude in spades. But they changed the presentation of the story and, as in *Cabaret*, they put it into a kind of a frame: the story of Roxie Hart, murderess, of how she escaped the noose and went on to a brief career as a stareable-at notoriety on the variety stage, was related in a series of intermittently announced numbers and scenes, as if it were a vaudeville program. This allowed the songwriters to fill their score with the kind of full-frontal performance material of which they had showed themselves to be the masters in the cabaret songs of *Cabaret* (and in various nightclub assignments), and the numbers that they turned out proved to be every bit as good and glittering as any of their earlier work. The oily lawyer of the piece hailed the use of "Razzle Dazzle" as an all-purpose smokescreen and turned his insincerity up to maximum as he assured "All I Care about Is Love," the lady inmates of the Cook County Jail related the circumstances of the crimes they didn't commit in a "Cell Block Tango," the most prominent of them walloped out a hymn to the most practiced vices of the age in "All That Jazz," and Roxie's see-through husband mourned his lack of importance in a "Mr Cellophane" which had a colorable echo of the once famous vaudeville song "Nobody" to it.

With Gwen Verdon (Roxie) and Chita Rivera (Velma Kelly)—Broadway's two outstanding actress-singer-dancers of the era—featured at the top of the bill in a show which gave full-blooded opportunities to all of their talents, and not least in the very individual dance routines in which Fosse specialized, *Chicago* scored a fine success, and if its run of 947 performances on Broadway did not come up to the totals of such shows as *The Wiz*, it—by contrast—put up an altogether better performance than most Broadway shows of its era in other parts of the world, becoming a hit in both Britain and Australia, and also getting a translated showing in Europe.

CHICAGO, a musical vaudeville in 2 acts by Fred Ebb and Bob Fosse, based on the play of the same name by Maurine Dallas Watkins. Lyrics by Fred Ebb. Music by John Kander. Produced at the 46th Street Theatre, New York, 3 June 1975.

Characters: Roxie Hart, Amos Hart, Velma Kelly, Billy Flynn, Mary Sunshine, Matron "Mama" Morton, Fred Casely, Liz, Annie, June, Hunyak, Mona, Go-To-Hell Kitty, &c.

Plot: Roxie Hart was having an affair with a salesman, and when he quit she shot him. To her amazement and horror she was arrested. Mama Morton, wardress of the Cook County Jail, offers—for a consideration—to help her get off. For there is a way. He's called Billy Flynn, he's a lawyer, and he never lost a case for a female client yet, but he costs. The money is raised, and Billy sets to fabricating a background and a story for Roxie which has the sob-sister of the local rag drooling, and which relegates the up-to-then interesting story of fellow murderess Velma Kelly right off the front pages. Roxie gets overconfident, is shocked back to reality when a possibly innocent but non-American-speaking and Flynn-less woman is convicted of murder in the very court in which she is to appear, and hanged, and she finally makes it through her well-orchestrated trial safely. But just before the "not guilty" verdict comes, some girl pulls off this sensational multiple murder in an adjoining divorce court. The journalists abandon Roxie and head for the big new story. All that's left for her in her publicity-stripped freedom is to join Velma Kelly in a mildly scandalous double act round the minor vaudeville houses of America.

Songs: "All That Jazz" (Velma &c.), "Funny Honey" (Roxie), "Cell Block Tango" (murderesses), "When You're Good to Mama" (Matron), Tap Dance, "All I Care About" (Billy), "A Little Bit of Good" (Mary Sunshine), "We Both Reached for the Gun" (Billy, Roxie, Mary Sunshine), "Roxie" (Roxie &c.), "I Can't Do It Alone" (Velma), "My Own Best Friend" (Roxie, Velma), "Me and My Baby" (Roxie), "I Know a Girl" (Velma), "Mr Cellophane" (Amos), "When Velma Takes the Stand" (Velma), "Razzle Dazzle" (Billy), "Class" (Matron, Velma), "Nowadays" (Velma, Roxie), reprise "All That Jazz."

Broadway of 1975 was the rocket-site, however, for a show that would both out-run *The Wiz* and put *Chicago* in the shade: a show that would become a phenomenon of the musical theater, and also the latest tenant of the musical-theater long-run record. *A Chorus Line* was the umpteenth musical about people in musicals, and it was also the latest in line of the "party" kind of show that had so recently proved so effective. But this time round the gathering that brought together the folk in whose fates and feelings we were invited to become interested wasn't one of social jollity; it was nothing more nor less than a search for work—a Broadway dance audition (albeit one that would have had Equity on the back of its director for misconduct had it ever really taken place). *A Chorus Line* gave a satisfying extra dimension to the "party" style of musical. In *Company* and in *Follies* the parade of people had been the be-all of the show: of action there was virtually none, and at the end of the evening, when the party finished and the characters went home, no one was very much if at all altered from what he or she had been at the beginning of the show. What action there was, or wasn't, had had no tangible result. In *A Chorus Line*, however, the display of personalities had a point—the dancers in question were showing themselves off in an attempt to get work—and at the end of their display there was indeed a result. A group of them were selected for an engagement in the show that wasn't within the show. *A Chorus Line*, for all that its essence was that of a "party" musical, did have a very definite beginning, quite a few middles, and an end. It also had one other notable difference from those two earlier shows: in contrast to the often irritating New Yorkers of *Company* and the exaggerated egos and showbizzily overblown emotions of the *Follies* folk, the people of *A Chorus Line* were a thoroughly likable bunch. They had faults, of course, but they were the faults of youth, the faults that come out when a person is trying so very hard to show the best of her- or himself. By and large, every one of those young dancers up there, working their pumps off in an attempt to sell themselves and their talent to the voice in the stalls, was an appealing character—something which made the ultimate selection of the "winners" a genuine climax, and the disaster of the muscular accident which strikes one of the most attractive of them into a moment much more genuinely moving than many a musical-theater death.

The characters of *A Chorus Line* and their case histories were based on real life, on the personalities and experiences of a group of dancers who had, in a series of working sessions, confided their lives to each other, to director-choreographer Michael Bennett (1943–1987), and to the trio of new-to-Broadway writers who, under his influence, would ultimately turn this mass of thoroughly raw material into a musical. The result was a gallery of individuals of all kinds — a group which had only their love of dance in common — with all kinds of feelings and experiences to relate: the girls who took up dancing for the escape it offered from a less than lovely family life, the dancer who wanted to be an actress but got put off by a trendy drama coach, another who was so good in the chorus she got promoted to featured parts but couldn't cope with them and had to come back, yet another who had to have plastic surgery to improve her looks before she started getting jobs; the boy who came to dance through drag shows, another who started his career because he knew he could outdo his sister's efforts, another who almost became a kindergarten teacher before realizing he could get stuck there, and another who is still suffering the effects of a puberty that is altogether as momentous for him as the chance to be in a Broadway show. And each of them got to express her or his feelings or tell her or his tale in a song and/or a dance, a series of numbers which was capped by a soaring hymn to a dancer's life, "What I Did for Love," and by the performance of the number for which they are auditioning, "One."

A *Chorus Line* was first produced — with some of the original group of dancers playing "themselves" and others not — at the same Public Theatre which had launched *Hair* and a remarkable number of other adventurous and/or trendy musicals, and it quickly showed up as a first-class hit. After a swift revamp to its ending to make it more conventionally appealing ("star" dancer Donna McKechnie, playing "herself" as the returnee to the chorus, was switched from being a "loser" to a "winner"), it was whisked up to Broadway, and there it settled in for the remarkable run which would make it a record-breaker. Curiously, however, it did not go on from here to win productions and success world-wide. An efficient but tame London production did only fairly well, and although Australia and several European countries welcomed the show, it created nothing like the impression made by a *Fiddler on the Roof* or a *My Fair Lady*. An opened-out and slickly modernized film version also had a mitigated effect. But *A Chorus Line*'s Broadway history alone has established it as one of the most memorable shows of all time, and as a landmark in musical-theater history.

A CHORUS LINE, a musical by James Kirkwood and Nicholas Dante. Lyrics by Edward Kleban. Music by Marvin Hamlisch. Produced at the Public Theatre, New York, 15 April 1975, and at the Shubert Theatre, 25 July 1975.

Characters: Zach, Larry, Sheila, Val, Cassie, Diana, Judy, Kristine, Maggie, Bebe, Connie, Mike, Don, Richie, Al, Paul, Mark, Greg, Bobby, &c.

Plot: A group of dancers are auditioning on the stage of a Broadway theater. The director thins them down to a final group of seventeen, and then asks each of those remaining to identify and talk about him or herself. The stories and the preoccupations of each of the dancers tumble out. The director holds two back for individual chats: Cassie, his one-time lover who went briefly on to bigger things and whom he finds it hard to see back in the chorus, and Paul, a superb if effeminate dancer whose personal history is too tough to tell in front of the others. The dancers resume their dancing, performing the steps of the number "One." Suddenly Paul falls to the ground with a wrecked carti-lage. He is carried out, his career over, and the others are left to think about what they will do when their dancing days are done. Then the successful dancers are named. It is over. But as a finale to the show the full cast appears in the spangles of showtime performing "One."

Songs: "I Hope I Get It" (ensemble), "I Can Do That" (Mike), "And . . ." (ensemble), "At the Ballet" (Bebe, Sheila, Maggie), "Sing!" (Kristine, Al), "Hello Twelve, Hello Thirteen, Hello Love" (ensemble), "Nothing" (Diana), "Dance: Ten, Looks: Three" (Val), "The Music and the Mirror" (Cassie), "One" (ensemble), Tap Combination, "What I Did for Love" (Diana), reprise "One" (ensemble).

The songs of *A Chorus Line* heralded the entry into the musical theater of the musician Marvin Hamlisch (b 1944), up to this time mostly occupied with writing for film, and Hamlisch was to go on to produce the songs for a second winning musical, of a very different kind, four years later. *They're Playing Our Song* was an up-to-date musical comedy, written by top comedy writer Neil Simon—whose musical-theater track record to date was an impeccable one of three shows and three hits—with songs from Hamlisch and Carôle Bayer Sager. It was said that the libretto was actually an autobiomusical, and that its story of the crazy personal and professional relationship between a popular music composer and his lyricist-cum-lover reflected the life of its songwriters. Whether this was so—or to what extent—Simon's book was certainly a hair-raisingly funny piece of writing. The largest number of songs were actually presented as the output of the two characters, and in consequence they were songs of a different tone from those heard in *A Chorus Line*—brittle, lively pieces of chartable words and music, orchestrated and arranged in the manner of the more adult type of modern popular music. But there were also some numbers that were written to be performed in the context of this up-to-date successor to the "operetta-within-the-operetta" style of piece favored by Novello and other such writers: the pair mused thoughtfully "If He/She Really Knew Me" and bounced around a restaurant dance floor to the show's merry title-song in two of the most effective moments of the evening.

They're Playing Our Song was a first-rate success in both America and Britain, and it found itself an unusually large number of foreign-language productions as well. A good number of these productions were encouraged, of course, by the show's dimensions—the cast comprised just the two huge star rôles and a half-dozen singers who played the stars' alter egos and supplied their backing vocals, and, although the show's original production was a large-stage affair, it proved an ideal musical for smaller theater productions and companies.

THEY'RE PLAYING OUR SONG, a musical in 2 acts by Neil Simon. Lyrics by Carôle Bayer Sager. Music by Marvin Hamlisch. Produced at the Imperial Theatre, New York, 11 February 1979.

Characters: Sonia Walsk, Vernon Gersch, voices of Vernon, voices of Sonia.

Plot: Vernon Gersch hasn't written a hit in a while and is looking for a new lyricist. So he meets with Sonia Walsk. She turns out to be—like him—a New Yorker, Jewish, and hyper-everything, and they even share the same psychiatrist. She also turns out to be maddeningly unpunctual, unreasonable, and into more isms than is decent. It isn't long before they are writing songs together and she moves in. But Sonia has an ex called Leon who takes this change of address badly. He has a borderline-breakdown, and he's inclined to ring up in the middle of the night for chat and counsel. The songwriting goes pretty well, but the relationship—with a bit of help from Leon—goes sour, especially when it seems that Sonia puts Leon before work. So they break up. But while Vernon is in the hospital with a broken leg Sonia comes to visit. She's actually come to see Leon who's upstairs, but she brings a gift for Vernon. Vernon's got to know Leon now, and Leon's got himself sorted out. It's not long before Vernon and Sonia have got sorted out too.

Songs: "Fallin'" (Vernon), "Workin' It Out" (Vernon, Sonia, boys, girls), "If He/She Really Knew Me" (Sonia, Vernon), "They're Playing Our Song" (Vernon, Sonia), "Right" (Sonia, Vernon), "Just for Tonight" (Sonia), "When You're in My Arms" (Sonia, Vernon, boys, girls), "I Still Believe in Love" (Sonia), "Fill in the Words" (Vernon).

They're Playing Our Song didn't find too many fellow hits with which to share the latter years of the 1970s. A very distinct shrinking in the number of productions, the number of new shows, the number of good new shows, and particularly the number of successful and good new shows had been becoming increasingly evident throughout the main theatrical centers of the world—and right now that meant Broadway and London. But there were a baker's half-dozen of winners mounted for the first time between 1976 and 1980, and, in contrast to the early part of the decade, when fine hit shows from unfamiliar names had been the order of the day, most of them were—worryingly, for those looking for the writers who would take over the baton and keep the genre sizzling—credited to more or less proven men, men who had been already the stars of the early seventies, the sixties, or even the fifties. Cy Coleman, Michael Stewart, Betty Comden and Adolph Green, Charles Strouse, and, of course, the latest addition to the ranks of musical-theater royalty, the young team of Rice and Lloyd Webber.

Coleman actually provided the music for no fewer than three fine and successful shows during this half-decade: one small-scale musical comedy, one brilliant burlesque operetta, and one lively "concept" biomusical. The musical comedy was a show based—in the best old tradition—on a piece of French farcical comedy, a little wife-swapping play with the inviting title *Viens chez moi, j'habite chez une copine.* Stewart remade the piece fairly thoroughly—in the best old tradition—pulling out anything that might have resembled actual sex and real infidelity, resetting the little romp in the purlieus of Trenton, New Jersey, rather than the dangerously French country of France, and topped it with the warning title *I Love My Wife.* Coleman decorated the happy, innocent little comedy with a jolly set of songs for the four characters and four on-stage musicians who made up the show's entire personpower, and the show was an endearing little success.

The following season, Coleman teamed with two more of Broadway's most successful and most enduring bookwriters, Comden and Green, on another adaptation. *On the Twentieth*

On the Twentieth Century: "I've got it all . . ." Lily Garland jubilates over her escape from the Svengali-like hold of the now-down-on-his-luck man who created her.

Century was a stage musical version of the 1932 comedy *Twentieth Century*, a piece which had already been transferred with much success to the cinema screen, where it had been played by John Barrymore and Carole Lombard. The "Twentieth Century" in question was nothing Orwellian, it was simply the name of a famous luxury train which linked Chicago and the East Coast of America, and it was on that train (a piece of period coachbuilding which allowed the show's designer some fine opportunities) that the crazy super-theatrical action of the play took place. Both play and film had been fine and funny works, but the musicalizing team managed to top both in effectiveness thanks to the use of an extra dimension, the music—music which heightened and colored the comedy to splendidly extravagant and comic effect. *On the Twentieth Century* was written and composed as a so-glamorous-it's-on-the-edge-of-absurdity piece, a megatheatrical comedy-burlesque, its super-romantic moments heightened by "bouffe" sub-operatic vocals, its comedy lifted by tunes and rhythms which rippled with fun. Coleman had displayed his winning musical sense of humor on the stage many times over since the beautiful burlesqueries of *Little Me*, but in *On the Twentieth Century* he really gave out his best. The piece's klutzy little piano-playing heroine was metamorphosed into a glamorous, dazzling singing star, pinging out stratospheric soprano notes as her Svengali rubbed up her ambitions to play the rôle of the melodramatic French streetsinger "Véronique." He baritoned out his determination—"I Rise Again"—after a scorching theatrical flop and, when all was darkest, gave out with "The Legacy"—a preposterous list of bequests that was a prelude to a phoney death. A contract was proposed to the strains of a driving sextet, a check was drooled over in four-part harmony, and the evening peaked in what is probably the musical theater's most magnificent solo dilemma scene of all time: the star, torn between two rôles, the gut-grinding drama of Mary Magdalene (which she knows she shouldn't take) and Somerset Maugham's witty, brittle "Babette," imagines herself in one play and the other before the two get all mixed up together in her brain and—leaping within a semi-quaver from soprano trills to plunging chest voice—she has to fight her way into the "right" decision.

On the Twentieth Century was a remarkable piece of musical-theater writing, a piece whose qualities—textual and musical—should have earned it an enduring place in the musical-theater repertoire, but although it won the accolades of Broadway's prizegivers, it succeeded in compiling a run of only 460 performances. In London, slightly revised and dazzlingly cast, it lasted just 165. Why? Because it fell into that category of shows that are just a bit too clever for their own good. Burlesque works only if the public can understand what is being burlesqued. References to the latest TV soap opera will bring hoots of recognition and appreciation, but sophisticated burlesque of styles and subjects which are less generally well known will end up winning over only a limited audience. *On the Twentieth Century* followed *Candide* and *Valmouth* and others of the ilk down that path. Whether the names attached to it are or will become fashionable enough to allow it the sort of resurrection that *Candide* achieved remains to be seen.

ON THE TWENTIETH CENTURY a musical in 2 acts by Adolph Green and Betty Comden, based on the play *Twentieth Century* by Charles MacArthur, Ben Hecht, and Bruce Milholland. Music by Cy Coleman. Produced at the St James Theatre, New York, 19 February 1978.

Characters: Mildred Plotka/Lily Garland, Oscar Jaffee, Owen O'Malley, Oliver Webb, Letitia Primrose, Bruce Granit, Conductor Flanagan, Dr Johnson, Imelda Thornton, Max Jacobs, Agnes, Congressman Lockwood, Anita, Maxwell Finch, &c.

Plot: Oscar Jaffee's latest production has bombed pocket-wrenchingly in Chicago, but the producer still has plans. He blackmails his way into a state-room on the train, the Twentieth Century, heading for New York and lays siege to the Hollywood star Lily Garland. She is going to be in his next play and make his fortune. Oscar created Lily. She was a gauche little piano-player called Plotka till he remade her as the star she has become. She was also his lover. But Lily broke free from her Svengali, went to Hollywood and upwards. She did it on her own, and she will never ever go back. Oscar went downwards. But, in the sixteen hours between Chicago and New York, sixteen hours with more hilarious ups and downs than the Empire State Building's elevators, Lily changes her mind. By the time the terminus is reached it is clear that her perfectly molded filmic escort and the sophisticated comedy offered her by a suave and successful producer are both going to be on the end of a resounding "no." Oscar Jaffee has risen again.

Songs: "Stranded Again" (ensemble), "Saddle Up the Horse" (Oscar, Owen), "On the Twentieth Century" (ensemble), "I Rise Again" (Oscar, Owen, Oliver), "Indian Maiden's Lament" (Imelda, Lily), "Véronique" (Lily &c.), "I Have Written a Play" (Conductor), "Together" (Oscar &c.) "Never" (Lily), "Our Private World" (Oscar, Lily), "Repent" (Mrs Primrose), "Mine" (Oscar, Bruce), "I've

Got It All" (Lily, Oscar), "Life Is Like a Train" (porters), "Five Zeroes" (Oliver, Owen, Oscar, Mrs Primrose), "Sign" (Oscar, Owen, Oliver, Lily, Mrs Primrose, Bruce), "She's a Nut" (ensemble), "Babette" (Lily &c.), "The Legacy" (Oscar), reprise "I Have Written a Play" (Dr Johnson), "Lily, Oscar" (Lily, Oscar), reprise "Life Is Like a Train," reprise "On the Twentieth Century."

If Coleman got less than his deserts with a rather too-sophisticated show, he more than made up for that disappointment with one which had all the obvious and wide appeal that *On the Twentieth Century* did not. *Barnum* was a biomusical, a sketchy skip through some of the events (true and just maybe true) of the life of the American showman whose name—with a little help from the cinema and from continuing exposure on the banderôles of "Barnum and Bailey's" way after his death—has become synonymous with the word circus. What made *Barnum* a winner, however, was not its content but its concept. Just as *Cabaret* and *Chicago* had been presented with parts of their tale "framed" in night-club and vaudeville situations, this show was staged in circus terms and in a circus ring. A small group of multi-talented players performed acrobatics, juggling, wire-walking, unicyling, and a whole variety of other circus-related feats—as well as a selection of supporting rôles—as part of the story of how Phineas Taylor Barnum made his way from showing imaginatively publicized freaks up to the very peak of his profession as a showman with Barnum and Bailey's Circus. We got to see Joice Heth, "the oldest woman in the world," whom Barnum proclaimed had been George Washington's nanny, we saw Tom Thumb dancing in front of giant scenery, and we saw the glamorous (well, that's dramatic licence for you!) Swedish soprano Jenny Lind, whom Barnum presented in America and who the authors of the musical would have us believe had an affair with her promoter (her faithless real-life husband, Goldschmidt, was presented in the show, but without being dubbed her husband), but above all we saw something that always has enormous appeal: the delightful versatility of the little group of artists who played "everybody else," singing, dancing, acting, creating scenery, performing all sorts of tricks in a production which stopped spinning colorfully along only to allow the odd, less mobile minute of the story of Barnum's married life to be given stage space.

The songs which Coleman and Michael Stewart supplied to the show were, however, no also-rans. They were a multicolored lot, topped by some of the merriest march music to have been heard on the musical stage in ages in the parade song "Come Follow the Band" and "Join the Circus." The star pattered out the showman's creed "There Is a Sucker Born Ev'ry Minute," dubbed himself "The Prince of Humbug," and galloped helter-skelter through a "Museum Song" describing the contents of the building that was his first big venture before joining his wife in a gentle debate on "The Colors of My Life." The featured characters also each had their musical moment, Tom Thumb asserting that "Bigger Isn't Better" as he whirled about the stage, Joice Heth declaring "Thank God I'm Old" at the sight of modern folks and modern ways, and Jenny Lind soaring out a sweet soprano "Love Makes Such Fools of Us All" in a delightful score in which energy and razzmatazz were to the fore.

Barnum had a fine run on Broadway, but it was in Britain—where the part of Barnum was introduced by Michael Crawford and decorated with a barrage of extra tricks and feats for that athletic actor—that the show scored its biggest success of all, establishing itself for several returns to the West End in the years that followed. By the time it returned, however, *Barnum* had notched itself up an impressive series of productions further afield, a series which turned it into one of the most widely seen Broadway musicals of its era.

BARNUM, a musical in 2 acts by Mark Bramble. Lyrics by Michael Stewart. Music by Cy Coleman. Produced at the St James Theatre, New York, 30 April 1980.

Characters: Phineas Taylor Barnum, Charity (Chairy) Barnum, The Ringmaster/Mr Goldschmidt/James A. Bailey, Joice Heth/Blues Singer, Tom Thumb, Jenny Lind, Amos Scudder, White-Faced Clown, Chester Lyman, Sherwood Stratton, Mrs Stratton, Wilton, Edgar Templeton, Humbert Morrissey, &c.

Plot: In spite of the disapproval of his wife, Phineas Taylor Barnum makes a career in the exhibition business, showing attractions such as "the oldest woman in the world" with a good deal of humbuggery. But his wife pulls up her sleeves and gives practical help when he builds his American Museum. When the Museum burns down, he goes on the road with a new topliner, the midget Tom Thumb, but then his Charity persuades him into trying a classier act—promoting the famous soprano Jenny Lind. The up-marketing process is a huge success, but Barnum gets a bit close to his star and he returns home ready to give into his wife's pleas to try a more legitimate form of business. Having failed as a clockmaker and as a building entrepreneur, he ends up in politics. Then his world falls apart. Charity dies, the politicians double-cross him, and he ends up being persuaded back into the one job he was good at. He joins Mr Bailey in launching Barnum and Bailey's Circus: the Greatest Show on Earth.

Songs: "There Is a Sucker Born Ev'ry Minute" (Barnum), "Thank God I'm Old" (Joice), "The Colors of My Life" (Barnum, Charity), "One Brick at a Time" (Charity &c.), "Museum Song" (Barnum), "I Like Your Style" (Charity, Barnum), "Bigger Isn't Better" (Tom Thumb), "Love Makes Such Fools of Us All" (Jenny), "Out There" (Barnum), "Come Follow the Band" (Barnum &c.), "Black and White" (Blues Singer, Charity, Barnum, &c.), reprise "The Colors of My Life" (Barnum, Charity), "The Prince of Humbug" (Barnum), "Join the Circus" (Bailey, Barnum, &c.), reprise "There Is a Sucker Born Ev'ry Minute" (Barnum).

Broadway's other two most internationally successful musicals of this era also came, at least partly, from practiced hands, and in fact Michael Stewart—teamed again with his *Barnum* collaborator Mark Bramble—scored a second time in the year of 1980. This time, however, it was with a barely original show. The cinema screen had served as a source of inspiration and/or texts and/or songs for the musical stage since before the days when it had learned to speak—as far back as 1919 Otto Harbach had filched the silent screen's *Miss George Washington* as the basis for his libretto *The Little Whopper*—and in recent years a selection of screenplays which had been written specifically for the cinema had been made up into musicals. Rather fewer original screen musicals, however, had been taken holus bolus from the screen and made into stage musicals. When they had, such pieces as Posford and Maschwitz's *Goodnight Vienna*, Rodgers and

Hammerstein's *State Fair*, and Lerner and Loewe's *Gigi* had not worked very well, and it was the 1974 London remake of the Danny Kaye *Hans Christian Andersen* written by and for Tommy Steele which had proved the most successful such experiment to date. But only to date. For Stewart and Bramble's new theatricalization of the classic 1933 film musical *42nd Street* proved to be easily the most effective screen-to-scene show that the world had seen.

The authors tacked together their show (they minimized their contribution, taking a credit for "lead in and crossovers" much as Paul Rubens had so disarmingly credited himself with "jingles and tunes" in earlier years) around the famous chorus-girl-to-instant-star story with maximum theatrical effect, concentrating on providing a series of opportunities for blazingly good-old-daisical dance-and-song routines, dressed up in blazingly glamorous and nostalgia-provoking costumes. Some of these routines and songs were presented in time-honored style as part of the show-within-the-show, the *Pretty Lady* in which Our Heroine is zinged to stardom, others as rehearsals or even auditions (the opening, with the curtain rising inch-by-inch on what looked like a hundred hopefully time-step-tapping feet was one of the most memorable Broadway had seen in a long time), but a handful were also actually eased into the action. All of the songs used, however, were the genuine period article, second-hand numbers culled not only from *42nd Street* but from other films for which *42nd Street* songwriters Al Dubin and Harry Warren had supplied material (the *Golddigger* films, *The Singing Marine*, *Go into Your Dance*, *Hard to Get*), in a nicely judged combination of the hugely familiar, the sort-of-familiar, and the mostly forgotten which stopped the show from turning into the indigestibly over-rich hit parade of numbers which some other pasticcio, compilation, and remade shows have been. "We're in the Money" was done as a large-scale tap-number with huge coins as tap-boxes, "Dames" became a costume parade, "Shuffle Off to Buffalo" a coochy comedy routine, and the title song became a dramatic dance scena—all as scenes from *Pretty Lady*—"About a Quarter to Nine" was used as a singing lesson, while "Lullaby of Broadway" was the number in which Our Heroine was wooed back to the theater and to stardom by the entire company, headed by the grim-voiced producer who was to tell her, in the film's most famous line, that "you're going out there a youngster, but you've got to come back a star."

42nd Street was a first-class Broadway hit through no fewer than 3,486 performances, filled London's Theatre Royal, Drury Lane, for four and a half years, and scored a further hit in Australia before being taken round the Continent in an English-language version, and it undoubtedly prompted the translation from screen to stage of a number of other classic musicals in the years that followed.

42ND STREET, a musical in 2 acts by Michael Stewart and Mark Bramble, based on the screenplay of the same name and the novel by Bradford Ropes. Lyrics by Al Dubin. Music by Harry Warren. Additional lyrics by Johnny Mercer and Mort Dixon. Produced at the Winter Garden Theatre, New York, 25 August 1980.

Characters: Julian Marsh, Dorothy Brock, Billy Lawler, Peggy Sawyer, Bert Barry, Maggie Jones, Pat Denning, Andy Lee, Anytime Annie, Lorraine, Phyllis, Oscar, Abner Dillon, &c.

Plot: Julian Marsh is staking his all on the musical *Pretty Lady*. But he's got his financial backing from kiddie-car magnate Dillon, who's sweet on leading lady Dorothy Brock, so he has to keep an eye on Brock. She's still mooning altogether too much over not-very-ex-boyfriend Pat Denning. When Denning gets too obvious, Marsh gets a friendly gangster to warn him off, but a change of schedule means that he's there in Philadelphia when the show is trying out, and Brock—who thinks he's eyeing chorine Peggy Sawyer—is putting everything at risk with her jealous behavior. Then, on the first tryout night, disaster strikes. A dancer stumbles and pushes Peggy into Brock. The star falls and doesn't get up—her leg is broken and the curtain has to come down. Peggy, of course, is sacked. It seems that the show's Broadway trip will have to be abandoned, but the chorus kids come up with an idea: Peggy Sawyer can play the lead! Marsh goes after the girl, persuades her back to the theater with visions of spotlights and tinsel, puts her to work to learn the lead rôle and, on opening night, she and the show triumph. As for Brock, she's found true happiness too—she's given up the theater and married Pat. So everybody has a happy ending.

Songs: "42nd Street" (audition), "I'm Young and Healthy" (Billy, Peggy), "Shadow Waltz" (Dorothy &c.), "Go into Your Dance" (Maggie, Peggy, Annie, Lorraine, Phyllis, Andy), "You're Getting to Be a Habit with Me" (Dorothy, Billy, Peggy, &c.), "Getting Out of Town" (Pat, Bert, Maggie, Annie, Dorothy, &c.), "Dames" (Billy &c.), "I Know Now" (Dorothy), "We're in the Money" (Billy, Annie, Peggy, Lorraine, Phyllis, &c.), "Sunny Side to Every Situation" (Annie &c.), "Lullaby of Broadway" (Julian), "About a Quarter to Nine" (Dorothy, Peggy), "Shuffle Off to Buffalo" (Bert, Maggie, Annie, &c.), "42nd Street" (Peggy, Billy, &c.), reprise "42nd Street."

Broadway's other hit of the later 1970s went even further than did *42nd Street*—in fact, it went to just about as many countries and languages (not to mention the screen) as any other post-war musical. *Annie* wasn't based on a play or a film or a book—it was based, of all things, on a newspaper comic strip. Perhaps surprisingly, it was far from the first musical so to be. There had been dozens since *Hogan's Alley* and *McFadden's Row of Flats* had walloped around America's less upmarket theaters in the dying days of the nineteenth century, some of which had even turned—like the strips—into series (*Bringing Up Father* was a notable one). In more recent years Broadway had had a visit from Superman and off-Broadway from two lots of "Peanuts," but the most successful attempts at cartoon-to-musical-stage up until the advent of *Annie* had been the British First-World-Wartime piece *The Better 'Ole* and *Li'l Abner*, a musical written around Al Capp's hayseedy Dogpatch inhabitants and produced on Broadway for 693 performances in 1956.

Annie was the story of Little Orphan Annie, Harold Gray's pop-eyed, curly-headed brat who'd made her début in the Chicago Tribune in 1924 and had since invaded hundreds of other journals world-wide. Little Orphan Annie was an institution, and the writers of the musical carefully kept her as what she was—a comic strip and an institution. The show and its little heroine were allowed to invoke one sentiment and one reaction only and that was "ahhhh." The villains were comic strip villains with altogether less real threat about them than Snow White's Wicked Queen, and one was never tempted to consider the implications, for example, to be found in the name of the multi-grillionaire who became the little orphan's deputy dad—the source of Daddy Warbucks's wealth might have been war profiteering, but such a shadow would have sat ill on the face of a show which didn't aspire to any such coloring, or to any more dimensions than those of a comic strip. The songs, too, were made in the same vein—a lot of sentiment, a dose of fun, and plenty of catchy melody as written by Charles Strouse, two decades down the road from *Bye Bye Birdie*. Little Annie bawled out her optimistic vision of what the world will bring "Tomorrow," her wardress hissed out her horror of "Little Girls," the villains dreamed greasily of "Easy Street," a radio group cooed out the maxim that "You're Never Fully Dressed without a Smile," "NYC" got the thumbs up and—in a rare moment of downbeat feeling—poor old President Hoover got the thumbs down, in a set of songs which were a perfect illustration to a tale of simple but rarely saccharine charm.

Annie played 2,377 performances on Broadway and three and a half years in London, and went on to be played in most corners of the English-speaking world, and a good number of those where other languages were spoken, as well as being made—with rather too much hype and rather less success—into a 1982 film, and provoking several attempts at a musequel. It holds its place, a decade and more down the line, as the world champion of cartoon musicals.

ANNIE, a musical in 2 acts by Thomas Meehan, based on the comic strip "Little Orphan Annie" by Harold Gray. Lyrics by Martin Charnin. Music by Charles Strouse. Produced at the Alvin Theatre, New York, 21 April 1977.

Characters: Annie, Miss Hannigan, Daddy Warbucks, Grace Farrell, Mrs Pugh, Rooster Hannigan, Drake, Lily St Regis, Bert Healy, Bonnie Boylan, Connie Boylan, Ronnie Boylan, FDR, the Brains Trust Molly, Pepper, Duffy, Tessie, July, Kate, &c.

Plot: Little Orphan Annie is determined to get out of the orphanage run by the febrile Miss Hannigan and find the parents who left her there so many years ago. She runs away and gets caught, but then succeeds in getting herself chosen as the lucky orphan whom the uncountably rich Daddy Warbucks is conscience-salvingly treating to a rich Christmas. Over the festive season, Annie makes herself so cute that Daddy offers to adopt her for good, but the child insists that her parents are still alive. Daddy gets the might of the nation into gear to carry out a search, and it seems that he has succeeded when a lowly pair turn up to claim Annie and the money Daddy has offered as a reward. Alas, they are only Miss Hannigan's rascally brother and his floosie in disguise. Annie's real parents are really dead, so she will stay and be Daddy Warbucks's little girl after all.

Songs: "Maybe" (Annie, orphans), "It's the Hard-Knock Life" (Annie, orphans), "Tomorrow" (Annie), "We'd Like to Thank You, Herbert Hoover" (chorus), "Little Girls" (Miss Hannigan), "I Think I'm Gonna Like It Here" (Grace, Annie, &c.), "NYC" (Warbucks, Grace, Annie), "Easy Street" (Miss Hannigan, Rooster, Lily), "You Won't Be an Orphan for Long" (Grace &c.), "You're Never Fully Dressed without a Smile" (Bert, Ronnie, Connie, Bonnie), reprise "Tomorrow" (Annie, FDR, Warbucks, the Brains Trust), "Something Was Missing" (Warbucks), "I Don't Need Anything But You" (Warbucks, Annie, Grace, &c.), "Annie" (Grace &c.), "A New Deal for Christmas" (Annie, Warbucks, Grace, FDR, &c.).

In 1977 Broadway got one of those musicals that come right out of left field, a one-off piece from non-Broadway-establishment folk and an unlikely venue, in an unlikely tone and style, which conquered by virtue not just of its novelty but also by its freshness and its quality. *The Best Little Whorehouse in Texas* was a country music musical. Once again, it was not the first— *Shenandoah* had been at least a semi-example of recent seasons—but without any doubt at all it was the most successful. The show began its life at the Actors' Studio, progressed to off-Broadway and ultimately to Broadway, and if it got a little bigger on the way, it never lost its originality and spontaneity during that climb to bigger and more lucrative venues.

During the history of the musical theater many, many a troupe of whores—with or without a madame and of all nationalities—had trouped their way across the stage, women usually presented as overpainted, overdressed, overloud, and invariably golden-hearted, and often pasted in to a story simply in order to allow some loud and lively song and dance. These two-dimensional, corny creatures had ended by becoming a really dreary musical-theater cliché. The inhabitants of *The Best Little Whorehouse in Texas*, however, were nothing like this. They were just modern working girls, with a working girl's personal and professional problems. Their main problem, in this piece, came from a posturing and poisonous media "personality" who is trying to close them down. The authors turned out a based-on-fact story full of warmly believable characters—the friendly, risen-from-the-ranks woman who runs the house with due care for the welfare of both her girls and her customers, the small-town sheriff who is just a touch more than her friend, the little waitress with a quickly suppressed yen to let herself go just for a moment, the farmgirl with a determination to be a good, working whore, and the single mother who turns from a dark-glasses, peroxide-blonde vamping on city corners to purveying the girl-next-door image in the easygoing country whorehouse—all of whose lives get messed up by the maniacal "investigative journalist" in the face of whose mediatic power even the soft-shoe-shuffling Governor of the state cannot stand up. It was a pointed and pleasing tale, but what made it more than just a pretty story was the dialogue that authors Peter Masterson and Larry L. King gave to their characters, and in particular to their leading man: the sheriff. Perhaps people really talk that way in Texas, but to folk outside that state the technicolored oaths and scatological similes that punctuated the show's speeches were an eye-opener and a rib-wrencher. Audiences were left with aching diaphragms after just an actful of some of the most hilarious below-the-navel humor in history.

Carol Hall's songs didn't go for that kind of humor. Mostly they were friendly pieces which either loped along in the most relaxing of country styles—the amiable description of the whorehouse in "Twenty Fans" and "A Li'l Ole Bitty Pissant Country Place," the motherly advice to a new professional "Girl, You're a Woman," or the memories of the "Bus from Amarillo"—or, when things got hotter, took on more driving rhythms, as in the accusatory "Texas Has a Whorehouse in It" or the Aggie Song, in which a bunch of young footballers let rip in merrily masculine dance.

The show was a splendid Broadway success through 1,584 performances, but—perhaps because of its very special flavor—it failed utterly to export. A British production, for some crazy reason mounted in the vastness of the Theatre Royal, Drury Lane, didn't catch on, and even Australia—where country music traditionally gets a good hearing—didn't respond. A film version, which messed the piece around, failed, and an attempt to write a musequel went the same way as the attempted follow-ups to *Bye Bye Birdie* and *Annie*. But the original show and its original production were one of the happiest highlights of the latter 1970s in a musical theater where international successes were rare, and hometown ones not that much more numerous.

THE BEST LITTLE WHOREHOUSE IN TEXAS, a musical in 2 acts by Larry L. King and Peter Masterson. Music and lyrics by Carol Hall. Produced at the Actors' Studio, New York, 20 October 1977, at the Entermedia Theatre 17 April 1978, and at the 46th Street Theatre 19 June 1978.

Characters: Mona Stangley, Sheriff Ed Earl Dodd, Melvin P. Thorpe, The Governor, Doatsey Mae, Edsel Mackay, Mayor Rufus Poindexter, C. J. Scruggs, Senator Wingwoah, Jewel, Angel, Shy, &c.

Plot: The Chicken Ranch (so called because in the old days the management accepted payment in kind) has functioned for years as a friendly neighborhood brothel, and under Miss Mona its best traditions continue. But a TV person called Melvin Thorpe sees in the Chicken Ranch a chance to spice up his show, and he turns his God-given powers and the cameras of KTEX-TV on the best little whorehouse in the state. Miss Mona's pal, the Sheriff, tries to whang him out of town, but Thorpe persists and drags the state Governor in to help him win his battle. The local functionaries can't cope with so much floodlight on them, Sheriff Ed Earl is out of his small-town league, and mighty little Melvin wins his glorious victory. The Chicken Ranch closes, the girls go off to find jobs in other, maybe less salubrious places, and Miss Mona says goodbye to Ed Earl—who was, after all, just a friend—and heads on to the next part of her life.

Songs: Prologue, "Twenty Fans" (ensemble), "A Li'l Ole Bitty Pissant Country Place" (Mona), "Girl, You're a Woman" (Mona), Watch Dog Theme, "Texas Has a Whorehouse in It" (Thorpe &c.), "Twenty-Four Hours of Lovin'" (Jewel), "Doatsey Mae" (Doatsey Mae), Angelette March, "The Aggie Song" (Aggies), "The Sidestep" (Governor), "No Lies" (Mona), "Good Old Girl" (Ed Earl), "Hard Candy Christmas" (girls), "Bus from Amarillo" (Mona).

There was one other hit musical produced in the late 1970s, however—the musical that was to be indubitably the biggest and most international hit of its era, and it was the new show from the creators of *Jesus Christ Superstar*. It was seven years between the initial production of *Superstar* and the arrival on the stage of the second musical from the team of Rice and Lloyd Webber, but those seven years had seen the gradual permeation of their first show through the world's theaters, the first attempts to make a professionally sized musical out of the little *Joseph and the Amazing Technicolor Dreamcoat*, and the preparation of the second musical in question. For, if *Jesus Christ Superstar* had started life as a gramophone recording only through the accident of its not originally having found a stage producer, *Evita*—a biomusical on the Argentinean dictator's wife Eva Peron—started its life as a gramophone recording on purpose. And why not? The system had worked well with the first show, and the fact of having the public come to a show happily knowing or recognizing the tunes they were about to hear had been a plus which was thoroughly in line with musical and theatrical tradition. This very curious humano-musical phenomenon—the preference for hearing a known tune or song rather than something new and unfamiliar—which had been at the root of the pasticcio tradition and of one aspect of the interpolation habit in the old days, had encouraged song-plugging to vast peaks in later years, and in more recent times has been the moving force behind the sorry spate of scissors-and-glue compilation shows which have displaced original shows from the world's stages. It had now found a fresh outlet, and, since *Superstar*, "concept recordings" of unstaged—and often unstageable—musicals had begun to appear.

When the double-disc recording of the complete score of the sung-through *Evita* came out in 1976, there were more than a few folk willing to commit themselves to saying that this one was unstageable. But not because, like so many of the others, it was bad. Quite the contrary. It was stunning. And stunningly popular. In February 1977, the monologue "Don't Cry for Me, Argentina" actually made its way to the very top of the British hit parades, a place which hadn't been inhabited by a show-song in eons, and never by an unproduced show-song, and a second item from the recording, the little ballad of dispossession "Another Suitcase in Another Hall," made it to number 18. But the series of scenes from the life of Mrs Peron seemed to present all kinds of staging problems. It is history now that those problems were solved, without very much in the way of rearrangement being practiced on the material heard on the record, and *Evita*, as staged by Hal Prince (director) and Larry Fuller (choreography) turned out a triumph.

The show's libretto followed the career of Eva Peron, née Duarte, from her native small-town Argentina, via a liaison with a tango singer which got her up to the capital, to her meeting with and appropriation of the military man Juan Peron, then on to greater things, and ultimately to a tragic death at the peak of what she apparently regarded as her achievement. That "achievement"—even if it earned the adoration of millions of the ordinary people who saw her as the "Santa Evita" who would steal from the rich and give to the poor—was shown here as really little more than a selfish revenge on the rich and social Argentineans who had never willingly allowed her, even as Mrs President, to rise into their closed-to-the-commoner circles. If Eva was subtly shown in a less than heroic light, however, the early death which allowed her to become an icon in the James Dean–Marilyn Monroe class also allowed her story to become a fine piece of personal tragedy, ready-made for that musical stage which the other pair would also inhabit, though with very much less success. The libretto used only five principal characters. There were Eva and Peron, and the ex-lovers of each—her tango-singer and his barely pubescent schoolgirl—plus a fifth character called Che. In spite of sporting the name of the terrorist who became a wallposter for one of the flakier generations of pre-adults, and in spite of the fact that when it came to the stage the actor who played the rôle was dolled up in jungle-warfare trappings, the character was not an attempt to represent the personality and politics of

Evita: Elaine Paige is Evita.

the man who called himself Che Guevara. It was, rather, simply an amalgam of anti-Evita feelings, taken from all sides and from all colors of opinion, and Che's function in the show was one of a jeering, leering critic, always negative, never with anything constructive to do or say, and—given what actually happened—ultimately impotent. Eva Peron is always going to defeat this power-less creature. Like all the best heroes, this woman is bested only by death. But what would have happened had she lived longer? What would have happened if she had toppled from her funambulistic perch? Or if Monroe had got old and blowsy or Dean become fat and bourgeois? Well, they wouldn't have had musicals written about them, to start with.

The score of *Evita* took its writers one step further on from *Joseph* and *Superstar*. Here, for the first time, the pair were dealing not with figures of biblical antiquity but with almost modern folk involved in a very different kind of drama. And here, again, for the first time, Lloyd Webber was composing a leading rôle for a female voice of the "rock-opera" fach. In *Superstar* only the men had ventured into this idiom, while the women stayed in a more traditional musical vein—now, for the first time, was introduced a rock-opera leading lady with vocal lines written to match those of the men. But not quite. The men's music in *Superstar* had made use of the full range of the male voice—the rock tenors scaling the tenor heights, the priests sailing up and down to the extremes available to the different kinds of male voices—but *Evita* did not do that. The music for the star rôle concentrated solely on one register of the female voice, the chest register—that area which had been featured in the coon-shouting of olden days, and the work of the Broadway belt artist in more recent years—to the complete exclusion of the head voice. The top octave of the female range was wholly ignored. This exclusion, however, this writing of the entire vocal part of the show's leading lady in chest voice, allowed for some fine dramatic effects. To sing an E natural or, Lord forbid, an F in chest voice, something which few coon-shouters or belters could do, is indeed beyond the range of most vocalists. Even many a fine jazz singer is obliged to move into the "soprano" tones of the head voice before F is reached, at the risk of rupturing her epiglottis. So the excitement in hearing a dramatic "rock-operatic" chest voice soaring into these demanding and difficult areas was every bit as frisson-making as hearing an operatic soprano spiralling into the F in alt, an octave higher. And the music of *Evita* frequently made those demands on its star.

The other rôles were less musically dramatic. The rôle of Che was written for a less raging rock-tenor of the Jesus/Judas kind, the little mistress was given the same kind of country tones that Mary Magdalene had used, the tango-singer was a parody of an old-fashioned vocalist, and Peron—whose singing was limited—was a rôle for an actor-who-sings staunchly. The odds in the uneven musical battle of the night were all on one side.

Filling this newly minted kind of rôle—the prima-donna-rockopera—for the first time was naturally going to be difficult. For the recording, the writers had used an actress-cum-pop-vocalist, and if her acting of the rôle, and her gritty performance of its music, had helped her big monologue to hitdom, it was nevertheless evident that for the theater something else was necessary. The search for the star who would play Evita became a veritable newspaper soap opera which almost rebounded on itself, particularly when it was announced that the rôle had gone to one of the supporting players from *Billy*, who was far from being a star. Before the show opened, anyway. Afterwards, there was no question about it. Prima-donna-rockopera was born, and Elaine Paige, who could claim to being the first of the species, has remained one of its outstanding examples for two decades. Ex-*Godspell* player turned pop star David Essex helped, as Che, to boost the marquee value and the tenorish music of "Oh! What a Circus" to number three on the post-opening hit-parades, but if *Superstar* had been the men's musical, this one was indubitably the lady's—rocketing up to the chesty heights as she declared herself "Rainbow High" or powering out the bewildering election address "Don't Cry for Me, Argentina."

Evita was an instant hit, but it aroused some amazing tantrums in the papers over its subject matter. For years, a certain color of the press had worked at giving the world an image of Mrs Peron that was blacker than black, and now that image was being threatened by, of all things, a musical. Committed journalists howled with a sometimes risible fury at this threat to their perceptions and power, but they howled to little effect. The public flocked to *Evita*, and it was quickly established as as big a hit as *Superstar* (2,900 performances). The howling was repeated in America, where the director hedged his bets by wicked-witching up the performance of his leading lady for the early part of the run, and once again to no effect. *Evita* proved, again, a first class hit (1,568 performances). The show went on to be performed all over the world, with producers unearthing new examples of the prima-donna-rockopera for the occasion from Brazil to Mexico to Australia to Hungary and even to South Africa. South Africa had banned *Superstar*, but it saw no reason to ban this one. Argentina, on the other hand, perhaps understandably, did. Oh well, it had happened—and, on that occasion, certainly with justification—all those years ago to *The King and I* in Thailand.

EVITA, a musical in 2 acts by Tim Rice. Music by Andrew Lloyd Webber. Produced at the Prince Edward Theatre, London, 21 June 1978.

Characters: Eva, Peron, Magaldi, Che, Mistress, &c.

Plot: Teenaged Eva Duarte gets out of her smalltown Argentinean existence between the sheets of a touring tango singer. Once he has got her to Buenos Aires she dumps him, and sets her sights on a more prominent and powerful man, the soldier-politician Peron. Evicting Peron's juvenile mistress, she moves into his life and his bed, and soon she is urging her lover towards taking supreme power in the Argentine. She is still only in her twenties when he becomes President, but the new first lady of the country has made herself a high profile with her campaigning and her enthusiastic promises of robbed-from-the-rich windfalls for the people. She is sanctified as the people's darling as she promotes the cockeyed kind of democracy in which she seems to believe, forcing the old aristocracy who have always disdained her to donate large sums to a foundation which is supposed to help the poor. Carried away on her own myth, she tries and fails to conquer Europe, but—in spite of the jeers and jealousies of those she has dispossessed—she is still solid at home. Until she is struck down by cancer. "She did nothing for years" is the epitaph the narrator gives her. It wasn't that she did nothing—but what did she achieve apart from a flaming and glamorous personal career that ended before her dreams and acts were seen to be hollow?

Songs: A Cinema in Buenos Aires July 26, 1952, "Requiem for Evita" (Eva, Che, &c.), "Oh! What a Circus" (Che, Eva &c.), "On This Night of a Thousand Stars" (Magaldi), Eva and Magaldi (Eva, Magaldi), "Eva Beware of the City" (Magaldi), "Buenos Aires" (Eva), "Goodnight and Thank You" (Eva, Che, &c.), "The Art of the Possible" (Peron, politicians), Charity Concert, "I'd Be Surprisingly Good for You" (Eva, Peron), "Another Suitcase in Another Hall" (Mistress), "Peron's Latest Flame" (chorus), "A New Argentina" (Che, Eva, Peron, &c.), On the Balcony of the Casa Rosada (Peron &c.), "Don't Cry for Me, Argentina" (Eva), "High Flying, Adored" (Che, Eva), "Rainbow High" (Eva &c.), Rainbow Tour (Che, Eva, Peron, &c.), "The Actress Hasn't Learned the Lines You'd Like to Hear" (Eva, Che), "And the Money Kept Rolling In" (Che), "Santa Evita" (chorus), Waltz for Eva and Che (Eva, Che), "She Is a Diamond" (Peron &c.), "Dice Are Rolling" (Peron, Eva), Eva's Final Broadcast (Eva), Montage, Lament (Eva, Che, &c.).

SOME NOTABLE MUSICALS 1970–1980

1970 PURLIE (Gary Geld/Peter Udell/Peter Rose, Ossie Davis) Broadway Theatre, New York, 15 March

APPLAUSE (Charles Strouse/Lee Adams/Adolph Green, Betty Comden) Palace Theatre, New York, 30 March

COMPANY (Stephen Sondheim/George Furth) Alvin Theatre, New York, 26 April

1971 FOLLIES (Stephen Sondheim/James Goldman) Winter Garden Theatre, New York, 4 April

GODSPELL (Stephen Schwartz/John Michael Tebelak) Cherry Lane Theatre, New York, 17 May

JESUS CHRIST SUPERSTAR (Andrew Lloyd Webber/Tim Rice) Mark Hellinger Theatre, New York, 12 October

1972 GREASE (Jim Jacobs, Warren Casey) Eden Theatre, New York 14 February

PIPPIN (Stephen Schwartz/ Roger O. Hirson) Imperial Theatre, New York, 23 October

1973 A LITTLE NIGHT MUSIC (Stephen Sondheim/Hugh Wheeler) Shubert Theatre, New York, 25 February

THE ROCKY HORROR SHOW (Richard O'Brien) Theatre Upstairs, Royal Court Theatre, London, 19 June

1974 BILLY (John Barry/Don Black/Ian Le Fresnais, Dick Clement) Theatre Royal, Drury Lane, London, 1 May

HANS ANDERSEN (Frank Loesser/Beverley Cross, Tommy Steele) London Palladium, London, 17 December

1975 THE WIZ (Charlie Smalls/William F. Brown) Majestic Theatre, New York, 5 January

SHENANDOAH (Gary Geld/Peter Udell/Peter Rose, James Lee Barrett) Alvin Theatre, New York, 7 January

A CHORUS LINE (Marvin Hamlisch/Edward Kleban/James Kirkwood, Nicholas Dante) Public (Newman) Theatre, New York, 15 April

CHICAGO (John Kander/Fred Ebb/Bob Fosse) 46th Street Theatre, New York, 3 June

1976 ANNIE (Charles Strouse/Martin Charnin/Thomas Meehan) Alvin Theatre, New York, 21 April

1977 I LOVE MY WIFE (Cy Coleman/Michael Stewart) Ethel Barrymore Theatre, New York, 17 April

1978 ON THE TWENTIETH CENTURY (Cy Coleman/Adolph Green, Betty Comden) St James Theatre, New York, 19 February

THE BEST LITTLE WHOREHOUSE IN TEXAS (Carol Hall/Peter Masterson, Larry L. King) Entermedia Theatre, New York, 17 April

EVITA (Andrew Lloyd Webber/Tim Rice) Prince Edward Theatre, London, 21 June

1979 THEY'RE PLAYING OUR SONG (Marvin Hamlisch/Carol Bayer Sager/Neil Simon) Imperial Theatre, New York, 11 February

SWEENEY TODD (Stephen Sondheim/Hugh Wheeler) Uris Theatre, New York, 1 March

1980 BARNUM (Cy Coleman/Michael Stewart/Mark Bramble) St James Theatre, New York, 30 April

42ND STREET (Harry Warren/Al Dubin pasticcio/Michael Stewart, Mark Bramble) Winter Garden Theatre, New York, 25 August

12 MODERN
TIMES

The huge and international success of *Evita*—coming, as it did, after the equally important effect made by *Jesus Christ Superstar*—marked Rice and Lloyd Webber out as the new men of the musical-theater 1970s who were the most likely to carry on succeeding. And they did. But not together. *Evita* was to be the last musical on which the two writers would team for many, many years, and their careers thereafter continued at different paces. Rice turned out the texts for two musicals in the 1980s, but Lloyd Webber composed the scores for five, and among those five were two of the biggest musical-theater hits of all time.

The first of the two was brought out in 1981, and it seemed at the time as unlikely a candidate for theatrical honors as there had ever been. *Cats* didn't have a librettist, for it didn't really need one—the words of the show were, quite simply, prefabricated, being culled directly (or as good as directly) from a series of cat poems which made up the more frivolous section of the opus of the respected poet and playwright T. S. Eliot (deceased). Originally, Lloyd Webber had set a handful of these whimsical little verses about curiously characterful cats just as isolated songs, and it was only subsequently that the idea of making them into a stage show was mooted. But as what? As a song cycle? A television program? As half of an evening's theatrical entertainment paired with something else, as the first professional productions of *Joseph* had been? With a choreographed version of the "Variations on a Theme of Paganini" which the composer had written for his 'cello-playing brother, perhaps? Eventually it was decided that *Cats* would be a full-length show. More bits of feline Eliot were put to music, and the cat-characters of the poems and their stories were strung onto a tiny bit of plotline in what was no less than the latest in the decidedly successful line of "party" musicals. The cat-characters of Eliot's *Old Possum's Book of Practical Cats* were seen gamboling all over a giant rubbish dump as they got themselves ready for their and Eliot's very own feline party, that Jellicle Ball which would bring the evening to its climax and the smidgin of story that it possessed into the show. But such story as there was was not the point or the attraction of the entertainment—it was the merry rogue's gallery of feline creatures and their songs and dances that were the raison d'être of the evening. Particularly their dances, for *Cats* had the unusual feature of being not only a sung-through show, but also a danced-through one. The rôle of each of its many personalities, with the exceptions only of the venerable paterfamilias of the rubbish dump, Old Deuteronomy, and—eventually—of the bedraggled glamour cat, Grizabella, who was to become the evening's singing heroine, was cast with a skilled dancer, and from the moment the animals made their first appearance, slinking around the auditorium in the dark, eyes aglow, while the overture played, their movement was choreographed.

Cats and its novel staging owed a good deal to the kind of chance that so often provokes novelty. Producer Cameron Mackintosh secured as a venue for the show the unloved New London Theatre, a building designed by the theater designer and architect Sean Kenny in the 1970s to be "the theater of the future." By the 1980s the house—which had barely seen a successful show in its seven years of existence—seemed to have no future at all. *Cats*, of course, would change all that. But the features that Kenny had included in his auditorium became an integral part of the original mounting of the musical that would save it: the three-quarters round auditorium, the floor-level stage with the revolving center, the connected levels that would become the show's cat-walks. Director Trevor Nunn and choreographer Gillian Lynne utilized each of these elements of the New London Theatre's interior in creating the entertainment.

The songs of *Cats* were, naturally, composed in a distinctly different tone from those of *Evita* and of *Jesus Christ Superstar*. There was nothing of the real-life drama of those two emotional life-stories to be found in the jolly cavortings of a bunch of pretty pussies. Lloyd Webber happily indulged his propensity for amiably gentle musical parody as each cat was given a tune and a style with just enough familiarity about it to help point up his parallel with a certain kind of human being. The Rum Tum Tugger—a sleek pop puss—went as Presleyish as the Pharoah of *Joseph* in his song, two little kitten-burglars bounced around the stage to the strains of a jaunty "Mungojerrie and Rumpleteazer," the plumply shiny and bespatted cat of the London gentleman's club bobbed jauntily if distinctly weightily along as "Bustopher Jones," a couple of girlcats belted out their bewareness of the dread "Macavity," and the highlight of the evening came when good old Gus, the Theatre Cat, launched into a description of that splendid piece of melodrama-to-music known as "Growltiger's Last Stand," himself playing the rôle of the piratical Growltiger to his companion's portrayal of the fluffy, white Lady Griddlebone in the story of a heroic cat unfairly taken prisoner by the filthy foreigners while he was making reasonably noisy love. There were some more imposing moments for the imposing Old Deuteronomy, but the musical moment which proved to be the takeaway hit of the show was a number written for the one more or less serious character in this gaggle of creatures, the shabby, disliked Grizabella. Alone and nostalgic, she looks back—in a number of which the flavor was altogether apart from the jolly pieces purveyed by her more lively companions—on the days when she was beautiful and sings of her "Memory." The difference in flavor was easily accounted for—this song, unlike the others, was not kosher Eliot. Its lyric was constructed by director Nunn from fragments and impressions of the poet's published and unpublished work to the outline of an existing tune. As performed by Elaine Paige, the creator of Grizabella, it became a top-ten hit soon after the show's opening.

Cats: The mighty Growltiger woos his fluffy love, the Lady Griddlebone, with the wowsing story of Billy Molloy, unaware that the beastly un-British foreigners are about to attack a man when he is in the middle of making love.

Cats became an extraordinary success, settling in at its no-longer unloved and unfamiliar home for what—at the time of writing—has been a record-breaking and still continuing run of some fifteen years. Following on the success of *A Chorus Line*, it confirmed the appeal both of the "party" kind of musical, in which its audiences (which seemed to be becoming more passive with the years) had no need to concentrate on the vagaries of a plot, and of the dance-based musical, and also of the "novelty" show—the kind of piece based on an idea, a mode of presentation, rather than on a linear script in the traditional musical-play vein. It was a trend that was to have its confirmation thoroughly in the years that followed as *Cats* went on to follow up its London triumph with an equivalent success on Broadway, and in multiple productions all around the world.

Those productions also put a seal on another trend which had been becoming more and more the norm in recent years, especially under the influence of more and more complex stagings and "creative" royalty arrangements (i.e., financial reward on a box-office percentage basis for director, choreographer, and—it now seemed—everyone down to the third assistant hairdresser, on every reproduction of their work in any country or restaging of a show). That trend was the breath-for-breath reproduction of a show's initial mounting in subsequent productions in other countries. For many years, London productions of successful Broadway shows had been given something of this treatment—often a dance captain was sent from America to reproduce, as near as was practical, the staging and/or steps of the original version. Now, an overseas producer no longer bought the rights to stage a show and then produce it as he wished: precise copies had become the rule, precise copies firmly controlled by the original producer and creative team. *Cats*, however, proved something of a problem in this respect: without tearing the insides out of a lot of conventional theaters, the show could not be mounted in the same version that had been shown at the New London. At first, it seemed that this might constrict the life of what was clearly a considerable hit, but eventually an alternative version, adapted for performance in a normal proscenium theater (and equally firmly controlled thereafter), was staged by the original creators, and—although a little of the show's original appeal was lost in this adaptation—*Cats* went on to the career which has probably made it, in real terms and as of this moment, the most successful musical in the history of the genre.

CATS, a musical in 2 acts, based on T. S. Eliot's *Old Possum's Book of Practical Cats.* Music by Andrew Lloyd Webber. Produced at the New London Theatre, London, 11 May 1981.

Characters: Asparagus [Growltiger], Bombalurina, Bustopher Jones, Demeter, Deuteronomy, Grizabella, Jellylorum [Griddlebone], Jennyanydots, Jemima, Macavity, Munkustrap, Mungojerrie, Mr Mistoffolees, Rumpleteazer, Rumpus Cat, Rum Tum Tugger, Skimbleshanks, Victoria, &c.

Plot: A cavalcade of cats disport themselves on a great rubbish heap: there's the Gumbie cat who teaches cockroaches self-improvement, the macho Rum Tum Tugger, the boiled-fronted Bustopher Jones, Old Deuteronomy, the grand master of the group, and Munkustrap, who relates the doggy story of "The Awefull Battle Between the Pekes and the Pollicles," which was, of course, resolved by a Cat. Only one cat stays at a distance: the torn and tawdry Grizabella, an overused outcast. We hear the grand theatrical story of "Growltiger's Last Stand," and see the cats make up a train from chunks of rubbish to illustrate a song about "Skimbleshanks the Railway Cat," we meet magical Mr Mistoffolees and don't quite meet Macavity the mystery cat, and finally—since tonight is the night of the Jellicle Ball—one cat is chosen to ascend to the Heaviside layer and there be given another chance, a kind of tenth life. It is Grizabella who is chosen and who gets apotheosized as everyone else brings the ball and the dancing to its close.

Songs: "Jellicle Songs for Jellicle Cats," "The Naming of Cats," "The Invitation to the Jellicle Ball" (Victoria, Mistoffolees), "The Old Gumbie Cat" (Jennyanydots, Cassandra, Jellylorum, Bombalurina), "The Rum Tum Tugger" (Rum Tum Tugger), "Grizabella the Glamour Cat" (Grizabella, Demeter, Bombalurina), "Bustopher Jones" (Bustopher Jones, Jennyanydots, Jellylorum, Bombalurina), "Mungojerrie and Rumpleteazer" (Mungojerrie, Rumpleteazer), "Old Deuteronomy" (Deuteronomy, Munkustrap, Rum Tum Tugger), "The Awefull Battle of the Pekes and the Pollicles" (Munkustrap), The Marching Song of the Pollicle Dogs, "The Jellicle Ball," "Grizabella" (Grizabella), "The Moments of Happiness" (Deuteronomy, Tantomile), "Gus: The Theatre Cat" (Gus, Jellylorum), "Growltiger's Last Stand"/"The Ballad of Billy McCaw" (Gus, Jellylorum), "Skimbleshanks, the Railway Cat" (Skimbleshanks), "Macavity" (Demeter, Bombalurina), "Mr Mistoffolees," "Memory" (Grizabella), "The Journey to the Heaviside Layer," "The Ad-dressing of Cats" (Deuteronomy). Alternative numbers included: "In questa tepida notte" (Gus, Jellylorum), "Mungojerrie and Rumpleteazer" (different version).

The year after the production of *Cats* saw the production of another musical with a score by Andrew Lloyd Webber. If this seemed rather a quick turnover, especially given the considerable gaps between the composer's new works in earlier years, this was easily explicable: the entertainment in question was, in fact, not wholly new. The idea of a two-part show which had been originally mooted when a home was being sought for the *Cats* songs did actually come to fruition, and the show in question did indeed use the 'cello "Variations" as one of its two halves. Reorchestrated for a full-sized theater orchestra in which four 'cellos were prominently featured, it served as the score for a variegated dance performance, choreographed by modern dance creator Anthony van Laast and giving vigorously exhibitionist opportunities to a small group of skilled, specialist performers. Although the dancers got the chance to create something of a character in their various routines, and some of the routines had a tiny breath of storyline to them, the piece was essentially pictorial and danceworthy and not in any way linear.

The other part of the program, the part which took the spot which might have been that of the *Cats* songs, was another song cycle—and one that was entirely different in character from anything that might have been made out of the Eliot poems. *Tell Me on a Sunday*, which had been produced, recorded, and televised and seen its title-song make it to number 3 in the pop charts two years before, was a modern piece, set in contemporary America and presenting a thoroughly worked-out young woman of today as its performer and its central character. You followed this rather foolish—but likable rather than irritating—English girl through her description, in a linear series of songs, of her attempts to get herself settled into a life and a love affair in far-off America. She doesn't make it. Each and every man she commits to finds a way out before long. But she doesn't run home and, even though she's distinctly middle-aging when we leave her at the end of the evening, you know that she's going to keep on trying. Good girl. The songs, written to words by well-established popular songwriter Don Black (b 1936) (whose top show credit to date had been on *Billy*), were a splendidly real lot. After and alongside the merry whimsies of *Cats*, the "real" contemporary numbers written to be performed by a real contemporary character presented a fine contrast. The singer determined that her present love would be "The Last Man in My Life" and promised "Nothing Like You've Ever Known," and as each romance went down the gurgler she reiterated, "It's Not the End of the World," as she went optimistically on to the next, and wrote home to tell Mum all about it. The title-song was a warmly sad little number in which the singer, knowing that the end of an affair is nigh, tries to pick the how and the when of its ending. The cycle was staged on a mobile island, with vivid back projections of urban America behind and the orchestra filling the rest of the stage, and the result was extremely effective.

The combination of the song cycle and the dance entertainment was, not unreasonably, called *Song and Dance*. Originally intended just for a limited season staging at London's Palace Theatre, it took off with an unexpected vigor and, as a result, ended up not only playing for two years in the West End but touring, being retelevised, revived twice, and seen—often in locally realigned versions—all round the world. Sometimes the remaking worked well, but the questionable and questioned wisdom of the breath-for-breath reproduction system was proven when the show was done over for Broadway: rechoreographed and with the character of the singer broadened and coarsened, it had little of the same appeal and did not succeed in the same way.

Cats had been a "party" musical with the tiniest bit of plot; *Song and Dance* had been not inaccurately called "a concert for the theater." Both had been entertainments rather than musical plays and both had been extremely successful on any terms. Therefore it was not surprising that Lloyd Webber's next work for the musical theater—a collaboration with the same director and designer with whom he had worked on *Cats*—was a piece built on similarly story-light lines, with the visuals, the ideas, the characters, and the music getting preference over any attempt at coherent playwriting in the once traditional manner of the musical stage. The characters of *Starlight Express* were another bunch of anthropomorphologs. After the whirling parade of dancing-singing cats of the earlier show, we were now given a squadron of dancing-singing trains. Since—give or take Auden's memorable bit of chuffery "The Night Mail"—none of the more readable poets of recent centuries had been inspired into locomotive verse, this piece did need a librettist, and telly-poet Richard Stilgoe, who had been livening the airwaves with his cheerful and reasonably impromptu topical doggerel, was the man chosen. The train-characters didn't come out as attractively or endearingly as their feline counterparts, but they were in any case slightly hampered by the unfortunately uncredible Good-Little-Engine tale to which they were tacked. Sweet-Little-Steam-Engine (black), with the support of gospel-singing-Poppa and his cohorts and belief in the big Starlight-Express in the sky, beats all the nasty modern engines—diesel and electric (white)—and wins a speed challenge race, and a pretty frilly little carriage (white) to boot. Go on, tell me another.

However, the story—as in *Cats*—wasn't what *Starlight Express* was all about. This was a train show, and trains the audiences were given. The entire cast of the show, fantastically dressed in what looked like futuristic motor cycle gear (with much padding in case of accidents), was put onto roller skates, and the highlight of the evening was the series of skated train-races which swooped from the stage up to a track running below the rim of the dress circle, over a hydraulic bridge above the stage and back down to stage level. The races were set with some driving, but carefully measured, music in the modern pop vein, raising the temperature of what (when you looked closely) were fairly peculiar races to high excitement point.

In fact, Lloyd Webber purposely went for a modern kiddie-pop sound in the score of this kiddie-aligned show, but although a number of the songs were written and orchestrated in this vein, those that came out most successfully were those where, yet again, the composer indulged in a bit of friendly parody: little Miss Carriage bewailing in Tammy Wynettish tones that she's been "U.N.C.O.U.P.L.E.D" from her faithless engine, or a couple of beat-up bits of rolling stock admitting to "One Rock and Roll Too Many." The poppy music, however, served finely as music to dance to. The trains were rather handicapped in comparison with the cats by having to do their dancing on wheels, but the sometimes athletic routines that they presented nevertheless kept the proceedings decidedly lively. Curiously, given its tone of music, the score of *Starlight Express* didn't produce a hit-parade song—the first full-sized Lloyd Webber musical not to do so—but that in no way hampered it in its ride to success.

The show was actually given some revisions during its early life—the uncredible plot was explained away as being the work of a child playing with his train set, the good-little-old-fashioned-black versus nasty-modern-skilled-whites bit was eased out by less racially angled casting and, as the show progressed, a whole series of sometimes considerable alterations were made. And there was plenty of time for them to happen, for although *Starlight Express* had only a limited life when it was produced on Broadway, its London production and another megaproduction staged in Bochum, Germany, both proved to be hugely enduring. London's *Starlight Express*, in fact, lasted so long (it is, at the time of writing, the second longest runner—after *Cats*—in West End history) that it was given the kind of facelift not seen in the West End since George Edwardes's days, when official "second editions" of shows were produced. *Starlight Express*, composed to be musically up-to-date, had stayed so long in its atmospherically train-decorated auditorium that it was now anything but up-to-date. And so it was given a new 1990s look, being reorganized, reorchestrated, and restaged without even being taken off, and in this up-to-date version, with less story but with more high-tech action than ever, it continues on, playing to vast audiences of delighted young and not so young, a dozen years down the track.

Having struck three times in succession with musicals that staunchly put aside the old musical-play format in favor of a more loosely constructed framework, the composer finally came back to a more traditional kind of book musical with his fourth show of the decade, a musical which was actually based on a celebrated novel. Gaston Leroux's nineteenth-century story *Le Fantôme de l'Opéra* has, however, reached us here in the English-speaking world, and in the last years of the twentieth century, not so much thanks to the printed page but through the medium of the cinema screen. Since the famous Lon Chaney movie of 1925, a grotesque classic of those silent screen days before the invention of the bloodier-than-thou kind of horror movie, *The Phantom of the Opéra* has been a favorite piece of rather more grand guignolesque romance than Leroux originally, perhaps, intended. A stage version of *The Phantom of the Opéra* (yes, it has an accent—it's the Paris Opéra building that's in question, not the genre "opera" in general), with Leroux's story illustrated by a pasticcio score of operatic excerpts, was produced in suburban London, and Lloyd Webber was struck by its possibilities as a vehicle for his then wife, dancer-singer Sarah Brightman. However, just as had happened nearly thirty years earlier when another composer-producer, Richard Rodgers, had ventured to stage a musical with a pasticcio score, the pasticcio score never made it to the stage. In the same way that Rodgers had ended up writing all the music for *The Sound of Music*, so Lloyd Webber ended up creating a wholly new musical show around *The Phantom of the Opéra*.

Since *Evita*, and even though both halves of *Songs and Dance* had received recorded exposure before the putting together of their combined show, the composer had renounced the practice of launching the entire musical as a recording. In the cases of both *Cats* and *Starlight Express*, pre-production singles had been issued, but in neither case to good effect: *Cats*'s big hit-parade success with "Memory" had, like that of "O What a Circus," come after the show's opening, and in the hands of an original cast star. The get-'em-into-the-theater-humming-the-score process was continued, however, with *The Phantom of the Opéra*, and this time—with the hit parade having moved into the age of the pop video—two portions of Lloyd Webber's score, released well before the show, got whistles widely whetted for the stage production. Steve Harley and Sarah Brightman's recording of "The Phantom of the Opéra," accompanied by a video showing the pair gliding on a gondola through the subterranean passages of the Opéra, made it to number 7, and Miss Brightman and Cliff Richard teamed on a version of the love song "All I Ask of You" that climbed right up to 3. Both duets (helped by their chosen singers) had a distinctly up-to-date pop sound to them, but both—in keeping with their story—were soaringly romantic in melody and in words. When the show was produced, however, it was seen that this kind of music did not dominate the score: rather, it was a mixture of the classical-pop-modern kind of music, which the composer had purveyed with such success since *Jesus Christ Superstar*, and of genuine operatic burlesque, which sometimes burlesqued with such agility that it verged on sounding like the real thing. It was a dichotomy which might have been awkward—but it worked. When the prima donna, Carlotta, let rip with a chunk of parody Massenet, all high zeds and fioratura, and the score then segued into Our Heroine performing the same rôle and the same song ("Think of Me") in an agile little soprano, but with a decidedly modern turn of phrase and accompaniment, the effect could have been almost comical—but it wasn't. The two styles merged particularly convincingly in the operatic excerpt from the Phantom's own opera, *Don Juan Triumphant*, which was seen as part of the last act.

As in *Evita*, the score produced a third hit-parade top-ten number to add to the two pre-production successes when the show opened. Michael Crawford, most recently seen playing Phineas Taylor Barnum in London's edition of the Broadway biomusical, created the rôle of the Phantom, and his emotionally charged performance of the seductive "Music of the Night" joined the two principal duos of the evening as a popular takeaway success. The most remarkable part of the score of *The Phantom of the Opéra* was, however, never going to be a hit-parade song, for it was the kind of piece which had, in recent decades, become a rarity on the musical stage, a thoroughly written section of dramatic ensemble work. The sextet "Prima Donna" was a notable and exciting bit of romantic musical-theater writing, a number composed in that operatic style where the voices of half a dozen people, expressing their passions and thoughts at one and the same time, are blended in such a fashion as to weave an impressive body of vocal sound while still allowing the "story" of the song to come through. Here, the managers of the theater are trying to woo the insulted star, Carlotta, to return to the Opéra stage, and while they plead and flatter, and while Carlotta gets back triumphantly among the high zeds at seeing

The Phantom of the Opéra: "... is here inside your mind." Christine Daäé seems as if she will fall under the spell of the masked man ...

them grovel, the Comte de Chagny, and Mme Giry and her daughter—who know what the Phantom can and will do if tried—wonder aghast at what will happen.

The Phantom of the Opéra was produced with all the colorful lavishness suitable to a romantic period melodrama, with the operas-within-the opera giving the opportunity for some super-lavish effects (beginning with an elephant and going on from there), and the big masquerade ball, which had been featured in surprising color in the old black and white silent film, including both a dazzling array of period costume and an apparently thousand-foot wide staircase. And for those—especially those in Row G—who didn't know that the Phantom sabotages the

Opéra chandelier, causing it to drop in deadly fashion into the auditorium (right around Row G), the finale of the first act with its plunging chandelier was another spectacular moment. This chandelier actually took a well-managed curve in its trajectory and landed, instead, on the front of the stage, but the effect was still theatrically stunning.

The show proved to have it all—a romantic-dramatic story of considerable power, molded into a libretto which only very occasionally went a-wandering away from its ever-forward plot, a score which mixed romance and power with a certain leavening of humor, a production of the most splendidly glamorous kind—and, with Crawford and the daintily Trilbyesque Miss Brightman giving definitive performances in their rôles, it became an instant hit. It has carried on being an instant hit ever since, installing itself for runs in the main centers which will doubtless challenge even its own composers' records in years to come, and covering the world from one end to the other and in a multitude of languages as it establishes itself as one of the musical-theater triumphs of all time.

THE PHANTOM OF THE OPÉRA, a musical in a prologue and 2 acts by Andrew Lloyd Webber and Richard Stilgoe, based on the novel of the same name by Gaston Leroux. Lyrics by Charles Hart. Additional lyrics by Richard Stilgoe. Music by Andrew Lloyd Webber. Produced at Her Majesty's Theatre, London, 9 October 1986.

Characters: The Phantom of the Opéra, Christine Daäé, Raoul Vicomte de Chagny, Monsieur Firmin, Monsieur André, Carlotta Guidicelli, Meg Giry, Madame Giry, Ubaldo Phangi, Joseph Buquet, Monsieur Reyer, Auctioneer, &c.

Plot: Paris Opéra chorine Christine Daäé is looked over and coached by a disjointed voice that she believes belongs to the Angel of Music, but when the vindictive "phantom" of the Opéra frightens prima donna Carlotta into refusing to perform, and the young girl is given the chance to stand in triumphantly, it soon becomes clear that "angel" and "phantom" are one and the same. In fact, the "phantom" is a man, a disfigured genius who lives in the subterranean dungeons below the Opéra and who there has composed an opera for his beloved Christine. He succeeds in forcing the Opéra management to mount his opera, with Christine starred, but his plans go awry when the young Vicomte de Chagny and Christine fall in love. He makes every kind of effort to keep them apart, severing the great chandelier of the Opéra from its moorings during a performance, appearing threateningly in a flaming death's head garb at the Opéra ball, and finally kidnapping the girl. But de Chagny goes after them, down to the Phantom's underground lair, and there the final confrontation takes place. Love triumphs, and when the mob falls upon his home the Phantom has vanished, leaving de Chagny and Christine to their happy ending.

Songs: "Think of Me" (Carlotta, Christine, de Chagny), "Angel of Music" (Christine, Meg), "Little Lotte"/The Mirror ["Angel of Music"] (Christine, de Chagny, Phantom), "The Phantom of the Opéra" (Phantom, Christine), "The Music of the Night" (Phantom), "I Remember"/"Stranger Than You Dreamed It" (Christine, Phantom), "Magical Lasso" (Buquet, Mme Giry, Meg, &c.), "Notes"/"Prima Donna" (André, Firmin, de Chagny, Carlotta, Mme Giry, Meg, Phantom), "Poor Fool, He Makes Me Laugh" (Carlotta), "Why Have You Brought Me Here?"/"Raoul, I've Been There"/"All I Ask of You" (de Chagny, Christine), reprise "All I Ask of You" (Phantom), "Masquerade"/"Why So Silent" (ensemble), "Notes"/"Twisted Every Way" (André, Firmin,

Carlotta, Phangi, de Chagny, Christine, Mme Giry, Phantom), Rehearsal of *Don Juan Triumphant* (Christine, Phangi, Carlotta, Reyer, Giry), "Wishing You Were Somehow Here Again" (Christine), "Wandering Child"/"Bravo, Monsieur" (Phantom, de Chagny), Before the première of *Don Juan Triumphant*, "The Point of No Return" (Phantom, Christine), "Down Once More"/"Track Down This Murderer" (ensemble), Final scene (Phantom, Christine, de Chagny).

Since starting small with the little *Joseph and the Amazing Technicolor Dreamcoat*, with its small cast of principals and its children's chorus, its simple songs simply accompanied, and its next-to-no physical production, the musicals of Andrew Lloyd Webber had grown to enormous proportions. *Cats, Starlight Express,* and *The Phantom of the Opéra* were each huge productions, employing large casts, large orchestras, and scenic designs and costumes that were ever more lavish and more technically complex. The composer was aware of this galloping expansion, and decided that for his next musical he would concentrate on writing something on a much less grandiose scale. The subject and source that he chose was one with which he had toyed for a number of years: an intimate study of pentagonal love in warmish places written by the British novelist David Garnett in 1955 and entitled *Aspects of Love*. Charles Hart, lyricist of *The Phantom of the Opéra*, and Don Black from *Tell Me on a Sunday* were entrusted with the words to the musical version, and *Aspects of Love* was created as a show with just nine principal players, a chorus large enough only to supply an understudy for each principal, and a small band—forces altogether suitable for the very real and personal story and characters of the piece, a story and characters which could not have contrasted more wholly with the luxuriant period melodrama of *The Phantom of the Opéra*. The show did not reach the stage in quite the same proportions as it had been conceived. As director, musical director, and designer took charge, the cast and orchestra both underwent inflation, and the often quick-changing scenes of the story were given a physical production which included as many moving parts—computerized!—as the most scenically complex show in town. By the time *Aspects of Love* opened, on the middle-sized stage of London's Prince of Wales Theatre, it had become a middle-sized musical rather than an intimate one. It had also hoisted a prereleased recording of its theme song—the tenor "Love Changes Everything"—into runner-up spot on the charts, the highest rung achieved by one of Lloyd Webber's songs since "Don't Cry for Me, Argentina."

The score of *Aspects of Love* was written recognizably in the mode which Lloyd Webber had made his own, and which he had featured so successfully in his only other show to date to deal with real, twentieth-century life and love—*Tell Me on a Sunday*. Like that piece, it was composed in a much smoother and more controlled tone than the raging rock-operatics of *Jesus Christ Superstar,* it did not take in the teenypop style and sounds of *Starlight Express* or the lusher romanticism of *The Phantom of the Opéra*'s high melodramopera, and it also avoided the moments of friendly parody which had been a feature of so many of Lloyd Webber's works to date. It did, however, rise to some splendid moments of modern-romantic musical theater, notably in the funeral sequence which brought the second act to its climax with the leading lady's desperate admission of her fear of loneliness ("Anything But Lonely") and the driving, dancing eulogy "Give Me the Wine and the Dice," both pieces written for the now smoothed-down version of the prima-donna-rock-opera style of voice which had become almost the standard in the musical theater, and both moments that were contrasted with such pleasingly gentle and unshowy ones as the paternally loving "The Last Man You Remember," delivered by the senior man of the show in a warmly creased basso, and a sweet-voiced "Song of Childhood."

The show aroused two different kinds of reaction. On the one hand, there were those who found its warmth and its narrow focus, and the fact that it dealt with real and modern sentiments in a real and fairly modern story, pleasing, and its comparatively reduced size something of a relief from the grandiose productions, glitzy designs, and exaggerated sentiments on show in so many other musicals of recent decades. On the other hand, there were those to whom the musical theater was synonymous with the glamorous, the glitzy, and the grandiose, and who felt that *Aspects of Love* didn't give them the same value for their money as pieces such as *Cats* or *The Phantom the Opéra*. As a result, it did not become the blockbuster that its more supersized predecessors had, contenting itself with a good London run, a modest Broadway stay, and a series of later productions round the world during which some progress was made towards returning the show to the dimensions that it had originally been intended to have. But the message was clear: the public in general did not want intimate musical plays from the man whose big, spectacular musicals were dominating the world's musical stages. They wanted more big, spectacular musicals. The message was received.

ASPECTS OF LOVE, a musical in 2 acts by Charles Hart and Don Black, based on the novel of the same name by David Garnett. Music by Andrew Lloyd Webber. Produced at the Prince of Wales Theatre, London, 17 April 1989.

Characters: George Dillingham, Alex Dillingham, Rose Vibert, Jenny Dillingham, Giulietta Trapani, Marcel Richard, Elizabeth, Hugo le Meunier, a circus chanteuse, &c.

Plot: Young Alex Dillingham falls for a French touring actress, Rose Vibert, and persuades her to join him for a week at "his" villa in Pau. It is not "his" villa, however—it belongs to his bon vivant uncle George, and when the charming, epicurean George puts in an appearance things change. Rose is soon "called back" to her company, and Alex is heartbroken. Several years later, Alex visits George in Paris and, to his fury, finds Rose there: they are living together. The two young people are soon back in bed together again, but Rose then sends Alex away: she prefers the easygoing if faithless love that George offers to the youthful passion of his nephew. She has to fight for it, though, following George to Italy and the home of his old flame Giulietta Trapani, before—when his financial affairs collapse—getting him to marry her. She bears him a child, Jenny, she becomes a successful actress, and then Alex comes back into their lives. Now it is George's turn to suffer jealousy as the growing Jenny starts to love Alex. His jealousy leads to his death. He collapses on the stairs below his daughter's bedroom, spying on the pair. Now it is Rose's turn to be desperate: George is gone—Alex must stay. But he does not. He leaves the too demanding love offered by Rose and Jenny, and departs instead with Giulietta.

Songs: "Parlez-vous français?" (Rose, Alex, Marcel, crooner), "Seeing Is Believing" (Rose, Alex), "A Memory of a Happy Moment" (George, Giulietta), "Chanson d'enfance" (Rose), "Everybody Loves a Hero" (chorus), "She'd Be Far Better Off with You" (George, Alex), "Stop, Wait, Please" (Giulietta, George), "Leading Lady" (Marcel &c.), "Other Pleasures" (George), "There Is More to Love" (Giulietta), "Mermaid Song" (Jenny, Alex), "The First Man You Remember" (George, Jenny), "Journey of a Lifetime" (chanteuse &c.), "Hand Me the Wine and the Dice" (Giulietta), "Anything But Lonely" (Rose).

The two musicals on which Rice worked, with composers other than his first partner, during the 1980s found varying fortunes. A piece about the medieval minstrel *Blondel*, told in a rather more sophisticated version of the tone and style of *Joseph and the Amazing Technicolor Dreamcoat* and set to music by Stephen Oliver, did not take off, in spite of containing some very merry pieces of lyric-writing, but a collaboration with Bjørn Ulvaeus and Benny Andersson—the two male quarters of the pop group ABBA—on the musical *Chess* did.

Chess followed the fortunes of two world-championship players, one American and one Russian, as they battled for their sporting crown in front of a background of political jiggery-pokery of all shades. They weren't very nice people. The American—who was not, of course, Bobby Fischer—was portrayed as a loud, neurotic, self-centered creep (a characterization which later caused some supertouchy Americans to wail that the libretto was anti-American!), the Russian—who, equally, didn't represent Spassky—as a dour sort of fellow who cheated on his wife, and the jiggery-pokers—a smooth American TV-cum-CIA man and a bullocking bear of a Russian secret policeperson—weren't much better. But their story was interestingly woven together and the unlikely topic of a boardgame made up into a fine and dramatically effective piece of theater.

Musically, the show combined the styles of *Superstar* and *Evita*: the rôles of the two players were both written in the "rock tenor" register which had been used for the parts of Jesus and Judas (the part of the American being, in fact, created by the same artist who had been the original recorded Judas), while the leading lady's rôle—the part of the Hungarian-American Florence Vassy, who switches her allegiance from the Westerner to the Easterner during the course of the evening—was written as a splendid prima-donna-rockopera part, and performed by Britain's ruling queen of the genre, Elaine Paige. All three shared in the musical highlights of a very appreciable score in the modern vein—the Russian soaring out his "Anthem" to the land that is his heart, and the American wallowing in self-pity and searing upper-register singing in "Pity the Child" and vaunting the perils of "One Night in Bangkok," but it was the lady who got the great gems of the evening, both in solo and in duo. Alone, she gave forth with the beautiful love-song "Heaven Help My Heart," but she also joined in two exciting duets—"The Mountain Duet" and "You and I"—with the Russian and, most notably, a third—with the Russian's wife—as the two each declared "I Know Him So Well." The romantic and dramatic rock-opera portions of the score were contrasted with some humorous moments in which the kind of musical parody that Rice and Lloyd Webber had enjoyed together got a showing—an opening

Chess: While Anatoly Sergeievsky struggles to concentrate on holding his World Championship, distractions such as the reproaches of his abandoned wife fill his head.

chorus which took a swing at the conventional merry-peasant opening chorus of old-days musicals and the world of Rodgers and Hammerstein, a jokey piece with false airs of the Red Army Choir about "The Soviet Machine," and a prissy duo for two embassy officials, piqued at having to stop their game of tiddlywinks and process a defection ("Oh, my dear, how boring, he's defecting . . ."). There was also a considerable dance element, headed by a leaping grotesque of a principal dancer playing the contest's Arbiter, an element which owed its presence largely to the fact that *A Chorus Line* director-choreographer Michael Bennett had originally been slated to mount the show. When—with a dancer-heavy cast engaged—he was unable to do so, the dance part was not reduced, although the whole of the intended choreography was never completed. Finally, there was some splendid ensemble music, which came to a peak in the climactic, pounding "Endgame" sequence in which the Russian strives to concentrate on winning his championship while the problems of wife, mistress, and conniving politicians all conspire to distract him from his game.

Chess followed the *Superstar* path by making its first appearance as a double-disc recording, and it won instant popularity, with the women's duet, as sung by Elaine Paige and Barbara Dickson, becoming the first show-song since "Don't Cry for Me, Argentina" to make it to number 1 on the English charts. Even in France, where the musical theater now exists only in a state of weary moribundity, the songs of *Chess* shot to popularity. It went on from there, again like *Superstar*, to be given performances as a concert musical, before the stage version of the show, set back by Michael Bennett's death and dazzlingly mounted instead by *Cats* and *Starlight Express* director Trevor Nunn, was produced in London. It also won a delighted reaction (although the levels of amplification, which were now reaching pain point in the musical theater, got their heaviest criticism to date here) and the show went on to run for 1,209 performances. Thereafter, however, things went wrong. Nunn had apparently been unhappy with having to put together a production on the bones already laid out by Bennett, and when the show went to America it was—unusually for this day and age—given a completely new production, a production which also involved some rewrites which weren't done just because of the changed status of Russia. Virtually every alteration turned out to be for the worse, and a fine musical fell from Broadway in disarray. Since then, *Chess* has been given a number of other English-language productions in more or less fiddled-with versions, none of which has come near to re-creating the mood and power of the original, a result which would seem to give support to the use of that "breath-by-breath reproduction" system of exporting musical shows which has always seemed such an unimaginative one.

CHESS, a musical in 2 acts by Tim Rice. Music by Bjørn Ulvaeus and Benny Andersson. Produced at the Prince Edward Theatre, London, 14 May 1986.

Cast: Frederick Trumper, Anatoly Sergeievsky, Florence Vassy, Alexander Molokov, Walter de Courcey, The Arbiter, Svetlana Sergeievsky, two civil servants, Mayor of Merano, Viigand, &c.

Plot: The world chess championship—F. Trumper (USA) vs. A. Sergeievsky (USSR)—is taking place in Merano, Italy. The press have loudmouthed Trumper cast as the bad guy. The KGB have Sergeievsky programmed to win. Gamesmanship reigns only second to the commercial and political considerations surrounding the event. Trumper stages a newsworthy walkout and his second, the ex-Hungarian Florence Vassy, has to go to Sergeievsky to try to negotiate a return to the tables. When Trumper joins them it is evident that something very personal has happened. Disoriented, the U.S. champion loses and takes out his frustration on Florence, and she walks out on him. When Sergeievsky follows his win by defecting, the loser's ex-girl is at the new champion's side. A year later, Sergeievsky defends his title against a new Russian challenger in Bangkok. As part of their game strategy, the KGB have sent the champion's abandoned wife to Thailand, and she and Florence meet. Both women are being pressured to influence the game, and Florence is made to believe that her father, who disappeared in 1956, is alive and can be released to America should the champion throw the match. But Trumper, commentating the event, comes to his old rival's aid. On a quiet Thai hillside he meets privately with Sergeievsky and hands on a game-play tip that can help him win. Among all the circus, the game can still be the winner. Sergeievsky wins, and returns to Russia. Everyone apparently has what they want now. Except perhaps Florence—for is her father really still alive? And maybe Sergeievsky. Well, all the politicians have what they want, anyhow.

Songs: "The Story of Chess" (ensemble/solo), "Merano" (ensemble)/"What a Scene! What a Joy!" (Trumper, Mayor, &c.), The Russian and Molokov/"Who Needs a Dream?" (Sergeievsky, Molokov), The Opening Ceremony: "No One Can Deny That These Are Difficult Times" (ensemble)/"I'm the Arbiter" (Arbiter)/"Whether You Are Pro- or Anti" (chorus), "A Model of Decorum and Tranquillity" (Molokov, Florence, &c.), "[Nobody's On] Nobody's Side" (Florence, Trumper), "Der kleiner Franz" (chorus), Mountain Duet: "This Is the One Situation" (Florence, Sergeievsky), Florence Quits (Trumper, Florence), "Pity the Child" (Trumper), Embassy Lament (two civil servants), "Heaven Help My Heart" (Florence), Anthem ["My Land"] (Sergeievsky), "One Night in Bangkok" (Trumper), "You and I" (Florence, Sergeievsky), "Soviet Machine" (Molokov &c.), "I Know Him So Well" (Svetlana, Florence), The Deal (ensemble), Endgame (ensemble), reprise "You and I" (Sergeievsky, Florence), reprise "My Land" (Florence). Additional and alternative numbers included: "Someone Else's Story (Florence), "No Contest" (Trumper, de Courcey), Lullaby (Florence, Gregor Vassy).

The rock-opera style of musical, as promoted by Rice, Lloyd Webber, and *Jesus Christ Superstar*, had been attempted by a number of writers since the early 1970s, but with a conspicuous lack of success in the hands of any but its creators. Finally, however, a musical did appear—a musical avowedly written under the influence of *Superstar*—which would ultimately prove to be every bit as successful as its model. The word "ultimately" is important there, for the career of *Les Misérables* nearly came to a premature end on two separate occasions before the show became the triumph that it is today.

The musical version of Victor Hugo's celebrated novel was written by three Frenchmen, writers Alain Boublil and Jean-Marc Natel, and popular songwriter Claude-Michel Schönberg. The first- and last-named of these had ventured,with another pair of collaborators, an earlier attempt at a theater musical: taking, as *Superstar* had done, a distinctly large topic as their playground, they had turned out a cockeyed rocky retelling of some of the events of *La Révolution française*. It had been issued, again *Superstar*-style, as a double-disc concept recording, and then given a brief theatrical season in Paris. Now, seven years down the line, they surfaced with a second recording, another piece of recorded musical theater that was the musicalization of a momentous work. Their *Les Misérables* followed the same course that the other had done, from disc to the Paris stage, and after a set season there it was folded away. And that might have been its end. But the show came to the attention of London producer Cameron Mackintosh, riding high on the success of *Cats*, and as a result it was given a second chance. It was also given a very considerable remake, a remake which turned it from a vast, straggling piece of musical theater meant for an audience of French folk to whom the story was as familiar as *Romeo and Juliet* is to the English, into a piece of rather more dramatically coherent musical theater for all nations.

The remaking included one or two theatrical decisions which were a touch shocking to the French authors—the virtual elimination of the irritatingly *Oliver*-ish but extremely celebrated character of the child Gavroche was one—but the result was a musical of extraordinary dramatic power which managed to include a surprising amount of the narrative of the vast novel. The score of the show as originally recorded and subsequently played in Paris was very largely supplemented by new numbers, to fit the new shape and layout of the show, and in one case a melody was even remade into a song for a different character, but, as with the script, the result proved remarkably of a piece.

The music of *Les Misérables* was, by and large, written for the "rock-opera" style of voice, although nowhere nearly as rockily as portions of *La Révolution française* or, indeed, *Superstar*, had been. As in the work of Lloyd Webber, the years had brought a smoothing down of the more aggressive rock elements—which now seemed more like mannerisms than manners—into a strong modern theater-music idiom. The rôles of the two main protagonists of the story, the runaway ticket-of-leave man Jean Valjean and the policeman Javert who pursues him, were written for strong modern "pop"-style voices of some range—Valjean reaching into the tenor register and Javert making a pleasantly contrasting sound in the medium baritone area—the part of the maltreated Fantine was composed in the equivalent feminine vein and color, and the juvenile Eponine was for a plaintive country-rock voice. The young men whose foolish attempt at a street rebellion against the government is the setting for much of the story's tragedy, and most particularly the central Marius, were, again, a set of stingingly modern voices, almost all of whose music was written for the top part of the male voice. There was little place for the bass-baritone in *Les Misérables*. However, the vocal layout of the show did include one surprise, one element which—at this stage—was foreign to the rock opera idiom. The rôle of Cosette, the child whom Valjean brings up and who becomes the ingénue of the show's second half, was altered between France and London from being a vaguely modern soprano to a wholly straight light opera voice. It was a kind of voice that hadn't been heard on the modern musical stage for years, and—as a result—casting the part proved a difficult job. Young singing artists, in this day and age, were trained to be prime-donne-rockopere, and not to sound like such past-era stars as Lisbeth Webb or Shirley Jones. The part of Cosette, joined soon after by that of *The Phantom of the Opéra*'s Christine, was to be instrumental in putting the young legitimate soprano back on the musical-theater map, and changing a good many singing teachers' habits.

The score of *Les Misérables*, written in an agreeably French-flavored version of the modern rock-opera style, mixed the dramatic, the romantic, and the comic in fair doses. The dramatic highlights came in the violent student songs ("Red and Black," "Do You Hear the People Sing") and the ensemble ("One Day More," ex-"Demain") in which the fighting is heralded, the romantic in such pieces as the juveniles' duet "In My Life" (ex-"Dans ma vie"), and the comic in the music given to the slatternly Innkeeper Thénardier and his wife. But the most effective moments were the less out-front ones—Valjean praying for Marius's safety in "Bring Him

Home," little Eponine pouring out her hopeless love in "On My Own" and dying gently to the strains of "A Little Bit of Rain," Javert's introspective "Stars" and "Who Is This Man?," and Marius's sad looking-over of "The Empty Chairs and Empty Tables" where his dead friends had planned their foolish fight.

Les Misérables was produced by Mackintosh in alliance with the Royal Shakespeare Company and initially staged at the company's home in the Barbican, and—in spite of a remarkable mise en scène—the initial reaction to it was not over the moon. In fact, it was distinctly downbeat. Even with the alterations that had been made, the long and relatively complex story, its darkly dramatic mood, and its bevy of unfamiliar characters seemed to combine in a musical that was much too much like hard work. Critics and audiences who didn't know Hugo's story were inclined to give up trying to follow its ins and outs. When the time came for the piece to be shifted from its subsidized house into the mainstream of the West End, there was a distinct pause. *Les Misérables* had reached its second crisis point. But it came through. Mackintosh decided to take the risk, and took this overlong, overcomplex, overdifficult musical into the West End's Palace Theatre, and there it has stayed now for over a decade, while productions have proliferated all around the world. And, as it establishes itself as one of the most important pieces of musical theater in history, no one anywhere would now dream of accusing the show of being overlong, overcomplex, or overdifficult.

LES MISÉRABLES, a musical tragedy by Alain Boublil and Jean-Marc Natel, based on the novel by Victor Hugo. Music by Claude-Michel Schönberg. Produced at the Palais des Sports, Paris, 17 September 1980. Produced in its revised, English-language version by Herbert Kretzmer at the Barbican Theatre, London, 30 September 1985, and at the Palace Theatre, 4 December 1985.

Characters: Jean Valjean, Javert, Fantine, Cosette, Thénardier, Mme Thénardier, Eponine, Marius, Enjolras, Gavroche, Bishop of Digne, &c.

Plot: Jean Valjean breaks his ticket-of-leave terms and runs away, and over the years that follow he becomes a prosperous factory-owner. But the policeman, Javert, whom he has eluded, a man with a deep belief in the sanctity of the law, never gives up his pursuit of the runaway criminal. When his factory-worker Fantine is dismissed and falls into prostitution and death, the repentant Valjean takes on the care of her child, Cosette, and he brings her up in well-to-do style in Paris. Cosette falls in love with the student, Marius, and when the students of Paris take to the streets to fight against the government troops, Valjean follows him, determined that the boy shall come to no harm. On the barricades, he encounters Javert, but when he is given the opportunity to kill his old enemy he holds his hand. Later, while bearing the scarcely alive body of Marius from the scene of the fighting, he again meets the policeman. But now Javert is himself shattered, his certainties of right and wrong inextricably mixed. He lets Valjean depart, and—tortured beyond endurance—drowns himself in the Seine. Marius recovers, and is wed to Cosette, and Jean Valjean—whose life since his escape has included very little peace—passes away in peace.

Songs: "Look Down, Look Down" (convicts, Valjean, Javert), "What Have I Done?" (Valjean), "At the End of the Day" (Fantine, Valjean, Foreman, chorus), "I Dreamed a Dream" (Fantine), "Lovely Ladies" (Fantine, whores, &c.), Fantine's Arrest (Batambois, Fantine, Javert, Valjean), The

Les Misérables: The students of Paris take to the streets in a death-dealing nineteenth-century demonstration.

Runaway Cart (Valjean, Javert, &c.), "Who Am I?" (Valjean), Fantine's Death: "Come to Me" (Fantine, Valjean), The Confrontation (Valjean, Javert), "A Castle on a Cloud" (Cosette), "Master of the House" (Thénardier, Mme Thénardier), The Bargain (Valjean, Thénardiers), Thénardier Waltz (Thénardier, Mme Thénardier), Beggars' chorus: "Look Down" (chorus), The Robbery and Javert's Intervention (ensemble), "Stars in Your Multitudes" (Javert), Eponine's Errand (Eponine, Marius), "Red and Black" (Enjolras, students), "Do You Hear the People Sing?" (Enjolras, students), "In My Life" (Cosette, Valjean), "A Heart Full of Love" (Marius, Cosette), The Attack on Rue Plumet (ensemble), "One Day More" (ensemble), "Here Upon These Stones" (ensemble), "On My Own" (Eponine), Javert's Arrival, "Little People" (Gavroche &c.), "A Little Drop of Rain" (Eponine, Marius), The Night of Anguish and the First Attack, "Drink with Me" (Grantaire &c.), "Bring Him Home" (Valjean), Dawn of Anguish (Enjolras &c.), The Second Attack and the Final Battle, "Dog Eats Dog" (Thénardier), "Who Is This Man?" (Javert), "Turning" (chorus), "Empty Chairs at Empty Tables" (Marius), "Every Day" (Marius, Cosette), Valjean's Confession (Valjean, Marius), Wedding Chorale (Marius, Thénardier, Mme Thénardier, &c.), "Beggars at the Feast" (Thénardier, Mme Thénardier), Finale Act 2 and Epilogue: "Alone I Wait in the Shadows" (Valjean, Cosette, Marius, Fantine, Eponine)/reprise "Do You Hear the People Sing?" (ensemble).

The superb qualities and vast success of *Les Misérables* led to hopes that another source of fine new musicals had been found in Boublil, Natel, Schönberg, and company, and so there was disappointment in some quarters when their next show appeared. *Miss Saigon* had all the signs of being a musical-made-calculatedly-to-order. It appeared to favor the scenically spectacular over the dramatically coherent in its text—something which *Les Misérables* had never done, in either of its versions—while its music, in contrast to the vibrant melody-filled score of its predecessor, seemed so bland and characterless as to be scarcely credible as coming from the same hand.

Miss Saigon was a remake of the *Madame Butterfly* story—play and opera—resituated in the far-enough-away-to-be-breastbeatingly-fashionable setting of the Vietnam war, in which Hollywood had recently been wallowing with considerable financial success. It was a setting which had the dubious quality of insisting that a play or a film be taken "seriously," for even decades down the line the Vietnam war was not an event to be considered lightly. The Cio Cio San, the Madame Butterfly, of this piece was a Hanoi tart called Kim, her Lieutenant Pinkerton was an American Embassy official who takes her home and falls in love with her between bedtime and the next morning, the marriage-broker of the opera became a Eurasian pimp with the airs of *Oliver!*'s Fagin, and the opposition to their relationship came not from the religious Bonze of the original tale, but from a jealous cousin to whom the little tart had been promised in prewar days. Our Hero's abandonment of his girl was put down to the precipitate withdrawal of American personnel, her suicide was justified by her ambition to get her son to the land of the greenback and McDonald's hamburgers. Somehow love didn't get much of a look in. The libretto, using sometimes crude would-be-realistic language which rapidly became boring, was a harsh and hacked-up affair, which went into second-act flashback in order to allow the show's spectacular showpiece—the departure of the helicopter taking Our Hero away from Hanoi while Kim tries in vain to get past the wire to join him, which actually fitted chronologically into the first act—to be seen at the theatrically correct climactic point of the evening. That helicopter—which was pointedly featured on the show's poster—became the symbol of *Miss Saigon*. It also, sadly, seemed to be the show's raison d'être. It also, clearly, helped the musical to become—if not a success on the scale of *Les Misérables*—at least a long-runner in the West End, while on Broadway it has, at the time of writing, already whirlybirded way past the total of performances and receipts achieved by such a piece as *Aspects of Love*, which favored warmth and content over spectacle, or the handful of fine examples of home-made musical theater which Broadway gave to the musical stage in the 1980s.

There were, unfortunately, only a handful. But, while London established itself as the principal source of the large-scale sung-through musical in these years, Broadway continued to be the most effective in turning out pieces on the traditional songs-and-scenes lines, even if on a distinctly slower and very much less cornucopic scale that it had done ten or twenty years earlier, and with minimum effect beyond those English-speaking boundaries which shows such as *The Phantom of the Opéra* and *Les Misérables* had thoroughly flattened. Some of the most successful writers of the Broadway of previous years were still on the scene, and it was one of them—Jerry Herman—who was responsible for the songs of the one Broadway musical successfully to follow *Barnum* to a wider selection of audiences. *La Cage aux folles* was built on the very best of well-used traditions, for, like *The Phantom of the Opéra* and *Les Misérables* and so many other musicals before them, it was "taken from the French." However, whereas those two musicals had been based on novels, this one—like shows from *The Yeomen of the Guard* to *Oh, Kay!*—was based on a play. More, like the last-named, it was based on a first-rate example of that once incomparable genre, the French farce. In an era when Paris is more inclined to import the best of its farcical comedy from England than write its own, the play *La Cage aux folles* was the biggest native-made farce hit to arrive on the French stage for ages. It ran for seven years, went on to be made into a highly successful film, and ultimately became a musical which repeated the success of the piece's first two incarnations.

La Cage aux folles was a merry tale about the problems faced by a couple of Saint Tropez homosexuals when their son (well, not biologically theirs, but sentimentally) gets engaged to the daughter of a local anti-gay crusader. The most picturesque elements of the show owed their inclusion to the fact that "maman," otherwise Albin, was also "Zaza," the in-drag star of the cabaret at the club of the show's title, and selections from the drag-show-within-the-show provided a usefully glitzy set of decorations to the main plotline of the musical. It was a far cry from the days when Ivor Novello and Noël Coward had presented the operetta-within-the-operetta or Cicely Courtneidge had played scenes from her musical-within-her-musical. We had had—from *La Belle de Cadix* to *42nd Street*—the movie-musical-within-the-musical, we had had the pop-songs-within-the-musical, as in *They're Playing Our Song*, cabaret-within-the-musical from *Die Wunder-Bar* and *Get a Load of This* to *Cabaret*, and just about every other version imaginable of stand-up performance included—for good reason or for very little—as part of a musical play. However, give or take the intergalactic suspenders and stockings in *The Rocky Horror Show*, *La Cage aux folles* was the first hit musical to boast the drag-show-within-a-musical—equipped with an exceptional chorus line of exceedingly long-legged chorines.

Herman supplied a well-judged set of songs as illustration to the show and its story. He let rip particularly with the material for Albin-Zaza, for in this character the musicalizer of *Dolly* and of *Mame* and of Giradoux's Countess Aurelia was supplied with the ultimate in grandes dames, a creature who was quite simply a grande-dame musical songwriter's dream. Zaza was no less than the over-the-top-extension, the super-apotheosis of every bespangled, wrinkle-smothered stardame of stage and film, and when she hurled her defiantly heart-chipped self-justification "I Am What I Am" at her on-stage and auditorium listeners, it was like a kind of mixture of "The Man That Got Away" and "I'm Still Here" rolled into one gigantic blow-torch song, teetering on the edge of parody without ever quite toppling over. Needless to say, the song very quickly found its way out of the show and into the repertoires of precisely those performers of whom Albin was the sweet, grotesque mimicry and, in their hands, rather than the deep brown baritone of its creator, it very often did topple. But Albin was more than just a travesty of aging femininity, and the blowtorch song was contrasted with some jollier moments—

a pick-me-up piece called "A Little More Mascara" in which the star transforms himself from Albin into Zaza, and a lively singalong celebrating "The Best of Times." There were gentler moments, too, as Georges, Albin's other half, serenaded his touchy friend in a Trenet-style chanson "Song on the Sand," or their son danced merrily along the promenade "With Anne on My Arm," and there was even an effective ensemble (Cocktail Counterpoint) in which the family does their disastrous best to entertain their prospective in-laws.

Directed by Arthur Laurents (who, sadly, seemed to have given up writing libretti) in a fine farcical style which threatened to get burlesquey only when the couple's improbable "black maid" got into the act, *La Cage aux folles* turned out a full-scale hit, running up 1,761 performances on Broadway before going out to the rest of the world. Oddly enough, it had a less than happy career in its other main English-language productions, spending just 301 performances swimming about on the large London Palladium stage, but it went on to a long list of further showings in Europe, where it became evident that it adapted excellently to smaller houses. The Austrian première, mounted in a space that amounted to little more than a village hall, re-created the atmosphere of the cabaret to great effect, and resulted in the show going on to further, perhaps unfortunately not always small, productions throughout the Continent.

LA CAGE AUX FOLLES, a musical in 2 acts by Harvey Fierstein, based on the play of the same title by Jean Poiret. Music and lyrics by Jerry Herman. Produced at the Palace Theatre, New York, 21 August 1983.

Characters: Georges, Albin, Jean-Michel, Jacob, Édouard Dindon, Madame Dindon, Anne, Francis, Jacqueline, Monsieur Renaud, Les Cagelles (Chantal, Monique, Dermah, Nicole, Hanna, Mercedes, Bitelle, Lo Singh, Odette, Phaedra, Angélique, Clo-Clo), &c.

Plot: Georges and Albin—lovers of long standing—run the Cage aux Folles nightclub in Saint Tropez, where Albin stars as the glittering Zaza in the drag cabaret. Not all the locals approve, and the politician Dindon is loud in his objections to these debauched ho-mo-sex-u-als. So, when the couple's son, Jean-Michel, comes home and says he wants to marry Anne Dindon, problems loom. Especially as the Dindons will have to meet his parents. Less than tactfully, the boy rearranges his home, but one of the rearrangements—an attempt at Albin's temporary replacement with the biological mother he's barely known—causes dreadful heartache. However, biological mother fails to show and Albin, dolled up in a neat tailored number, stands in. All goes well until the owner of the restaurant where they are dining requests a number from her "star" guest: Albin obliges and automatically whips off his wig at the end of the song. Disaster. But by now the youngsters have their priorities in place. They stand by Georges and Albin, and Dindon, caught in the company of the very folk he has so often decried, has to give in.

Songs: "We Are What We Are" (Cagelles), "A Little More Mascara" (Albin), "With Anne on My Arm" (Jean-Michel), reprise as "With You on My Arm" (Georges, Albin), "The Promenade," "Song on the Sand" (Georges), "La Cage aux Folles" (Albin, Cagelles), "I Am What I Am" (Albin), reprise "Song on the Sand" (Georges), "Masculinity" (chorus), "Look Over There" (Georges), Cocktail Counterpoint (ensemble), "The Best of Times" (Albin, Jacqueline, &c.), reprise "Look Over There" (Jean-Michel &c.), reprise "Song on the Sand."

The show-within-a-show syndrome, in its various variations, was at the base of several other successful musicals of the period. In 1981 Michael Bennett, the creator of *A Chorus Line*, masterminded the spectacularly high-tech staging of another gotta-make-it-good-in-showbiz musical. Instead of focusing on the musical theater, as *A Chorus Line* had done, or on the movies, as *42nd Street* had done, *Dreamgirls* followed the lines taken by pieces from *Expresso Bongo* to *They're Playing Our Song* and chose the world of pop music as its setting. But whereas the last-named show had involved itself with the ups-and-downs in the personal and professional lives of a pair of writers of pop music, this time the action centered on the career of a group of performers and on the behind-the-scenes finagling which has so long dictated who shall succeed and who fail in the pop world. The performers were a 1960s girl group, a trio of staunch-voiced, professionally packaged singers who made one think (as one was probably supposed to do) of the successful real-life group The Supremes, and the music with which they were provided was in a zingily Motownish vein. Much of Henry Krieger's score was devoted to the songs sung by the group, but the musical highspot of the evening was the show's big emotional number, a piece which brought down the curtain on Act 1 with the same effect as "I Am What I Am" would do in *La Cage aux folles*. The overweight, overpowering, overdemanding Effie has been sacked from the group by the man who has been her lover, and she lets all her overcooked feelings out in a searing, soaring, shrieking piece of powerful pop-soul music — "And I'm Telling You I'm Not Going" — which wrought huge demands on the voice of the singer, and which brought the act to a stunning musical climax. *Dreamgirls* had a splendid Broadway run (1,522 performances) and a brief revival, but its appeal did not spread wider, and its only showings outside America were given by a touring troupe sent out from home base. In 1983 Krieger supplied the songs for another gotta-make-it-good-in-showbiz musical — this one charting the rise to stardom of a tot known as *The Tap Dance Kid* — but curiously he did not become a fixture on a Broadway which would have seemed a natural habitat for him.

London, too, turned out another successful show-within-a-show musical when the staged version of *42nd Street* was succeeded by a staged version of the even more famous musical film *Singin' in the Rain*. This time the ingénue made her way to stardom and the arms of the leading man not by tapping her little heart out, but by loaning her pretty singing voice to a glamorous but nails-on-the-blackboard-voiced star of the silent screen at the advent of the sound cinema. *Singin' in the Rain* stuck rather more closely to the original screenplay and song-schedule than *42nd Street* had done, and — with the famous "rain" sequence sung and danced with boundless energy and verisimilitude by the same Tommy Steele who had ridden *Half a Sixpence* to triumph a quarter of a century earlier — it proved an enormous hit. The show was exported from London to several other important theater centers, but Broadway missed out. Wheels within wheels led to the successful London version being barred from American stages, and a sadly feeble "new" version written by the famous authors of the original screenplay —

none other than the venerable Comden and Green—being mounted instead. It proved one of the most expensive flops ever to have visited Broadway.

Over the years, a number of shows had been mounted which were produced in the terms of the late Victorian English music-hall, their story "framed" and colored by what the modern world understands as being the style of the popular entertainments of that period. 1985 brought one of the most successful of the kind—a new musical retelling of Charles Dickens's famously unfinished *The Mystery of Edwin Drood*. The show that this show was set inside was a performance at London's "Music Hall Royale," and it was the hall's chairman and the members of its company who were cast in burlesquey versions of the characters of Dickens's novel: the schizophrenic, drug-addicted village choirmaster, the hot-tempered Edwin, the purer than possible Rosa whom both of them love, a mysterious brother-and-sister pair from dark-dyed Ceylon, and a raddled drug-mistress with a secret in her heart. The story proceeded up to the point where—with Edwin gone missing in a Christmas-night storm, and presumed dead—the mystery seemed about to be elucidated—and then it stopped, as Dickens had done, and the show became a "solve-it-yourself" one. The audience was invited to vote as to the probable ending and pick its own guilty party, and the musical then ended in accordance with their choice.

This merry bit of burlesque-comical musical theater, with its interactive ending, was illustrated with some delightful numbers by songwriter Rupert Holmes in a score that ranged from the cod music-hall ("Off to the Races," "The Wages of Sin") to some highly characterful and even adventurous solos for the melodramatic characters—the choirmaster's hot-and-cold "A Man Could Go Quite Mad," the heroine's silvery, pre-Raphaelite hymn to "Moonfall," or the drolly comical number for a bit-part player given his one big chance ("Never the Luck")—and some fine bits of ensemble writing.

The show had a respectable Broadway run, but an ill-cast London edition foundered, and it never reached success of the proportions that might have been expected in days less dominated by the spectacular musical stage.

Another popular songwriter—Roger Miller of "Little Green Apples" and "King of the Road" fame—also turned out the songs for a successful musical play in the 1980s. *Big River* was the latest in the line of country-music musicals, and its country music was attached to a chunk of the story of Mark Twain's *Huckleberry Finn* story. There had been, over the years, umpteen attempts at transferring the Mississippi stories of Tom Sawyer and Huck Finn to the stage, musical and non-musical, but this one finally brought it off with a success which took it to 1,005 performances on the Broadway stage and considerable popularity in Australia.

Two of the most successful—and certainly two of the best—musicals of the 1980s scenes-and-songs shows were pieces which could be counted as the up-to-date inheritors of the opéra-bouffe tradition: musicals which mixed the wit and comedy of parody with a light and bright musical score which reflected that burlesque fun. The first of these came from off-Broadway—an area of the theater with a tradition in burlesque musicals of the *Little Mary Sunshine* or

Dames at Sea kind—and it took the endlessly popular world of the cinema, with its exaggerated characters and manners, as its butt and as its source.

The 1960 *Little Shop of Horrors* had been a hilariously horrible B-movie about a person-eating plant, which had become something of a cult. It was an absolute sitter for burlesque treatment, and, in the hands of author Howard Ashman and musician Alan Menken, it got it in spades. Ashman gave the show's characters the true burlesque touch—a nerdier than nebbish little hero, a vacuously wide-eyed heroine whose intellectual capacities would have made Gilbert's Yum-Yum look like a Rhodes scholar, a supervicious leather-clad dentist with a loin-stirring passion for doing painful things with his drills, and a rock 'n' rolling plant whose night isn't complete until it has digested the entire cast—and Menken compounded the effect with a score of 1960s-flavored songs. A trio of impossibly sixtiesish harmony-hooting girls booped out the show's title-song, the heroine longed for sweet suburbia "Somewhere That's Green," the hero pleaded with his recalcitrant flower "Grow for Me" and got rhapsodic with his beloved in "Suddenly Seymour," and the evening came to its musical highspot when the plant—which is actually not a plant at all, but a creature from outerspace masquerading as a plant—started demanding, in scalding rock tones, that the boy "Feed Me!"—with human blood, of course.

The small-cast, small-scale *Little Shop of Horrors* was a 2,209 performance success off-Broadway, went nearer than any off-Broadway show in history to making ends meet in a suitably middle-sized West End theater, and went on not only to win productions all round the world, but to return to the cinema screen whence it had come in its new, bouffe, and musical shape.

LITTLE SHOP OF HORRORS, a musical in 2 acts by Howard Ashman, based on the screenplay of the same name by Charles Griffith. Music by Alan Menken. Produced at the WPA Theatre, New York, 6 May 1982, and at the Orpheum Theatre, 27 July 1982.

Characters: Seymour Krelbourne, Audrey, Orin Bernstein, Mr Mushnik, Ronnette, Chiffon, Crystal, Audrey II, Derelict.

Plot: Skid Row shopboy Seymour finds this strange and interesting plant during a total eclipse. He brings it back to Mr Mushnik's flowershop, names it Audrey after his adored assisted-blonde workmate, tends it tenderly, and finds that it's making him a celebrity. Then he discovers that the plant thrives on blood. He gives it a bit of his own, but that's not enough. Then, one day, he goes to visit the beastly dentist who is assisted-blonde Audrey's sadistic suitor. Before beginning the thrilling drilling, the dentist helps himself to a happy whiff of gas, but the mask gets stuck and the beast laughs himself to death. So Seymour—whose fame and fortune are growing daily—feeds him to the demanding plant. It is the beginning of the end: before the curtain falls Mushnik, Audrey, and Seymour have all fallen into the maw of the monster—for the plant is actually an aggressive alien and world domination is its aim. So look out!

Songs: "Little Shop of Horrors" (Ronnette, Crystal, Chiffon), "Skid Row" ["Downtown"] (ensemble), "Da-Doo" (Seymour, Crystal, Ronnette, Chiffon), "Grow for Me" (Seymour), "Ya Never Know" (Seymour, Mushnik, Ronnette, Crystal, Chiffon), "Mushnik and Son" (Mushnik, Seymour), "Dentist!" (Orin, Crystal, Ronnette, Chiffon), "Somewhere That's Green" (Audrey), "Feed Me" (Audrey II, Seymour), "Now" (Seymour, Orin), "Closed for Renovation" (Mushnik,

Seymour, Audrey), "Suddenly Seymour" (Audrey, Seymour, Crystal, Ronnette, Chiffon), "Suppertime" (Audrey II), "The Meek Shall Inherit" (ensemble), "Sominex"/"Suppertime" (Audrey, Audrey II, Seymour), "Don't Feed the Plants" (ensemble).

Filmland came in for another dose of burlesque treatment in a large-scale musical which arrived on Broadway in 1989, bringing back two of the musical theater's most remarkable writers: author Larry Gelbart, who had been away too long since contributing to the extremely skillful libretto to *A Funny Thing Happened on the Way to the Forum,* and the Great White Way's most outstanding and most outstandingly successful songwriter of his generation, Cy Coleman. The combination didn't disappoint, for the show that the pair turned out together proved to be the wittiest, cleverest piece of musical-theater entertainment since Coleman's *On the Twentieth Century* more than a decade earlier. The Hollywood genre which was the starting point for the burlesque of *City of Angels* was the gumshoe detective movie: the kind of film that starts off with a downbeat, laid-too-far-back voice-over, introducing grubby streets and a shabby private detective—grandfather of Columbo—who we know will bump his way through a selection of black-and-white dangers, and up against both authority and a bunch of busty broads, until the show is over and the crime and the criminal are uncovered. He might raise his fists from time to time, but hardly ever his voice or his hourly rate.

City of Angels utilized the ubiquitous show-within-a-show technique, but it used it with a degree of sophistication rarely before attempted. This show ran on two tracks at once. On the one hand, the audience was shown the progress of a novelist turned screenwriter called Stine who is (a) trying to adapt his slightly pretentious cop novel as a screenplay and (b) keep his marriage in order. On the other, it saw scenes from the screenplay-in-progress as it was written by the author, and/or rewritten by what he regards as an insensitive, box-office-blinded producer whom the authors named, in the old burlesque-descriptive style, Buddy Fidler. The two parts of the show—the real-life and the novel/screen-fiction—ran in parallel, with the same actors appearing both as the real-life characters of the real-life part and also as the characters in the filmplay. In case this was potentially confusing for an inattentive audience member, the show's production color-coded the real-life scenes in full-color scenery and costumes and dressed the film scenes in black and white. The real-life characters were burlesqued with varying degrees of enthusiasm: there was the vaguely liberal writer of cop-potboilers who gets all het up about the "social content" being taken out of his dime novel on its way to the screen, and his wife who works in publishing yet clucks on about the authorial "integrity" her husband is selling out by working for the megabucks of Hollywood—but there were also such highly colored characters as the beastly producer, a broadly mocking caricature of the sweethearting, finagling, unzipped film executive, or the ingénue who is willing to do just ANYTHING to get on and who has the size of lips needed to make sure she does. At the center of all this was "our hero," the gruffly mostly-macho cop who is the hero of the novel and screenplay as seen within the mind of its author, and as seen by us within the musical—until the climactic moment when we see that the rôle has been cast not with this Bogartian bravo, but with a poncy, pop-singing poseur.

The story of the screenplay-within-the-musical progressed throughout the evening, told sometimes in the form that author Stine imagined it and then in its rewritten-by-the-boss form, but always keeping a forward impetus as it took in all the "necessary" elements of its genre—the sex and the violence, of course, fashionably to the fore—on its way through the tale of a ruthless, double-crossing, well-endowed dame out to murder her iron-lungbound munitions-monger husband and pin the blame on a dopey dick. And, as he watched the development and/or disintegration of his work, author Stine was seen trying—in parallel—to play the filmland game and still keep his pants on. Unsuccessfully.

City of Angels the film-within-the-musical was not a musical film, which ought to have meant that the songs of *City of Angels* the musical were attached to the real life characters—but it didn't quite turn out that way. The film characters were equally as liable to burst into a number as the real-life ones, in a selection of jazzy-cum-swingy numbers that went from the moody to the jolly to the crisply parodic. The moody part of the score was topped by a cabaret song—presented as such—performed by the woman the detective loved and lost, "With Every Breath I Take," the jolly moments included the duo "You're Nothing without Me," between the author and his creation, and a smartly rueful "You Can Always Count on Me," sung by the kind of girl who's just a pal until she judges the moment right to jump, and the parodic was topped by the producer's description of his method of work in "The Buddy System" and by a heavy-breathed number for the cop and the villainess of the screenplay swapping filmland clichés with a tennis flavor ("The Tennis Song").

City of Angels was an undoubted hit, but its success remained limited. Like *On the Twentieth Century*, it proved to be too "difficult" to attract wide audiences. Wit and clever comic construction were not à la mode at the end of the 1980s: the musical theater was becoming angled almost wholly towards the romantic and the dramatic and, of course, the physically spectacular. This dilemma came to a peak when *City of Angels* played London. When, after only a fair run, the show's closure was announced, some of the newspaper critics rose up in a manner never witnessed in the history of the musical stage and roasted their readers for their lack of discernment. *City of Angels* rallied enough to last a few months more, but that was all. It was one of the most discouraging moments in the history of the musical stage.

CITY OF ANGELS, a musical in 2 acts by Larry Gelbart. Lyrics by David Zippel. Music by Cy Coleman. Produced at the Virginia Theatre, New York, 11 December 1989.

Characters: Stine, Stone, Gabby/Bobbi, Oolie/Donna, Jimmy Powers, Buddy Fidler/Irwin Irving, Munoz, Pancho Vargas, Yamoto/Cinematographer, Alaura Kingsley/Carla Heywood, Mallory Kingsley/Avril Raines, Announcer/Mahoney/Del Dacosta, Officer Pasco/Gene/Orderly, Angel City Four, &c.

Plot: Author Stine is adapting his cop novel for Hollywood producer Buddy Fidler. Fidler makes such alterations as he sees fit and Stine and his hero Stone grumble. The film centers on private dick Stone who lost his cop job when he took the rap for a girlfriend who murdered an overhard film producer, and who now survives on freelance work. He gets an unbelievably rich commission to find a missing little heiress, but it turns out to be just a blind. The gold-digging stepmother of the girl in question wants him around the house to take another rap—when she murders her vastly wealthy husband. Buddy introduces all sorts of corny rewrites, extends the rôle of an amenable actress, and finally casts the part of the detective with a box-office star of a singer with whom his wife has usefully been having an affair. Stine throws in his hand and his job, and heads back to the world of publishing where integrity is prized and respected and where no one would dream of politically correcting a writer's work.

Songs: Theme from *City of Angels*, "Double Talk Walk," "What You Don't Know about Women" (Gabby, Oolie), "You Gotta Look Out for Yourself" (Jimmy Powers, Angel City Four), "The Buddy System" (Buddy), "With Every Breath I Take" (Bobbi), "The Tennis Song" (Alaura, Stone), "Everybody's Gotta Be Somewhere" (Angel City Four), "Lost and Found" (Mallory), "All You Have to Do Is Wait" (Munoz), "You're Nothing without Me" (Stone, Stine), "Stay with Me" (Jimmy Powers, Angel City Four), "You Can Always Count on Me" (Oolie), Alaura's Theme, "It Needs Work" (Gabby), "L.A. Blues," reprise "With Every Breath I Take" (Bobbi, Stone), "Funny" (Stine), reprise "You're Nothing without Me" (Stine, Stone), Epilogue: Theme from *City of Angels* (Stone).

For all its intelligence and wit, *City of Angels* was by no means a "small" or even a "middle-sized" musical. Like its fellow screenland musical *On the Twentieth Century* before it, it boasted scenery of considerable glamour and moving parts to add to its textual and musical attractions, but, again like the earlier show, the spectacular part of the entertainment was kept in its place as a supporting attraction, rather than as the main event of the evening. The same, it was sad to say, could not be said for an increasing number of the musicals that made their way to the stages of New York and London during, in particular, the later 1980s. Vast, multi-million pound or dollar budgets were lavished on boosting mostly worthless pieces of writing into spectacular productions—from rocking ships to futuristic cities, space travel, and practical helicopters—that it was hoped would fool enough of the public some of the time. It fooled them very little of the time, and nearly all of these whistle-the-scenery shows went fairly quickly down the drain. However, there was little doubt that the "megamusical"—the scenery-laden spectacular—was upon us. When there were hits, they were almost always in the grandiose manner and, as *Aspects of Love* had proven, a writer or producer lowered the level of production values at his peril. The new public that the musical theater was attracting, more and more, in the 1980s was a public that wanted visual entertainment, first and foremost. But it was not—not yet, anyhow—a public that was willing to give up all care for content.

Among the megamusicals, there was—in the earlier 1980s at least—still space for a smaller show to make itself a name and a place on the stages of the world. *Little Shop of Horrors* had been one such. Another—on an even smaller scale—was an amusing little musical-concert of country songs which purported to be sung by a group of *Pump Boys and Dinettes*. An agreeable study of three couples who are (or aren't) about to have a *Baby* also won some fond friends if a less wide showing, and *March of the Falsettos*, a trendy little piece about a neurotic New York Jewish chap, his wife, his son, his boyfriend, and his psychiatrist, also found an appreciative off-Broadway audience. Each of these smaller-sized musicals prospered, if and when they prospered, in small-house circumstances, but there was one small and very unshowy musical play which actually took up residence in the West End and on Broadway and succeeded in staying afloat for a remarkably long time among the dreadnoughts of the musical-theater world. But it took it more than a little time to do so.

Blood Brothers, which began its life at Britain's Liverpool Playhouse, was—particularly in the beginning—more like a play with a handful of incidental songs. Written by the successful playwright Willy Russell, it was a little fable which used the favorite old musical-theater element of the long-lost child as its central motif. This being a modern play set in modern times, it was, of course, not possible to have a mother going round losing her children in the way so many folk seemed to do in earlier centuries: this child was "lost" knowingly. The lost child was actually one of two: a pair of twins who are separated at birth and brought up with different mothers under different conditions. The one who stays with his own stoically rueful and sometimes working mother is charming, lazy, irresponsible, gets the girl, and is led into crime; the one who is given away to be brought up by a middle-class family is less obviously attractive, hard-working, serious, doesn't get the girl, and makes a success of his life. When the truth of the two boys' relationship comes out, the stay-at-home cries furiously, "I could have been him," if his mother had given him away to be brought up as his twin had been. He is, of course, wrong: his personality would have let him down no matter which side of town he'd lived on, but he doesn't see it that way. All he wanted was an easy life like you see people having on the telly, and he thinks his brother had it easy. He's really rather thick. But nonetheless tragic.

The focus of the piece was not, however, fixed largely on the boys—it was fixed on their mother, a not-very-bright, daydreamy, used-up kind of woman of thirty-going-on-fifty who makes the best of a rather shabby life, which centered on dancing and movies until it became centered on making ends meet and her seven fast-fathered children. It was to the mother that the bulk of the musical moments of the evening fell: a series of plangent, folksy little numbers among which her appraisal of life on "Easy Terms" and her broken, final "Tell Me It's Not True" were the most effective. The early scenes of *Blood Brothers*, in which adult actors played the two boys as children, were both delightful and effective, and if the later scenes saw the characters becoming a little less "real" as people, and a touch more the mouthpieces for ideas, the music supported the characterizations and the story effectively through to its end.

The show was not a success when it was produced in the West End in 1983. However, its small cast and small staging demands won it many provincial productions and, finally, the same producer whose endless touring of *Joseph and the Technicolor Dreamcoat* had built up that show into the hit it eventually became brought a touring production of *Blood Brothers* back to the West End. And this time the show caught on. At the time of writing it is in its eighth year in the West End, and has also made the trip to Broadway, where it seems to have settled in for a run.

BLOOD BROTHERS, a musical in 2 acts by Willy Russell. Produced at the Liverpool Playhouse, 8 January 1983, and at the Lyric Theatre, London, 11 April 1983.

Characters: Mrs Johnstone, Mickey, Eddie, Sammy, Linda, Mr Lyons, Mrs Lyons, Narrator, &c.

Plot: Mrs Johnstone has seven children, no husband, and works as a daily for lonely Mrs Lyons, who has no children and a husband who is always away. When Mrs Johnstone finds she is expecting twins, Mrs Lyons eagerly offers to take one of the babies. She will pretend that it is her own child, and cares nothing for the curse that is said to hover over twins torn apart should they ever find out the truth of their relationship. And so, Mickey and Eddie grow up apart, but they meet nevertheless and become friends and childish "blood brothers." When Mrs Lyons discovers that "her" child has found his way to his real family, she cracks up and insists on moving to another part of town, but fate will not let the tale rest there. The Johnstones are rehoused not far from the Lyonses, and the now growing youngsters meet again. Both boys fall for the same Linda, but Eddie goes away to university and Mickey marries the girl. While hard-working Eddie's life and career head upwards, envious and untalented Mickey's go downwards, and in the end he turns thief, taking part in a robbery where a man is killed. He goes to jail. And while he is there it is Eddie who comforts Linda. His jealousy wound up to an unbearable point, the out-of-jail Mickey confronts his blood brother — who, he now knows, is more than just that — with a gun. He didn't mean it to go off. Not really. But the curse has come home to roost.

Songs: Narration (Narrator), "Marilyn Monroe" (Mrs Johnstone), "My Child" (Mrs Johnstone, Mrs Lyons), "The Devil's Got Your Number" (Narrator), "Easy Terms" (Mrs Johnstone), "Shoes Upon the Table" (Narrator), "Kids" ["Just a Game"] (Mickey, Eddie, Linda, Sammy, &c.), "Long Sunday Afternoon"/"My Friend" (Mickey, Eddie), "Bright New Day" (Mrs Johnstone &c.), reprise "Marilyn Monroe" (Mrs Johnstone), "One Summer" (Narrator), "That Guy" (Mickey, Eddie), "There's a Few Bob in Your Pocket" (Mickey, Eddie, Linda), "I'm Not Saying a Word" (Eddie), "Take a Letter, Miss Jones" (Mr Lyons &c.), "Prison Song" (Mrs Johnstone), reprise "Marilyn Monroe" (Mrs Johnstone), "Light Romance" (Mrs Johnstone), "There's a Man Gone Mad" (Narrator), "Tell Me It's Not True" (Mrs Johnstone).

Some of the stars of the previous decade(s) fared less well in the 1980s. In the shadow of the big hits, Kander and Ebb turned out the numbers for a grande-dame musical based on the 1942 Katharine Hepburn/Spencer Tracy film *Woman of the Year*, which posted up 770 performances on Broadway, but another musical devoted almost wholly to its feminine stars, the story of the mother and daughter whose lives centered on *The Rink*, in spite of boasting two of the best-loved and grandest dames of the musical-theater world in Chita Rivera and Liza Minnelli at its billhead, failed to catch on. Its reduced proportions, and the continuing success of *Cabaret* and *Zorba*, helped it win several regional productions overseas, but *The Rink* — with its downbeat story and rather irritatingly self-centered characters — didn't ever manage to establish itself.

The most successful unsuccessful writer of the period, however, was undoubtedly Stephen Sondheim. He was unsuccessful in that the three shows for which he wrote the music and lyrics during the 1980s failed to become commercial successes or to catch the public imagination in the way that the hits of the era did, but he was successful in establishing himself a cult and co-terie reputation on a wide scale, a reputation which was to earn his apparently commercially un-viable shows repeated productions in theaters where the money of the unable-to-try-protesting many was available to be spent in mounting musicals and plays for the benefit of the few. Those few, however, were and are a very devoted and very vocal few (and a lot of them seemed to have jobs as subsidized theater directors and managers), and as a result the musicals written by Sond-heim since his rejection of the kind of mainstream musical theater for which he had written be-tween *West Side Story* in 1957 and *A Little Night Music* in 1973 have had a showing on a scale way above the level that would have been normal following their fair-to-lousy original runs.

The first of the three Sondheim musicals of the 1980s had a really lousy run (16 performances), and—in spite of a number of attempts to get it moving again on the back of the strongly devel-oping Sondheim legend in later years—it eventually floundered away into the same limbo in-habited by the songwriter's earlier and other full-scale flop, *Anyone Can Whistle*. *Merrily We Roll Along* didn't actually look or sound like anything very complex. It was a musical version of George S. Kaufman and Moss Hart's sad 1934 story of youthful dreams turned to shiny ashes, a show which is remembered mostly because of the theatrical gimmick central to its construc-tion. The story is told backwards. It wasn't a bad trick, for it allowed the audience to begin with the slick and disabused scenes and build progressively backwards-forwards to more positive and enjoyable moments, even though the taste of what the happy young people of the final scenes had become stayed sourly in one's mind. George Furth's musical version of the play was per-formed by a group of youngsters who "aged up" for the early scenes and was decorated with a set of simple-sounding songs including an attractive ballad ("Not a Day Goes By") and a musi-cal television interview (Franklin Shepard Inc.), but there was nothing in the score which showed off the exceptional skills, textual or musical, that had won the writer such an enthusias-tic following in his earlier shows. And then we were told that the music was—like the play—writ-ten backwards. Who would have guessed it? Perhaps it was the fact that *Merrily We Roll Along* was more an intellectual exercise than a theatrical musical that stopped it from succeeding.

Merrily We Roll Along was succeeded by *Sunday in the Park with George*, and this time the composer and his librettist, James Lapine, went thoroughly out on a limb, constructing and writing a very oddly shaped musical which seemed more like a one-act musical play with one act of more or less relevant discussion following it. The key to the show was a good old tableau vivant of the kind that had been so popular as home-made entertainment more than a century earlier: a grouping of costumed performers in a representation of a famous scene or work of art. The work of art in this case was the well-known painting "Un dimanche d'été sur l'île de la Grande Jatte," painted by the French pointillist artist Georges Seurat. The tableau vivant came at the end of the first act, and the act itself was spent introducing us to the various people in the picture, all of whom were eventually "improved" by the artist when he fixed them on canvas. We also witnessed the falling to bits of the self-centered artist's relationship with his mistress-model: he is too wound up in his creative activity—and talking about it, endlessly—to pay much attention to anyone else, so she goes off with a kindly baker instead. And, from what we can see, good old pain-in-the-ear George (as he's called here) is going to be perfectly happy indulging in his orgies of intellectual introspection and theory-filled art without her.

The musical, however, did not finish here. Act 2 presented us with a second George, a modern American one. He is also an artist and, rather than theories, he has the commercial gift of the gab that gets him commissions from those with handouts to devote to the arts. He's used some trustee's handout to construct a piece of mechanical performance art (which gave a performance to rival *Miss Saigon*'s helicopter), and the party at which this is launched is the setting of the act. Nothing actually happens during this rather different kind of "party musical." People talk a lot, fencing adeptly with cocktail-party gimme-ness, and art patronage and criticism and the misuse of both get dissected. In a final scene George II visits the island where George I painted the picture in Act 1.

The musical score of *Sunday in the Park with George* was not made up of numbers as such. Only rarely did a character get to have a lengthy solo say. It seemed, rather, to be made up of conversations constructed—perhaps purposely—in reflection of the painting style of the first George: hundreds and thousands of tiny colored dots which—if you stand back far enough—come together to give what the artist hoped was a special view of color and light. The music, which rarely allowed itself to flow into an obvious melody, was, in its turn, made up of what seemed to be many small pieces—including thematically repetitive ones—all put together to make up a whole. The result was, again perhaps as with George, intellectually satisfying to those who could understand its nature, but not immediately or obviously attractive to those who didn't. They had to make do with such pieces as the mistress's warmly amusing and impatient monologue as she models motionlessly but sweatily in the sun, or the merry number in which the characters of the painting celebrated "Sunday."

Sunday in the Park with George drew strongly varied reactions. Some found it both intellectually pretentious and (apart from the creation of the painting and its Act 2 equivalent, the Chromolume show) untheatrical, awkwardly constructed, musically unattractive, and—worst—incomprehensible. Others welcomed extravagantly its discursive nature, its departure from normal shape and sound and kind of coherence. There didn't seem to be any half measures. It wasn't what a normal musical-theater audience, even a reasonably open-minded one, expected or wanted—but those who wanted the musical theater to go somewhere different were delighted. Even if they weren't all quite sure precisely where *Sunday in the Park with George* was going, and why. The show ran for 604 performances on Broadway, and it has subsequently been played in a number of subsidized theaters around the world, confirming itself as a piece which does not pull the modern theatergoing audience, but which has special attractions for those audiences to whom its writer's works are the supreme examples of modern musical theater.

Another favorite form of Victorian theater was put into modern dress in the next of Lapine and Sondheim's shows, the 1988 *Into the Woods*. This time it was the fairy-tale burlesque or extravaganza that got the 1980s treatment. The show was, like *Sunday in the Park with George*, a two-part affair, but this time the two parts hung together rather more coherently, as part of one and the same story. The first half was a quest—less the sort of quest followed by the *Man of La Mancha* and more like that of the merry soubrets of the French hit *Andalousie*, who spend their operettic evening trying to get together the elements to mix their love potion. This one followed the efforts of the childless Baker and his Wife to gather together the necessary ingredients to produce a magical glass of milk which will return the local witch to youth and beauty, after which she will take off the nasty spell she has put on them that's stopping them from breeding. By the end of Act 1, their quest—which has involved Jack of the Beanstalk's cow, Cinderella's slipper, Rapunzel's hair, and Little Red Riding Hood's topcoat—is done, and everyone has his or her happy ending. Act 2 went past the happy endings to look at their consequences and then watched each happy ending fall to bits. It got dangerously near being precisely what the old fairy-tales themselves had been—a Piece with a Moral. The Moral, in this case, being more of a question: if we stick at nothing to get what we want, are we going to pay for it later? And it doesn't stop short of giving an answer. That answer is: you bet your life you are.

Into the Woods, particularly in its first act, was an altogether more attractive and amusing piece than *Sunday in the Park with George* had been. It was less aggressively intellectual, generally comprehensible, often wittily and imaginatively amusing, and such subtexts and morals and things as were involved were pretty optional. The musical stood up as a piece of clever fairy-tale burlesque which could be taken at face value, or with just as much of a dose of Meaningfulness as the audience wished. In the second act, which was painted in dourer colors, the options became progressively fewer, the story sourer, and the characters less attractive. For *Into the Woods* was a fairy-tale burlesque for the age of the Psychoanalyst, and all those merry folk of Act 1 turn out pretty much second-raters in Act 2.

The music and lyrics in the show also proved more accessible than those of the previous piece, and the wordfully witty Sondheim of earlier days got back into gear in some of the evening's most appreciable comic numbers—Red Riding Hood's encounter with a dirty old wolf who leers "Hello, Little Girl" at her, the miserere of two lustful Princes suffering "Agony" at not being able to get their rocks off with the girl of the moment (and, when they have, suffering the same agony over the next unattainable female), and Cinderella's description of her Prince's up-to-date dirty tricks—laying pitch on the palace steps to hamper her too-well-known midnight flight. Elsewhere, however, to the detriment of general comprehension but the pleasure of the committed, the songwriter was inclined to favor a more "modern poetry" style of lyrics and a less frank use of melody.

Doubtless thanks to its familiar characters and its higher level of accessibility, *Into the Woods* won a little wider acceptance than *Sunday in the Park with George* had done, but although the musical stayed on Broadway for 764 performances, it flopped in a commercial production in London, and has otherwise found itself a berth mostly in those same subsidized theaters which continue to offer a home to these works.

SOME NOTABLE MUSICALS 1980–1994

1980   LES MISÉRABLES (Claude-Michel Schönberg/Alain Boublil, Jean-Marc Natel) Palais des Sports, Paris, 17 September

1981   WOMAN OF THE YEAR (John Kander/Fred Ebb/Peter Stone) Palace Theatre, New York, 29 March

    CATS (Andrew Lloyd Webber) New London Theatre, London, 11 May

    MARCH OF THE FALSETTOS (William Finn) Chelsea Westside Arts Theatre, New York, 13 October

    DREAMGIRLS (Henry Krieger/Tom Eyen) Imperial Theatre, New York, 20 December

1982   PUMP BOYS AND DINETTES (John Floey, Mark Hardwick, Debra Monk, Cass Morgan, John Schimmel, Jim Wann) Princess Theatre, New York, 4 February

    SONG AND DANCE (Andrew Lloyd Webber/Don Black) Palace Theatre, London, 26 March

    LITTLE SHOP OF HORRORS (Alan Menken/Howard Ashman) WPA Theatre, New York, 6 May

1983   BLOOD BROTHERS (Willy Russell) Liverpool Playhouse, Liverpool, 8 January

    SINGIN' IN THE RAIN (Arthur Freed/Nacio Herb Brown pasticcio/Tommy Steele) London Palladium, London, 30 June

    LA CAGE AUX FOLLES (Jerry Herman/Harvey Fierstein) Palace Theatre, New York, 21 August

    BABY (David Shire/Richard Matlby/Sybille Pearson) Ethel Barrymore Theatre, New York, 4 December

    THE TAP DANCE KID (Henry Krieger/Robert Lorick/Charles Blackwell) Broadhurst Theatre, New York, 21 December

1984   STARLIGHT EXPRESS (Andrew Lloyd Webber/Richard Stilgoe) Apollo Victoria Theatre, London, 27 March

    SUNDAY IN THE PARK WITH GEORGE (Stephen Sondheim/James Lapine) Booth Theatre, New York, 2 May

1985   BIG RIVER, the Adventures of Huckleberry Finn (Roger Miller/William Hauptmann) Eugene O'Neill Theatre, New York, 25 April

    THE MYSTERY OF EDWIN DROOD (Rupert Holmes) Delacorte Theatre, New York, 4 August

LES MISÉRABLES (English version) (Claude-Michel Schönberg/Herbert Kretzmer) Barbican Theatre, London, 30 September

1986   CHESS (Bjørn Ulvaeus, Benny Andersson/Tim Rice) Prince Edward Theatre, London, 14 May

1987   THE PHANTOM OF THE OPÉRA (Andrew Lloyd Webber/Charles Hart, Richard Stilgoe) Her Majesty's Theatre, London, 9 October

INTO THE WOODS (Stephen Sondheim/James Lapine) Martin Beck Theatre, New York, 5 November

1989   ASPECTS OF LOVE (Andrew Lloyd Webber/Don Black, Charles Hart) Prince of Wales Theatre, London, 17 April

MISS SAIGON (Claude-Michel Schönberg/Alain Boublil, Richard Nelson) Theatre Royal, Drury Lane, London, 20 September

CITY OF ANGELS (Cy Coleman/David Zippel/Larry Gelbart) Virginia Theatre, New York, 11 December

1991   THE WILL ROGERS FOLLIES (Cy Coleman/Adolph Green, Betty Comden) Palace Theatre, New York, 1 June

1993   SUNSET BOULEVARD (Andrew Lloyd Webber/Don Black/Christopher Hampton) Adelphi Theatre, London, 12 July

1994   BEAUTY AND THE BEAST (Alan Menken/Tim Rice, Howard Ashman) Palace Theatre, New York, 18 April

13
ENDPIECE

$\mathcal{T}$he big musical-theater hits of the 1980s were the biggest hits that the theater had ever known. They have gone through vast runs in their original productions in London and/or New York, and they have traveled all around the world, being reproduced in all sorts of languages and countries and being seen by more people, including many people who had never previously been theatergoers, than any shows in history. But that is only to be expected, for the nature of theatergoing has changed very noticeably over recent years. Not so very long ago, a solid core of theater seats was sold to a solid core of regular theatergoers: folk to whom the theater was their most or at least one important form of entertainment and leisure. Some of these regular playgoers would go to anything and everything that was produced; others—the bulk—were a little more selective, but would rarely miss a good or successful show. Some would go to the theater every week, some more than once a week; all were regulars. And these people, this kind of theatergoer—or of musical-theatergoer, since that's what we're talking about here—is now a threatened species.

Why? Because the theater has changed. The hits may be bigger and longer, but they are also fewer. And they are fewer at least partly because, largely for economic but also for product reasons, there are fewer shows produced. And even among those "fewer" there is an important sector that has largely disappeared: the middle-range show. There are big hits, there are double-quick flops, but the show in between—the show which perhaps just recoups its investment after a year or two (once upon a time a month or two would have done) in town—that kind of show is becoming rarer and rarer. Why?

Going to the theater has now become an "event." You don't just go to the theater where there is a hit show running and buy yourself a ticket: you book six months, perhaps even twelve months in advance, and spend your time thinking how good it's going to be before you get there. And all those new theatergoers, those folk who perhaps attend the theater a couple of times a year, are not going to take a risk on anything less than the Biggest and the Best available. They'll wait, rather than spend their "event" on something which might not be top drawer. Or, at least, that they can tell the neighbors was top drawer. And so, the big hits get bigger, and the not-so-big hits struggle.

And as the big hits get bigger, and the middle-range show gets rarer, the theater as an investment gets less attractive, and production levels sink. In the 1920s, when Broadway or the West

End could be counted upon to harbor a dozen or more nicely sized hits a season, forty or fifty or sixty new musicals might make their way to the stage: more than enough for the regular theatergoer to feast on unstintedly. Nowadays the stage has arrived when Broadway and the West End between them are doing well to première half a dozen musicals a year. All may be failures. And the regular musical-playgoers, with nothing to get their teeth into, are abandoning the theater for other entertainments. Their abandoning isn't going to hurt the big hits, but it will be the death of the lesser shows. And, of course, if the lesser shows aren't produced, where will the writers of the next generation of big hits come from?

The end-of-this-century musical theater—it is turning 1996 as I write this—is largely a spectacular, megamusical kind of theater. Just occasionally a small musical show of the *Blood Brothers* kind can make a mark, but by and large the book musicals of this era are big, extravagant, expensive shows. On the one hand, there is the solid phalanx of modern musical-theater hits— such as *Cats*, *Les Misérables*, or *The Phantom of the Opéra*—which have become the backbone of the modern musical-theater repertoire. And, on the other, there are the nostalgia shows: revivals, pasticcios, and compilation shows. At the moment, with producing a new musical being such a multi-millions-risky affair, productions such as these have become the latest fashion. In the 1990s, extravagantly scenic remountings of famous old and not so old musicals (originally produced with much, much less in the way of hydraulics and flim flam), often featuring "drawing" name artists from other now more name-making media such as television or film, make up a significant part of the musical theater on show in the main centers. Some of these old to middle-aged musicals have made it back to the stage unharmed and in fine shape, but others—less well looked after by those who control such things on behalf of their writers, dead or alive— have been given the kind of go-over which allows a goer-over to claim a new copyright. Some, too, have been "politically corrected" to suit the tastes of the most pressing of pressure groups or of today's linguistic fascists, while others have had their scores infiltrated by songs taken from other sources, or even from cut-outs, in a way unimagined by the original writers and songwriters. Sometimes, of course, but just sometimes, this kind of remaking works—the revision practiced on the 1937 piece *Me and My Girl* was a notable example—on other occasions the damage is minimal, but mostly it is the remakers who are best served by the process (royalty-wise) rather than the show. Or than the audiences, who are unaware that they are being served up "improved," "corrected" classics in the Shakespeare-improved-by-Cibber vein.

The same kind of friendly familiarity which inspires the public to visit a revival of a well-known (and well known to have been successful) show also helps the survival of the pasticcio musical, an often unsophisticated kind of musical theater which has endured—in better or worse health—down through the centuries, and its younger, less talented, and lazier sister, the compilation show. Recent years have seen continuing examples of both kinds of work as Broadway launched such pieces as *My One and Only*, *Crazy for You*, and the compilation shows *Sophisticated Ladies* and *Jerome Robbins' Broadway*, and London devoted itself to repackaging

1950s and 1960s pop music into soi-disant biomusicals of once-upon-a-youthday performers designed to appeal to the now grown-up and wallet-filled children of the 1950s and the 1960s.

A good, faithful revival of a classic musical is a joy not to be missed, pasticcio shows on the present lines and compilations can be enjoyed as concerts, but at the heart of the musical theater—its chief attraction—will always be the brand new musical. And so, what have the 1990s brought us so far in the way of original new musicals? And what can they be expected to bring in what remains to us of the twentieth century? With the decade more than half gone, the score-sheet is not looking terribly healthy. In fact, not since the dawn of the modern era of the musical theater in the middle of the last century have five or six years passed in which so little that is appreciable or likely to be enduring has been introduced to the public, and awards ceremonies have become an ought-to-be-abolished embarrassment. To date, the "old guard" have kept themselves to the fore: there has been one new musical each from Andrew Lloyd Webber and Cy Coleman (with Comden and Green), while Stephen Sondheim has turned out two, and Kander and Ebb have produced another grande-dame piece to add to a list of credits which hasn't looked masculine since *Zorba*. Otherwise, there has been a noticeable orientation towards the young of all ages, to family musicals for that "event" occasion—a prettily staged musical version of the kiddie tale *The Secret Garden*, a cartoon-to-stage version of the Disney film *Beauty and the Beast*, a TV-to-stage version of the juvenile gotta-make-it-good-in-showbiz series *Fame*—and, for those same grown-up children of the sixties who patronize the pop-music shows, a new record-to-stage version of The Who's previously stage-unsuccessful concept musical *Tommy*.

Both Coleman's show and Lloyd Webber's musical were pieces which looked back to a bygone and rather more thoroughly thriving-on-originality age of entertainment business. Coleman, Comden, and Green, in team with librettist Peter Stone, produced a piece called *The Will Rogers Follies*, written around the personality of the popular cowboy humorist of the 1910s and 1920s. It served much as the revivals and pasticcio shows had done—and an unfortunate London extravaganza on *Ziegfeld* produced shortly before had done more glitzily and more precisely—to allow the re-creation of numbers using the styles and fashions of those peak years of the musical stage, while profiting from modern technical facilities. The result wasn't anything in the class of Coleman's previous piece, *City of Angels*, but it provided agreeable old-fashioned entertainment of the kind which it was becoming increasingly obvious, three-quarters of a century down the line, that the public was still keen to see.

Lloyd Webber's show was a piece written, to a libretto by playwright Christopher Hampton and lyrics by Don Black, with rather more dramatic intent than Stone's light-hearted entertainment. Following on from the successful translation to the musical stage of the grotesque cinematic *The Phantom of the Opéra*—and with the lesson of *Aspects of Love* having shown that grandiose subjects and scenes were much more likely to win approval—the composer again devoted himself to putting to music a piece of classic cinema with a grotesque, larger than life central character. In his first ever grande-dame musical, Lloyd Webber introduced to the musical

Sunset Boulevard: Where the grande-dame musical met the composer of The Phantom of the Opéra.

stage one of the cinema's most classic grandes dames of all: the silent film-star Norma Desmond, unforgettably portrayed by Gloria Swanson in the 1950 movie *Sunset Boulevard*.

Transferring *Sunset Boulevard*, with its dark, claustrophobic feeling, to the musical stage— and, above all, to what was obliged in this day and age to be the spectacular musical stage— cannot have been an easy task. On the screen, the star had been able to create the dominating and powerful personality of Norma Desmond with the aid of close camera work. On a large stage, full of spectacular scenery, such a performance would be much more difficult. But this Norma Desmond had music with which to power up her personality, music which ran the gamut of the entire rock-opera prima-donna range and then some, and Lloyd Webber was able to pull out one of those broad, beautiful, between-the-eyes melodies which are his speciality, and which have helped make his songs and his shows so very singable and so very popular all around the world, for the crucial character-explaining number which was central to Norma's rôle. "With One Look I Can Break Your Heart," she sings of the art of the silent film actor, and you know that she can. Or that she could.

Sunset Boulevard was not built quite on the usual lines of a Lloyd Webber musical, effectively sung through and with the "numbers" encased in—but extractable from—the rest of the musical body of the work. This script held more dialogue than had been normal, almost as much as a regulation songs-and-scenes show, but it moved into long sung portions throughout the evening. The obviously extractable number was, indeed, Norma's big song, but—as had happened in *Aspects of Love* with the splendid but ill-recorded "Anything But Lonely"— a pre-production try for the top of the charts went wrong when the song was lackadaisically rearranged for Barbra Streisand's cover version. With its dramatic tension gone, the song meant nothing. In the show, however, it was stunning. The other principal musical moments were the leading man's disabused vision of "Sunset Boulevard," Norma's radiant return to the studio with "Everything's as If We Never Said Goodbye," and her equally self-deluding vision of "The Perfect Year" that she is about to have—a year that ends in mayhem and murder. The body of the work, however, showed up some changes in the composer's style, and the most notable of these was one which had already been noticed (and not approved by all) in the score of *Aspects of Love*: thematic repetition. Not just once or twice, but more times than the tune of "Ol' Man River" gets played in *Show Boat*. At some stages of the show's opening number, which repeated the same musical phrase over and over through a very long piece of introductory scene-setting, one had the feeling of having wandered into a Philip Glass opera. In that particular number, the repetition served to reproduce the effect of the numbing workaday routine it portrayed, but elsewhere it was found by some to be less apt or enjoyable.

Sunset Boulevard picked up where *The Phantom of the Opéra* had left off, establishing itself as the first—and, so far, the only—international hit of the 1990s, but it did its picking up equipped with a considerable problem. A problem which was also one of its principal strengths. The rôle of Norma Desmond is one of the most demanding in the modern musical theater, for it demands both an enormous star presence—if the woman isn't utterly, compellingly powerful and reeking of star quality then she's on the verge of repulsive—and a singing voice with the power and the range of an Evita. It's going to be difficult finding the tenth take-over.

SUNSET BOULEVARD, a musical in 2 acts, based on the screenplay by Billy Wilder, Charles Brackett, and D. M. Marsham Jr. Book and lyrics by Christopher Hampton and Don Black. Music by Andrew Lloyd Webber. Produced at the Adelphi Theatre, London, 12 July 1993.

Characters: Norma Desmond, Joe Gillis, Betty Schaefer, Max von Mayerling, Cecil B. De Mille, Artie Green, Manfred, &c.

Plot: On-the-down writer Joe Gillis runs his car into an empty LA drive while escaping his creditors and finds himself in the timewarped mansion of aging silent film-star Norma Desmond. He also finds himself a job, for Miss Desmond is planning a comeback and she has written a vast film-play in which she will star as the teenaged Salomé. It needs work. So Joe stays in the house and fiddles a bit with the impossible script. Only, when it is done, Norma will not have him leave: she is falling in love. But Joe still has contact with the real world, and one contact is his best friend's girl, Betty Schaefer, with whom he is writing a screenplay. While Norma is falling in love with Joe, Joe and Betty are falling in love with each other. Norma takes her screenplay to De Mille at the studios, and the famous producer is kind to her. She has her moment of glory when she is recognized by an old hand on the lot, and she goes home happy to prepare herself for her comeback. But then she finds out about Betty. When she challenges Joe, he lets rip at her with the truth, and all the comfortable lies with which Max, now her butler, once her director and husband, has surrounded her over the years are torn away. Norma goes over the edge and, taking a gun, she shoots Joe Gillis dead. The last reel is finished.

Songs: Introduction ["I Guess It Was Five a.m."] (Joe), "Let's Have Lunch" (ensemble), "No More Wars to Fight" (Norma), "With One Look" (Norma), "Salomé, What a Woman, What a Part" (Norma, Joe), "She Is the Greatest Star of All" (Max), "Movies" (ensemble), scene: "I Just Re-Read 'Blind Windows'" (Betty, Joe), "New Ways to Dream" (Norma, Joe), "The Lady's Paying" (Manfred, Joe, Norma, &c.), "The Perfect Year" (Norma, Joe), "This Time Next Year" (ensemble), "Sunset Boulevard" (Joe), "Everything's as If We Never Said Goodbye" (Norma), "Eternal Youth" (beauticians), "Too Much in Love to Care" (Betty, Joe), reprise "New Ways to Dream" (Max), reprise "With One Look" (Norma).

Kander and Ebb, allied with the same librettist, Terrence McNally, who had created the book for *The Rink*, also turned to the world of the cinema for their new musical. It was something that was becoming increasingly obvious: where once the cinema had fed on the stage both for its subject-matter and for its larger-than-life characters, from Lily Garland and Oscar Jaffee to Peggy Sawyer and Julian Marsh, via hundreds and hundreds of others, now the process was reversed. The stage, and the musical stage in particular, was these days feeding almost desperately from the cinema, even to the extent, with a piece like *Beauty and the Beast*, of trying to put life into its animated characters. The fantasy-drama *The Kiss of the Spiderwoman* had, indeed, made much of its fame as a film (although it had been a book and a play first), but it was not the piece's connection with the modern cinema that was the preponderant one, it was its connection with that earlier era of cinema, the era before the development of the modern trends for "realism," raw flesh, and bloodbathing on the movie screen, an era which had now become both a realm of otherworldly, other-timely, good-old-daisical enjoyment and inspiration. The "Spiderwoman" of the title wasn't a relation of television's "Spiderman," she was another Norma Desmond character: a grotesquely exaggerated screen goddess. This one was able to be all the more grotesque and exaggerated in that she existed only in the imagination of the central character. Like Billy Fisher, like Tillie who had the Nightmare, Molina—from his South American jail—could fly away into fantasies where he could find solace in the company of the over-the-top creature of his imagination. The nature of *The Kiss of the Spiderwoman* allowed a mixture of realism and dream while also being almost a parody of the grande-dame musical. Produced in London—always less in love with the grande-dame genre than Broadway—it failed, but a subsequent Broadway production did predictably better and, in a period when good new musicals come along less and less frequently, the show succeeded in finding itself a continuing run.

Stephen Sondheim continued his run of dark-toned and/or downbeat musicals into the 1990s, but still without managing to find success. In 1991 he teamed with John Weidman of *Pacific Overtures* on a curious kind of "party" musical which had for its characters some of the most grotesque and pitiful people yet to have be seen on the musical stage. *Assassins* presented the audience with a singing selection of those folk who have, up to this time, murdered or attempted to murder American presidents. It seemed to have little raison d'être except as a piece of sensationalism akin to that displayed in the less salubrious supermarket magazines or serial-killer movies, and it provoked little interest.

Passion, however, saw both author and composer moving on to a decidedly more positive track. The piece was, once again, dark in color and tragic in tale, but this time it was an end-to-end story, a powerful love-story which saw a man giving up a light love with an easy and easygoing girl for one with a plain, dying, but infinitely passionate woman. The subject and its characters—real people with real feelings to express—allowed Sondheim to spread himself and his music with markedly more lyricism and considerably more force than in recent shows, but, sadly, *Passion* proved to be even less to the taste of Broadway audiences than his shows of the 1980s, and it closed in 280 performances.

So what can we expect from the rest of the 1990s? Lloyd Webber, Sondheim, Coleman, Kander and Ebb, Black, Gelbart, Simon, Hamlisch, and two of the writers of *Les Misérables*—Boublil and Schönberg—are still on the scene and still, with luck, have more musicals to offer us. But there seems to be a disturbing lack of new writers snapping at their heels. It is, of course, difficult for a new writer to get launched under the megamusical conditions of these days. It is easier for a producer to count on proven talent or a proven show when investing his and/or other people's fistfuls of millions. But normally, in the past, when the musical theater has been attacked by the sort of gigantism that reigns today, new writing talent has come from smaller theaters producing small-scale musicals. That kind of small-scale musical and the kind of theater which would present such a musical seem to be in crisis right now. Or is it the public that is in crisis? Has the stage musical as we know it outlived its useful life? Should it become crystallized as, for example, circus has been, or as opera has effectively been: repeating its best bits of from-the-past over and over to audiences who whistle the tunes as they come into the theater? Surely not. The theaters of London and New York and the other main musical-theater centers are still full. The musical has a high profile—in some ways higher than ever. But if the second half of the 1990s brings us—like the first half—only one or two successful and/or appreciable new shows, what can we expect from the 2000s? One per decade? Or something new. Who knows? But it should be fun finding out.

PHOTO CREDITS

INDEX